T0181898

Lecture Notes in Computer Science 14057

The series Lecture Notes in Computer Science (LNCS), including its subseries Lecture Notes in Artificial Intelligence (LNAI) and Lecture Notes in Bioinformatics (LNBI), has established itself as a medium for the publication of new developments in computer science and information technology research, teaching, and education.

LNCS enjoys close cooperation with the computer science R & D community, the series counts many renowned academics among its volume editors and paper authors, and collaborates with prestigious societies. Its mission is to serve this international community by providing an invaluable service, mainly focused on the publication of conference and workshop proceedings and postproceedings. LNCS commenced publication in 1973.

Vincent G. Duffy · Heidi Krömker ·
Norbert A. Streitz · Shin'ichi Konomi
Editors

HCI International 2023 – Late Breaking Papers

25th International Conference on Human-Computer Interaction
HCII 2023, Copenhagen, Denmark, July 23–28, 2023
Proceedings, Part IV

 Springer

Editors
Vincent G. Duffy
Purdue University
West Lafayette, IN, USA

Heidi Krömker
Technische Universitat Ilmenau
Ilmenau, Germany

Norbert A. Streitz 🆔
Smart Future Initiative
Frankfurt am Main, Germany

Shin'ichi Konomi
Kyushu University
Fukuoka, Japan

ISSN 0302-9743   ISSN 1611-3349 (electronic)
Lecture Notes in Computer Science
ISBN 978-3-031-48046-1   ISBN 978-3-031-48047-8 (eBook)
https://doi.org/10.1007/978-3-031-48047-8

This Springer imprint is published by the registered company Springer Nature Switzerland AG
The registered company address is: Gewerbestrasse 11, 6330 Cham, Switzerland

Paper in this product is recyclable.

Foreword

Human-computer interaction (HCI) is acquiring an ever-increasing scientific and industrial importance, as well as having more impact on people's everyday lives, as an ever-growing number of human activities are progressively moving from the physical to the digital world. This process, which has been ongoing for some time now, was further accelerated during the acute period of the COVID-19 pandemic. The HCI International (HCII) conference series, held annually, aims to respond to the compelling need to advance the exchange of knowledge and research and development efforts on the human aspects of design and use of computing systems.

The 25th International Conference on Human-Computer Interaction, HCI International 2023 (HCII 2023), was held in the emerging post-pandemic era as a 'hybrid' event at the AC Bella Sky Hotel and Bella Center, Copenhagen, Denmark, during July 23–28, 2023. It incorporated the 21 thematic areas and affiliated conferences listed below.

A total of 7472 individuals from academia, research institutes, industry, and government agencies from 85 countries submitted contributions, and 1578 papers and 396 posters were included in the volumes of the proceedings that were published just before the start of the conference. Additionally, 267 papers and 133 posters were included in the volumes of the proceedings published after the conference, as "Late Breaking Work". The contributions thoroughly cover the entire field of human-computer interaction, addressing major advances in knowledge and effective use of computers in a variety of application areas. These papers provide academics, researchers, engineers, scientists, practitioners and students with state-of-the-art information on the most recent advances in HCI. The volumes constituting the full set of the HCII 2023 conference proceedings are listed on the following pages.

I would like to thank the Program Board Chairs and the members of the Program Boards of all thematic areas and affiliated conferences for their contribution towards the high scientific quality and overall success of the HCI International 2023 conference. Their manifold support in terms of paper reviewing (single-blind review process, with a minimum of two reviews per submission), session organization and their willingness to act as goodwill ambassadors for the conference is most highly appreciated.

This conference would not have been possible without the continuous and unwavering support and advice of Gavriel Salvendy, founder, General Chair Emeritus, and Scientific Advisor. For his outstanding efforts, I would like to express my sincere appreciation to Abbas Moallem, Communications Chair and Editor of HCI International News.

July 2023   Constantine Stephanidis

HCI International 2023 Thematic Areas and Affiliated Conferences

Thematic Areas

- HCI: Human-Computer Interaction
- HIMI: Human Interface and the Management of Information

Affiliated Conferences

- EPCE: 20th International Conference on Engineering Psychology and Cognitive Ergonomics
- AC: 17th International Conference on Augmented Cognition
- UAHCI: 17th International Conference on Universal Access in Human-Computer Interaction
- CCD: 15th International Conference on Cross-Cultural Design
- SCSM: 15th International Conference on Social Computing and Social Media
- VAMR: 15th International Conference on Virtual, Augmented and Mixed Reality
- DHM: 14th International Conference on Digital Human Modeling and Applications in Health, Safety, Ergonomics and Risk Management
- DUXU: 12th International Conference on Design, User Experience and Usability
- C&C: 11th International Conference on Culture and Computing
- DAPI: 11th International Conference on Distributed, Ambient and Pervasive Interactions
- HCIBGO: 10th International Conference on HCI in Business, Government and Organizations
- LCT: 10th International Conference on Learning and Collaboration Technologies
- ITAP: 9th International Conference on Human Aspects of IT for the Aged Population
- AIS: 5th International Conference on Adaptive Instructional Systems
- HCI-CPT: 5th International Conference on HCI for Cybersecurity, Privacy and Trust
- HCI-Games: 5th International Conference on HCI in Games
- MobiTAS: 5th International Conference on HCI in Mobility, Transport and Automotive Systems
- AI-HCI: 4th International Conference on Artificial Intelligence in HCI
- MOBILE: 4th International Conference on Design, Operation and Evaluation of Mobile Communications

Conference Proceedings – Full List of Volumes

https://2023.hci.international/proceedings

25th International Conference on Human-Computer Interaction (HCII 2023)

The full list with the Program Board Chairs and the members of the Program Boards of all thematic areas and affiliated conferences of HCII2023 is available online at:

http://www.hci.international/board-members-2023.php

HCI International 2024 Conference

The 26th International Conference on Human-Computer Interaction, HCI International 2024, will be held jointly with the affiliated conferences at the Washington Hilton Hotel, Washington, DC, USA, June 29 – July 4, 2024. It will cover a broad spectrum of themes related to Human-Computer Interaction, including theoretical issues, methods, tools, processes, and case studies in HCI design, as well as novel interaction techniques, interfaces, and applications. The proceedings will be published by Springer. More information will be made available on the conference website: http://2024.hci.international/.

General Chair
Prof. Constantine Stephanidis
University of Crete and ICS-FORTH
Heraklion, Crete, Greece
Email: general_chair@2024.hci.international

https://2024.hci.international/

Contents – Part IV

HCI in Automated Vehicles and Intelligent Transportation

Sustainable Green Smart Cities and Smart Industry

Digital Human Modeling, Ergonomics and Safety

Bibliometric Literature Analysis and Systematic Review of Occupational Ergonomics

Matthew Chang and Vincent G. Duffy[✉]

Purdue University, West Lafayette, IN 47906, USA
{chang841,duffy}@purdue.edu

Abstract. This report seeks to understand the topic of occupational ergonomics through a comprehensive bibliometric analysis and systematic literature review. To conduct this analysis, three primary key terms were utilized across a variety of online databases where data was collected and analyzed through the lens of engagement, trend, cluster, and word cloud analyses. Using appropriate quantitative and qualitative research tools, inferences and conclusions are developed to better understand the industries in which occupational ergonomics plays a role, identify risks, and provide strategic recommendations in prevent future injury. From the analyses performed, findings include increasing understanding and engagement with workplace ergonomic related keywords, as seen in Figs. 5 and 6. Additionally, organizations and employees are becoming more aware of industry-standard terms including ergonomics, musculoskeletal disorder/disease, risk, and more as seen through an increased cluster frequency in Figs. 11 and 12. This project also highlights ongoing and future potentials for research in this area of study.

Keywords: Occupational Ergonomics · Safety · Musculoskeletal Disorders

1 Introduction and Background

1.1 Introduction

Defined by the Occupational Safety and Health Administration (OSHA) as the study of work, occupational ergonomics can be explained as the development of tools and other techniques that fit the task at hand to the employee, rather than altering the worker for the role. Structured by ten principles, occupational ergonomics involves 1) working in a neutral. Comfortable position, 2) reducing the need for excessive force, 3) keeping materials within reaching distance, 4) working at the proper height for the employee, 5) decreasing unnecessary movement, 6) minimizing fatigue levels caused by the role, 7) reducing contact stress, 8) allowing for clearance, 9) moving and stretching throughout the day, and 10) working in a comfortable environment [9]. Despite this framework, musculoskeletal disorders (MSDs) and related injuries still occur and can be attributed to both physical and cognitive reasons. Physically, examples of MSDs include limb strain injuries from repetitive motions, cumulative trauma disorders, numbness in the joints or limbs, posture-related injuries from manual material handling, and more. Cognitively,

V. G. Duffy et al. (Eds.): HCII 2023, LNCS 14057, pp. 3–19, 2023.
https://doi.org/10.1007/978-3-031-48047-8_1

visual and mental fatigue are two common causes of injury in addition to decreased mental alertness level, incorrect perceived usability of products, user experience design failures and more. According to the World Health Organization (WHO), over 1.7+ billion people live with MSDs globally and this number is continually increasing and often leads to significant limitations in mobility, dexterity, and general well-being [18]. Similar, in the United States in 2018, 30% of injuries causing days missed from work were as a result of MSDs. Shown in the figure below from the U.S. Bureau of Labor Statistics, while the number of missed work days due to musculoskeletal disorders has been decreasing since 2011, it still remains a problem in today's workplace, accounting for 250,000+ missed days [2] (Fig. 1).

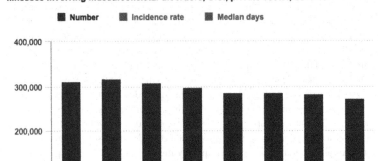

Chart 1. Number, incidence rate, and median days away from work of injuries and illnesses involving musculoskeletal disorders, U.S., private sector, 2011-18

Fig. 1. U.S. Bureau of Labor Statistics Missed Work Days from MSDs Chart

Understanding the root causes of musculoskeletal disorders and looking at mitigation factors and how ergonomics can play a role is significant to today's workforce. As workers get older and certain jobs become more automated, this should lead to a reduction in MSDs, but with over 1.5 billion people still affected globally, this is still a pertinent issue that requires remediation.

There are several factors that have been driving this factor to importance over the past few years and currently. Obviously, workers are suffering from repetitive and long-lasting injuries and in certain cases, death. Another significant factor is the financial cost of injury. Seen in Fig. 2 below, in 2021, the total cost of work injuries equated to $167 billion dollars in the United States where wages lost were $47.4 billion, medical expenses $36.6 billion, and administrative costs $57.5 billion [10].

Ergonomics and human anthropometry are a large facet of Industrial Engineering and thus occupational hazards, and musculoskeletal injuries fall within these categories.

These topics are important to industrial engineers as they seek to improve process efficiencies, promote productivity, keep systems within their control limits, and ultimately drive organizational and financial growth.

Outside the Industrial Engineering industry, several steps have already been taken to automate and digitize processes that may pose risks to employees. Additionally, certain industries like manufacturing and construction specifically have begun looking to incorporate new technologies like robots to replace individuals roles that may have been hazardous or leading influences of musculoskeletal disorders in the past.

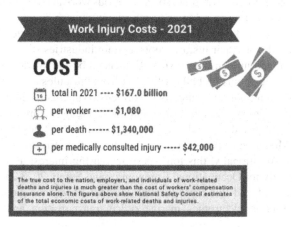

Fig. 2. 2021 Work Injury Costs in the United States

While the field of ergonomics and workstation design is not new, research has only recently begun to gain prominence into musculoskeletal disorders, their causes, and how to mitigate them. Further funding should be provided to better understand these risks, identify methods of preventing them, and to developing new technologies that would protect individuals. Additionally, organizations should begin adapting their systems and implementing new systems and protocols to protect their employees.

The safety-related community and industrial engineers globally have begun to address this issue of musculoskeletal disorders head on. From investing more into research of these causes and creating new recommendations for change to speaking about it more frequently at industry conferences to even educating their classrooms and organizations about this issue has assisted in addresses this topic.

1.2   Problem Statement and Scope of Analysis

In this project, a bibliometric literature analysis and systematic review was conducted on the topic of occupational ergonomics, a field of increasing interest and prominence. Commonly referred to as the creation and usage of tools, platforms, systems, and more that allow employees to perform work with higher degrees of safety, comfortability, and efficiency, this analysis seeks to understand where various industries stand with this topic, identify hazards and risks employees face in different work environments, and provide recommendations on mitigation strategies.

To better understand and gain a holistic view of occupational ergonomics, several key words were considered in this analysis. These include occupational ergonomics, safety, and musculoskeletal disorders and their corresponding terms. Techniques used to perform these analyses and create recommendations include Google Ngram, Vicinitas, VOSViewer, maxQDA, Harzing, CiteSpace, BibExcel, and more.

1.3 Statement of Relevance and Applicability

As technology has improved over time, so have various work and industry environments. From increased automation to robotics to others, employees have had to evolve from what work was previous known as. However, while several industries have made this change and evolved from their historic roots, certain industries still require significant human interaction and human-based work. Evidenced by the World Health Organization, over 1.7+ billion people globally still suffer from musculoskeletal disorders today, illnesses derived from poor and dangerous work environments. Seen through the 2023 HCI International Conference, job design and the changing nature of work remain as one of the primary topics discussed within the DHM: 14th International Conference on Digital Human Modeling & Applications in Health, Safety, Ergonomics & Risk Management section. Additionally, this topic is of increasing interest as seen through the International Society for Occupational Ergonomics and Safety 2023 conference, where researchers have analyzed this topic through the lens of various industries including aerospace, construction, electronics, marine, office, transportation, and more.

2 Bibliometric Analysis and Literature Review

In this section of the report, various techniques will be used to perform a comprehensive bibliometric analysis and literature review. These include search term, Vicinitas Engagement, Google Ngram, VOS Viewer, CiteSpace Cluster and Citation Burst, MAXQDA Word Cloud, Harzing, and BibExcel related analyses. These methodologies were derived from a bibliometric analysis performed by researchers from the University of Almeria [19].

2.1 Data Collection Methodologies and Summary of Search Terms

To better understand the topic of occupational ergonomics, select key words were identified, including occupational ergonomics, safety, and musculoskeletal disorders. In doing so, a basic lexical search was performed on each key word individually, and again collectively within the online databases of Google Scholar, Scopus, and Web of Science. As seen below in Tables 1, 2 and 3, these represent the individual search results for each database where in Table 4 the results are shown for the collective search. Similarly, in Fig. 3, the data is represented graphically for the individual words while Fig. 4, represents the total search data results.

As seen in Tables 1, 2, 3 and 4 and Figs. 3 and 4, there is a large disparity between individual key word search and collective, indicating there may be discrepancies when identifying related terms in research of this topic. It can also be seen in Fig. 3 that there

Table 1. Summary of Search of 'Occupational Ergonomics' in Various Databases

Summary of Occupational Ergonomics in Various Databases	
Database	Number of Results
Google Scholar	1,010,000
Scopus	10,057
Web of Science	7,075

Table 2. Summary of Search of 'Safety in Various Databases

Summary of Safety in Various Databases	
Database	Number of Results
Google Scholar	4,890,000
Scopus	1,939,956
Web of Science	1,687,355

Table 3. Summary of Search of 'Musculoskeletal Disorders' in Various Databases

Summary of Musculoskeletal Disorders in Various Databases	
Database	Number of Results
Google Scholar	1,290,000
Scopus	44,446
Web of Science	43,822

may be a correlation between occupational ergonomics and musculoskeletal disorders. Lastly, it is evident that Google Scholar provides the greatest number of results while Scopus and Web of Science are relatively comparable.

2.2 Vicinitas Engagement Analysis

The first analysis performed in this report was using Vicinitas to understand trend results and how the identified key words are discussed in the community. Vicinitas is a software that partners with Twitter to analyze user information from the past ten days. To generate these results, key word 'workplace ergonomics' was used a synonym of 'occupational ergonomics' as this did not generate any results but can be concluded to be of similar prominence. Shown in Fig. 5, 91 users made 100 posts that resulted in an influence of over 790K+, indicating that this topic is of increasing interest. Additionally, further

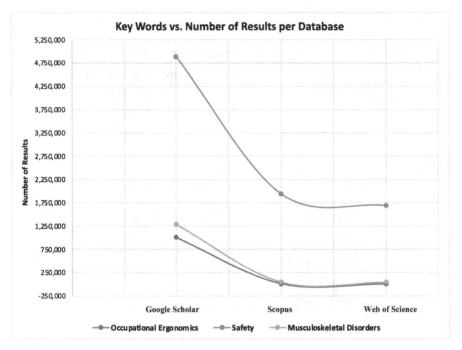

Fig. 3. Graphical Representation of Individual Key Word Search per Database

Table 4. Summary of Search for All Key Words in Various Databases

Summary of All Keywords Searched Together in Various Databases	
Database	Number of Results
Google Scholar	65,900
Scopus	607
Web of Science	910

supported in the graphs seen in Fig. 6, the engagement, and posts timeline both display a positive trend over this analysis period.

2.3 Google Ngram Analysis

Figures 7, 8, 9 and 10 represent an additional trend analysis as conducted through Google Ngram. The individual key words are mapped on Figs. 7, 8, 9 and Fig. 10 displays the results for all terms combined. Google Ngram is an online viewing analysis tool that charts frequencies of search terms using the annual count of n-grams within the printed sources. To generate these results, the year range for sources was defined to be from 2000 to 2019 (most recent year available) to ensure recent and reliable results/Seen in Fig. 7, there has been variable interest in the term 'Occupational Ergonomics' while

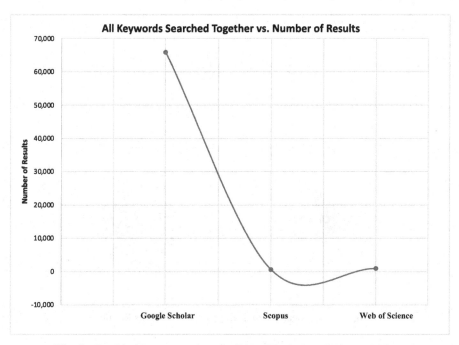

Fig. 4. Graphical Representation of All Key Words Searched per Database

Fig. 5. Vicinitas Engagement Analysis Results

there has been a slight decrease for terms like 'Safety' and 'Musculoskeletal Disorders'. Perhaps the most shocking result from this analysis is the variance between the key words when searched together. Demonstrated in Fig. 10, key word 'Safety' resulted in significantly greater analysis compared to 'Occupational Ergonomics' and 'Musculoskeletal Disorders'.

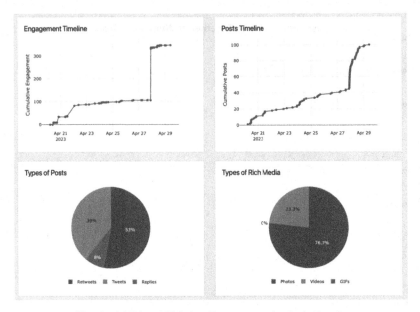

Fig. 6. Additional Vicinitas Engagement Analysis Results

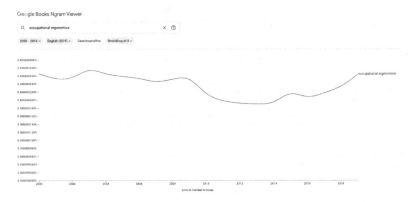

Fig. 7. Google Ngram Analysis for Key Word 'Occupational Ergonomics'

2.4 VOS Viewer Cluster Analysis

To further understand the topic of occupational ergonomics, a bibliometric cluster analysis was performed in VOS Viewer using key word 'Occupational Ergonomics'. Using data generated from Scopus, this resulted in 6,000+ related keywords and when threshold limits were added to show the top 1,000 words who had a minimum occurrence of five, the diagram in Fig. 11 was constructed. As seen in the figure, terms of significance that can be derived from this analysis include 'Ergonomics', 'Occupational Health', 'Musculoskeletal Disease', 'Occupational Risk', and others.

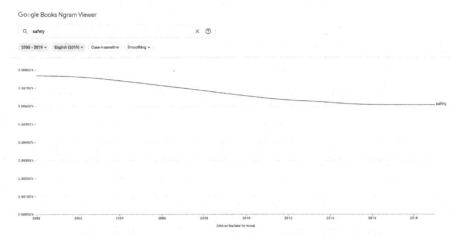

Fig. 8. Google Ngram Analysis for Key Word 'Safety'

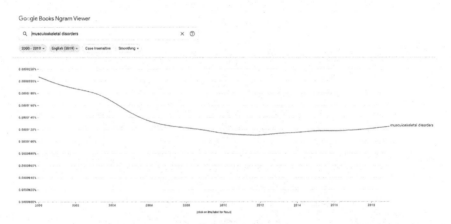

Fig. 9. Google Ngram Analysis for Key Word 'Musculoskeletal Disorders'

2.5 CiteSpace Cluster and Citation Burst Analysis

In addition to the VOS Viewer analysis seen in Fig. 12, an additional cluster map was created using CiteSpace, which identifies key groupings of terms within the data provided. In this analysis, 900+ sets of data were provided from Web of Science to generate the result seen above, resulting in important clusters including 'Health and Security Hazards', 'Musculoskeletal Pain', 'Vibration', 'Work-Related Musculoskeletal Disorders', and 'Risk Assessment'. Using these results, further research and analysis can be conducted on these related terms to better understand the field of occupational ergonomics. It is important to note that within these 900+ sources, CiteSpace has identified one reference that resulted in the strongest citation burst.

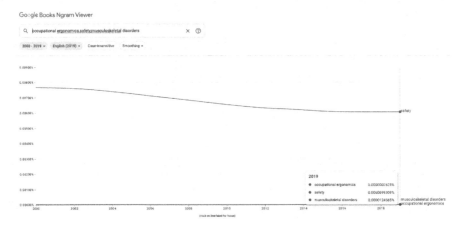

Fig. 10. Google Ngram Analysis for All Key Words Combined

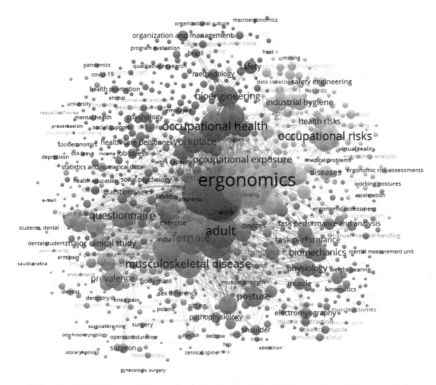

Fig. 11. VOS Viewer Cluster Analysis for Key Word 'Occupational Ergonomics'

2.6 MAXQDA Word Cloud and Trend Analysis

Following the cluster analysis, a word cloud was generated using MaxQDA to identify content topics of significance within seven leading articles in this field. These articles

Top 1 References with the Strongest Citation Bursts

References	Year	Strength	Begin	End	2013 - 2023
Wang D, 2015, J CONSTR ENG M, V141, P0, DOI 10.1061/(ASCE)CO.1943-7862.0000979, DOI	2015	3.09	2019	2020	

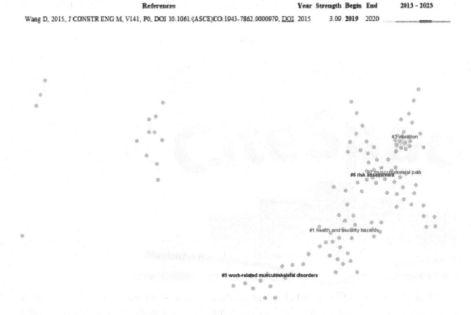

Fig. 12. CiteSpace Cluster Map with Citation Burst Analysis

Fig. 13. MaxQDA Word Cloud Analysis

were located through Google Scholar using key words 'Occupational Ergonomics', 'Safety', and 'Musculoskeletal Disorders'. To create a concise and fully representative word cloud, the minimum word occurrence in each article was set to 15 showing a total of 100 words. Seen in Fig. 13, these terms of influence include 'Ergonomics', 'Work', 'Study', 'Design', 'Health', 'Factors', 'Occupational', and many more (Fig. 14).

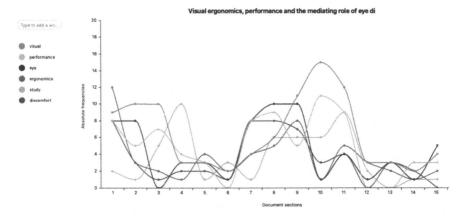

Fig. 14. MaxQDA Word Trend Analysis

Following the MaxQDA word cloud analysis, the same software was used to perform a word trend analysis on the identical set of data, displaying trends of key words within the articles. Seen in Fig. 13, six key terms were identified including 'Visual', 'Performance', 'Eye', 'Ergonomics', 'Study', and 'Discomfort'. Plotted against the number of sections they are apparent in within the data provided, this resulted in a graph that does not clearly display any correlation. From these results, it can be concluded that there are no individual or group of terms that correlate directly with occupational ergonomics.

2.7 Harzing and BibExcel Analysis

After a comprehensive literature review using software and techniques including engagement and trend, citation burst, and word cloud analysis, the final evaluation tool using in this project was conducted using BibExcel to create a leading table of authors publishing within the space of occupational ergonomics. To generate these results, a lexical search was performed in Harzing, and the results are shown in Fig. 16. BibExcel, a literature analysis tool used to evaluate the performance and impact of researchers, was then used to generate a leading table to researchers in this field. Using 100 results from the Harzing search which were limited to the years 2003 to 2023, this resulted in 44 individual authors of which one published three papers, eight wrote two, and the remaining one. Sorted using BibExcel to remove unnecessary information, this data was then inputted into Excel to create a PivotChart as seen in Fig. 17 (Fig. 15).

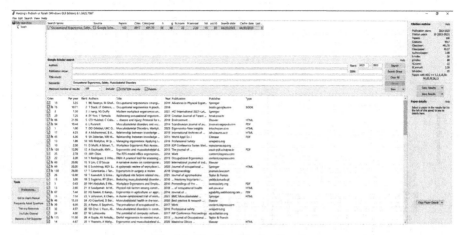

Fig. 15. Harzing Citation Results

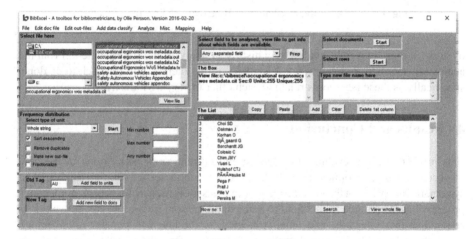

Fig. 16. BibExcel Analysis Using Harzing Data

3   Discussion and Analysis

Occupational ergonomics is an emerging topic of interest for researchers here and abroad. From understanding the various responsibilities of employees, to the environments these individuals operate in, to the risks and hazards they face, and even strategies in preventing these injuries, researchers have made significant progress in reducing musculoskeletal and related disorders, however, there is still important work to be done in decreasing the number of people facing these challenges globally.

Evaluating the various key words used in this analysis to better understand occupational ergonomics as a whole, it is clear that the term 'occupational ergonomics' is still in its infancy stages evidenced through the decreased number of articles and researchers in this field. However, 'safety' and 'musculoskeletal disorders' are both massive fields

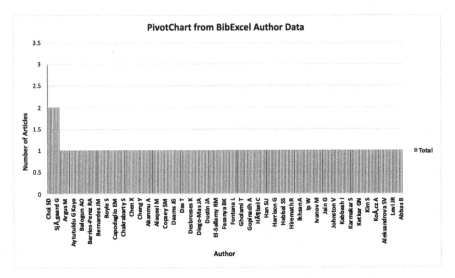

Fig. 17. Graphical Representation of BibExcel Leading Table Analysis

of study in their own right, with a long history of analysis and improvement. From the analyses performed in this project, it is apparent that there is still research to be done, specifically as these key words relate to each other in varying industries.

4 Results and Conclusion

This project seeks to evaluate the interest and current work being done in the field of occupational ergonomics through the lens of a bibliometric literature analysis and systematic review. Seen through the various analysis tools used in this report, tremendous progress has been made in this field to understand the root causes of risk, how workers respond to these hazards, and what strategies can be taken to prevent future injury. Throughout this analysis, several trends were identified, from the correlation of key words 'safety' and 'musculoskeletal disorders' to clustered terms in published articles, this report serves to provide a diverse and balanced perspective of ergonomics, particularly as it pertains to occupational safety and health.

5 Future Work

Despite the comprehensive analysis provided in this report, there is still future improvement to be done in this field, as seen through the continuous research efforts. Highlighted in Fig. 18 is a nearly $700,000 research grant awarded by the National Science Foundation to investigate the effects of worker-robot interactions in the construction industry and how they can be used to mitigate common work hazards. Awarded in 2021, this research is being conducted through San Diego State University and is scheduled to be completed by 2026. Similarly, as a result of this grant, the scholarly article seen in Fig. 19

Award Abstract # 2047138
CAREER: Co-Adaptation and Trust in Worker-Robot Interactions: Scalable Adoption of Collaborative Robots in Construction

NSF Org:	CMMI Div Of Civil, Mechanical, & Manufact Inn
Recipient:	SAN DIEGO STATE UNIVERSITY FOUNDATION
Initial Amendment Date:	March 22, 2021
Latest Amendment Date:	February 23, 2023
Award Number:	2047138
Award Instrument:	Standard Grant
Program Manager:	Alex Leonessa aleoness@nsf.gov (703)292-0000 CMMI Div Of Civil, Mechanical, & Manufact Inn ENG Directorate For Engineering
Start Date:	September 1, 2021
End Date:	August 31, 2026 (Estimated)
Total Intended Award Amount:	$691,328.00
Total Awarded Amount to Date:	$801,751.00
Funds Obligated to Date:	FY 2021 = $691,328.00 FY 2022 = $65,282.00 FY 2023 = $45,141.00
History of Investigator:	Reza Akhavian (Principal Investigator) rakhavian@sdsu.edu
Recipient Sponsored Research Office:	San Diego State University Foundation 5250 CAMPANILE DR MC1947 SAN DIEGO CA US 92182-1901 (619)594-5731
Sponsor Congressional District:	51
Primary Place of Performance:	San Diego State University 5500 Campanile Drive San Diego CA US 92182-1324
Primary Place of Performance Congressional District:	51
Unique Entity Identifier (UEI):	H59JKGFZKHL7

Fig. 18. NSF Award for Future Work in the Field of Occupational Ergonomics

was published. Written to understand the implications of using robots and new technology such as artificial intelligence and machine learning in the architecture, engineering, and construction industries, these researchers are evaluating the usages of technology and innovation in improving work safety and hazard mitigation. Seen through these recent research efforts, it can be concluded that the topic of occupational ergonomics remains prominent, significant to various industries, and will continue to result in future research and work.

Contents lists available at ScienceDirect

Automation in Construction

journal homepage: www.elsevier.com/locate/autcon

Review

Trustworthy AI and robotics: Implications for the AEC industry

Newsha Emaminejad [a], Reza Akhavian [b,*]

[a] *Department of Civil, Construction, and Environmental Engineering, San Diego State University, 5500 Campanile Dr., San Diego, CA 92182, USA*
[b] *Department of Civil, Construction, and Environmental Engineering, San Diego State University, 5500 Campanile Dr., San Diego, CA 92182, USA*

ARTICLE INFO

Keywords:
Artificial intelligence
robotics
AEC industry
trust
technology adoption

ABSTRACT

Human-technology interaction is concerned with trust as an inevitable user acceptance requirement. As the applications of artificial intelligence (AI) and robotics emerge in the architecture, engineering, and construction (AEC) industry, there is an immediate need to study trust in such systems. This paper presents the results of a systematic review of the literature published in the last two decades on (1) trust in AI and AI-powered robotics and (2) AI and robotics applications in the AEC industry. Through a thorough analysis, common trust dimensions are identified and the connections to the existing AEC applications are determined and discussed. Furthermore, major future directions on trustworthy AI and robotics in AEC research and practice are outlined. Findings indicate that although AEC researchers and industry professionals increasingly study and deploy AI and robotics, there is a lack of systematic research that studies key trust dimensions such as explainability, reliability, robustness, performance, and safety in the AEC context

Fig. 19. Research Article Published from NSF Future Work Award

References

1. Anwer, S., Li, H., Antwi-Afari, M.F., Wong, A.Y.L.: Associations between physical or psychosocial risk factors and work-related musculoskeletal disorders in construction workers based on literature in the last 20 years: a systematic review. Int. J. Ind. Ergon. **83**, 103113 (2021)
2. Aziz, F.A., Ghazalli, Z., Mohamed, N.M.Z.N., Isfar, A.: A future framework of knowledge-based ergonomics assessment system at workplace in automotive assembly plant. In: Goossens, R.H.M. (ed.) Advances in Social & Occupational Ergonomics. AISC, vol. 487, pp. 93–105. Springer, Cham (2017). https://doi.org/10.1007/978-3-319-41688-5_9
3. https://www.bls.gov/iif/factsheets/msds.htm
4. Broszkiewicz, R.: Affluence, occupational safety and ergonomics: are they interdependent? Int. J. Occup. Saf. Ergon. **22**(4), 577–579 (2016)
5. Chintada, A., Umasankar, V.: Improvement of productivity by implementing occupational ergonomics. J. Ind. Prod. Eng. **39**(1), 59–72 (2022)
6. Choi, S.D.: A study of trade-specific occupational ergonomics considerations in the US construction industry. Work **42**(2), 215–222 (2012)
7. Crawford, J.O.: Working until 70, government policy, economic need and the role of ergonomics and occupational health. In: International Congress Series, vol. 1280, pp. 29–34. Elsevier (2005)
8. Emaminejad, N., Akhavian, R.: Trustworthy AI and robotics: implications for the AEC industry. Autom. Constr. **139**, 104298 (2022)
9. Fasanya, B.K., Shofoluwe, M.: Occupational ergonomics: emerging approaches toward improved worker productivity and injury reduction. In: Goonetilleke, R.S., Karwowski, W. (eds.) AHFE 2018. AISC, vol. 789, pp. 385–395. Springer, Cham (2019). https://doi.org/10.1007/978-3-319-94484-5_40
10. Gangopadhyay, S.: Occupational ergonomics: a special domain for the benefit of workers' health. Indian J. Occup. Environ. Med. **26**(3), 135 (2022)

11. https://injuryfacts.nsc.org/work/costs/work-injury-costs/#:~:text=The%20total%20cost%20of%20work,administrative%20expenses%20of%20%2457.5%20billion
12. https://www.who.int/news-room/fact-sheets/detail/musculoskeletal-conditions
13. Jahangiri, H., Kazemi, R., Mokarami, H., Smith, A.: Visual ergonomics, performance and the mediating role of eye discomfort: a structural equation modelling approach. Int. J. Occup. Safety Ergon. **29**(3), 1075–1079 (2022). https://doi.org/10.1080/10803548.2022.2111885
14. Karwowski, W., Marras, W.S. (eds.): The Occupational Ergonomics Handbook. CRC Press, Boca Raton (1998)
15. Kaur, H., et al.: Workers' compensation claim rates and costs for musculoskeletal disorders related to overexertion among construction workers—Ohio, 2007–2017. Morbidity Mortality Weekly Rep. **70**(16), 577 (2021)
16. Keyserling, W.M., Chaffin, D.B.: Occupational ergonomics-methods to evaluate physical stress on the job. Ann. Rev. Public Health **7**(1), 77–104 (1986). https://doi.org/10.1146/annurev.pu.07.050186.000453
17. Lim, S., D'Souza, C.: A narrative review on contemporary and emerging uses of inertial sensing in occupational ergonomics. Int. J. Ind. Ergon. **76**, 102937 (2020)
18. Palikhe, S., Yirong, M., Choi, B.Y., Lee, D.-E.: Analysis of musculoskeletal disorders and muscle stresses on construction workers' awkward postures using simulation. Sustainability **12**(14), 5693 (2020). https://doi.org/10.3390/su12145693
19. Ruiz-Real, J.L., Uribe-Toril, J., De Pablo Valenciano, J., Gázquez-Abad, J.C.: Worldwide research on circular economy and environment: a bibliometric analysis. Int. J. Environ. Res. Public Health **15**(12), 2699 (2018). https://doi.org/10.3390/ijerph15122699
20. Sanjog, J., Patel, T., Karmakar, S.: Occupational ergonomics research and applied contextual design implementation for an industrial shop-floor workstation. Int. J. Ind. Ergon. **72**, 188–198 (2019). https://doi.org/10.1016/j.ergon.2019.05.009
21. Schwartz, A., et al.: Janitor ergonomics and injuries in the safe workload ergonomic exposure project (SWEEP) study. Appl. Ergon. **81**, 102874 (2019)
22. Smets, M.: A field evaluation of arm-support exoskeletons for overhead work applications in automotive assembly. IISE Trans. Occup. Ergon. Human Fact. **7**(3–4), 192–198 (2019)
23. Stack, T., Ostrom, L.T., Wilhelmsen, C.A.: Occupational Ergonomics: A Practical Approach. John Wiley & Sons, Hoboken (2016)
24. Svendsen, M.J., Schmidt, K.G., Holtermann, A., Rasmussen, C.D.N.: Expert panel survey among occupational health and safety professionals in Denmark for prevention and handling of musculoskeletal disorders at workplaces. Safety Sci. **131**, 104932 (2020). https://doi.org/10.1016/j.ssci.2020.104932
25. Taifa, I.W.R.: A student-centred design approach for reducing musculoskeletal disorders in India through Six Sigma methodology with ergonomics concatenation. Safety Sci. **147**, 105579 (2022). https://doi.org/10.1016/j.ssci.2021.105579
26. Upasani, S., Franco, R., Niewolny, K., Srinivasan, D.: The potential for exoskeletons to improve health and safety in agriculture—perspectives from service providers. IISE Trans. Occup. Ergon. Human Fact. **7**(3–4), 222–229 (2019)

Ergonomics in Transportation Vehicles: A Comprehensive RAMSIS Study on Design Optimization for Enhanced Comfort and Safety

Ritika Hada and Vincent G. Duffy[(✉)]

Purdue University, West Lafayette, IN 47906, USA
{rhada,duffy}@purdue.edu

Abstract. Ergonomics is a critical factor in the design of transportation vehicles, as it can significantly impact comfort, safety, and overall user experience. This study aims to conduct a systematic review of the current literature on the topic of ergonomics in transportation vehicles and to perform an in-depth RAMSIS analysis of the design optimization process. The study will explore the various factors driving the importance of ergonomics in transportation vehicles and the initiatives being undertaken to address this challenge. The review will also examine the role of human factors and ergonomics (HFE) and human-computer interaction (HCI) communities in developing user-centered design methodologies, advanced interfaces, and simulation tools for transportation systems. Furthermore, the study will analyze the use of RAMSIS software in evaluating the ergonomics of transportation vehicle designs and optimizing the design process for enhanced comfort and safety. The systematic review will be based on a comprehensive search of relevant databases and will include both qualitative and quantitative studies. The study findings will provide valuable insights into the current state of research on ergonomics in transportation vehicles and will highlight the importance of design optimization for enhancing comfort and safety.

Keywords: RAMSIS · Ergonomics · Design optimization · Transportation vehicles · Safety

1 Introduction and Background

The objective of this study is to optimize the design of transportation vehicles for enhanced comfort and safety by applying a comprehensive RAMSIS analysis of ergonomics. Through this analysis, various design changes can be made to improve the overall ergonomic conditions of vehicle seats, pedals, and steering wheels, as well as ensure that back seats can accommodate a wide range of body types. The analysis also includes sight and reflection analysis to reduce glare and improve visibility for passengers. The goal of this study is to create transportation vehicles that are safer, more comfortable, and better suited to a wide range of human body types and sizes.

© The Author(s), under exclusive license to Springer Nature Switzerland AG 2023
V. G. Duffy et al. (Eds.): HCII 2023, LNCS 14057, pp. 20–42, 2023.
https://doi.org/10.1007/978-3-031-48047-8_2

1.1 Transportation and Ergonomics

Vehicles, whether they be cars, buses, trains, or planes, are essential to modern society. They allow people to move quickly and efficiently from one place to another, but they can also cause discomfort and even injury to passengers and operators if they are not designed with ergonomics in mind. Ergonomics is the science of designing tools, machines, and systems to fit the human body and maximize efficiency, comfort, and safety. In transportation, omics are crucial for the well-being of passengers and operators, who spend hours sitting or standing in confined spaces.

Research has shown that poor ergonomics in vehicles can lead to musculoskeletal disorders, such as back pain, neck pain, and shoulder pain. For example, long-distance truck drivers are at high risk of developing lower back pain due to prolonged sitting posture and lack of lumbar support.

Designers of vehicles should prioritize ergonomics to ensure the well-being of passengers and operators. This involves considering posture, support, accessibility, vibration, and noise, as well as lighting and climate in the design process. Seats and controls should encourage a relaxed posture and provide proper support to different body sizes and shapes. Controls should be easily reachable and operated without requiring excessive force or awkward postures. Excessive vibration and noise should be minimized, and adequate lighting and climate control are necessary to ensure a comfortable and safe environment. By incorporating these principles, transportation vehicles can provide a safer, more comfortable, and more efficient mode of transportation.

2 Research Methodology

2.1 Literature Review

Ergonomics is a crucial factor to consider while designing transportation vehicles since it greatly impacts user comfort, safety, and overall experience. A rising number of people are now interested in using RAMSIS software to assess the ergonomics of transportation vehicle designs and to streamline the design process for increased comfort and safety. RAMSIS was used in a study by Kuo et al. (2015) to assess the ergonomics of a bus driver's workspace and pinpoint potential improvement areas, like the gear shift and steering wheel placement. RAMSIS was utilized in a different study by Marler et al. (2016) to optimize the design of an agricultural tractor cabin, which increased operator comfort and decreased tiredness.

Much attention has been paid to developing user-centered design techniques for transportation systems in addition to using RAMSIS. For instance, Stanton et al.'s (2017) work emphasized the value of integrating users in the design process and identified a number of user-centered design techniques that can be applied to enhance the ergonomic design of transportation systems. The ergonomics of transportation vehicles have also been significantly improved by the introduction of cutting-edge interfaces and displays. The use of touchscreens in vehicle cabins was explored in the study by Ahlström et al. (2018), and it was discovered that when they are thoughtfully built, they can increase user productivity and enjoyment.

In tackling the issue of ergonomics in transportation vehicles, the human factors and ergonomics (HFE) and human-computer interaction (HCI) communities have a well-established role. The research by Smith-Jackson et al. (2016) highlighted the significance of incorporating HFE into the design of transportation systems and outlined different HFE concepts that may be used to enhance ergonomics in transportation vehicles.

Overall, the literature emphasizes the significance of design optimization for boosting comfort and safety as well as the crucial function of ergonomics in transportation vehicles. Creating more user-friendly, effective, and safe transportation systems can benefit from the application of RAMSIS software, user-centered design techniques, cutting-edge interfaces and displays, and the incorporation of HFE principles into the design process.

2.2 Data Collection

At the initial stage of conducting the literature review, multiple databases were searched using similar search terms. It is worth noting that the terms "efficiency" and "productivity" were sometimes used interchangeably in the search. Table 1 presents the databases that were searched, the corresponding search terms used, and the resulting outcomes.

Table 1. Database search table for Scopus, Dimensions, and SpringerLink with search term

Search Term	Database		
	Scopus	ProQuest	Google Scholar
"Ergonomics"	54,883	218,416	1,880,000
"RAMSIS"	128	3037	6410
"Safety"	1,937,841	43,313,401	4,960,000
"Transportation Vehicles"	109,302	4,055,454	4,380,000
"Design Optimization"	569,693	1,792,241	6,230,000

2.3 Trend Analysis

The trend analysis for this topic is completed on Scopus and nGram Viewer. When analyzing search results, the publishing year was filtered from 1970–2023 in Scopus and from 1980–2019 in nGram Viewer.

Figure 1(A) shows the results from the Scopus search stating how a lot of research was done on the safety and ergonomics of transportation vehicles. Figure 1(B) shows significant study was done by researchers in the engineering and computer science disciplines (Fig. 2).

2.4 Relevant Statistics

"Leading" lists are useful for identifying the most influential authors, journals, universities, and other entities that publish articles related to a specific topic. BibExcel software

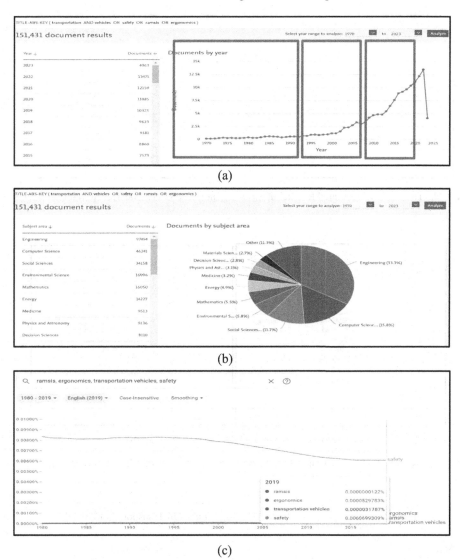

Fig. 1. (a) Trend analysis for "Ergonomics and Safety in Transportation Vehicles" from 1970 to Present on Scopus, (b) Documents on "Ergonomics and Safety in Transportation Vehicles" across subject areas. (c) N-Gram Viewer Results for the Keywords- RAMSIS, Human Modeling Design, and Ergonomics Bibliometric Analysis

with metadata obtained from Google Scholar via Harzing was used to create such lists, researchers used. Also, Scopus analytics provides insights into the leading documents by country and authors (Fig. 3, Table 2 and 3).

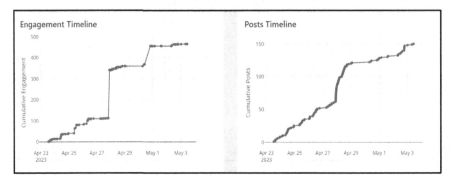

Fig. 2. The timeline generated for Vicinitas for Ergonomics, Safety, and Transportation vehicles

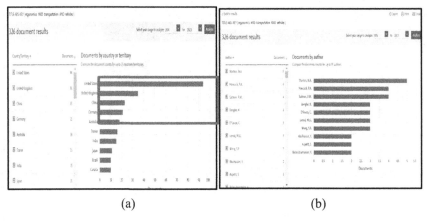

(a)   (b)

Fig. 3. (A) Leading countries and (B) authors working in the area of "Ergonomics in Transportation Vehicles"

Table 2. Leading Table of Authors for Ergonomics in Transportation Vehicles

Authors	Years	No of Articles
NA Stanton	1998–2019	13
J.D. Lee	2001–2012	10
L.N. Boyle	2006–2017	8
B. Donmez	2008–2018	7
WJ Horrey	2007–2014	7

Table 3. Leading Table of Institutes for Work on Ergonomics in Transportation Vehicles

Institutes	Years	No of Articles
University of Iowa	1996–2013	18
Universite Gustave Eiffel	2002–2021	16
Monash University	1980–2020	15
Loughborough University	1980–2019	14
Technical University of Munich	2002–2021	14

3   Results

3.1   Co-citation Analysis

A co-citation analysis was conducted using Web of Sciences in VOS Viewer software. Co-citation analysis is an important bibliometric technique that allows researchers to analyze the relationships and influence among scholarly works (Figs. 4 and 5).

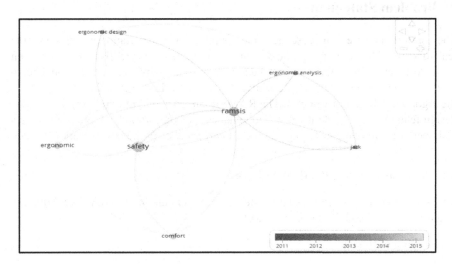

Fig. 4. Network Visualization in VOS Viewer with Web of Science search result

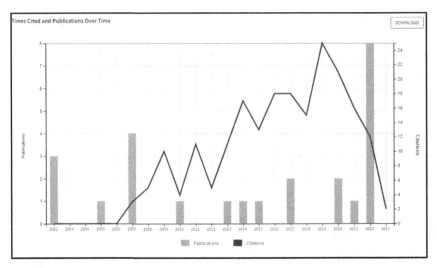

Fig. 5. Network Visualization in VOS Viewer with Web of Science search result

4 Problem Statement

The comfort and safety of passengers and operators in transportation vehicles are critical concerns. The poor ergonomic design of vehicles can lead to discomfort and even musculoskeletal disorders, resulting in decreased productivity and increased healthcare costs. To address this issue, it is essential to conduct a RAMSIS analysis to evaluate the ergonomic design of vehicles. The RAMSIS analysis will provide insights into the design features that can be improved to enhance the comfort and safety of passengers and operators, thereby improving the overall performance of the transportation system.

4.1 Analysis Through RAMSIS Software

This section covers the entire step-by-step process for running the RAMSIS Software as guided by Andre and Martin in the lecture.

A. **Loading of the car**

   In this step, the "Future Car Model" that was provided by Andre and the team was loaded into the RAMSIS system (Fig. 6).

B. **Create Boundary Manikins, reposition boundary manikin(s), and locate manikin(s) in vehicle seats**

   The first step towards analyzing the geometry is using the Bodybuilder function to create different manikins. Six different Manikins were created i.e., 5th percentile Female, 50th percentile Female, 95th percentile Female, 5th percentile Male, 50th percentile Male and 95th percentile. Figure 8 shows 5th percentile Females, 50th percentile Males, and 95th percentile Males.

Fig. 6. Loading the initial setup Car file on the RAMSIS tool

Procedure- Ideally there are two ways of creating Manikins- using the prebuilt Manikins (with pre-defined torso) or using the bodybuilder feature. We used the latter as it enabled us to choose by "Value" in the bodybuilder feature. Below are the key steps highlighted-

1. We used the "Project Manager" plugin, Role definition i.e. Driver, "Bodybuilder" plugin, "Anthropometric" database, Typology, and Control Measurements (shown below) to create the Manikins.
2. Used "Next Gen- Define Restriction" and "Posture calculation" to create restrictions for Manikin. (Shown in Fig. 7 below). This was required to place Manikin inside the car and was done for both driver and passenger.
3. We also visualized through the skin lines for a better understanding of their posture.
4. Save the session in a new folder.

NextGen - Restriction Overview (Max_perc_Male-Passenger)										
Target	Limit Surface	Fixations	Direction	Pelvis Rotation	Pelvis Translation		Torso Angle	Joint	Manu	
	Manikin Comp.	Env. Object	Tangentiality	Status	Distance	Optional ID		Condition		
1	H-point	sgrp_rear_r	Off	active	0.0 mm	-------	-------			
2	LeftHeel	floor	Off	active	0.0 mm	-------	-------			
3	RightHeel	floor	Off	active	0.0 mm	-------	-------			
4	LeftBall	floor	Off	active	0.0 mm	-------	-------			
5	RightBall	floor	Off	active	0.0 mm	-------	-------			

Posture Calculation...   Define Restriction...   Close

Fig. 7. Defining typology and restriction overview of the Manikins in RAMSIS

Significance- Creating different Manikins helped us understand the utility of different equipment and features in the car model and design a more universal design (Fig. 8).

C. **Evaluating the location and comfort and doing adjustments for the seat, pedal position, and steering wheel for enhanced comfort**

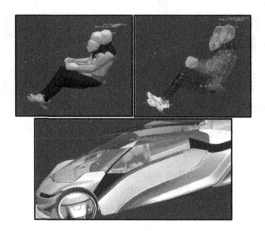

Fig. 8. Duplicating the Manikins to create a driver and a passenger

As we can see from the figure above, the driver has been positioned in the car but is not comfortable owing to many reasons- the seat is very back for the 5th percentile Female due to which she has to sit on the edge of the chair, low space between the head of 50% Male and the ceiling of the car which means they will easily hit the roof in case of any jerks in the car. In other words, the setup defined is not reachable for the Manikins. They should be shifted a bit closer to the steering wheel translating into a reachability envelope which will improve the Ergonomics and overall comfort for the Manikin.

The below images show the changes that were done to the car equipment positioning to enhance the comfort of the driver.

D. **Readjustment of Seat, Pedal, and Steering wheel (shift wheel and run posture)**

a) Moving the steering wheel towards Manekin 100 mm in the x-axis (Relatively/Vector)- As seen in the case of the 5th percentile female, she has to sit on the edge of the seat to access the steering wheel and also has to lean back to rest on the back. Hence, the first change done was moving the steering wheel forward 100 mm in the x-axis (relatively/ Vector). After this, "Posture Calculation" was re-run so that the Manekin re-adjusts itself.

The figure below highlights (a) Before the position of Manekin (b) the Readjustment of the steering wheel and (c) the post-re-adjustment position of Manekin (d) the post-re-adjustment of All active Manikins (Fig. 9).

b) Adjusting the Pedal and seat to enhance it for the female
Post steering wheel re-adjustment, repositioning was done for the pedal and seat in the below form-

i. Shifted the Seat upwards and forward (across the x-axis and z-axis) to make it more upright.
ii. Shifted the Pedal and Footrest backward (Accel_de_centerline) by 90mm each.

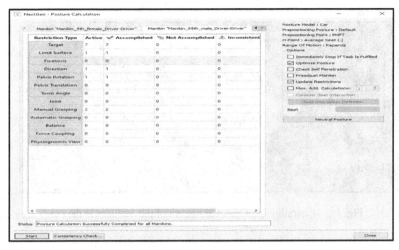

Fig. 9. Illustrating Adjustment analysis of the Manikin in the RAMSIS tool

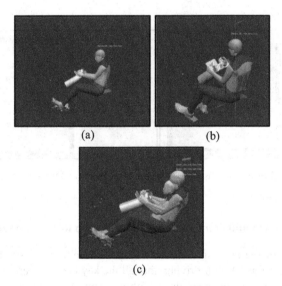

(c)

Fig. 10. The figure highlights (a) Before positioning of Manekin (b) the Readjustment of the steering wheel and (c) the post-re-adjustment position of Manekin post-re-adjustment of All active Manikins

The procedure for doing this was similar to the last readjustment, i.e., change the position using the toolbar, Run "Posture calculation" and review "Comfort" in the Analysis tool. Figure 10 below signifies the original position and post-adjustment position for a uniform comparison (Fig. 11 and 12).

c) Comfort analysis (Reduced from Shoulders, Right leg, and left leg area)- The impact of the above rearrangements was analyzed through the "Comfort" feature within the "Analysis" tab. The figure below shows the Comfort analysis before and after the

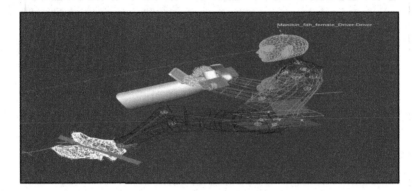

Fig. 11. Illustrating the Final Adjustment of the Manikin in the car

re-positioning to assess the impact. As we can see from the Figure below, the comfort has increased for the Shoulders, Right leg, and Left leg area.

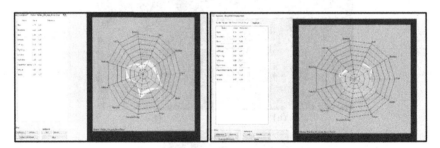

Fig. 12. Illustrating "Comfort Analysis" for Manikins

E. **Evaluate the reach and comfort of the touch screen for the passenger**

The next part of the analysis is to review the reachability of the driver Manikin. It's crucial for the safety of their driving, that all the key elements are well within their reach. Hence, an analysis has been done with an example of the touch screen or the display dashboard. Using the "Pre-defined reach envelopes", we have done the "Reach analysis" to analyze the present state. As demonstrated in Fig. 13, a major section of the display dashboard is outside the reach of all Manikins, especially 5% of females. Owing to the shorter torso, she's significantly outside the reach of the dashboard as compared to 50% & 95% of males.

This implies, that, to reach the display board/ control panel, the driver will have to lean to a great extent which will pose a serious threat to safety.

a) Defining a comfortable reach- Post reviewing the current challenges with reachability, we defined a "Comfort" reach in which the driver will not have to stretch their arm completely and easily access the features of the control panel. Our reach goes from the

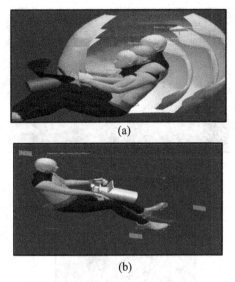

Fig. 13. The figure illustrates (a) the dashboard is out of reach for the Manikin. (b) Manikins reach on various installments within the car

shoulder joint to the middle finger joint (maximum reach including shoulder movement) which ensures better comfort (Fig. 14).

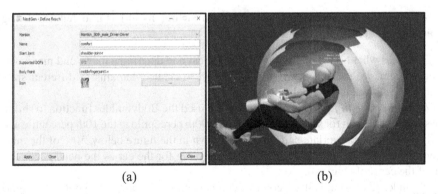

Fig. 14. (a) Defining reach for the Manikin. (b) Applying Adjustment points to the Manikin in the car

b) Shifting the control panel to move within the comfortable reach - To address these reachability challenges, changes were made to the position of the control panel so that it falls within the comfortable reach. The control panel was shifted in the x and y axis (towards the driver) so that she can reach a major part of it without leaning or reclining. Doing this translation of the Control panel, we can see through the figures below that it now falls within the reachability of all the manikins (Fig. 15).

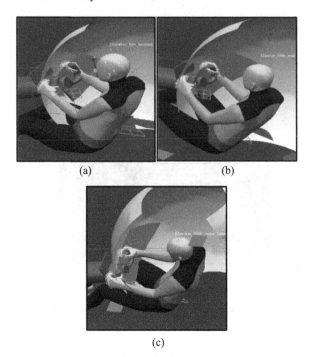

Fig. 15. (a), (b), (c) Manikins can reach the dashboard post adjustment

F. Determining the maximum percentile in sitting height (torso length) being accommodated in the rear seat

To assess what body heights can fit into the car and determine the % and maximum sitting height, we use the Bodybuilder function to create Manikins of different sizes using the Anthropometric tool.

a) Finding the fit for Male passengers- We used the Bodybuilder function to shrink the size of the person for sizes ranging from the 90th percentile to the 10th percentile and analyzed for the appropriate percentile. As shown in the figure below, 50% of the male is not fitting into the car. It reflects that he is too big for the car as the head is coming out of the car roof (Fig. 16).

To understand what is the recommended percentile, the person's typology (height) was reduced to 30%–10%. Figure A, B, and C below show that C i.e. 10th percentile Male is a good fit for the car as only he can fit properly (Fig. 17).

b) Finding the fit for female passengers- We used the Bodybuilder function to shrink the size of the Females for sizes ranging from the 90th percentile to the 50th percentile and analyzed for the appropriate percentile. As shown in the figure below, 75% of females are fitting into the car. Additionally, a more comfortable percentile seems to be 50% as shown below (Fig. 18).

c) Scale the car to fit the person

As we saw that only the 10th percentile of Males and ~ 70% of Females are a good fit for the car, we can scale the car "Uniformly" to adjust it according to the Manekin.

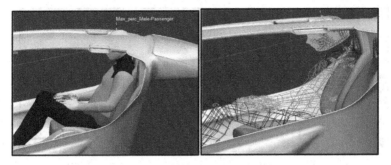

Fig. 16. Illustrating Male Passenger is too big for the car

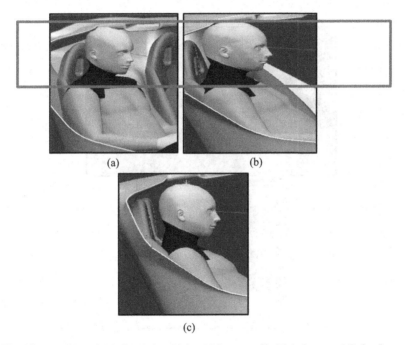

(a)   (b)

(c)

Fig. 17. (a), (b), and (c) shows that (c) i.e. 10th percentile Male is a good fit for the car

The figure above shows how the car has been scaled up uniformly to adjust the Manekin (Fig. 19).

G. **Evaluate the visibility (obstructions and acuity) of the instrument cluster for the driver**

The procedure followed for evaluating the visibility is- Creating a point on screen-> Move eye to focus on the point > Vision Analysis within the Cognitive plugin. The figure below shows the left and right eye view of the driver and the passenger respectively (Fig. 20).

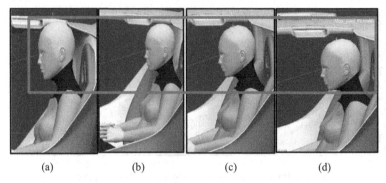

(a)   (b)   (c)   (d)

Fig. 18. (a), (b), and (c), (d) show that (d) 50th percentile Female is a good fit for the car

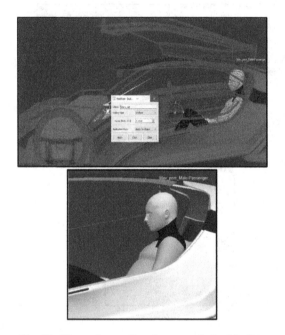

Fig. 19. Illustrating scaling the car to fit the Manikin

a) Sight Analysis- This was achieved by using "Sightlimits" to understand the obstruction created by the steering wheel (as shown by the yellow sight cone in image 1). It is done to check whether the driver can see the display clearly or is getting behind the steering wheel.

The figure below shows how to set "Sight Limits" i.e. when the driver is viewing directly at the new point created on the control panel, is there any portion that is getting blocked by the steering wheel? It builds the Sightcones that provides insight into the vision which is getting blocked due to the steering wheel (Fig. 21).

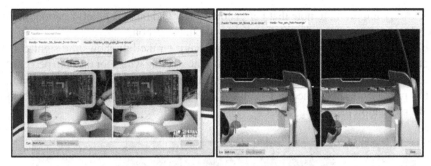

Fig. 20. Illustrating Visibility Analysis of Manikins

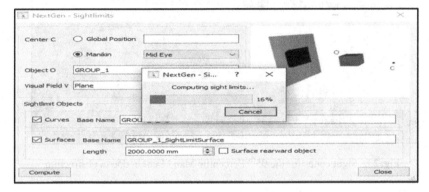

Fig. 21. Adjusting sight limits for the Manikin

b) Sight analysis for 5th percentile Female- The figure on the left shows the sight cones which are being created due to the obstruction of the steering wheel for the 5th percentile female (Fig. 22).

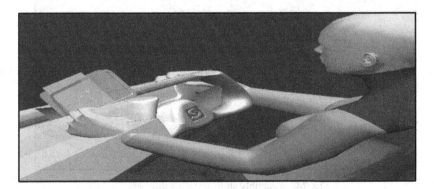

Fig. 22. Sight cones for the Manikin

It is very important to note that her vision is clear and there is no obstruction on the control panel. This shows there is no problem with the vision.

c) Sight analysis for 95% of Males- The figure on the left shows the sight cones which are being created due to the obstruction of the steering wheel for the 95th percentile male. It is very important to note that his vision is not clear getting obstruction on the control panel. This shows there is a problem with the vision and the driver is not able to see the navigation panel (Fig. 23).

Fig. 23. Sight cones for the 95th Percentile Man Manikin due to obstruction

d) Shifting the display board up to clear Vision for the 95th percentile Male- Shifting the assembly of the display panel and the steering gear upwards enables a clear vision of the 95th percentile male. The sight cones are now being formed below the steering wheel and not obstructing his vision (Fig. 24).

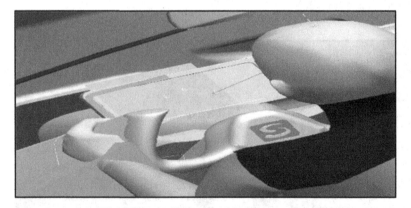

Fig. 24. Assembly shift of the display panel

H. Acuity analysis

The acuity analysis's purpose is to see what should be the sizes of the characters on the display board. It shows three features- Acceptable, Recommended, and Minimum. All three have been created here for two Manikins i.e., 5th percentile Female and 95th percentile Male. And the figure below shows the difference between both. Here we can also see that the line of vision is pointed at the mirror. As we see in the figure below, the size of the character increased in seconds. The big torso male mostly sits at the back i.e. positioned at the back of the seat. Hence, we see that the character size required for readability is more (Fig. 25).

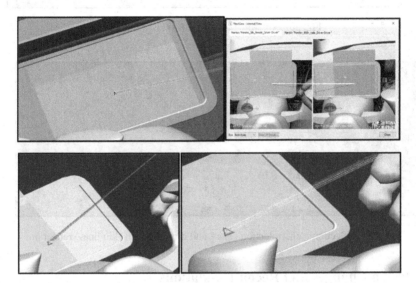

Fig. 25. Illustrating readability of characters by the Male Manikin

I. Reflection analysis

There are two kinds of reflections- Night time reflection and daytime reflection.

a) Night-time reflection -Here the emitting light source resides inside the vehicle. It gets reflected inside from the display to the windshield and finally hits the driver's eye as shown below (Fig. 26).

b) Daytime reflection- Daytime reflections mean the reflection that occurs during the daytime. The source of light is outside the car (Rear window in this case). The light travels from the rear window and reflects through the display glass. The figure below shows the reflection path, reflection cones, and driver's (with skin lines) reflection (Figs. 27, 28, 29 and 30).

c) Rotation to reduce the obstruction from reflection- Since it creates discomfort, we rotated the display panel to reduce the reflection to the driver's eye. This will enable them to see the display panel. As seen below, we have rotated the geometry which reduces the light entering the car.

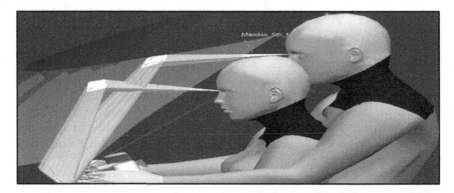

Fig. 26. Nighttime reflection for the Manikins

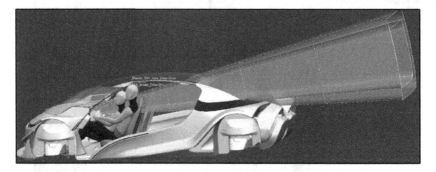

Fig. 27. Reflection path, reflection cones, and driver's (with skin lines) reflection

5   Design Changes and Recommendations

To enhance the ergonomic conditions of transportation vehicles there should be multiple factors that could be considered to make the solution robust. There are multiple transportation systems like cars, heavy-duty vehicles, military vehicles, aircraft, and ships. Each of these transportation vehicles should be designed to accommodate the climatic conditions, environment, terrain, and countries they are being used in. It also boils down to the nature of the job being done while using these transportation vehicles. The pedal adjustment, steering wheel, and seat cushion all contribute to the ergonomics and the comfort of the driver and the passengers. These factors need to be additionally kept in mind while designing the system.

6   Discussion

As a computer science engineer with a background in the oil and gas industry, my focus has primarily been on developing software solutions. However, an assignment on safety engineering challenged me to explore a new subject outside of my area of expertise. This experience pushed me beyond my comfort zone and required me to learn

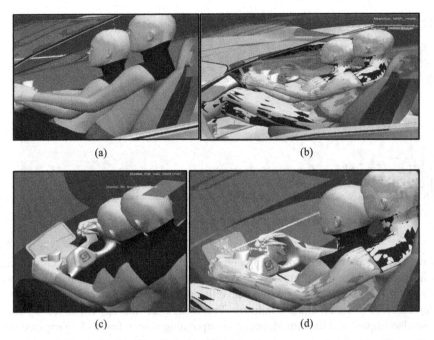

Fig. 28. **(a)**, **(b)**, **(c)**, **(d)**: Illustrating the reflections geometry for the Manikins

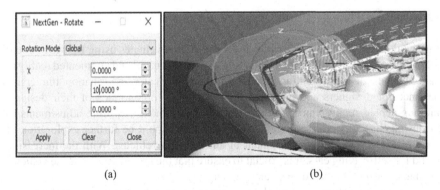

Fig. 29. (a) Defining rotation axis (b) Illustrating the impact of change in rotation

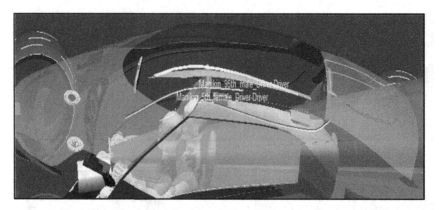

Fig. 30. Illustrating the final impact of change in geometry

a new perspective on human modeling and the significance of considering ergonomic conditions during the design process. I gained a comprehensive understanding of how tools like RAMSIS can improve safety and efficiency in various industrial applications, including those in the oil and gas industry. This experience not only expanded my skill set but also emphasized the importance of incorporating human factors into engineering design.

7 Future Work

Future work in the field of Ergonomics in transportation vehicles using RAMSIS could involve the integration of advanced technologies such as virtual and augmented reality to enhance the design and evaluation process. Virtual reality can provide a more immersive experience for designers and engineers to evaluate the ergonomics of their designs, while augmented reality can help them visualize and make real-time adjustments to their designs in a physical setting. Additionally, there could be further exploration of the use of RAMSIS in the development of autonomous vehicles. With the increasing demand for self-driving cars, it is crucial to ensure that the ergonomics of these vehicles are suitable for both human drivers and passengers.

A sample project topic related to this field could be "Ergonomic Design of Autonomous Vehicle Interiors Using RAMSIS and Virtual Reality". This project could explore the use of RAMSIS and virtual reality in the design of autonomous vehicle interiors that are comfortable, safe, and efficient for passengers and human drivers. A relevant source obtained from NSF.gov is a grant awarded to the University of Michigan for research on "Human Factors of Automated Driving". This project aims to investigate the human factors and human-machine interaction involved in the development of automated vehicles, with a focus on safety, comfort, and trust. The project could potentially use RAMSIS in the evaluation and design of ergonomic features for automated vehicles.

References

1. Beatty, J.: Task-evoked pupillary responses, processing load, and the structure of processing resources. Psychol. Bull. **91**, 276 (1982)
2. Brackel, T.: Adaptive Control of Flexible Workshop Production Systems: Use of Modern Information and Communication Technologies for Efficient Production Control Under Real-Time Conditions. Gabler Verlag, Wiesbaden (2009)
3. Breese, J.T., Fuhrmann, A.M., Duffy, V.G., Luebke, A.: Developing ergonomic design recommendations using human-centric RAMSIS analysis. In: Duffy, V.G., Rau, PL.P. (eds) HCI International 2022 – Late Breaking Papers: Ergonomics and Product Design. HCII 2022. Lecture Notes in Computer Science, vol. 13522. Springer, Cham (2022). https://doi.org/10.1007/978-3-031-21704-3_7
4. Bretschneider-Hagemes, M., Korfmacher, S., Lipinski, K.R.: The role of standardization for occupational safety and health (OSH) and the design of safe and healthy human-computer interaction (HCI). In: Duffy, V.G. (ed.) DHM 2018. LNCS, vol. 10917, pp. 19–28. Springer, Cham (2018). https://doi.org/10.1007/978-3-319-91397-1_2
5. Broy, M. (ed.): Cyber-physical systems. In: Innovation through Software-Intensive Embedded Systems, pp. 17–32. Springer, Berlin (2010)
6. Buchner, A., Baumgartner, N.: Text-background polarity affects performance irrespective of ambient illumination and colour contrast. Ergonomics **50**(7), 1036–1063 (2007)
7. Buettner, R.: Cognitive workload of humans using artificial intelligence systems: towards objective measurement applying eye-tracking technology. In: Timm, I.J., Thimm, M. (eds.) KI 2013. LNCS (LNAI), vol. 8077, pp. 37–48. Springer, Heidelberg (2013). https://doi.org/10.1007/978-3-642-40942-4_4
8. Byers, C., Bittner, C., Hill, G., Zaklad, L., Christ, E.: Workload assessment of a remotely piloted vehicle (RPV) system. In: Proceedings of the Human Factors Society 32nd Annual Meeting, pp. 1145–1149. Human Factors and Ergonomics Society, Santa Monica (1988)
9. Cegarra, J., Chevalier, A.: Theoretical and methodological considerations in the comparison of performance and physiological measure of mental workload. In: Harris, D. (ed.) Engineering Psychology and Cognitive Ergonomics. 7th International Conference, EPCE 2007 (2007)
10. Duffy, V.G.: Chapter 29, Digital Human Modeling in Design. The Handbook of Human Factors and Ergonomics titled "Human Digital Modeling in Design", 5th edn, pp. 761–781 (2012)
11. Chapter 8, Social and Organizational Foundation of Ergonomics: Multi-Level Systems Approaches. Of the Handbook of Human Factors and Ergonomics titled "Human Digital Modeling in Design", 5th edn, pp. 227–235 (2012)
12. Brauer, L.: Environmental and occupational ergonomics. In: Safety and Heal (2014)
13. Erol, R., Ozkan, T.: Ergonomic design of a cabin for a construction equipment. J. Constr. Eng. Manag. **145**(8), 04019050 (2019)
14. Etezadi-Amoli, J., Babalhavaeji, F., Sharifi, M.: Ergonomic evaluation of driver's seat in off-road vehicles. Int. J. Ind. Ergon. **58**, 1–8 (2017)
15. Gómez-Jacinto, L., Monsalve-Jáimez, J.: Ergonomic evaluation of the driving posture of truck drivers in Colombia. Transp. Res. F: Traffic Psychol. Behav. **73**, 223–234 (2020)
16. Hocker, A., Duffy, V.G.: Boundary comfort: A RAMSIS perspective. In: Duffy, V.G., Rau, PL.P. (eds.) HCI International 2022 – Late Breaking Papers: Ergonomics and Product Design. HCII 2022 (2022)
17. Kuo, T., Simeonov, P., Mokhtarzadeh, H.: Effect of seat position on driver injury risk in rear-end crashes: a RAMSIS study. Traffic Inj. Prev. **16**(6), 557–564 (2015)
18. Modeling Safety Criticality in Aviation Maintenance Operations to Support Mastery of Human Factors Linking Context to Evaluation in the Design of Safety Critical Interfaces

19. National Science Foundation. Award Abstract #1939889 Collaborative Research: Advancing Understanding of Disturbance Interactions and Nutrient Cycling in the Face of Global Change in Northern Hardwood Forests. Accessed 4 May 2023

20. Brauer, L.: Occupational biomechanics and human factors engineering. In: Safety and Health for Engineers, 3rd edn., p. 235. John Wiley & Sons, Inc. (2014)

21. Parasuraman, R.: Designing automation for human use: empirical studies and quantitative models. Ergonomics **43**(7), 931–951 (2000)

22. Salvendy, G., Karwowski, W.: Handbook of Human Factors and Ergonomics, 5th edn. Wiley, Hoboken (2021)

23. Wang, Z., Chen, Y., Liu, J., Chen, Q.: An ergonomic evaluation of sitting postures and seat discomfort in a high-speed train. Appl. Ergon. **88**, 103197 (2020)

24. Wickens, C.D., Gordon, S.E., Liu, Y., Lee, J.: An Introduction to Human Factors Engineering. Pearson Prentice Hall, Upper Saddle River (2004)

25. Wickens, C.D.: Multiple resources and performance prediction. Theor. Issues Ergon. Sci. **3**(2), 159–177 (2002)

Integrating Industry 4.0 Technologies for Enhanced Safety Engineering: A Comprehensive Review and Analysis

Savannah Hutchins[✉], Niral Jhaveri, and Vincent G. Duffy

Purdue University, West Lafayette, IN 47907, USA
{hutchi15,njhaver,duffy}@purdue.edu

Abstract. Advancements in technology over the past few decades have led to rapid changes in manufacturing and process industries. This industry-wide shift towards automation and digitization is better known as Industry 4.0, or the fourth industrial revolution. As new Industry 4.0 technologies are adopted and "smart factories" become commonplace, the impact on the health and safety of manufacturing workers needs to be understood. The aim of this systematic review is to understand how Industry 4.0 technologies can be integrated without introducing new risks to worker health and safety through a literature review and database, content, and co-citation analyses. The literature analysis revealed publications analyzing connections between Industry 4.0 and worker health and safety, however, as an emerging field, relevant studies and publications are limited. More funding and research into the relationship between Industry 4.0 and worker OHS will be critical to the advancement, implementation, and acceptance of new technologies. Future research should likely concentrate on establishing concepts that incorporate human factors considerations into the design of integrated safety systems.

Keywords: Industry 4.0 · Smart Factory · Health · Safety Engineering · Automation

1 Introduction and Background

Manufacturing industries across the world are critical to global employment, trade, and technological advancements. Industry 4.0, short for Fourth Industrial Revolution, is a broad push to improve the manufacturing industry "on the basis of advanced digitalization within factories, the combination of internet technologies and future-oriented technologies in the field of 'smart' objects..." (Lasi et al. 2014). The introduction of Industry 4.0 technologies has had a significant impact on industrial settings, opening new avenues for enhanced productivity, efficiency, and automation. In a 2020 article, Coulibaly and Foda highlight the importance of the industry 4.0 agenda "'Industry 4.0' technologies—are poised to reshape the global manufacturing landscape, with important consequences for the traditional role of manufacturing in economies' structural transformation, growth, and job creation." Industry 4.0 is a broad concept, but it can be summarized by two objectives: to implement advanced technologies and to decentralize

© The Author(s), under exclusive license to Springer Nature Switzerland AG 2023
V. G. Duffy et al. (Eds.): HCII 2023, LNCS 14057, pp. 43–58, 2023.
https://doi.org/10.1007/978-3-031-48047-8_3

production. The implementation of new technology is driven by the "recent developments that have resulted in higher availability and affordability of sensors, data acquisition systems and computer networks" as well as steady competition in the manufacturing industry (Lee et al. 2015). Decentralizing production through Industry 4.0 technologies like automation and digitization is driven by the need for increased production flexibility and efficiency to meet "customer demands for tailored product" (Almada-Lobo 2016). (Lasi et al. 2014) summarizes the drivers of Industry 4.0 decentralization as drivers as "general social, economic, and political changes".

According to the U.S. Bureau of Labor Statistics, "Industrial engineers devise efficient systems that integrate workers, machines, materials, information, and energy to make a product or provide a service" (2023). This topic is important to Industrial Engineering because Industry 4.0 is and will alter manufacturing production through the automation of machinery, the evolving roles of workers in manufacturing, and the digitization of factory data and layouts to name a few. Beyond the realm of Industrial Engineering, there has been significant Industry 4.0 development in the fields of computer science, internet and information technology (IT), mechanical design and modeling, and automation. "Smart manufacturing" is a reality due to the collaboration among these fields. Increased data and analysis capabilities in the IT sector will enable manufacturers to identify process issues that could be resolved through smart manufacturing technologies including artificial intelligence and automation (Qi and Tao 2018). However, as these technologies become more integrated into industrial processes, safety concerns have grown in importance. Worker safety and accident prevention remain essential priorities in industrial settings, and safety engineers are responsible for creating and implementing safety measures that can keep up with the rapid changes in technology and industry. During past industrial growth, or "booms", worker health and safety was often neglected and only considered after issues arose, in other words, the manufacturing industry response reactive rather than proactive (Badri 2018). Over the last 30 years, however, the frequency of deaths and injuries in process industries has decreased, indicating a shift in how individual companies and industry view the health and safety of manufacturing workers (Lee et al. 2019). In the first chapter of his textbook, Goetsch provides multiple examples of progress in the field of safety engineering during prior "industrial revolutions" include worker's compensation, National Council of Industrial Safety, and the Occupational Safety and Health Act (OSH Act) (2019). These critical milestones for industrial worker health and safety beg the question: what will the fourth industrial revolution contribute to safety engineering?

2 Purpose of Study

The purpose of this study is to understand the connection between Industry 4.0 technologies and safety engineering through a systematic literature review. New Industry 4.0 technologies will challenge the manufacturing industry to prioritize the health and safety of its workers while also redefining current health and safety guidelines and mentalities to align with an Industry 4.0 world. Furthermore, the report intends to provide a comprehensive review of the current state of safety engineering and to identify the challenges that safety engineers face when implementing safety measures in industrial settings. It also seeks to provide practical insights into how Industry 4.0 technology might be used to tackle these difficulties and improve worker safety.

Analysis tools including Cite Space, VOS Viewer, Scite.ai, MAXQDA, and Vicinitas were used to analyze publication data and create information visuals.

3 Research Methodology

3.1 Data Collection

We used academic databases such as Google Scholar, Springer Link, Web of Science & Scopus to conduct a comprehensive literature search. Industry 4.0 and safety engineering were among the search terms we used. In addition, we manually checked the reference lists of relevant papers to guarantee that no relevant studies were overlooked. Our search was restricted to peer-reviewed journal articles, conference presentations, and book chapters published between 2010 and 2023.

Table 1. Keyword search in various databases and the number of results

Database	Number of Articles
Web of Science	21,299
Scopus	25,579
Google Scholar	299,000
Springer Link	430,178

Table 1 shows the number of articles found using the search term "Industry 4.0". The information was gathered from four primary databases that were specifically chosen for this purpose. According to the table, Springer Link and Google Scholar produced the most articles. We chose the most relevant studies for full-text review after assessing the titles and abstracts of the search results. The important data from the selected papers was then retrieved, including the research methodology, key findings, and implications of Industry 4.0 on safety engineering.

To ensure the validity of our research methods, we referred to the study conducted by Gobbo et al. 2018 titled "Making the links among environmental protection, process safety, and Industry 4.0." In their research, they adopted a similar approach to ours in visualizing bibliometric networks. By examining their findings, we discovered that Gobbo et al. highlighted the advantages of using Google Scholar, which offers a broader coverage compared to Web of Science and Scopus. Furthermore, they found that the Scopus database provides a more extensive range of resources compared to Web of Science. Their study also revealed that citation analyses, co-citation analyses, keyword co-occurrences etc. were among the most commonly studied types of bibliometric network relations. Incorporating these findings into our methodology helps to strengthen the reliability and relevance of our research.

3.2 Trend Analysis

The data extracted from Web of Science using the search terms "Industry 4.0" and "Safety Engineering" was used to create the trend diagram shown in Fig. 1. The number of publications relating to these topics has increased significantly over the last thirteen years, indicating that the safety engineering aspect of Industry 4.0 are emerging areas.

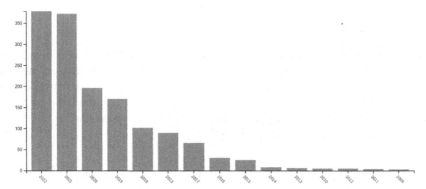

Fig. 1. Web of Science trend diagram of the 1473 publications related to search term "Industry 4.0" and "Safety Engineering" from 2009–2022. ("Web of Science", n.d.)

Figure 2 shows a trend plot built with data from Scopus by searching for "Industry 4.0". The diagram demonstrates that the number of publications on the topic has increased exponentially over the last ten years, indicating that the industry 4.0 has gained a lot of prominence.

Overall, the trend analysis identifies the growing demand for industrial safety measures, the expansion of Industry 4.0 technologies, and the incorporation of these technologies into safety engineering. It also delves into the issues that safety engineer face and how Industry 4.0 technology may help overcome them. Furthermore, the trend analysis identifies emerging trends in safety engineering, such as the use of AI-based predictive maintenance and the use of smart sensors for worker safety monitoring.

3.3 Engagement Measure

Vicinitas was used to measure the engagement level of Twitter users on Industry 4.0. Using the "hashtag/keyword tweets" search tool, tweets containing the keywords "industry 4.0", "smart factory", "factory", and "manufacturing" within the last ten days were analyzed. Figure 3 shows the engagement data and word cloud extracted from this search and Fig. 4 shows the engagement trend. The engagement trend indicates an increasing interest in this area over the past ten days.

Another Vicinitas report is shown in Fig. 5. This report identifies the other hashtags used in addition to "#smart factory" in the analyzed tweets. This information is useful, as it helps identify what other areas related to Industry 4.0 may be trending as well. In these tweets, some of the common Industry 4.0 technologies like AI and 5G are being used.

Documents by year

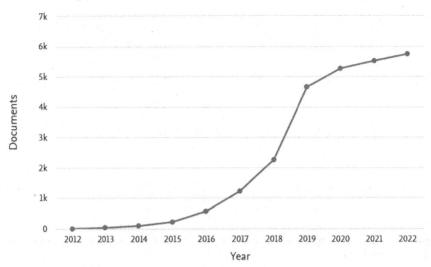

Fig. 2. Scopus trend diagram of the 25,579 publications related to search term "Industry 4.0" from 2012–2022. ("Scopus", n.d.)

Fig. 3. Vicinitas search of #smart factory in tweets over a ten day span. ("Vicinitas." n.d.)

Engagement Timeline

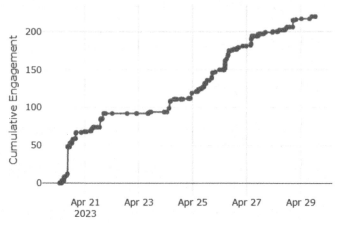

Fig. 4. Vicinitas engagement trend showing the use of "#smart factory" in tweets over a ten day span ("Vicinitas." n.d.).

Hashtags

☑ #smartfactory	228	
☑ #ai	64	
☑ #manufacturing	57	
☑ #innovation	45	
☑ #5g	45	
☑ #industry40	43	
☑ #tech	42	
☑ #technology	41	
☑ #digital	40	
☑ #machinelearning	38	

Fig. 5. Vicinitas report of hashtags used in addition to "#smart factory in tweets over a ten day span ("Vicinitas." n.d.).

4   Results

4.1   Co-citation Analysis

Co-citation analysis is a popular bibliometric technique that analyzes the co-citation patterns of publications to provide insight into the intellectual structure of a topic. Co-citation analysis is a valuable tool for researchers who are interested in understanding the intellectual structure of a field and identifying key publications and authors.

A dataset of 320 articles carefully picked from Scopus using relevant keywords was used to conduct co-citation analysis on the topic of "Industry 4.0." Only articles cited at least 3 times were included in the resulting cluster after the data was exported in CSV format for analysis. This approach ensures that the co-citation analysis is conducted on a robust dataset, and the resulting cluster (Fig. 6) provides a comprehensive and insightful overview of the most cited publications on the topic.

Fig. 6. Co-citation analysis using "VOS viewer" software ("VOS viewer," n.d.)

8 articles were chosen from the cluster for an In-depth review in the discussion section. Figure 7 shows the key articles identified using the software.

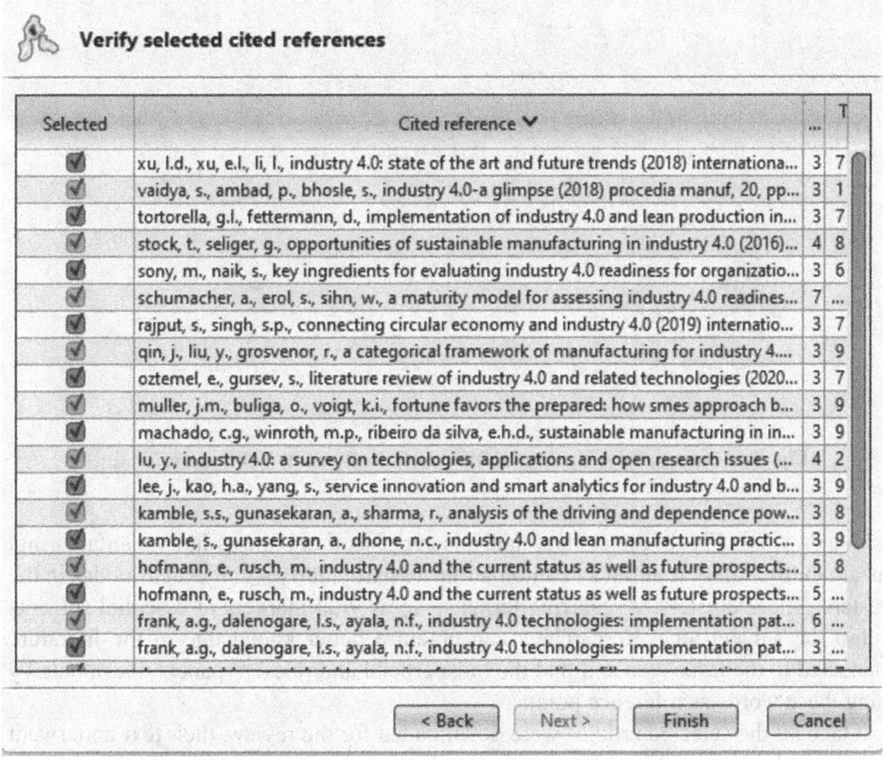

Verify selected cited references

Selected	Cited reference ⌄	...	T
☑	xu, l.d., xu, e.l., li, l., industry 4.0: state of the art and future trends (2018) internationa...	3	7
☑	vaidya, s., ambad, p., bhosle, s., industry 4.0-a glimpse (2018) procedia manuf, 20, pp...	3	1
☑	tortorella, g.l., fettermann, d., implementation of industry 4.0 and lean production in...	3	7
☑	stock, t., seliger, g., opportunities of sustainable manufacturing in industry 4.0 (2016)...	4	8
☑	sony, m., naik, s., key ingredients for evaluating industry 4.0 readiness for organizatio...	3	6
☑	schumacher, a., erol, s., sihn, w., a maturity model for assessing industry 4.0 readines...	7	...
☑	rajput, s., singh, s.p., connecting circular economy and industry 4.0 (2019) internatio...	3	7
☑	qin, j., liu, y., grosvenor, r., a categorical framework of manufacturing for industry 4....	3	9
☑	oztemel, e., gursev, s., literature review of industry 4.0 and related technologies (2020...	3	7
☑	muller, j.m., buliga, o., voigt, k.i., fortune favors the prepared: how smes approach b...	3	9
☑	machado, c.g., winroth, m.p., ribeiro da silva, e.h.d., sustainable manufacturing in in...	3	9
☑	lu, y., industry 4.0: a survey on technologies, applications and open research issues (...	4	2
☑	lee, j., kao, h.a., yang, s., service innovation and smart analytics for industry 4.0 and b...	3	9
☑	kamble, s.s., gunasekaran, a., sharma, r., analysis of the driving and dependence pow...	3	8
☑	kamble, s., gunasekaran, a., dhone, n.c., industry 4.0 and lean manufacturing practic...	3	9
☑	hofmann, e., rusch, m., industry 4.0 and the current status as well as future prospects...	5	8
☑	hofmann, e., rusch, m., industry 4.0 and the current status as well as future prospects...	5	...
☑	frank, a.g., dalenogare, l.s., ayala, n.f., industry 4.0 technologies: implementation pat...	6	...
☑	frank, a.g., dalenogare, l.s., ayala, n.f., industry 4.0 technologies: implementation pat...	3	...

< Back   Next >   Finish   Cancel

Fig. 7. Key Articles identified using VOS viewer ("VOS viewer," n.d.)

4.2   Content Analysis

VOS viewer was used to perform content analysis on the metadata from Scopus. A keyword search of "Industry 4.0" in Scopus generated 25,579 results, out of which 103 results were subsequently exported in CSV format. The generated file was opened in VOS viewer, and the content was analyzed by selecting the "create map based on network data" option. The link strength was set to zero and the minimum number of occurrences of a term was set to 5 to capture as many words as feasible. After applying this criterion, 206 words met the threshold, out of which 124 relevant terms were selected as shown in Fig. 8.

Fig. 8. Content analysis using "VOS viewer" software ("VOS viewer," n.d.)

As shown in Fig. 8, the content analysis suggests that phrases like manufacturing, sustainability, safety training and automation are particularly significant as nodes in the clusters. These clusters of recurring terms serve as vital markers of essential subjects within the subject area. Researchers can obtain a better knowledge of the literature connected to the issue area and find the most crucial and relevant papers to evaluate by using these words as reference points.

Once all the selected articles were downloaded for the review, their text underwent content analysis using MaxQDA software, which enabled the creation of a word cloud that displays the most common keywords found within the set of articles. Figure 9 presents the word cloud which was then used to identify appropriate keywords for the literature review.

MaxQDA software provided easy text analysis capabilities, including visualizing keywords and their frequency across the set of documents. Figure 9 shows the top five most frequent words identified were Industry, Technology, Safety, Health, and Manufacturing. The built-in features of MaxQDA software made it a valuable tool for analyzing the text and identifying the most important keywords for the literature review (Fig. 10).

Fig. 9. Word Cloud using MaxQDA software ("MAXQDA," n.d.)

4.3 Cluster Analysis

Cite Space is a robust cluster analysis tool that provides various benefits to academics in the scientific community. Its capacity to find and depict correlations between clusters of linked scientific papers is one of its key advantages. Cite Space can identify major publications and authors within a given subject by studying co-citation patterns, making it an essential tool for scholars interested in mapping the intellectual structure of a specific domain.

Data was collected from Scopus in plain text file format for cluster analysis using the keywords "Industry 4.0" and "Safety Engineering," yielding a total of 100 results. The results were then subjected to cluster analysis using Cite Space. Figure 11 shows a large central cluster, indicating a dominant or central theme within the field. The smaller clusters within the main cluster represented different articles and subtopics within the domain, providing researchers with a comprehensive overview of the most relevant publications and subtopics in the field. With its advanced features and robust capabilities, Cite Space is an invaluable tool for researchers seeking to explore and analyze the relationships between scientific publications in each field.

4.4 Citation Burst

A citation burst analysis was conducted to identify the most influential and impactful papers in the field of safety engineering and Industry 4.0. This analysis helped to identify

Word Cloud: Word frequencies

16 documents (201 analyzed words)   19 different words

Display top ranks ∨   Min. frequency 3

Word	Word length	Frequency	%	Rank	Documents	Documents %
Industry	8	31	15.42	1	16	100.00
safety	6	19	9.45	2	8	50.00
technologies	12	12	5.97	3	3	18.75
health	6	6	2.99	4	2	12.50
manufacturing	13	6	2.99	4	4	25.00
future	6	5	2.49	6	4	25.00
impact	6	5	2.49	6	3	18.75
applications	12	4	1.99	8	4	25.00
industry	8	4	1.99	8	3	18.75
management	10	4	1.99	8	2	12.50
Occupational	12	4	1.99	8	3	18.75
systems	7	4	1.99	8	3	18.75
work	4	4	1.99	8	1	6.25
Data	4	3	1.49	14	3	18.75
environment	11	3	1.49	14	3	18.75
identified	10	3	1.49	14	2	12.50
industrial	10	3	1.49	14	2	12.50
Process	7	3	1.49	14	2	12.50
production	10	3	1.49	14	3	18.75

Fig. 10. Keywords from word Cloud using MaxQDA ("MAXQDA," n.d.)

Fig. 11. Cluster analysis using "Cite space" software ("Cite Space," n.d.)

emerging trends and areas of research that are gaining momentum, as well as the most influential authors and institutions. By examining the citation patterns and burst rates of papers within the field, we were able to gain insights into the impact of certain publications and the networks of researchers who are driving the field forward.

A citation burst was generated using Cite space software. Figure 12 shows the top 5 references which are experiencing the strongest citation burst from a list of 100 articles. It is because "Industry 4.0" is an emerging concept with publications not yet having received widespread attention or recognition from other researchers.

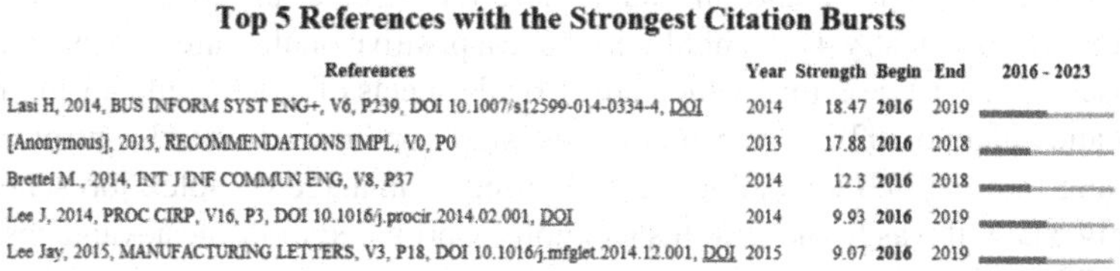

Top 5 References with the Strongest Citation Bursts

References	Year	Strength	Begin	End	2016 - 2023
Lasi H, 2014, BUS INFORM SYST ENG+, V6, P239, DOI 10.1007/s12599-014-0334-4, DOI	2014	18.47	2016	2019	
[Anonymous], 2013, RECOMMENDATIONS IMPL, V0, P0	2013	17.88	2016	2018	
Brettel M., 2014, INT J INF COMMUN ENG, V8, P37	2014	12.3	2016	2018	
Lee J, 2014, PROC CIRP, V16, P3, DOI 10.1016/j.procir.2014.02.001, DOI	2014	9.93	2016	2019	
Lee Jay, 2015, MANUFACTURING LETTERS, V3, P18, DOI 10.1016/j.mfglet.2014.12.001, DOI	2015	9.07	2016	2019	

Fig. 12. Citation Burst using "Cite space" software ("Cite Space," n.d.)

4.5 Pivot Table

A pivot table was used to analyze the leading authors in the field of safety engineering and Industry 4.0, based on the number of cited publications. The pivot table analysis allowed us to quickly and easily identify the most influential authors in the field, as well as the institutions they are affiliated with and the topics they are/were researching. This analysis can serve to guide future research and provide insights into the most important and influential research being undertaken in the domain area.

Metadata from VOS viewer helped us gain access to the number of cited articles by different authors to create a pivot table in Microsoft Excel. Table 2 helped us identify the authors who have contributed the most in the given research topic.

Table 2. Leading authors table using VOS Viewer ("VOS viewer," n.d.)

Authors with most citations	No. of Cited Publications
Schumacher a.	7
Hofmann e.	6
Frank A.G.	6
Stock T.	4
Xu L.D.	3

5 Discussion

The manufacturing industry and its workers are critical to global trade, employment, and consumers. As the manufacturing industry adopts Industry 4.0, there will be advancements and acceptance of new technologies that will drastically impact social life (Oztemel and Gursev 2020). These technologies, however, are incredibly complex and pose problems when it comes to implementation and industrial performance (Frank et al. 2019). Implementation concerns combined with the fact that a significant number of process related accidents are still occurring, give rise to additional concerns that Industry 4.0 technologies could introduce more risk (Lee et al. 2019). One literature review found that Industry 4.0 technologies have a positive on the safety management of warehouses and logistic sectors, which are critical aspects of any manufacturing facility (Forcina and Falcone 2021). For example, in a study on how advanced control models, a promising Industry 4.0 technology, can be used to manage complex job scheduling and supply chain, it was found that this technology provided multiple advantages. (Dolgui et al. 2019) Other literature reviews, however, highlight the potential risks of new Industry 4.0 technologies. In the cyber-physical space, "security and safety problems in the areas of industrial automation, control systems and critical infrastructure" are major concerns and budding focus areas (Gajek et al. 2022). Another Industry 4.0 technologies that will alter the manufacturing industry is automation. Automation is necessary to execute complex tasks and increase efficiency but is also beneficial to the health and safety of manufacturing workers. Brauer highlights this in Chapter 33 of Safety and Health for Engineers, "The new methods may reduce errors and accidents by recognizing the capabilities and limitations of humans and new capabilities of machines" (2016). On the other hand, increased automation also poses new risks for manufacturing workers due to the "absence of standards and regulations for human–machine interaction" (Zorzenon et al. 2022). While automation can relieve workers from cumbersome tasks, it also increases human-robot interaction and greater mental stress (Veruscka, n.d.). From automation to big data, Industry 4.0 technologies span a broad spectrum, so it is not surprising that opinions regarding its impact on safety engineering vary. What does not vary from publication to publication is that additional work is needed to understand the full impact.

More research and studies into how Industry 4.0 will impact manufacturing workers is required, as current health and safety legislation, training, guidelines, and practices do not account for the risks associated with these integrating these technologies into a functioning manufacturing facility (Popovic et al. 2020). Despite Industry 4.0 being one of the most widely discussed topics across multiple fields and industries, the majority of available publications do not highlight the occupational health and safety benefits or risks. (Polak-Sopinska et al. 2020) There has been minimal research into how Industry 4.0 impacts the occupational health and safety (OHS) of manufacturing workers, but the number of studies is relatively small and inconclusive on whether Industry 4.0 technologies improve worker health and safety (Zorzenon 2022). More research into the relationship between Industry 4.0 and worker OHS will be critical to the advancement, implementation, and acceptance of new technologies.

6 Conclusion

In conclusion, our comprehensive review and analysis demonstrates that the integration of Industry 4.0 technologies can significantly enhance safety engineering in various industries. Organizations can attain improved levels of safety, productivity, and efficiency by using modern technologies such as the Internet of Things (IoT), artificial intelligence (AI), and Automation. Our research also uncovered the significant obstacles and opportunities related with the implementation of Industry 4.0 technologies in safety engineering, such as the requirement for a qualified workforce, higher investment, and the possibility of new business models and value propositions. Automation is an important feature of Industry 4.0 technologies because it has the potential to improve safety engineering by minimizing the need for human interaction in hazardous conditions. Our research focuses on the potential advantages of automation in safety engineering, such as increased safety, productivity, and cost-effectiveness. However, it also emphasizes the importance of exercising caution and careful consideration when implementing automated systems, as well as ensuring that humans retain control and are able to intervene in the event of an emergency or unexpected event. As a result, incorporating automation into safety engineering must be addressed with a balanced and strategic approach, harnessing the benefits while reducing the dangers. Additionally, as Industry 4.0 technologies expand and become more widely used in industrial settings, it is critical for safety engineers to keep up with these innovations and use them to improve safety procedures. By addressing the obstacles of integrating new technologies, safety engineers may play an important role in guaranteeing worker safety in the industry 4.0 era.

7 Future Work

Investigating the role of human factors in the design and implementation of integrated safety systems is one potential future work that can be pursued in the framework of Industry 4.0 and its connection with safety engineering. While Industry 4.0 technologies provide significant opportunities for improving workplace safety, the human factors involved in their operation and maintenance must not be overlooked. Future research might thus concentrate on establishing design concepts that incorporate human factors considerations into the design of integrated safety systems. This may entail performing user studies to better understand the needs and requirements of operators and maintenance workers, as well as designing training programs to guarantee that they can properly use the integrated safety systems. Furthermore, research can focus on developing decision support systems to help operators and maintenance personnel make informed decisions about safety-related issues. Incorporating human factors into the design and implementation of Industry 4.0-based safety systems can help to ensure that these systems are effective and efficient in improving workplace safety.

To determine whether the National Science Foundation (NSF) is investing in the development of automation and smart manufacturing in the context of Industry 4.0, a search was conducted on their website using the relevant keywords. The search yielded a study proposal approved by the NSF, focused on smart manufacturing and its transformation for the future. The proposal is depicted in Fig. 13, suggesting that this research area holds significant potential for the future and requires further exploration to evaluate its effectiveness.

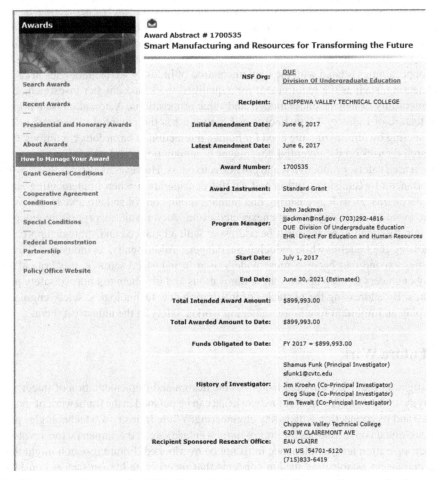

Fig. 13. A screenshot from the NSF website showing approval of a research project that focusses on Smart Manufacturing and transforming it for the future.

References

Almada-Lobo, F.: The industry 4.0 revolution and the future of manufacturing execution systems (MES). J. Innov. Manag. **3**(4), 16–21 (2016). https://doi.org/10.24840/2183-0606_003.004_0003

Gobbo, J.A., Busso, C.M., Gobbo, S.C.O., Carreão, H.: Making the links among environmental protection, process safety, and industry 4.0. Process. Saf. Environ. Prot. **117**, 372–382 (2018). https://doi.org/10.1016/j.psep.2018.05.017

Badri, A., Boudreau-Trudel, B., Souissi, A.S.: Occupational health and safety in the industry 4.0 era: a cause for major concern? Saf. Sci. **109**(November), 403–411 (2018). https://doi.org/10. 1016/J.SSCI.2018.06.012

Brauer, R.L.: Safety and Health for Engineers, John Wiley and Sons, Incorporated (2016). ProQuest Ebook Central. http://ebookcentral.proquest.com/lib/purdue/detail.action?docID=4513082

CiteSpace. n.d. http://cluster.cis.drexel.edu/~cchen/citespace/

Coulibaly, B., Foda, K.: The future of global manufacturing. Brookings. Brookings. Accessed 4 Mar 2020. https://www.brookings.edu/blog/up-front/2020/03/04/the-future-of-global-manufa cturing/

Dolgui, A., Ivanov, D., Sethi, S.P., Sokolov, B.: Scheduling in production, supply chain and industry 4.0 systems by optimal control: fundamentals, state-of-the-art and applications. Int. J. Prod. Res. **57**(2), 411–432 (2019). https://doi.org/10.1080/00207543.2018.1442948

Forcina, A., Falcone, D.: The role of industry 4.0 enabling technologies for safety management: a systematic literature review. Procedia Comput. Sci. **180**(January), 436–445 (2021). https:// doi.org/10.1016/J.PROCS.2021.01.260

Frank, A.G., Dalenogare, L.S., Ayala, N.F.: Industry 4.0 technologies: implementation patterns in manufacturing companies. Int. J. Prod. Econ. **210**(April), 15–26 (2019). https://doi.org/10. 1016/j.ijpe.2019.01.004

Gajek, A., Fabiano, B., Laurent, A., Jensen, N.: Process safety education of future employee 4.0 in industry 4.0. J. Loss Prev. Process Ind. **75**(February), 104691 (2022). https://doi.org/10.1016/ j.jlp.2021.104691

Goetsch, D.L.: Occupational Safety and Health for Technologists, Engineers, and Managers, 9th edn. Pearson, Boston (2019)

Harzing Publish or Perish. n.d. https://harzing.com/resources/publish-or-perish/windows

Industrial Engineers: Occupational Outlook Handbook. U.S. Bureau of Labor Statistics. U.S. Bureau of Labor Statistics. Accessed 6 Feb 2023. https://www.bls.gov/ooh/architecture-and-engineering/industrial-engineers.htm

Lasi, H., Fettke, P., Kemper, H.-G., Feld, T., Hoffmann, M.: Industry 4.0. Bus. Inf. Syst. Eng. **6**(4), 239–242 (2014). https://doi.org/10.1007/s12599-014-0334-4

Lee, J., Bagheri, B., Kao, H.-A.: A cyber-physical systems architecture for industry 4.0-based manufacturing systems. Manuf. Lett. **3**(January), 18–23 (2015). https://doi.org/10.1016/j.mfg let.2014.12.001

Lee, J., Cameron, I., Hassall, M.: Improving process safety: what roles for digitalization and industry 4.0? Process. Saf. Environ. Prot. **132**(December), 325–339 (2019). https://doi.org/10. 1016/j.psep.2019.10.021

MAXQDA. n.d. https://www.maxqda.com/

Mendeley. n.d. https://www.mendeley.com/

National Science Foundation. Smart Manufacturing and Resources for Transforming the Future. Award Abstract #1700535. Accessed 30 June 2021

Oztemel, E., Gursev, S.: Literature review of industry 4.0 and related technologies. J. Intell. Manuf. **31**(1), 127–182 (2020). https://doi.org/10.1007/s10845-018-1433-8

Polak-Sopinska, A., Wisniewski, Z., Walaszczyk, A., Maczewska, A., Sopinski, P.: Impact of industry 4.0 on occupational health and safety. In: Karwowski, W., Trzcielinski, S., Mrugalska, B. (eds.) AHFE 2019. AISC, vol. 971, pp. 40–52. Springer, Cham (2019). https://doi.org/10. 1007/978-3-030-20494-5_4

Popovic, A., Milijic, A., Popović, A., Milijić, A.: Impact of reshoring in industry 4.0 on economic development in the wake of covid-19 crisis digital economy: chances, risks, sustainable development impact of reshoring in industry 4.0 on economic development in the wake of covid-19 crisis (2020). https://www.researchgate.net/publication/353822254

Qi, Q., Tao, F.: Digital twin and big data towards smart manufacturing and industry 4.0: 360 degree comparison. IEEE Access **6**, 3585–3593 (2018). https://doi.org/10.1109/ACCESS.2018.279 3265

Scopus. n.d.

Veruscka, Leso Luca, Fontana Ivo, Iavicoli. n.d. The Occupational Health and Safety Dimension of Industry 4.0.

Vicintas. n.d.

VOS viewer. n.d. https://www.vosviewer.com/

Web of Science. n.d.

Zorzenon, R., Lizarelli, F.L., de A. Moura, D.B.A.: What Is the potential impact of industry 4.0 on health and safety at work? Saf. Sci. **153** (2022). https://doi.org/10.1016/j.ssci.2022.105802

Human Modeling in Design for Reducing Human Error in Product Lifecycle

Rebecca Kasner[✉] and Vincent G. Duffy

Purdue University, West Lafayette, IN 47907, USA
{rkasner,duffy}@purdue.edu

Abstract. Human error is inevitable to some degree, though in many cases it can lead to a significant risk of human injury or illness. Because of this, designers and engineers need to be aware of many considerations to ensure that their products and processes are safe. To do this, they must consider human error throughout the lifecycle, including design, manufacturing, and product in use. Especially as technology advances and processes become more optimized, risk potential should be studied and analyzed before an incident can occur. Simulation and human modeling tools provide essential information to improve products and reduce risks. This paper discusses the importance of understanding and reducing human error through a systematic review of the topic and through exemplifying one of many tools, RAMSIS, that aids in analyzing such risk. Specifically, the tool is used to study user interaction with a vehicle, which can help designers identify potential areas of concern that could lead to unsafe driving conditions.

Keywords: Human Error · Human Reliability · Human Modeling · Ergonomics · Human Factors · Simulation · RAMSIS

1 Introduction and Background

1.1 Human Error and Reliability Overview

An important topic within the space of safety and health is human error and reliability. In many cases, especially in industry, injuries and illnesses are related to or a direct result of human error. In the aircraft industry, human error has attributed to 70% of accidents and incidents, and its importance is universally understood to be a significant contributory factor (Feggetter 1982). Additionally, in the medical industry, human error is the dominant cause of anesthesia mishaps (Cooper et al. 1984). Even in software systems safety, "human errors impact the design and development of software-controlled systems," which can lead to critical safety failures (Brown 1988).

This topic has always been relevant, as humans are prone to mistakes. Articles published as early as the mid-1900s refer to studies related to human errors/human factors. However, in recent years advanced automation and programming mistakes can lead to increased risks as they create new varieties of human error (Ogle et al. 2008). Implications of these industry changes need to be further studied and understood, especially by process or industrial engineers and product designers.

V. G. Duffy et al. (Eds.): HCII 2023, LNCS 14057, pp. 59–77, 2023.
https://doi.org/10.1007/978-3-031-48047-8_4

Several solutions have been created to reduce the incidence or occurrence of human errors. Human Reliability Analysis (HRA) has become more prevalent with the creation of the Cognitive Reliability and Error Analysis Method (CREAM), which works to classify and study erroneous actions to predict and describe how errors can potentially occur (Hollnagel 2005). Risk analysis and accident causation theories often discuss human error, such as the human factors theory that attributes accidents to events ultimately caused by human error (Goetsch 2019, 32). Human reliability and safety risk reduction are improved by understanding these methodologies and creating more standardization. With proper utilization, they can act as a potential safeguard against human error and provide additional opportunities to explore possible risks.

1.2 Relevant Definitions

Some key terms are summarized in Table 1 to aid in understanding the topic of human error. Notably, human error discusses a failure to perform a task, while human reliability is the probability of the task being successful.

Table 1. Relevant definitions for the topic of human error and reliability.

Key term	Definition
Human error	"(T)he failure to perform a specified task (or performance of a forbidden action) that could lead to disruption of scheduled operations or result in damage to property and equipment" (Dhillon 1989)
Human reliability	"(T)he probability of accomplishing a job or task successfully by humans at any required stage in system operation within a specified minimum time limit (if the time requirement is specified)" (Dhillon 1989)
Risk	"(R)isk event (e.g., an "accident") is the product of the probability of that event and (a unified measure of) the (assumed negative) consequences that necessarily accompany that event" (Sheridan 2008)

2 Systematic Literature Review

2.1 Purpose and Methods

This report aims to understand the topic of human error through a systematic review, then utilize an ergonomic vehicle design software, RAMSIS, as an example of an analysis tool. In general, the purpose of a systematic review is to provide a "comprehensive, unbiased synthesis of many relevant studies in a single document" (Aromataris and Pearson 2014). Many examples from various industries, such as medical, construction, and product design, reference the goal and methodology. One such example related to the field of design is included in the references, "Design for manufacturing and assembly methods in the product development process of mechanical products: a systematic literature review" (Formentini et al. 2022).

The first step in the process is to understand the purpose or question of the review. In this case, the goal is to understand human error and its applicability to product design. Next, relevant studies are searched and selected to fit the inclusion criteria (Aromataris and Pearson 2014). This must be a thorough process where each search is refined based on quality (Khan et al. 2003). Then, the data is summarized and interpreted, and the topic is synthesized and thoroughly understood.

For this paper, data mining and bibliometric analysis tools were utilized to understand the correlation between human error and product design.

2.2 Procedure

Research related to the topic of interest was found initially by searching various databases, such as Scopus and Google Scholar. From this, many analyses were done, such as a trend review, co-citation, and word map. This provided insight into common areas within the topic, highly cited papers, and frequent authors. Next, selected articles were searched in Scite, a tool that shows the citations and references of the paper (Scite n.d.). This provides additional studies that give insight into the topic. A summary of the initial article search terms (before those extracted from secondary data mining tools) and the databases used are shown in Table 2 below.

Table 2. Initial article search terms and databases used.

Search term	Database
human AND error	Scopus
human AND reliability	Scopus
human AND error AND methods	Scopus
human AND error AND terms	Scopus
human AND error AND risk	Scopus
human AND error AND design	Scopus
human error	Google Scholar
human reliability	Google Scholar
human error terms	Google Scholar

2.3 Trend Analysis

To understand the importance and relevance of the topic of human error, trend patterns were explored. First, the Google Ngram tool was used to compare trends with the keywords: "human error," "risk analysis," and "ergonomic design" (Google Books n.d.). The graph in Fig. 1 shows that all keywords have an upwards trend of relevance over the last 80 years.

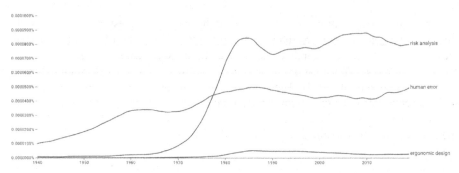

Fig. 1. Ngram Viewer result showing the comparison of the keywords: "human error," "risk analysis," and "ergonomic design" (Google Books n.d.).

Next, the academic database, Scopus, was searched for document trends (Elsevier n.d.). Figure 2 shows a pronounced upward trend of interest in this topic from the keyword search "human AND error." The total number of documents related to this subject is well over 450,000, with the majority in the last 20 years. This data is also summarized in Table 3, which validates the identified trend of an increase in academic interest.

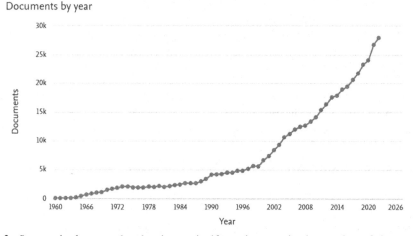

Fig. 2. Scopus database results showing a significant increase in the number of documents containing the keywords "human AND error" since 1960 (Elsevier n.d.).

Additionally, social media was searched for term usage and related keywords. Vicinitas is a tool that searches Twitter for recent word trends on posts and hashtags (Vicinitas 2023). Figure 3 shows the results of searching "human error" in the program. There are a considerable number of posts and a high level of engagement on this topic, as seen at the top of the image. Additionally, this tool can be used to identify similar areas of interest based on the word cloud provided. The related topics center around learning, data, waste, and cybersecurity.

Table 3. Summary of Scopus database results showing an increase in the number of documents by decade containing the keywords "human AND error" since 1960 (Elsevier n.d.).

Year	Number of Documents
2020	24094
2010	14108
2000	6638
1990	4133
1980	2144
1970	1468
1960	39

Fig. 3. Vicinitas results showing significant engagement and influence with the term "human error," as well as identified related words (Vicinitas n.d.).

Lastly, a text data map was created on the VOSviewer program from the search results of "human error AND methods" on Scopus (Fig. 4) (Elsevier n.d.) (Jan van Eck and Waltman n.d.). Originally, a search was made for only "human AND error," but it outputted too broad of results that were not relevant to the topic. Two large clusters are identified from the map: methodologies and technology/learning. The top words are related to analysis (experiments and case studies), work (quality, efficiency, etc.), and safety (accident, detection, etc.). These words were then utilized in subsequent searches to identify further areas of study related to the topic.

From the trend analysis, it is clear that human error is a growing topic of interest that needs to be explored and understood in fields of related research, especially safety and product design.

2.4 Co-citation Analysis

Co-citation indicates that a particular source is highly impactful in a given area, especially if it has been cited more than twice. For this analysis, a bibliographic data map was created using the VOSviewer software (Fig. 5) (Jan van Eck and Waltman n.d.). This information is also summarized with the number of co-citations in Table 4.

The co-citation map contains data compiled from the top 5,000 documents from the Scopus database search of the keywords "human error AND methods." The data

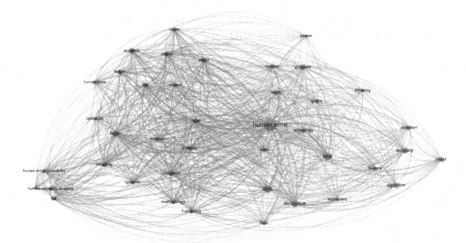

Fig. 4. VOSviewer word map created from "human error AND methods" search showing 2 main clusters of words (Jan van Eck and Waltman n.d.).

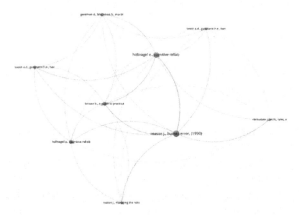

Fig. 5. Co-citation bibliographic map created using the VOSviewer software showing the 9 most-cited sources from searching the Scopus database for the keywords "human-error AND methods" (Jan van Eck and Waltman n.d.).

was exported to VOSviewer with the minimum number of co-citations set to 25. The analysis identified nine papers as frequently co-cited, most related to reliability and error analysis methods or risk management and assessment tools. The most commonly cited reference was "Cognitive Reliability and Error Analysis Method (CREAM)," by Erik Hollnagel with 177 citations (Hollnagel 2005). Authors Erik Hollnagel and James (J.T.) Reason appear twice in the list for different papers or books, indicating that they are top researchers in the topic.

Table 4. Summary of the 9 most-cited sources from searching the Scopus database for the keywords "human-error AND methods" (Jan van Eck and Waltman n.d.).

Cited Reference	Citations
Hollnagel, Erik. *Cognitive Reliability and Error Analysis Method (CREAM)*. Oxford u. a.: Elsevier, 2005	177
Reason, James. *Human Error*. Cambridge: Cambridge Univ. Pr., 1990	142
Swain, A D, and H E Guttmann. "Handbook of Human-Reliability Analysis with Emphasis on Nuclear Power Plant Applications." Applied Ergonomics 16, no. 1 (1985). https://doi.org/10.2172/5752058	76
Kirwan, Barry. *A Guide to Practical Human Reliability Assessment*. 1st ed. London: Taylor & Francis, 1994	50
Gertman, David I., Harold S. Blackman, J. L. Marble, J. C. Byers, and C. L. Smith. *The SPAR-H Human Reliability Analysis Method*. Washington, D.C.: U.S. Nuclear Regulatory Commission, 2005	38
Reason, J. T. *Managing the Risks of Organizational Accidents*. 1st ed. London: Routledge, 1997	26
Rasmussen, Jens. "Skills, Rules, and Knowledge; Signals, Signs, and Symbols, and Other Distinctions in Human Performance Models." IEEE Transactions on Systems, Man, and Cybernetics SMC-13, no. 3 (1983): 257–66. https://doi.org/10.1109/tsmc.1983.6313160	26
Bell, Julie, and Justin Holroyd. "RR679 - Review of Human Reliability Assessment Methods." Health and Safety Laboratory. Accessed April 21, 2023. https://www.hse.gov.uk/research/rrhtm//rr679.htm	23
Hollnagel, Erik. *Human Reliability Analysis: Context and Control*. London u.a.: Academic Press, 1993	21

2.5 Results and Discussion

Historical Contribution. Many important early references were identified through the co-citation, though a deeper historical analysis was needed. The term "human error" only started appearing in documents around the 1960s, when it rapidly increased in research and interest. Prior, some studies refer to "human factors," i.e. "aircraft accidents… caused by human factors," such as maintenance, supervisory or pilot errors, from "Human factors that cause aircraft accidents," published in 1956 (Moseley 1956).

In the widely referenced book (published in 1990), "Human Error," James Reason states that in the past, human error was largely only studied in the vicinity of major accidents or disasters (Reason 1990). Similarly, the article "Introduction: Human Errors and Error Handling," by the same author (as well as Dieter Zapf), published in 1994, states: "Error research increased with the appearance of cognitive theories in the 1970s and 1980s" (Zapf and Reason 1994).

Reappraisal. From the analysis, a reappraisal was performed to understand related subtopics. Some of these areas were selected from the VOSviewer word map (Fig. 4), while others were commonly noted topics within the reviewed references. These are summarized in Table 5 below.

Table 5. Sub-topics related to human error based on the clusters identified from the word map.

Methodologies	Technology/Learning
Safety	Human factors
Probability	Design

Safety. At the root of human error is the evaluation and enforcement of safety. Unsafe conditions and accidents resulting from mistakes can and should be eliminated. As this is such a key subtopic, nearly all sources in this paper refer to safety in some regard. Methodologies for detecting and reducing human error target improving safety. Some of these, or their applications, are discussed in this report, such as CREAM or HRA in general (Hollnagel 2005) (Hollnagel 1993).

Probability. Predicting accidents and related risks is essential in reducing their severity and occurrence. Numerous methodologies analyze human reliability or human error probability to prevent incidents. Some references in this report discuss these, such as SPAR-H and A Guide to Practical Human Reliability Assessment, though many others exist (Gertman et al. 2005) (Kirwan 1994). Each utilizes a nuanced approach that highlights different characteristics or aspects of analyses.

Human Factors. In an industry-specific definition, Barry Beith defines human factors as focusing "on system usability and designing system interfaces to optimize the users' ability to accomplish their tasks error-free in a reasonable time and, therefore, to accept the system as a useful tool" (Beith 1999). Human factors studies aim to reduce human error so users can complete targeted tasks. Additionally, as previously discussed, this term was a precursor to the existence of human error analyses.

Design. The relationship between human error and design is the main focus of this paper. Human error is often studied in accidents related to manufacturing or healthcare, though poor designs can also lead to unsafe conditions for users. This can be observed in the design itself or in the way that a user chooses to use the product. In either case, designers and engineers need to safeguard against human error to prevent unsafe conditions. As Roger Brauer discusses, "processes require planning and design to reduce opportunities for human error … That also emphasizes reducing accidents" (Brauer 2016, 10). By understanding potential failure modes early in product or process design, solutions can be made more reliably (Soria Zurita et al. 2018).

Conclusions and Future Work. This systematic review provides insights into the history and continued interest in the topic of human error. The bibliometric analysis reveals that there are many methods and related sub-topics that have already been widely explored, largely through the lens of quantifying risk and the causes of accidents. Existing methodologies and tools allow designers and engineers to study and understand risk potential, though these need to advance to provide solutions in times of new technology and growing advancement.

As discussed, advanced research and development on the topic of human error is still recent. Some tools and methodologies for analyzing accidents resulting from human error have been developed, such as CREAM, which can be studied to understand cause-and-effect relationships (Hollnagel 2005). However, prevention and risk-elimination tools need further development. Additionally, with increasing applications of complicated automation, more tools are being developed to reduce human error. However, many of these technologies are still in the early phases of development and need to be better understood as they could bring new sources of risks.

Currently, there are some ongoing and early efforts to reduce limitations in the field. A recent project, funded by the National Science Foundation (NSF), is working to improve human-automation interaction (HAI) evaluation and repair to "eliminate many kinds of potential interaction errors while minimizing the risk of introducing additional human errors" (NSF n.d.). The project provides a further understanding of identifying risks before an accident can occur, particularly from the lens of process automation.

Additionally, in the healthcare industry new tools have been created to aid in the precision and efficiency of complicated surgeries. Robots are being used to assist in surgeries, which "causes less damage to the patient's body, less pain and discomfort, shorter hospital stays, quicker recovery times, smaller scars, and less risk of complications" (Fosch-Villaronga et al. 2022). With this new technology, robots reduce human error but could potentially increase other concerns or risks due to the narrow understanding of their capabilities and limitations.

3 Advanced RAMSIS Software Implementation

3.1 RAMSIS Software Overview

As identified, there are many tools to analyze safety or health risks. One of these programs based on digital human modeling is RAMSIS. The software allows designers to simulate human-vehicle interaction and interior ergonomics to create efficiency models in early product development (Human Solutions n.d.). The tool can reduce the incidence of human error-related accidents by allowing designers to identify problems before they occur, such as glare or ergonomic issues when operating the vehicle.

The following subsections of this report outline the procedures and results of various ergonomic analyses of a vehicle, with a specific focus on redesign. This particular exercise was supported by experts from the Human Solutions team. Through provided suggestions, human error can be reduced for future drivers, as well as for engineers later in the product development process.

3.2 Initial Setup

The first step in accessing the RAMSIS software is downloading the required links from the Human Solutions website. This analysis pertains to a vehicle analysis, which can be seen when the file is opened (see Fig. 6).

Fig. 6. An image showing the car geometry used in the demonstration.

3.3 Boundary Manikins Creation

For human-vehicle interactions to be studied, manikins were created. The driver role was made first using the *Role Definition* menu. Then, manikins were created using the *Body Builder* menu and *Anthropometry*. Using the *Control Measurement* window, the dimensions of the manikin were modified by *type*. With these changes, the following manikins were created to represent potential extremes of the population:

1. 50th percentile male with a medium torso
2. 5th percentile female with a long torso
3. 5th percentile female with a short torso
4. 95th percentile male with a long torso
5. 95th percentile male with a medium torso
6. 95th percentile male with a short torso

3.4 Reposition and Locate Manikin in Vehicle

The manikins next needed to be assigned to the vehicle. This was done using the *Define Restrictions* tool. The following table (Table 6) summarizes the restrictions placed on each manikin to restrain them to the driver's seat.

With the completed restrictions, the *Posture Calculation* was made to apply the settings to each manikin. The resulting positions are shown in Fig. 7 below.

Reviewing the manikins' positions in the vehicle revealed further restrictions needed. For example, the heads of the taller manikins protruded outside the roof of the vehicle. Additionally, the shorter manikins needed to be able to see over the hood to the road. These were both corrected with limit restrictions (see Fig. 8).

3.5 Location and Comfort Analysis – Overall Driving Position

Comparing the posture of the manikins to the neutral position revealed that the manikins were not in an ergonomic orientation. The manikins were sitting more inclined with their legs very extended and necks strained (see Fig. 9).

Some design changes were made to re-position the manikins closer to the desired posture. The initial state of discomfort was measured with the *Comfort Feeling* tool. To improve the condition, the steering wheel was moved toward the front of the car, and

Table 6. Summary of restrictions applied to each manikin to constrain them to the driver's seat of the vehicle

Manikin Component/Restriction Type	Environment Object/Fixation
H-point	seat_travel
LeftHeel	floor
RightHeel	floor
LeftBall	footrest
RightBall	accel_de_centerline
Pelvis Rotation	Tilt Sideways/Long Axis Rotation
Line-of-vision	−0.99 −0.00 −0.12
H-point Fixation	Current Position (after *Posture Calculation*)
HAR_3_10	stw_r
HAL_3_10	stw_l
Manual Grasping (both hands)	Grasp softly

Fig. 7. Manikins located in the driver's seat after initial restrictions have been applied.

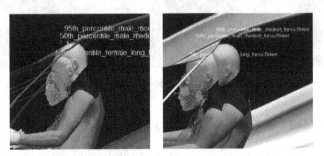

Fig. 8. Before and after change of taller manikin heads interfering with the roof of the vehicle.

the acceleration pedal was moved toward the back of the car. This greatly reduced the discomfort of the manikins, as shown for Manikin 3 in Fig. 10.

The improvement can also be seen by comparing again to the neutral position of each manikin (see Fig. 11).

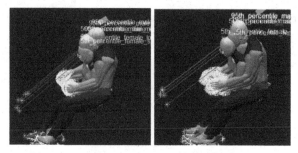

Fig. 9. Manikin posture in the current position (left) and the ideal/neutral position (right).

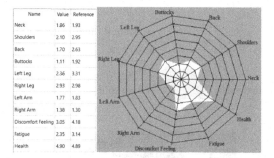

Fig. 10. Discomfort reductions for Manikin 3 compared to the reference before design modifications were made.

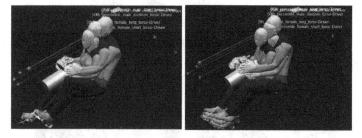

Fig. 11. Manikin posture in the modified position (left) and the ideal/neutral position (right).

3.6 Location and Comfort Analysis – Touch Screen for Passenger

The next set of analyses was performed on a passenger, rather than a driver. A new role was created and the manikins were assigned as *passengers*. Then, they were relocated to the passenger seat of the car and fixed within the vehicle by defining restrictions on the H-point, pelvis, and both heels.

A reachability analysis was created to understand the distance from each manikin to the display. Using the *Compute Reachability* tool, *Arm Right* was activated to study the right arm (see Fig. 12).

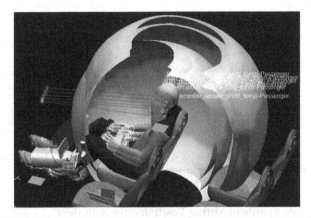

Fig. 12. Right arm reachability analysis for each passenger manikin.

The reach analysis showed that the two manikins with the reach covering the least of the display were Manikins 1 (50th percentile male with a medium torso) and 4 (95th percentile male with a long torso). Because of this, these manikins were prioritized for the reach and comfort analysis, as they will have the most difficulty accessing the display.

A point was created on the display as a sample contact point for the manikins. Both manikins were able to reach the screen but needed to distort their bodies. To improve reachability, the display was moved. First, it was rotated about a point aligned with the steering column toward the driver and moved toward the back of the car. The posture improvements are shown in Fig. 13 below.

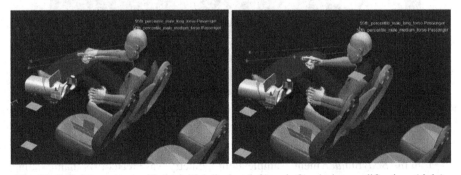

Fig. 13. Manikin posture with the initial display (left) and after design modifications (right).

These improvements are also validated with a new comfort analysis, shown in Fig. 14 below.

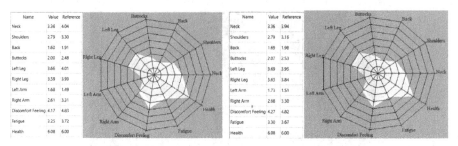

Fig. 14. Discomfort reductions for Manikin 1 (left) and Manikin 4 (right) compared to the reference before design modifications were made.

3.7 Maximum Percentile in Sitting Position – Body Builder

The next analysis aims to determine the maximum size of a manikin that can fit within the backseat of the vehicle. Initial male and female manikins were created with medium settings and located to the backseat. The male manikin's head interferes with the roof of the car while the female's head has excess clearance (see Fig. 15).

Fig. 15. Position showing male manikin's head interfering with roof (left) and female manikin's head with excess clearance (right).

From the *BodyBuilder* menu, sample anthropometry was created. By manipulating the sitting height, applying it to the manikin, and re-calculating the posture, the maximum height of each manikin could be iteratively discovered. The results show that the maximum sitting height for the male and female manikins is the 10th (879 mm) and 60th percentile (882 mm), respectively.

3.8 Visibility of Instrument Cluster – Driver

To analyze the visibility of the instrument cluster, the steepest and shallowest viewing angles of the manikins were used to understand the full range. The line of sight of Manikin

2 (5th percentile female with a long torso) has the steepest angle, while Manikin 6 (95th percentile male with a short torso) has the shallowest. A point was created on the center of the screen and using the *Move Eye* function, both manikins focused their eyes on the point. The *Internal View* analysis was run to visualize what the manikins were seeing (Fig. 16 and 17). Both manikins could see the screen and no design modifications were needed.

Fig. 16. Left and right eye visualization of Manikin 2 looking at the screen.

Fig. 17. Left and right eye visualization of Manikin 6 looking at the screen.

Next, potential screen obstructions were studied, namely the steering wheel. Running the *Sight Limit* analysis showed that no design modifications were needed to eliminate an obstruction (Fig. 18).

Lastly, an *Acuity* analysis was run to evaluate text and symbol size on the screen. In the study, only the furthest manikin from the screen (Manikin 4: 95th percentile male with a long torso) was used, as it will need the largest size to safely interpret the information. A letter character was added to the recommended size (Fig. 19), showing that because it is similar to the text on the image, the display is acceptable for the driver to interpret.

3.9   Reflections on Windshield and Glare – Driver's Cover Glass

The last vehicle analysis performed was understanding potential reflections on the manikins. For the study, the male and female manikins with short torsos (Manikins 3 and 6) were chosen because they sit the lowest in the vehicle and experience the most critical reflections. First, the *Reflection* analysis was run on simulated daytime

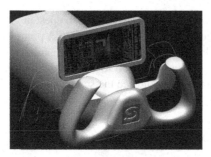

Fig. 18. Obstruction analysis of the steering wheel on the screen showing the outline of the shadow outside the bounds of the screen.

Fig. 19. Text character "A," of the recommended size for Manikin 4 compared to the screen display.

reflections/glare (light from the rear window bouncing off the screen into the driver's eyes). The result showed that both manikins experienced considerable reflection from the screen (Fig. 20).

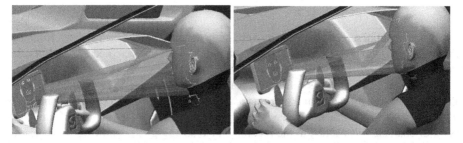

Fig. 20. Reflection from the rear window off the screen for Manikins 3 (left) and 6 (right).

To eliminate the reflection, the screen was rotated 15 deg in the negative y-direction to angle light from the rear window up to the roof. Additionally, the screen was still angled in a way that allowed the manikins to read easily.

Reflections from the windshield due to the screen light at nighttime were also analyzed. Some light will cause a glare in the eyes of both manikins (Fig. 21). In this analysis, the windshield cannot be modified, though the design recommendation would be to change the angle to reduce reflection into the eyes of the driver.

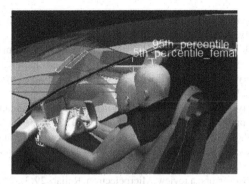

Fig. 21. Reflection from the screen light off the windshield for Manikins 3 and 6.

3.10 Summary

The vehicle analysis above identified numerous design changes that should be made to accommodate various users (summarized in Table 7 below).

Table 7. Summary of design recommendations made through these analyses

Vehicle Component	Redesign Recommendation	Explanation
Cab/Roof	Increase height	Interference with user's heads
Steering wheel	Move toward front of car	Improve driver ergonomics
Acceleration pedal	Move toward back of car	Improve driver ergonomics
Display	Rotate toward driver	Improve display reachability
Display	Move toward back of car	Improve display reachability
Instrument Cluster Screen	Rotate toward roof	Reduce glare to driver
Windshield	Rotate toward back of car	Reduce reflection from screen

In failing to perform such studies early in the design process, projects will move inefficiently and can fall victim to human error later. Additionally, if these problems are never identified before launching the product, users can be exposed to increased human-error-related risks.

References

1. Aromataris, E., Pearson, A.: The systematic review: an overview. AJN Am. J. Nurs. **114**(3), 53–58 (2014). https://doi.org/10.1097/01.naj.0000444496.24228.2c

2. Award # 1918140 - FMITF: Collaborative Research: Track I: Preventing Human Errors in Cyber-Human Systems with Formal Approaches to Human Reliability Rating and Model Repair. NSF. Accessed 21 Apr 2023. https://www.nsf.gov/awardsearch/showAward?AWD_ID=1918140

3. Beith, B.H.: Human Factors and the Future of Telemedicine. Medical Device & Diagnostic Industry. Accessed 1 June 1999

4. Bell, J., Holroyd, J.: RR679 - Review of Human Reliability Assessment Methods. Health and Safety Laboratory. Accessed 21 Apr 2023. https://www.hse.gov.uk/research/rrhtm//rr679.htm

5. Brauer, R.L.: Safety and Health for Engineers. John Wiley & Sons, Incorporated, New York (2016). Accessed 21 Apr 2023. ProQuest Ebook Central

6. Brown, M.L.: Software systems safety and human errors. In: Computer Assurance, 1988. COMPASS 1988, pp. 19–28 (1988). https://doi.org/10.1109/cmpass.1988.9634

7. Cooper, J.B., Newbower, R.S., Kitz, R.J.: An Analysis of major errors and equipment failures in anesthesia management. Anesthesiology **60**(1), 34–42 (1984). https://doi.org/10.1097/000 00542-198401000-00008

8. Dhillon, B.S.: Human errors: a review. Microelectron. Reliab. **29**(3), 299–304 (1989). https://doi.org/10.1016/0026-2714(89)90612-4

9. Elsevier. "Scopus." Elsevier. Accessed 19 Apr 2023. https://www.elsevier.com/en-gb/soluti ons/scopus

10. Feggetter, A.J.: A method for investigating human factor aspects of aircraft accidents and incidents. Ergonomics **25**(11), 1065–1075 (1982). https://doi.org/10.1080/001401382089 25065

11. Formentini, G., Rodríguez, N.B., Favi, C.: Design for manufacturing and assembly methods in the product development process of mechanical products: a systematic literature review. Int. J. Adv. Manuf. Technol. **120**(7–8), 4307–4334 (2022). https://doi.org/10.1007/s00170-022-08837-6

12. Fosch-Villaronga, E., Khanna, P., Drukarch, H., Custers, B.: The role of humans in surgery automation. Int. J. Soc. Robot. **15**(3), 563–580 (2022). https://doi.org/10.1007/s12369-022-00875-0

13. Gertman, D.I., Blackman, H.S., Marble, J.L., Byers, J.C., Smith, C.L.: The SPAR-H Human Reliability Analysis Method. U.S. Nuclear Regulatory Commission, Washington, D.C. (2005)

14. Goetsch, D.L.: Occupational Safety and Health: For Technologists, Engineers, and Managers, 9th edn. Pearson, Boston (2019)

15. Google Books Ngram Viewer. Google Books. Google. Accessed 19 Apr 2023. https://books. google.com/ngrams/

16. Hollnagel, E.: Cognitive Reliability and Error Analysis Method (CREAM). Elsevier, Oxford (2005)

17. Hollnagel, E.: Human Reliability Analysis: Context and Control. Academic Press, London (1993)

18. Human Solutions - Products - RAMSIS General. Accessed April 21, 2023. https://www. human-solutions.com/en/products/ramsis-general/index.html

19. Jan van Eck, N., Waltman, L.: VOSviewer. Leiden University's Centre for Science and Technology Studies. https://www.vosviewer.com/20

20. Khan, K.S., Kunz, R., Kleijnen, J., Antes, G.: Five steps to conducting a systematic review. JRSM **96**(3), 118–121 (2003). https://doi.org/10.1258/jrsm.96.3.118

21. Kirwan, B.: A Guide to Practical Human Reliability Assessment, 1st edn. Taylor & Francis, London (1994)

22. Moseley, C.H.G.: Human factors that cause aircraft accidents. SAE Technical Papers (1956). https://doi.org/10.4271/560285

23. Ogle, R.A., "Trey" Morrison, D., Carpenter, A.R.: The relationship between automation complexity and operator error. J. Hazard. Mater. **159**(1), 135–141 (2008). https://doi.org/10.1016/j.jhazmat.2008.01.065

24. Rasmussen, Jens: Skills, rules, and knowledge; signals, signs, and symbols, and other distinctions in human performance models. IEEE Trans. Syst. Man Cybern. **SMC-13**(3), 257–266 (1983). https://doi.org/10.1109/TSMC.1983.6313160

25. Reason, J.T.: Managing the Risks of Organizational Accidents, 1st edn. Routledge, London (1997)

26. Reason, J.: Human Error. Cambridge Univ. Pr, Cambridge (1990)

27. Scite: See How Research Has Been Cited. scite.ai. Accessed 19 Apr 2023. https://scite.ai/

28. Sheridan, T.B.: Risk, human error, and system resilience: fundamental ideas. Human Fact. J. Human Fact. Ergon. Soc. **50**(3), 418–426 (2008). https://doi.org/10.1518/001872008x250773

29. Soria Zurita, N.F., Stone, R.B., Demirel, O., Tumer, I.Y.: The function-human error design method (FHEDM). In: SME 2018 International Design Engineering Technical Conferences and Computers and Information in Engineering Conference, vol. 7 (2018). https://doi.org/10.1115/detc2018-85327

30. Swain, A.D., Guttmann, H.E.: Handbook of Human-Reliability Analysis with Emphasis on Nuclear Power Plant Applications. Appl. Ergon. **16**(1) (1985). https://doi.org/10.2172/5752058

31. Twitter Analytics Tool for Tracking Hashtags, Keywords, and Accounts. Vicinitas. Accessed 19 Apr 2023. https://www.vicinitas.io/

32. Zapf, D., Reason, J.T.: Introduction: human errors and error handling. Appl. Psychol. **43**(4), 427–432 (1994). https://doi.org/10.1111/j.1464-0597.1994.tb00838.x

Systematic Literature Review on the Advances of Wearable Technologies

Daniel Kuratomi[✉], Chanho Shin, and Vincent G. Duffy

Purdue University, West Lafayette, IN 47906, USA
{dkuratom,shin243,duffy}@purdue.edu

Abstract. This literature review examines the emerging field of wearable technologies and their impact on various industries, including healthcare, fitness, and ergonomics. Using advanced research techniques such as CiteSpace, VOS Viewer, and Scite.ai, we identified the most relevant and current information on wearable technologies. The review reveals that wearable technologies are becoming increasingly popular due to their potential to enhance human health and well-being. Wearable devices can monitor a range of health metrics such as heart rate, sleep quality, and physical activity, helping individuals to better understand and manage their health. Additionally, wearable technologies are being used in various industries to improve performance and productivity. Furthermore, the review highlights the importance of job design in the implementation of wearable technologies. The integration of wearable technologies in the workplace can enhance job performance and improve employee well-being, but it also requires careful consideration of job design to avoid potential negative impacts on job autonomy, privacy, and work-life balance. Overall, this literature review underscores the potential benefits of wearable technologies and the need for further research to fully realize their potential in improving human health and well-being and enhancing workplace productivity. The review also highlights the importance of considering job design when implementing wearable technologies in the workplace.

Keywords: Wearable Technologies · Human Factors · Ergonomics

1 Introduction and Background

Wearable devices are becoming more popular because they can help improve human health. They can track things like heart rate, sleep, and activity, which helps people understand their health better. Businesses like fitness, healthcare, and sports also use wearable devices to help people perform better. However, these benefits can also translate well to the business world by tracking and aiding workers perform their tasks. Wearable devices can make it easier to stay connected with others and get information quickly. More and more people are getting long-term illnesses and need to be monitored from home, so wearable health devices have been created to help. Further, the population of most of all the developing countries is aging and there is a need to reduce healthcare costs through all systems. Wearables technologies can aid in this by providing better

V. G. Duffy et al. (Eds.): HCII 2023, LNCS 14057, pp. 78–95, 2023.
https://doi.org/10.1007/978-3-031-48047-8_5

prevention through monitoring of the patients at home. There are also more people who want to stay fit and healthy, so there are more wearable devices for them too. Wearable devices are possible now because the sensors and batteries are small enough to fit on your body and work well.

Wearable technologies can provide real-time feedback on worker performance and safety, this helps prevent workplace injuries and accidents. Additionally, wearable devices can assist in the automation of industrial processes, leading to greater efficiency and productivity, for example in factory or construction settings. Outside of industrial engineering, there are various efforts to address challenges in wearable technologies, including improvements in battery life and the miniaturization of sensors. Further, advances in artificial intelligence and machine learning are being applied to the data being recorded by wearable devices and provide more accurate and appropriate insights in health monitoring. Finally, wearables are being developed to not only track basic physiological features like heart rate but more complex ones like sweat and brain waves. This will allow us to apply this technology to tackle more advanced diseases and illnesses.

To better respond to wearable technologies, society needs to provide funding for research and development of new devices and technologies, while also considering mitigation strategies to address potential risks and challenges. It is necessary to define the privacy risks that will come with the technology and where to set limits to what to track. Additionally, society should adapt to the changing landscape of wearable technologies by promoting digital literacy and ensuring equitable access to these de-vices and their benefits. The human factors and ergonomics and human-computer interaction communities have been working to address the topic of wearable technologies by conducting research on user needs and preferences, as well as usability testing of wearable devices. Additionally, these communities have been developing guidelines and standards for the design of wearable technologies that prioritize user safety and comfort. Finally, the safety-related community has been collaborating with wearable technology manufacturers to develop safety protocols and regulations for the use of wearable devices in industrial settings.

2 Methodology

To perform this systematic review, a previously published methodology was followed that include the implementation of powerful computational tools to find the most relevant documents for the topic (Sodhi et al. 2023). The methodology aims to find and filter the most appropriate documents for review. This includes standard database search with different filters, advanced trend analysis using raw information from said databases and artificial intelligence analysis tools.

2.1 Databases

To perform the initial search, 3 academic databases were used: Google Scholar, Scopus and Web of Science. In all 3 databases, the term Wearable Technologies was searched with and without quotations. When possible, the results were organized by number of citations or relevance. For the Web of Science database, the core collection was used to improve compatibility with other analysis tools.

2.2 Analysis Tools

With the results of the database searches, the raw data was analyzed using advanced analysis tools to provide insights into the main topic and relevant subtopics. A quick overview of the different tools is presented in the following section.

Google Ngram

Google Ngram Viewer is a web-based tool that allows users to search and analyze the frequency of words and phrases in Google's vast collection of digitized books. This massive corpus of text spans centuries, making it a useful resource for linguistic and cultural analysis. The tool enables users to visualize how language usage has changed over time, and also allows them to compare the usage of multiple words or phrases at once. Additionally, Google Ngram Viewer can be used to identify trends, patterns, and historical events that have influenced language usage.

To perform a search in Google Ngram Viewer, the user inputs one or more words or phrases separated by commas into the search bar on the homepage. The user can also specify a date range, language, and corpus. After clicking "Search," the tool generated a graph that showed the frequency of the searched words or phrases over time.

Harzinz's Publish or Perish

Harzing's Publish or Perish is a software program designed to help academics and researchers assess their research impact. It works by using various metrics to analyze a researcher's publication output and citation record, including the h-index, g-index, and the number of citations per paper. The tool also allows users to search for and analyze publications by other researchers in their field.

To perform a search in Harzing's Publish or Perish, the user inputs the name of the author or search query into the search bar on the homepage. They could also refine their search by selecting various options such as the database, years of publication, and document type. After clicking "Search," the tool generated a list of publications that matched the search criteria, along with various citation metrics for each publication. This tool is useful to download the raw data from Google Scholar, as the normal interface of said database does not allow it.

VOS Viewer

VOS Viewer is a free software program designed for visualizing and analyzing bibliometric networks, such as those based on scientific publications. The tool allows users to create and manipulate network visualizations, using techniques such as clustering, density visualization, and pathfinder networks. It also includes features for analyzing and comparing network data, such as network indicators and pathfinder measures.

To perform a search in VOS Viewer, the user imports a dataset into the tool, such as a bibliographic file exported from a citation database. They can then create a network visualization by selecting different options for the nodes and edges, such as author names or publication keywords. After generating the visualization, the user could explore the network and identify patterns and trends using various tools and techniques available in

VOS Viewer. For this research, the database Scopus results were used and the first 2000 top articles based on the number of citations were selected.

CiteSpace

CiteSpace is a software tool for visualizing and analyzing trends and patterns in scientific literature. It allows users to create and manipulate network visualizations of co-citation and co-occurrence relationships between publications. The tool also includes features for identifying emerging trends, influential authors, and key research themes within a particular field of study.

Scite.ai

Scite.ai is a web-based platform that uses artificial intelligence and natural language processing to evaluate the credibility of scientific publications. It works by analyzing the citation context of a publication and assigning a "smart citation" that indicates whether the citing work provides supporting or contradicting evidence. The platform also includes features for searching and browsing scientific publications and tracking the impact of a researcher's work.

Vicinitas.io

Vicinitas.io is a web-based platform designed for analyzing and visualizing scientific literature. It allows users to search for and explore relationships between different publications, authors, and keywords within a particular field of study. The tool includes features for generating network visualizations, analyzing citation data, and identifying emerging trends and research themes.

3   Results

3.1   Initial Search Results

Three databases were searched for the topic of wearable technologies. Scopus, Web of Science and Google Scholar, the latter using Harzing's Publish or Perish software. The results of the number of articles are presented in the following table (Table 1).

Table 1.   Academic databases reviewed, terms utilized and number of results.

Database	Wearable Technologies	"Wearable Technologies"
Scopus	40,722	25,706
Web Of Science	22,916	1,708
Google Scholar	971,000	34,200

3.2 Relevant Definitions

Wearable device: an electronic gadget that is embedded within clothing, watches, or accessories and can be worn on the body. These devices can have various functions, ranging from basic features such as heart rate monitoring and pedometer capabilities to advanced "smart" functions and features (Kumar et al. 2020).

Wearable sensor: a device that is attached externally to a person's body to measure physiological parameters of interest. These sensors can monitor vital signs like heart rate and blood pressure during daily activities and be used for continuous health monitoring, movement analysis, rehabilitation, and evaluation of human performance. Additionally, wearable sensors can be integrated with wireless power supplies and data communication systems to allow real-time, continuous sensing. (Nag et al. 2015).

Flexible electronics: electronic components and devices that retain their functionality even when they are stretched, bent, folded, or twisted. These electronics are lightweight, low-cost, conformable, and can be easily tailored to fit different applications. As a result, they are gaining popularity in various fields such as healthcare, communication, safety, security, and aerospace, among others (Corzo et al. 2020).

3.3 Trends

Using the keyword "wearable technologies", a search was performed in Scopus for journal articles and conference proceedings. Analyzing said results, you can see a trendline that shows the exponential growth of the topic over the last couple of decades. With less than 200 articles per year in the years 2000's, the topic became extremely popular in the early 2010's and reached its current maximum output at around 3500 articles per year in the year 2017 (Fig. 1).

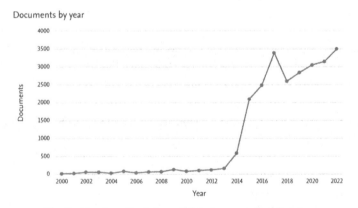

Fig. 1. Number of articles published per year per Scopus.

Google Ngram Viewer can be used to identify trends, patterns, and historical events that have influenced language usage. Searching only the term "wearable technologies" shows the emergence of interest in this topic around the year 2014 (Fig. 2).

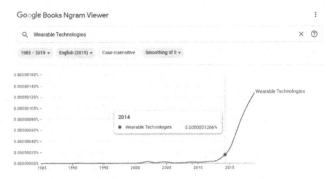

Fig. 2. Google Ngram trend of the topic of wearable technologies.

However, when comparing to other established topics such as Human Factors and Ergonomics, the topic of wearable technologies is still in its infancy at least in regard to books (Fig. 3).

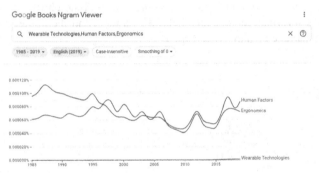

Fig. 3. Google Ngram trend of the topic of wearable technologies compared to Human Factors and Ergonomics.

For a quick overview, the top 10 articles from Scopus, Web of Science and Google Scholar were downloaded as pdfs for further analysis. These pdf files were then ingested into maxQDA and a word cloud was generated in the form of HF to explore the most common subtopics discussed in these articles (Fig. 4).

3.4 Cluster Analysis (VOS Viewer/CiteSpace)

After performing the search in Scopus, the metadata of the search results was exported in plain text format. This metadata was then ingested into VOS Viewer to perform different analysis of said results. The first was a Co-ocurrence analysis with a minimum threshold of 15 value. A total of 433 keywords were reviewed and 4 clusters were identified using the tool. In the figure, the 4 different clusters are differentiated using the colors red, green, blue, and yellow. This analysis allows us to see the main keywords that are shared within the articles of the search results and visualize the most common ones. The green cluster

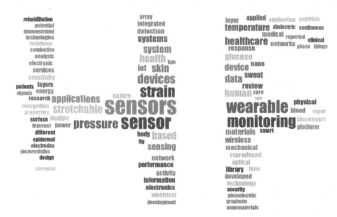

Fig. 4. Word cloud of the top 10 articles from the 3 databases. (Color figure online)

represents the applications of wearable technologies while the red represents articles focusing on the specific of the wearable sensors. The yellow cluster shows keywords related to the wireless communication subtopic and the blue cluster shows electrical subtopics. This information was very helpful to understand the underlying subtopics that relate to wearable technologies (Fig. 5).

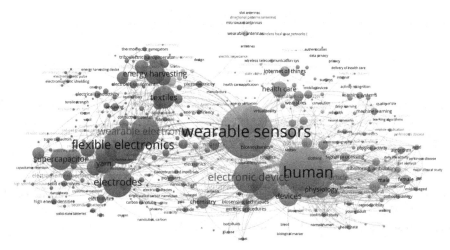

Fig. 5. VOS Viewer with Scopus results, Co-occurrence analysis, 15 minimum thresholds. 433 keywords, 4 clusters

Similarly, the same metadata of the results was used to perform a co-citation analysis using VOS Viewer. This analysis had a minimum threshold of 20 and resulted in 40 items in 3 clusters. This cluster analysis shows the relationship between papers that reference other papers in the search results. The most important articles from this analysis were selected for further review as they represent important nodes in the topic of wearable technologies. Further, co-authorship and co-authorship by countries was also explored.

Finally, the last figure represents the most popular journals in the co-citation analysis (Figs. 6 and 7).

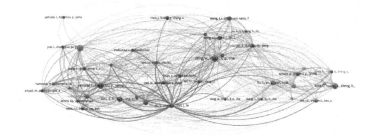

Fig. 6. VOS Viewer with Scopus results, Co-citation analysis, 20 minimum threshold, 40 items, 3 clusters.

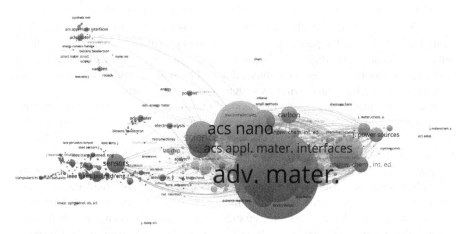

Fig. 7. VOS Viewer with Scopus results, co-citation analysis, cited sources, minimum threshold 20, 559 elements, 8 clusters.

3.5 Co-citation Analysis

Using the co-citation analysis, the top 10 articles were selected using the VOS Viewer software. The articles were selected based on the link number instead of just the raw number of citations as to select only the articles with the most quality (Fig. 8).

From those 10 articles, the top 3 articles were further explored to understand the topics they relate to. The first text discusses the development of bio-integrated wearable systems that can measure a variety of biological and environmental signals, offering insights into human health and performance. The article outlines recent advancements in material science, chemical analysis techniques, device designs, and assembly methods that make this technology unique, non-invasive, and able to intimately integrate with the human

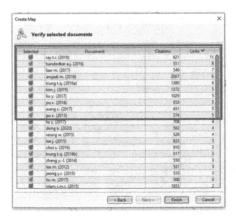

Fig. 8. List of most relevant papers according to the co-citation analysis

body. The article summarizes the latest advances in this emerging field and connects fundamental developments in chemistry, material science, and engineering with sensing technologies that have the potential for widespread deployment and societal benefit in human health care. The article also discusses the design considerations for sensors and associated platforms, highlights the most advanced biosensors, and provides strategies for achieving fully integrated, wireless systems (Ray et al. 2019).

The second article provides an overview of the challenges and gaps in developing effective wearable chemical sensor systems, including materials, power, analytical procedure, communication, data acquisition, processing, and security. The paper discusses potential solutions to these key problems encountered by wearable chemical sensors via advances in related fields and routes to incorporate them onto such sensor platforms. The authors also discuss the future prospects of this emerging sensor field and its ability to open up new avenues in the field of wearable electronics (Bandodkar et al. 2016).

The final article identified with the co-citation analysis presents a study on the fabrication of wearable, healable, and adhesive epidermal sensors using mussel-inspired conductive hybrid hydrogel framework. The sensors are designed for ultrasensitive human-machine interaction and healthcare monitoring and are assembled from conductive and human-friendly hybrid hydrogels with reliable self-healing capability and robust self-adhesiveness (Liao et al. 2017).

3.6 CiteSpace Clusters

After performing the search of the keywords in the database Web of Science, the metadata results were exported as a plain text file and ingested into the CiteSpace software. CiteSpace allows the analysis of the results from Web of Science and divides the articles into clusters and labels the clusters based on shared keywords. The analysis was based using the references as nodes with a g-index of 15. This allows the classification of the clusters based on subtopics of the wearable technologies topic and allows for further analysis on them. In the figure, the main clusters are shown in different colors. Similarly, to the VOS Viewer analysis, some clusters focus on mobile applications, others focus on electronics, others focus on specific sports data and others in selective sensor groups (Fig. 9).

Fig. 9. CiteSpace keyword clusters.

It is also possible to export the cluster information from CiteSpace into table format. Here, the different clusters are specified. It is possible to analyze the size, the average year that the cluster appears, and the labels related to the cluster (Table 2).

Using the labels classified by CiteSpace, the main clusters were identified as Longitudinal monitoring, Stretchable sensors and Transdermal sensors. These relevant subtopics were further explored:

Longitudinal monitoring is a method of continuous monitoring of an individual's health over an extended period of time (Mukhopadhyay et al. 2015). This method involves the collection of data at multiple time points, allowing for the detection of changes in an individual's health status over time. Wearable devices are a popular tool for longitudinal monitoring, as they can provide continuous physiological data (Ajami et al. 2015). Longitudinal monitoring can be used for precision health, disease risk assessment, and early detection of preclinical conditions (Mukhopadhyay et al. 2015).

Stretchable sensors are a type of wearable technology that can be attached to clothing or directly mounted on the human skin for real-time monitoring of human activities. Stretchable sensors must fulfill several minimum requirements, including high stretchability, flexibility, durability, low power consumption, biocompatibility, and lightweight (Amjadi et al. 2016). These sensors can measure and quantify electrical signals generated by human activities and can provide a new opportunity for human-activity monitoring and personal healthcare (Trung et al. 2016). Stretchable sensors can be made from a variety of materials, including silver nanowires, carbon nanotubes, and conductive elastomers (Amjadi et al. 2014).

Table 2. CiteSpace Cluster results

ClusterID	Size	Mean (Year)	Label (LLR)
0	49	2014	**longitudinal monitoring** (3.43, 0.1); conducting polymers (3.43, 0.1); performance parameters (3.43, 0.1); pilocarpine (3.43, 0.1); ambient assisted living (3.43, 0.1)
1	49	2017	wearable electronics (6.97, 0.01); **stretchable sensors** (5.69, 0.05); soft robotics (4.6, 0.05); flexible electronics (4.6, 0.05); iot (2.84, 0.1)
2	31	2014	technology (9.69, 0.005); additive manufacturing (4.82, 0.05); healthcare technologies (4.82, 0.05); **transdermal sensing** (4.82, 0.05); diabetic foot ulcers (4.82, 0.05)
3	29	2015	wearables (7.3, 0.01); physiolytics (6.23, 0.05); acceleration (6.23, 0.05); q-methodology (6.23, 0.05); qualitative analysis (6.23, 0.05)
4	25	2016	triboelectric nanogenerators (12.38, 0.001); electromagnetic energy (6.15, 0.05); triboelectric nanogenerator (6.15, 0.05); wind energy (6.15, 0.05); textrodes (6.15, 0.05)
5	22	2018	health and safety (9.3, 0.005); ubiquitous sensing (9.3, 0.005); security (9.3, 0.005); human-machine interaction (5.68, 0.05); accuracy (4.63, 0.05)
6	18	2019	wearable robot (4.56, 0.05); artificial intelligence (4.56, 0.05); wearable device (4.56, 0.05); prevention (4.56, 0.05); population health (4.56, 0.05)
8	12	2016	health insurance (6, 0.05); perceived benefit (6, 0.05); smart services (6, 0.05); smart watch (6, 0.05); theory of planned behavior (6, 0.05)
9	12	2014	external load (7.28, 0.01); prescribing performance (7.28, 0.01); gps (7.28, 0.01); training technology (7.28, 0.01); internal load (7.28, 0.01)

Transdermal sensors are a type of wearable technology that can be attached to the skin to monitor physiological signals, such as glucose levels, alcohol consumption, and vital signs (Teymourian et al. 2021). These sensors can detect changes in the skin's interstitial fluid, which can provide valuable information about an individual's health status. Transdermal sensors can be made from a variety of materials, including graphene, gold nanoparticles, and conductive hydrogels (Pu et al. 2016). Wearable transdermal sensors can be used for remote health monitoring, early diagnosis of diseases, and fall risk assessment in older adults (Mirjalali et al. 2021).

3.7   CiteSpace Citation Bursts

CiteSpace is also able to analyze the data based on the time domain, as such it is able to detect when the articles were cited and by whom. This allows the software to select the articles that spark important discussions surrounding a specific topic. This is called a citation burst. These bursts show which papers generated an increase in co-citation during a short period of time and as such can be considered of special interest during the literature review. As such, they were also selected for further review (Fig. 10).

Top 16 References with the Strongest Citation Bursts

References	Year	Strength	Begin	End	2013 - 2023
Chan M, 2012, ARTIF INTELL MED, V56, P137, DOI 10.1016/j.artmed.2012.09.003, DOI	2012	4.97	2015	2017	
Stoppa M, 2014, SENSORS-BASEL, V14, P11957, DOI 10.3390/s140711957, DOI	2014	5.94	2016	2019	
Bower M, 2015, COMPUT EDUC, V88, P343, DOI 10.1016/j.compedu.2015.07.013, DOI	2015	4.46	2016	2017	
Swan M, 2013, BIG DATA-US, V1, P85, DOI 10.1089/big.2012.0002, DOI	2013	2.58	2016	2018	
Sultan N, 2015, INT J INFORM MANAGE, V35, P521, DOI 10.1016/j.ijinfomgt.2015.04.010, DOI	2015	3.03	2017	2018	
Piwek L, 2016, PLOS MED, V13, P0, DOI 10.1371/journal.pmed.1001953, DOI	2016	2.72	2018	2019	
Patel MS, 2015, JAMA-J AM MED ASSOC, V313, P459, DOI 10.1001/jama.2014.14781, DOI	2015	2.52	2018	2019	
Sonner Z, 2015, BIOMICROFLUIDICS, V9, P0, DOI 10.1063/1.4921039, DOI	2015	2.52	2018	2019	
Mukhopadhyay SC, 2015, IEEE SENS J, V15, P1321, DOI 10.1109/JSEN.2014.2370945, DOI	2015	2.84	2019	2020	
Chuah SHW, 2016, COMPUT HUM BEHAV, V65, P276, DOI 10.1016/j.chb.2016.07.047, DOI	2016	2.83	2019	2021	
Liu Y, 2017, ACS NANO, V11, P9614, DOI 10.1021/acsnano.7b04898, DOI	2017	2.83	2019	2021	
Amjadi M, 2016, ADV FUNCT MATER, V26, P1678, DOI 10.1002/adfm.201504755, DOI	2016	2.83	2019	2021	
Khan Y, 2016, ADV MATER, V28, P4373, DOI 10.1002/adma.201504366, DOI	2016	2.59	2019	2021	
Peake JM, 2018, FRONT PHYSIOL, V9, P0, DOI 10.3389/fphys.2018.00743, DOI	2018	2.93	2020	2023	
Miyamoto A, 2017, NAT NANOTECHNOL, V12, P907, DOI 10.1038/nnano.2017.125, 10.1038/NNANO.2017.125, DOI	2017	4.34	2021	2023	
Kim J, 2019, NAT BIOTECHNOL, V37, P389, DOI 10.1038/s41587-019-0045-y, DOI	2019	3.94	2021	2023	

Fig. 10. CiteSpace Citation Burst.

The 3 main articles that caused a citation burst were selected to review the topic they are covering. The articles were selected based on the Strength of the citation burst. The first article relates to wearable electronics and smart textiles. The review focuses on recent advances in the field of smart textiles, paying particular attention to the materials and their manufacturing process. The document discusses the convergence of electronics and textiles into fabrics that are able to sense, compute, communicate, and actuate (Stoppa et al. 2014).

The second article discusses the development and challenges of smart wearable systems (SWS) for health monitoring (HM), which are becoming increasingly important due to rising healthcare costs and technological advancements. The article reviews the current research and development of SWS for HM, focusing on multi-parameter physiological sensor systems and activity and mobility measurement system designs that can provide real-time decision support processing for disease prevention, symptom detection, and diagnosis. The article describes the state of the art in SWS, recent implementations of wearable healthcare systems, current issues, challenges, and prospects of SWS, and future challenges facing this technology (Chan et al. 2012).

The final article explores the educational affordances of wearable technologies for mobile learning design. It draws upon a wide sample of knowledgeable educators from around the world as well as the literature to provide a comprehensive conceptualization of ways that wearable technologies may be utilized, and the key issues that need to be considered in their learning designs (Bower et al. 2015).

3.8 Authors, Countries and Journals

Using Scopus, the leading table for authors was produced. This information, combined with the cluster analysis and the citation burst, provided valuable insights into the most relevant authors of the field (Fig. 11).

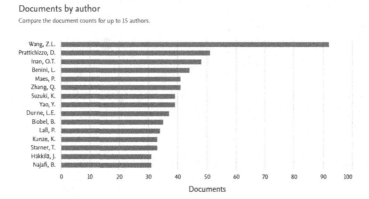

Fig. 11. Leading authors for the topic of wearable technologies according to Scopus

Similarly, the leading countries for the publication of articles related to wearable technologies were taken from Scopus. The main producers of academic articles in this topic are the US and China with the rest of the countries far away from sais output (Fig. 12).

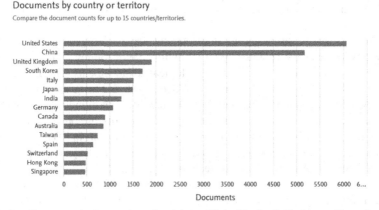

Fig. 12. Leading countries by number of articles published in the field of wearable technologies.

From the affiliation's perspective, it is clear that the publications from China are concentrated in a few research centers, as the research from the US appears to be more scattered across a lot of different entities (Fig. 13).

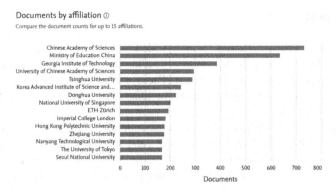

Fig. 13. Leading affiliations by number of articles published in the field of wearable technologies.

3.9   Engagement Results (Vicinitas)

Using Vicinitas, the engagement of the wearable technologies' topic was measured using twitter data. Using the free tool, an account was connected to the service and the hashtag Wearable Technologies was analyzed. A word cloud was generated from the tweets and replies related to the topic and the engagement timeline and post timeline were generated. In these figures, it is possible to see the cumulative engagement and cumulative posts related to wearable technologies in the twitter space. It is also possible to review the type of post and the type of media that is being discussed in this topic (Fig. 14).

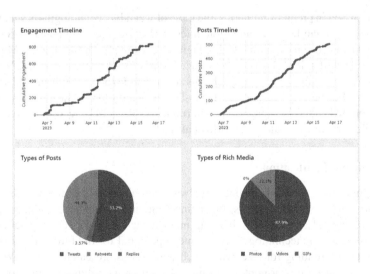

Fig. 14.   Vicinitas.io engagement results for twitter.

4 Discussion

The initial search of the literature review yielded several thousand articles related to the topic of wearable technologies. After excluding duplicates and irrelevant articles, 50 articles were selected for further review. These articles were analyzed in depth, and a cluster analysis was performed to detect the most relevant sub-topics in the field of wearable technologies.

The cluster analysis revealed that the most common sub-topics in wearable technologies are health monitoring, fitness tracking, and smart clothing. Health monitoring includes the use of wearable devices to monitor various physiological parameters such as heart rate, blood pressure, and blood glucose levels. Fitness tracking refers to the use of wearable devices to track physical activity, including steps taken, distance traveled, and calories burned. Smart clothing refers to the use of wearable devices that are integrated into clothing, such as shirts or pants, to track various physiological parameters.

Other sub-topics identified in the literature review include the use of wearable technologies for remote patient monitoring, sleep tracking, and stress management. Additionally, the review found that advances in wearable technologies are driving innovation in other fields, such as sports performance and military applications.

Overall, the literature review found that wearable technologies are rapidly advancing, with new devices and applications emerging constantly. The field is highly interdisciplinary, involving experts from diverse fields such as engineering, medicine, and computer science. Further research is needed to fully understand the potential of wearable technologies and to develop devices that meet the needs of consumers and healthcare providers alike.

As discussed in previous numerals, the topic of wearable technologies is very related to job design, human factors, and ergonomics. Therefore, there are many topics in the course text that relate to wearable technologies. For example, in Chapter 22: Managing Low-Back Disorder Risk In The Workplace, Sect. 7.6 - Exoskeletons and Wearable Robotics, Page 619, the topic of exoskeletons and wearable robotics is discussed. (Marras et al. 2021). Further, in Chapter 11: Three-Dimensional (3d) Anthropometry And Its Applications In Product Design, Sect. 1 – Introduction, Page 283, the topic of ergonomics and mobile computing is addressed (Ma et al. 2021).

4.1 Academic Justification

The development of wearable devices involves a combination of different technologies from fields such as human factors, bioengineering, and biomedical engineering. Due to its wide range of applications, there are many areas where wearable devices can be utilized. As wearable technology has enormous potential for the future, there is likely to be substantial funding for research, which will increase research interest. Wearable technology is currently worn outside of the body, but in the future, it could potentially be embedded inside the human body, further expanding its potential applications.

Wearable technologies can have multiple applications that are extremely relevant to job design and human factors and ergonomics. For example, they allow the monitoring and reduction of risk of incorrect postures by using sensor systems that can detect the orientation and movements of different parts of the body and can provide feedback to the user. They can also evaluate and control certain physical loads using force sensors to detect pressures in the body or limps. Finally, they can also improve the workers' efficiency by tracking the mood, stress level, fatigue and/or cognitive performance of the workers in a personalized manner. As such, application of wearable technologies is very important for the development of many solutions in the areas of health care, industry, job design and sports.

Wearable technologies are a unique topic because they explore the intersection between technology and human behavior in a very interrelated manner. Slowly, the miniaturization of processors and sensors has allowed the commercialization of many devices that are now ubiquitous in our daily life. Although currently used for sports and basic health tracking, they have the potential to revolutionize all aspects of human life.

5 Future Work

Wearable technology has greatly advanced in recent years, offering features such as health monitoring, information access, and message reception through watches. This progress is due to the reduction in the size of sensors and other hardware. However, there are still some limitations, such as the battery life and sensor size, that need to be improved. Users may find it inconvenient to charge the device frequently due to battery limitations, but this could be addressed through the use of solar panels or flexible batteries embedded in watch straps or smart cloth which all correspond to future developments required.

For example, NSF grant #1849243 titled "Center for the Advancement of Wearable Technologies (CAWT): Engineered (Bio)Interfaces, Energy Harvesting/Storage and Data Analytics for Health and Diagnostic Monitoring" has three main goals that aims that they are currently working towards (Cunci et al. 2021):

1) Advance the fundamental and applied science of biosensors, portable power and storage, and data analytics;
2) Provide an engaged and diverse workforce for the nation's wearable technology sector; and.
3) Stimulate economic development together with PR's medical device industry.

References

Ajami, S., Teimouri, F.: Features and application of wearable biosensors in medical care. J. Res. Med. Sci. **20**(12), 1208 (2015). https://doi.org/10.4103/1735-1995.172991

Amjadi, M., Kyung, K.-U., Park, I., Sitti, M.: Stretchable, skin-mountable, and wearable strain sensors and their potential applications: a review. Adv. Func. Mater. **26**(11), 1678–1698 (2016). https://doi.org/10.1002/adfm.201504755

Amjadi, M., Pichitpajongkit, A., Lee, S., Ryu, S., Park, I.: Highly stretchable and sensitive strain sensor based on silver nanowire-elastomer nanocomposite. ACS Nano **8**(5), 5154–5163 (2014). https://doi.org/10.1021/nn501204t

Bandodkar, A.J., Jeerapan, I., Wang, J.: Wearable chemical sensors: present challenges and future prospects. ACS Sensors **1**(5), 464–482 (2016). https://doi.org/10.1021/acssensors.6b00250

Bower, M., Sturman, D.: What are the educational affordances of wearable technologies? Comput. Educ. **88**, 343–353 (2015). https://doi.org/10.1016/j.compedu.2015.07.013

Chan, M., Estève, D., Fourniols, J.-Y., Escriba, C., Campo, E.: Smart wearable systems: current status and future challenges. Artif. Intell. Med. **56**(3), 137–156 (2012). https://doi.org/10.1016/j.artmed.2012.09.003

Corzo, D., Tostado-Blázquez, G., Baran, D.: Flexible electronics: status, challenges and opportunities. Front. Electron. **1**, 59403 (2020). https://doi.org/10.3389/felec.2020.594003

Cunci, L., et al.: Multicolor fluorescent graphene oxide quantum dots for sensing cancer cell biomarkers. ACS Appl. Nano Mater. **4**(1), 211–219 (2021). https://doi.org/10.1021/acsanm.0c02526

Kumar, K., Paul, A., Chen, J.I.-Z.: Special issue on "Wearable computing techniques for smart health." J. Ambient Intell. Human. Comput. **11**(11), 4305–4305 (2020). https://doi.org/10.1007/s12652-020-01786-6

Liao, M., et al.: Wearable, healable, and adhesive epidermal sensors assembled from mussel-inspired conductive hybrid hydrogel framework. Adv. Func. Mater. **27**(48), 1703852 (2017). https://doi.org/10.1002/adfm.201703852

Ma, L., Niu, J.: Three-dimensional (3D) anthropometry and its applications in product design. In: Handbook of Human Factors and Ergonomics, pp. 281–302 (2021). https://doi.org/10.1002/9781119636113.ch11

Marras, W.S., Karwowski, W.: Managing low-back disorder risk in the workplace. In: Handbook of Human Factors and Ergonomics, pp. 597–629 (2021). https://doi.org/10.1002/9781119636113.ch22

Mirjalali, S., Peng, S., Fang, Z., Wang, C.-H., Shuying, W.: Wearable sensors for remote health monitoring: potential applications for early diagnosis of Covid-19. Adv. Mater. Technol. **7**(1), 2100545 (2022). https://doi.org/10.1002/admt.202100545

Mukhopadhyay, S.C.: Wearable sensors for human activity monitoring: a review. IEEE Sens. J. **15**(3), 1321–1330 (2015). https://doi.org/10.1109/JSEN.2014.2370945

Nag, A., Mukhopadhyay, S.C.: Wearable electronics sensors: current status and future opportunities. In: Mukhopadhyay, S.C. (ed.) Wearable Electronics Sensors: For Safe and Healthy Living, pp. 1–35. Springer, Cham (2015). https://doi.org/10.1007/978-3-319-18191-2_1

Pu, Z., et al.: A continuous glucose monitoring device by graphene modified electrochemical sensor in microfluidic system. Biomicrofluidics **10**(1), 011910 (2016). https://doi.org/10.1063/1.4942437

Ray, T.R., et al.: Bio-integrated wearable systems: a comprehensive review. Chem. Rev. **119**(8), 5461–5533 (2019). https://doi.org/10.1021/acs.chemrev.8b00573

Stoppa, M., Chiolerio, A.: Wearable electronics and smart textiles: a critical review. Sensors **14**(7), 11957–11992 (2014). https://doi.org/10.3390/s140711957

Teymourian, H., Tehrani, F., Mahato, K., Wang, J.: Lab under the skin: microneedle based wearable devices. Adv. Healthcare Mater. **10**(17), 2002255 (2021). https://doi.org/10.1002/adhm.202002255

Sodhi, D., Duffy, V.: A systematic literature review of virtual reality education and COVID-19 safety. In: Duffy, V.G., Lehto, M., Yih, Y., Proctor, R.W. (eds.) Human-Automation Interaction: Manufacturing, Services and User Experience, pp. 627–647. Springer International Publishing, Cham (2023). https://doi.org/10.1007/978-3-031-10780-1_35

Trung, T.Q., Lee, N.-E.: Flexible and stretchable physical sensor integrated platforms for wearable human-activity monitoringand personal healthcare. Adv. Mater. **28**(22), 4338–4372 (2016). https://doi.org/10.1002/adma.201504244

Alrige, M., Chatterjee, S.: Toward a taxonomy of wearable technologies in healthcare. In: Donnellan, B., Helfert, M., Kenneally, J., VanderMeer, D., Rothenberger, M., Winter, R. (eds.) New

Horizons in Design Science: Broadening the Research Agenda: 10th International Conference, DESRIST 2015, Dublin, Ireland, May 20-22, 2015, Proceedings, pp. 496–504. Springer International Publishing, Cham (2015). https://doi.org/10.1007/978-3-319-18714-3_43

Borthwick, A.C., Anderson, C.L., Finsness, E.S., Foulger, T.S.: Special article personal wearable technologies in education: value or villain? J. Digital Learn. Teach. Educ. **31**(3), 85–92 (2015). https://doi.org/10.1080/21532974.2015.1021982

Brophy, K., Davies, S., Olenik, S., Çotur, Y.: The future of wearable technologies, London UK (2021). https://www.guderesearch.com/wp-content/uploads/2021/12/IMSJ8878-Wearable-Tech-Briefing-Paper-210601.pdf

Çiçek, M.: Wearable technologies and its future applications. Int. J. Electr. Electron. Data **3**, 45–50 (2015). https://www.academia.edu/download/37446358/wearable.pdf

Optimization of Driver Cabin Human Factors Design for Sweeper Truck Based on Ramsis: Enhancing Driver Comfort and Safety

Shoupeng Li, Zhisheng Zhang[✉], and Wanrong Han

School of Mechanical Engineering, Southeast University, Nanjing 211189, China
{220214957,oldbc,220214971}@seu.edu.cn

Abstract. This study utilizes ergonomics principles and RAMSIS software to optimize the analysis of driver posture in the sweeper cabin and constructs 18 different Chinese human body models of varying genders and sizes. Firstly, parameters such as H30 and H-point X-axis travel (L95) are determined based on vehicle type, platform, and benchmark vehicle data. Seat back angle, ankle comfort angle, and seat slide rail inclination are also set. Subsequently, RAMSIS software is employed to create a 3D model for simulating driver posture, and the cabin layout is optimized based on human comfort evaluation results. Next, spatial and reachability analyses are conducted to ensure that components such as the steering wheel and operating handles are within reach. Finally, evaluators are organized to conduct subjective evaluations of the driving cabin to verify the effectiveness of the optimization scheme. Through simulation analysis and subjective evaluation, the final optimization scheme is determined to be "steering wheel position moved back by 30 mm and raised by 10 mm" and "seat slide rail moved forward by 25 mm." This scheme improves the comfort of drivers with different heights and sitting heights during driving, thus meeting the driving requirements of the vast majority of people. This study provides valuable references for the ergonomics design of sweeper cabins and demonstrates the accuracy of RAMSIS simulation results.

Keywords: Ergonomics · Ramsis · Sweeper cabin design · Patial analysis · Reachability analysis

1 Introduction

In recent years, the importance of the driving work environment for sweeper truck operators has been increasingly recognized, with growing demands for aspects such as seat comfort, steering control ergonomics, workspace adequacy, and visual safety. Ergonomic design for sweeper trucks involves the rational arrangement and optimization of various in-cabin components, including control levers, mirrors, knobs, instrument panels, and seats, taking into account factors

V. G. Duffy et al. (Eds.): HCII 2023, LNCS 14057, pp. 96–111, 2023.
https://doi.org/10.1007/978-3-031-48047-8_6

such as the driver's physiological and psychological characteristics, movement patterns, and habits [14]. However, the adoption of layout schemes based on the American SAE-J826 standard in cabin development by many automotive companies may not adequately address the ergonomic requirements of different ethnic groups, particularly in the context of Chinese drivers [11].

Currently, several simulation software tools are available in the field of ergonomics, including RAMSIS, JACK, ANTHROPOS, SAMMIE, and CAVA. Among these, RAMSIS is the most widely applied, being utilized by over 70% of global passenger car manufacturers [7]. This study aims to explore the application of RAMSIS software in the ergonomic design of sweeper truck cabins, focusing on the unique requirements of Chinese drivers, and providing valuable insights for future ergonomic design in sweeper trucks.

2 Introduction to Human-Machine Layout Methods

The setting of the driver's seating posture is an essential component of ergonomics, involving the selection of human body percentiles, the definition of driver posture seating parameters, and the determination of the steering wheel position [6]. To better understand the definition of driver posture, paper introduces the following nine key concepts:

- H-point: This is the key point for determining the position of the driver or passenger in the seat, which is the pivot point where the human model's torso and thigh are connected. In the medical field, it is called the Hip Point, abbreviated as H-point.
- H30: This is the vertical distance from the driver's H-point to the heel point.
- L95: This is the horizontal distance from the driver's H-point to the pedal point, with different sitting heights corresponding to different horizontal distances.
- A40: This is the driver's seat back angle, with different sitting heights corresponding to different seat back angles.
- A46: This is the driver's ankle angle, characterizing the angle between the driver's ankle and the vertical line when initially pressing the accelerator pedal.
- SWC point: This is the steering wheel rotation center point, which is the intersection of the steering column axis and the upper surface of the steering wheel rim.
- H90: Vertical distance from the SWC point of the steering wheel to the ground.
- A18: This is the steering wheel tilt angle, which is the angle between the upper surface of the steering wheel rim and the Z-axis.
- A19: This is the slide rail tilt angle, which is the angle between the seat slide rail and the horizontal plane.

This chapter sets the driver's sitting posture through these key concepts. The human-machine attitude is shown in Fig. 1. First, select an appropriate driver

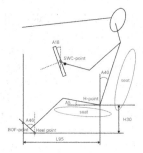

Fig. 1. Explanation diagram of human posture position parameters.

model based on human body percentile data. Then, define the driver posture seating parameters, including H-point, H30, L95, A40, A46, etc [13]. Next, determine the steering wheel position (SWC point) and tilt angle (A18) to ensure that the driver can comfortably operate the steering wheel during driving. Finally, adjust the seat slide rail tilt angle (A19) according to the driver's height and sitting height [8].

2.1 Selection of Human Body Percentiles

This study uses fixed sample human body size parameters and employ human body models for analysis. According to the functional requirements of the product, there are typically three categories of human body ranges considered in the design process [9]: Category 1: 5% female to 95% male, using the upper and lower limit percentiles of human body size as the basis for product design; Category 2: 5% female or 95% male, using the upper or lower limit of human body size as the design basis; Category 3: using the 50% human body size as the design basis. Since automotive design needs to accommodate the driving and riding needs of people with different heights, Category 1 is usually used as the design basis, with the SAE 95% human body as the design benchmark [1].

2.2 Determination of Seat and Steering Wheel Position

The steering wheel position is mainly determined by the steering wheel center point and the steering wheel tilt angle. Paper referred to the empirical formula of a Japanese company to preliminarily determine the steering wheel position [2]. The steering wheel center point SWC (W_X, W_Y, W_Z) relative to the heel point coordinate (as shown in Fig. 2) can be calculated using formulas (1) and (2):

$$W_X = -0.786\Delta(H30) + 676 \tag{1}$$

In the formula, W_X represents the horizontal distance between the steering wheel center point and the heel point, and H30 represents the vertical distance from the H-point to the heel point.

$$W_Z = -0.903\Delta W_X + 1063 \tag{2}$$

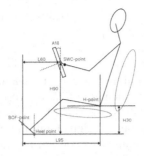

Fig. 2. The steering wheel center point SWC (W_X, W_Y, W_Z) relative to the heel point coordinate.

Fig. 3. The relationship between the center point and H-point of the steering wheel and W_Y.

In the formula, W_Z represents the vertical distance between the steering wheel center point and the heel point, and W_Z represents the horizontal distance between the steering wheel center point and the heel point. W_Y is generally consistent with the driver's Y-coordinate or within a 10mm range inside the vehicle (as shown in Fig. 3). The steering wheel tilt angle can be determined with reference to formula (3)

$$A18 = 0.08\Delta(H30) + 4.5 \tag{3}$$

In the formula, A18 represents the steering wheel tilt angle, and H30 represents the vertical distance from the H-point to the heel point. Taking a three-box sedan as an example, the steering wheel center point coordinates are (357.67, 10, 740.02), and the steering wheel tilt angle is 36.9°.

2.3   Definition of Driver Posture Seating Parameters

Setting of H30 and L95. In the actual setting process, H30 and L95 are a set of interrelated parameters, with H30 being determined first. H30 can be determined based on factors such as vehicle type, platform, and benchmark vehicle data. Vehicles are divided into the following categories [4]:

Category A vehicles - H-point height (H30) less than 405 mm. This category includes passenger cars, multi-purpose passenger vehicles, and light passenger vehicles.

Category B vehicles - H-point height (H30) between 405 mm and 530 mm. This category includes medium and heavy trucks and buses.

After determining H30, it calculated L95 according to the recommended formula in SAE J4004. It is worth noting that the SAE standard plays a significant role as a reference in the ergonomic design of automobiles in our country. The currently valid standard for H-point travel design recommendations is SAE J4004. The method for determining the H-point travel in this standard first requires determining the X-coordinate L95 of the H-point [10]. The SAE J4004 standard provides a detailed statistical analysis of the comfortable positions of drivers' bodies at different percentiles, and the resulting curve represents the horizontal distance between the H-point and the BOF point (L95) as a quadratic function of the seat height H30 [12]. Typically, we use the 95% vehicle body as the design reference point, as shown in formula (4).

$$L95 = 718 - 0.24 * (H30) + 0.41 * (L60) - 18.2 * t \tag{4}$$

In the formula, L95 is the horizontal distance from the pedal point to the H-point; H30 is the vertical distance from the H-point to the heel point; L60 is the distance from the BOF point to the SWC point; t is the transmission type parameter, with automatic transmission $t = 0$ and manual transmission $t = 1$. This sweeper is a manual transmission, $t = 1$. L60 is the distance from the steering wheel center point to the BOF point, which is not specified. According to experience, its value is generally 480–600 mm. The final H30 of the sweeper is determined to be 405 mm, and L95 is determined to be 749.2 mm.

Setting of Seat Back Angle A40. The seat back angle is related to the sitting height H30, and the initial definition is based on formula (5).

$$A40 = -0.024 * (H30) + 30 \tag{5}$$

In the formula, A40 is the driver's seat back angle; H30 is the vertical distance from the H-point to the heel point. According to experience and SAE recommendations, the seat back angle of a sedan is usually set to 25°, and the seat back angle of an SUV is set to 23°. After calculation, the seat back angle of the sweeper is set to 20.3°.

Determination of Driver's Ankle Angle. The comfortable ankle joint angle range is 87° to 105°. To ensure the comfort of the entire vehicle's pedal travel, major automakers uniformly set the initial position of the accelerator pedal ankle angle to 87°. The sweeper's ankle angle initial position is set to 87°.

Determination of Seat Slide Rail. The seat slide rail tilt angle can be determined according to formula (6).

$$A40 = -0.024 * (H30) + 30 \tag{6}$$

In the formula, A19 represents the seat slide rail tilt angle; H30 represents the vertical distance from the H-point to the heel point. Sedans are usually set to 5°, and SUVs are usually set to 0° to 2° [3]. The angle of the seat surface is the horizontal angle of the seat cushion. After calculation, A19 is equal to 1°. Since most of the sweeper's work requires the driver to bend forward to observe the near road surface, the seat tilt angle is minimized to facilitate body work, temporarily set to 0°, which can ensure that the body does not slide forward and reduce muscle tension, thus reducing the likelihood of fatigue.

The length of the seat slide rail should meet the riding requirements of 5% to 95% passengers, as shown in Fig. 4.

Fig. 4. Schematic diagram of the range that can meet the seating requirements of 5% to 95% of passengers.

It is known that the adjustment range of the driver's seat of this model of sweeper is as follows: suspension travel ±40mm, up and down travel ±30 mm, front and rear travel ±80 mm. Steering wheel adjustment travel: front and rear travel ±20°, high and low travel 0 to 80 mm. The model is shown in the Fig. 5.

Fig. 5. Model diagram of adjustable seat structure.

3   RAMSIS Software Optimization Analysis

RAMSIS is a software developed by the Technical University of Munich specifically for human posture research [13]. Its data mainly comes from the driving habits and joint angles of most drivers during driving and can predict the next few years based on the current size of the human body.

3.1   Creation of 3D Models

At present, although most foreign car companies are using RAMSIS software to analyze driving postures, there are relatively few related studies in domestic car companies, and many studies only follow foreign or local optimization [5]. The SAE human body model mainly comes from the North American market. Since SAE does not specify the average height of men and women, it only specifies the height (including shoe thickness of 2.5 cm) and other related dimensions of large (95% male body), medium (50% male and female mixed body), and small (5% female body) human bodies. Therefore, this study converts the Chinese human body sizes in RAMSIS into small (5%), medium (50%), and large (95%) human body sizes and compares them with SAE, as shown in Fig. 6. Using net height (minus shoe thickness of 2.5 cm), sitting height (trunk length), thigh length, and calf length as the four dimensions to compare the SAE human body parameters, the small (5%), medium (50%), and large (95%) human body sizes of Chinese human bodies in the RAMSIS human body database are shown in Table 1. As can be seen from Table 1, the height, thigh length, and calf length of the Chinese human body in RAMSIS are all smaller than those of the SAE human body, but the sitting height (trunk length) is larger than that of the SAE human body. Therefore, the sitting height is also taken into consideration. When using

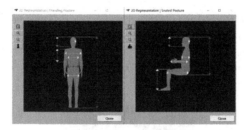

Fig. 6. Ramsis can view dimensional data of various positions of the human body.

Table 1. Difference between Chinese RAMSIS manikin data and SAE Mannequin.

	Gender	Net height	Thigh length	Calf length	Sitting high
RAMSIS-5%	female	1496.8	836.4	519.5	415.9
SAE-5%	female	1525	798	524	470
RAMSIS-50%	mix	1633.2	899.8	553.8	460
SAE-50%	mix	1690	879	586	530
RAMSIS-95%	male	1803.7	963.8	592.7	536.9
SAE-95%	male	1880	960	648	614

the RAMSIS module in CATIA V5 R19 software, RAMSIS software can create specific human bodies with certain age ranges, years, nationalities, heights, waist circumferences, and sitting heights as needed. In this study, we customized the human body size items and set them through the RAMSIS >Manikin >Define Manikin option in the main menu. The year used is 2020, which is close to the year of this study. Since the sweeper developed in this study is specifically designed for the Chinese market, we chose the country as "China". This paper mainly demonstrates posture, excluding the influence of waist circumference, and creates a total of 18 human bodies with "2020", "18 to 60 years old", "China", "two genders", "large, medium, and small human body heights (including shoe thickness of 2.5 cm) and other related dimensions", and "three sitting heights: high, medium, and low", as shown in Fig. 7.

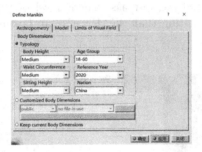

Fig. 7. Select the required Mannequin from Ramsis

In the CATIA environment, we established models of the steering wheel, seat, and operating handle and assembled them into the main simulation platform (driver's cab framework). Such a good simulation platform can be used for driving simulation tests, as shown in Fig. 8. During the driving operation, the driver needs to perform various tasks, such as turning the steering wheel and operating the handle, to predict the driving posture. By using the comfort standards automatically provided by the software for the human body model, it can adjust the layout of the driver's cab to improve the comfort of the human body model.

Using the forward kinematics method, it can adjust the position angle and limb angle position of the human body model using the RAMSIS Motion function, and dragged the slider to change the limb state, as shown in Fig. 9. Then, the human body model was deployed to the corresponding position of the designed driver's cab 3D model. The evaluation results are given in numerical form combined with bar charts. The smaller the value, the higher the comfort level. It is generally believed in the industry that a value less than 2.5 is very ideal, 2.5 to 5.5 is acceptable but needs modification, and greater than 5.5 is unreasonable.

Fig. 8. Overall 3D model of sweeper.

The shorter the bar chart, the better the comfort. Evaluation indicators include overall body maladaptation, partial body maladaptation, and spinal health. Figure 9 shows the initial comfort assessment level of the driver's cab design before adjustment, indicating that the driver's cab layout scheme needs to be modified.

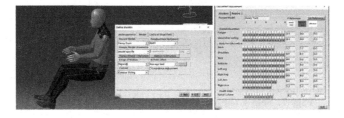

Fig. 9. Drag the slider to change the limb state of the mannequin and Rating of discomfort.

3.2   Space and Reachability Analysis

The reachability of the driver's hands is used to determine the rationality of the position and adjustment range of the control parts of the sweeper and to judge whether the steering wheel and operating handle of the cleaning vehicle are within the reach of the hands. For example, as shown in Fig. 10, the steering wheel is located within the transparent orange space, which means that the steering wheel is within the reach of the hands in a comfortable sitting position, providing better ergonomics.

Fig. 10. Simulation of hand accessibility of Mannequin.

Adding Constraints. To ensure that the driver's posture is as close to reality as possible, certain constraints need to be added (as shown in Fig. 11). The constraint descriptions are shown in Table 2.

Fig. 11. Add constraints to the Mannequin.

Table 2. Add constraints to various parts of the Mannequin.

Serial Number	Name	Meaning
1	Head constraint	Ensure there is a certain amount of space between the head and the ceiling
2	Hand constraints	Ensure that the hand is within the adjustment range of the steering wheel
3	Right heel point constraint	Ensure that the heel point is on the carpet surface
4	Right Foot Tread Constraint	Ensure that the pedal is on the accelerator pedal
5	Left Foot Tread Constraint	Ensure that the pedal is on the resting pedal surface
6	Left heel point constraint	Ensure the heel point is on the carpet
7	H-point constraint	Ensure that the H-point is within the seat travel frame

Simulation Results. The human body model posture is automatically set by the RAMSIS plugin, making the human body model posture adapt to the seat, steering wheel, center console, and other components and adding constraints. When the comfort evaluation results of the human body model are displayed again as Fig. 12, the evaluation results will change according to the different human body models.

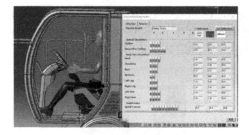

Fig. 12. The comfort evaluation results of the Mannequin will change with the adjustment.

The discomfort of various human bodies is shown in Fig. 13. It can be seen that for taller drivers (Tall), the discomfort of female human bodies is lower than that of male human bodies; for medium-height drivers (Middle), the discomfort of male human bodies is lower than that of female human bodies; for shorter drivers (Short), the discomfort of male human bodies is lower than that of female human bodies.

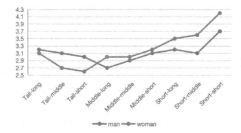

Fig. 13. Comfort score of Mannequin with different figures.

By comparing the simulation results, it can be found that: a. There are significant differences between Chinese and Western human bodies, and it is not entirely appropriate to use the empirical formulas of Western driving postures. b. The simulation results of RAMSIS software are highly consistent with reality, such as comparing the hand grip points, where some tall personnel's hand grip points are concentrated in the lower part of the adjustment range, which is consistent with the feedback from the prototype vehicle that "some tall personnel report the steering wheel distance is too far"; comparing the H-points, the H-points of short (5%) female human bodies are concentrated at the front end of the seat travel frame, and some have exceeded the range, which is consistent with the feedback that "short-statured personnel cannot obtain a suitable seat position".

Optimization Analysis. Considering various influencing factors, it is suggested to "move the steering wheel position 30 mm backward and 10 mm upward" to address the issue of "tall personnel reporting the steering wheel position is too far forward"; and "move the seat travel frame 25 mm forward" to address the issue of "short-statured personnel not being able to obtain a suitable seat position", and conduct simulation analysis with RAMSIS software.

The optimization analysis of "moving the steering wheel position 30 mm backward and 10 mm upward" takes the "Tall" and "Middle" heights of male human bodies as the research objects, ensuring that other constraint conditions remain unchanged, and only moving the steering wheel position 30 mm backward and 10 mm upward. The comparison of human body discomfort is shown in Fig. 14. The discomfort of the improved scheme has significantly decreased, indicating that the ergonomics of the human body has been greatly improved.

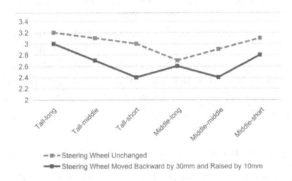

Fig. 14. Comfort score when only changing the steering wheel.

The optimization analysis of "moving the seat travel frame 25 mm forward" takes the "Short" and "Middle" heights of female human bodies as the research objects, ensuring that other constraint conditions remain unchanged, and only moving the seat travel frame 25 mm forward. The comparison of human body discomfort is shown in Fig. 15. The discomfort of the human body has significantly decreased, indicating that the ergonomics of the human body has been greatly improved.

The final comparison of human body discomfort determines the improvement plan as "moving the steering wheel position 30 mm backward and 10 mm upward" and "moving the seat slide rail 25 mm forward". The discomfort of different heights and different sitting heights of "male" and "female" human bodies has decreased, and the ergonomics of the human body has improved [7].

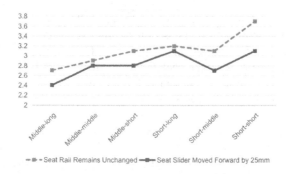

Fig. 15. Comfort score when only changing seat.

4 Subjective Evaluation of the Driver's Cabin

Determining the driving posture is one of the essential tasks in the field of human-machine interaction. Subsequent adjustments may have a significant impact on the project timeline and development costs. To ensure that the driving posture can meet the requirements of the vast majority of drivers, a subjective evaluation should be conducted in the test vehicle model after the initial determination of the human-machine posture.

4.1 Selection of Evaluators

The selection of subjects for the evaluation experiment is as follows:

(1) The height range of the evaluators should include various heights, with no less than three people for each height.
(2) Evaluators should have at least 2 years of driving experience and a certain understanding of automobile structures to ensure they can provide reasonable suggestions for the project. Considering these factors, three groups of evaluators, totaling nine people, were selected. Detailed information is shown in Table 3.

Table 3. Testers are divided into "high, medium, and low" groups based on their different body sizes.

Group	High stature group			Middle stature group			Short stature group		
Evaluators	1	2	3	4	5	6	7	8	9
Height/mm	181	182	184	175	174	176	163	162	159
Upper body length/mm	90.5	91	92	87.5	87	88	81.5	81	79.5
Driving experience/year	3	4	7	03	6	1	7	5	4

4.2   Evaluation Process

The evaluation experiment steps are as follows:

(1) All evaluators adjust their preferred driving position in the actual vehicle based on their personal preferences and provide assessment scores according to their actual feelings and scoring criteria.
(2) Adjust the seat position of the human-machine test bench model to be consistent with the actual vehicle, move the steering wheel 30 mm backward and 10 mm upward, and organize all evaluators to conduct subjective evaluations.
(3) Adjust the steering wheel position of the human-machine test bench model to be consistent with the actual vehicle, and move the seat slide rail 25 mm forward, then organize all evaluators to conduct subjective evaluations.
(4) Adjust the human-machine test bench model, move the steering wheel 30 mm backward and 10 mm upward, and move the seat slide rail 25 mm forward, then organize all evaluators to conduct subjective evaluations.
(5) All evaluators use the same scoring criteria, adopting a "7-likert system". 1 represents "very dissatisfied", 7 represent "very satisfied", and the intermediate scores are assigned accordingly. Evaluators receive training before the assessment to ensure that under the same conditions, the assessment scores of different evaluators for the same project are as consistent as possible.

4.3   Evaluation Results

The evaluation results of the three groups of evaluators are shown in Fig. 16.

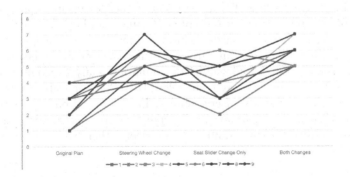

Fig. 16. Score of each tester under different adjustment methods.

(1) In the original scheme, the second group had the highest score, while the first and third groups had lower scores. This indicates that the original human-machine driving posture is more satisfactory for people of medium height, while taller and shorter individuals have complaints, requiring improvement.

(2) The first group of evaluators had a significant increase in evaluation scores for the "steering wheel backward scheme"; the third group of evaluators had a significant increase in evaluation scores for the "seat travel frame forward scheme". This indicates that the complaints of taller and shorter individuals have been well addressed.

(3) All evaluators had significantly increased scores for the final determined scheme ("steering wheel position backward + seat travel frame forward"), indicating that the human-machine posture can meet the driving requirements of the vast majority of people. The evaluation results of the human-machine test bench model prove the effectiveness of the optimization scheme for the vehicle's human-machine posture and indirectly confirm the accuracy of the RAMSIS simulation results, which can be applied more in-depth in the subsequent project development process.

5   Conclusion and Outlook

This study utilized ergonomics principles and RAMSIS software to optimize the driver's posture in the cabin of a sweeper truck, constructing 18 different gender and size Chinese human body models. Through simulation analysis and subjective evaluation, the final optimization scheme was determined as "steering wheel position moved backward by 30 mm, raised by 10 mm" and "seat slide rail moved forward by 25 mm". This scheme improved the comfort of drivers with different heights and sitting postures during driving, thus meeting the driving requirements of the vast majority of people. The research provides valuable reference for the ergonomic design of sweeper truck cabins and verifies the accuracy of RAMSIS simulation results, offering an effective tool for future similar studies.

In future research, the application of ergonomics can be further expanded in other types of vehicles and scenarios to meet the needs of more people. Additionally, more human body models and driver posture parameters can be explored to enhance the accuracy and applicability of simulation analysis. Combining other simulation software, such as JACK and ANTHROPOS, can also contribute to a more comprehensive study of ergonomics. Lastly, attention can be given to drivers' physiological and psychological responses during actual driving to better optimize the working environment for drivers, thereby improving driving safety and comfort.

References

1. Buisson, P., Duffy, V.G.: Simulation and ergonomic analysis of a very tall male driving an excavator in RAMSIS. In: Duffy, V.G., Rau, P.L.P. (eds.) HCII 2022. LNCS, vol. 13522, pp. 113–126. Springer, Cham (2022). https://doi.org/10.1007/978-3-031-21704-3_8

2. Chi, C., Xu, Y., Xu, G., Cheng, B., Shen, J.: Modular design and analysis of the x-by-wire center point steering independent suspension for in-wheel electric vehicle. Adv. Mech. Eng. **10**(6) (2018). https://doi.org/10.1177/1687814018777587

3. Hao, S., Cheng, C.T., Wang, J.N., Zhang, J.Y., Yu, Y.: Ergonomic optimization and test evaluation of sports SUV cockpit layout design. Jilin Daxue Xuebao (Gongxueban)/J. Jilin Univ. (Eng. Technol. Ed.) **52**(7), 1477–1488 (2022). https://doi.org/10.13229/j.cnki.jdxbgxb20210125. Cockpit layout; Layout designs; Layout schemes; Optimisations; RAMSIS; Style designs; Subjective evaluation test; Test evaluation; Vehicle engineering; Vehicle layout

4. He, J., Yang, C., Zhu, T., Wang, X., Hu, Y.: Comparative study on cab's H point design model based on human factors engineering. In: Long, S., Dhillon, B.S. (eds.) MMESE 2018. LNEE, vol. 527, pp. 305–313. Springer, Singapore (2019). https://doi.org/10.1007/978-981-13-2481-9_35

5. Macuzic, S., Lukic, J., Glisovic, J., Miloradovic, D.: Pedal force determination respect to ride comfort. In: International Congress of Automotive and Transport Engineering - Mobility Engineering and Environment (CAR2017). IOP Conference Series-Materials Science and Engineering, vol. 252 (2017). https://doi.org/10.1088/1757-899X/252/1/012010

6. Mansfeld, A., Luebke, A., Duffy, V.G.: Review and assessment of excavator operations using RAMSIS ergonomic engineering software. In: Duffy, V.G., Rau, P.L.P. (eds.) HCII 2022. LNCS, vol. 13522, pp. 275–295. Springer, Cham (2022). https://doi.org/10.1007/978-3-031-21704-3_18

7. van der Meulen, P., Seidl, A.: Ramsis – The Leading Cad Tool for Ergonomic Analysis of Vehicles. In: Duffy, V.G. (ed.) ICDHM 2007. LNCS, vol. 4561, pp. 1008–1017. Springer, Heidelberg (2007). https://doi.org/10.1007/978-3-540-73321-8_113

8. Mourad, L., Claveau, F., Chevrel, P.: Design of a two DOF gain scheduled frequency shaped LQ controller for narrow tilting vehicles. In: Proceedings of the American Control Conference, American Control Conference (ACC), Montreal, CANADA, 27–29 June 2012, pp. 6739–6744 (2012)

9. Ni, C.: Computer-aid ergonomic analysis of excavator driver's body posture model. In: Duffy, V.G. (ed.) HCII 2022. LNCS, vol. 13319, pp. 100–111. Springer, Cham (2022). https://doi.org/10.1007/978-3-031-05890-5_8

10. Parkinson, M.B., Reed, M.P.: Optimizing vehicle occupant packaging. SAE Trans. 890–901 (2006)

11. Paul, G., Wang, X., Yang, J.: An introduction to the special issue on digital human modeling (DHM) in ergonomics 4.0 introduction. IISE Trans. Occup. Ergon. Hum. Factors **9**(3–4), 107–110 (2021). https://doi.org/10.1080/24725838.2021.2027508

12. Stojanovic, N., Grujic, I., Glisovic, J., Abdullah, O.I., Vasiljevic, S.: Application of new technologies to improve the visual field of heavy duty vehicles' drivers. In: Karabegović, I. (ed.) NT 2019. LNNS, vol. 76, pp. 411–421. Springer, Cham (2020). https://doi.org/10.1007/978-3-030-18072-0_48

13. Vogt, C., Mergl, C., Bubb, H.: Interior layout design of passenger vehicles with RAMSIS. Hum. Factors Ergon. Manuf. **15**(2), 197–212 (2005). https://doi.org/10.1002/hfm.20022

14. Wang, X., Zhang, J., Ban, X.J., Tan, D.: Dynamic feature extraction method of driver's propensity under complicated vehicle group. Adv. Mech. Eng. (2013). https://doi.org/10.1155/2013/287653

Designing Hazard Mitigations for Workers with Limited Mobility: A Review and Bibliometric Analysis

Alder Philipps[✉] ⓘ and Vincent G. Duffy

Purdue University, West Lafayette, IN 47907, USA
{philipp0,duffy}@purdue.edu

Abstract. Work-related health and safety hazards affect adults with mobility-limiting disabilities disproportionately more than non-disabled adults. Conditions that expose adults with disabilities to greater health and safety risk include employers failing to implement effective workplace ergonomic adaptations and hiring discrimination leading to unstable employment. A systematic review and bibliometric analysis were conducted to evaluate the sources of work-related hazards for workers with mobility-limiting disabilities, the impact of exposure to those hazards, hazard mitigations with design, and measures of mitigation effectiveness. Bibliometric methods implemented included textual concept analysis and scientific mapping of co-citation analysis, and key articles were selected for detailed review. Two key sources of hazards identified are (1) the work environment (workstation, work tools, and interaction with people and machines) and (2) hazards related to employment (transportation to work, safe clothing, and unemployment). Human factors engineering and Digital Human Modeling are two existing design approaches implemented to address these hazards. Design solutions include ergonomic workstations, prosthetics for performing tasks, and robotic devices. The primary measures of mitigation effectiveness are participation in the workplace and safety. Despite existing design solutions, there is still a need to mitigate work-related hazards for physically disabled people. There is a growing demand for innovation as employment rates continue to improve for adults with disabilities.

Keywords: Physical Disability · Limited Mobility · Workplace · Ergonomics

1 Introduction and Background

In 2020, 11.1% of the United States (US) civilian population had a mobility-related disability [1], and the employment rate for people with disabilities in the US was 21.3% [2]. Therefore, the population of employed people in the US with a disability is approximately 8 million. Worldwide, it is estimated that 1.3 billion people experience significant disabilities [3]. Many workers with physical disabilities experience hiring discrimination and rejection from the employer to realize workplace adaptations [4]. These barriers put these workers at greater risk of workplace injury related to inadequate ergonomics and

V. G. Duffy et al. (Eds.): HCII 2023, LNCS 14057, pp. 112–129, 2023.
https://doi.org/10.1007/978-3-031-48047-8_7

health and safety issues associated with inconsistent employment. Work-related injuries affect millions of workers each year and significantly negatively impact the economy due to productivity losses and healthcare costs [5]. There have been efforts to prevent and treat work-related injuries for workers with and without disabilities. Efforts to address work-related injuries for people with disabilities include accommodations such as rotating work tasks, flexible scheduling, scheduling during less busy shifts, and physical therapy [6].

Hazard mitigation for workers with mobility related disabilities is critical now due to the increased proportion of workers with disabilities and changes resulting from the COVID-19 pandemic. The percentage of persons with a disability employed in 2022 is the highest on record and has steadily increased since comparable data was first collected in 2008 [2]. Additionally, with the advent of the COVID-19 pandemic, many workers, including workers with physical disabilities, transitioned to work-from-home settings where employers provided minimal support for setting up an optimal ergonomic workstation. Inadequate ergonomic workstations at home have worsened employees' musculoskeletal health [7]. As of February 2023, only approximately 50% of US workers have returned to in-office work [8].

Hazard mitigation through design for workers with physical disabilities is an essential topic in the field of Industrial Engineering. Within Industrial engineering, safety risk management improves operational efficiency in an industrial setting. The safety risk management process applied to workers with disabilities involves identifying and preventing hazards and measuring the effectiveness of hazard mitigations [9, pg. 600]. Hazard mitigations in the field of ergonomics that have already been implemented for this topic include adjustable ergonomic desks and seating and Digital Human Modeling design analysis [10].

Previous literature reviews on ergonomic design for people with disabilities showed very little research involving human subjects. Instead, most research is extrapolative or theoretical [11]. Therefore, further studies are required to identify the needs of the physically disabled working population and design solutions to mitigate safety hazards accordingly. There is also a need for employers and government agencies to address sustaining barriers that people with disabilities face when seeking employment [4].

2 Problem Statement

This review seeks to evaluate how work-related hazards impact workers with physical disabilities related to limited mobility. The focus of this review is twofold: (1) how design mitigates work-related hazards for people with disabilities and (2) how to measure the effectiveness of hazard mitigations regarding workplace participation and safety.

3 Method

Bibliometric analysis is a widely used methodology for research assessment in various scientific fields, and it supports objective and transparent review of literature [12, pg. 243–244]. The bibliometric methodology implemented in this review is described in van Raan [12, pg. 267], which includes textual concept analysis and scientific mapping of co-citation analysis. These methodologies have been used in prior publications in the field of Ergonomics, including [13] and [14].

A trend analysis using Google Ngram [15] was used to identify search terms that are relevant and emerging. Based on the results of the trend analysis, an initial keyword search was conducted in Springer Link [16] and Google Scholar [17] using the keywords "physical disability" OR "limited mobility" AND workplace AND ergonomics AND design." An initial search was also conducted in the journal Applied Ergonomics. Due to the smaller article set, broader keywords were used: "workplace" AND "disability" AND "design." Five articles were selected from the results based on the relevance of their abstract.

Next, an advanced search of Google Scholar was repeated with the same search terms, using the software Harzing Publish or Perish [18], which provides a ranked list of the top 100 articles and information on the number of citations per year. The search was limited to 2019 to 2023, focusing on the most recent relevant articles. BibExcel [19] software was used to identify the authors with the most published articles in the search results. One article from the leading author was selected based on the relevance of the abstract.

A search in Web of Science (WOS) [20] was conducted, for which co-citation analysis with VOSviewer [21] produced 20 articles that were cited together. From the co-cited articles, one article was selected based on the relevance of the abstract. The leading author from the co-citation article list was reviewed for current publications in Research Gate [22], and two relevant articles were selected. CiteSpace [23] was used to generate a citation burst with four leading authors, and the authors' recent publications were reviewed in Research Gate. One additional article was selected. Finally, a search in Scopus [24] was conducted, and results were filtered by the relevant topic area of engineering. Four articles were selected based on the relevance of its abstract.

Scopus results were used to collect trend analysis of the number of publications in this research area over time. Social trend analysis of this topic's emergence on Twitter was also performed using Vicinitas [25].

Next, a keyword analysis was performed. A CiteSpace keyword cluster diagram was generated, showing the main topic areas that appeared in the WOS literature search. A Word Cloud and a table of key terms for the selected articles were generated in MAXQDA [26]. A lexical search was performed in MAXQDA to determine the prevalence of select phrases and co-occurring words. Four main themes were identified based on the keyword analysis results. Detailed content analysis of each theme in the selected articles was performed using MAXQDA Word Explorer.

4   Results and Discussion

4.1 Defining Keywords

Keywords identified for data collection are limited mobility, physical disability, physical impairment, ergonomic design, and workplace accessibility. Physical impairment is defined as "a physiological disorder or condition, cosmetic disfigurement or anatomical loss impacting one or more body systems" [27]. For this analysis, limited mobility, physical disability, and physical impairment are synonymous. Accessible is defined as "a site, facility, work environment, service, or program that is easy to approach, enter, operate, participate in, or use safely and with dignity by a person with a disability" [28]. Ergonomics is the "science of conforming the workplace and all its elements to the worker" [9, pg. 206].

4.2 Selection of Search Terms Using Trend Analysis

First, the terms "limited mobility," "physical disability," and "physical impairment" were compared using Google Ngram (Fig. 1). "Physical disability" and "physical impairment" are more popular terms compared to "limited mobility." Physical impairment" emerged more recently than "physical disability." However, both terms are still used today. Next, topic areas of "workplace accessibility," "design for disability," and "workplace ergonomics were compared" (Fig. 2). While "workplace ergonomics" is no longer an emerging trend, there is an emergence in "workplace accessibility" and "design for disability." Based on the results of this trend analysis, the search terms "physical disability" OR "limited mobility" capture both the specific research topic and a synonymous term that may be more broadly used for the topic. The terms "ergonomics" and "workplace" were selected based on their greater popularity in comparison to the phrase "workplace accessibility." Finally, the search term "design" was included by itself instead of in the phrase "design for disability," due to the likelihood to yield a broader set of article results that may be related to the topic of interest. This trend analysis is also evidence that Ergonomic design for limited mobility in the workplace is an emerging and unique topic relevant for further research.

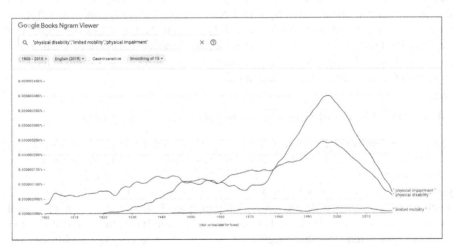

Fig. 1. Google Ngram results comparing the terms "physical disability," "limited mobility," and "physical impairment."

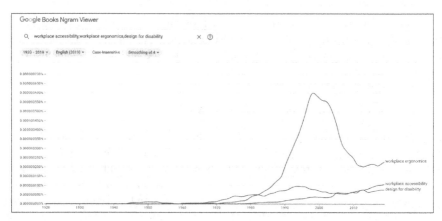

Fig. 2. Google Ngram results comparing terms "workplace ergonomics," "workplace accessibility," and "design for disability."

4.3 Keyword Search and Article Selection

In the initial keyword search, SpringerLink yielded 584 results. Two articles were selected "Industrial Manufacturing Workstations Suitability for People with Disabilities: The Perception of Workers" by Teixeira, E. et al. [29] and "The Influence of Human Factors in the Functional Analysis of the Support Device for Users with Upper Limb Agenesis." by Okumura et al. [30]. Google Scholar yielded 2,820 results, and two articles were selected, "Digital human modeling (DHM) for improving work environment for specially abled and elderly" by Charu M. Maurya et al. [10] and "The Effect of Functional Capacity Related Ergonomic Risk Factors on Quality of Life of People with Physical Disability" by Beliz Kaygisiz et al. [31]. Applied Ergonomics yielded 324 results, and the following article was selected: "History of Inclusive Design in the UK" by P. John Clarkson and Roger Coleman [32].

4.4 Advanced Keyword Search on the Impact of Ergonomic Design

The Harzing Publish or Perish search was conducted, and the search results were analyzed in BibExcel. Figure 3 below shows the most frequently published authors in the top 100 search results. The author Alida Esmail was selected based on the most articles yielded, and each article has frequent citations of 4 or more per year. The Esmail et al. article "Fashion Industry Perceptions of Clothing Design for Persons with a Physical Disability: The Need for Building Partnerships for Future Innovation" was selected as an additional reference for this review after checking the relevancy of the abstract [33].

A search was conducted in the database Web of Science (WOS) using the original search: "physical disability" OR "limited mobility" AND workplace AND ergonomics AND design, and 7533 results were yielded. These results were refined by filtering for articles in the categories of "rehabilitation," "engineering biomedical," "ergonomics," and "industrial relations labor," published within the past five years, yielding 213 results.

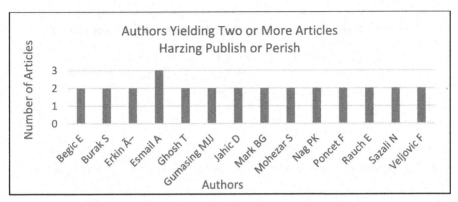

Fig. 3. Most frequently published authors in the top 100 search results from Harzing Publish or Perish Google Scholar advanced search.

Co-citation analysis results using VOSViewer for the WOS are shown in Fig. 4 below. From the WOS results, an article that was co-cited along with seven other articles was reviewed for the relevance of its abstract and selected: "Broadening the Conceptualization of Participation of Persons with Physical Disabilities: A Configurative Review and Recommendations" [35]. The co-citation search yielded the highest author occurrence for Kathleen Martin Ginis. The author was searched on Research Gate for more recent publications. The articles "The Participation of People with Disabilities in the Workplace Across the Employment Cycle: Employer Concerns and Research Evidence" [36] and "Experiential Aspects of Employment and Their Relationship with Work Outcomes: A Cross-Sectional Study Using a Novel Measure of Participation in Workers with and without Physical Disabilities" [37] were selected.

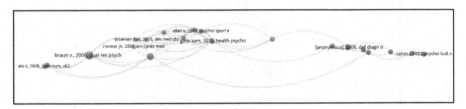

Fig. 4. Co-citation analysis using VOSViewer, for the Web of Science search data.

The citation burst analysis in CiteSpace using the same WOS data yielded four authors with the most substantial citation bursts (Fig. 5). Publications for the authors were reviewed in Research Gate, and the article "Economic Wellbeing and Life Satisfaction Among Working and Non-Working Adults with Disabilities" [38] was selected based on relevance to the research topic.

A search was conducted in the database Scopus using the keywords "workplace" AND "disability" AND "design" and yielded 801 results. Broader search terms were selected compared to the previous search because the initial search terms greatly limited the results. Many documents for the Scopus search were in the field of medicine

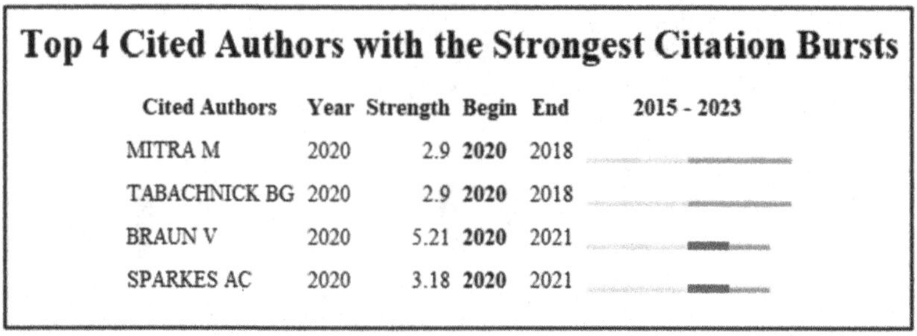

Top 4 Cited Authors with the Strongest Citation Bursts
Cited Authors Year Strength Begin End 2015 - 2023
MITRA M 2020 2.9 2020 2018
TABACHNICK BG 2020 2.9 2020 2018
BRAUN V 2020 5.21 2020 2021
SPARKES AC 2020 3.18 2020 2021

Fig. 5. Leading authors from CiteSpace citation burst analysis for the Web of Science search data.

(Fig. 6). To select articles most relevant for ergonomics and design, the Scopus search was narrowed to the field of Engineering, yielding 75 results. Based on a review of abstracts, the following four articles were selected: "Toward Adaptive Human–Robot Collaboration for the Inclusion of People with Disabilities in Manual Labor Tasks" [39], "Inclusive Design of Workspaces: Mixed Methods Approach to Understanding Users" [40], "Beyond the Pandemic: The Role of the Built Environment in Supporting People with Disabilities Work Life" [41], and "Development and Validation of Disability Management Indicators for the Construction Industry" were selected [42]. Table 1 summarizes the search terms used for all databases and the number of article results yielded.

Documents by subject area
Other (6.9%)
Arts and Humani... (1.7%)
Environmental S... (2.3%)
Nursing (3.4%)
Psychology (4.5%)
Computer Scienc... (5.7%)
Engineering (6.0%)
Business, Manag... (7.3%)
Health Professi... (9.3%)
Social Sciences... (13.1%)
Medicine (39.8%)

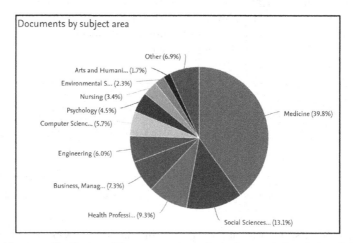

Fig. 6. Subject area distribution of Scopus search results for keywords "workplace," "disability," and "design."

Table 1. Search terms used for all databases and the number of articles yielded.

Database/Journal	Search Terms	Number of Articles Yielded
SpringerLink	"physical disability" OR	584
Google Scholar	"limited mobility" AND workplace AND ergonomics AND design	2820
Applied Ergonomics	"workplace" AND "disability" AND "design"	324
Google Scholar Using Harzing Publish or Perish	"physical disability" OR "limited mobility" AND workplace AND ergonomics AND design	Limited to 100
Web of Science	"physical disability" OR "limited mobility" AND workplace AND ergonomics AND design	7533
Web of Science narrowed the search	Above search terms + limited to categories "rehabilitation," "engineering biomedical," "ergonomics," and "industrial relations labor."	1,128
Scopus	"workplace" AND "disability" AND "design"	801
Scopus narrowed search	"workplace" AND "disability" AND "design" + limit to engineering	75

4.5 Trend Analysis Based on Publications and Social Media Search

Research Publication Trend Analysis
A publication trend diagram for the Scopus searches for keywords "workplace" AND "disability" AND "design" is shown in Fig. 7. There is an upward trend in the volume of articles published on this topic, beginning in the late 1990s and steadily increasing until 2023. Figure 8 shows the relative increase in the number of articles published by leading countries between 1997–2010 and 2010–2023 in the Scopus search results. Based on these emergence indicators, there is foreseeable growth in this research area.

Social Engagement Trend Analysis Through Vicinitas Analytics
Figure 9 summarizes the Vicinitas analysis of trends in social engagement for the keyword "disability" in 2080 Twitter posts over the last ten days before April 24, 2023. The topic of disabilities has received significant engagement on Twitter in a 10-day analysis. According to the Vicinitas Twitter content analysis tool, 1,800 users created 2,100 posts,

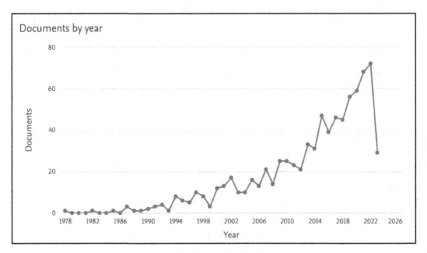

Fig. 7. Publication trend diagram for the Scopus searches for keywords "workplace" AND "disability" AND "design"

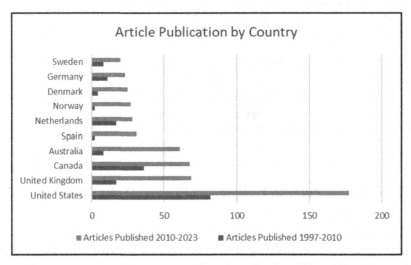

Fig. 8. Scopus search results show the relative increase in articles published by leading countries between 1997–2010 and 2010–2023.

which engaged 3,000 and influenced 10 million people. The posting and engagement both showed an upward trend during the ten days.

A VOSviewer text data co-occurrence map was generated from Vicinitas data for the keyword "disability" (Fig. 10). Notably, jobs, benefits, and healthcare are trending topics related to the keyword "disability" on Twitter. Common linkages include job, benefit, barrier, and proof. The high co-occurrence of the term job with disability suggests that the topic of disability in the workplace has relevant social engagement on Twitter, just as it is an emerging topic in literary publications.

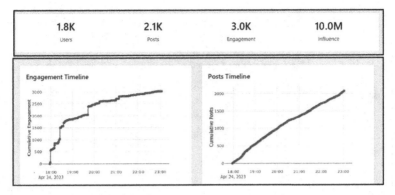

Fig. 9. Vicinitas social engagement trend analysis for the keyword "disability."

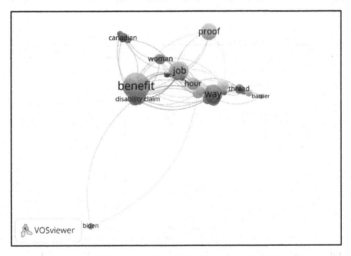

Fig. 10. Text data co-occurrence map for Vicinitas data on the keyword "disability."

4.6 Keyword Analysis of WOS Search Results and Selected Key Articles

CiteSpace keyword cluster diagram, showing the main topic areas that appeared in the WOS literature search, is shown in Fig. 11. Assistive technology is identified as the most relevant cluster, and keywords from the cluster include adjustment, rehabilitation, activities of daily living, assistive technology, stroke, cerebral palsy, and quality. The Word Cloud and associated top keyword table generated in MaxQDA from the list of previously selected key reference articles are shown in Fig. 12. Keywords and phrases which are drawn from the lexical analysis are then checked using the search tool in MaxQDA to determine the percentage of the articles which contain the keyword or phrase, as shown in Fig. 13. Notably, "disability" and "work" occurred in 100% of articles. The remaining topic areas in Fig. 13 are subtopics that include disabilities and work.

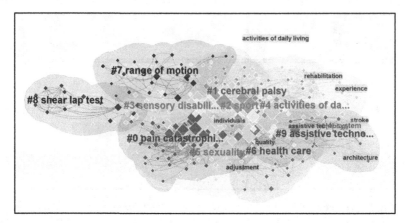

Fig. 11. CiteSpace keyword cluster diagram, showing main topic areas that appeared in the WOS literature search.

Fig. 12. MAXQDA Word Cloud and Associated Top Keyword Table.

4.7 Content Analysis of Themes Using Lexical Search

From the keyword analysis performed on the WOS search results and selected key articles, four themes were identified for content analysis in the area of design for disabilities or limited mobility in the workplace. The following themes were selected based on relevance and occurrence in at least 60% of the key articles: (1) ergonomic design to mitigate safety hazards, (2) design of devices to mitigate safety hazards, (3) participation as metric, and (4) safety as metric of hazard mitigation effectiveness.

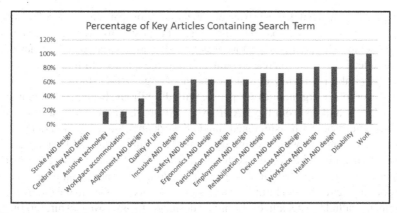

Fig. 13. Percentage of Key Articles containing search terms and phrases, calculated with MAXQDA lexical search.

For the four key themes identified, a lexical search was conducted in MAXQDA to find specific article references to each theme. The content for each theme is summarized in the following sections. The most frequent word combinations for each topic aided in the focus of the summary and are shown in Table 2, which was generated in the MAXQDA lexical search.

Table 2. Most frequent word combinations for each central theme generated in MAXQDA.

Theme 1: Ergonomic	Theme 2: Participation
24 ergonomic risk	12 employment participation
13 ergonomic risk factors	5 social participation
9 ergonomic analysis	4 canadian disability participation
6 ergonomic design	4 disability participation
4 ergonomic evaluation	4 effective participation
Theme 3: Devices	**Theme 4: Safety**
12 support devices	3 design safety
10 prosthetic support devices	3 safety behaviors
6 assistive devices	2 occupational safety
5 prosthetic devices	2 safety awareness
2 devices using	1 safety awareness positively influences

Theme 1: Ergonomic Design to Mitigate Safety Hazards

Kaygisiz et al. [31] found that the most prevalent ergonomic risk for people with disabilities is working primarily in a computerized work area. Fifty-two participants with physical disabilities (42 male and 12 female) were evaluated for ergonomic risk factors at work using several metrics. All participants worked full-time (40 h per week) for either a government agency or a private organization. Most participants (88.5%) worked in a high-risk posture, exacerbated by the length of exposure for workers in a stationary computer setup. The high-risk posture was linked to an increased risk of developing musculoskeletal disorders, increased pain, and reduced quality of life.

Maurya et al. [10] review digital human modeling (DHM) studies to improve the industrial workplace ergonomics for people with disabilities. Scenarios evaluated with DHM include manikins from the HADRIAN software database with various physical constraints interfaced with a simulated standard work environment compared to a modified work environment with accommodations. Manikins in the HADRIAN database were validated against actual users performing tasks. The evaluated physical constraints include a wheelchair, limited joint degrees of freedom, arm and leg amputations, inaccurate pointing, and strength limitations. Design concepts assessed in the modified work environment included specialized furniture designed to improve posture ergonomics for people with limited joint mobility. Transportation to and from work has also been evaluated with DHM, where manikins representing elderly and disabled people were interfaced with standard public bus designs and vehicles to assess suitability and design needs.

Theme 2: Device/Product Design to Mitigate Safety Hazards
Okumura et al. [30] reviews the influence of human factors on the design of prosthetic support devices for people with disabilities in the workplace as part of safety mitigation. The effect of human factors includes considerations of workplace interactions between humans, machines, and equipment, and environmental factors, all of which can impact safety. The study measured the preference for activities performed with and without using a prosthetic device and activities where using the device enhances safety. The study concluded that the end user's involvement in the design process has positive outcomes for the user's adoption and long-term use of the device.

Clarkson et al. [32] also emphasized the importance of a human-centered design process for developing products for people with disabilities, including using tools like the IDEO Human-Centered Design Toolkit [34]. Several organizations that promote human-centered design for disabilities were also compiled, including the European Institute for Design and Disability (now EIDD Design for All Europe), European Design for Ageing Network (DAN), International Association for Universal Design (IAUD), Design for All Institute of India, and Institute for Human Centered Design.

A comprehensive survey of 222 workers in the processing industry evaluated the adequacy of currently available workstation designs and assistive devices for people with physical disabilities by Okumura et al. [30]. Results showed that, although assistive devices are already available, workstations are rarely being adapted with assistive devices for people with physical disabilities due to the average perception that there is no need to implement distinct workstations for people with disabilities. Similarly, Mandischer et al. [39] discuss the availability of robotic assistive devices for workers with disabilities but the lack of implementation due to the cost barriers associated with customizing devices. The study proposes that assistive systems with higher levels of user control are more easily adapted into work environments without needing customization.

Work clothing is a potential source of safety hazards for people with disabilities, and adaptive clothing design seeks to mitigate that hazard. Loose clothing is a hazard when working in environments with machines [9, pg. 325], and protective clothing are common safety mitigations for contaminated environments [9, pg. 642]. Since clothing is generally mass-produced and standardized, people with disabilities have challenges with finding clothing that fits properly and meets their needs for fully participating in the workplace. A growing number of designers are making clothing adapted for people with disabilities, and challenges include the lack of partnership between academic research on this subject and the fashion industry [33].

Theme 3: Participation Metrics for Measuring Hazard Mitigation Effectiveness
Per the lexical search, measuring participation is a common way to evaluate the impact of a particular design implemented for workers with disabilities. For instance, in a review of the design of adaptive clothing for people with disabilities, improving participation in life activities, including work, was the primary objective [33]. Participation is linked directly to safety outcomes because decreased participation in the workplace can lead to depression, chronic stress, and poverty associated with reduced access to proper nutrition, shelter, and healthcare [38].

The concept of participation in workplaces for people with disabilities is reviewed in Martin Ginis et al. [35], including both objective (time spent on paid work and performance) and experiential (mastery, sense of autonomy, belonging, meaning, engagement, and challenge). Standard experiential metrics which can be implemented to measure workplace participation include the Basic Needs Satisfaction and Work Scale and the Job Characteristic Framework.

Objective aspects of participation, including employment rates and poverty rates, were evaluated for working-age adults with disabilities, showing significantly higher rates for adults with disabilities [38]. The experiential aspects of participation were assessed for people with and without physical disabilities [37]. For people with disabilities, participation measured by greater engagement was associated with fewer job disruptions, while this association was not seen with those without disabilities. Other areas that were measured included greater autonomy and greater belongingness. The overall experiential participation scores were lower for the subgroup with disabilities.

Theme 4: Safety Metrics for Measuring Hazard Mitigation Effectiveness
Standard work-related safety metrics include measures for ergonomic safety risks, including Rapid Upper Limb Assessment (RULA) and Okawo Working Posture Analysis System (OWAS) [31]. These can be used to measure the influence of workstation design solutions for people with disabilities. As discussed in the previous section, metrics of employment rate are also important for measuring safety outcomes, and unemployment is associated with increased safety risk. For cases where a prosthetic assistive device is implemented for the performance of specific tasks, safety effectiveness metrics will be custom to the particular tasks involved. It can be measured with user testing [30].

The implementation of these metrics to measure hazard mitigation effectiveness is better for workers with disabilities compared to those without. According to Bonaccio et al. [36], workers with disabilities are likelier to report minor safety incidents and generally have a higher awareness of safety than their non-disabled coworkers, which increases the safety awareness of organizations.

4.8 Discussion

Discussion on Mitigation of Safety Hazards for Workers with Disabilities
In the reappraisal of this review, several insights have been collected on how design for people with disabilities in the workplace is used to mitigate hazards contributing to safety risks. First, consideration of various occupational risks for workers with physical disabilities can be used to prioritize mitigations. For example, computerized works stations are the largest source of ergonomic-related safety incidents for workers with disabilities. Computer workstation design is an important area of focus for risk reduction. Also, the scope of safety-related hazards is broader than workstations, machines, or even the workplace. Other sources of hazards include transportation to and from work, social interaction, work clothing, and lack of employment. There is an opportunity for more comprehensive designs for hazard mitigation that account for some of these broader hazards, which may have yet to be fully considered in the past.

Digital human modeling (DHM) has been implemented as a tool for evaluating how humans with disabilities interact with their work environment and informing the design needs for various types of physical limitations. DHM can also assess public and private transportation, an essential aspect of access to work environments for people with physical disabilities. There is an opportunity for DHM to be used to evaluate the ergonomics of other design solutions in the workplace, like clothing and prosthetic design.

Another tool used in design to mitigate safety hazards is human factors analysis. Including the end user in all phases of the product development process is essential to ensure that the design meets the end user's needs and will be effectively implemented.

Discussion on Measuring Effectiveness of Hazard Mitigations
When measuring the effectiveness of hazard mitigation while designing for people with disabilities, two standard endpoints are participation outcomes and safety outcomes. When measuring participation outcomes, it is recommended to consider both objective and experiential results. When measuring safety outcomes, important considerations are the effect on safety for performing particular tasks, the effect measured by standardized ergonomic metrics, and the related impact on safety outside of the workplace.

5 Conclusion and Future Work

5.1 Conclusion

In conclusion, a systematic review and bibliometric analysis were conducted to evaluate the sources of work-related hazards for workers with disabilities, the impact of exposure to those hazards, hazard mitigations with design, and measures of mitigation effectiveness. Sources of hazards were identified as those in the work environment (workstation, work tools, and machines, interaction with people and machines) and hazards outside of the work environment (transportation to and from work, safe clothing, unemployment). While many of these hazards are also experienced by non-disabled people, the impact of the hazards has a disproportionate effect on disabled people. Design approaches for hazard mitigation include human factors considerations and Digital Human Modeling, and design efforts have included ergonomic workstations, prosthetics for performing tasks, and robotic devices. Two primary measures of mitigation effectiveness are participation in the workplace and safety.

5.2 Future Applications

There is emerging research on workplace ergonomic design for workers with disabilities. Recent NSF grants awarded in 2022–2023 include subtopics of developing wearable prosthetic robots to restore mobility [43], mechanisms for enhancing the symbiotic relationship between a user and their mobility system [44] and developing safer and more comfortable prosthetic attachment systems [45]. These research areas are promising because they address the need to include human subjects in research on the ergonomic needs of people with physical disabilities, and improving the person's comfort and connection with their movement directly impacts safety.

References

1. Centers for Disease Control and Prevention Website, National Center on Birth Defects and Developmental Disabilities, Division of Human Development and Disability. Disability and Health Data System (DHDS) Data. https://dhds.cdc.gov. Accessed 30 Apr 2023
2. Bureau of Labor Statistics Website, Persons with a Disability: Labor Force Characteristics (2022). https://www.bls.gov/news.release/pdf/disabl.pdf. Accessed 30 Apr 2023
3. World Health Organization Website, Disability. https://www.who.int/news-room/fact-sheets/detail/disability-and-health. Accessed 30 Apr 2023
4. Corrigan, P.W., et al.: Disability and work-related attitudes in employers from Beijing, Chicago, and Hong Kong. Int. J. Rehabil. Res. **31**(4), 347–350 (2008). https://doi.org/10.1097/MRR.0b013e3282fb7d61
5. Seabury, S.A., Terp, S., Boden, L.I.: Racial and ethnic differences in the frequency of workplace injuries and prevalence of work-related disability. Health Aff. **36**(2), 266–273 (2017). https://doi.org/10.1377/hlthaff.2016.1185
6. Padkapayeva, K., Posen, A., Yazdani, A., Buettgen, A., Mahood, Q., Tompa, E.: Workplace accommodations for persons with physical disabilities: evidence synthesis of the peer-reviewed literature. Disabil. Rehabil. **39**(21), 2134–2147 (2017). https://doi.org/10.1080/09638288.2016.1224276
7. MacLean, K.F.E., Neyedli, H.F., Dewis, C., Frayne, R.J.: The role of at home workstation ergonomics and gender on musculoskeletal pain. Work **71**(2), 309–318 (2022). https://doi.org/10.3233/WOR-210692
8. Washington Post Website: America's offices are now half-full. They may not get much fuller. https://www.washingtonpost.com/business/2023/02/04/return-to-office-occupancy-status/. Accessed 30 April 2023
9. Goetsch, D.L.: Ergonomic hazards, musculoskeletal disorders (MSDs) and cumulative trauma disorders (CTDs), 9th edn. In: Occupational Safety and Health for Technologists, Engineers, and Managers. Pearson, Boston, MA (2019)
10. Maurya, C.M., Karmakar, S., Das, A.K.: Digital human modeling (DHM) for improving work environment for specially-abled and elderly. SN Appl. Sci. **1**(11), 1–9 (2019). https://doi.org/10.1007/s42452-019-1399-y

11. Vujica Herzog, N., Buchmeister, B.: Workplace design and ergonomic analysis for workers with disabilities. In: Karwowski, W., Goonetilleke, R.S., Xiong, S., Goossens, R.H.M., Murata, A. (eds.) AHFE 2020. AISC, vol. 1215, pp. 127–134. Springer, Cham (2020). https://doi.org/10.1007/978-3-030-51549-2_17

12. van Raan, A.: Measuring science: basic principles and application of advanced bibliometrics. In: Glänzel, W., Moed, H.F., Schmoch, U., Thelwall, M. (eds.) Springer Handbook of Science and Technology Indicators. SH, pp. 237–280. Springer, Cham (2019). https://doi.org/10.1007/978-3-030-02511-3_10

13. Roach, A.L., Duffy, V.G.: Emerging applications of cognitive ergonomics: a bibliometric and content analysis. In: Stephanidis, C., Harris, D., Li, W.-C., Schmorrow, D.D., Fidopiastis, C.M., Antona, M., Gao, Q., Zhou, J., Zaphiris, P., Ioannou, A., Sottilare, R.A., Schwarz, J., Rauterberg, M. (eds.) HCII 2021. LNCS, vol. 13096, pp. 77–89. Springer, Cham (2021). https://doi.org/10.1007/978-3-030-90328-2_5

14. Enebechi, C.N., Duffy, V.G.: Virtual reality and artificial intelligence in mobile computing and applied ergonomics: a bibliometric and content analysis. In: Duffy, V.G. (ed.) HCII 2020. LNCS, vol. 12199, pp. 334–345. Springer, Cham (2020). https://doi.org/10.1007/978-3-030-49907-5_24

15. Google Website: Google Ngram Viewer. https://books.google.com/ngrams/. Accessed 25 Apr 2023

16. Springer Nature Website: Springer Link. https://link-springer-com.ezproxy.lib.purdue.edu/. Accessed 25 Apr 2023

17. Google Website, Google Scholar. https://scholar.google.com/. Accessed 25 Apr 2023

18. Harzing, A.W.: Publish or Perish. https://harzing.com/resources/publish-or-perish. Accessed 28 Apr 2023

19. Persson, O.: BibExcel. https://homepage.univie.ac.at/juan.gorraiz/bibexcel/. Accessed 28 Apr 2023

20. Clarivate: Web of Science. https://apps.webofknowledge.com. Accessed 28 Apr 2023

21. Centre for Science and Technology Studies, VOSViewer: Visualizing Scientific Landscapes, https://www.vosviewer.com/. Accessed 28 April 2023

22. Research Gate, Share, and Discover Research. https://www.researchgate.net/. Accessed 28 April 2023

23. Chen, Chaomei. CiteSpace: Visualizing Patterns and Trends in Scientific Literature. http://cluster.cis.drexel.edu/~cchen/citespace/. Accessed 28 Apr 2023

24. Elsevier B.V. Scopus. https://www.scopus.com/home.uri. Accessed 28 Apr 2023

25. Twitter, Vicinitas: Twitter Tracking Tool. https://www.vicinitas.io/. Accessed 28 Apr 2023

26. Verbi. MAXQDA. https://www.maxqda.com/. Accessed 29 Apr 2023

27. ADA Website: ADA Tool Kit, Chapter 1, Statutes and Regulations. https://archive.ada.gov/pcatoolkit/chap1toolkit.htm. Accessed 29 Apr 2023

28. ODR website: ADA 101 - ADA Glossary - Legal and Practical Terms A-B | Odr. https://odr.dc.gov/book/ada-101-ada-glossary-legal-and-practical-terms/ada-101-ada-glossary-legal-and-practical-terms-b. Accessed 29 Apr 2023

29. Teixeira, E.S.M., Okimoto, M.L.L.R.: Industrial manufacturing workstations suitability for people with disabilities: the perception of workers. In: Rebelo, F., Soares, M. (eds.) AHFE 2017. AISC, vol. 588, pp. 488–497. Springer, Cham (2018). https://doi.org/10.1007/978-3-319-60582-1_49

30. Okumura, M.L.M., da Silva, G.A.P., Junior, O.C.: The influence of human factors in the functional analysis of the support device for users with upper limb agenesis. In: Canciglieri Junior, O., Trajanovic, M.D. (eds.) Personalized Orthopedics, pp. 289–310. Springer, Cham (2022). https://doi.org/10.1007/978-3-030-98279-9_10

31. Kaygisiz, B.B., Uyanik, M., Kayihan, H: The effect of functional capacity related ergonomic risk factors on quality of life of people with physical disability. Ergoterapi ve Rehabilitasyon Dergisi **8**(2), 113–122 (2020). https://doi.org/10.30720/ered.617387

32. Clarkson, P.J., Coleman, R.: History of inclusive design in the UK. Appl. Ergon. **46**(Part B), 235–247 (2015). https://doi.org/10.1016/j.apergo.2013.03.002

33. Esmail, A., et al.: Fashion industry perceptions of clothing design for persons with a physical disability: the need for building partnerships for future innovation. Int. J. Fash. Des. Technol. Educ. **15**(1), 77–85 (2022). https://doi.org/10.1080/17543266.2021.2004243

34. IDEO Website: Design Kit: The Human-Centered Design Toolkit. https://www.ideo.com/post/design-kit. Accessed 01 May 2023

35. Martin Ginis, K.A., Evans, M.B., Ben Mortenson, W., Noreau, L.: Broadening the conceptualization of participation of persons with physical disabilities: a configurative review and recommendations. Arch. Phys. Med. Rehabil. **98**(2), 395–402 (2017). https://doi.org/10.1016/j.apmr.2016.04.017

36. Bonaccio, S., Connelly, C.E., Gellatly, I.R., Jetha, A., Martin Ginis, K.A.: The participation of people with disabilities in the workplace across the employment cycle: employer concerns and research evidence. J. Bus. Psychol. **35**(2), 135–158 (2019). https://doi.org/10.1007/s10869-018-9602-5

37. Martin Ginis, K.A., Jetha, A., Gignac, M.A.M.: Experiential aspects of employment and their relationship with work outcomes: a cross-sectional study using a novel measure of participation in workers with and without physical disabilities. Disabil. Health J. **16**, 101448 (2023)

38. Henry, A.D., Mitra M., Gettens, J., Zhang, J.: Economic wellbeing and life satisfaction among working and non-working adults with disabilities. For health consulting publications, UMass Chan Poster (2013). https://doi.org/20.500.14038/27080

39. Mandischer, N., et al.: Toward adaptive human–robot collaboration for the inclusion of people with disabilities in manual labor tasks. Electronics (Basel) **12**(5), 1118 (2023). https://doi.org/10.3390/electronics12051118

40. Narenthiran, O.P., Torero, J., Woodrow, M.: Inclusive design of workspaces: mixed methods approach to understanding users. Sustain. (Basel, Switzerland) **14**(6), 3337 (2022). https://doi.org/10.3390/su14063337

41. Martel, A., Day, K., Jackson, M.A., Kaushik, S.: Beyond the pandemic: the role of the built environment in supporting people with disabilities work life. ArchNet-IJAR **15**(1), 98–112 (2021). https://doi.org/10.1108/ARCH-10-2020-0225

42. Quaigrain, R.A., Issa, M.H.: Development and validation of disability management indicators for the construction industry. J. Eng. Des. Technol. **16**(1), 81–100 (2018). https://doi.org/10.1108/JEDT-04-2017-0032

43. National Science Foundation: Adapting to the human body: shape-adaptive attachment for parallel wearable robots using jamming. Award Abstract #2240508 (2023)

44. National Science Foundation: SCC-IRG track 1: advancing human-centered sociotechnical research for enabling independent mobility in people with physical disabilities. Award Abstract #2124857 (2022)

45. National Science Foundation: Electromagnetic attachment of assistive devices. Award Abstract #2144015 (2022)

Ergonomics in Transportation: A Comprehensive Review and Analysis

Adithya Rajesh$^{(\boxtimes)}$, Karthick Kumaravel, and Vincent G. Duffy

Purdue University, West Lafayette, IN 47906, USA
{rajesh9,kkumara,duffy}@purdue.edu

Abstract. This study looks at the importance of ergonomics in transportation as well as the contributions of the human factors and ergonomics (HFE), human computer interface (HCI), and safety-related organizations to this critical area of focus. The study provides an outline of the problems with transportation ergonomics, such as the physical and mental tiredness caused by extended travel, subpar infrastructure, and distracted driving. It considers how these concerns impact the safety, efficiency, and sustainability of transportation systems as well as how industrial engineering, HFE, HCI, and safety groups are addressing these issues. The paper focuses on the contributions made by these communities in identifying ergonomic concerns, developing plans for risk reduction, and developing technology that enhances the effectiveness and safety of transportation. The findings show that even while significant progress has been made in addressing ergonomics-related transportation challenges, more research and development are still needed to ensure that transportation systems meet user needs and promote sustainability and safety. The research provides a helpful overview of the importance of ergonomics in transportation and the contributions made by many groups in addressing this significant area of concern, highlighting the necessity of developing transportation systems that prioritize passenger safety, comfort, and productivity. A review of many studies found that incorporating ergonomics into transportation design can significantly reduce accidents, fatigue, and musculoskeletal issues among commuters and transportation workers.

Keywords: Ergonomics · Transportation · Comfort Analysis · Human factors · Human Computer Interface

1 Introduction and Background

As knowledge of the interaction between people and their workplaces grow, ergonomics and human factors have attracted a lot of interest in a variety of sectors. The automobile industry is one sector where the use of ergonomics has proved crucial. Ergonomics has developed into an important field of research and development for automobile makers with the goal of boosting safety and enhancing the driving experience [1].

Ergonomics and human factors are important in many other industries than the automotive sector, such as industrial engineering, human-computer interaction, and safety-related organizations. Ergonomics and related fields have a considerable influence on

© The Author(s), under exclusive license to Springer Nature Switzerland AG 2023
V. G. Duffy et al. (Eds.): HCII 2023, LNCS 14057, pp. 130–144, 2023.
https://doi.org/10.1007/978-3-031-48047-8_8

the transportation sector. The safety, efficiency, and sustainability of transportation operations are directly impacted by the design and optimization of transportation networks. The creation of user-friendly, safe, and environmentally friendly transportation systems has gained importance in recent years. As a result, research in transportation ergonomics has become more well-known, with an emphasis on creating creative solutions to satisfy the rising need for effective, safe, and sustainable transportation systems [2].

The HFE, HCI, and safety-related communities have made major contributions in this field by identifying ergonomic risks associated with transportation, creating plans to reduce these risks, and creating technology to improve both the safety and effectiveness of transportation. To guarantee that transportation networks serve consumers' demands and advance sustainability and safety, there is still more work to be done. The purpose of this study is to examine the difficulties with ergonomics in the transportation industry, the contributions of the communities of industrial engineering, HFE, HCI, and safety, and the possibilities for more research and development in this field of transportation systems. Technologies like driverless cars, smart infrastructure, and traffic control systems are examples of ITS.

Documents by year

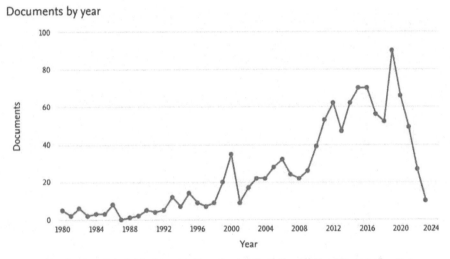

Fig. 1. Trend analysis Scopus - Ergonomics in transportation ("Scopus," n.d)

Figures 1, 2, and 3 show a comparable pattern in the trend analysis between driver ergonomics, vehicle ergonomics, and transportation ergonomics. As people started to understand the significance of ergonomic transportation in the years following 1980, there has been a noticeable increase in research interest in these areas. The surge in research activity in the twenty-first century is another evidence that this subject is still important and has room for more investigation and advancement. Therefore, it is clear that ergonomic transportation research is still crucial and needs to be continued in order to improve the safety and wellbeing of workers in the transportation sector.

Documents by year

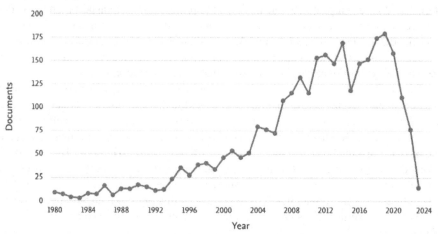

Fig. 2. Trend analysis Scopus - Vehicle ergonomics ("Scopus," n.d)

Documents by year

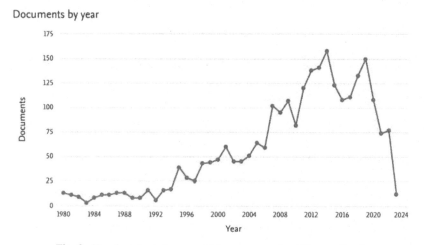

Fig. 3. Trend analysis Scopus - Driver ergonomics ("Scopus," n.d)

2 Purpose of Study

This study aims to investigate the role of ergonomics in transportation and its effects on the sustainability, effectiveness, and safety of transportation systems. The architecture of cars, infrastructure, and communication systems, as well as other aspects of building and improving transportation networks, all depend on ergonomics to make driving comfortable, safe, and effective. Also included in the study's objectives are the identification of the major difficulties and opportunities related to the application of ergonomic solutions in the transportation industry as well as the investigation of the potential benefits of cutting-edge technologies like human-computer interfaces, automation, and artificial intelligence in improving transportation ergonomics. The results of this study will aid in the creation of efficient and environmentally friendly transportation systems that can fulfill the rising demand for mobility while lowering their negative effects on the environment and enhancing user happiness and safety.

The study also intends to analyze the many techniques and approaches utilized in transportation ergonomics research, such as simulation-based design, field investigations, and user-centered design, to pinpoint each approach's advantages and disadvantages as well as the possibility of integrating them. The research also aims to investigate the part played by stakeholders in the development and use of ergonomic transportation solutions, such as drivers, passengers, policymakers, and transportation providers. Transportation systems may be adjusted to the unique requirements of various users and environments by integrating stakeholders in the design process and taking into consideration their wants, preferences, and input, resulting in more inclusive and efficient solutions. Finally, the study aims to offer useful suggestions and recommendations for transportation practitioners, decision-makers, and researchers in order to enhance transportation ergonomics and encourage the adoption of novel solutions in the transportation industry. In addition to initiatives for removing adoption obstacles and scaling up effective treatments, these recommendations can include best practices for the design, assessment, and use of ergonomic solutions.

3   Procedure

The primary aim of this study has guided the methodology for investigating existing literature and discovering new insights. While course textbooks acted as the main source during the initial stages of obtaining background knowledge, supplementary course materials such as the handbook of human factors and ergonomics [3] and the handbook of human-machine interaction [4] helped to gain information about the practical aspects of ergonomics in transportation. The chapter on Transportation from Brauer's Safety and health for engineers [5] as well as the chapter Computers.

Automation and Robots from Goetsch's course textbook [6] both proved invaluable resources. A method article [7] was chosen to provide guidelines for the systematic review and reappraisal process. The following sections detail the steps that were taken as well as the information gathered from each one. A similar methodology was adopted in articles dealing with the bibliometric analysis of topics related to ergonomics and musculoskeletal injuries. While [8] uses general literature search and tools such as MAXQDA and Vicinitas to identify the potential risks and address musculoskeletal disorders in the workspace, [9] provides new light on ergonomic analysis and company investment benefits through term analysis, database search and co-citation/co-occurrence analysis. We have used several of these methods to aid our understanding of the current trends and developments in the transportation domain from an ergonomic viewpoint.

3.1 Literature Review

The safety, comfort, and well-being of passengers and drivers are directly impacted by ergonomics, making it a crucial component of transportation design [10]. For transportation systems to be safer and more effective, human factors and ergonomics (HFE) concepts must be included. Additionally, the advancement of cutting-edge technologies like human-computer interfaces (HCI) has the potential to improve the functionality and security of transportation systems. The goal of this literature review is to give the readers a general understanding of the significance of ergonomics in the transportation industry as well as the contributions made by different organizations in addressing ergonomics-related transportation issues.

Automobile seat design should take into account the target population's expectations for comfort as well as ergonomic standards based on physiology and anthropometry. This claim is confirmed by a study that involved 12 people testing five different small vehicle seats. The results showed differences between the stated anthropometric accommodation requirements and the individuals' desired lumbar height, seatback breadth, cushion length, and cushion width. The authors [11] draw the conclusion that while ergonomics principles serve as the foundation for seat design, they cannot be used arbitrarily because they do not guarantee pleasant chairs. The problem can be addressed with modern techniques such as Finite Element Modeling which can be applied for Analysis of Seat Comfort [12]. On the other hand we can use digital human modeling software such as RAMSIS along with a mixture of other variables like Joint Angles, Seat Pressure and Tissue Loads to bring more multi-factor analysis for our current problem [13].

In transportation, inclusive design and ergonomics are connected since both seek to increase passenger comfort and safety [14]. Designing the job, equipment, and the workplace with the workers' surroundings as a priority in order to provide more comfortable working circumstances is known as ergonomics [14]. The goal of ergonomics in transportation is to minimize pain and harm by customizing the vehicle to the user's body [16]. On the other side, inclusive design attempts to provide products and environments that are accessible to everyone, regardless of their skills or limitations [14]. The term "inclusive design" refers to the process of designing automobiles and transportation systems that are accessible to those with disabilities, such as those who use wheelchairs or have vision impairments [14]. Thus, ergonomics and inclusive design share a goal of enhancing the comfort, safety, and accessibility of transportation for all passengers.

Table 1. Publications with respect to database

Database	Search term	No. of Publications
Scopus	Ergonomics in transportation	1,157
Scopus	Vehicle ergonomics	3,122
Web of Science	Ergonomics in transportation	779
Web of Science	Vehicle ergonomics	2,129
Dimensions.ai	Vehicle ergonomics	1,729

It can be deduced from the above Table 1 that various databases have a diverse collection of data for the same search terms, such as 'Vehicle ergonomics' and 'Ergonomics in transportation'. We may use this analysis to decide which databases to consider and to see which databases are conservative. It is without a doubt evident that the Scopus provides a greater collection of data for our study given the current topic and search terms. To get a holistic view, we include all the high-quality research data from Dimensions.ai, Web of Scopus, and Scopus into our present study.

Documents by country or territory
Compare the document counts for up to 15 countries/territories.

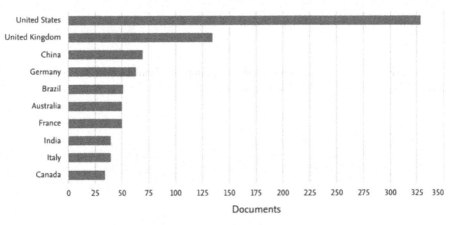

Fig. 4. Number of documents in the topic of review by country ("Scopus" n.d.)

From the above Fig. 4 it can be inferred that the country wise analysis of publications conducted utilizing the tools offered from Scopus database. Results show that the United States, United Kingdom, China, and Germany are the pioneers in this topic as they are seen in top rankings in this list. This result is not surprising as we know these countries are leading manufacturers as well as avid customers of the automobile industry in the world. Along with their interest in the auto industry, these nations have made significant investments in R&D, allowing them to stay on the cutting edge of new developments in the transportation industry. Future research efforts may be guided by this information, which is useful for identifying the industry's key players.

3.2 Engagement Measures

For obtaining important insights from huge datasets, data mining has significantly increased in popularity. Vicinitas is a data mining tool created particularly to assess levels of involvement by examining Twitter activity pertaining to a given subject. To gauge Twitter users' level of involvement with transportation safety in this study, the tool was used. All tweets with "Transportation Safety" as a hashtag or keyword were included in the search. Figure 5 illustrates the results of the data set in a graphical format, showcasing the level of interest and conversation surrounding the subject. By using data mining techniques, the research offers insightful information about how the public views transportation safety, which may be helpful in creating programs and policies to improve safety in the transportation industry.

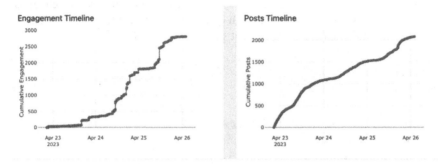

Fig. 5. Vicinitas Keyword related tweet graph for Transportation Safety

Fig. 6. Word cloud generated using Vicinitas search ("Vicinitas," n.d.)

The word cloud created using Vicinitas Fig. 6 shows that words like convenience, quality, safety, and unreliability are prioritized by Twitter users when it comes to transportation safety. This shows that these subjects are being actively discussed in relation to transportation safety. According to the results, there is room for development in terms of transportation safety, convenience, quality, and reliability. These findings highlight how crucial it is to concentrate on these issues in order to increase everyone's level of transportation safety.

3.3   Trend Analysis

The Google Ngram graph below in Fig. 7 displays the frequency of the terms, "Human Factors in Transportation," "Vehicle Ergonomics," and "Driver Comfort and Safety" in books that were published between 1980 and 2019. These subjects have grown significantly in popularity and gained attention in the twenty-first century. The graph shows a dramatic increase in the use of these keywords after the year 2000, showing an increasing interest in the topic. This demonstrates the significance of these issues and their connection to current academic study. To increase the security and comfort of transportation for everyone, further study and research into these areas is required.

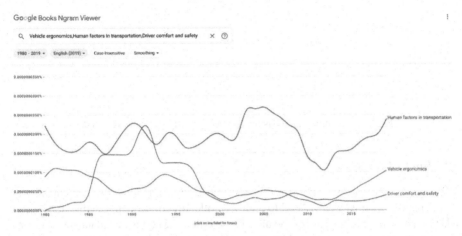

Fig. 7. Google Ngram ("Google Books NGram Viewer" n.d.)

3.4 Citation Analysis

Multiple tools were used to analyze the data obtained from literature review to identify clusters of similar work. This included co-occurrence and co-citation analysis using vosviewer as well as citespace. By looking deeper into the articles identified using these tools more insight was gained in the topic of interest. Automation was a keyword that came up frequently during the literature review of ergonomics in transportation. The influence of automation as well as the dangers of misuse of the technology was talked about in detail by Parasuraman, R & Riley, V [17]. While driving comfort is an important factor in modern ergonomics, driving safety is also paramount. Automobile driving requires quick and efficient information processing by the driver [18]. Automation reduces this burden by reducing the tasks that are required by the driver. Research by See and Lee [19] looked into how automation can be improved with active involvement by the user. Figure 8 shows the co-citation analysis linking some of the major articles in this domain.

Citespace was also employed to find and generate clusters of articles that are related to each other in the field of transportation with a focus on ergonomics and automation. The source data to generate the clusters were exported from the Scopus database using the search term "Vehicle Ergonomics". Figure 9 shows the clusters named using extracted keywords. Among these, some of the most prominent clusters are "comfort", "autonomy" "HMI" and "human automation interaction". This corresponds to the other methods used in this systematic review as cements the relevance of the abovementioned terms in modern research related to ergonomics in transportation.

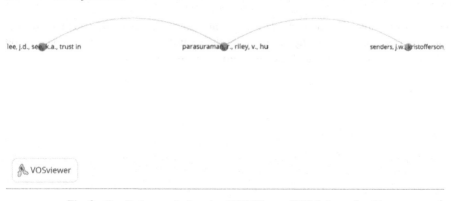

Fig. 8. Co-citation analysis using VOS Viewer ("VOSviewer," n.d.)

3.5   Content Analysis

VOS viewer software was used in this research study to analyze the content of academic papers. Scopus was utilized to gather a collection of academic publications, and a keyword search produced 2000 results. These articles' Scopus metadata was exported in WoS format after extraction. The dataset was imported into VOS viewer, and content analysis was carried out using the "create map based on network data" option. The connection strength was adjusted to zero to collect as many pertinent terms as feasible. Subsequently, 24 words satisfied the required criterion. Figure 4 displays the findings of the content analysis. Using this method, we were able to find patterns and correlations within the information, providing key insights into how academic works are related. Our findings have important ramifications for ongoing research in this area and lay the groundwork for the creation of fresh diverse solutions to challenging issues.

Similarly, after downloading all the articles chosen for the evaluation, a content analysis based on their text was carried out. This involves creating a word cloud to represent the important keywords in the chosen articles visually. The created word cloud in Fig. 5 was used to carry the literature review. Notably, technology, automation, comfort and transportation emerged as the four most important terms from the investigation.

In the cluster analysis, it was shown that the keywords "Automation," "Comfort," "Posture," and "Seat" are key nodes in the clusters. The terms used most often in the sample are highlighted in Fig. 6. These terms are significant in the subject of discussion since they are present in the clusters. Researchers who are researching the literature on the subject might use these important phrases as a point of reference. By highlighting these key phrases, academics may better comprehend the field's theoretical underpinnings and current state of scientific inquiry, which will help to foster the creation of fresh perspectives and solutions to challenging issues.

MAXQDA offers useful data on the frequency of terms used in the text, in contrast to content analysis performed with VOS viewer, which prioritizes link strength as the major criteria. The ability to find the most prevalent keywords associated with the subject of interest provided by this function is especially useful for our investigation. The articles chosen for the discussion portion of our literature review were then searched using these identified keywords. We were able to concentrate our attention on the exact areas of

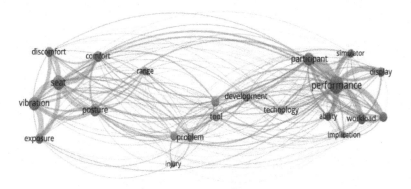

Fig. 9. Co-occurrence map generated in VOS Viewer using 2000 articles exported from Scopus database ("Scopus," n.d.; "VOSviewer," n.d.).

Fig. 10. Word cloud generated using maxQDA ("MAXQDA," n.d.)

the articles that were most pertinent to our study issue by using a lexical search. We were able to better comprehend the primary points that were made in the chosen articles thanks to this technique, which also influenced how we developed our literature review.

Citespace also allows for the creation of citation bursts, which shows the most highly cited articles along with the time period in which they were active (Fig. 10). This helped identify the research done by Young et al., [20] which focused on the fundamental ergonomic principles for the design of in-vehicle information systems that are part of smart and sustainable future transportation systems. Another article that focused on the automation aspect of transportation by Fagant and Kockelman [21] discussed the potential of Autonomous vehicles.

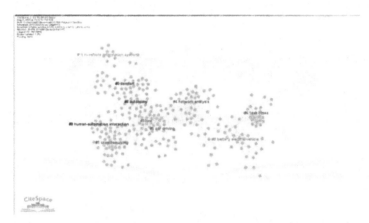

Fig. 11. Cluster Analysis using citespace. Keyword used - "Vehicle Ergonomics" ("CiteSpace," n.d.).

Top 5 References with the Strongest Citation Bursts

References	Year	Strength	Begin	End	2013 - 2023
Young MS, 2011, APPL ERGON, V42, P533, DOI 10.10165j.apergo.2010.08.012, DOI	2011	2.96	2013	2016	
Stanton NA, 2011, APPL ERGON, V42, P502, DOI 10.1(16;j.apergo.2010.08.016, DOI	2011	2.07	2014	2016	
Franke T, 2012, APPL PSYCHOL-INT REV, V61, P368, DOI 10.1111/j.1464-0597.2011.00474.x, DOI	2012	2.76	2016	2017	
Fagnant DJ, 2015, TRANSPORT RES A-POL, V77, P167, DOI 10.1016/j.tra.2015.04.003, DOI	2015	2.89	2019	2020	
Ackermann C, 2019, TRANSPORT RES F-TRAF, V62, P757, DOI 10.1016/j.trf.2019.03.006, DOI	2019	2.76	2021	2023	

Fig. 12. Citation burst generated using citespace for articles having keyword "Vehicle Ergonomics" ("CiteSpace," n.d.).

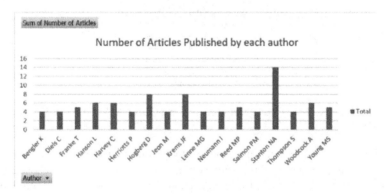

Fig. 13. Pivot chart showing number of articles by authors with 4 or more research articles ("BibExcel," n.d.)

In addition to using VOS viewer, we also examined the information taken from Harzing's Publish or Perish using BibExcel, a potent bibliometric analysis tool. To determine the top writers in the subject area under consideration, we specifically created a pivot table in BibExcel (Fig. 11). The most significant researchers in the discipline and their contributions to the research landscape may be identified by looking at the publication output of individual writers.

We import the metadata from Harzing's Publish or Perish into BibExcel and perform the analysis to create the "leading authors" table. The chart was then created by exporting the results to an excel file. The results of this investigation are shown in Figure. Using BibExcel, we were able to comprehend the research output of specific academics in the field better for this study. Future research projects can be informed by this data, which can also be used to locate possible partners and learn more about the research environment in the area. Additionally, by locating the most significant academics in the area of interest, this method can aid in the development of fresh interdisciplinary approaches to difficult problems (Figs. 12 and 13).

4 Discussions

4.1 Intelligent Transportation Systems (ITS)

Intelligent transportation systems (ITS) are cutting-edge technologies that improve the efficiency, safety, and sustainability of transportation networks by utilizing information, communication, and sensor technology. Smart infrastructure, autonomous cars, and traffic management systems are a few examples of ITS technology [22]. ITS is important for increasing safety, lowering congestion, and boosting transportation efficiency. More recently, research investigating the suitability of using various parameters such as deceleration rate to improve the safety of autonomous vehicles has shown great promise [23]. Enhancing the safety of drivers and pedestrians is one of the primary aims of implementing ITS.

4.2 Active Transportation

There are several health and environmental advantages to active transportation, which includes human-powered modes of mobility including walking, cycling, and wheelchair use. It encourages more exercise, lowers greenhouse gas emissions, and enhances air quality. Active transportation has been linked to lower obesity rates in some areas, according to studies [24]. A more sustainable and healthful society can result from promoting active transportation via infrastructure development and policy implementation.

4.3 Sustainable Transportation

An approach to transportation that prioritizes the needs of all users, including those who utilize public transit, bicycles, and foot traffic, is known as sustainable transportation. In order to create a cleaner and healthier environment, it tries to lower greenhouse gas emissions and encourage the use of renewable energy sources. Long-term planning, creative design, and eco-friendly technology must all be prioritized in the development of sustainable transportation [25].

4.4 Universal Design

The idea of universal design is to provide spaces and products that can be used and accessed by anybody, regardless of their physical or mental disabilities. In the realm of transportation, universal design refers to the process of creating transportation systems that are usable by all users, including people with impairments or mobility issues. It is the goal of universal design to give everyone, regardless of ability, access to equal opportunities and means of transportation [26]. Digital Human modeling is an important tool in ensuring universal design principles can be implemented in automobile design and manufacturing [27]. This can be done in multiple ways. Comfort analysis can be used to understand how joint angles and driving postures contribute negatively to ergonomics in a vehicle [28]. Other research focusing on developing statistical models to analyze driving postures has also gained popularity [29].

A crucial component of creating intelligent transportation systems is human computer interaction (HCI). HCI is essential to the design and development of technology that improves user experience and guarantees accessibility for all users. By incorporating HCI into transportation systems, it is ensured that technology is created with the user in mind, resulting in more effective, accessible, and user-friendly transportation systems. In conclusion, the creation of effective, secure, and accessible transportation systems depends on the combination of intelligent transportation systems, active transportation, sustainable transportation, universal design, and HCI. A cleaner, healthier, and more egalitarian society may result from the design and development of transportation systems that promote accessibility, sustainability, and the user experience.

5 Conclusion

The literature review on ergonomic transportation highlights the necessity of developing transportation systems that prioritize passenger safety, comfort, and productivity. A review of many studies found that incorporating ergonomics into transportation design can significantly reduce accidents, fatigue, and musculoskeletal issues among commuters and transportation workers. To offer transportation that is ergonomically effective, however, designers, engineers, and legislators must collaborate. The evaluation highlights how advanced technologies, like autonomous automobiles, virtual reality, and artificial intelligence, have the potential to revolutionize ergonomic transportation. With this technology, travel experiences can be more flexible and personalized. Therefore, putting ergonomic design first in transportation is crucial for ensuring everyone travels safely and comfortably. It is critical to think about how ergonomic design may improve the security, comfort, and effectiveness of transportation systems as we anticipate the future of transportation.

6 Future Work

In the upcoming years, the widespread use of autonomous and semi-autonomous cars is anticipated to transform the transportation sector. The significance of ergonomics in transportation will only increase as more people use these cars. The user experience and human-machine interaction in these vehicles therefore have to be the primary topics of future study. To make sure that these cars are user-friendly, pleasant, and safe for passengers, studies must be done to assess their ergonomic design. Additionally, it is crucial to create rules and guidelines that place a high priority on the ergonomics of autonomous and semi-autonomous vehicles [30]. Future research must also look at how these cars affect society, including how they affect energy use, the environment, and traffic congestion. To the benefit of both passengers and the environment, it is crucial to make sure that these vehicles are ergonomically constructed as they become more widely used.

References

1. Márquez, M.A., Garcia, J.M., Venezuela, S.C.T.: Ergonomics of urban public passangers transportation. 9th **23** (2004)
2. Dobson, K.: Human Factors and Ergonomics in transportation control systems. Procedia Manuf. **3**, 2913–2920 (2015)
3. Salvendy, G., Karwowski, W. (eds.): Handbook of Human Factors and Ergonomics. Wiley (2021)
4. Boy, G.A. (ed.): The Handbook of Human-Machine Interaction: A Human-Centered Design Approach. CRC Press (2017)
5. Brauer, R.L.: Transportation. In: Safety and Health for Engineers, pp. 213–236. Wiley, New Jersey (2006)
6. Goetsch, D.L.: Computers, automation and robots. In: Occupational Safety and Health for Technologists, Engineers, and Managers, pp. 526–537. Pearson, Boston (2019)
7. Moher, D., Liberati, A., Tetzlaff, J., Altman, D.G., PRISMA Group: preferred reporting items for systematic reviews and metaanalyses: the PRISMA statement. Ann. Internal Med. **151**(4), 264–269 (2009)
8. Asokan, S., Duffy, V.G.: Using bibliometric analysis, ergonomic principles and a perching stool to prevent injuries in the workplace. In: Duffy, V.G., Rau, PL.P. (eds.) HCI International 2022 – Late Breaking Papers: Ergonomics and Product Design, HCII 2022. LNCS, vol. 13522, pp. 23–33. Springer, Cham (2022). https://doi.org/10.1007/978-3-031-21704-3_2
9. Evans, B., Duffy, V.G.: Ergonomic analysis through targeted industrial case review and company investment benefit. In: Duffy, V.G., Rau, PL.P. (eds.) HCI International 2022 – Late Breaking Papers: Ergonomics and Product Design. HCII 2022. Lecture Notes in Computer Science, vol. 13522, pp. 190–206. Springer, Cham (2022). https://doi.org/10.1007/978-3-031-21704-3_13
10. Gowtham, S., et al.: Seating comfort analysis: a virtual ergonomics study of bus drivers in private transportation. IOP Conf. Ser. Mater. Sci. Eng. **912**(2), 022018 (2020)
11. Kolich, M.: Automobile seat comfort: occupant preferences vs. anthropometric accommodation. Appl. Ergon. **34**(2), 177–184 (2003)
12. Ma, K., Li, B., Yan, Z., Liu, Q.: Finite element modeling and analysis of seat comfort. In: Kountchev, R., Patnaik, S., Shi, J., Favorskaya, M.N. (eds.) Advances in 3D Image and Graphics Representation, Analysis, Computing and Information Technology. SIST, vol. 180, pp. 347–351. Springer, Singapore (2020). https://doi.org/10.1007/978-981-15-3867-4_40
13. Siefert, A.: Occupant comfort-a mixture of joint angles, seat pressure, and tissue loads. No. 2016-01-1438. SAE Technical Paper (2016)
14. Angeleska, E., Sidorenko, S., Jankovic, A., Rizov, T.: Application of virtual ergonomic tools for evaluating an inclusive autonomous vehicle interior. South East Eur. J. Archit. Des. **2022**, 1–8 (2022)

15. Mat, S., Salim, M.A., Wan, W.M.F., Yusop, M.S.M.: Design and ergonomics analysis of cutter machine locking device in aerospace industry. J. Mater. Sci. Eng. **5**(2), 145 (2011)
16. Woodcock, A.: New insights, new challenges; person centred transport design. Work **41**(Suppl. 1), 4879–4886 (2012)
17. Parasuraman, R., Riley, V.: Humans and automation: use, misuse, disuse, abuse. Hum. Factors **39**(2), 230–253 (1997)
18. Senders, J.W., Kristofferson, A.B., Levison, W.H., Dietrich, C.W., Ward, J.L.: The attentional demand of automobile driving. Highw. Res. Rec. **195**, 15–33 (1967)
19. Lee, J.D., See, K.A.: Trust in automation: designing for appropriate reliance. Hum. Factors **46**(1), 50–80 (2004)
20. Young, M.S., Birrell, S.A., Stanton, N.A.: Safe driving in a green world: a review of driver performance benchmarks and technologies to support 'smart'driving. Appl. Ergon. **42**(4), 533–539 (2011)
21. Fagnant, D.J., Kockelman, K.: Preparing a nation for autonomous vehicles: opportunities, barriers and policy recommendations. Transp. Res. Part A Policy Pract. **77**, 167–181 (2015)
22. Barbaresso, J., et al.: USDOT's Intelligent Transportation Systems (ITS) ITS strategic plan, 2015–2019. No. FHWA-JPO-14-145. United States. Department of Transportation. Intelligent Transportation Systems Joint Program Office (2014)
23. Ackermann, C., Beggiato, M., Bluhm, L.-F., Löw, A., Krems, J.F.: Deceleration parameters and their applicability as informal communication signal between pedestrians and automated vehicles. Transp. Res. F Traffic Psychol. Behav. **62**, 757–768 (2019)
24. Bassett, D.R., Pucher, J., Buehler, R., Thompson, D.L., Crouter, S.E.: Walking, cycling, and obesity rates in Europe, North America, and Australia. J. Phys. Act. Health **5**(6), 795–814 (2008)
25. Litman, T.: Well Measured-Developing Indicators for Sustainable and Livable Transport Planning - 5 March 2021 (2021)
26. Steinfeld, E., Maisel, J.: Universal Design: Creating Inclusive Environments. Wiley (2012)
27. Bubb, H., Grünen, R.E., Remlinger, W.: Anthropometric vehicle design. In: Bubb, H., Bengler, K., Grünen, R.E., Vollrath, M. (eds.) Automotive Ergonomics, pp. 343–468. Springer, Wiesbaden (2021). https://doi.org/10.1007/978-3-658-33941-8_7
28. Peng, J., Wang, X., Denninger, L.: Ranges of the least uncomfortable joint angles for assessing automotive driving posture. Appl. Ergon. **61**, 12–21 (2017)
29. Park, J., Ebert, S.M., Reed, M.P., Hallman, J.J.: A statistical model including age to predict passenger postures in the rear seats of automobiles. Ergonomics **59**(6), 796–805 (2016)
30. Wan, J., Wu, C.: The effects of vibration patterns of take-over request and non-driving tasks on taking-over control of automated vehicles. Int. J. Hum. Comput. Interact. **34**(11), 987–998 (2018)
31. CiteSpace (n.d.). http://cluster.cis.drexel.edu/~cchen/citespace/
32. Google Books NGram Viewer (n.d.). https://books.google.com/ngrams/
33. Vicinitas (n.d.). https://www.vicinitas.io/
34. Scopus (n.d.). https://www.scopus.com/
35. MAXQDA (n.d.). https://www.maxqda.com/
36. VOSviewer (n.d.). https://www.vosviewer.com/
37. Dimensions (n.d.). https://www.dimensions.ai/

Proposal of a Multi-parametric Ergonomic Assessment Protocol Integrating Intra-operative Use of Wearable Technology to Evaluate Musculoskeletal Discomfort for Surgeon During Laryngeal Surgery

Emma Sala[1] , Marco Mazzali[2], Emilio Paraggio[2] , Gianluca Rossetto[3] ,
Giorgio Cassiolas[4] , Emilia Scalona[2] , Francesco Negro[5],
Giuseppe De Palma[1,2] , Cesare Piazza[2] , and Nicola Francesco Lopomo[3(✉)]

[1] Unit of Occupational Medicine, Hygiene, Toxicology and Occupational Prevention, ASST
Spedali Civili di Brescia, Brescia, Italy
[2] Department of Medical and Surgical Specialties, Radiological Sciences and Public Health,
University of Brescia, Brescia, Italy
[3] Department of Information Engineering, University of Brescia, Brescia, Italy
nicola.lopomo@unibs.it
[4] Complex Structure of Surgical Sciences and Technologies, IRCCS Istituto Ortopedico Rizzoli,
Bologna, Italy
[5] Department of Clinical and Experimental Sciences, University of Brescia, Brescia, Italy

Abstract. Musculoskeletal disorders (MSDs) represent a cross-cutting problem among healthcare workers; particular attention should be given to surgeons who are involved in mentally and physically demanding tasks. This work aimed to propose a multi-parametric ergonomic approach able to exploit different wearable devices to estimate cervical discomfort and the muscular fatigue sustained by an otolaryngology (ENT) surgeon during the execution of laryngeal surgeries. The proposed protocol includes the use of both inertial measurement units (IMUs) and surface electromyography (EMG) probes to monitor head movement and muscle activation during the surgical procedures. IMUs were placed on the forehead and at the C7 level, while EMG probes were positioned on relevant bilateral upper body muscles involved in the surgical tasks. Data analysis encompassed the extraction and examination of flexion/extension, bending, and axial rotation joint angles and EMG signals were scrutinized to assess muscle activation and fatigue. The proposed protocol was preliminary validated involving one expert surgeon, who realized 28 surgeries, employing either a conventional microscope or an advanced exoscope; the setup was well-tolerated, with only minor discomfort reported. The protocol effectively captured detailed information regarding head movement and muscle activation patterns throughout the surgeries, revealing notable features in surgical approaches. The ergonomic assessment protocol provides a solid foundation for future investigations and the development of tailored surgical training programs aimed at mitigating the risk of MSDs among surgeons.

Keywords: Ergonomics assessment · risk assessment · otolaryngology surgery · ENT · wearable technologies · inertial measurement units · electromyography

V. G. Duffy et al. (Eds.): HCII 2023, LNCS 14057, pp. 145–154, 2023.
https://doi.org/10.1007/978-3-031-48047-8_9

1 Introduction

Musculoskeletal disorders (MSDs) are a cross-cutting problem among healthcare workers, whose prevalence varies depending on the occupation and the departments in which they work [1].

Among these operators, scientific literature clearly reports that surgeons are overall involved in some of the most both mentally and physically demanding tasks [2]. Indeed, all the specialists in surgery could be at high risk of developing MSDs and, the overload they perceive could directly impact also on the overall quality of the surgical performance, the clinical outcomes, and – in extrema ratio –the safety of the patients themselves [2–4]. In fact, among surgeons, the most commonly reported issues mainly involve the upper body, including the neck, lower back, shoulders, and upper back; indeed, the cervical track of the spine appears to be one of the most affected regions [2].

Due to the impact of repetitive tasks and sustained muscular activities while maintain awkward postures, otolaryngology (or ENT – Ear, Nose and Throat) surgeons result to be at high risk of developing MSDs, with a reported prevalence between 47 and 90%, a percentage that is indeed in line with other surgical specialties but much higher with respect to the general population [5–7]. Typical disorders affecting ENT surgeons include musculoskeletal pain, swelling, stiffness, restricted movement, and fatigue; further, typical disease are tendonitis and carpal tunnel syndrome [5]. It is worth underlining that it is fundamental to identify the effective musculoskeletal overload since musculoskeletal disorders can contribute to shortening the length of surgeons' careers [8, 9].

In order to overcome these issues, during the last decades, several improvements have been proposed addressing both the surgical procedure, equipment and supporting tools [10]. In fact, the type of instrumentation used by the surgeons during an ENT procedure affects the posture they assume while performing the task and with repercussions on the engagement of their muscles [11–13]. To counteract some of these issues, the introduction of the exoscope in ENT surgery – for instance - has been representing a very recent innovation; the field of application of this technology is microsurgery for benign and malignant pathologies, in both adult and children's surgeries [14–16]. Indeed, the approach on the neck lesion with exoscope presents the advantage of reducing the iatrogenic risk of injury and improves the correct exeresis of neoformations [14].

Focusing on risk assessment, studies presenting an evaluation of musculoskeletal overload conducted with questionnaires and observational methods are mainly reported in the literature with little information about data validity [17]. In fact, most of the used approach to actually assess risk exposure in this context is related to the use of qualitative tools/scales and surveys, such as the NASA-TLX, which was developed to ascertain a subject's level of cognitive and physical load [18].

For the past few years, improvements in technology have made it possible to use wearable solutions so as to objectify the risk and support a multifactorial quantitative approach [19]; indeed, wearable devices integrate well into the surgeon's activities with minimal impact on her/his/their work, also intra-operatively [2, 10, 18, 20].

In this study, we hypothesized that it was fundamental to integrate information concerning both kinematics and kinetics to assess the overall musculoskeletal risk related ENT surgery. For this reason, this work aimed to propose a multi-parametric ergonomic approach able to exploit different wearable technologies (i.e., inertial measurement units and surface electromyography probes) so as to estimate the cervical discomfort and the muscular fatigue sustained by an ENT surgeon during the execution of laryngeal surgeries.

2 Materials and Methods

2.1 Participants

The presented preliminary study involved for 12 months one expert surgeon. All the involved patients were specifically diagnosed with pathologies at laryngeal level. The study was conducted at the ASST Spedali Civili, Brescia, Italia, according to the values expressed in the Declaration of Helsinki and the principles of good worker health surveillance.

2.2 Experimental Setup

In order to assess the discomfort of the postures and the muscular fatigue during the surgery, we introduced specific wearable devices that allowed us to track both the kinematic of the head with respect to the trunk and the muscular activation of several muscles of the upper body involved in the realization of the surgical tasks.

In particular, for the kinematic acquisitions, we include two wireless inertial measurement units (IMUs, WaveTrack Inertial System, Cometa System), whereas 8 wireless probes for surface electromyography (EMG, Mini Wave Infinity, Cometa System) were used to acquire muscular electrical activity.

IMUs were placed on the forehead by means of an elastic headband and at C7 level via adhesive tape, respectively; IMUs provide raw data (acceleration, angular rate, magnetic field), fused data (quaternion), and relative joint angles at a sampling rate of 140 Hz; joint angles were available after having realized the static calibration process as suggested by the manufacturer. Position of the IMUs is reported in Fig. 1.

EMG probes were placed on the belly of several bilateral muscles including:

- right/left sternocleidomastoid muscles;
- right/left cervical splenii;
- right/left upper trapezii;
- right/left anterior deltoids.

Before placing the probe, the skin was deeply cleaned with alcohol. All these muscles represented - in our hypothesis after having performed a preliminary analysis - the muscular structures mainly involved during the surgery. In order to compare across different sessions, a maximal voluntary contraction (MVC) task in isometric conditions was included in the protocol at the beginning of each session and specifically performed for each defined muscular group. The MVC tasks were selected in order to estimate the maximal activation of all the investigated muscles; all the EMG signals were then normalized with respect to the MVC so as to obtain a signal included in the range $[-1, 1]$. The 8 probes were recorded and sampled at 2000 Hz according the specifications of the used hardware. Position of the EMG probes is depicted in Fig. 2.

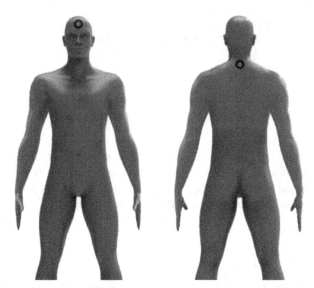

Fig. 1. Experimental setup: position of the wireless inertial measurement units on the head and cervical spine (C7 level) are highlighted in red (Color figure online).

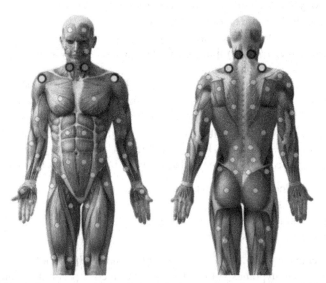

Fig. 2. Experimental setup: position of the wireless proves for the acquisition of surface electromyography signals. Right/left sternocleidomastoid muscles are highlighted in magenta, right/left cervical splenii in blue, right/left upper trapezii in green, and right/left anterior deltoids in yellow (Color figure online).

All the wearable devices were tested before their use within the operating room so as to assess the corresponding risks for the surgeon and the patients in terms of electrical and electromagnetic compatibilities and the overall usability of the approach.

2.3   Data Analysis

Both three-dimensional joint angles and EMG signal for each muscle were extracted from
*.c3d files via custom processing and analysis pipeline (Matlab R2022a; MathWorks
Inc.).

Joint angles (flexion/extension, bending, and axial rotation) were filtered by using
a moving average digital filter (rectangular time window of 250 ms) to get smoother
signals; any drift was compensated before extracting the data by identifying the time
frame with the head in the neutral position. From the signals we specifically extracted
maximum and minimum values, overall range, average value and standard deviation;
the latter parameter was defined to estimate the head "stillness" during the surgery.

Before performing any further analysis, all the EMG signals were compensated for
DC component, filtered with a notch digital filter ($f = 50$ Hz with harmonics, q-factor
$= 35$), and a band-pass digital system ($f_{high-pass} = 20$ Hz; $f_{low-pass} = 250$ Hz; $n = 50$;
Hann window-based zero-phase FIR filter). Onset for each muscle was identified using
the Taeger-Kaiser energy operator ($k = 5$ and threshold defined on MVC baseline level)
[21] and kept into account to recognize the burst with an overall temporal duration of at
least 5 s. Within each identified muscular burst, on a time window of 250 ms, we evaluated
the median frequency of the corresponding power spectrum, RMS value, and the integral
under the signal curve. As an index of fatigue, we estimated also the median frequency
percentual drop on the whole burst considering the difference between the average value
of the last 3 s with respect to those of the first 2 s; when the drop was higher than 8%
we identified the burst with a possible evidence of fatigue [22]. Overall, we analysed the
number of recognized bursts and the number of bursts with possible muscular fatigue
and normalized them with respect to the temporal length of the intervention.

The whole set of available parameters proposed for the analysis is reported in Table 1
for joint angles and Table 2 for EMG, respectively.

Table 1.   Parameters used to analysis head movement with respect to trunk.

Flex/Ext				
Bending				
Ax. Rotation				
Angle Max [deg]	*Angle Min [deg]*	*Angle Range [deg]*	*Angle Average [deg]*	*Angle STD [deg]*

3   Results and Discussion

In order to validate the approach, the proposed protocol was applied on 12 different whole
surgery days on the defined period by involving a single experienced ENT surgeon who
performed 28 laryngeal surgeries by means either of a conventional transoral approach
via an operating microscope system or a commercial exoscope (Endoskope, Karl Storz).

Table 2. Parameters used to analysis EMG signals.

N. Activation > 5 s		
N. Activation with Possible Fatigue (when Med Freq Drop > −8%)		
% N. Activation with Fatigue/N. Activation [%]		
N. Activation/Surgery Duration [#/min]		
N. Activation with Possible Fatigue/Surgery Duration [#/min]		
Mean Activation Duration [s]	*Overall*	Mean
		STD
	Fatigue	Mean
		STD
	No Fatigue	Mean
		STD
Mean RMS	*Overall*	Mean
		STD
	Fatigue	Mean
		STD
	No Fatigue	Mean
		STD
Mean Median Freq Drop [%]	*Overall*	Mean
		STD
	Fatigue	Mean
		STD
	No Fatigue	Mean
		STD
Mean Signal Integral	*Overall*	Mean
		STD
	Fatigue	Mean
		STD
	No Fatigue	Mean
		STD

The setting up lasted on average less than 5 min and the overall setup was quite well tolerated by the surgeon, who reported a slight discomfort due to the headband, but only when the surgeries lasted more than 30 min, overall, with an average time of the surgeries of 29.7 ± 16.2 min.

From the kinematic point of view, the protocol allowed us to estimate the flexion/extension, axial rotation, and bending of the head with respect to the trunk and the variations in the head posture during the execution of different surgeries. On a few occasions the calibration procedure was sub-optimal, thus reporting angular values with a systematic bias; anyhow, the overall range and the variation can be considered as reliable values. An example of the obtained information is reported in Fig. 3.

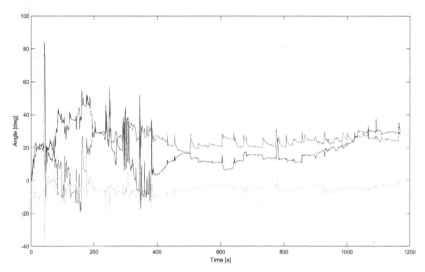

Fig. 3. Example of joint angles obtained for the head movement with respect to the trunk; flex/ext angle is highlighted in red, bending in green and axial rotation in blue (Color figure online).

Furthermore, the protocol allowed us to assess the muscular activation in terms of onsets, number, and duration of the activations, and estimation of muscular fatigue through median frequency analysis. An example of muscular burst identification is reported in Fig. 4 for the right anterior deltoid muscle and Fig. 5 for the left sternocleidomastoid muscle.

As highlighted by the previous figure, the identification of the onset was easier on the "bigger" muscle (i.e., deltoids and trapezii), whereas there were some critical issues for the cervical splenii and sternocleidomastoid muscles due to a lower signal-to-noise ratio.

The preliminary analysis of the data suggested that there are several differences in the performed surgical approaches, which affect the head postures and the development of fatigue of upper limb muscles indeed, despite demonstrating similar patterns in muscle activations.

4   Conclusions

The proposed ergonomic assessment protocol resulted in being easy to set up and well accepted by the surgeon during the realization of the laryngeal surgeries considering both the used procedure, i.e., the conventional operating microscope and exoscope.

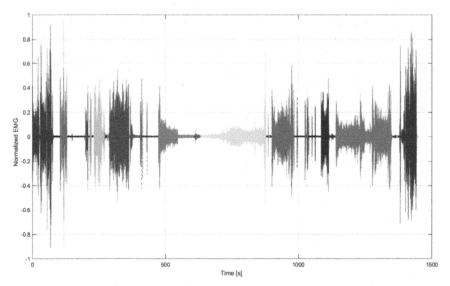

Fig. 4. Example of identification of the muscular burst on right anterior deltoid muscle; every color is a different muscular activation that lasted, continuously, at least 5 s. EMG signal is normalized and reported in the range [−1, 1].

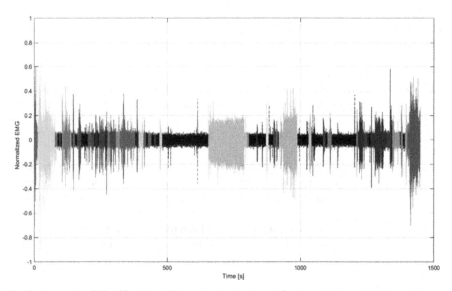

Fig. 5. Example of identification of the muscular burst on left sternocleidomastoid muscle; every color is a different muscular activation that lasted, continuously, at least 5 s. EMG signal is normalized and reported in the range [−1, 1].

The main findings of this study represent a first basis for further ergonomic studies, including standard assessments, and the acquired information can be used to develop specific surgical training programs so as to minimize the overall risk of developing MSDs.

References

1. Epstein, S., et al.: Prevalence of work-related musculoskeletal disorders among surgeons and interventionalists. JAMA Surg. **153**, e174947 (2018). https://doi.org/10.1001/jamasurg.2017. 4947
2. Yang, L., Wang, T., Weidner, T.K., Madura, J.A., Morrow, M.M., Hallbeck, M.S.: Intraoperative musculoskeletal discomfort and risk for surgeons during open and laparoscopic surgery. Surg. Endosc. **35**, 6335–6343 (2021). https://doi.org/10.1007/s00464-020-08085-3
3. Abbruzzese, K., et al.: Physical and mental demand during total hip arthroplasty. Orthop. Clin. North Am. **53**, 413–419 (2022). https://doi.org/10.1016/j.ocl.2022.06.005
4. Galaiya, R., Kinross, J., Arulampalam, T.: Factors associated with burnout syndrome in surgeons: a systematic review. Ann. R. Coll. Surg. England **102**, 401–407 (2020). https://doi.org/10.1308/rcsann.2020.0040
5. Storey, B., Verkerk, M., Hashtroudi, A., Golding-Wood, D.: A systematic review of interventions to prevent work-related musculoskeletal disorders in ENT surgeons. J. Laryngol. Otol. **136**, 622–627 (2022)
6. Szeto, G.P.Y., Ho, P., Ting, A.C.W., Poon, J.T.C., Cheng, S.W.K., Tsang, R.C.C.: Work-related musculoskeletal symptoms in surgeons. J. Occup. Rehabil. **19**, 175–184 (2009). https://doi.org/10.1007/s10926-009-9176-1
7. Bolduc-Bégin, J., Prince, F., Christopoulos, A., Ayad, T.: Work-related musculoskeletal symptoms amongst otolaryngologists and head and neck surgeons in Canada. Eur. Arch. Otorhinolaryngol. **275**, 261–267 (2018). https://doi.org/10.1007/s00405-017-4787-1
8. Giagio, S., Volpe, G., Pillastrini, P., Gasparre, G., Frizziero, A., Squizzato, F.: A preventive program for work-related musculoskeletal disorders among surgeons. Ann. Surg. **270**, 969–975 (2019). https://doi.org/10.1097/SLA.0000000000003199
9. Dianat, I., Bazazan, A., Souraki Azad, M.A., Salimi, S.S.: Work-related physical, psychosocial and individual factors associated with musculoskeletal symptoms among surgeons: implications for ergonomic interventions. Appl. Ergon. **67**, 115–124 (2018). https://doi.org/10.1016/j.apergo.2017.09.011
10. Choi, H.S., In, H.: The effects of operating height and the passage of time on the end-point performance of fine manipulative tasks that require high accuracy. Front. Physiol. **13**, 944866 (2022). https://doi.org/10.3389/fphys.2022.944866
11. Chen, T., Dailey, S.H., Naze, S.A., Jiang, J.J.: The head-mounted microscope. Laryngoscope **122**, 781–784 (2012). https://doi.org/10.1002/lary.21877
12. Statham, M.M., Sukits, A.L., Redfern, M.S., Smith, L.J., Sok, J.C., Rosen, C.A.: Ergonomic analysis of microlaryngoscopy. Laryngoscope **120**, 297–305 (2010). https://doi.org/10.1002/lary.20686
13. Maxner, A., Gray, H., Vijendren, A.: A Systematic review of biomechanical risk factors for the development of work-related musculoskeletal disorders in surgeons of the head and neck. Work **69**, 247–263 (2021). https://doi.org/10.3233/WOR-213474
14. Ferlito, S., et al.: High definition three-dimensional exoscope (VITOM 3D) in E.N.T. surgery: a systematic review of current experience. J. Clin. Med. **11**, 3639 (2022). https://doi.org/10.3390/jcm11133639
15. Carlucci, C., Fasanella, L., Maccarini, A.R.: Exolaryngoscopy: a new technique for laryngeal surgery. Acta Otorhinolaryngol. Ital. **32**, 326–328 (2012)

16. Chebib, E., Benoit, C., Bois, E., Teissier, N., Van Den Abbeele, T.: New surgical frontiers for 4k 3D-exoscope in paediatric head and neck surgery. Eur. Arch. Otorhinolaryngol. **280**, 2033–2041 (2023). https://doi.org/10.1007/s00405-022-07785-x

17. Hansson, G.-Å., et al.: Questionnaire versus direct technical measurements in assessing postures and movements of the head, upper back, arms and hands. Scand. J. Work Environ. Health **27**, 30–40 (2001). https://doi.org/10.5271/sjweh.584

18. Arrighi-Allisan, A.E., et al.: Ergonomic analysis of functional endoscopic sinus surgery using novel inertial sensors. Laryngoscope **132**, 1153–1159 (2022). https://doi.org/10.1002/lary.29796

19. Meltzer, A.J., et al.: Measuring ergonomic risk in operating surgeons by using wearable technology. JAMA Surg. **155**, 444 (2020). https://doi.org/10.1001/jamasurg.2019.6384

20. Thurston, T., et al.: Assessment of muscle activity and fatigue during laparoscopic surgery. Surg. Endosc. **36**, 6672–6678 (2022). https://doi.org/10.1007/s00464-021-08937-6

21. Solnik, S., DeVita, P., Rider, P., Long, B., Hortobágyi, T.: Teager-Kaiser operator improves the accuracy of EMG onset detection independent of signal-to-noise ratio. Acta Bioeng. Biomech. **10**, 65–68 (2008)

22. Whittaker, R.L., La Delfa, N.J., Dickerson, C.R.: Algorithmically detectable directional changes in upper extremity motion indicate substantial myoelectric shoulder muscle fatigue during a repetitive manual task. Ergonomics **62**, 431–443 (2019). https://doi.org/10.1080/00140139.2018.1536808

Bibliometric Analysis and Systematic Review for Ergonomics in Transportation

Jacob Short[✉] and Vincent G. Duffy

Purdue University, West Lafayette, IN 47907, USA
{short77,duffy}@purdue.edu

Abstract. Ergonomics in transportation is an essential area of research with the potential to enhance the safety and comfort of many individuals. By incorporating ergonomic principles into transportation systems, they can become safer, more comfortable, and more efficient. In this paper, a bibliometric analysis and systematic review are conducted to identify trends and areas of interest within the field. Leading authors and leading institutions are identified. Co-occurrence and co-citation analyses are performed. Word clouds are generated from relevant literature. Data was first exported from sources such as Scopus, Google Scholar, Web of Science, Dimensions, and Harzing's Publish or Perish. The data was then analyzed with a variety of tools including VOSviewer, CiteSpace, BibExcel, Vicinitas, and MAXQDA. A brief procedure for conducting content analyses in each tool is provided. Potential future work is identified and discussed. Overall, the use of various bibliometric analysis tools is demonstrated for use in a systematic literature review and the importance of incorporating ergonomic principles into transportation systems is discussed.

Keywords: Ergonomics · Transportation · Bibliometric Analysis

1 Introduction

The topic of ergonomics in transportation is important to individuals and society since it directly impacts the comfort, safety, and well-being of all those who use transportation systems in one form or another, which in certain countries (particularly the United States), is nearly every individual. Poor ergonomics in transportation can lead to physical discomfort and injury while addressing the issue has the potential to reduce healthcare costs while enhancing overall quality of life. Several factors are driving the importance of ergonomics in transportation today including commuting times, an aging population, advances in technology, and a growing concern for sustainability. Therefore, it has become increasingly important to design and maintain transportation systems that are comfortable, safe, and efficient for all individuals.

For industrial engineering, the field is of particular interest since it involves designing, optimizing, manufacturing, and maintaining systems that interact between people and their environment on the industrial scale. Outside the realm of industrial engineering, various efforts are being made to address the challenge of ergonomics in transportation.

V. G. Duffy et al. (Eds.): HCII 2023, LNCS 14057, pp. 155–175, 2023.
https://doi.org/10.1007/978-3-031-48047-8_10

This includes public awareness campaigns, government regulations, and industry initiatives. Although significant work exists for motor vehicles in particular, many human factors problems apply to all modes of transportation (rail, marine, pedestrian, aviation) (Eby 2006).

Society needs to respond to the role ergonomics plays in transportation by paying greater attention to the impact it has on individual well-being. Companies and regulatory agencies should prioritize the implementation of ergonomic design principles, while individuals can contribute by advocating for better ergonomics and adopting better ergonomic practices in their own lives. In many cases, ergonomics and comfort have been linked to perceptions of service quality, particularly within the airline industry (Brochado et al. 2019). This perception incentivizes transportation industries to implement ergonomic principles. Human factors, ergonomics, and safety-related communities have contributed significantly to addressing the topic. These communities have conducted vast amounts of research to better understand the effect of poor ergonomics and have developed standards and guidelines for the design of ergonomic transportation systems. Additionally, these communities have worked with companies to implement practical solutions while raising awareness for the field.

1.1 Key Definitions

Ergonomics – Ergonomics is a broad field that relates human capabilities and limitations to the design of products, systems, and environments. There are three major relationships: performance, safety and health, and satisfaction. Performance improves output and reduces errors. Safety and health minimize accidents and injuries resulting from human limitations. Satisfaction designs items that are comfortable, desirable, convenient, and pleasing. (Brauer 2006).

It is defined similarly by (Goetsch 2013). Ergonomics is a multidisciplinary science that seeks to confirm the workplace and all of its physiological aspects to the worker. Ergonomics involves: Using special design and evaluation techniques to make tasks, objects, and environments more compatible with human abilities and limitations. Seeking to improve productivity and quality by reducing workplace stressors, reducing the risk of injuries and illnesses, and increasing efficiency.

Transportation Systems – Combination of elements and their interactions, which produce the demand for travel within a given area and the supply of transportation services to satisfy this demand (Cascetta 2001).

Cognitive Workload – The user's perceived level of mental effort that is influenced by many factors, particularly task load and task design (NASA 2021).

Musculoskeletal Disorders – Disorders of the muscles, nerves, tendons, ligaments, joints, cartilage, and spinal discs that do not result from slips, trips, falls, motor vehicle accidents, or other similar accidents (Brauer 2016).

1.2 Bibliometric Analysis and Systematic Review Overview

Systematic reviews and bibliometric analysis methods have been previously discussed in the literature. For instance, one author broke down bibliometric analysis into the categories of performance analysis and science mapping (Donthu et al. 2021). As seen below, this includes many of the analysis techniques included in this paper such as co-citation analysis, citation-related metrics, and citation-and-publication-related metrics.

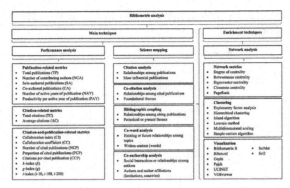

Fig. 1. Bibliometric analyses are composed of primary techniques and enrichment techniques. Some examples of mapping are citation, co-authorship, and co-citation analysis (Donthu et al. 2021)

In the paper "Five Steps to Conducting a Systematic Review", the authors identified the five following key steps (Khan et al. 2003).

1. Frame the Question
2. Identify Relevant Work
3. Assess the Quality of Studies
4. Summarize the Evidence
5. Interpret the Findings

1.3   Ergonomics in Transportation in Safety Engineering

As defined previously by Brauer, ergonomics is a broad field that relates human capabilities and limitations to the design of products, systems, and environments. Goetsch similarly defined it as using special design and evaluation techniques to make tasks, objects, and environments more compatible with human abilities and limitations. Both of these authors have addressed both ergonomic and transportation-related topics within their textbooks, which verifies the legitimacy of ergonomics in transportation as a safety-related topic.

Transportation
Optimizing equipment to fit the human body's requirements is an essential factor in transportation safety. The table below was taken from Chapter 14: Transportation of (Brauer, 2016) and shows safety-related design aspects of vehicles that are contained within the Federal Motor Vehicle Safety Standards. Two of these in particular are 101: Controls and displays and 111: Rearview mirrors. To address these standards, the ergonomics analysis tool Ramsis can be used to analyze the design of the controls and displays as well as rearview mirrors in a vehicle. For example, Ramsis can evaluate the layout and

positioning of controls to ensure they are easily accessible and visible to the driver, reducing the likelihood of distraction or error. Similarly, Ramsis can assess the rearview mirrors' location and size to ensure it provides adequate visibility (Table 1).

Table 1. Excerpt from (Brauer 2016) Chapter 14: Transportation, Page 178, Table 14-1 Federal Motor Vehicle Safety Standards.

Number	Topic
CRASH AVOIDANCE	
101	Controls and displays
102	Transmission shift lever sequence, starter interlock, and transmission braking effect
103	Windshield defrosting and defogging systems
104	Windshield wiping and washing systems
105	Hydraulic and electric brake systems
106	Brake hoses
108	Lamps, reflective devices and associated equipment
109	New pneumatic bias ply and certain specialty tires
110	Tire selection and rims for motor vehicles
111	Rearview mirrors
113	Hood latch system
114	Theft protection

Ergonomics

Since ergonomics relates human and machine capabilities, an important comparison to be made is to analyze the strengths of each. In the field of transportation, the "machine" can be thought of as the vehicle and any corresponding interfaces with the people inside that are performing a vehicle-related function. With the trend of giving machines greater responsibilities (autonomy, self-driving, voice-interface systems, etc.), the interface between the two is becoming increasingly important. The integration of these technologies into transportation systems in particular was previously identified as an emerging area in the CiteSpace timeline analysis. By comparing machine and human capabilities, and by defining a machine to be a vehicle or vehicle interface, the table further supports that ergonomics in transportation is a safety-related area of study (Table 2).

Table 2. Excerpt from (Brauer 2016) Chapter 33: Ergonomics Page 463, Table 33-1 Comparison of Functional Capabilities of People and Machines.

People are Better at:	Machines are Better at:
Detecting signals in high noise environments	Responding with minimum lag time (Machines have microsecond lags, whereas people have lags of 200 ms or more.)
Recognizing objects over varied conditions of perception	Precise, repetitive operations
Handling unexpected occurrences	Storing and recalling large amounts of data
Ability to reason inductively	Monitoring kinds of functions
Ability to profit from experiences	Deductive reasoning ability
Originality	Sensitivity to stimuli. (The range of human sensitivity is limited.)
Flexibility of reprogramming	Exerting force and power
Ability to perform when overloaded and to adjust to compensate for the overload	

Two ergonomics hazards are musculoskeletal disorders (MSDs) and cumulative trauma disorders (CTDs). Goetsch has a dedicated chapter for these hazards in Chapter 10: Ergonomics Hazards: Musculoskeletal Disorders (MSDs) and Cumulative Trauma Disorders (CTDs) of his textbook (Goetsch 2013). In the topic of ergonomics in transportation, musculoskeletal pain was found to be present in 81% of professional truck drivers in a self-reported questionnaire (Robb and Mansfield 2007). For these reasons, safety engineering plays a critical role in this topic of interest.

2 Research Methodology

2.1 Data Collection

References were found from many sources throughout this paper. Google Scholar is a free search engine that provides access to a wide range of literature and was used extensively to find articles and to search keywords. Scopus, Dimensions, and Web of Science are databases that provide access to literature that were similarly used extensively throughout this paper. Harzing's Publish or Perish is a software program that can retrieve and analyze citation information from these sources and was used to perform and consolidate sources in one place.

The keywords "Ergonomics" AND "Transportation" were searched in various databases. Web of Science had the least number of results at 803. Scopus had slightly more at 1,250. Dimensions and Google Scholar had significantly more results. The Dimensions results include 51,466 articles, 45,867 Chapters, 12,323 Edited Books, and 8,672 Proceedings, with the rest being miscellaneous sources (Table 3).

Table 3. Number of results after searching keywords in corresponding database

Database	Number of Results
Web of Science	803
Scopus	1,250
Dimensions	126,151
Google Scholar	200,000

To perform the data analysis, a variety of software tools were used. These include Vicinitas, database analysis tools (Scopus, Dimensions, WoS, Scite.ai, Publish or Perish), Google nGram, VOSviewer, CiteSpace, MAXQDA, and BibExcel. The tools and methods presented have been previously used for similar purposes. Three example articles that utilized or discussed these tools are (Simsek et al. 2023), (Donthu et al. 2021), and (Zhang et al. 2021). Additional tools mentioned in these papers include AuthorMapper, Gephi, HistCite, Biblioshiny, and SciMat.

2.2 Social Media Engagement

Vicinitas was used to analyze Twitter trends. Searching the phrase transportation ergonomics came up with less than a dozen results. Searching only for the term ergonomics came up with 1599 results. The trend from the 10 days from April 5th through April 15th, 2023, showed a consistent upward trend with over 4000 cumulative

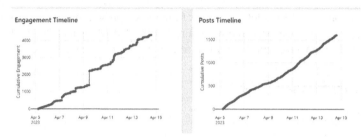

Fig. 2. Vicinitas engagement and posts trends between April 5th and April 15th

engagements and over 1500 posts. The trend from April 20th to April 26th was similar (Fig. 2).

The topic of ergonomics remained a topic of interest at least throughout the month of April 2023 on Twitter. Longer periods of analysis were not available through the tool for the free version. The interest can be explained by the inclusion of interesting images that get passed around social media as well as the unique relevance that ergonomics has in daily life. One example found from this analysis was a picture of a unique-looking chair that had thousands of retweets. An additional example is the tweet shown below that shares the ideal posture for an individual working on a computer which received nearly 195,000 engagements (Fig. 3).

Fig. 3. A Twitter user shared the ideal desk posture targeted at programmers and received nearly 195,000 engagements.

2.3 Trend Analysis

The keywords "Ergonomics" AND "Transportation" were searched in Scopus and Dimensions to generate trend diagrams (Fig. 4) for documents by year. Both databases show a similar overall increasing trend and a decrease after 2020. Dimensions shows a significant spike in 2007 whereas Scopus shows a small increase in 2006. The lower bound for years was set to 1995 since before this date the number of publications was relatively consistent and low volume.

Looking at the trend diagrams it appears the number of documents has been steadily increasing over time. This implies that the topic of ergonomics in transportation is an

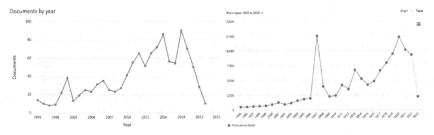

Fig. 4. Trend diagram from 1995 to 2023 for 1,115 documents (Scopus, Left) and 126,151 publications (Dimensions, right)

emerging area of study. Dimensions in particular shows a rapid increase in publications, with the number of documents rising from roughly 2,500 in the year 2000 to about 12,500 in 2020. However, both sources do show a decrease around 2019 and on, which could be due to the newer works not being analyzed or fully included in the data analysis.

The consistent increase in the number of publications over time can be attributed to the potential applications in the field. The potential benefits range from improving driver and passenger comfort to reducing stress levels, improving safety, and reducing the likelihood of long-term injury and associated healthcare costs. With the constant advancements in technology, new opportunities are arising for ergonomics research to improve transportation systems. For instance, the emerging development of autonomous vehicles presents unique challenges that can be addressed through the application of ergonomic principles to the design of the vehicle's interface and control systems. The growing number of environmentally conscious individuals continues to grow, leading to an increasing interest in sustainable transportation solutions which additionally require ergonomic considerations to optimize design and operation. These potential applications highlight the importance of the field and explain the steady increase in the number of publications related to this emerging area.

A Google nGram analysis was then performed with the topic of interest and related topics (Fig. 5). Looking at the trends there appears to be a cyclical pattern and periods of popularity. Vehicle ergonomics for instance was especially popular in 2011. Car ergonomics and transportation ergonomics cycle over time. Car comfort appears to be decreasing with plateaus.

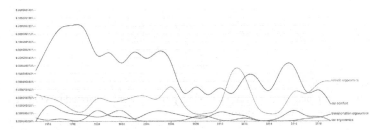

Fig. 5. Google nGram shows cyclical patterns for car ergonomics, transportation ergonomics, and car ergonomics. Vehicle ergonomics appears to increase over time.

In addition to Google nGram, Scopus, Dimensions, and Vicinitas, Scite.ai can also be used to generate trends. The figure below shows the distribution of citations over time. The colors represent the breakdown of what percentage of citation statements support (green), mention (gray), or contrast (blue) claims made by the papers they reference. Note the chart is not to scale. The chart has a maximum number of total citations of 1,165 in the year 2013, but visually peaks in the year 2018 with 843 citations. Contrasting claims were present in the years 2003–2006, 2011–2012, 2016, 2018, 2019, and 2021 (Fig. 6).

Fig. 6. Scite.ai distribution of citation statements from 1979 through 2023

3   Results

3.1   Co-citation Analysis

Co-citation is when two or more documents are cited together by other documents (Small 1973). Co-citation analysis examines the relationships among cited publications and can reveal foundational themes. Co-authorship analysis is similar but is used to examine relationships among authors (Fig. 1). Searching the keywords "Ergonomics" AND "Transportation" in Scopus returned 1,250 documents. These were exported into a csv file and used for analysis in VOSviewer. Two types of analysis were then performed which are co-authorship and co-citation. Co-authorship used a minimum of 2 documents per author; of the 1175 authors, 25 met the threshold. Co-citation used a minimum of 4 citations of a cited reference; of the 23309 cited references, 50 met this threshold. The largest set of connected items is 31 which is shown in the figure (Fig. 7).

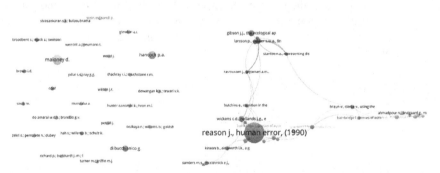

Fig. 7. Co-authorship map (left) and co-citation map (right) were generated in VOSviewer from 1,250 most relevant articles exported from Scopus.

10 articles of interest were identified from the co-citation analysis performed in VOSviewer and are shown in the table below. The range of work is quite extensive. For

instance, ergonomics research was applied to the design of traffic symbols and several other authors discussed human-automation interaction. One co-citation even discussed ergonomics in the context of submarines returning to periscope depth (Table 4).

Table 4. Top 10 articles of interest identified from co-citation analysis

Article Title	Reference
Road Transport in Drift? Applying Contemporary Systems Thinking to Road Safety	(Salmon, McClure, and Stanton 2012)
Book Review: Cognitive Work Analysis. Toward Safe, Productive and Healthy Computer-Based Work	(Dreyfus 2000)
Representing Distributed Cognition in Complex Systems: How a Submarine Returns to Periscope Depth	(Stanton 2014)
The Need for a Systems Theory Approach to Road Safety	(Larsson, Dekker, and Tingvall 2010)
Risk Management in a Dynamic Society: A Modelling Problem	(Rasmussen 1997)
Human Factors in Engineering and Design	(McCormick and Sanders 1987)
Traffic Sign Symbol Comprehension: A Cross-Cultural Study	(Shinar et al. 2003)
Humans and Automation: Use, Misuse, Disuse, Abuse	(Parasuraman and Riley 1997)
Trust in Automation: Designing for Appropriate Reliance	(Lee and See 2004)
Possibilities to Improve the Aircraft Interior Comfort Experience	(Vink et al. 2012)

3.2 Content Analysis

A co-occurrence analysis was performed similarly to that of the co-citation and co-authorship maps in VOSviewer. The minimum number of term occurrences was set to 30, which of 25,178 terms resulted in 109 terms for the 60% most relevant (Fig. 8).

The keywords "Ergonomics" AND "Transportation" were then searched in Web of Science. The top 500 most relevant articles were exported with Full Record and Cited References information. The articles were then analyzed in CiteSpace to generate clusters of keywords (Fig. 9). Some of these clusters are human factors, risky behaviors, design assessment, autonomy, and railway. A connection to the previous analysis done in VOSviewer is present in the themes of these keywords. For instance, the yellow cluster in the co-occurrence map shows human-factors-related keywords such as risk, posture, and musculoskeletal disorder which lines up with both the human-factors and risky

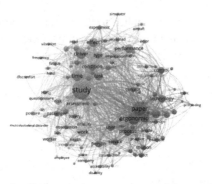

Fig. 8. Co-occurrence map for 60% most relevant terms at a minimum of 30 occurrences generated in VOSviewer from 1,250 most relevant articles exported from Scopus

behavior clusters here. Additionally, the autonomy cluster lines up with the red cluster in the co-occurrence map which has words such as technology, computer, and simulation. Analyzing an additional 500 articles sorted by the newest in Web of Science adds a more complete picture to the previous analysis. In the new keyword cluster analysis, clusters such as digital human modeling, artificial intelligence, and voice interface are added.

Using the timeline visualization in CiteSpace adds even more context to these keywords. From the 1995–2013 timeline in Fig. 10, it can be seen that areas of interest include whole-body vibration and workload. Analyzing from 2010–2023 in Fig. 11 shows a new emphasis on elderly, wearable devices, driving experience, driving simulation, and stages of automation. The Google nGram timeline in Fig. 12 provides support for the timeline shift after 2010 which reveals an increasing interest in driving simulation and digital human modeling.

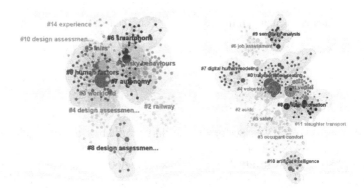

Fig. 9. Keyword clusters generated in CiteSpace for top 500 relevant articles (left) and top 500 relevant and 500 newest (right) from Web of Science for 2013–2023

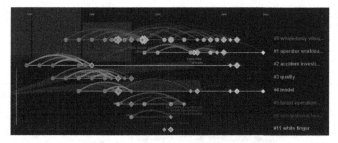

Fig. 10. 1995–2013 timeline view for 1000 articles in CiteSpace

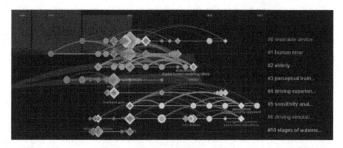

Fig. 11. 2010–2023 timeline view for 1000 articles in CiteSpace

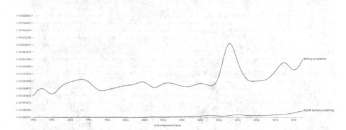

Fig. 12. Google nGram for driving simulation and digital human modeling showing increasing interest over time

3.3 CiteSpace Bursts

Analyzing the burst information in CiteSpace resulted in the identification of 10 Journals (Table 5) and 4 authors (Table 6) with citation bursts. Trying to analyze the information with keywords, references, and institutions resulted in CiteSpace stating that no burst information was found. Joose de Winter has the strongest author burst at a value of 4.08. This author specializes in transportation, human factors, human-robot interaction, and applied statistics (Joost ResearchGate 2023).

The timeline for CiteSpace (Fig. 13) provides further context for the journal bursts identified. The table corresponds to the timeline, where it can be seen that the Journal of Applied Ergonomics in 2011 had 104 references to it later in time. Most of the strongest journal bursts are located in the top left of the timeline view, which corresponds to the keywords transportation seating, vehicle, and ac/dc (Table 7).

Table 5. Ten journals were identified to have had citation bursts through CiteSpace.

Top 10 Cited Journals with the Strongest Citation Bursts

Cited Journals	Year	Strength	Begin	End	2013 - 2023
ACCIDENT ANAL PREV	2010	5.8	2013	2015	
THESIS	2008	4.87	2013	2018	
SAFETY SCI	2012	4.64	2013	2015	
WORK	2009	3.35	2013	2017	
HUM FACTORS	2012	3.74	2016	2019	
TRANSPORT RES A-POL	2015	4.8	2018	2021	
PLOS ONE	2013	3.18	2018	2020	
PROCEDIA MANUF	2015	4.81	2019	2020	
ADV INTELL SYST	2016	3.23	2020	2021	
SUSTAINABILITY-BASEL	2019	4.5	2021	2023	

Table 6. Four authors were identified to have had citation bursts.

Top 4 Authors with the Strongest Citation Bursts

Authors	Year	Strength	Begin	End	2013 - 2022
SHERIDAN TB	2020	2.47	2020	2016	
HANCOCK PA	2020	3.33	2020	2019	
DE WINTERJCF	2020	4.08	2020	2020	
NAUJOKS F	2020	2.55	2020	2022	

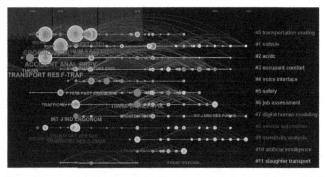

Fig. 13. Timeline of journals and keywords in CiteSpace showing large bursts in the top left area

3.4 Word Cloud

The first word cloud (Fig. 14) was generated in Vicinitas, which is a tool that analyzes Twitter trends. The term "ergonomics" was searched which came up with 1599 results. Some of the words found are ergonomics, noise, human, chair, cognitive, office, gaming, and productivity.

A second word cloud (Fig. 15) was generated in Maxqda. Eight articles in addition to Chapter 14: Transportation (Brauer 2006) were used to generate it. Words shown have a minimum frequency of four. Some of the keywords shown are ergonomics, transportation, data, design, drivers, safety, and workload.

The table corresponding to the Maxqda word cloud is shown below. The words human, data, control, design, ergonomics, and transportation are used most frequently

Table 7. Cited journals and their citation count showing Applied Ergonomics at the top with 104 references to 2011

Count	Centrality	Year	Cited References	Cited Journal...
104	0.00	2011	APPL ERGON
83	0.00	2009	ERGONOMICS
83	0.00	2010	ACCIDENT ANAL PREV
65	0.00	2009	TRANSPORT RES F-TRAF
58	0.00	2012	HUM FACTORS
34	0.00	2012	SAFETY SCI
30	0.00	2011	INT J IND ERGONOM
23	0.00	2011	TRANSPORT RES C-EMER
21	0.00	2008	THESIS
19	0.00	2015	TRANSPORT RES A-POL
17	0.00	2009	WORK
17	0.00	2011	TRANSPORT RES REC
16	0.00	2012	P HUM FACT ERG SOC A
16	0.00	2016	ADV INTELL SYST
15	0.00	2010	TRAFFIC INJ PREV
15	0.00	2013	PLOS ONE
13	0.00	2015	PROCEDIA MANUF
13	0.00	2018	FRONT PSYCHOL
12	0.00	2009	IEEE INT VEH SYM
11	0.00	2012	P HUMAN FACTORS ERGO
11	0.00	2015	J TRANSP HEALTH
11	0.00	2020	INT J ENV RES PUB HE
10	0.00	2011	HUM FACTOR ERGON MAN

Fig. 14. Vicinitas word cloud corresponding to a search of "ergonomics"

Fig. 15. Word cloud generated in Maxqda from 8 articles and textbook chapter

throughout the 8 literature sources and textbook chapter reviewed. Ergonomics and transportation have the highest document percentage, which makes sense because the articles were found by searching those keywords (Table 8).

3.5 Leading Authors

To identify leading authors, the first approach used was to search scite.ai for related articles with (Ergonomics) AND (Transportation). The table below was transcribed from

Table 8. Maxqda word cloud results show human, data, and control as the most commonly used words.

Word	Word length	Frequency ▾	%	Rank	Documents	Documents %
• human	5	117	0.88	1	5	50.00
• data	4	111	0.84	2	6	60.00
• control	7	96	0.73	3	4	40.00
• design	6	76	0.57	4	6	60.00
• ergonomics	10	76	0.57	4	8	80.00
• transportation	14	76	0.57	4	8	80.00
• train	5	73	0.55	7	4	40.00
• transport	9	70	0.53	8	4	40.00
• carts	5	63	0.48	9	1	10.00
• safety	6	60	0.45	10	5	50.00
• factors	7	59	0.45	11	6	60.00
• systems	7	58	0.44	12	4	40.00
• system	6	57	0.43	13	3	30.00
• methods	7	56	0.42	14	2	20.00
• workload	8	55	0.42	15	3	30.00
• performance	11	54	0.41	16	4	40.00

scite.ai and shows the top five researchers with the most work related to the search (Table 9).

Table 9. Top five researchers and corresponding publication count from Scite.ai

Researcher	Publication Count
Neville a Stanton	6
Luis Montoro	4
Sergio a Useche	4
Alberto De Vitta	3
Boris Candales	3

The second approach was to use BibExcel. The top 500 articles from Harzing's Publish or Perish were identified using a google scholar search. The results were then exported into BibExcel for trend analysis. The results from BibExcel were then put into Excel for formatting. The top 9 authors and their number of articles published are shown in Fig. 16.

The third and final approach to identify leading authors was to use the search terms in Scopus (Fig. 17). The only author present in all three is Neville Stanton. Hancock is present in the scite.ai and Scopus search, but not BibExcel. Similarly, Vink is in both the scite.ai and Scopus tables, but not BibExcel.

Neville Stanton is a British Professor of Human Factors and Ergonomics at the University of Southampton. As stated in his profile, he is conducting research "into improving and optimizing human performance in systems, especially with the introduction of new technology and automation" (Professor Neville Stanton 2023). Much

Leading Authors and Number of Articles
Published

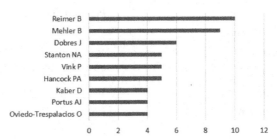

Fig. 16. Leading authors identified with BibExcel from the top 500 most relevant articles exported from Harzing's Publish or Perish using Google Scholar

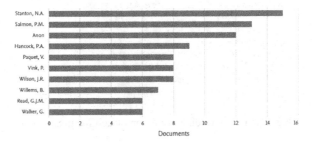

Fig. 17. Top 10 leading authors according to Scopus

of his work is also focused on accident prevention. One of his works was found in the co-citation analysis which applied three network models to interactions in the sound and control room in a submarine (Stanton 2014). His more recent work used systems analysis tools to investigate new control room configurations and reduce crew size (Stanton and Roberts 2019).

3.6 Leading Institutions

A similar approach was taken to identify leading institutions. The top five leading institutions with the most supported papers are in the table below. It is unclear how scite.ai defines most supported regarding institutional publications (Table 10).

The top 10 leading institutions were identified in Scopus using the same search terms (Fig. 18). There is no overlap between scite.ai and the Scopus leading institutions, which is likely due to a difference in where each platform sources information.

Table 10. Leading institutions and their publication count from scite.ai

Institution	Publication Count
Anhanguera Uniderp University	1
Arizona State university	1
Arthritis Research Uk	1
Bloomberg	1
Catholic University of America	1

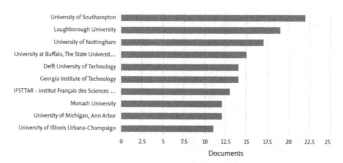

Fig. 18. Top 10 leading institutions according to Scopus

4 Discussion

From the results, it is clear that there is an emerging area of study within the topic of ergonomics in transportation for automated and computer-based systems. The CiteSpace keyword cluster for instance had phrases such as autonomy and smartphone. Analyzing an additional 500 articles sorted by newest introduced phrases such as digital human modeling, vehicle automation, voice interface, and artificial intelligence. The Google nGram of digital human modeling supports this by showing an increasing interest as of 2014. The timeline views in CiteSpace show a shift from traditional areas of study such as operator workload, occupational health, and whole-body vibration to computer-based areas such as wearable devices, driving simulation, and automation.

The results can then be used to inform lexical search terms related to the topic. The table was put together from the word clouds (Maxqda, Vicinitas), the co-occurrence map (VOSviewer), keyword cluster, and timeline views (CiteSpace). The words are in no particular order (Table 11).

The co-citation analysis revealed several key areas of study that are consistent with the other forms of analysis. The first area of interest is passenger comfort. In aircraft applications, Vink (who was also identified as a leading author) found a clear relationship between comfort, legroom, hygiene, and seat space to the passenger's perception of a comfortable aircraft interior (Vink 2012). This is supported by research conducted by Ana Brochado who had similar conclusions (Brochado et al. 2019). More general work has also been done for both office and automotive applications. One article in particular

Table 11. Collection of important keywords identified from analysis tools

Ergonomics	Transportation	Voice Interface
Safety	Human factors	Digital Human Modelling
Workload	Performance	Artificial Intelligence
Simulation	Wearable Device	Automation

states a distinction between comfort and discomfort, in which comfort is associated with a sense of well-being and aesthetics, whereas discomfort is related to biomechanics and fatigue factors (Helander and Zhang 2010).

The second area of interest is in automation. John Lee and Katrina See state that trust guides reliance in complex and unanticipated situations when a full understanding of automation is impractical. Their work developed a conceptual model that integrated existing research on trust in automation and the influence of display characteristics (Lee and See 2004). John Lee additionally found that the increase in automation is requiring more work in training, interface design, and interaction design rather than less (Lee 2008).

The third and last major area of interest identified in the co-citation analysis is road safety. One article studied traffic signs used in different cultures to identify underlying rules that affect comprehension. The authors found that the highest levels of comprehension were present for signs that integrated ergonomic design principles such as familiarity, standardization, and physical representation (Shinar et al. 2003). In 2006, Shinar continued the work and established a set of specific ergonomic guidelines for traffic sign design (Bassat and Shinar 2006). There has also been extensive work in applying systems theory to road safety (Salmon, McClure, and Stanton 2012; Larsson, Dekker, and Tingvall 2010; Rasmussen 1997). Two of the leading authors identified, Paul Salmon and Neville Stanton wrote one of the papers and found human factors methodologies can be applied to road safety through links they found to their work on complex systems theory. The field of Human factors has been heavily researched since at least 1957 and is present in both course textbooks (Goetsch 2013) (Brauer 2016) (McCormick and Sanders 1987). This field of study appeared throughout the analysis performed previously.

5   Ramsis Ergonomics

One ergonomics analysis tool in particular is Ramsis. This is a powerful and widely used ergonomics analysis tool within the automotive industry. Its usefulness lies in its ability to evaluate and optimize various vehicle design aspects for various characteristics including human reachability and visibility while accounting for a variety of body types. Human-machine interaction, posture, and glare are additional tools available in Ramsis. Being able to analyze these factors allows designers and engineers to make informed design changes and optimizations throughout the development of the vehicle. As a result, customers can potentially be more satisfied with the product and experience lower injury rates as well as improved safety. An example that was previously done is the creation of manakins of varying body types and their positioning inside a vehicle. The 95th percentile male for example would not comfortably fit in the vehicle at the given position due to the low ceiling height. The seat should be lowered or feature adjustability to accommodate this individual. Visibility and reachability are examples of analyses that were previously performed within Ramsis in Lab 3 (Fig. 19).

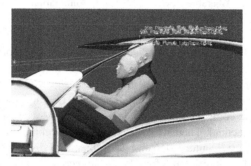

Fig. 19. Several manakins of varying body types were created and positioned in a vehicle. In industry applications, this can help designers accommodate a wide range of people.

Ramsis has a wide variety of analysis tools available for users. This tool can address many of the keywords noted in the cluster and timeline analysis performed in VOSviewer and CiteSpace. Two keywords identified in these are transportation seating and occupant comfort. Ramsis can address the seating by analyzing the reachability of the digital human models as well as by analyzing the visual field. The occupant comfort can be addressed through a discomfort analysis, which is based on the angle of joints over different periods of time.

6   Future Work

A keyword search of transportation "ergonomics" was performed on the National Science Foundation's website to identify current and future work being conducted in this field. One of the more interesting awards was to the University of Arizona in 2018 for the study of Cyber Transportation Systems (CTS), shown in the figure below. The abstract states the goal is to develop a computational framework for human-CTS interactions which will enable the derivation of design requirements and optimal parameter settings for connected and automated vehicles to maximize human safety. The goal of the research is to ultimately develop the first tool "to understand the fundamental mechanisms of human-CTS interaction by predicting the effects of technology on driver behavior". This is consistent with the emerging trends identified throughout the analysis, particularly with the aspects of autonomy and human-technological interactions (Fig. 20).

Along the same lines as the NSF Award mentioned, work is being conducted to understand the role of humans in autonomous Maritime operations. As more systems become automated, it is critical to understand the interactions between humans and computer-based systems. The article, published in the Journal of Ergonomics, found

Fig. 20. The National Science Foundation awarded a $138,342 grant to the University of Arizona for the study of Cyber Transportation and Human Interaction. (NSF Award 2023)

four themes: Trust, Awareness and Understanding, Control, and Training and Organization of Work (Mallam 2019). Another group of researchers studied the applicability of human factors and ergonomics systems analysis tools for intervening in global systems (Thatcher 2019). It is clear that a significant amount of future work is related to autonomous systems and integrating different fields of study.

7 Conclusion

The research process for bibliometric analysis has greatly supported project insight. The first step of a bibliometric analysis was the identification of the research question and selection of relevant databases and sources. The articles retrieved from these sources were screened and selected based on specific criteria (relevance, year, etc.). Bibliographic information was then extracted and analyzed using various tools. The tools helped to visualize the literature, identify leading authors and institutions, and map trends over time. By going through this process, insight into the field of ergonomics in transportation was gained. Trends in the field, emerging topics, key authors, and influential institutions have been identified. The tools used (Vicinitas, VOSviewer, BibExcel, CiteSpace) have facilitated this process. Without performing the bibliometric analysis process, many of the insights into ergonomics in transportation would be significantly harder to come by.

References

Ben-Bassat, T., Shinar, D.: Ergonomic guidelines for traffic sign design increase sign comprehension. Hum. Fact. J. Hum. Fact. Ergon. Soc. **48**(1), 182–195 (2006). https://doi.org/10.1518/001872006776412298

Brauer, R.L.: Safety and Health for Engineers, 2nd edn. (2006). https://doi.org/10.1002/047175093X

Brauer, R.L.: Safety and Health for Engineers, 3rd edn. Wiley (2016)

Brochado, A., Rita, P., Oliveira, C., Oliveira, F.: Airline passengers' perceptions of service quality: themes in online reviews. Int. J. Contemp. Hosp. Manage. **31**(2) (2019). https://doi.org/10.1108/IJCHM-09-2017-0572

Cascetta, E.: Transportation systems BT - transportation systems engineering: theory and methods. In: Transportation Systems Engineering: Theory and Methods (2001)

Donthu, N., Kumar, S., Mukherjee, D., Pandey, N., Lim, W.M.: How to Conduct a Bibliometric Analysis: An Overview and Guidelines. J. Bus. Res. **133**, 285–296 (2021). https://doi.org/10.1016/j.jbusres.2021.04.070

Dreyfus, S.: Book Review: cognitive work analysis. Toward safe, productive and healthy computer-based work. Bull. Sci. Technol. Soc. **20**(6), 481–482 (2000). https://doi.org/10.1177/027046760002000607

Eby, D.W., Kantowitz, B.H.: Human factors and ergonomics in motor vehicle transportation. In: Handbook of Human Factors and Ergonomics, pp. 1538–1569 (2006). https://doi.org/10.1002/0470048204.ch59

Goetsch, D.L.: Occupational safety and health for technologists, engineers, and managers. Ind. Fabr. Prod. Rev. **87** (2013)

Helander, M.G., Zhang, L.: Field studies of comfort and discomfort in sitting. Ergonomics **40**(9), 895–915 (1997). https://doi.org/10.1080/001401397187739

Joost De Winter | Professor (Full) | Ph.d. - Researchgate. https://www.researchgate.net/profile/Joost-De-Winter. Accessed 1 May 2023

Khan, K.S., Kunz, R., Kleijnen, J., Antes, G.: Five steps to conducting a systematic review. J. R. Soc. Med. **96**(3), 118–121 (2003). https://doi.org/10.1177/014107680309600304

Larsson, P., Dekker, S.W.A., Tingvall, C.: The need for a systems theory approach to road safety. Saf. Sci. **48**(9), 1167–1174 (2010). https://doi.org/10.1016/j.ssci.2009.10.006

Lee, J.D., See, K.A.: Trust in automation: designing for appropriate reliance. Hum. Factors **46**, 50–80 (2004). https://doi.org/10.1518/hfes.46.1.50_30392

Lee, J.D.: Review of a pivotal human factors article: 'humans and automation: use, misuse, disuse, abuse.' Hum. Factors J. Hum. Factors Ergon. Soc. **50**(3), 404–410 (2008). https://doi.org/10.1518/001872008x288547

Mallam, S.C., Nazir, S., Sharma, A.: The human element in future maritime operations – perceived impact of autonomous shipping. Ergonomics **63**(3), 334–345 (2019). https://doi.org/10.1080/00140139.2019.1659995

McCormick, E.J., Sanders, M.S.: Human Factors in Engineering and Design. McGraw-Hill, New York (1987)

NASA 2021: NASA-STD-3001 Technical Brief: Cognitive Workload, 15 December. https://www.nasa.gov/sites/default/files/atoms/files/cognitive_workload_technical_brief_ochmo_06232020.pdfQuery

NSF Award Search: Award # 1812899 - CHS: Small: Modeling cyber transportation and human interaction in connected and autonomous vehicles. https://www.nsf.gov/awardsearch/showAward?AWD_ID=1812899&HistoricalAwards=false. Accessed 30 April 2023

Parasuraman, R., Riley, V.: Humans and automation: use, misuse, disuse, abuse. Hum. Factors **39**(2), 230–253 (1997). https://doi.org/10.1518/001872097778543886

"Professor Neville Stanton B.Sc. (Hons), Ph.d., Fbpss, Fergss, Miet, MCIHT." Professor Neville Stanton | Engineering | University of Southampton. https://www.southampton.ac.uk/engineering/about/staff/ns4c08.page. Accessed 1 May 2023

Rasmussen, J.: Risk management in a dynamic society: a modelling problem. Saf. Sci. **27**(2–3), 183–213 (1997). https://doi.org/10.1016/S0925-7535(97)00052-0

Robb, M.J.M., Mansfield, N.J.: Self-reported musculoskeletal problems amongst professional truck drivers. Ergonomics **50**(6) (2007). https://doi.org/10.1080/00140130701220341

Salmon, P.M., McClure, R., Stanton, N.A.: Road transport in drift? Applying contemporary systems thinking to road safety. Saf. Sci. **50**, 1829–1838 (2012). https://doi.org/10.1016/j.ssci.2012.04.011

Shinar, D., Dewar, R.E., Summala, H., Zakowska, L.: Traffic sign symbol comprehension: a cross-cultural study. Ergonomics **46**(15), 1549–1565 (2003). https://doi.org/10.1080/0014013032000121615

Şimşek, A.İ., Taşdemir, B.D., Koç, E.: A bibliometric analysis and research agenda of the location of electric vehicle charging stations. Bus. Manage. Stud. Int. J. **11**(2), 610–625 (2023). https://doi.org/10.15295/bmij.v11i2.2246

Small, H.: Co-citation in the scientific literature: a new measure of the relationship between two documents. J. Am. Soc. Inf. Sci. **24**(4), 265–269 (1973). https://doi.org/10.1002/asi.4630240406

Stanton, N.A.: Representing distributed cognition in complex systems: how a submarine returns to periscope depth. Ergonomics **57**(3), 403–418 (2014). https://doi.org/10.1080/00140139.2013.772244

Stanton, N.A., Roberts, A.P.: Better together? Investigating new control room configurations and reduced crew size in submarine command and control. Ergonomics **63**(3), 307–323 (2019). https://doi.org/10.1080/00140139.2019.1654137

Thatcher, A., Nayak, R., Waterson, P.: Human factors and ergonomics systems-based tools for understanding and addressing global problems of the twenty-first century. Ergonomics **63**(3), 367–387 (2019). https://doi.org/10.1080/00140139.2019.1646925

Vink, P., Bazley, C., Kamp, I., Blok, M.: Possibilities to improve the aircraft interior comfort experience. Appl. Ergon. **43**(2), 354–359 (2012). https://doi.org/10.1016/j.apergo.2011.06.011

Zhang, Z., Duffy, V.G., Tian, R.: Trust and automation: a systematic review and bibliometric analysis. In: HCI International 2021 - Late Breaking Papers: Design and User Experience, pp. 451–464 (2021). https://doi.org/10.1007/978-3-030-90238-4_32

Coupling the Vehicle Design Phase with an Ergonomic Simulation to Accommodate Different Driver Shapes in the United States in 2023

Frederik A. Weber[1]([✉]), Martin Pohlmann[2], and Vincent G. Duffy[1]

[1] Purdue University, West Lafayette, IN 47906, USA
{weber215,duffy}@purdue.edu
[2] Human Solutions of North America, Morrisville, NC 27560, USA
mpohlmann@human-solutions.com

Abstract. RAMSIS is a highly realistic and time-efficient software tool that is designed to support manufacturers in improving customer satisfaction by finding design flaws and hence, improving the well-being of the customer. In this paper, the need for continuous redesigning of the passenger cabin in automobiles is discussed. A new design of a car is tested by seating a manikin inside and simulating its optimal posture for the given constraints of the car and manikin. The applied method is a digital simulation of the human interacting with the passenger cabin interior. The demonstration was performed on RAMSIS a CAD-based simulation tool. In this work, Furthermore, this study explores multiple discussion points such as the benefits and future applications of the software, results of the simulation, and how obstacles or limitations could be resolved. In this project, the following analyses are conducted: discomfort analysis, reach analysis, max-size backseat-passenger calculation, obstructive vision, and reflective vision. One main result is the incompleteness of the car design in terms of ergonomic design. Additionally, many of the conducted analyses showed significant ergonomic design faults for the current design. Lastly, future work extending the RAMSIS analysis is explored.

Keywords: RAMSIS · Mass customization · Obesity epidemic · Simulation · Human Modeling · Design · Ergonomic

1 Introduction and Background

Engineers strive to create the most efficient product for the consumer. For instance, cars have been evolving in cycles, with each change triggering the next round of innovations. More specifically, a horse-drawn carriage was a slow means of transportation and contributed to manure-filled streets. After the introduction of gasoline vehicles, the next leap was focused on driver safety, resulting in the development of features such as the safety belt, the rearview mirror, and later, the airbag [1, 2]. Today, the industry is undergoing a mass personalization revolution, as described by Wang et al. [3]. Similarly, Zhang et al. describe the present focus on designing cars to cater to the unique

V. G. Duffy et al. (Eds.): HCII 2023, LNCS 14057, pp. 176–191, 2023.
https://doi.org/10.1007/978-3-031-48047-8_11

needs of individual customers [4]. One aspect of mass customization is the passenger cell. To meet the current trend of personalization and customization, car designers are constantly rethinking the interior of cars. For example, the design is being reconsidered to accommodate the changing shapes of the American population. According to data from the Centers for Disease Control and Prevention (CDC), 41.9% of American adults aged 20 and above were obese in 2017 [5]. This figure is expected to rise in the coming years, highlighting the need to design cars that can accommodate the special needs of the growing population of overweight individuals [6, 7].

This paper is an application of the RAMSIS software. Applications have two justifications in research. Applications like [8, 9] show the necessity for applications because of the multiplicity of possible applications, here an excavator and a magnified view on a seat simulation. This is the first reason for justifying applications - providing and reproving the method's validity and actuality. Another justification can become relevant when applications lead to the implementation of new functionality, or the missing functionality becomes apparent. Another less significant aspect is the demonstration of ergonomic software to make people realize the necessity for functionality and ergonomic comfort rather than investing in design. This vehicle could be the workplace of a taxi driver or chauffeur service. Therefore, the driver seat is within the scope of the subject of job design. More, the drivers' discomfort is not the only metric measured in RAMSIS. It can also simulate the impact of sitting in the car for a prolonged time on the driver's health and simulate the impact of the sitting posture on the fatiguing probability of the driver. These are central in the job design research of the subject's safety, hazard, and long-term health.

The objective of this research is, as stated in the research question: "**Objective: Consider Ergonomic Analysis for Manikin in Industrial Setting using RAMSIS Analysis tools.** Consider the task list. In the lab report, a. demonstrate proficiency at using the software related to the task list on the following page, and b. demonstrate the use of analysis tools; explain methods, results and assess (in discussion)."

2 Literature Review

The literature review is performed in the form of bibliometric analysis. Three approaches were undertaken to sort and visualize the data: (A) a word-cloud was created, (B) a graphical analysis was performed using the VOSviewer software [10], and (3) a yearly publication frequency overview for keywords was created using Google Ngram Viewer [11].

2.1 Word-Cloud

To generate a word-cloud, a small number of publications was collected. A word-cloud lists common words in one or multiple papers and shows the common terms by frequency of usage. More specifically, the most frequently used word will be the largest, and words under a threshold chosen by the designer will not be part of the cloud. The keywords for the word-cloud were "human", "modeling" and "automotive". The keywords were chosen from the presentations of "Human Solutions" [12]. Further, the year of publication was limited to the years 2019 to 2023 to encompass the most recent developments on the topic. Two publications were chosen from database search on Google Scholar [13] which yielded the papers [14, 15] and Scopus [16], yielding [17, 18]. Additionally, chapter 29 "Digital human modeling in design [19]" of the book "Handbook of Human Factors and Ergonomics" [20] was included. Also, chapter 27 "Modeling and Simulation of human systems" of the same book is used [21]. The final word-cloud figure, displayed below in Fig. 1, has been stripped of unnecessary words and limited to the 50 most frequently used words.

Fig. 1. Word-cloud generated with wordcloud.com based on the sources [14–21]

2.2 VOSviewer cloud

In the second part of this analysis, the VOSviewer software is used. In the first step, the key phrases "human modeling" and "customization" were searched in the Web of Science resource [22]. The complete set of 328 papers resulting from the search is exported as a "plain text file" and the 15 manuscripts were added to the reference list. Then VOSviewer [10] using Java 8 is used to analyze the sources. VOSviewer detects multi-occurrences of terms in the titles and abstracts of papers. In this scenario, the occurrences threshold is chosen to three, which yields a result of 83 terms. Then, a relevance algorithm of the VOSviewer selects 60% of the 83 terms, which reduces the terms to a total of 50. An alternative version is presented in Fig. 2 with a threshold of 4 and 45 terms, which is reduced to 31 terms for the word-cloud. Figure 3 highlights the interconnections that are linked to the keyword "human". Another good test of significance of a topic is analyzing peoples talking about a subject. Therefore, the Dimensions AI search engine was used (see Fig. 4). Dimension AI counts the number of times a keyword is mentioned on Twitter.

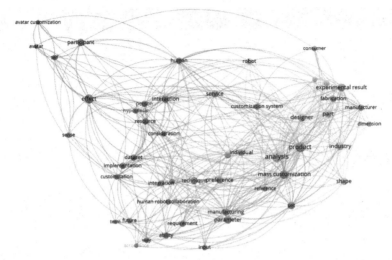

Fig. 2. VOSviewer results for 3 times multi-occurrences in the collected articles.

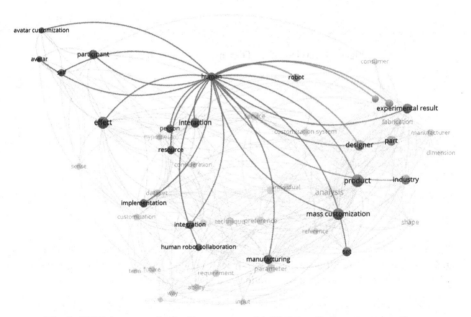

Fig. 3. VOSviewer results for 3 occurrences highlighting the human connections.

2.3 Frequency of Publication

The last bibliographic analysis conducted in this work investigates the frequency of publication using the Google Ngram Viewer. The keywords for this analysis were chosen as follows: (1) "human modeling", (2) "mass customization", and (3) "obesity epidemic". The result of this bibliographic search is presented in Fig. 5.

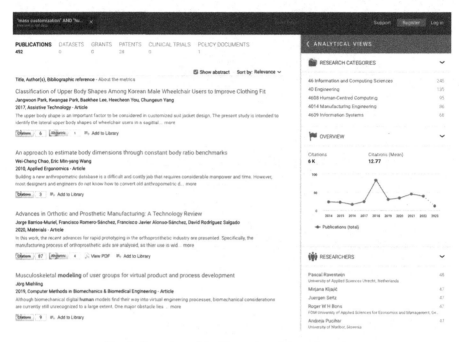

Fig. 4. Overview of the Dimensions AI search engine.

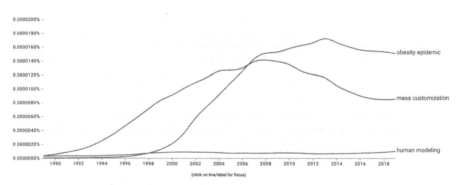

Fig. 5. Google Ngram result highlighting the share of publications over the years including the keywords human modeling, mass customization, and obesity epidemic.

2.4 Results of Bibliographic Analysis

The multi-part bibliographic analysis showed that (1) multiple research approaches are currently undertaken to understand and improve current designs (radar, augmented reality, cad, human participants, etc.), (2) a share of participant studies are performed, (3) human modeling for mass customization is a relevant subject, (4) there is a mismatch between the research about mass customization on one side and the manufacturer on the other, and (5) obesity, mass customization, and human modeling are currently relevant in research. This is validated through the modeling idea of chapter 27 of the *Handbook of Human Factors and Ergonomics* [21], as can be seen in Fig. 6 from the chapter.

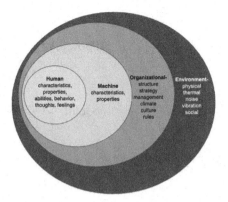

Fig. 6. Building up a human-centered design approach by Paul et al. [21]

3 Methodology

The following analysis was performed in the CAD modeling software RAMSIS. Within the software, a human's movement, posture, realistic behavior, and comfort are simulated. The simulation analyzes the human within a novel car. The functions used are joint capacity analysis and reach analysis.

The demonstrations are performed with the help of external data input, a car design that has been provided by an unknown seller. This car is still in its.zip shell and needs to be extracted and saved in the data location of RAMSIS. In the second step, one must declare this car design to RAMSIS.

3.1 Human Comfort

The comfort of a human can be measured by finding the optimal position of a human. This general position can be split into separate limb angles. For example, it is considered most comfortable if the knee is kept at an angle of 103° [23] . The relevant limb angles can be seen in Fig. 7. Vogt et al. have provided a table with all the angles necessary for the driver's seat position, see Table 1.

3.2 View Angle

Another aspect of human variability is the view angle for humans. To drive safely, the vision of a driver should not be obstructed and rather, one should have a perfect line of vision around the vehicle. The looking-out view as described by Trivedi et al. must have a good view, especially for the front view and side view, including the low visibility in front of the vehicle [24]. The viewing line including the head tilt angle is described by Vogt et al. as 12.8° [23]. A complete vision including the relevant car geometry can be seen in Fig. 8.

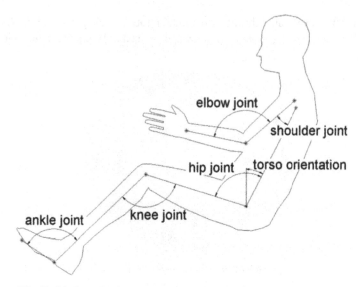

Fig. 7. Limb angles for the human in the driver seat (taken from [23])

Table 1. Recommendations for angles of joints (taken from [23]).

	RAMSIS	Bubb (1992)	DIN 33408	Dupuis (1983)	HdE (1989)	Rebiffé (1969)
Torso orientation	27°	—	—	—	—	—
Angle of shoulder joint	22°	9°–69°	38°	—	—	0°–25°
Angle of elbow joint	127°	134°–158°	120°	—	—	80°–120°
Angle of hip joint	99°	101°–113°	95°	105°–115°	110°	95°–120°
Angle of knee joint	119°	142°–152°	125°	110°–120°	145°	95°–135°
Angle of ankle joint	103°	77°–115°	90°	—	100°	90°–110°

4 Procedure/Analysis

In this paper, a future vehicle design purchased for demonstration and publication is analyzed, with a purpose of studying the ergonomic benefits and limitations of the car. The vehicle can be seen in Fig. 9. The vehicle is not specially chosen nor designed by the RAMSIS owner. Seven methods are used to test the car: (1) discomfort analysis, (2) reach analysis, (3) internal vision, (4) object view obstruction analysis, (5) night vision reflection, (6) daylight vision glare on surfaces, and (7) sizing limitations for passengers on the back seats. These methods are applied to test the suitability of the vehicle for all shapes, heights, and sexes.

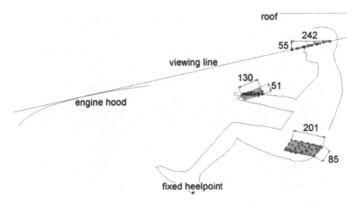

Fig. 8. Minimal allowed driver's view angle over the hood of the vehicle (taken from [23])

Fig. 9. The provided future car model in CAD.

4.1   Creation of Boundary Manikins

In this paper, there are ten manikins created to test the future vehicle. There are two sets, including the female and male sexes. A data set storing the age and shape-related data is supplied incorporating demographic data from Germany from the year 2004. These data can be used to create boundary manikins, or manikins that represent the majority of the population, excluding outliers. For the reference year of 2004 and the age group of 18–70, the three categories can be defined as follows: (1) length, (2) corpulence, and (3) proportion. These three can each be defined by type "short", "medium", and "large", or by value as a percentage of the population. Here, the body masses are chosen by value in the fields of "height", and "corpulence". For most tests, these manikins are chosen. The resulting manikin parameter can be seen in Table 2. Two additional manikins are later added for the back-seat passenger calculation.

Table 2. Parameter describing boundary manikins.

Sex	Height	Height percentile	Corpulence percentile
Female	1558 mm	8th	8th
Female	1567 mm	8th	95th
Female	1664 mm	50th	50th
Female	1810 mm	95th	8th
Female	1816 mm	95th	95th
Male	1595 mm	8th	8th
Male	1599 mm	8th	95th
Male	1745 mm	50th	50th
Male	1891 mm	95th	8th
Male	1899 mm	95th	95th

4.2 Manikin Placement in the Vehicle

Placing the manikins into the car requires target limitations similar to CAD restrictions. First, the door, chassis, and seat of the car are hidden. This allows better access to the seating area of the driver. Next, the manikin view is changed to a wire view, exposing the skeletal frame and body points of the human. Here, the H-point, the sitting base is visible, which is linked by "Target restriction" to the adjustable seat field of the vehicle. This field simulates all seat positions available, allowing movement in the x-axis and the z-axis. The same target restrictions are performed for the pairs Left Heel-floor, Right-Heel-floor, Right Ball-acceleration pedal in the pushed position, Left Ball-Footrest, Lefthand-Steering wheel, and Righthand-Steering Wheel. These connections can be seen in Fig. 10a. Next, the posture is calculated which yields the result seen in Fig. 10b.

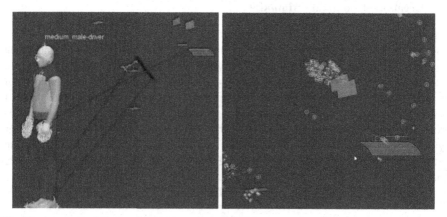

Fig. 10. (a) on the left, manikin with target restrictions to vehicle locations, (b) on the right, manikin seating in the car showing the target restrictions in action.

These restrictions can be copied from one manikin to all the others via "Special copy" and "special Paste", only pasting the "reference points".

4.3 Discomfort Analysis

The first iteration of posture calculation places the manikin inside the car and gives a baseline for the discomfort analysis. It shows that the stress on the manikin is significant, specifically that there is stress on the left and right leg, and on "discomfort Feeling" and "Health". "Discomfort Feeling" is the superposition of all the separate body parts. To create a comfortable driving experience, the stress on the body parts was minimized and these actions influence on the "discomfort feeling" tested. The manikins with the highest discomfort feelings were chosen to be the exemplary manikin for which a bodily stress reduction analysis was conducted. This was performed by shifting the vehicle's interiors placement. It is assumed that these small movements can be accommodated by the general frame of the car.

As the placements of the manikins in the car foreshadowed, there are 5 relevant points of limitation in the car. The main position is the seat, then there are the hands on the steering wheel, the floor/the roof of the car, and the gas and brake pedal. These are therefore the only measures to change the discomfort of the human. All items can be moved in all axes but should stay within an acceptable range of their current position. The focus of the movement was placed on the smallest (female) individual and the tallest (male) person with respect to the leg, arm, and body posture. A second focus lay on the people with a large corpulence.

4.4 Reach Analysis

After seating the driver in the main seat, the question arose about how easily the driver can access the middle console. This reach is relevant since the middle console regularly includes elements like the radio or climate control. Reaching all necessary car modules without compromising the driving position and subsequent control over the vehicle is essential. Therefore, the "comfortable reach" is defined as the range of motion originating in the clavicula and ending in the center of the index finger. Here, the clavicula is chosen as that allows for movement without fully disconnecting the human back from the seat. The middle of the index finger is chosen because of the extra motion range to perform actions like turning a dial or pushing a button.

The range of motion analysis can be accessed through either the analysis tab in ergonomics or by double clicking the range of motions analysis line for the extremity of choice in the object tree within the class "New Project" and "Reachability Definition". When opening the object information, the origin and endpoint can be changed. To reach the middle console easily, the console is moved slightly. The range of motion is limited to the x-axis, rotation in the z-axis, and y-axis.

4.5   Internal Vision

Internal vision is a method supplied by RAMSIS that shows the vision a human driver would have for a given position and line of sight. The line of sight can be independently moved while considering the driving posture. It is accessed through "Operations", and subsequent "Move eyesight". There are three options to originate the movement from (1) mid-eye, (2) neck, and (3) shoulders. Here, the neck is chosen as it is important to see the movement of the whole head and the same is important for subsequent measurements.

The line-of-sight analysis shows the left and right eye view on a separate screen. There are three views chosen to represent the line of sight for the boundary manikins: (1) the low point view over the vehicle's hood as explained in the methods, (2) the direct view on the vehicle's driver's screen, and (3) the human's view when checking the rearview mirror.

4.6   View Obstruction Analysis

When looking at the ergonomics and safety of the car, viewing obstruction is an important measure. Everything obstructing the driver from attending to the important driving tasks is a safety issue. Therefore, RAMSIS has a function producing view shade, a linear extrapolation of the object as if the object would extend everywhere where the light cannot shine anymore into the eyes of the human. These are represented with cones.

4.7   Vehicle Backseat Passenger Height Limitation

The car design is very sportive but attempts to accommodate backseat passengers. This analysis is designed to simulate the maximal height of males and females that can sit in the backseat. Further, these data allow insight into how much of the male and female population could fit into the backseat and sit comfortably.

First, another neutral, average-height manikin is created, one male and one female. Going forward, the only size change is the torso height as this height is dominant for seated positions [Vogt]. This manikin is placed into the backseat with the target limitation functions (1) h-Point and lower-seat-cushion, (2) left and right Ball each on the ground, and (3) left and right Heel on the ground. This simulation tool does not fixate the back of the manikin to the back of the seat. Also, at this point, there is a target Limitation created for the human vertex to the ceiling. Even with this measure for calculating the height, the process is tedious. Even with the approximate human height one has to analyze the posture for correct posture rather than self-distortion. The local optimal posture for the manikin is calculated and updated. In order to measure the available torso height, a ceiling plane is created and attached to the lower side of the ceiling, exactly at the position of the manikin's head from the preliminary optimal posture calculation. Next, the distance is measured with a standard CAD measuring method and used as input to the new torso length of the manikin. For that, one activates the bodybuilder module and updated the topology. After that, the data is transferred into all active manikins with "apply for all active manikins" in the "Set Boundary conditions"-tab. After that, the posture is updated. For the new posture, the now activated (but not fulfilled) target Limitation will show the offset (under or over mismatch). This mismatch is deducted from the manikins and the posture recalculated, with a deactivated vertex-ceiling limitation. This last procedure is repeated if there is a positive or zero mismatch.

4.8 Reflection Analysis

While in a car, reflection on surfaces is a safety risk as the light can situationally blind the driver. A one-second-long blindness can, including the time of readjustment, disrupt the driver's attention to the road for a multitude of seconds. This is hazardous, especially at higher speeds. Therefore, this analysis tries to reduce the possibility of blinding by reflection. For this, all reflective surfaces are analyzed so that no ray of refracted rays could blind the driver. The reflective surfaces are: (1) the driver screen, (2) the center console, (3) the side mirrors, and (4) the rearview mirror. For reflection, there is the necessity of light sources; for this paper, it is assumed that all windows are perfect sources, as there is a multitude of light sources outside the car, for example (1) sun, (2) moon, (3) other cars, and (4) street lighting. RAMSIS has the functionality in the "Odontology Module" choosing "analysis", and the function "reflection". For one reflection surface, this method calculates all possible rays, including primal and secondary rays ending in the human's eye. Additionally, a cone is created to highlight all directions that light can come from to be redirected, again from one reflection surface, and into the eye of the driver. Tilting the reflective surface can reduce the amount of light being redirected into the eye of the driver.

5   Results

The discomfort analysis results does not show consistent results. While it was possible to find a generally better arrangement for all boundary manikins, further changes to the benefit of some manikins lead to more discomfort for others. The best improvements were made for the female at 8th percentile in size and 95th percentile in circumference. The comfort distribution can be seen on the left in Fig. 11 and the right of Fig. 11 shows the final posture of the manikin. The discomfort is shown in yellow, while the original positioning (before moving the pedal/seat/steering wheel) is displayed in white. The overall improvement, which is less than ideal, is also shown in Fig. 11. The best condition was formed by moving the gas pedal and the footrest 40 mm closer to the manikin, increasing the distance of the gas pedal and footrest by 20 mm, moving the gas pedal and footrest down by 30 mm, and moving the seat up by 10 mm.

The second analysis, the reach analysis, showed that a slight movement (30 mm X-axis, 12° turn around the y-axis and 5° turn around the z-axis) was enough to move the center console in reach of the human. Additionally, this movement achieved an unobstructed line of sight on both the street and onto the screen. This was also confirmed, as no steering wheel cone obstructed the view on the driver's screen (Fig. 12).

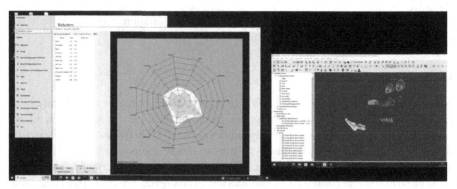

Fig. 11. Female driver including the discomfort analysis result.

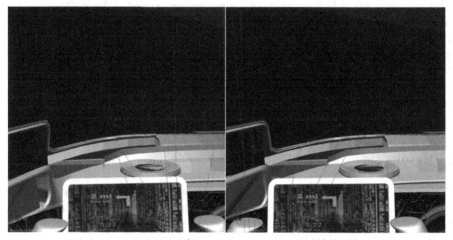

Fig. 12. Internal view of the female 8th percentile (height) and 95th percentile (weight) when looking onto the hood of the vehicle.

The reflection analysis showed that the driver screen's design, position, and angle are well suited for the chosen boundary manikin as the rays mostly get blocked by the manikin's body. A slight tilting of $+10°$ in the y-axis of the driver's screen can be an improvement since it would completely redirect the rays to the ceiling of the car. An analysis of the windshield showed that no reflection surface could blind the driver. The minimum height of a passenger can be seen in Fig. 13. In this case, 98% of males are not able to sit comfortably in the backseat of this vehicle (Fig. 13a), while 60% of females cannot sit in the backseat, see Fig. 13b. There are two limiting factors, namely the heightened backseat area and the hinges of the door, that do not directly impact the height but are unsafe when trying to fit into this small area.

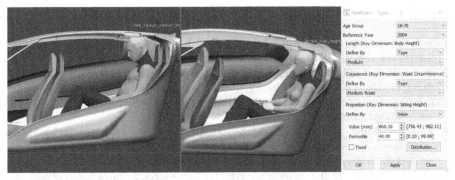

Fig. 13. (a) a discomfortable oversized male in the backseat of the vehicle, (b) a female with the maximal height possible in the backseat of the vehicle, (c) the corresponding date to the female in the backseat.

6   Discussion and Outlook

The result of the discomfort analysis shows a strong improvement for individual boundary manikin but is not an overall success as the overall discomfort is still high. It is not finally proven that the high discomfort is completely traceable back to the imperfect vehicle design or a local minimum. One aspect can be that the analysis compares two extreme cases, or a very short person to a very tall person. Also, the focus was strongly placed on the angle of the knees and slightly on the hip flexor. The other joints are similarly relevant. The reach analysis has been proven successful; all manikins can reach the designated area. However, just the ability to comfortably, and therefore, safely, reach the center console is only part of the ergonomic analysis. The next question concerns longer reach: what can be reached by removing the back from the back of the seat? Is that an encouragement? The reflections are mostly - and with little changes to the design - easily removable. The most efficient way to calculate the height of the backseat passenger is by defining the height a torso can have in the backseat, using this height as a torso length, and then verifying by using a target limitation, as seen in the analysis in 4.7.

   Future analysis should be focused on identifying the human joint angle corresponding lengths: approaching a knee angle of 103° is a good task but is less complicated if the length between the gas pedal and the seat is too long. Also, the posture calculation function needs to be further investigated. All manikins were initialized with a strong backward-angled back. It is unclear if this is the best posture. Another aspect of the discomfort analysis that was not fully elucidated is the "health" classification. One aspect that should be looked at is the reach analysis for the full break analysis. Will the reach be enough for the driver to perform an emergency brake? The analysis of uncomfortable reach could also be a future endeavor. A collaboration could be undertaken with the developer team [25]. To do so, one could change the RAMSIS software into the next stage, a partial or full extended reality. A restricted motion condition as described in task 2.8 can be attempted to be resolved by creating a forced boundary around surfaces that are not limited/connected to each other. If there is a connection/breach of boundary, the potential risk is high.

References

1. Jiang, R., Liu, Z., Li, H.: Evolution towards optimal driving strategies for large-scale autonomous vehicles. IET Intel. Transp. Syst. **15**(8), 1018–1027 (2021)
2. Ebsworth, M. A., Ebsworth, E.: History of the Automobile. Salem Press Encyclopedia (2015)
3. Wang, Yi., Ma, H.-S., Yang, J.-H., Wang, K.-S.: Industry 4.0: a way from mass customization to mass personalization production. Adv. Manufact. **5**(4), 311–320 (2017). https://doi.org/10.1007/s40436-017-0204-7
4. Zhang, X., Ming, X., Liu, Z., Zheng, M., Yuanju, Q.: A new customization model for enterprises based on improved framework of the customer to business: a case study in the automobile industry. Adv. Mech. Eng. **11**(3), 1687814019833882 (2019)
5. CDC 2017-March 2020 examination survey. https://www.cdc.gov/nchs/fastats/obesity-overweight.htm
6. Kelly, T., Yang, W., Chen, C.-S., Reynolds, K., He, J.: Global burden of obesity in 2005 and projections to 2030. Int. J. Obes. **32**(9), 1431–1437 (2008)
7. McGuire, S.: Institute of Medicine. 2012. Accelerating progress in obesity prevention: solving the weight of the nation. Washington, DC: The National Academies Press. Adv. Nutr. **3**(5), 708–709 (2012)
8. Raymer, W., Luisa C.: Advanced RAMSIS. Analysis of excavator operator. In: Duffy, V.G., Rau, P.L.P. (eds.) Proceedings of the HCI International 2022–Late Breaking Papers: Ergonomics and Product Design: 24th International Conference on Human-Computer Interaction, HCII 2022, Virtual Event, 26 June–1 July 2022, vol. 13522, pp. 308–335. Springer, Cham (2022). https://doi.org/10.1007/978-3-031-21704-3_20
9. Bubb, H., et al.: The development of RAMSIS in past and future as an example for the cooperation between industry and university. Int. J. Hum. Factors Model. Simul. **1**(1), 140–157 (2006)
10. VOSViewer Application. https://www.vosviewer.com/. Accessed 01 May 2023
11. Google Ngram Viewer Homepage. https://books.google.com/ngrams/. Accessed 01 May 2023
12. Human Solutions Homepage. https://www.human-solutions.com. Accessed 01 May 2023
13. Google Scholar Homepage. https://scholar.google.com/. Accessed 01 May 2023
14. Silva da, A.G., Mendes Gomes, M.V., Winkler, I.: Virtual reality and digital human modeling for ergonomic assessment in industrial product development: a patent and literature review. Appl. Sci. **12**(3), 1084 (2022)
15. Demirel, H.O., Salman, A., Duffy, V.G.: Digital human modeling: a review and reappraisal of origins, present, and expected future methods for representing humans computationally. Int. J. Hum. Comput. Interact. **38**(10), 897–937 (2022)
16. Scopus Homepage. https://www.scopus.com/search/form.uri?display=basic#basic. Accessed 01 May 2023
17. Baskaran, S., et al.: Digital human and robot simulation in automotive assembly using Siemens process simulate a feasibility study. Procedia Manuf. **34**, 986–994 (2019)
18. Deep, Y.: Radar cross-sections of pedestrians at automotive radar frequencies using ray tracing and point scatterer modelling. IET Radar. Sonar Navig. **14**(6), 833–844 (2020)
19. Duffy, V.G.: Digital human modeling in design. In: Handbook of Human Factors and Ergonomics, pp. 761–781 (2021)
20. Salvendy, G.: Handbook of Human Factors and Ergonomics, 4th edn, pp. 1615–1638. Wiley, Hoboken (2012)
21. Paul, G.E.: Modeling and simulation of human systems. In: Handbook of Human Factors and Ergonomics, pp. 704–735 (2021)
22. Web of Science Homepage. https://www.webofscience.com/. Accessed 01 May 2023

23. Vogt, C., Mergl, C., Bubb, H.: Interior layout design of passenger vehicles with RAMSIS. Hum. Factors Ergon. Manuf. Serv. Ind. **15**(2), 197–212 (2005)

24. Trivedi, M M., Gandhi, T., McCall, J.: Looking-in and looking-out of a vehicle: computer-vision-based enhanced vehicle safety. IEEE Trans. Intell. Transp. Syst. **8**(1), 108–120 (2007)

25. NSF awarded grants Homepage. https://www.nsf.gov/awardsearch/showAward?AWD_ID= 1850055&HistoricalAwards=false. Accessed 01 May 2023

26. Xu, X., et al.: Enabling hand gesture customization on wrist-worn devices. In: Proceedings of the 2022 CHI Conference on Human Factors in Computing Systems, pp. 1–19 (2022)

27. Kim, S., Lee, K.: The paradigm shift of mass customisation research. Int. J. Prod. Res. **61**(10), 3350–3376 (2023)

28. Cuadrado, J., Lugris, U., Mouzo, F., Michaud, F.: Musculo-skeletal modeling and analysis for low-cost active orthosis customization and SCI patient adaptation. In: Zahariev, E., Cuadrado, J. (eds.) IUTAM Symposium on Intelligent Multibody Systems – Dynamics, Control, Simulation. IB, vol. 33, pp. 41–54. Springer, Cham (2019). https://doi.org/10.1007/978-3-030-005 27-6_2

29. Luo, W., Wang, J., Wang, C., Li, Z.: Redesign of glasses customization service process based on analysis of influencing factors in customer purchase decision-making process. In: 2021 IEEE International Conference on Industrial Engineering and Engineering Management (IEEM), pp. 1164–1168. IEEE (2021)

30. Zeng, D., Guan, M., He, M., Tian, Z.: An interactive evolutionary design method for mobile product customization and validation of its application. Int. J. Comput. Intell. Syst. **15**(1), 1–17 (2022). https://doi.org/10.1007/s44196-022-00075-8

31. Lohmann, M., Anzanello, M.J., Fogliatto, F.S., da Silveira, G C.: Grouping workers with similar learning profiles in mass customization production lines. Comput. Ind. Eng. **131**, 542–551 (2019)

32. Suginouchi, S., Mizuyama, H.: Scheduling auction: a new manufacturing business model for balancing customization and quick delivery. In: Ameri, F., Stecke, K.E., von Cieminski, G., Kiritsis, D. (eds.) APMS 2019. IAICT, vol. 567, pp. 109–117. Springer, Cham (2019). https:// doi.org/10.1007/978-3-030-29996-5_13

33. Husain, K.N., et al.: Procedure for creating personalized geometrical models of the human mandible and corresponding implants. Tehnički vjesnik **26**(4), 1044–1051 (2019)

34. Arpaia, P., et al.: Preliminary experimental identification of a FEM human knee model. In: 2020 IEEE International Symposium on Medical Measurements and Applications (MeMeA), pp. 1–6. IEEE (2020)

35. Li, J., Tanaka, H., Miyagawa, S.: Applying the programmable modeling tool to support the hospital infection control staff in customizing the filtering face-piece respirators for health care worker. In: Karwowski, W., Trzcielinski, S., Mrugalska, B., Di Nicolantonio, M., Rossi, E. (eds.) AHFE 2018. AISC, vol. 793, pp. 270–279. Springer, Cham (2019). https://doi.org/ 10.1007/978-3-319-94196-7_25

36. Lucci, N., Monguzzi, A., Zanchettin, A M., Rocco, P.: Workflow modeling for human–robot collaborative assembly operations. Rob. Comput. Integr. Manuf. **78**, 102384 (2022)

37. Zhang, J., Luximon, Y., Shah, P., Zhou, K., Li, P.: Customize my helmet: a novel algorithmic approach based on 3D head prediction. Comput. Aided Des. **150**, 103271 (2022)

38. Xi, W., Bao, Y., Qiao, L., Xia, G., Xiaoming, T.: Parametric modeling the human calves for evaluation and design of medical compression stockings. Comput. Meth. Programs Biomed. **194**, 105515 (2020)

39. Chen, G.Y.H., Chen, P.-S., Tsai, T.-T.: Applying the task-technology fit model to construct the prototype of a medical staff scheduling system. Technol. Health Care **30**, 1055–1075 (2022)

40. Yetkin, B.N., Ulutas, B.H.: A skill-based MILP model in cellular manufacturing systems with human-robot collaboration. IFAC-PapersOnLine **55**(10), 1728–1733

A Systematic Review of Enhancing Aerospace Safety with Augmented Reality

Ray Wu[✉], Molly Moore, and Vincent G. Duffy

Purdue University, West Lafayette, IN 47906, USA
{wu1161,moore262,duffy}@purdue.edu

Abstract. A flight simulator is a device that replicates the experience of flying an aircraft realistically, without actually leaving the ground. It consists of a cockpit with various systems and instruments that simulate the flight environment through the use of augmented reality. Augmented reality is a technology that overlays virtual elements onto the real world, enhancing the user's perception and interaction with their environment in real time. Flight simulators have been identified as valuable tools to provide safe and cost-effective ways to train pilots and simulate emergencies. This form of augmented reality can improve safety training by allowing the trainees, or pilots, to visualize and interact with potential hazards in a controlled environment, which can help them understand and retain safety procedures. By doing a bibliometric analysis, we conducted a deep dive into the uses of flight simulators and how it impacts flight training and engineering design.

Keywords: Flight simulator · safety · aerospace · human factors · augmented reality · certification

1 Introduction and Background

In recent years, the use of Augmented Reality (AR) technology has gained popularity across various professional fields, including aerospace. In the aviation industry, flight simulators are widely used to train pilots before they fly a real plane with passengers. This training method provides a safe and controlled environment for pilots to practice real-world scenarios without risking lives or causing damage to expensive aircraft (Lofaro et al. 2011). The use of flight simulators is also cost-effective, allowing for more frequent and comprehensive training, which contributes to improved safety in aerospace operations.

With the help of AR, pilots have gained more experience and confidence while training, leading to better situational awareness, decision-making skills, and crew resource management. Flight simulators are also used for research purposes, allowing researchers to study human performance in high-stress environments and develop new safety procedures and protocols (Minaskan et al. 2022). The continuous improvement of flight simulators requires the collaboration of various disciplines, including Industrial Engineering (IE), Aerospace, Electrical, and Mechanical Engineering, as well as Human Factors and Ergonomics (HFE) and Human-Computer Interaction (HCI). Potential risks associated with flight simulators can be mitigated by implementing strict safety regulations and guidelines to ensure proper training for pilots. Ultimately, the use of flight simulators and AR in aerospace contributes significantly to improved safety and more efficient training for pilots.

1.1 Purpose of Study

The purpose of this study is to create a bibliometric analysis and systematic review with topics related to flight simulators and safety engineering, conduct a content analysis of secondary data, and compile a comprehensive report that includes visualizations, a reference list, and summaries of definitions, historical aspects, methods, results, and future work related to the topic.

From the Merriam-Webster Dictionary, a flight simulator is "an airplane pilot-training device in which the cockpit and instruments of an airplane are duplicated and the conditions of actual flight are simulated" (Merriam-Webster, flight simulator). Augmented reality is, "an enhanced version of reality created by the use of technology to overlay digital information on an image of something being viewed through a device", (Merriam-Webster, augmented reality). "Human Factors is a body of knowledge about human abilities, human limitations, and other human characteristics that are relevant to design. Human factors engineering is the application of human factors information to the design of tools, machines, systems, tasks, jobs, and environments for safe, comfortable, and effective human use", (Chapanis, 1991).

Below is a table showing searches performed in Scopus with the number of articles per year since 2016 for various search terms per the topic, such as, "augmented reality AND safety" and "flight simulator AND safety". The number of articles increases year over year, meaning the topic is becoming more and more relevant.

Table 1. Number of Articles per year for various search term combinations in Scopus

Year	2016	2017	2018	2019	2020	2021	2022
Search: digital twin AND safety	1	7	17	76	149	223	416
Search: augmented reality AND safety	68	103	123	187	235	256	286
Search: digital twin AND aerospace	2	5	7	28	39	57	55
Search: flight simulator AND safety	78	75	101	117	104	102	119

2 Research Methodology

We conducted a bibliometric analysis using the analysis tools in the chart listed below.

Through this study, we concluded that the fields of human factors and ergonomics, as well as human-computer interaction (HCI), have contributed significantly to flight simulation and safety in the aerospace industry. The use of augmented reality plays a significant role in the accessibility, efficiency, and reliability of learning how to fly an aircraft (Rigas et al. 2019). Errors and crashes that could potentially damage the aircraft

Table 2. Descriptions of bibliometric analysis tools

Analysis Tool	Description
Web of Science	Online research database to access scholarly literature, track citations and analyze research trends[36]
Scopus	Citation database used for academic research[33]
Purdue Libraries	Library database used for Purdue University to support research needs[20]
Scite.AI	AI platform used to evaluate the reliability and context of scientific articles[32]
Google Scholar	Web-based search engine for scholarly literature[34]
VOS Viewer	Software used to create bibliometric networks[37]
Google nGram	Search engine used to relate frequencies of research vocabulary in printed sources[6]
Harzing	A bibliometric tool used to analyze publication records, citations, and related metrics[17]
Citespace	Software used to visualize and analyze scholarly literature[8]
MaxQDA	A software program used for qualitative data analysis[23]
Springer	Database for scholarly research articles[21]
Research Gate	Platform to share research collaboration[30]
NSF	National Science Foundation database used to promote scientific publication[28]

or harm the passengers can now be safely simulated and experienced without any risk. This holds significant importance as it allows pilots to train in a safe environment without risking lives or multimillion-dollar aircraft.

2.1 Data Collection

Several steps were taken to conduct a systematic review and collect bibliometric data related to flight simulators and safety engineering. First, relevant keywords related to the topic were identified, such as "flight simulator," "safety engineering," "aviation safety," "digital twin," and other such words. These keywords can then be used to search various databases, such as Scopus, Scite.ai, Web of Science, and Google Scholar. The search results can then be screened using inclusion and exclusion criteria to select articles that meet the study's objectives. Bibliometric analyses were conducted to identify trends and patterns in the selected articles, such as authorship, publication dates, citation counts, and keywords. The data was visualized using software tools such as VOSviewer or Scite.ai to identify clusters of related articles and co-citation networks. The results of the systematic review and bibliometric analysis were then compiled into a comprehensive report, including a reference list of selected articles and summaries of the key findings.

2.2 Trend Analysis

The three diagrams below are trend information pulled from the Scopus database used to highlight which years, affiliations, and subject areas are most popular with the search terms "flight simulator" and "safety", as well as "digital twins" and "safety" (Fig. 1).

The Scopus search shown above is a trend diagram highlighting the increased documentation rising over the past decade for the search terms "digital twin" and "safety", starting to rise from 2017 to the present (Fig. 2).

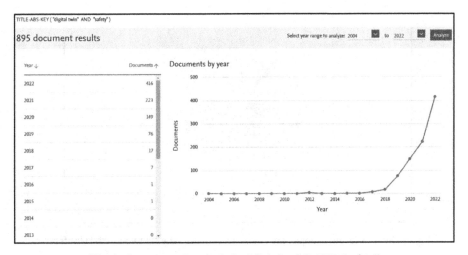

Fig. 1. Scopus trend analysis for "digital twin" AND "safety"

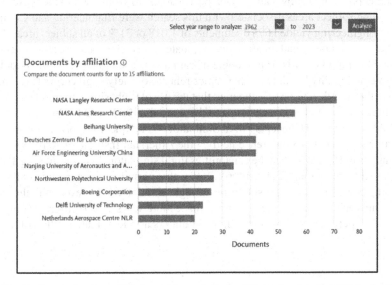

Fig. 2. Scopus leading affiliation table analysis for "flight simulator" AND "safety"

The Scopus search shown above yielded 1,518 results from 1962 to the present. The main leading affiliations associated with this search were NASA and several institutes from China. All these affiliations had 20 or more articles, mostly from 1990 and on (Fig. 3).

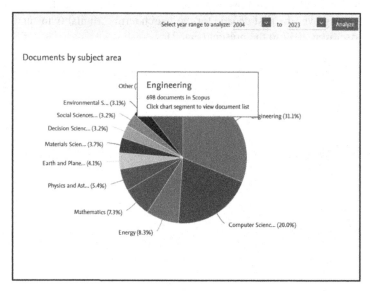

Fig. 3. Scopus leading subject area table analysis for "digital twins" AND "safety"

The Scopus search shown above yielded 1,018 results from 2004 to the present. The main leading subject areas associated with this search were Engineering and Computer Science. Engineering yielded 698 documents of 1,018 or 31% of all subject areas. Other subject areas included: mathematics, energy, materials science, and social sciences.

The line graph below is from Google nGram and is used to compare the popularity of "augmented reality" with two other topics related to safety engineering (Fig. 4).

From the Google nGram, it's apparent that the use of flight simulators and augmented reality in research articles began being used between the 1980s-1990s. One article found, "The NASA Advanced Concepts Flight Simulator – A unique transport aircraft research environment" refers to a conference held by the American Institute of Aeronautics and Astronautics in 1996 to look at the capabilities flight simulators have in studying aviation safety and human factors (Blake, 1996). Before that period, computers did not have the processing power to create realistic forms of flight simulators. However, with the advent of cheap microchips, computing power was made more accessible to different companies who could experiment with making flight simulators as a legitimate method of training pilots.

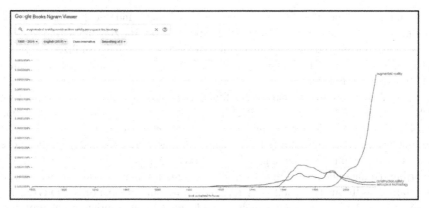

Fig. 4. Google nGram comparing "augmented reality" to "construction safety" and "aerospace technology"

3 Procedure and Results

3.1 Co-citation Analysis

We performed a co-citation analysis using the Harzing and Vos Viewer software to compare and contrast different citations on the subject of aerospace, safety, and augmented reality. To import data from Harzing to VOS Viewer, we exported the publication data related to flight simulators from Harzing. This was done by selecting the publications and exporting them as exportable files. Once we had the file, we opened the VOS Viewer

Fig. 5. Harzing Search Table, a search of "aviation" and "ergonomics"

and imported the exportable file by going to the "File" menu and selecting "Import bibliographic data". We then selected the file we exported from Harzing in the import dialog box. After importing the data, we analyzed it in VOS Viewer and visualized the bibliometric networks. Below is a screenshot of the Harzing search performed on "aviation and ergonomics" (Fig. 5).

To conduct a co-citation analysis for flight simulators and safety engineering using VOSviewer, the first step was to collect a set of relevant articles related to the topic. This was done by conducting a systematic review and bibliometric analysis as discussed earlier. Once a set of relevant articles is identified, they were exported from the chosen database in the required format (e.g.,.bib,.ris, or.txt) and imported into VOSviewer. After importing the data, the next step is to create a co-citation map. To do this, we selected "co-citation" as the analysis method, selected the minimum number of citations required for an article to be included in the analysis, and edited the appropriate number of items to be displayed on the map.

The resulting co-citation map showed clusters of articles that were frequently cited together, with each cluster representing a distinct research topic. In addition to the co-citation map, VOSviewer also generates a variety of other visualizations, such as a timeline showing the publication year of each article and a density visualization showing the frequency of keywords in the article set. These visualizations were useful for identifying trends and patterns in the research field and providing insights into the evolution of the topic over time. The results of the co-citation analysis were used to identify key research themes and gaps in the literature, which informed us of future research directions in the field of flight simulators and safety engineering (Fig. 6).

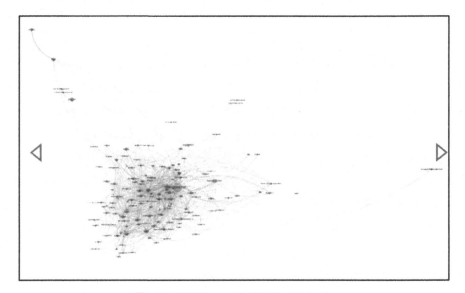

Fig. 6. VOS Viewer Co-Citation Analysis

In the figure below, several informative clusters were formed in the CiteSpace tool, but not many applied to the topic of this paper, other than "education", which can apply to flight simulation for pilots. The data uploaded into CiteSpace was a search in the Web of Science database for "Augmented Reality" (Fig. 7).

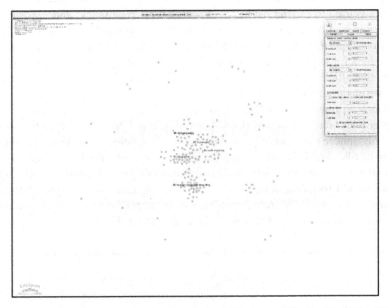

Fig. 7. Cite Clusters from CiteSpace for the search of "Augmented Reality" in Web of Science

Several references from the Top 4 Strongest Citation Bursts related directly to the topic relating to flight simulation or aerospace. When performing the search on the Web of Science, searching "safety" and "augmented reality" didn't yield several articles to work with in CiteSpace. See the figure below for the Citation Burst History results (Fig. 8).

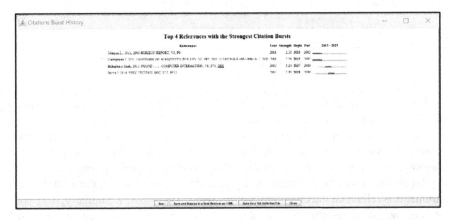

Fig. 8. Citation Burst from CiteSpace for a search of "Augmented Reality" in Web of Science

3.2 Content Analysis Results from MAXQDA

The research was conducted in aviation ergonomics by using several resources from Max QDA, VOS viewer, and Harzing data/excel to find relevant articles and search topics. Harzing was used to expand the keyword search for "ergonomics" and "aviation" and the minimum occurrences of a term were set to 10 and the number of words to 151. The Harzing data was then imported into VOS Viewer. This gave us a broad view of what words to look for while conducting general research relating to aviation ergonomics.

With five articles related to "ergonomics" and "aviation" based on the Harzing data search, we made sure that each of these articles was from a wide spread of sources from the textbook, Springer, Google Scholar, and ResearchGate to have diverse sources. Once the five articles were put into Max QDA, we could find the most common words and remove any unnecessary words. The word cloud shown below has 100 words. The most common words were flight, disorientation, illusions, spatial, orientation, and other such words that related to aviation human factors. Doing this gave a blueprint on what specifically we should focus on, which in the case of ergonomics were "flight", "displays", and "instrument". All of this relates to the use of augmented reality for flight simulators. Below is a visual of the Max QDA word cloud generated (Fig. 9).

Fig. 9. Max QDA Word Cloud

There were correlations between the use of augmented reality and training. Training new pilots in an aircraft is a very dangerous and costly activity, especially if it's their first time flying (Moesl et al 2023). In most aircraft accident cases, pilots cannot read their instruments properly and often make fatal decisions based on their improper reading (Dariusz, 2018). For example, if an aircraft is flying at an angle through clouds and the pilot doesn't know he's at such an angle, having a clear sight of the aircraft angle instruments is reliant on the ergonomics of his seat (Li et al 2015). Similarly, if a pilot's seat is not adjusted properly and the pilot has to take evasive maneuvers, the extra 0.2 s spent trying to find the control and reaching for it is a matter of life and death (Balaj et al. 2018). Having proper research in a pilot's seat, line-of-vision, and reachability is an essential part of aviation human factors and can be simulated through the use of flight simulators.

4 Discussion

4.1 Flight Simulators for Training

As technology advances in the future, augmented reality (AR) has the unique ability to teach different advanced topics quickly and reliably. They provide a safe and cost-effective way for users to train in a variety of different scenarios, without putting themselves or others at risk (Minaskan et al. 2022). Augmented reality (AR) has the potential to revolutionize training for future work by providing immersive and interactive experiences that blend the physical and virtual worlds, allowing for realistic simulations, hands-on learning, and personalized training in various fields such as healthcare, engineering, manufacturing, and more, enhancing skills acquisition, performance, and productivity. Chapter 12, "Safety and Health Training" on page 255, from David Goetsch's text, *Occupational Safety and Health for Technologists, Engineers, and Managers*, dives into different safety and health training techniques but does not explicitly mention the use of augmented reality used as training. (Goetsch, 2019).

4.2 Flight Simulators and Safety

Flight simulation and augmented reality can be used for training and flight testing in the field of safety engineering. Flight simulators can be used for pilot training, aircraft design and testing, and safety analysis. By using flight simulators, safety engineers can conduct experiments to evaluate the safety of different aircraft systems, procedures, and scenarios without exposing real pilots or passengers to potential risks. Flight simulation also allows safety engineers to identify and address safety hazards, evaluate the effectiveness of safety measures, and optimize safety protocols in a controlled and safe environment (Ancel et al. 2022). The course material in Professor Duffy's class, IE 558, *Occupational Safety and Health for Technologists, Engineers, and Managers*, by David Goetsch, represents safety and health training techniques in Chapter 12, which aligns nicely with flight simulators for pilots (Goetsch, 2019). Chapter 4 of Goetsch's text, "Roles and Professional Certifications for Safety and Health Professionals" also relates to this topic as it highlights safety in different professions (Goetsch, 2019).

4.3 Importance of Augmented Reality

The growing popularity of Augmented Reality and the advancement of technology has led to an increased interest in exploring the potential of Augmented Reality in various professional fields, especially aerospace. Nearly all airlines have pilots go through special training using flight simulators before flying an actual plane with passengers. Using a flight simulator as a training tool enhances the accessibility, efficiency, and reliability of learning how to fly an aircraft. Errors and crashes that could potentially damage the aircraft or harm the passengers can now be safely simulated and experienced without any risk. This holds significant importance as it allows pilots to train in a safe environment without risking lives or multimillion-dollar aircraft.

The use of flight simulators has become increasingly important in aerospace for several key reasons, such as real-world training, cost savings, and improved safety. Flight simulators provide a safe and controlled environment for pilots to perform realistic training without the risks and hazards associated with an actual flight. Flight simulation training allows pilots to gain extensive practice in various real-world and potential emergencies. Additionally, the pilots can gain more experience and confidence using an augmented reality version of the training.

Aviation organizations can also save money by using flight simulators. Training in real aircraft is expensive, especially for complex aerospace systems. Flight simulators offer a cost-effective alternative by reducing the need for actual flight time and associated expenses, such as fuel costs, maintenance, and insurance. This cost-effective approach allows for more frequent and comprehensive training, which ultimately contributes to improved safety in aerospace operations.

Flight simulators also allow for the simulation of potentially dangerous scenarios, such as adverse weather conditions, engine failures, and system malfunctions, without putting real pilots or passengers at risk. This helps identify potential safety risks, develop appropriate procedures, and mitigate hazards before they occur in real-world operations while also creating the opportunity to address human factors, such as human error, which is a leading cause of aviation accidents (Mistry, 2021). Training in flight simulators can help pilots and aerospace professionals develop situational awareness, decision-making skills, and crew resource management, which are critical factors in enhancing safety.

4.4 Flight Simulation in Engineering

Flight simulation and different forms of augmented reality that can be used for training are important for Industrial Engineering because they can help Industrial Engineers analyze and optimize specific processes and make improvements where necessary. The simulations allow for testing various scenarios, identifying potential issues, and making informed decisions about system design and capacity planning.

Outside of the IE realm a lot of initiatives are being implemented in aerospace with flight simulators. Airlines use flight simulators to train their pilots are particular types of planes. At Boeing, pilots are sent from various airlines to the simulator to learn how to fly specific aircraft. Flight simulators are an effective tool for allowing pilots to get familiar with different types of aircraft, like a Boeing 737 versus an Airbus A320, that may not be possible or safe to practice in real aircraft (Şentürk et al. 2021). Engineers in several disciplines such as Aerospace, Electrical, and Mechanical also use flight simulators to test new aircraft designs and systems. This can also help cut down on costs and time associated with the design engineering phases of a project. Flight simulators are also used for research purposes, particularly in the areas of human factors and aviation safety. For example, three research scientists and engineers from California simulated with the National Aeronautics and Space Administration Ames Research Center (NASA ARC) and the U.S. Army Aviation Development Directorate (ADD) used augmented reality to study spatial auditory displays for obstacle avoidance in flight (Miller et al. 2018).

Additionally, researchers can use simulators to study human performance in high-stress environments and to develop new safety procedures and protocols.

HFE and HCI have contributed to flight simulation safety by focusing on the application of user-centered design principles. They do this by considering the abilities and limitations of the pilots to make sure that the simulators are designed to be usable and most effective. They also consider the design of user interfaces when designing displays and controls. To improve safety, human factors, and ergonomics, the designs of these systems for pilots must revolve around cognitive workload, situational awareness, and visual attention (Oberhauser, 2017). Overall, HFE and HCI play a very important role in the development, implementation, and continuing improvements of flight simulators by improving the design, usability, and training associated with flight simulators.

5 Conclusion

In conclusion, bibliometric analysis is a powerful tool for exploring research trends and patterns in the field of flight simulators and safety engineering. By analyzing publication data, we identified key areas of focus, major contributors to the field, and emerging topics of interest. This information informed us of future research directions and to make evidence-based decisions about the design, development, and implementation of flight simulators and safety engineering systems. Additionally, the applications of flight simulation in engineering and the contributions of human factors and ergonomics to flight simulator safety demonstrate the importance of interdisciplinary collaboration in ensuring the safe and effective operation of aircraft. Continued research and innovation in flight simulation and safety engineering will be critical for advancing aviation safety and improving the performance of aircraft systems.

6 Future Work

The aviation industry should continue to invest in developing and improving flight simulators to make them more realistic and accurate. Pilots need to be properly educated and trained to handle various situations in flight. Governments and aviation regulators should increase their oversight and regulation of training programs that involve flight simulators by making sure programs are up to date-and meet the latest safety standards. The NSF-funded project, "Collaborative Research: Networked Multi-Player Flight Simulators for Improved Pilot Training and Air Traffic Management," is an example of ongoing efforts to improve flight simulator training programs and enhance aviation safety through the development of new technologies and collaboration tools for pilots and air traffic controllers (Glinert, 2003). Funding can support research and development of new technologies that can improve flight simulators. Society can mitigate potential risks associated with flight simulators by implementing strict safety regulations and guidelines, ensuring proper maintenance of simulators, and providing adequate training to pilots and simulator operators (Wise, 2019). Regular evaluations and audits can also help address any issues before they become significant problems. The development of a virtual reality simulator for training unmanned aircraft systems pilots has been funded by the National Science Foundation (Gruner, 2023). To ensure relevance and effectiveness in preparing pilots, society must adapt to the continually changing pilot training needs and requirements.

The application of augmented reality (AR) technology in aerospace safety has significant potential for future work. As the aviation industry continues to grow, safety measures will evolve to keep up with the complex and challenging demands of flying (Alarcon et al, 2020). AR has the potential to improve safety by enhancing situational awareness and providing real-time information to pilots (Iizuka et al, 2019). The technology can also be integrated with other safety measures, such as automation and predictive analytics, to enhance safety further. Future research is needed to develop AR systems that are specifically designed for aviation, as well as to explore the best ways to train pilots and other aviation personnel to use AR effectively and safely.

The NSF article titled "The Use of Augmented Reality for Aerospace Safety" provides valuable insights into the potential applications of AR technology in the aviation industry (Forbes, 2019). The article highlights the historical development of AR technology and its recent affordability and accessibility, which has made it a viable option for aerospace safety.

The article also discusses the potential benefits of AR in enhancing situational awareness and improving safety for pilots and passengers. AR technology can provide pilots with real-time information about their surroundings, such as weather conditions, traffic, and potential hazards (Dhief et al. 2022). This information can be overlaid in their field of view, allowing them to maintain a clear picture of their environment while keeping their attention focused on critical tasks. Moreover, the article identifies several key areas of future research that are crucial in realizing the full potential of AR technology in the aviation industry. These areas include the development of AR systems that are specifically tailored for aviation, the integration of AR with other safety measures such as automation and predictive analytics, and effective training methods for pilots and other aviation personnel.

Overall, the NSF article provided valuable insights into the potential of AR technology in enhancing safety in the aviation industry. The article highlighted the need for continued research and development in this area to ensure that AR technology is effectively integrated into aviation safety systems and that pilots and other aviation personnel are trained to use AR technology effectively and safely (Forbes, 2019).

References

Alarcon, R., et al.: Augmented reality for the enhancement of space product assurance and safety. Acta Astronaut. **168**, 191–199 (2020). https://doi.org/10.1016/J.ACTAASTRO.2019.10.020

Ancel, E., et al.: Design and Testing of an Approach to Automated In-Flight Safety Risk Management for sUAS Operations. AIAA Aviation 2022 Forum (2022). https://doi.org/10.2514/6.2022-3459

"Augmented reality." Merriam-Webster.com Dictionary, Merriam-Webster, https://www.merriam-webster.com/dictionary/augmented%20reality. (Accessed 18 Apr 2023)

Bałaj, B., et al.: Spatial disorientation cue effects on gaze behaviour in pilots and non-pilots. Cogn. Technol. Work. Technol. Work **21**(3), 473–486 (2018). https://doi.org/10.1007/s10111-018-0534-7

Blake, M.W.: The NASA advanced concepts flight simulator: a unique transport aircraft research environment. In: 1996 Flight Simulation Technologies Conference, pp. 385–392 (1996). https://doi.org/10.2514/6.1996-3518

Books Google Ngrams. https://books.google.com/ngrams/ (Accessed 10 July 2023)

Chapanis, A.: To communicate the human factors message, you have to know what the message is and how to communicate it. Hum. Factors Soc. Bull. **34**, 1–4 (1991)

CitNetExplorer. https://citespace.podia.com/ (Accessed 10 July 2023)

Dariusz, B.: Spatial disorientation simulator. Safety Defense **4**, 10–16 (2018). https://doi.org/10.37105/sd.3

Dhief, I., Alam, S., Lilith, N., Mean, C.C.: A machine-learned go-around prediction model using pilot-in-the-loop simulations. Trans. Res. Part C: Emerging Technol. **140** (2022). https://doi.org/10.1016/J.TRC.2022.103704

"Flight simulator." Merriam-Webster.com Dictionary, Merriam-Webster. https://www.merriam-webster.com/dictionary/flight%20simulator. (Accessed 18 Apr 2023)

Forbes, J.: National Science Foundation. "The Use of Augmented Reality for Aerospace Safety." Award Search: flight simulators (2019). https://www.nsf.gov/awardsearch/showAward?AWD_ID=1841563 (Accessed 01 May 2023)

Glinert, E.: National Science Foundation. "Collaborative Research: Advancing Simulations and Research on Optical and Radar Remote Sensing for Airborne Environmental Applications." Award Search: flight simulators, last modified December 3 (2003). https://www.nsf.gov/awardsearch/showAward?AWD_ID=0325074

Goetsch, D.L.: Chapter Twelve: in Occupational Safety and Health for Technologists, Engineers, and Managers. Pearson, 9th edn., p. 255 (2019)

Goetsch, D.L.: Chapter Four: Roles and Professional Certifications for Safety and Health Professionals", in Occupational Safety and Health for Technologists, Engineers, and Managers, Pearson, 9th edn. p. 59 (2019)

Gruner, D.: Development of a Virtual Reality Simulator for Training of Unmanned Aircraft Systems Pilots," National Science Foundation, Award Number: 1818519. https://www.nsf.gov/awardsearch/showAward?AWD_ID=1818519 (Accessed 1 May 2023)

Harzing.com: Publish or Perish. https://harzing.com/resources/publish-or-perish (Accessed 10 July 2023)

Iizuka, K., Takahashi, H., Kurosu, M.: Enhancing airline pilot training with virtual-reality simulators: a study of human-computer interaction. Interact. Comput. **31**(2), 205–217 (2019). https://doi.org/10.1093/iwc/iwz014

Li, W.-C., Chung-San, Y., Greaves, M., Braithwaite, G.: How cockpit design impacts pilots' attention distribution and perceived workload during aiming a stationary target. Procedia Manufact. **3**, 5663–5669 (2015). https://doi.org/10.1016/j.promfg.2015.07.781

Lib.purdue.edu. https://www.lib.purdue.edu/ (Accessed 10 July 2023)

Link.springer.com. https://link.springer.com/ (Accessed 10 July 2023)

Lofaro, R.J., Smith, K.M.: The aviation operational environment: Integrating a decision-making paradigm, flight simulator training, and an automated cockpit display for aviation safety. Technol. Eng. Manag. Aviation: Advanc. Dis. **241–282** (2011). https://doi.org/10.4018/978-1-60960-887-3.CH015

MaxQDA. https://www.maxqda.com/ (Accessed 10 July 2023)

Miller, J. D., Godfroy-Cooper, M., Wenzel, E.M.: Arsad: an augmented-reality spatial auditory display for obstacle avoidance during all phases of flight. In: Annual Forum Proceedings - AHS International, 2018-May (2018).

Minaskan, N., Alban-Dromoy, C., Pagani, A., Andre, J.-M., Stricker, D.: Human intelligent machine teaming in single pilot operation: a case study. In: Schmorrow, D.D., Fidopiastis, C.M. (eds.) Augmented Cognition: 16th International Conference, AC 2022, Held as Part of the 24th HCI International Conference, HCII 2022, Virtual Event, June 26 – July 1, 2022, Proceedings, pp. 348–360. Springer International Publishing, Cham (2022). https://doi.org/10.1007/978-3-031-05457-0_27

Mistry, K., Bhatt, M.: Augmented reality in aerospace: a review on flight simulation training. Int. J. Innovative Technol. Exploring Eng. 10(12), 1307–1312 (2021)

Moesl, B., Schaffernak, H., Vorraber, W., Braunstingl, R., Koglbauer, I.V.: Multimodal Augmented Reality Applications for Training of Traffic Procedures in Aviation. Multimodal Technol. Interact. 7(1) (2023). https://doi.org/10.3390/MTI7010003

National Science Foundation (NSF). https://www.nsf.gov/ (Accessed 10 July 2023)

Oberhauser, M., Dreyer, D.: A virtual reality flight simulator for human factors engineering. Cogn. Technol. Work 19(2–3), 263–277 (2017). https://doi.org/10.1007/s10111-017-0421-7

ResearchGate. https://www.researchgate.net/ (Accessed 10 July 2023)

Rigas, D., Boile, M.: Human Factors considerations for the design and evaluation of augmented reality applications in aviation. In: Proceedings of the Human Factors and Ergonomics Society Annual Meeting, vol. 63(1), 1655–1659 (2019). https://doi.org/10.1177/1071181319631468

Scite.ai. https://scite.ai/ (Accessed 10 July 2023)

Scopus. https://www.scopus.com/ (Accessed 10 July 2023)

Scholar.Google.com. https://scholar.google.com/ (Accessed 10 July 2023)

Şentürk, B., Çagiltay, N.E., Goul, E.B.: Augmented reality applications in aviation. J. Air Trans. Manag. 92, 102057 (2021). doi:https://doi.org/10.1016/j.jairtraman.2020.102057

The Web of Science Core Collection. https://www.webofscience.com/wos/woscc/basic-search (Accessed 10 July 2023)

VOSviewer. https://www.vosviewer.com/ (Accessed 10 July 2023)

Wise, J.A., David Hopkin, V.: Virtual flight simulation: a safe and effective training tool for pilots. J. Aviation/Aerospace Educ. Res. 28(1), 26–40 (2019). doi:https://doi.org/10.15394/jaaer.2019.1403

HCI in Automated Vehicles
and Intelligent Transportation

Guardian Angel – Using Lighting Drones to Improve Traffic Safety, Sense of Security, and Comfort for Cyclists

Anna-Sofia Alklind Taylor[1] (ID), Kajsa Nalin[1] (ID), Jesper Holgersson[1(✉)] (ID), Andreas Gising[2] (ID), Bruce Ferwerda[3] (ID), and Lei Chen[2] (ID)

[1] School of Informatics, University of Skövde, Skövde, Sweden
jesper.holgersson@his.se
[2] RISE Research Institutes of Sweden, Gothenburg, Sweden
[3] Department of Computer Science and Informatics, Jönköping University, Jönköping, Sweden

Abstract. Active mobility, such as biking, faces a common challenge in Swedish municipalities due to the lack of adequate lighting during the dark winter months. Insufficient lighting infrastructure hinders individuals from choosing bicycles, despite the presence of well-maintained bike paths and a willingness to cycle. To address this issue, a project has been undertaken in the Swedish municipality of Skara for an alternative lighting solution using drones. A series of tests have been conducted based on drone prototypes developed for the selected bike paths. Participants were invited to cycle in darkness illuminated by drone lighting and share their mobility preferences and perception. This paper summarizes the users' perception of drone lighting as an alternative to fixed lighting on bike paths, with a special focus on the impact on travel habits and the perceived sense of security and comfort. Most participants were regular cyclists who cited bad weather, time, and darkness as significant factors that deterred them from using bicycles more frequently, reducing their sense of security. With drone lighting, the participants appreciated the illumination's moonlight-like quality and its ability to enhance their sense of security by illuminating the surroundings. On the technology side, they gave feedback on reducing the drone's sound and addressing lighting stability issues. In summary, the test results showcase the potential of drone lighting as a viable alternative to traditional fixed lighting infrastructure, offering improved traffic safety, sense of security, and comfort. The results show the feasibility and effectiveness of this innovative approach, supporting transformation towards active and sustainable mobility, particularly in regions facing lighting challenges.

Keywords: Active mobility · Drone lighting · UX · Traffic safety · Perceived safety

1 Introduction

In the journey of mobility transformation to more active mobility, such as cycling and walking, a common challenge faced by most municipalities in Sweden is the

© The Author(s), under exclusive license to Springer Nature Switzerland AG 2023
V. G. Duffy et al. (Eds.): HCII 2023, LNCS 14057, pp. 209–223, 2023.
https://doi.org/10.1007/978-3-031-48047-8_13

long period of the year, where most hours of the day do not have proper day-light. If combined with a lacking lighting infrastructure, such conditions may be a barrier that prevents people from cycling after dark [12], even with good bike paths and a motivation to use the bicycle for traveling (e.g., to work). In the research project "Skara - Guardian Angel[1]", we use a bike path in the Swedish municipality of Skara as a test case for using drones instead of a fixed lighting infrastructure to provide lighting to its users. The project aims to develop an innovative and economically viable solution with drones for lighting bike paths and providing companion support to improve cycling safety, security, and com-fort, thus supporting changing travel habits toward sustainable mobility. As a major study topic, the project conducted user studies to analyze how cyclists perceive drones as a viable alternative to fixed lighting in terms of a perceived sense of safety, security, and comfort.

1.1   Background

Mobility is under transformation where active mobility, such as biking, is encour-aged for healthier and emission-free travel. However, despite the excellent bike paths that have been built, installing and maintaining lighting systems is expen-sive, and it may not be possible to have good lighting conditions on all bike paths, especially in rural areas. Under such circumstances, even if people prefer to take their bikes as much as possible, they may avoid riding in darkness. This may be because of the reduced safety and comfort in the darkness or the reduced perceived sense of security. To deal with this and support the travel behavior change to active mobility, a natural question is how to find economically viable solutions for bike path lighting. Besides, bicycle-related traffic accidents have become more significant in recent years, requiring potential infrastructure sup-port to improve cyclist safety. This project addresses those challenges and targets the needs of cyclists in the Nordic regions, especially in rural areas. Instead of investing in the traditional fixed lighting infrastructure, the project develops and tests on-demand infrastructure solutions that use drones to provide lighting and potentially more companion services to improve traffic safety, perceived sense of security, and comfort. The aim of this project is to analyze how cyclists perceive drones as a viable alternative to fixed lighting in terms of a perceived sense of safety, security, and comfort.

1.2   Related Research

To develop and test a successful drone-based lighting alternative, understanding cyclists is essential, and User Experience (UX) is thus one of four key factors the project bases its work on – along with trust, safety, and societal impact. In addition to being the foundation of the test study design, the four factors are also used to analyze the data collected from the tests. The work is loosely based on the

---

[1] https://www.ri.se/en/what-we-do/projects/on-demand-infrastructure-services-for-active-mobility.

USUS (abbreviation of: usability, social acceptance, user experience, and societal impact) evaluation framework for user-centered Human-Robot Interaction (HRI) that Weiss et al. [15] developed for the assessment of interaction scenarios with humanoid robots, with adaptations to suit the project's circumstances better. A description of the factors; *UX, trust, safety*, and *societal impact*, and how they relate to the four factors of the USUS evaluation framework are described as follows.

UX
The ISO definition of UX is "user's perceptions and responses that result from the use and/or anticipated use of a system, product, or service" [5]. This definition can encompass many aspects related to perception, and a useful description and distinction are made by Hassenzahl [4], who describes people's perceptions of interactive products as *pragmatic* or *hedonic*. Pragmatic is mainly product-focused, referring to more traditional usability aspects such as the perceived ability of the product in terms of making the interaction effective and efficient. Hedonic focuses on the person and how the product is perceived to support the person's emotional needs and desires. In this project, as for [4], the UX concept encompasses both pragmatic and hedonic aspects, meaning that usability is included in the UX concept. In contrast, Usability and UX were separate factors in the USUS evaluation framework.

Trust
The factor trust in this study concerns, for example, *perceived safety, perceived self-efficacy* [13,14], *attitude towards drones* [3,8], as well as *perceived visibility by others* [16]. The common trait of these aspects is that they relate to the cyclist's perceptions and emotions, specifically concerning perceived safety and the drone. In the USUS evaluation framework, several of these aspects were included in the *social acceptance factor*.

Safety
The safety factor concerns more practical aspects such as *drone predictability* [6], and traffic safety, e.g., (the cyclist's) *visibility of road and surroundings* along with *speed* and how the cyclist's speed can decrease safety.

Societal impact
As in the USUS evaluation framework [15], societal impact is an important factor, however, with a slightly different focus here: contributions towards a more sustainable society. The four first indicators of the societal impact factor relate to four of the UN's sustainable development goals [11]: The health aspect of *active mobility* (SDG 3), *sustainable travel habits* (SDG 11), increased *gender equality* (SDG 5), and improved *infrastructure* (SDG 9). The fifth indicator, *Traffic safety*, relates to Vision Zero[2].

Altogether, building on the four factors; UX, trust, safety, and societal impact, this study aims to analyze how users perceive drones as a viable alternative to fixed lighting infrastructure.

---

[2] https://bransch.trafikverket.se/en/startpage/operations/Operations-road/vision-zero-academy/This-is-Vision-Zero/.

2 Research Approach

The research approach started with developing a technical solution to allow test persons to experience a drone light solution in a realistic environment, followed by evaluating user experience via questionnaires, interviews, and observations. To be able to collect data in the early phases of development, we complemented the real-world environment tests with virtual reality (VR) environment tests.

2.1 Progress Outline

In 2022, the initial technical solution was developed where a commercial drone equipped with a spotlight that could follow a smartphone application utilizing global navigation satellite system (GNSS)[3]. During a first pilot test of the system in early spring 2022, one project member tested the solution, resulting in several improvements to the prototype and the test setup design. A 360-video was recorded in different light configurations during the pilot test, and this was later used in two focus groups, with a total of 13 participants, held during the summer of 2022.

Before recruiting participants to the focus groups, a questionnaire was created, and the link was distributed through different municipality channels, posters, and the network of the project team. The questions related to demographic data, current travel habits, preferences, motives for choosing a bicycle instead of, for example, a car, and motives for choosing another mode of transport before a bicycle, as well as questions on the sense of security and general thoughts on using drones in different situations. A total of 32 persons answered this questionnaire. However, since no questions were asked regarding the drone lighting solution, these answers have not influenced the continued development of the drone solution, nor have they been included in the results presented in this paper. The 13 focus group participants answered a variation of the questionnaire, but more importantly, they experienced the VR-video recording during the first pilot and answered questions related to this.

Feedback from the focus group interviews suggested, among other things, that the concept as such was interesting though the range of the enlightened area was too short and that a second drone simulating 'next light pole' would improve the experience. This feedback generated another technical iteration where a second drone was added to the solution. In November 2022, the improved drone solution was tested with two cooperative drones enlightening the bike path. Five test persons experienced the solution.

In February and March 2023, another 24 test persons experienced bicycling in the dark with the aid of two drones illuminating the bike path.

2.2 Test Setup

As mentioned, the study was conducted using a selected bike path in the Swedish rural municipality of Skara. The total length of the test track (back and forth)

---

[3] Satellite positioning often referred to as GPS.

is about one kilometer, and the test times were chosen to represent the typical darkness of Swedish winter. The tests were conducted in two periods from 2022-11-23 to 2022-11-24, and from 2023-02-27 to 2323-03-20. Figure 1 illustrates the test configuration and procedure. As described earlier, two drones were used to cover the lighting areas directly above the cyclists and further ahead. The drones were synchronized and followed the cyclist based on the position signals from a smartphone equipped with the test bicycle.

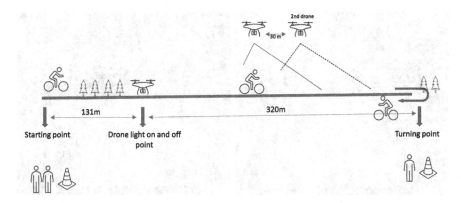

Fig. 1. Overview of the test track and procedure

Each test session was divided into three parts; a questionnaire, a test on the bike path, and an interview. The test sessions started at a conference hotel with the test participant filling out the same questionnaire as in the focus groups with questions relating to demographic data, current travel habits, preferences, motives for choosing a bicycle instead of, for example, a car, and motives for choosing another mode of transport before the bicycle, as well as questions on the sense of security and general thoughts on using drones in different situations.

After completing the questionnaire, the test participant was driven by car to the bike path where the drone test was to be conducted. The chosen location is far from other light sources and becomes very dark as the sun sets. The illumination of the city of Skara could be seen on the horizon, but other than that, there are no lights. The test participant was handed an electric bike, a helmet, and instructions to ride the bike along the bike path to a traffic cone placed around 450 m away from the starting point, then turn around and cycle back. Each test took about 5 min, around 30 s for preparations such as putting on the helmet, and about 4–5 min of biking.

In the test setup, the drones were waiting (spotlight turned off) for the cyclist to enter the flight area, approximately 130 m from the starting point at the end of an extra dark tree alley (i.e., *the drone light on and off point* in Fig. 1). The bicyclist started the journey through the tree alley, and after *the drone light on and off point*, each drone's light was turned on, and the drones started to follow the bicyclist to provide lighting. The 'above' drone reference position was 25 m above the cyclist, and the'ahead' drone reference was the same altitude but 30m ahead of the cyclist. As the test person reached the traffic cone, 450 m away from the starting point, the test person turned around, and the drones rearranged and followed the test person back. Finally, as the cyclist approached *the drone light on and off point* (see Fig. 1), the drones turned off the lighting one by one. After that, the test person continued through the tree alley back to the starting point. Figure 2 show the lighting conditions without and with the drone lights.

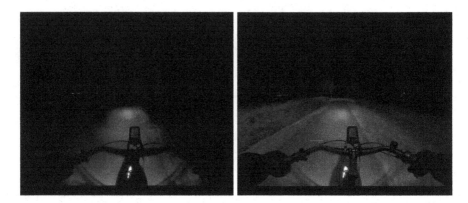

Fig. 2. Lighting conditions with bike lighting only (left) vs with also drone lighting (right)

After the bike path test, the test participant was driven back to the hotel where the interview was conducted. The interview explored the test person's perceptions of the drone lighting system, focusing on their sense of security, emotional comfort, thoughts of possible drawbacks, and improvements. When designing the interview guide, a semi-structured interview approach was chosen [9] since we wanted flexibility and balance between structure and openness. In doing so, we chose a small set of predefined questions focusing on the test person's sense of security, comfort, thoughts of possible drawbacks, and improvements. In addition, we asked questions for further clarification in specific areas of interest. For instance, when discussing possible improvements, some of the test persons discussed adjustments, e.g., the lighting. In contrast, others discussed a much broader view of possible future usage areas of drones and different business models for how to use lighting drones for other purposes when noting lighting up bike paths. The interviews were recorded and then transcribed before being analyzed by the research team. Data analysis was conducted using content analysis [2,7,10]. In its essence, content analysis yields "a relatively systematic and comprehensive summary or overview of the data set as a whole" [10, p. 182], by observing repeating themes and categorizing them using a coding system that is developed inductively during the coding process. The coding process was not entirely inductive since we, in advance had identified the four factors: UX, trust, safety, and societal impact. However, when analysing the factors, several themes within each factor were identified by the research team. For example, when analysing the trust factor (i.e., the test persons' perception or feeling that the lighting drones are reliable and safe for cycling during dark conditions), we found several themes. These themes are hereafter called indicators and include, for example, attitudes toward drones and perceived self-efficacy.

3   Results and Analysis

A total of 29 participants participated in the tests, 5 in November 2022 and 24 in February/March 2023. Of these, 20 identify as men (69%) and 9 as women (31%). Most of them (93%) were between 26 and 66+ years of age. One was under 18 and one was between 19 and 25 years. The majority of the participants go cycling often, and most use their bike primarily for errands and commuting. The most common reasons for *not* taking the bike are weather and time (around 67% each), with 37% indicating darkness as a reason, and only 19% indicating uncertainty or worry about safety issues. Most of the participants are positive towards delivery drones (93% positive, 0% neutral, 7% negative), whereas there is greater division when it comes to surveillance drones, though still mainly positive attitudes (62% positive, 20% neutral, 17% negative).

In the following sections, we describe our findings based on the four factors UX, trust, safety, and societal impact. It should be noted that the indicators found for each factor do overlap, and should, therefore, not be interpreted as exclusive. All quotes used in the results and analysis have been translated from Swedish into English by the research team.

3.1   User Experience

In the context of the current project, UX is the cyclists' perceptions and responses that result from the use and/or anticipated use of lighting drones. The initial analysis of the cyclists' UX was based on traditional usability goals, such as effectiveness and efficiency, but the analysis also revealed a number of other indicators related to UX. The following five indicators were identified: 1) effectiveness, 2) efficiency, 3) spatiality and embodiment, 4) flexibility, and 5) emotion.

In this context, *effectiveness* refers to the accuracy and completeness with which the cyclist can see the bike path and its surroundings using drone lighting. Data from the early focus groups showed that some people prioritized clear sight far ahead, while others emphasized the necessity of being able to see well to the sides of the path. We decided that both viewpoints were equally valid; by seeing far ahead, the cyclist can anticipate bike path turns and potential dangers, and by having a fair perception of the side of the path, they can spot any dangers lurking there. Thus, the prototype was adapted to include two drones, one that lights up a bit ahead of the cyclist and one that lights up the cyclist and their close surroundings. During the early pilot test, we also found that the height by which the drones are flying affects the effectiveness of the lighting. If the drones fly at a low altitude (approximately 15 m above ground), the cyclist experiences the light as too bright, negatively affecting their night vision. The lighting was described as being under a spotlight, where everything outside the cone of light became very dark. By flying the drones at a higher altitude (ca. 25 m above ground), the light is more dispersed and, thus, does not affect night vision as much. Three participants from the tests independently described the experience as "cycling under a full moon", and none mentioned feeling as if being under a spotlight or being blinded by the lights.

Efficiency, in this context, refers to, for instance, the drones' responsiveness to the cyclist's movement. For the cyclist to ride at their own pace and to maintain clear sight even when turning, slowing down, speeding up, or stopping, the drones have to sense the cyclist's location in real-time. In the prototype, we used the GPS signal from a smartphone placed on the bike (or the cyclist) to track the cyclist's movement. In the tests, the participants did not mention any negative experiences with the drones' responsiveness except for a few comments regarding the feeling that the drones "wobbled" a bit when the cyclist did the 180-degree turn on the test track. This was improved in a later version of the prototype. All in all, efficiency was deemed satisfactory.

Spatiality and embodiment have to do with the relationship between our bodies and the (physical) space in which we are moving. In this case, the cyclist moves through a dark area and must feel that the movement forward is safe and predictable. However, one participant points out that moving on a bike differs from walking in the same space. Were they to walk, they would have liked to have the bike path behind them well lit too: "On the other hand, I turned my head a few times because I wanted to look back, but then it's pitch black there, so when you're cycling it's okay that it's like that. But if I were to walk, if we say that I'm walking, I'd like to have the rear [light] turned on as well". Thus, understanding how users move their bodies to the physical space is essential to how and where to direct the light.

Flexibility is an indicator that emerged during the analysis of the interviews. Although the focus of the project was on lighting for cyclists, several participants suggested further uses of the drones, indicating that flexibility was an important aspect of the final solution. For instance, one participant mentioned they would like to use the lighting drones for walks, not just cycling. Similarly, another participant wanted lighting drones to be able to go skiing off-track in the winter. Yet, another said "I envision future expansions of [the drone lighting system] how it can be applied to other areas. I have been involved in searching for people in [the volunteer organisation] Missing People. A bunch of drones would make a difference". Several participants also brought up new features that would increase the drones' usefulness during cycling, such as recording the cyclist or keeping track of their position. One participant said "What I was thinking before, if I should change my travel behavior and start cycling more and do it in the dark. That's how I feel anyway. Would I ride my bike out there by myself anyway and be illuminated so that people from far away could see me riding by myself. It would still create a slightly insecure feeling for me. That was it, in case someone was filming or who knew that I was there. Some such a function possibly. So that you know that the drone is my little bodyguard here".

Emotion is a broad indicator that refers to the emotional experience of cycling with lightning drones. Some emotions have already been mentioned, such as feeling as if cycling under a full moon or thinking of the drone as a bodyguard or guardian angel. A more direct emotional response was observed during one of the tests, where one of the participants let out a loud squeal of joy as the drone lights turned on. Most participants expressed positive feelings towards the drone lighting, with varying degrees of excitement. None expressed negative feelings towards the drone lighting specifically, although some did not like the sound that the drones made. It should be noted, however, that some participants found the sound neutral or reassuring. For instance, one participant mentioned during the interview that they felt more safe hearing the drones, knowing that they were there.

3.2   Trust

Trust is about the user's perception or feeling that the lighting drones are reliable and safe for cycling during dark conditions. When analyzing this dimension, five indicators have been identified: 1) perceived safety, 2) perceived self-efficacy, 3) attitudes towards drones, 4) perceived visibility by others, and 5) reliability.

Perceived safety is about how the test persons perceived a sense of control when cycling. The general perception among the test persons was that if compared to a standard bike light, the drone light was way much better. The drone light offered an overview that cannot be accomplished with a standard bike light or fixed lighting infrastructure. Not least, a better wide-angle is highlighted by the test persons as an important promoter for perceived safety, as the following quotes exemplify: "You feel safe when you have the wide-angle view," and "It feels much safer when you can see around you."

Perceived self-efficacy is a factor that emerged during the analysis. High perceived self-efficacy occurs when cyclists feel they are in control of the situation and believe they can reach their goals [1]. However, if they lack self-efficacy, it can result in low perceived ease-of-use, anxiety, and mistrust in the system [13]. As we did not specifically measure participants' perceived self-efficacy, we have to rely on observational data. One observation we made was among some of the older women in our study. As we were transporting them to the bike path, they expressed worry about cycling in the dark since they normally only cycle during daytime. We observed a noticeable change in the way that they talked about cycling after the test, with more confidence and optimism. Since this was observed during transport to and from the bike path, no quotes were recorded to assess this change properly. Thus, these results are speculative, but perceived self-efficacy seems to us to be relevant as an indicator of trust.

Attitudes towards drones is about the test persons' general attitudes towards using drones for various purposes. Among the test persons, there was a generally positive attitude towards using drones, e.g., last-mile goods deliveries, filming, or photographing objects. One test person with a military background was a bit more explicit regarding this matter than most other test persons and pointed out that there are always pros and cons when using drones and that there are aspects that need to be taken into consideration and carefully analyzed, such as what will happen if someone bicycles close to a military-protected object, or other possible scenarios where drones are not permitted to fly, or when personal integrity aspects come into play.

Perceived visibility by others concerns the test persons' perception of their visibility by others, e.g., other cyclists, pedestrians, or car drivers. In general, the test persons perceived their visibility as positive because they were seen from a relatively long range by others when lit up by the drones.

Reliability relates to the test persons' perception of how reliable the drone is and to what extent the drone behaves as expected by the test persons. Whereas most test persons only have positive experiences, some test persons pointed out that the synchronization between the two drones and the cyclist could be improved in the sense that if the speed of the cyclist changed, for example, through a sudden break or acceleration, the drones had a slight delay for some of the test persons. Another aspect discussed among a few of the test persons was the technical performance of the drones, such as the somewhat limited battery capacity that most conventional drones suffer from.

3.3 Safety

Safety concerns the test persons' perception of the level of traffic safety obtained when using lighting drones for cycling during dark conditions, i.e., how the test persons perceive the usage of lighting drones to prevent accidents and possible injuries when cycling during the dark. When analyzing this dimension, three indicators have been identified: 1) Predictability, 2) Visibility of road and surroundings, and 3) (travel) Speed.

Predictability concerns to what extent the test persons perceive they can foresee possible upcoming happenings when cycling, i.e., pedestrians, animals, or physical objects. The test persons pointed out that with the light from the drones, the likelihood of seeing things and having the possibility to react to unexpected events in time was excellent. In addition, the test persons also pointed out that the drone light resulted in fewer shadows and dark spots, increasing visibility and predictability. The following quotes from the test persons serve as illustrating examples of such predictability: "It was as cycling under the full moon" and "It was beyond expectations. It felt as safe as when cycling during the day".

Visibility of road and surroundings is about the test persons' perception of how well they could see the bike path and the surroundings when bicycling. The test persons were very much in agreement that the drone lighting provided good visibility. Not least, the usage of two drones with a combined light was pointed out as very positive since it was easy to see the bike path ahead simultaneously with seeing to the side of the bike path close to the test persons. We use the following quotes as examples: "Not as daylight but very close" and "If there had come an animal from the side, there would have been no problem seeing it".

Speed concerns to what extent the perceived safety affects the speed of the test persons, i.e., how fast they dare to go concerning perceived control and visibility of the bike path and the surroundings. During the tests, none of the test persons exhibited any concerns about limited speed. This comes as no surprise since the test persons perceived the light provided by the drones as satisfactory.

3.4   Societal Impact

The societal impact is defined by the effect of an activity on a community [15]. In the context of the current study, we have defined the societal impact as the effect of drone lighting on the activities of cyclists in rural areas, particularly concerning the UN's sustainable development goals (SDG) [11] and Vision Zero. The SDGs addressed in this study are the health aspects of active mobility (SDG 3), increased gender equality (SDG 5), improved infrastructure (SDG 9), and sustainable travel habits (SDG 11), as well as contributions towards traffic Safety and Vision Zero. When analyzing this dimension further, five indicators were identified: 1) active mobility, 2) sustainable travel habits, 3) gender equality, 4) infrastructure, and 5) traffic safety. The first four indicators relate to SDGs and the fifth to Vision Zero, which is indicated through mentioning the related SDG or Vision Zero in the text below.

The health aspect of *active mobility (SDG 3)* refers to the promotion of healthy lives and well-being by supporting behavior changes toward active mobility. Within this study, we looked at how drone lighting in rural areas can be realized in a way that is accessible for all users so that a healthier lifestyle can be adopted during darkness. As discussed by the test persons, the usage of drone lightning will have a positive impact on their willingness and motivation to cycle also during the darker periods of the year since the improved lighting conditions are perceived as nearly similar to cycle in daylight. By providing drone lighting, overall safety can be improved in dark areas, such as better visibility of the roads and surroundings. Thereby, the overall cycling behaviors can be sustained even during the darker periods of the year. The outcomes contribute to SDG 3 to reduce traffic accidents as well as health risks.

Sustainable travel habits (SDG 11) refers to fostering of sustainable travel habits by providing access to safe, inclusive, affordable, accessible and sustainable transport systems for all, with special attention to the needs of those in vulnerable situations, women, children, persons with disabilities and older persons. The project targets the mobility needs in the Nordic rural areas and investigates on-demand infrastructure solutions to support the sustainable mobility mode, that is active mobility. The results provide insights and experiences for municipalities to understand the mobility needs, and challenges and provide the necessary support for changing travel habits.

Increased *gender equality (SDG 5)* refers to the equality of all genders through the empowerment of vulnerable groups. By facilitating lighting in rural areas that are experiencing excessive darkness, we have aimed to address the vulnerability of certain communities. As observed during the tests, we observed a notable change among women regarding cycling in darkness after participating in the test. Before the test, several women were reluctant to cycle during dark conditions. After the test, they exhibited a higher level of self-confidence and optimism about using the bike also during darkness.

Improved *infrastructure (SDG 9)* refers to the promotion of sustainable cities and society. The focus of this study is to increase the accessibility of rural areas that experience excessive darkness. By providing drone lighting, we can attempt to improve the current cycling infrastructure within societies. Based on the results from the analysis, we can conclude that using drones as an alternative to fixed light infrastructures may be an essential asset, not at least for smaller municipalities with limited budgets. The proof of feasibility, as well as the test persons' experiences, support the introduction of drones for municipality services, which contributes to the rapid development of drone-based infrastructure introduction.

Improved *traffic safety (Vision Zero)* refers to the goal of reducing traffic incidents. Vision Zero states that no human should be killed or seriously injured in traffic-related incidents. By providing improved lighting both ahead of the cyclist and to the sides, the cyclists' opportunity to see other cyclists or obstacles is enhanced. This, together with the increased visibility of the person cycling, contributes towards Vision Zero.

3.5 Summary

After summarizing the 29 interviews on using drones for lighting during cycling, it can be concluded that most of the test persons felt safe and comfortable with the light provided by the drones. The test persons noted that the light was sufficiently strong and broad, and the distribution of light was effective in enhancing visibility during the bike ride. There was agreement among the test persons that the drones were stable, although some jerky movements were observed, suggesting that using two drones during curvy cycling routes would be preferable. Some of the test persons also mentioned that they found it enjoyable to see the drone and that the sound it produced but rather comforting.

The four key factors (UX, Trust, Safety, and Societal impact) the project is based on were all found to be positively acknowledged throughout the results, and during analysis, several new indicators emerged to give more insight into each of the factors. The factors and their respective indicators that we identified in the study are summarized in Table 1.

Regarding potential improvements for drone lighting, some interviewees suggested enhancing the drone's stability during curvy cycling routes or when speed is changed. Others had no suggestions for improvements, as they felt the lighting was well-balanced and sufficient. One of the test persons expressed curiosity about the battery life of the drones and their potential application in search and rescue operations for missing individuals. In one of the interviews, the need for better lighting to enhance safety in rural areas and urban settings was discussed. It was also acknowledged that it may not always be feasible or desirable to have lighting everywhere. Overall, the interviewees exhibited a positive attitude towards using drones for lighting during cycling and believed it could contribute to a safer and more comfortable biking experience in darkness.

Table 1. Summary of the factors and indicators identified in the study.

Factors	Indicators
UX	Effectiveness Efficiency Spatiality and embodiment Flexibility Emotion
Trust	Perceived safety Perceived self-efficacy Attitudes towards drones Perceived visibility by others Reliability
Safety	Predictability Visibility of road and surroundings Speed
Societal impact	Active mobility (health) Sustainable travel habits Gender equality Infrastructure Traffic safety

4   Conclusions and Future Work

To tackle the common challenge of long and dark winters in Nordic countries and to support behavior changes towards sustainable travel, this study presented an innovative drone-based bike path lighting solution and the user study results. As summarised in the results and analysis, the tests, accompanied by the collected data, show that using lighting drones as a flexible alternative to a fixed lighting infrastructure is indeed a promising alternative. The unanimous positive response from the test persons shows that lighting drones provide good UX, can be trusted, promote traffic safety, and have a positive societal impact on many aspects. The study demonstrates the feasibility of using drones for rural bike path lighting, providing a potentially cost-efficient alternative to lighting infrastructure. The positive feedback indicates a potential high-level of acceptance and the solution contribution to support behavior changes towards sustainable travel, especially in rural areas.

Despite the positive results, we have just scraped the surface of this innovation project, and many research initiatives are left to be thoroughly investigated. It should also be noted that the test participants represent a selection of the Swedish population who already use their bikes quite frequently. Most of them were also interested in or curious about technology, which likely skewed the results toward a more positive attitude toward our solution. It would be beneficial to study how people who never or rarely cycle react to it since part of the project aimed to increase sustainable and emission-free transportation. Nonetheless, raising awareness among people in this group and recruiting them for future studies requires innovative activities.

The tests have been designed on the vision that drones are unpiloted and unmanned aerial vehicles (UAVs). During the tests, we had to simulate this setting by having a pilot ready to take control of the drone at any second, i.e. we didn't have a real UAV, simply because it is not legally permitted in Sweden. Future research on how civilian UAVs can be used and how legislation should be adjusted to fit the needs must be performed to make it realizable to continue with more extensive tests of lighting drones. The testing will be carried out in accordance with the development of harmonized drone operations in the European Union.

In addition, UAV technology must be improved regarding increased reach and working capacity. As for now, the drones used in the test had very limited battery capacity that has to be improved dramatically. This is an aspect discussed among the test persons. They would like to use drones for longer rides or other purposes where light is required, such as cross-country skiing. Still, they also were aware of the limited battery capacity of today's commercial UAVs. This leads to the interesting topic of infrastructure planning, including questions about where to place the drone and the charging infrastructures and how to schedule the drone usage based on battery levels.

Another interesting future research area that is strongly correlated to the HCI research field is how a user should be able to order and use a lighting drone. The most likely approach is for the user to use a smartphone app to order, control, and release a drone when not needed anymore. However, numerous aspects need to be considered to make this a positive UX experience. One such aspect is the issue of privacy. While having a drone as a guarding angel could increase cyclists' sense of safety, it could also intrude on their privacy. In addition, business model aspects must be carefully researched, i.e., if so, how much users should pay for lighting drones or if such a service would be free.

Acknowledgment. The study is supported by the Swedish innovation agency Vinnova through the project "Skara Guardian Angel - On-demand infrastructure services for active mobility" with project number 2021-03044. The authors thank the municipality of Skara for providing support on the test site selection and preparation as well as test participants recruiting; and the test participants for spending their time sharing their experiences and opinions for improving rural mobility. We especially want to thank Maria Nordström (Skara Municipality), Henrik Svensson (University of Skövde), Mahdere DW Amanuel (RISE), Kristoffer Bergman (RISE) and Rasmus Lundqvist (RISE).

References

1. Bandura, A.: Self-Efficacy: The Exercise of Control. W. H. Freeman, New York (1997)
2. Berelson, B.: Content Analysis in Communication Research. Free Press (1952)
3. Çetin, E., Cano, A., Deransy, R., Tres, S., Barrado, C.: Implementing mitigations for improving societal acceptance of urban air mobility. Drones **6**(2), 28 (2022)
4. Hassenzahl, M.: The hedonic/pragmatic model of user experience. In: Law, E., Vermeeren, A., Hassenzahl, M., Blythe, M. (eds.) Towards a UX Manifesto, vol. 10, pp. 10–14. Cost, Lancaster, UK (2007)
5. ISO: Ergonomics of human-system interaction - Part 11: Usability: Definitions and concepts (2018)
6. Kim, H.Y., Kim, B., Kim, J.: The naughty drone: a qualitative research on drone as companion device. In: Proceedings of the 10th International Conference on Ubiquitous Information Management and Communication, pp. 1–6. Association for Computing Machinery, New York (2016)
7. Krippendorff, K.: Reliability in content analysis: some common misconceptions and recommendations. Hum. Commun. Res. **30**(3), 411–433 (2004)
8. Oksman, V., Kulju, M.: Nordic study on public acceptance of autonomous drones. In: Stephanidis, C., Antona, M., Ntoa, S., Salvendy, G. (eds.) HCII 2022. LNCS, vol. 1655, pp. 532–539. Springer, Cham (2022). https://doi.org/10.1007/978-3-031-19682-9_67
9. Patton, M.Q.: Qualitative Evaluation and Research Methods, 2nd edn. Sage, Newbury Park (1990)
10. Silverman, D.: Interpreting Qualitative Data: Methods for Analysing Talk, Text and Interaction. Sage, London (2001)
11. UN General Assembly: Transforming our world: the 2030 Agenda for Sustainable Development, 21 October 2015, A/RES/70/1. https://www.refworld.org/docid/57b6e3e44.html. Accessed 9 June 2023
12. Uttley, J., Fotios, S., Robbins, C.J., Moscoso, C.: The effect of changes in light level on the numbers of cyclists. Light. Res. Technol. (2023)
13. Venkatesh, V.: Determinants of perceived ease of use: integrating control, intrinsic motivation, and emotion into the technology acceptance model. Inf. Syst. Res. **11**(4), 342–365 (2000)
14. Venkatesh, V., Morris, M.G., Davis, G.B., Davis, F.D.: User acceptance of information technology: toward a unified view. MIS Q. 425–478 (2003)
15. Weiss, A., Bernhaupt, R., Tscheligi, M.: The USUS evaluation framework for user-centered HRI. In: New Frontiers in Human-Robot Interaction, vol. 2, pp. 89–110 (2011)
16. Wood, J.M., Lacherez, P.F., Marszalek, R.P., King, M.J.: Drivers' and cyclists' experiences of sharing the road: incidents, attitudes and perceptions of visibility. Accid. Anal. Prev. **41**(4), 772–776 (2009)

Development of Urban Air Mobility (UAM) Vehicles for Ease of Operation

Vernol Battiste[1]([✉]) and Thomas Z. Strybel[2]

[1] San Jose State University Research Foundation, NASA Ames Research Center, Moffett Field, CA 94035, USA
vernol.battiste@nasa.gov
[2] Department of Psychology, California State University, Long Beasch, 1250 Bellflower Blvd., Long Beach, CA 90840, USA

Abstract. To date the air transportation system has been developed with the incremental introduction of new technology and with highly experienced air transport pilots and air traffic controllers overseeing flight operations. Thus, we currently have one of the safest commercial aviation systems in the world. General Aviation (GA) in the United States, however, has not always followed the same cautious and monitored approach to implementation; consequently, the GA safety record does not meet the high standards of commercial aviation. Recently, a new system known as Urban Air Mobility (UAM), is attracting considerable interest and investment from industry and government agencies. UAM refers to a system of passenger and small-cargo air transportation vehicles within an urban area with the goal of reducing the number of times we need to use our cars, thus improving urban traffic by moving people and cargo from crowded single passenger vehicles on our roads to personal and on-demand air vehicles. These UAM vehicles will be small and based on electric, Vertical-Take-Off-and-Landing (eVTOL) systems. A significant component of UAM is offloading of flight-management responsibilities from human pilots to newly-developed autonomy. Currently, over 100 UAM vehicles are either in development or production. Most, if not all, have a goal of fully autonomous vehicle operations, but fully autonomous flying vehicles are not expected in the near future. Therefore, we are developing concepts for UAM vehicles that will be easy to fly and/or manage by operators with minimal pilot training. In this paper we will discuss our human-automation teaming approach to develop an easy-to-operate VTOL aircraft, and some of the fly-by-wire technology needed to stabilize the vehicle so that a simple ecological mental model of the flying task can be implemented. We will discuss the requirements for a stability augmentation system that must be developed to support our simple pilot input model, and also present design guidelines and requirements based on a pilot input and management model. Finally, our approach to vehicle development will involve considerable operator testing and evaluation: improving pilot model, inceptors, displays and also work on a plan for how a UAM vehicle can be integrated with terminal area air traffic control airspace with minimal impact on controller workload.

Keywords: Urban Air Mobility · eVTOL · Stability Augmentation

This is a U.S. government work and not under copyright protection in the U.S.; foreign copyright protection may apply 2023
V. G. Duffy et al. (Eds.): HCII 2023, LNCS 14057, pp. 224–236, 2023.
https://doi.org/10.1007/978-3-031-48047-8_14

1 Why UAM?

A pressing issue in global ground transportation is traffic congestion in major metropolitan areas. In modern cities and suburbs drivers today spend hours in traffic during short trips. A global traffic scorecard published by INRIX in 2018 [1] showed that five of the most congested cities in the world are located in the United States. Also, according to INRIX, Los Angeles is the most congested city and drivers in Los Angeles spent an average of 102 h annually in traffic jams during peak congestion hours, costing drivers $2,828 each and the city $19.2 billion from direct and indirect costs. Direct costs relate to the value of fuel and time wasted, and indirect costs refer to freight and business fees from company vehicles idling in traffic. Those fees are then passed on to households through higher prices.

The congestion data provides a view into each city's unique set of transportation problems and how they might be solved, or made worse, with technology and new forms of transportation such as ride-hailing, car-sharing, and eventually autonomous vehicles, both ground and air. Urban Air Mobility (UAM) is a term used to describe a system that enables on-demand, highly automated, passenger or cargo-carrying air transportation services within and around a metropolitan environment. It is expected that UAM vehicles will utilize electric vertical takeoff/landing (e-VTOL) procedures, fly at relatively low altitudes and require very high degrees of automation, up to and including full automation (self-piloted).

1.1 Current and Proposed UAM Areas of Operations

In the latest survey of UAM operations, UAM systems are now operational in no less than 64 towns and cities globally. UAM airspace has recorded the launch of operational and research programs around the world. Below are four examples, most notability is the program in Iceland [2].

AHA and Flytrex Reykjavik, Iceland
AHA and Flytrex have become the world leaders in UAM. The companies fly 13 routes, making deliveries to public pickup areas and backyards across Reykjavik. In 2015, AHA, one of Iceland's largest eCommerce companies, contracted with Flytrex, an Israeli company, to develop a global positioning system tracker and logistics system to support its drone delivery service concept. Their drones were not fitted with any sensors for traffic avoidance, cameras, radar or any vision systems. The drone flies a GPS coordinate path along routes certified clear of obstacles from where the food is prepared to their delivery location. Using the drone delivery service reduces delivery time from 25 min by road, to 4 min by air. AHA received the go ahead for the delivery operation from the Icelandic authorities in 2018. AHA's drone delivery approach would not be approved in most parts of the world and seems to violate the FAA's beyond visual line of sight rules for drone operation [3].

Airbus Singapore, Malaysia
Airbus recently signed an agreement with Civil Aviation Authority of Singapore (CAAS) to continue testing its Skyway air traffic manage (ATM) concept that uses autonomous

technology to deliver 3D parts to ships docked in Singapore, and to deliver packages to a parcel station network on the campus of Singapore University. Through this network users will be able to send and receive important or urgent items, such as documents or small parcels. According to the Airbus "Wayfinder" Project Lead, the shift from automation to autonomy is not an all or none thing, but a tailored combination of humans and machines evolving over time to maintain or improve required levels of safety. Similar to the Boeing philosophy (see 2.0 Automation and Aviation Safety), systems are being managed by automation which allow the pilot to focus on dynamic situation assessment and decision making [4].

Tokyo Japan
In Japan, Bell is partnering with Japan Airlines and Sumitomo, a global conglomerate with businesses in aerospace, transportation, construction and more. The group plans to use their individual business portfolios to support the development of the necessary infrastructure and business use cases for air mobility in Japan. In addition to building the aircraft, Bell is building the digital infrastructure to support the operation, maintenance and booking of air taxi services through its AerOS UAS Traffic Management (UTM) services. Since Japan does not allow individually-owned ride-sharing services, they expect to partner with taxi companies. These partnerships offer a great opportunity to move UAM from concept to implementation [2].

Uber USA
Bell is also one of Uber's many partners in the Elevate UAM Ecosystem concept that plans to bring airborne ride-sharing to Los Angeles, Dallas and Melbourne by 2023, with plans to later expand into Uber's global ridesharing network [2].

1.2   UAM Vehicle Design and Assumptions About Autonomy

Even though the talk of the UAM industry has been on the development of autonomous ridesharing and package delivery vehicles, all systems currently being developed to support these operations are expected to have either a ground or an onboard pilot. However, unlike ridesharing drivers who own and are licensed to operate their own vehicles, future UAM rideshare or ground pilots will need significant training to become certified for urban mobility operations. Given the pilot shortage forecasted by Boeing and the considerable time needed to train commercial pilots, we need to develop different approaches to shorten the training time to certification. One approach that our group is working on that was postulated by Goodrich and Schutte [5] was to reduce the complexity of the flying task. In the next section we will describe our human-centered model for controlling the aircraft and its implementation in our Cave Virtual Reality simulator.

2   Automation and Aviation Safety

The safety record of the U.S. commercial aircraft fleet has seen a steady improvement in safety with the incremental introduction of flight deck automation. With increased automation we have seen improvements in both economics and flight efficiency. Automation has allowed airlines to reduce the number of flight-crew-members and to improve all weather operations. According to Stoll from Boeing Commercial, during his presentation at a 1988 NASA/FAA/Industry workshop on Flight Deck Automation, there is no question that the reduction in human error rates and thus improvements in flight safety, are due in part to the introduction of automation on the flight deck [6]. The consensus of the workshop participants was that automation along with crew resources management improved systems' overall efficiency and reduces errors in the aggregate. Stoll, who presented Boeing's philosophy for transport automation, reported that Boeing follows a very straightforward approach to automation; simplicity first, followed by redundancy then finally automation. Norman [6] chaired the workshop and presented a number of examples of how automation and simplicity were used to reduce human error. One example that stood out was the automating of system functions necessary to fire wall the engines (advance throttles to max power) during go-around. After simplifying and automating subsystems, the pilots only needed to advance the throttles to full power during this critical phase of flight. Another member of the workshop, John Miller from Douglas Aircraft, emphasized the role of the pilot in any decision to automate functions on transport aircraft. Miller reported that Douglas' philosophy was that any irrevocable action required a manual pilot input. Both manufacturers' (Boeing and Douglas) design philosophies emphasize that the pilot should primarily be responsible for flying the aircraft, and that a minimum number of crew procedures will facilitate this philosophy.

Over the years Boeing has followed the automation philosophy outlined above except on their recent introduction of the maneuvering characteristics augmentation system (MCAS) in the 737 Max which has been blamed for two crashes in 2018 and 2019 [7]. Despite a few exceptions like this one, the aviation system has seen steady improvement in safety and efficiency.

Automation such as FMS, EICAS, and ECAM, has contributed to the reduction in the number of manual tasks performed by flight crews: increasing passenger comfort, improving flight path controls and expanding operations under reducing weather minimums. Automation has also played a central role in reducing the number of repetitive tasks, which humans are ill-suited for, through its ability to perform these tasks precisely when needed. For example, one of the many jobs of the flight engineer was to maintain cabin temperature; for the communication officer one task was position reporting during a trip. These tasks and jobs were eliminated by automation. Good automation has aided in reducing pilots' workload, freeing attentional resources to focus on other higher-level tasks. On the flipside, poorly designed automation has been shown to reduce pilots' situational awareness, particularly as it relates to monitoring and data entry, which places additional load on the pilot and may increase workload. Automation can be a real problem when misunderstood or misused; in the case of MCAS, automation could get the aircraft into undesirable states from which it is impossible to recover, when the pilot is hand-flying the aircraft.

2.1 Automation Philosophies

Woods [6] who also participated in the workshop, identified two automation philosophies: Human-centered and automation-centered. In his discussion of automation-centered technology, the human is a sub-component or an interchangeable part of the system, and the human or system agent can be substituted for one another without adverse impact on the system. On the other hand, for human-centered automation, Woods identified three important factors that make the automation human-centered. First the human must have the locus of control: 1) effective authority and responsibility, 2) control of the machine resources – ability to change or direct lower order machine agents, and 3) the automation should always provide support to the human – avoid cases where the system forces fully automated or fully manual operation. Second, the general role of the human is to supervise or monitor the activities of lower order processes. This role requires greater situation awareness to support situation assessment which allows the human to track the machine's state and to predict future states. Third, the automation should support the human's role in error detection and mitigation.

2.2 Function Allocation

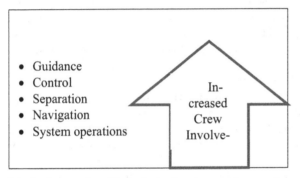

Miller and Stroll [6] also presented a chart similar to the one below which illustrates their automation philosophy by pilot function allocation. They postulated that subsystem management should be most amenable to automation because of the highly procedural nature of these tasks. Their philosophy also suggests that guidance and control would be the least amenable and should remain with the pilot because of the dynamic nature of these tasks (Fig. 1).

Fig. 1. Automation philosophy by function: guidance and control will be the most difficult to automate.

Although, most of the discussion about urban air mobility (UAM) has centered on autonomous-vehicle operations in urban environments, which will be discussed more later (see 4.0 UAM Vehicle Design and Assumptions about Autonomy), we should make clear the meaning of full autonomy. We should first define what we mean by autonomous flight operations, since we tend to use the terms "highly automated" and "autonomous" interchangeably. Lacher, Grabowski and Cook [8] in their paper on autonomy and trust in transportation, state, "autonomous systems decide for themselves what to do and when to do it." Given this definition we can easily distinguish between a highly automated and an autonomous system. For example, many describe Global Hawk UAV flights as autonomous because after takeoff it can conduct a flight without interacting with a ground operator. More appropriately, the Global Hawk should be thought of as fully automated, given that it follows a pre-scripted mission plan, but cannot change its mission plan based on unanticipated changes in the aircraft or environment. We will use the term autonomous to mean a vehicle that requires no human interaction. Goodrich and Schutte [5] provided an assessment of the state of the art on autonomous vehicles from knowledgeable demonstration passengers who reported that while the technology was impressive, it had a long way to go before it achieved widespread public use.

Given the state of the art in autonomous vehicle technologies, most companies are resigned to the fact that UAM vehicles will need onboard or ground pilots for the foreseeable future. This factor presents an additional challenge to UAM implementation in the near term: the availability of appropriately trained UAM pilots.

3 Pilot Shortage

According to Boeing, the aviation industry will need 804,000 new airline pilots worldwide between now and 2038 based on their aviation forecast [9]. This shortage will be due to fleet growth, retirement and attrition. This 20-year forecast shortage is based on the demand for commercial aviation aircraft with over 30 seats, business jets and commercial helicopter pilots. The shortage does not include the demand for UAM pilots over the same period. And since the projections for a fully autonomous UAM vehicle is not expected until ~ 2034 at the earliest, according to some estimates, it should be. Therefore, the success of UAM will depend on the success of recruitment and training efforts, combined with designing UAM vehicles that are easy to fly.

3.1 Time and Expense to Training Commercial Pilot

The cost to earn a pilot license can range between $5K dollars and $16K, and require ~60 h of flight time, depending on the school that you attend and the type of license you want to earn. Typically, a student starts with the private pilot license. To obtain a private pilot's license requires knowledge, skills and risk management in pre/post flight planning, airport operations, slow flight and stalls, navigation, and air space operations. The cost including airplane rental fees, flight instructor time, ground school training, FAA test fees, other supplies and, to reduce airplane time, simulator cost. To carry passengers in visual meteorological conditions (VMC) a pilot needs a private license plus a commercial-license endorsement, another $6K and ~250 flight hours with an instructor. To carry passengers in all weather conditions, an instrument endorsement will be needed, another $7K and ~50 h with an instructor. Based on today's requirements to safely operate a passenger-carrying helicopter in marginal weather conditions (special visual flight rules), one statue mile visibility, our pilot would have to spend $18K and ~350 h of flight time. In addition to the commercial pilot certificate, the pilot must fly for a company that holds a Part 119 certificate for the operation or the pilot can obtain this certification for themselves [10]. Through our human-centered vehicle design and interfaces, we can reduce pilot training time and the cost to train UAM pilots.

3.2 Rotorcraft Pilot

Training for rotorcraft pilots is more critical: The Joint Helicopter Safety Analysis Team (JHSAT) reported that 68% of calendar year 2006 helicopter accidents were attributed to poor pilot judgement." It was also found that 18% of all accidents occurred during training, highlighting the need for more training. Also, Rao and Marais [11] analyzed 5051 accidents between 1982–2008. The top-five hazardous states were caused by inflight loss of control, control flight into terrain, weather and failure to maintain physical clearance/altitude from objects.

3.3 Type Ratings

At the present time it is difficult to estimate what training will be required to manage the first generation of urban air vehicles given that over 100 different vehicles are being proposed and/or already in production. Additionally, the procedures needed for interfacing with the air traffic management system in today's national airspace have yet to be established. A number of concepts have suggested that two separate systems need to be developed, given the increased volume of traffic. However, there will be points where the systems will come together and need to coordinate separation and control responsibility. If UAM vehicles will be transporting goods and passengers to and from major airports, there will be places where the systems will need to either transfer control responsibility or coordinate to maintain current levels of safety. To support aircraft conducting visual flight rules with the vehicles providing self-separation, new rules will need to be developed. In addition, new protocols for digital or verbal communication will be required to transition between the two systems. At a minimum, however, simplifying the UAM vehicle aviate and tactical navigation tasks, with simplified interfaces augmented with automation, will be an important step in freeing up pilot resources so that they can take on the additional communication and coordination tasks.

4   UAM Vehicle Design and Assumptions About Autonomy

4.1   Aerial Vehicle Model

We modelled the virtual aircraft as an enlarged quadcopter that can take off and land vertically [12]. The vehicle was modified from a hexacopter 3D drone model available through the Professional Drone Pack (Professional Assets, Unity Asset Store [13]). The interior and the exterior of the original drone model were modified using open-source 3D computer graphics software, Blender, to create a quadcopter that is scaled to fit 2–4 passengers with cockpit displays of heading and speed for the pilot. It is important to note that the dynamics of the vehicle are based on a simple rigid body model. Several modifications were made to the exterior of the vehicle, including moving the propellers above the pilot's line of sight and using a darker color to increase its visibility when flying around and over buildings.

4.2   Initial Flight Control Inceptor Implementation

Goodrich et al. [5] in their discussion of haptic-multimodal flight controls suggested that loss of control and avoiding hazardous weather, terrain, obstructions and traffic would eliminate approximately 80% of current fatal accidents. Moreover, the key to achieving the desired increase in safety is preventing loss of control. They also suggested that the most important component of training is the amount of effort spent becoming proficient at basic flying skills. These skills are learning to manipulate flight control (stick and rudder) and throttle to make the vehicle go where directed. Our simplified ecological, human-centered model for controlling the quadcopter focuses on mapping action/inputs to the pilot world view.

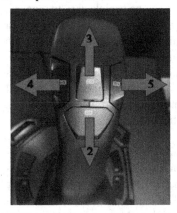

Fig. 2. Hover Mode vehicle controls.

The model supports two modes. The first mode "Hover" allows the operator to maneuver the vehicle during operations at speeds below 5kts. In Hover mode, no winds, the aircraft can climb or descend or rotate around the vertical using buttons 2–5, see Fig. 2. To climb press and hold button 3, to descend press button 2, to turn right press the right button 5 and to turn left press the left button 4 on the joystick [12]. These controls support hovering in the vehicle's current location while rotating around the vertical axes. For example, if the vehicle was heading/pointing north and the right joystick button was pressed the heading would change in an easterly direction; if the left button was pressed the heading would change in a westerly direction. In the hover-only mode, when the pilot pulls back on the stick the vehicle moves rearward; when the stick is pushed forward the vehicle moves forward. These controls map onto the pilots' world view of the movement of the vehicle and were easy to learn, with the sky being back or up and the ground being forward or down (see Fig. 2, for a depiction of the controls) (Fig. 3).

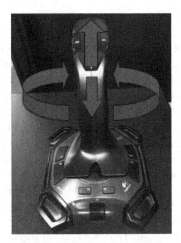

Fig. 3. Flight Mode Stick inputs.

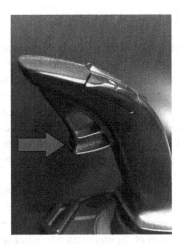

Fig. 4. Trigger to set current forward speed.

The second mode is the "Flight" mode which integrates the throttles for forward speed into the forward deflection of the joystick. This allows the operator to point the vehicle in the direction they want to go while increasing forward speed. When the vehicle reaches the desired speed the operator/pilot uses the trigger on the joystick, (see Fig. 4), to set the speed and direction of the vehicle with one simple input. To increase speed the operator just pushes forward on the stick or to reduce speed pulls back on the stick; and again, when the desired speed is reached the operator toggles the trigger to again set the forward speed. With the vehicle moving in the desired direction at the desired speed the operator can remove all forces from the stick, again making the vehicle easy to manage.

Until we reach full autonomy, pilot-in-the-loop flight will be the norm and we must design flight deck interfaces to reduce the effort of managing the flight tasks so we can reduce training time. Our initial design configuration that supports the aviate and tactical navigation tasks primarily is very much in line with our initial Concept-of-Operations (ConOps) where the operator/pilot manages the vehicle along a predefined route in visual meteorological conditions (VMC) using visual references in the terrain (pilotage); i.e., Bay Bridge, highways, San Francisco Bay at Candlestick point, Oracle Towers and the SFO Control Tower.

Current day VFR pilots have three primary tasks: Aviate, Navigate and Communicate. This paper will primarily focus on the Aviate and Navigate tasks and offer considerations for making the vehicle easy to fly and manage. According to the Boeing philosophy, we can either build a vehicle and then define the training required to manage it or start with a concept of a very stable vehicle and then design a human-centered interface that matches the new operator's mental model? As the discussion above shows, we started with a good mental model of the operator and the task to be performed and now we are beginning the process of mapping the operational concept and pilot model onto the UAM vehicle.

5   Vehicle Stability Augmentations

5.1   Stability Augmentation

An important task for any pilot is aviate. Therefore, making the UAM vehicle easy to fly and safe, will require vehicle stability augmentation. In our discussion so far, we have not dealt with low speed operations in windy conditions. When flying in major cities our UAM vehicle and pilot may experience rapid changes in wind direction and velocity due to urban canyons. Wikipedia describes an Urban Canyon as a place where the street is flanked by buildings on both sides creating a canyon-like environment. Such human-built canyons are created when streets separate dense blocks of structures, especially skyscrapers. This topic is important for UAM because UAM vertiports will be located in and around the city centers, where UAM vehicles will be picking up and delivering passengers and cargo. Some of the unusual flight characteristics of Urban Canyons are rapid changes in winds, temperature and views of the sky which will affect the stability of the vehicle and its access to GPS positioning data. For this paper we will only address the effects of rapidly changing wind speed and direction. The unique thing about urban canyons is that these changes can happen at any street intersection, and due to changes in temperature may occur mid-block. To anticipate these rapid or sudden changes, a stability augmentation system will be needed. Goodrich et al. [5] discussed the need for a stability augmentation system to make the vehicle easy to fly. They cited multiple simulation studies that have shown the benefits of pathway-in-the-sky displays to intuitively show where the vehicle should be flown combined with flight-by-wire (FBW) or -by-light (FBL) controls that significantly reduce the complexity of the manual control task of flying the vehicle. A FBW system is the complete replacement of the mechanical linkages between the pilot's stick and the control surface actuators using electrical signal wires. As aircraft have become more complex and unstable, manufacturers have added increased stability augmentation to reduce the complexity of the flight control task and cognitive demands on the pilot. For a history of stability augmentation and how the systems have evolved see Garg, Linda, and Chowdhury, [14].

5.2 No Augmentation

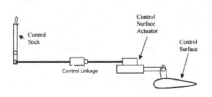

Stability augmentation systems (SAS) have been used in the past to allow us to fly even the most unstable vehicles. However, before discussing the first systems we will describe a system without stability augmentation where there is a single path to the controlling surface linked to a stick controlled by the pilot (Fig. 5) [15].

Fig. 5. Simple illustration of single path control system.

5.3 Initial Stability Augmentation System

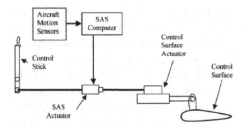

SAS was the first feedback control system design intended to improve dynamic stability characteristics of an aircraft. In a SAS system there are two paths to the SAS Actuator and thus, to the control surface – input from aircraft motion sensors, and input from pilot/flight stick. SAS was implemented in several century series fighters (F4, F104, T38, etc.) and was found to be very effective but SAS had its drawbacks: pilot input and SAS

Fig. 6. Simple illustration of Stability Augmentation System.

computer input sometimes were in conflict and limited control authority (no more than 10%) was given to the SAS computer (Fig. 6).

5.4 Control Augmentation System

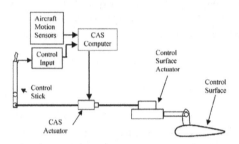

An improvement to SAS was the implementation of a Control Augmentation System (CAS). This system also had two paths to the flight control actuator but had two significant improvements to the SAS; flight stick input also went directly into the CAS computer and CAS control authority was increased to 50%. With CAS, the aircraft's dynamic motion response was well-damped, and control response is scheduled with the control system gains to main-

Fig. 7. Simple illustration of Control Augmentation System.

tain desirable characteristics throughout the flight envelope. CAS provided dramatic improvements in aircraft handling qualities. Both dynamic stability and control response characteristics could be tailored and optimized to the mission of the aircraft. CAS was implemented in aircraft such as the A-7, F-111, F-14, and F-15 (Fig. 7).

5.5 Fly-By-Wire Augmentation

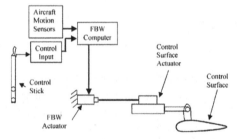

The last augmentation system, one in use on most new fighter and commercial jet and propeller aircraft, is the Fly-By-Wire or By-Light system. In this system all pilot input, as well as information on dynamic motion, goes through the FBW computer which controls the FBW actuator/flight controls, thus reducing the need to schedule inputs since the FBW computer has full control authority based on pilot input and dynamic motions of the aircraft, See

Fig. 8. Simple illustration of Fly By Wire Augmentation: no direct stick input.

Fig. 8. With full authority to dampen all undesirable motion in Roll, Pitch, Yaw, Load and Angle of attack due to environmental factors, the vehicle can be made stable in most flight regimes. The two major commercial aircraft manufacturers have two very different philosophies to implement their augmentation systems. For Airbus the final control authority is given to the FBW computer that tries to make sure that the vehicle does not get into any unusual altitudes (stall, fly into the terrain, or other malfunctions). Conversely, Boeing gives final control authority to the pilot allow them to push through FBW Computer inputs that are designed to prevent stalls and system malfunctions.

With a stable platform, our next task is to design a user interface that is ecologically aligned with the pilot/operator mental model for moving the vehicle through all flight regimes from departure to landing.

6 Conclusions: UAM Vehicle and Mission

If our industry is to meet the demand for UAM pilots to support the current vision of on-demand ride sharing and UAM package delivery we must reduce the time required for pilots to achieve full proficiency in the many envisioned UAM vehicles proposed. In this paper we highlighted an approach to UAM vehicle design that will make the vehicle easy to operate, reducing training time and time to certification. It is important, we believe, to make the vehicle easy to fly. We proposed a human-centered approach by teaming the automation with the human pilot through an intuitive mental model of tasks and direct mapping of inceptor input to task goals so as to directly command the velocity vector of the aircraft coupled with stability augmentation to create a stable platform that is easy to fly and will be acceptable to UAM ride-sharing passengers.

Our initial design of the input controls that make the vehicle easy to fly has only been evaluated by its developers and will be tested in our near-term studies. We expect these initial concepts will evolve to support a true operator-centered system for controlling and managing the vehicle and the strategic navigation and communication tasks of the UAM pilot. And we hope that by highlighting the need for FBW control systems, others will also see the need to build these systems into the design. Although we did not explicitly discuss Human Autonomy Teaming, it will be this coupling of humans with well-designed human-centered automation that will eventually aid us in achieving truly autonomous UAM flight.

References

1. INRIX 2018 Global Traffic Score Card. https://inrix.com/scorecard/
2. Unmanned Airspace. Accessed 10 Dec 2018. https://www.unmannedairspace.info/urban-air-mobility/urban-air-mobility-takes-off-63-towns-cities-worldwide/
3. AHA and Flytrex. https://dronebelow.com/2018/09/28/aha-drone-delivery-tested-in-iceland/
4. CAAS Airbus Skyway Agreement. https://www.caas.gov.sg/who-we-are/our-organisation/our-publications/publication-details/publication/caas-collaborates-with-industry-to-support-aviation-growth
5. Goodrich, K.H., Schutte P.C.: Haptic-multimodal flight control system update. In: 11th AIAA Aviation Technology, and Operations Conference, Virginia Beach, VA, 20–22 September 2011 (2011)
6. Norman, S.D., Orlady, H.W.: Proceedings of NASA/FAA/Industry workshop on Flight Deck Automation: Promises and Realities, Carmel California, 1–4 August 1988 (1988)
7. Boeing 737 Max Accident. https://www.businesstravelnews.com/Transportation/Air/Despite-Boeing-737-Max-Accident-Commercial-Aviation-Fatalities-Dropped-in-2019
8. Lacher, A.R., Grabowski, R., Cook, S.: Autonomy, trust, and transportation. Association for the Advancement of Artificial Intelligence (2014). www.aaai.org
9. Boeing Pilot Outlook. https://www.boeing.com/commercial/market/pilot-technician-outlook/
10. FAA Issues Charter Guidance to Pilots and Passengers. https://www.faa.gov/news/updates/?newsId=94849&omniRss=news_updatesAoc&cid=101_N_U
11. Roa, A.H., Marais, K.: Comparing hazard states and trigger events in fatal and non-fatal helicopter accidents. In: Proceeding of 16th AIAA Aviation Technology, Integration, and Operations Conference, Washington, DC, June 2016 (2016)

12. Marayong, P., Shaukar, P., Wei, J., Nguyen, H., Strybel, T.Z., Battiste, V.: Urban air mobility system testbed using CAVE virtual reality environment. In: IEEE 2020 Conference, Yellowstone, Wyoming (2020)
13. https://assetstore.unity.com/
14. Garg, A., Linda, R.I., Chowdhury, T.: Evolution of aircraft flight control system and fly-by-light flight control system. Int. J. Emerg. Technol. Adv. Eng. 3(12), 60–64 (2013)
15. Kaviyarasu, A.: Aircraft stability and control augmentation. Department of Aerospace Engineering. Madras Institute of Technology, Chromepet, Chennai

Intersection Roadway Marking Design: Effects Over Cyclist's Safety Perception

Marina V. Carvalho[1](✉) ⓘ, Paulo Noriega[1,2] ⓘ, David Vale[3] ⓘ,
and Francisco Rebelo[1,2] ⓘ

[1] CIAUD, Research Centre for Architecture, Urbanism and Design, Lisbon School of
Architecture, Universidade de Lisboa, Lisbon, Portugal
{marina.carvalho,pnoriega}@edu.ulisboa.pt, frebelo@fa.ulisboa.pt
[2] Interactive Technologies Institute/LARSyS, Universidade de Lisboa, Lisbon, Portugal
[3] Faculty of Architecture of the University of Lisbon, Lisbon, Portugal

Abstract. Bicycles as a transport mode, has many advantages to improve quality of urban life for carbon less cities, traffic congestion reduction and good for
resident's health. Despite these advantages, the number of new cyclists does not
increase in cities with low cycling maturity. There is a large percent of residents
interested but concerned about safety to cycling in urban streets. We developed an
experiment with images simulating a cyclist's route in an urban road intersection
to evaluate the level of safety perception in different types of cycling infrastructure. Three variables were studied: traffic density, cycleway types and intersection
designs. A set of images was shown to 300 individuals online who rated each
image in a four-point scale related to their perception of safety. Safety perception
was higher for: low traffic density, painted cyclist lane and separation of cyclists
from traffic. The simple presence of colored markings increased the safety perception relatedly with no design in the intersection environment. The more complex
studied intersection design increased even more the safety perception. Naturally,
the interventions of cycle design that include specific measures for cyclists needs
increase not only the level of their safety perceived, but the likelihood of using
bicycles. The complex design (Dutch model safety intersection design) is a good
approach to increase security awareness. In conclusion, there is a clear interaction
between the visual design on roads and the cyclist, this interaction has a positive
effect on the perception of safety and to improve cycling.

Keywords: Bicycle · Cycling Infrastructure · Safety Perception · Road
Intersection · Interaction Design

1 Introduction

Cities have the challenge to promote sustainable transport with bicycles and one of the
main barriers is the concern with the safety for cyclists in urban journeys. To increase
cycling in cities, this deterrent must be overcome to increase safety traffic for cyclists on
urban trips [1–3], particularly in countries with no cycling culture and limited cyclable
infrastructure where the barriers are higher. In order to increase cycling in cities, especially on those ones with low cycling maturity, it is necessary to overcome cycling
information deficiency concerning needs of current and potential cyclists [4].

© The Author(s), under exclusive license to Springer Nature Switzerland AG 2023
V. G. Duffy et al. (Eds.): HCII 2023, LNCS 14057, pp. 237–247, 2023.
https://doi.org/10.1007/978-3-031-48047-8_15

We start based on the premise if individuals feel safe, this will have a positive effect over their choices of modes of transport. Thus, a positive perception of safety of cyclists over urban environment, can increase cycling in urban environments [5].

Several studies evaluated environmental perceptions of urban spaces with infrastructure, using several tools such as photos, models, videos, virtual reality or local exposure. All offer advantages and disadvantages in different degrees of realism and experimental extent control they allow [6]. In these studies, there are aspects related to cycling situations and environmental perceptions that used virtual reality [7, 8], manipulated photos [9], videos [10] and realistic images [11]. According to [12], simulations allow to explore design options to test the safety, aesthetics or desirability, to determine which combinations are most effective at the urban microscale.

The current study, was inspired by the Fixmyberlin survey [11]. The survey which featured 21,000 participants, evaluated over 1000 combination on variations of street scenarios with many structural feature variables. All were evaluated through a four-point scale concerning safety perception. The Fixmyberlin study presented the preferred situation with 99% in the sample's preference (see Fig. 1a) and the least secure, with only 11% of the sample feeling safe (see Fig. 1b).

Fig. 1. a. Safer situation in Fixmyberlin. Font image: Fixmyberlin [11] **b.** Dangerous situation.

2   Methodology

To understand and articulate the closer link of cycle design qualities [9, 13] to transport planning and infrastructure interventions, we used a survey with the purpose of examining the effect from visual design to the safety of cycling infrastructure, assessing the perceived level of safety in the characteristics of each type of bicycle lane in the cyclist's route at an urban intersection. An online survey was responded by 300 residents most in cities with low cycling maturity [4], with low cycling rates and poor infrastructure for cyclists fifty four percent was male, and 46% female, aged between 18 years to 30, (14%) and more than 30 years corresponding to 86% of the sample. Most, held a bachelor or post-graduate degree.

The 24 study images, showing the section of the cyclist's route in an urban road intersection environment, were modeled in the Twinmotion software. The assessment was carried out by asking participants to express their perception of safety by evaluating a scene from the cyclist's point of view, when presented with different bicycle design configurations. Images were rated using a four-point scale according to perceived safety as (1) fairly unsafe, (2) unsafe, (3) safe, or (4) fairly safe.

The 24 images used was a product of a within design with 2*4*3 conditions:

a . Low traffic volume

b. High traffic volume

Fig. 2. a. Low traffic volume. **b.** High traffic volume

– 2 Traffic densities (see example Figs. 2a and 2b):

  – Low (a) and high (b);

– 4 Bicycle lanes (see example Figs. 3a, 3b, 3c and 3d).

a . Street without bicycle lane.

b. Large bicycle lane separated with garden pots and no parking.

c. Bicycle lane separated with parking lot on the left side.

Fig. 3. a. Street without bicycle lane. **b.** Large bicycle lane separated with garden pots and no parking. **c.** Bicycle lane separated with parking lot on the left side. **d.** Bicycle lane between motorized traffic lane and parking along.

d. Bicycle lane between motorized traffic lane and parking along.

Fig. 3. (*continued*)

a) a condition without bicycle lane;
b) a bicycle lane between motorized traffic lane and parking along;
c) a separated bicycle lane between the car parking lot on the left and the sidewalk on the right;
d) a separated large bicycle lane with garden pots and no parking on the left and a sidewalk on the right side.

– 3 Intersection design:

a) without design;
b) with marked lines and color (see example Fig. 4a);
c) with safety intersection design model (see example Fig. 4b).

Images was presented in google forms and the order of the presentation was randomized. A consent form was added to the survey, as well biographic data in order to characterize the sample. Data was gathered during 4 months between December 2021 and April 2022. Images from 2 to 4 are examples of the images related to independent variables studied, evaluated in the perceived level of safety from the cyclist perspective.

a. Intersection line and color design

b. Intersection safety design with line and color

Fig. 4. a. Intersection line and color design. **b.** Intersection safety design with line and color

3   Results and Discussion

The results presented in this paper concern's a global treatment for each of the levels of the independent variables studied. Thus, for the traffic density, the averages of the 12 images with low density and the 12 images with high density were calculated. For the second variable, Bicycle lanes, averages of 6 images were calculated for each of the four levels of this variable. For the variable, intersection design, which had three levels, the averages of the 8 images were calculated for each of the levels. Non parametric statistics was performed for each variable, to evaluate if safety perception was affected by each level of the variables.

3.1 Traffic Densities

Low traffic density safety perception, was higher (x = 2.94) than high traffic density (x = 2.67). The non-parametric test for two dependent samples (Wilcoxon) was chosen. The test result revealed the existence of a statistically significant difference (z = -11.84 p < 0.001) in the variation of traffic density on the road.

This result confirms that when the volume of traffic is high, the perception of risk for the cyclist increases [1, 14]. Traffic density, conjointly with speed, is the most influential variable in studies of stated preference in choosing routes by American cyclists [1, 15]. Concluding, perception of safety is inversely proportional to the traffic flow density on the road.

3.2 Bicycle Lanes

For the variable, Bicycle lane, we opted for a non-parametric Friedman test for dependent samples. The result revealed the existence of a statistically significant difference between the different levels of the variable Bicycle lane (χ^2 (3,n = 298) = 651.97, p < 0.001). Post tests revealed statistically significant differences between all levels of the bicycle lanes variable. In the a-b comparison (z = -7.88 p < 0.001); a-c (z = 17.27 p < 0.001); on a-d (22.74 p < 0.001); in b-c (z = 17.27 p < 0.001); in b-d (z = 14.86 p < 0.001); and in c-d (z = 5.4 p < 0.001) (Check Fig. 3 to have a reference of the different bike lanes). The non-existence of a bicycle lane (Fig. 3 a) is the situation perceived as the least safe (x = 1.8), followed by the (b) cycling lane (x = 2.7). In situations where there is a separation from the bicycle lane (c and d), the value of perceived safety was higher. In positioning the bicycle lane to the side of the crosswalk and separated from motorized traffic by the parking lot it is the second situation perceived as more safety (c, x = 3.3), and the situation of the separated bicycle lane with garden pots (d, x = 3.8) was the situation perceived as safer.

The Fig. 5, shows the mean ranks of the Friedman test for each level of the variable bicycle lane. It is very clear in this graphic the positive evolution of the safety perception from left bicycle lane type (a) to the right bicycle lane type (d).

According to [1] the preferred route types for cyclists are cycle lanes along main roads, as long as they are separated from traffic, and cycle lanes on residential streets with traffic moderation.

3.3 Intersection Line Design

The third variable under consideration is line and color design at the intersection. A non-parametric Friedman test for dependent samples was used. The results revealed the existence of a statistically significant difference between the different levels of the design variable in the intersection (χ^2(3, n = 300) = 325,27, p < 0.001). Post tests revealed statistically significant differences between all levels of the intersection line design variable (Check list of variables 3): 3a–3b (z = -13.04 p < 0.001); 3a–3c (z = 15.55 p < 0.001); 3b–3c (z = 2.51 p = 0.036).

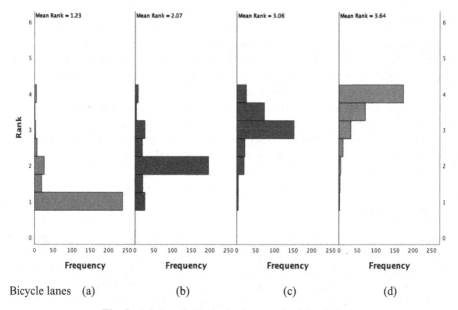

Fig. 5. Friedman's Ranks for intersection bicycle lane

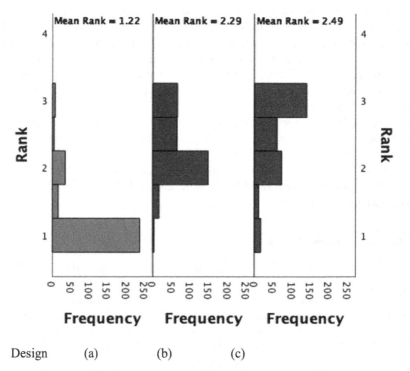

Fig. 6. Friedman's Ranks for intersection design

Design

In terms of average values, the analysis showed that the non-existence of design at the intersection was considered the least safe situation in the perception of the cyclist (3a, x = 2.5). The existence of a marked line and colored, was the situation perceived as intermediate (3b, x = 2.9) and the safe intersection design model, was considered the safest (3c, x = 3).

The Fig. 6, shows the mean rank of the Friedman test for each variable level of line and color design at intersection. It is very clearly in the graphic the perception of safety is much lower when there is no design (see Fig. 6a). However, in the situations with design intervention (see Fig. 6b and 6c) there are great overlap of rankings, but still the higher ranks related to human higher safety perception are on the safety intersection model Dutch.

4 Conclusion

All three variables studied (traffic densities, bike lanes and intersection design) have an impact on perceived safety. According to previous studies [1, 14, 16–18], it was already expected that the first two variables would have an impact on the safety perception. Again, high traffic densities generated a lower perception of safety and the segregation of bicycle lanes increased the perception of safety. Thus, the methodology used proved to be valid, as the results are similar to previous studies.

Therefore, we can reinforce the conclusion that the main variable under study, Intersection Design, also has an effect on the cyclists' perception of safety.

Consequently, the present study suggests that intersection design solutions be implemented, as they will have a positive effect on the perception of safety and can attract the potential cyclists. Even the simplest intervention, placing marked lines and color continuation at the intersection, had a positive effect on safety perceptions. Thereby, if the economic conditions of the municipalities do not allow the implementation of safe intersection design model solution (Dutch model), at least the marked lines and color, are simple and cost-effective solution that should be implemented at intersections.

We know that the norm [19] recommends that intersections should have uneven level crossing passages, but recognizing the costs of these solutions. Eventually, another compromise solution, which was not evaluated in this study, could be the simplified and more economical Dutch model, having only the paintings without the waiting crossing islands. The urgency imposed by climate change for sustainable mobility solutions, we can conclude that intersection design measures with colored lines and colors placed at intersections are commitment to increase the perceived safety to increase cycling on cities streets.

According to [2], design as an element of urban enhancement to increase the level of safety, comfort and attractiveness of the urban infrastructure environment, plays an important role in attracting new cyclists. Marked lines and color at intersections are safer routes from the cyclist's point of view and the experienced and cautious cyclists. Disconnected infrastructure often means that cyclists have to share the street space with pedestrians or motor vehicles and must negotiate [21], which is a risk for cyclists on the roads and a barrier to the growth of cycling. Indeed, the intersection design increased the level of safety perception in all types of bicycle lanes situations analyzed in the approach that perceived environmental conditions contribute to the likelihood of cycling [16] and appear to be an individual choice. Traffic density is an issue for cyclists, especially for less experienced ones. Density is inversely proportional to the perceived safety of cycling. And there are evidences that infrastructural aspects influence the desire to cycle [20, 22, 23]. Cyclists should avoid high-traffic roads, and routes on these high-density roads where should be physically separated from the faster traffic. It is confirmed in the literature [2, 9, 10, 24, 25]. Although previous cycling research had linked the presence of bicycle lanes and low-density traffic to cycling [16], they have found a non-linear relationship between the odds of bicycling and the perception of the car-oriented traffic environment. Affects cyclists. But when there is a route chance of choice, the separated bicycle lanes as well as low-traffic streets are the preferred. Thus, policy and urban intervention to increase cycling must take into account real and perceived environmental conditions.

This study, also provides important future clues for the application of interaction design in the management, planning and practice of the smart cities for sustainable mobility. An intelligent system that can dynamically adapt road design to the needs of each moment. For example, if the flow of cyclists increases in a certain period, the road can dynamically adapt to this new flow, changing the design of the horizontal signage, to primarily serve cyclists.

Acknowlegment. This work is financed by national funds through FCT – Fundação para a Ciência e a Tecnologia, I.P., under the Strategic Project with the references UIDB/04008/2020 and UIDP/04008/2020. 2020 and Interactive Technologies Institute -LARSyS-FCT Pluriannual funding's 2020–2023 (UIDB/50009/2020).

References

1. Winters, M., Teschke, K.: Route preferences among adults in the near market for bicycling: findings of the cycling in cities study. Am. J. Health Promot. **25**, 40–47 (2010). https://doi.org/10.4278/ajhp.081006-QUAN-236
2. McNeil, N., Dill, J., MacArthur, J., Broach, J., Howland, S.: Breaking barriers to bike share: insights from residents of traditionally underserved neighborhoods (2017). https://doi.org/10.15760/trec.176
3. Marshall, W., Ferenchak, N.: Why cities with high bicycling rates are safer for all road users. J. Transp. Health **13**, 285–301 (2019). https://doi.org/10.1016/j.jth.2019.03.004
4. Félix, R., Moura, F., Clifton, K.: Maturing urban cycling: comparing barriers and motivators to bicycle of cyclists and non-cyclists in Lisbon, Portugal. J. Transp. Health **15**, 100628 (2019). https://doi.org/10.1016/j.jth.2019.100628
5. Dill, J., Voros, K.: Factors affecting bicycling demand: initial survey findings from the portland, oregon, region. Transport. Res. Rec. **2031**(1), 9–17 (2007). https://doi.org/10.3141/2031-02
6. Nasar, J.L.: Assessing perceptions of environments for active living. Am. J. Prev. Med. **34**(4), 357–363 (2008). https://doi.org/10.1016/j.amepre.2008.01.013
7. Nazemi, M., Van Eggermond, M., Erath, A., Schaffner, D., Joos, M., Axhausen, K.: Studying bicyclists' perceived level of safety using a bicycle simulator combined with immersive virtual reality. Accid. Anal. Prevent. **151**, 105943 (2021). https://doi.org/10.1016/j.aap.2020.105943

8. Mouratidis, K., Hassan, R.: Contemporary versus traditional styles in architecture and public space: a virtual reality study with 360-degree videos. Cities **97**, 102499 (2020). https://doi. org/10.1016/j.cities.2019.102499

9. Mertens, L., et al.: The effect of changing micro-scale physical environmental factors on an environment's invitingness for transportation cycling in adults: an exploratory study using manipulated photographs. Int. J. Behav. Nutr. Phys. Activity **11**, 1–12 (2014). https://doi.org/ 10.1186/s12966-014-0088-x

10. Cabral, L., Kim, A.: An empirical reappraisal of the level of traffic stress framework for segments. Travel Behav. Soc. **26**, 143–158 (2022). https://doi.org/10.1016/j.tbs.2021.09.007

11. Fixmyberlin. Mobility Plataforma with "open data" for cycling planning combining transport planning, software development, TI, data analysis and user-centered design and communication (2020). https://fixmyberlin.de

12. Cunningham, G.O., Michael, I.L.: Concepts guiding the study of the impact of the built environment on physical activity for older adults: a review of the literature. Am. J. Health Promot. **18**(6), 435–443 (2004). https://doi.org/10.4278/0890-1171-18.6.435

13. Liu, G., Krishnamurthy, S., Wesemael, P.J.V.: Conceptualizing cycling experience in urban design research: a systematic literature review. Appl. Mobil. **6**, 1–17 (2018). https://doi.org/ 10.1080/23800127.2018.1494347

14. Teschke, K., et al.: Route infrastructure and the risk of injuries to bicyclists: a case-crossover study. Am. J. Public Health **12**, 2336–2343 (2012). https://doi.org/10.2105/AJPH.2012. 300762

15. Winters, M., Gavin, D., Kao, D., Teschke, K.: Motivators and deterrents of bicycling: comparing influences on decisions to ride. Transportation **38**, 153–168 (2011). https://doi.org/10. 1007/s11116-010-9284-y

16. Moudon, A.V., et al.: Cycling and the built environment, a US perspective. Transport. Res. Part D: Transp. Environ. **10**(3), 245–261 (2005). https://doi.org/10.1016/j.trd.2005.04.001

17. Dill, J., McNeil, N.: Four types of cyclists? examination of typology for better understanding of bicycling behavior and potential. Transport. Res. Rec. **2387**(1), 129–138 (2013). https:// doi.org/10.3141/2387-15

18. Dill, J., Nathan, M.: Revisiting the four types of cyclists: findings from a national survey. Transport. Res. Rec. **2587**(1), 90–99 (2016). https://doi.org/10.3141/2587-11

19. Crow, Design manual for bicycle traffic. Ede, Netherlands (2007). https://crowplatform.com/ product/design-manual-for-bicycle-traffic/

20. Hull, A., O'Holleran, C.: Bicycle infrastructure: can good design encourage cycling? Urban Plan. Transp. Res. **2**, 369–406 (2014). http://dx.doi.org/10.1080/21650020.2014.955210

21. Kircher, K., Ihlström, J., Nygårdhs, S., Ahlstrom, C.: Cyclist efficiency and its dependence on infrastructure and usual speed. Transport. Res. F: Traffic Psychol. Behav. **54**, 148–158 (2018). https://doi.org/10.1016/j.trf.2018.02.002

22. Buehler, R., Pucher, J.: Walking and cycling in Western Europe and the United States: trends, policies, and lessons. TR News **280**, 34–42 (2012). http://onlinepubs.trb.org/onlinepubs/trn ews/trnews280WesternEurope.pdf

23. Dill, J.: Bicycling for transportation and health: the role of infrastructure. J. Public Health Policy **30**, S95–S110 (2009)

24. Broach, J., Dill, J., Gliebe, J.: Where do cyclists ride? a route choice model developed with revealed preference GPS data. Transport. Res. Part A: Policy Pract. **46**, 1730–1740 (2012). https://doi.org/10.1016/j.tra.2012.07.00

25. Parkin, J., Ciaran, M.: The effect of cycle lanes on the proximity between motor traffic and cycle traffic. Accid. Anal. Prev. **42**(1), 159–165 (2010). https://doi.org/10.1016/j.aap.2009. 07.018

Systematic Review on Safety of Artificial Intelligence and Transportation

Sai Chandrahas Reddy Biddala, Omolara Ibikunle, and Vincent G. Duffy[✉]

Purdue University, West Lafayette, IN 47907, USA
{sbiddala,oibikun,duffy}@purdue.edu

Abstract. Artificial intelligence is growing fast, and it is becoming important due to advances that allow complex algorithms or software to be used in transportation. AI technologies are beneficial for all kinds of industries, including transportation. The development of AI in transportation engineering for autonomous vehicle (AV) control is a rapidly growing field. The introduction of AVs on the market, along with the development of related technologies, will have a potential impact not only on the automotive industry but also on urban transport systems, new mobility-related businesses will emerge, whereas existing ones will have to adapt to changes. However, there are also challenges associated with AI in transportation, including safety concerns, cybersecurity threats, and job displacement.

Surely technology can be a useful tool in promoting safety, but its effectiveness may depend on factors such as interactivity, equipment complexity, and adaptation of social behavior. System safety is the application of technical and managerial skills to the systematic, forward-looking identification, and control of hazards throughout the life cycle of a system like an AI [24]. In this paper a systematic literature review of the Safety of Artificial Intelligence and Transportation was performed by searching the keywords on the SCOPUS, Web of Science, and Google Scholar through Harzing software, many papers related to AI and transportation were explored. Searches were refined and led to VOS viewer to analyze the connection between authors and what papers come under similar topics. Next was a thorough analysis of engagements, which was done through Twitter trend analysis which collaborates a further justification of research into this topic. Overall, the findings from the systematic analyses of the four articles selected from various databases, including Google Scholar, SpringerLink, and ResearchGate, two chapters from Rogers L. Brauer's book Safety and Health for Engineers, Third Edition and David L. Goetsch Occupational Safety and Health for Technologists, Engineers, and Managers, 9th Edition with three more articles derived from the co-citation analysis led to interesting discoveries in integrating AI into transportation systems, with AI mitigating some risks while new ones come up which points to the importance of funding for future work into analyzing AI in systems, to increase sustainability, while mitigating AI's risks.

Keywords: Artificial Intelligence · Transportation · Safety

V. G. Duffy et al. (Eds.): HCII 2023, LNCS 14057, pp. 248–263, 2023.
https://doi.org/10.1007/978-3-031-48047-8_16

1 Introduction and Background

Artificial Intelligence and transportation are important to individuals, to society, and to the earth in many areas with some of it shown here: First is safety, where AI can improve transportation safety by predicting potential accidents and providing timely alerts to drivers, while also, enabling self-driving cars to eliminate the risk of human error. AI also has the potential to control traffic lights and even parking lots. Next is efficiency, where AI can optimize traffic flow. This also links to sustainability, where the optimized traffic flow can lead to lowered idle time. AI can also help with traffic management by suggesting to drivers alternate routes which helps reduce carbon emissions and environmental pollution. Overall, AI and transportation have the potential to improve safety, efficiency, and sustainability for individuals, society, and the earth. Artificial intelligence is becoming increasingly important in transportation due to its ability to address issues like rising travel demand, CO2 emissions, safety problems, and environmental damage. In addition, advances in AI and machine learning allow more complex algorithms and software which can optimize transportation systems and improve efficiency. Furthermore, the advancement in AI allows for self-driving cars.

In industrial engineering, AI can be used to streamline processes, optimize production, and improve quality control. AI helps to optimize complex systems and processes for maximum efficiency. AI can also automate tasks that come under the purview of an industrial engineer. This can be transportation route planning, scheduling, and maintenance. Additionally, AI can integrate different systems, allowing seamless workflow. AI has the potential to revolutionize industrial engineering through a full-on digital transformation. By automating repetitive tasks, optimizing processes, and reducing human error. Outside the IE realm, Continuous Improvement of Information technology is evolving daily to address the onset challenges concerning AI in transportation, also governments are reacting to the new AI technology and developing rules and regulations to ensure the safety of all security-related concerns. Also, automotive companies are collaborating with software companies to integrate AI in future vehicle developments.

Governments and the private sector can contribute by increasing funding for the research and development of AI and transportation. Society must encourage greater data access for researchers without compromising users' privacy. Society must also promote new models of digital education and AI workforce development so employees have the skills needed in the 21st-century economy. Next, society must address the risk associated with AI and transportation, like job losses, safety risks, and cyber risks. Society must also prioritize sustainability with the development of AI-powered transportation systems, where AI can reduce carbon emissions by developing sustainable transportation infrastructure.

Finally, HFE and HCI can help by researching user behavior and acceptance to better understand how users interact with AI-powered transportation systems. Safety-related communities can develop safety guidelines for the development and use of AI-powered transportation systems. Additionally, HFE and safety-related communities can develop training programs to educate operators, stakeholders, and drivers on the use of AI-powered transportation systems. All this can help to ensure that users can use these systems safely and effectively.

2 Purpose

This study aims to conduct a systematic review of the safety of AI implementation in the transportation industry. To essentially understand the integration of AI into transportation systems and how to deal with safety issues that come with AI utilization. Overall, the purpose is to conduct a systematic literature review on the topic of AI and transportation with a subset topic of safety and provide a meticulous summary of all the available primary research. This review is conducted with various software and tools for analyzing metadata like MaxQDA, VOS viewer, Cite Space, and Bib Excel.

3 Research Methodology

3.1 Data Collection

Data collection was carried out by multiple databases, with SCOPUS, Google Scholar through Harzing software, Vicinitas by Twitter, and Web of Science.

Table 1. Search terms and Databases

Search terms	Databases/Software	No. Articles
Artificial Intelligence and Transportation	SCOPUS, WOS, Harzing (Google Scholar)	6,719
Artificial Intelligence	SCOPUS	472,309
#AI, Transportation	Vicinitas -Twitter	1,752

Table 1 shows the search terms used in the 4 different databases and the number of total articles received from those databases. The main results used to export the data were Scopus and Harzing. The data that were exported were titles, authors, sources, abstracts, and cited references. Furthermore, Scopus data was exported via CSV file format and Harzing data was exported through WOS format. Each worked better with specific software. Scopus worked better with VOS viewer and Harzing worked better with Cite Space and BibExcel.

3.2 Engagement

The main way to get engagement data was to search the topic through Vicinitas, a data mining tool for Twitter, which gave results of the search #AI, Transportation. The results are shown in Figs. 1 and 2.

In addition, Fig. 1 shows the countries with the most publications on the topic of AI and Transportation. It is interesting to see China on the top with US and India beating the other countries out of the water. Additionally, Japan, known for its robotics and AI is not in the play. This may be due to their isolationist policies or that SCOPUS does not have permission to view Japanese publications.

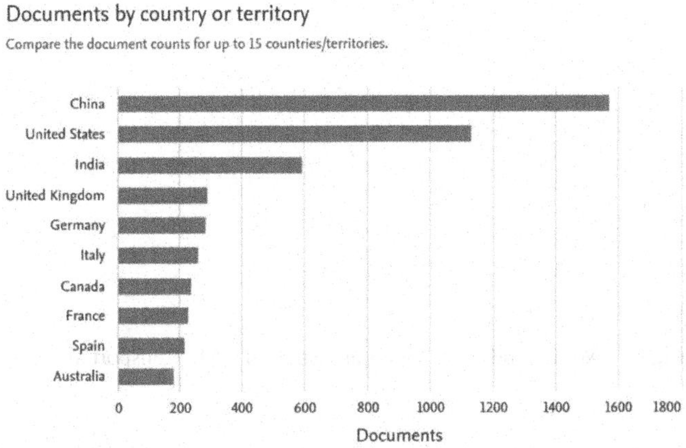
Documents by country or territory
Compare the document counts for up to 15 countries/territories.
China
United States
India
United Kingdom
Germany
Italy
Canada
France
Spain
Australia
0
200
400
600
800
1000
1200
1400
1600
1800
Documents

Fig. 1. SCOPUS country source on Artificial Intelligence and Transportation [5]

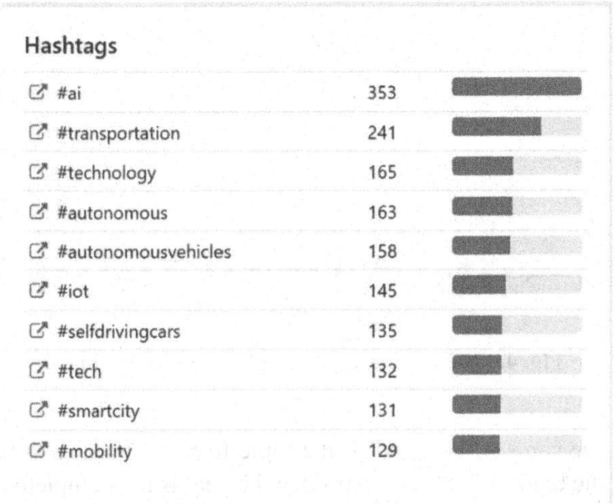
Hashtags
#ai 353
#transportation 241
#technology 165
#autonomous 163
#autonomousvehicles 158
#iot 145
#selfdrivingcars 135
#tech 132
#smartcity 131
#mobility 129

Fig. 2. Top hashtags result from Vicinitas search of #AI, Transportation

Figure 2 shows the hashtag trend of the topic in tweets within the past 10 days.

The figure above shows the most tweeted topic within the past 10 days. As we can see, transportation and AI are at the top. This coincides with the search #AI, Transportation. Furthermore, AI and transportation are linked to many other topics on Twitter, like healthcare, businesses, delivery, and industry Fig. 3.

3.3 Trend Analysis

Metadata was analyzed by the Web of Science. The analysis was to see papers published per year and to understand if the topic was justified to be emerging.

Word Cloud

Fig. 3. Word cloud from Vicinitas search of #AI, Transportation

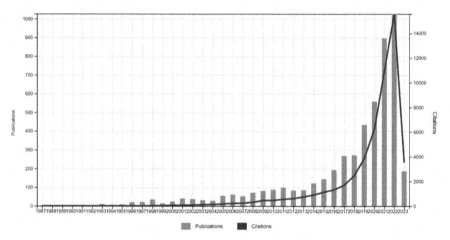

Fig. 4. WOS Publications and Citations over Time

From Fig. 4 we can see the trend of the topic to be increasing over time with the year 2022 being the highest. 2023 is a dip since the year is not completed yet at the time of publishing this paper, if we follow the previous trend, an upward increase would be expected for this year as well.

4   Results

4.1   Co-citation/Authorship Analysis

Co-citation analysis was used in this paper to understand the connection between articles that have cited each other, and Vos Viewer was used for this analysis.

Fig. 5. VOS Viewer articles from SCOPUS co-citation analysis

From the VOS viewer co-citation analysis in Fig. 5, we can see the bridge linking the software-heavy AI development to the applicative articles on the right past the blue, with smart city and intelligent systems applications. The most important point to take out is the article by Adadi, where they summarize AI and explain it in a way that allows AI to be understood and used in other industries than software development [9].

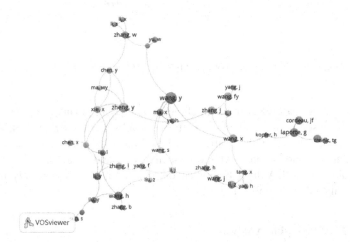

Fig. 6. VOS Viewer 1000 articles from Harzing co-author analysis

From the VOS viewer co-authorship analysis in Fig. 6, we can see authors linked to each other and forming bridges within the project topic. This justifies the further in-depth analysis of the project topic since many authors are working together on AI and transportation.

4.2   Content Analysis

Content analysis of keywords was done through VOS viewer and Cite space. Data was taken from Harzing for VOS viewer and Cite Space [14, 26]. Essentially 997 articles' metadata was utilized in content analysis, which was carried out to create links and clusters to understand the connection between contents in the articles.

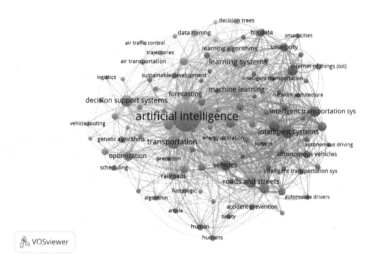

Fig. 7. VOS viewer keyword results from 1000 articles by Harzing [6]

From Fig. 7, we can see artificial intelligence is linked to many different sectors in the industry. These sectors can be from software development to transportation to data and system optimization. With AI affecting these industries, it is important to analyze and understand the integration of AI into these industries and make sure it is done safely and sustainably. Overall, AI has a big impact on society and must be carefully and safely observed, analyzed, and applied to industries.

4.3   Pivot Leading Table Analysis

Metadata from Harzing (Google Scholar) search was used in Bibexcel to create a leading table. Bibexcel is software that allows the analysis of many data within these articles [1]. Table 2 is an example of Author analysis and Table 3 is an example of keyword analysis. Additionally, Table 2 helps in finding prominent authors within the topic by analyzing papers authors have written. On the other hand, Table 3 helps in analyzing what most of the papers are about.

Table 2. Bibexcel Author leading table

Articles	Authors
17	Wang Y
9	Zheng Y
8	Wang H
8	Laporte G
7	Cuturi M
7	Trivedi MM
7	Wang FY
7	Cordeau JF
7	Wang X
6	Karaboga D
6	Stone P
6	Karlaftis MG
6	Zhang J
6	Gendreau M
6	Li Z

The leading table above is sorted by articles being authored by each author. For example, Wang Y is the author of 17 articles.

Table 3. Bibexcel Keyword leading table

Articles	Keywords
28	transportation
25	Transportation Science
21	on intelligent transportation
14	surveys &tutorials
14	Transportation
13	Transportation Research
13	Science
13	Intelligent Transportation
11	Transportation Research Part C
11	Artificial Intelligence

(continued)

Table 3. (*continued*)

Articles	Keywords
10	Proceedings of the
10	on intelligent transportation systems
10	IEEE Transactions on
10	Transportation Research Part C: Emerging
10	Journal of artificial intelligence research
10	International Journal of
9	Nature
9	IEEE

The leading table in Table 3 is sorted by the number of articles including the keywords. For example, transportation is seen in 28 articles.

4.4 Cluster Analysis

Cluster analysis was conducted by Cite Space and Harzing data. Cite space clusters were clustered by keywords connections in the articles' abstract.

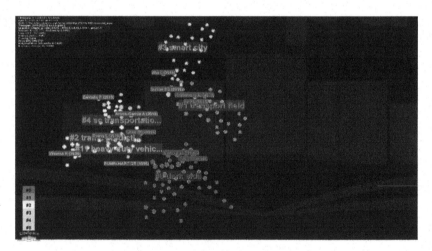

Fig. 8. Cite Space cluster by keywords [2]

Figure 8 further shows clusters by keywords in abstracts. Most articles were related to the implementation of AI like smart cities, or transportation.

Top 1 References with the Strongest Citation Bursts

References	Year	Strength	Begin	End	2007 - 2022
Lv YS, 2015, IEEE T INTELL TRANSP, V16, P865, DOI 10.1109/TITS.2014.2345663, DOI	2015	2.96	2018	2020	

Fig. 9. Cite space cluster burst with keyword clustering [7]

Figure 9 shows a citation burst with one article. This helps in finding articles relevant to the project topic. This also shows that AI use in Transportation is new and unexplored.

Summary

Time of creation: Mon Apr 17 17:15:56 EDT 2023

Introduction

This summary is automatically generated. To maximize the level of details in the summary, complete the following tasks before running this function:

- clustering and labeling by using the **All in One** button
- run the burst detection function from the **Burstness** tab in the Control Panel
- compute the betweenness centrality from the Nodes menu
- save the current visualization as a PNG image in the project folder

The summary highlights major clusters first, including citing articles and cited references. The importance of nodes will be summarized in terms of citation-based metrics such as citation counts and citation bursts, network-based metrics such as degree centrality and betweenness centrality. Sigma is a combination of both types, i.e., burst and betweenness centrality.

There are other features that are not included in the current summary, for example, structural variation analysis, analysis of uncertainties, concept trees, and dual-map overlays.

MAJOR CLUSTERS

The network consists of 4 clusters. The largest 4 clusters are summarized as follows.

Table 1. Summary of the largest 4 clusters.

ClusterID	Size	Silhouette	Label (LSI)	Label (LLR)	Label (MI)	Average Year
0	46	0.933	literature review	artificial intelligence (20.35, 1.0E-4)	new artificial intelligence infrastructure (2.78)	2019
1	29	0.973	artificial intelligence	component selection (20.7, 1.0E-4)	crossing traffic (1.29)	2017
2	27	0.996	artificial intelligence	business logistics system (18.95, 1.0E-4)	pavement crack detection (0.09)	2015
7	10	0.997	fourth industrial revolution	fourth industrial revolution (19.35, 1.0E-4)	new artificial intelligence infrastructure (0.09)	2019

Fig. 10. Cite Space summary page

The Cite space summary page above shows the most cited articles and how they are all connected. Using the summary page, we can pick relevant articles that have many cites attributed to them.

10 Articles used for further in-depth analysis were chosen by cluster keyword and co-citation analysis. All articles chosen were sent to Mendeley reference manager [4] Additionally, 2 chapters from Brauer and Goetsch was cited to support the discussion of course topics.

4.5 Content Analysis Via MaxQDA

After in-depth analysis articles were downloaded, MaxQDA was used to generate a word cloud from all the articles in Fig. 11.

The top keywords from Fig. 10 were Safety, Design, Data, Systems, and AI. MaxQDA also supports frequency lexical search which allows in-depth analysis of terms that were frequently seen in articles. In addition, it allows one to pinpoint where in the article to focus analysis on. An example of lexical search is shown in Fig. 12.

Fig. 11. MaxQDA Word cloud generation [3]

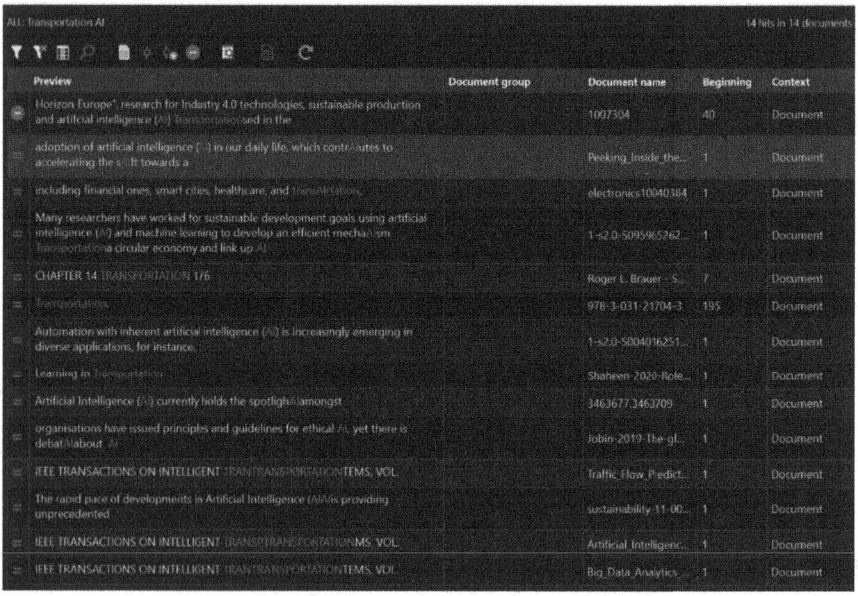

Fig. 12. MaxQDA lexical search of AI, Transportation

5   Discussion

Overall, the systematic review of the safety of artificial intelligence and transportation has been an excellent eye-opening and learning curve. The extraction and analysis of articles from various research databases have shed more light on the number of researchers, authors, publications, and countries of research as well as their interrelationship with other sectors.

According to the published paper ref. (8) AI methods that are finding their way to the transport field include Artificial Neural Networks (ANN), Genetic algorithms (GA), Simulated Annealing (SA), Artificial Immune system (AIS), Ant Colony Optimiser (ACO), and Bee Colony Optimization (BCO) and Fuzzy Logic Model (FLM) The successful application of these different AI requires a good understanding of the relationships between them and the application of the obtained data to tackle some challenges of the transportation system safely. Safe implementation of AI in transportation is crucial, quoted from Roger Brauer's textbook page 220 motor vehicle (a form of transportation) illustrates the importance of safety in transportation. According to the World Health Organization (WHO), 1 each year about 1.2 million people die on roads around the world. That amounts to about 3,400 each day reason why any new technology introduction should incorporate safety to reduce this alarming number. Article [27] highlighted the significant increase of embedded technology in automobiles which is now a key driver for automakers to prioritize areas such as ergonomics and user experience.

Furthermore, published work by Adadi [9], a key impediment to the use of AI-based systems is that they often lack transparency. Indeed, the black-box nature of these systems allows powerful predictions, but they cannot be directly explained. This issue has triggered a new debate on explainable AI (XAI). A research field holds substantial promise for improving the trust and transparency of AI-based systems. The crucial need for explaining AI outcomes becomes fully apparent, especially in life-changing decisions such as disease diagnosis; it is important to know the reasons behind such a critical decision, likewise in the transportation sector that has allocated with it a very high number of casualties according to https://www.nhtsa.gov/press-releases/early-estimate-2021-traffic-fatalities - Newly released estimates show traffic fatalities reached a 16 year high in 2021. XAI research field aims to make AI systems results more understandable to different sectors for their implementation in sectors like Safety and Transportation. Publication [15] explores how firms systematically foster trust regarding applied AI, it provides tangible approaches to increase trust in AI technology and illustrates the necessity of a democratic development process for applied AI. The paper shows an example of a survey of 1003 car buyers in Germany conducted by Plus (plus, 2015) in 2015 revealed that almost half of the respondents were skeptical regarding the topic of autonomous driving. Concerning the actual use of such vehicles, approximately 49% of respondents preferred traditional driving, and 43% preferred semi-autonomous driving. Only 5% of respondents preferred fully autonomous driving. This shows clearly that trust is important in human social interactions. If AI continues to build and prioritize safety in its implementation it will evolve trust which is mainly driven by the predictability of the technology.

At the onset of this project, it was tasked to collate relevant articles related to the keywords and locate one that connects safety to AI for transportation, this was overcome after exposure to various data analysis databases tools like SCOPUS, Google Scholar through Harzing software, Vicinitas by Twitter, and Web of Science, also prior knowledge from the chapter on Safety System and transportation from Rogers Brauer textbook further aids in the integration of safety into this great research topic.

In addition, Ballester's article talks about the definition of the article and how it helps in bringing the understanding of AI into the common public field [10]. Next, Di talks about autonomous vehicles and how AI developed from physics to use in cars [11]. Furthermore, Hagendorff analyses the ethics of AI and the issues that crop up due to AI integration in society [13]. Jabbapour also talks more about the consequences of AI and analyses the dark side of AI [16]. Finally, Jobin states a more global view on the ethics of AI and its benefits and costs to society [17]. Overall, these articles help in understanding AI and its integration, with sub-analyses on ethics and safety.

5.1 Project Uniqueness

This topic is unique due to the emerging AI situation. At present, AI is becoming more and more complex and allowing industries to utilize AI to optimize their systems. In this paper's case, we will focus on transportation systems and AI implementation. Compared to other literature like "Smart Manufacturing" by Kusiak, where the focus is on the manufacturing side of the industry, deep learning by Zhao, and the use of AI in automotive vehicles by Henstler [15, 18, 25]. This project topic considers all transportation and focuses on how AI can safely integrate, the issues that may crop up from AI integration, and the benefits AI can provide.

5.2 Course Justification

AI In Transportation Integration

"A trend started in the 2010s to incorporate smart or intelligent systems into vehicles. Various terms describe the new technologies: the autonomous car, piloted driving, and vehicle-to-vehicle (V2V) technology" (24, pg 180). This quote further justifies the project as an emerging topic. Abduljabbar's article talks about the application of AI in transportation [8]. The article is about the emerging topic of AI and transportation and the quote helps justify the topic by stating the trend of smart and intelligent systems integrating into vehicles. Brauer goes further and talks about autonomous cars, which are a huge subset of transportation with many companies affecting it, like Tesla.

Artificial Intelligence and Safety

"Now, with the speed of technical development being what it is, the safety and health problems associated with automation, particularly stress-related problems, are likely to increase." [12]. This quote is related to the safety aspect of AI in transportation and how the challenge of safety increases with AI use. Abduljabbar's article is about the application of AI in transportation, which also includes the risk of AI use [8]. Goetsch has a chapter on automation which also includes the issues that crop up with automation and what steps can be taken to mitigate these issues. Overall, the article is justified by Goetsch in terms of safety within AI and how to deal with it.

5.3 Additional Subtopics from Article Insights

User Experience in Automobiles
Using scite.ai, we can further analyze the topic of AI and transportation. Furthermore, we can see other articles that have supported the topic. One interesting article is by Renaud. Renaud states, "The literature reveals that in recent years, various authors have focused on the user experience" [22]. This quote is meant to justify the emerging topic of user experience in industrial applications with AI. Overall, Ribeiro's article helps in justifying further AI user experience research and justifying the focus [23].

Automobile Corporate Ergonomics
The next article is about Peugot's approach to Ergonomics. Using Scite.ai, we know that this article was cited nine times. One article comes to mind. Neuman's article utilizes Moreau's article where Neuman states, "Summarizing Peugeot's approach to ergonomics noted that "denser" task cycles (presumed to provide a productivity benefit) lead to increased MSDs in operators…" [19]. From this quote, we can see the use of Moreau's article as a note to further justify bad practices in task cycles. It even says the use of denser task cycles leads to problems for the operators. Overall, Moreau's article is referenced to justify better ergonomics and better practices in the workplace, which AI can help in optimizing task cycles and automating them.

6 Conclusion

In conclusion, AI can be integrated into transportation systems and other sectors. However, risks occur with AI use and must be mitigated by various safety practices. These practices can be researched in the future to better integrate AI and allow for safe use by operators and drivers in the transportation industry. This review shows the immense value Artificial intelligence has in the transportation industry, by optimizing traffic routes for drivers in the truck industry. AI can also replace the need for drivers and operators of complex systems, reducing the risk of human injury. However, artificial intelligence integration is expensive and is in its infancy. Researchers are studying AI and companies are further developing more complex AI which can be used in various sectors of society. Additionally, further research will make AI cheaper to implement and improve safety while using AI.

7 Future Work

Exploring the database of NSF.gov awards there is ongoing research titled "Encoding Dynamic Traffic Flow Analysis into AI for Network-Wide Early Alarming of Traffic-Demand-Influencing Events and Their Impacts" in University of Florida Lili Du (PI), Hongcheng Liu (Co-PI). This future work has started researching the integration of dynamic traffic flow analysis into artificial intelligence to provide early alarm of significant traffic-demand-influencing events (DIEs) and the associated traffic impacts. Urban traffic can deviate from normal states due to various scheduled and unscheduled DIEs,

Fig. 13. NSF Awards Search [20]

such as sports, commercial promotions, and festivals. These events often induce a surge in traffic demand, cause hours of congestion, and affect multiple traffic infrastructures. Early awareness of DIEs and their traffic impact will benefit many stakeholders, including travelers, government, and transportation-related service providers, in taking proactive actions to manage traffic congestion. In the future, the plan is to develop a network-wide online DIE monitoring system, which can automatically provide early alarm of the DIEs and forecast the resulting congestion. The research outcomes can be directly employed to mitigate traffic network congestion and become an essential component of future smart city technologies.

There is also a current ongoing workshop that will gather researchers from transportation, computer science, and other relevant disciplines to explore the frontiers of artificial intelligence (AI)-empowered methods, solutions, and future research directions to address urban transportation challenges by the same University of Florida (Fig. 13).

References

1. "BibExcel." n.d. https://homepage.univie.ac.at/juan.gorraiz/bibexcel
2. "CiteSpace." n.d. http://cluster.cis.drexel.edu/~cchen/citespace/
3. "MAXQDA." n.d. https://www.maxqda.com/
4. "Mendeley." n.d. https://www.mendeley.com/
5. "Scopus."n.d. https://www.scopus.com/
6. "VOSviewer." n.d. https://www.vosviewer.com/
7. "WebOfScience." N.d. https://clarivate.com/
8. Abduljabbar, R., Dia, H., Liyanage, S., Bagloee, S.A.: Applications of artificial intelligence in transport: An overview. Sustainability (Switzerland) 11(1). MDPI (2019). https://doi.org/10.3390/su11010189
9. Adadi, A., Berrada, M.: Peeking inside the black-box: a survey on explainable artificial intelligence (XAI). IEEE Access **6**, 52138–52160 (2018). https://doi.org/10.1109/ACCESS.2018.2870052

10. Ballester, O.: An artificial intelligence definition and classification framework for public sector applications. In: ACM International Conference Proceeding Series, pp. 67–75 (2021). https://doi.org/10.1145/3463677.3463709
11. Di, X., Shi, R.: A Survey on Autonomous Vehicle Control in the Era of Mixed-Autonomy: From Physics-Based to AI-Guided Driving Policy Learning. arXiv:2007.05156 (2020)
12. Goetsch - The_Safety_and_Health_Handbook. (n.d.)
13. Hagendorff, T.: The ethics of AI ethics: an evaluation of guidelines. Mind. Mach. **30**(1), 99–120 (2020). https://doi.org/10.1007/s11023-020-09517-8
14. Harzing, A.W.: Publish or Perish (2007). https://harzing.com/resources/publish-or-perish
15. Hengstler, M., Enkel, E., Duelli, S.: Applied artificial intelligence and trust-The case of autonomous vehicles and medical assistance devices. Technol. Forecast. Soc. Chang. **105**, 105–120 (2016). https://doi.org/10.1016/j.techfore.2015.12.014
16. Jabbarpour, M.R., Saghiri, A.M., Sookhak, M.: A framework for component selection considering dark sides of artificial intelligence: a case study on autonomous vehicle. Electronics **10**(4), 384 (2021). https://doi.org/10.3390/electronics10040384
17. Jobin, A., Ienca, M., Vayena, E.: Artificial Intelligence: the global landscape of ethics guidelines (2019)
18. Kusiak, A.: Smart manufacturing. Int. J. Prod. Res. **56**(1–2), 508–517 (2018). https://doi.org/10.1080/00207543.2017.1351644
19. Moreau, M.: Corporate ergonomics programme at automobiles Peugeot-Sochaux. Appl. Ergon. **34**(1), 29–34 (2003)
20. NSF: Encoding Dynamic Traffic Flow Analysis into AI for Network-Wide Early Alarming of Traffic-Demand-Influencing Events and Their Impacts. Sponsor: National Science Foundation. Award CMMI 2213459, $300,000 (10/01/2022–9/30/2025). Lili Du (PI), Hongcheng Liu (Co-PI)
21. Patrick Neumann, W., Dul, J.: Human factors: spanning the gap between OM and HRM. Int. J. Oper. Prod. Manag. **30**(9), 923–950 (2010). https://doi.org/10.1108/01443571011075056
22. Renaud, J., et al.: Product manual elaboration in product design phases: Behavioral and functional analysis based on user experience. Inter. J. Indust. Ergon. **71**, 75–83 (2019). https://doi.org/10.1016/j.ergon.2019.02.003. (Has missing data)
23. Ribeiro, T.M., Camâra, J.J.D.: Ergonomic approach of the influence of materials and the user experience in the interior of automobiles. In: Bagnara, S., Tartaglia, R., Albolino, S., Alexander, T., Fujita, Y. (eds.) Proceedings of the 20th Congress of the International Ergonomics Association (IEA 2018): Volume VI: Transport Ergonomics and Human Factors (TEHF), Aerospace Human Factors and Ergonomics, pp. 325–331. Springer International Publishing, Cham (2019). https://doi.org/10.1007/978-3-319-96074-6_35
24. Roger, L.: Brauer - Safety and Health for Engineers-Wiley (2016). (n.d.)
25. Zhao, Z., Chen, W., Wu, X., Chen, P.C.Y., Liu, J.: LSTM network: a deep learning approach for Short-term traffic forecast. IET Intel. Transport Syst. **11**(2), 68–75 (2017). https://doi.org/10.1049/iet-its.2016.0208
26. Zimmermann, N., Duffy, V.G.: Systematic literature review of safety management systems in aviation maintenance operations. In: Duffy, V.G., Landry, S.J., Lee, J.D., Stanton, N. (eds) Human-Automation Interaction. Automation, Collaboration, & E-Services, vol 11. Springer, Cham (2023). https://doi.org/10.1007/978-3-031-10784-9_19

Acceptability and Inclusivity of CCAM: What Strategies and Methods Should be Used to Engage Stakeholders?

Silvia Chiesa(✉), Dario Irrera, and Stefania Aguzzi

RE:Lab, Reggio Emilia 42122, RE, Italy
{silvia.chiesa,dario.irrera,stefania.aguzzi}@re-lab.it

Abstract. In all social studies and research, the involvement of users and citizens is fundamental in order to build products and carry out research that truly considers the user at the centre of construction and definition of the research process.

But what are the different strategies used to keep users involved throughout the entire research? And what are the best engagement strategies for their involvement? Obviously, there is not a single answer to this question, but the engagement strategies depend on the characteristics of the users to be reached and the objectives to be achieved.

In this article, a literature review on this topic will be presented and the main engagement strategies that are used for user engagement will be described and analysed. This investigation of the literature will constitute the basis of the research methodologies that will be followed within the SINFONICA project, a EU-funded project that foresees co-creation and co-design processes using effective engagement methodologies that foster the exchange of visions and knowledge involving citizens and relevant stakeholders.

Keywords: Social Engagement · Autonomous Vehicle · Engagement Strategies

1 Introduction

In the marked acceleration of technological research and evolution witnessed during the last few decades globally and in all sectors, the transport domain has not been left unscathed. On the contrary, mobility by its nature lends itself to being fertile ground for innovation and the development of cutting-edge technological solutions that succeed in improving the quality of life in terms of safety, comfort, accessibility, and social inclusion. Connected, Cooperative and Automated Mobility (CCAM) has become the trending topic in the automotive domain. CCAM fits into the broader domain of so-called Cooperative Intelligent Transport Systems (C-ITS). This definition stands for a set of solutions that enable digital technology to be applied to transport, in order to facilitate a rapid, low-latency, seamless exchange of information between vehicles

This study is part of the SINFONICA project that has received funding from the European Union under the Horizon Europe Research and Innovation Program (Grant Agreement n° 101064988).

and between them and infrastructures throughout the transport network. Some scholars [1] tend to consider C-ITS a subclass of the broader category of Intelligent Transport System (ITS). Under the umbrella of C-ITS, it is customary to include all the evolutionary trends involving connectivity, technology integration and communication technologies in traffic networks and transport systems for goods and people. In recent years, the topic has attracted a great deal of interest on a multidisciplinary level, as it involves not only the industrial and automotive worlds, but also related sectors such as air transport and shipping, Original Equipment Manufacturers (OEMs), telecommunications, service providers, the digital sector, etc.

In this framework, CCAM encompasses revolutionary technologies that are leading the transition to a new era of mobility: by combining the power of advanced sensors, distributed control algorithms, machine learning, 5G and connectivity technologies, and digital infrastructures, it is possible to deliver a high level of standards for security and safety. CCAM stakeholders, an alliance of cross-sectoral actors, are working to develop and implement a shared, coherent, and long-term R&D agenda. The ultimate goal is to create a more user-centered, multimodal, seamless, and inclusive mobility systems, increasing road safety while reducing traffic congestion and environmental footprint [2].

CCAM technologies are likely to have significant development and impacts on our economy and society. Several positive effects on future mobility are at stake, such as improved safety, transportation options for children, the elderly, and people with disabilities, reduced parking spaces, ways to reduce road congestion and improve the efficiency of public transport mobility systems. Furthermore, autonomous driving, electrification and shared models pave the way for more sustainable mobility solutions [3].

However, although the mentioned benefits, there is still insufficient demand of CCAM solutions, as society does not yet fully understand the potential positive repercussions of these enhanced mobility concepts [4]. Therefore, it is important to capitalize on knowledge collected through research to accelerate development and deployment of CCAM solutions, examining the long-term implications, benefits and impacts of integrating them into the mobility system. From this perspective, further development in this domain represents an important opportunity to shape and orient the mobility of the future, in order to make it more inclusive and respectful of the needs of all the road users and population. At the same time this innovative mobility needs to be understandable by all the possible users and groups, in order to be easily accepted and implemented.

For this reason – and taking in to account these elements – the main important aspects to take in consideration are, on the one hand, the needs of the different categories of users, on the other hand the urgence to individuate the main inclusive methodologies to collect and share information and key elements among all the involved stakeholder, to make CCAM usable, safe and acceptable.

2 How to Collect User Needs and Opinion

In light of the aforementioned reasons, it is fundamental to understand how people could take advantage from CCAM, ensuring that no one is left behind, thus collecting also opinion and ideas from different categories of users, especially from the vulnerable ones.

According to Grippenkoven and colleagues [5], the ultimate success of CCAM will largely depend on user adoption. The category of vulnerable road users includes those who are not behind the wheel of a car or truck, including pedestrians, cyclists, motorcyclists, and other no-transport users. As a result, these subjects are more prone to serious injury or fatality in the event of an accident. To properly address the needs of this special category of users, it is necessary to examine the root cause of this vulnerability and its consequences. For example, research has identified three demographic groups among walkers, cyclists, and motorcyclists as particularly vulnerable: children, people with disabilities, and the elderly [6, 7]. Furthermore, there is also a significant body of research on vulnerable road users, and while there is no single comprehensive theory of vulnerability in transport research, it is evident that vulnerable road users have different needs compared to those of non-vulnerable road users [8, 9]. With a view to introducing innovative mobility solutions that are equitable and socially inclusive, it is crucial that these unique needs are taken into account in order to ensure the safety of most disadvantaged categories.

Therefore, understanding the needs of vulnerable road users is a challenge that must be met in order to achieve a broad acceptance of CCAM solutions by pedestrians, cyclists, and powered two-wheeler riders. This is especially true considering that these individuals are more likely than others to be injured in the event of a vehicular collision, hence also potentially the most mistrustful of the deployment of novel and unseen mobility options.

To reach a more informed overview of the current situation, researchers have utilized data from the second edition of the E-Survey of Road Users' Attitudes (ESRA) survey, which is a survey on road users' attitudes that collected data from more than 35,000 road users across 32 countries. This survey revealed that vulnerable road users often put themselves in dangerous situations, such as crossing the street at a place other than a nearby pedestrian crossing, reading a text message or checking social media while walking on the streets, cycling without wearing a helmet, and riding a powered two-wheeler without wearing a helmet [10]. With this knowledge in mind, it is possible to better define and shape vulnerable road users' category, outlining its profile and characteristics, and acting accordingly. To do this, solutions such as infrastructure interventions, use of protective equipment, and training and educational campaigns must be implemented.

Different methodologies are already in place and have been adopted by researchers to investigate more in-depth user needs and request, including surveys (that can provide a broad understanding of user attitudes and perceptions towards autonomous vehicles) and focus groups (for an in-depth insights into user attitudes and perceptions towards autonomous vehicles, as well as for an identification of specific areas of concern or interest or ethnographic research). Such methodologies allow to observe how people interact with autonomous vehicle technology in their natural environment.

It is generally recommended to combine the above methods for a more comprehensive understanding of user viewpoints. The research should be conducted with a diverse group of participants to account for different perspectives and experiences. This can lead to a comprehensive knowledge on the possible implications and ways to improve usability and acceptance of CCAM, eventually understanding possible ideas, expectations and opinions of future users of this kind of mobility.

Kassens-Noor and colleagues [11] found significant divergences between different categories of users with special needs. While respondents with visual impairments, reduced mobility, or multiple accommodation were more likely to rely on public transportation than those without special needs, their willingness to use Autonomous Public Transit (APT) varied. Respondents with low vision were more likely to use APT, whereas drivers with reduced mobility were less prone to adopt this mobility option. Additionally, their findings indicated that respondents with special needs had mostly negative perceptions of Autonomous Vehicles (AVs). This is especially true for users with reduced mobility. Respondents with multiple accommodation needs are more concerned about the safety of APT than those with no special needs, while those with reduced mobility are more skeptical about self-driving technology. This study improves our understanding of perceptions and acceptance of APT among different special needs populations and supports policy makers in developing inclusive policies and practices that bring the promised benefits of AVs to these populations [11].

Parents' intentions to travel with an AV and their technical readiness, as well as parent (gender, location) and child demographics (age, restraint), are important determinants of AV's potential acceptability and impact. Lee and Mirman [12] identified two groups of potential AV users: curious and practitioners. Their study fills a gap in the literature by assessing parents' views on the use of AVs to transport for children [13].

A recurring theme in the media is the issue of perceived safety for autonomous driving. Therefore, in addition to the technical challenges involved in setting up autonomous mobility services, perceived security by potential users must be seen as a necessary prerequisite for success from the outset. Based on the results of a workshop with potential users of an autonomous public transport system, an online survey was developed to analyze concerns about using the system. The identified fears can be divided into three groups: (1) fear of other passengers, (2) fear of lack of transparency in the system, and (3) fear of technical failure.

3 Inclusive Methodologies for Participatory Inclusion

Stakeholder engagement is an essential component of any research project, as it raises awareness of the activities, themes, and scope of the researchers, it allows for the effective exchange of ideas and opinions and represents a mean to identify and assess the interests and needs of all stakeholders.

In participatory research, the study becomes a collaborative work where researchers and participants have the same objective to achieve action-orientated goals [14]. Following this non-hierarchical research, the outcomes permit to the society to be included in the research design and to produce alternative knowledge [15].

To pursue a successful stakeholder engagement, it is important to develop a plan that outlines the various methods and strategies that can be used to involve stakeholders and possibly stimulate and appeal them. This plan should include different communication channels, such as online surveys, and focus groups, as well as in-person meetings, legislative hearings, notice and comment opportunities [16], which enable stakeholders to provide feedback and voice their opinions. In addition to direct engagement, it is also strategically important to exploit the various media channels to give visibility to the research carried out, so as to foster the dissemination of information and create new fora in which people can discuss and exchange ideas. It is well known how social media and online communities, nowadays, represent an important space for participation and interaction between individuals belonging to more or less articulated and defined categories. Ray and colleagues [17] emphasized how important engagement is – especially in digital environments – to stimulate a proactive approach by people in the domain of online community behavior.

When involving a multidisciplinary and cross-sectoral audience, it is important to consider the power and influence of different stakeholders, as well as their diverse needs. It is also advisable to ensure that the right stakeholders are achieving the appropriate level of engagement. Finally, it is essential to identify existing relationships and interests as well as to communicate with stakeholders to ensure that everyone is on the same page. How can users', providers', and public administrations' needs, desires, and concerns be collected and understood? Also other authors as Fung (2004) [18] elaborated some key questions as guidelines helpful to organize the procedure and methods for the stakeholder engagement, in particular who should be involved, with which method and their impact and influence on the results.

When working together, an effective collaboration necessarily passes through a reciprocal and shared understanding of the themes at stake among users, providers, and public administration, ensuring that everyone is fine-tuned. Hence, communication is a component of utmost importance to achieve an effective engagement strategy. It is the responsibility of the researcher to understand and take into account the needs and perspectives of the stakeholders. This is a complex process that involves listening to them and making sure their needs, desires, and concerns are collected and well perceived. People wish to feel understood and that their opinions are valued. Exploiting the correct engagement strategy make this a relevant step in the collaboration process, as it ensures that all parties involved converge on the same concepts and that everyone's voice is heard and taken into consideration. An effective engagement methodology provides people the opportunity to share their insights and opinions with the group.

A concept examined in the research by Ray and colleagues [17] in the context of online communities – but which we believe is more broadly applicable when analyzing the engagement strategies – is that of the satisfaction of people involved. When considering active participation and proactive attitude being part of engagement, word of mouth and prior satisfaction play a mediating role. Ensuring that participants are satisfied during engagement processes is therefore an influential objective. The management of stakeholders one-on-one have to be part of the activities, to prevent their negative opinions from influencing the rest of the audience. In this sense, when the feedback crosses the line from constructive to negative, it is best to isolate the individual and handle the situation privately. This ensures that the negative opinion does not spread and affect the entire group. Additionally, within the group of people engaged it should always be reminded and clarified that everyone's opinion is valid, even if it is different from the group's opinion. Thus, it is important to respect everyone's opinion and work together to come up with the best solutions.

The two most important question to promote the participatory approach are "who should be involved, and how?" [19]. Indeed, for each group of participants the most appropriate methodology needs to be individuated to maximize the inclusion and engagement.

In order to reach all member of the society it is good to identify some questions that must be asked to identify the best methodology to implement for the involvement of specific categories of users. Indeed, usually in the participatory research some specific categories of the society have more probability to be engaged. Inclusion and exclusion are often influenced by some parameters such as the ethnic, racial, gender or socioeconomic affiliation of the people participating in public participation. It is therefore convenient to identify new ways of inclusion and engagement practices [20]. In fact, inclusion implies active negotiation between individuals with differences in perspectives, identities, institutional boundaries or problem definitions [21].

Various are the questions that would help in the identification of the correct methodology to be used for the engagement of a specific groups. These questions should be oriented to investigate the characteristics of this group and the potential barriers for their engagement.

According to Pytlik Zillig and Tomkins [16] the pertinent points for a correct involvement of participants are related to the effectiveness, as there are a number of potential effectiveness criteria that would influence the social engagement.

The important questions to improve the social engagement are different in the various phases of the engagement. In the preparation phase are related to the information and the stakeholder selection, in the execution phase refer to the concern whether the process selection is effectively carried out and acceptable to stakeholders and finally, some questions related to the outcomes that deal with the trust and satisfaction of the engaged public. Moreover, different kind of methods should be adopted according to the typology of audience, when they have to be engaged, to the type of project and the duration of the engagement. According to the previous characteristics Lindenau and Böhler-Baedeker (2014) [22] individuated different kind of engagement technique from the less interactive to the more participatory.

Other questions are related to the objective that researchers want to reach through the involvement of participants, for example whether the aim is to include individual or group and also the characteristics of involvement from the social-cognitive psychological point of view [23]. Moreover, the stakeholders' interests, motivation or eventual barriers in participation would help in identifying the best approach for their engagement.

Here, some engagement strategies for the participation of CCAM initiatives are reported, in relationship to specific groups of civil society representants and their specific characteristics.

According to the technological level of participants, in-person and online mechanisms in engagement can be selected. They have pro and cons: for example, in-person methodologies may use both large or small group format and permit to obtain immediate feedback [24]. Online processes differ in terms of spatiotemporal characteristics and procedure [24, 27]. Finally, the citizen engagement interventions are more likely to be successful in particular when the plan targets a service that citizens access directly, as for example association or organizations [27].

To engage society and users in mobility related research, traditional methods have recently been accompanied by innovative tools such as Virtual Reality (VR) technology and simulations. For example, public transportation (a complex and vast field) cannot be studied with a single design method. Preliminary results suggest that a traditional approach respecting universal design principles ensures CCAM and site accessibility, usability, and comprehensibility. Some studies have identified VR as a suitable tool for industrial designers to evaluate communication concepts between CCAM and pedestrians. This confirms that such digital tools improve traditional design methods, especially in terms of technologies that are not yet available in the market [28].

VR could be used to engage vulnerable road users, as for example elderly people, that can use the VR to imagine themselves in the context and in the reality with autonomous vehicles.

Distler et al. used in their study various participatory approach. They have conducted different workshops, held public discussions, and taken experimental self-driving shuttle rides. In doing this, they adopted mixed methodologies, characterized by multiple phases: a pre-immersion evaluation of acceptability, an immersive journey on an autonomous shuttle and a post-immersion evaluation of acceptance. They measured pre-immersion adoption before immersing participants in an on-demand transport scenario, and finally measured post-immersion adoption of Autonomous Mobility on Demand (AMoD). The results showed that while participants felt comfortable with the security issues, they found the AMoD experience to be ineffective. Their findings highlight key factors to consider when designing an AMoD experience [29]. Town hall meeting, for example, have the positive characteristics to be quite inexpensive [16].

Another engagement initiative that has been used to improve user engagement is the Living Lab. Already studied for decades [e.g., 32, 33] a Living Lab is a specific experiment that aims at harnessing the creativity and capabilities of different stakeholders and users, bringing them together to work on specific issues, «an environment in which people and technology are gathered and in which everyday context and user needs stimulate and challenge both research and development». Just to mention one example of living lab applied in the context of automated driving, Pucihar et al., 2019 describes the creation of a living lab where users participated in a survey and expressed their attitudes toward AVs. In April 2018, on the occasion of the official opening of the AV Living Lab on the premises of BTC City in Ljubljana[1], in Slovenia, TEN-T Days event was organized by the European Commission, BTC and AV Living Lab. The main purpose of the event was to provide AV demos, test Cars on Miles prototypes and assess attendees' readiness for autonomous driving solutions. The results provide initial insights into the readiness of citizens for autonomous driving implementation and indicate future actions needed to accelerate the adoption of AVs and future mobility solutions. Originally, the Living Lab concept was mentioned by MIT's Professor William Mitchell, Media Lab and School of Architecture and Urban Planning (in the context of physical development). The main

---

[1] From Pucihar et al. (2019): «BTC City is one of the largest business, leisure and shopping centers of Europe. With 21 million yearly visitors, 38,000 cars per day, spread over 475,000 m2, with 450 shops and services, and 3000 businesses, BTC City provides a physical and virtual environment for AV Living Lab. It provides the physical and technical infrastructure and ecosystems to experiment, develop proof of concepts, demonstrations and pilot operations of innovative new products, applications, services and business models»

goal of this concept is to identify and provide the possibility for users to contribute to successful innovations in production-consumption systems. The living laboratory concept refers to a human-centered approach to research and development where (ICT-based) innovations (services, products or applications) are created and validated in a collaborative, multi-context and real-world environment. Another important feature of the living lab is that it involves various stakeholders, such as universities and research institutes, small and medium enterprises (SMEs), industry, ICT companies, public sector and public partners, engaging them in the co-creation of innovations. Autonomous Vehicle Living Lab provides a complete infrastructure for autonomous driving experiences, artificial intelligence, cybersecurity, blockchain for retail applications, infotainment and vehicle-to-any communication. In addition to the development process, living laboratories can make a significant contribution to raising awareness of certain topics among different groups of participants.

End user engagement are also possible through the use of gamification strategies [32]. Gamification has become a possible solution to motivate people to contribute to society and this methodology could be used to involve participants. The idea is to use game elements in serious situations, to give people involved in a gamified scenario an incentive to perform certain actions in order to continue playing. Based on these principles, fun apps could be used to engage people, in particular young and students.

The interest on this procedure is evidenced by the availability of gamification platforms also in the mobility context, especially in relationship to the aspect of consuming. Development and use of Serious Games can also be used to raise awareness and build engagement [33]. Gamification can make the experience of using autonomous vehicles more engaging and motivating for users.

4   The Future of Mobility in the SINFONICA Project: Stakeholder Engagement Proposal

The domain of transport and mobility – and specifically the automotive – represents a focal point of research and development in the European Union even prior to the international level. Alonso Raposo and colleagues [34] highlight how much important is this strategic sector for the Member States, particularly in terms of labor market, trade and EU's Gross Value Added. In addition, Europe still represent a leader player in the automotive value chain; this sector plays a pivotal role in the international market and is one of those in which there is the largest amount of private investment in research and development and technological advancement.

Therefore, the European Union has long drawn attention to the innovation trends affecting the transport domain. Through its Framework Programs dedicated to research and development, the European Commission has been investing large sums in research in transport for some time, funding projects revolving around the topic of sustainable and inclusive mobility. This is, in fact, a very transversal topic, that could have significant impacts on several domains such as that of sustainability, circular economy, tourism, social inclusion, economic development, knowledge transfer and technology advancement.

The SINFONICA project has been recently funded under the current Horizon Europe Framework Programme 2021–2027. It responds to a specific topic outlined by the European Commission through a "top-down" approach, titled specifically: "Analysis of socio-economic and environmental impacts and assessment of societal, citizen and user aspects for needs based CCAM solutions (CCAM Partnership)". Already from the title, it is easy to guess the characteristics and research directions that will be pursued within the project.

SINFONICA aims to develop practical, efficient and innovative strategies, methods and tools to engage CCAM users, providers and other stakeholders (i.e., citizens, including vulnerable users, transport companies, public administrations, service providers, researchers, vehicles and technology providers), with the ambition of collecting and understanding their needs, wishes and concerns related to CCAM. The purpose is to be able to structure the collected data in a manageable and usable way, so that useful information, guidelines, and recommendations can be drawn for development, implementation, and deployment of innovative, connected and autonomous mobility solutions. Additionally, The SINFONICA project will include the development of decision support tools for designers and decision makers to improve the seamless and sustainable delivery of CCAM to be inclusive and equitable for all citizens. The particular nature of this research project – requiring input from both technical expertise and social innovation needs, led to the establishment of a consortium of private organizations, universities and public authorities that will have to address the several challenges posed by the topic.

The special attention within the SINFONICA project on co-creation and co-design processes evidently requires the careful development of effective engagement methodologies that foster and leverage the exchange of visions and knowledge between the people involved in the planned activities. This point will be applied involving and engaging citizens and relevant stakeholders.

But what are the best engagement strategies to use with citizens to maintain their participation at all stages of the research process? The literature research that has been conducted on engagement strategies will be used within the SINFONICA project to involve people and in particular vulnerable road users in all phases of the project. Some of the previously exposed engagement methodologies, indeed, will be used and validated in order to involve users and new methodologies will be tested for specific categories and groups of citizens.

In particular, the research will be oriented towards those categories of users who, from a literature review carried out in the early stage of the project, are under-researched. In this sense, particular attention will be reserved to the Vulnerable Road Users (VRUs), precisely because SINFONICA's ambition is for effective inclusiveness, exploiting the new frontiers of technological innovation in mobility to break down barriers and remove the obstacles that currently afflict the vulnerable categories, depriving them of adequate mobility solutions and the possibility of making the most of public transport services.

Therefore, at the core of the SINFONICA project will be the activity of data collection and analysis carried out through these engagement strategies, which will be conducted within four specific territories, chosen to adequately reflect the diversity and typicality that characterize the European territory, which will represent the so-called "Groups of Interest". Specifically, these territories will correspond to the municipality of Hamburg, in Germany; the West Midlands in the United Kingdom; the province of Noord-Brabant in the Netherlands and the municipality of Trikala in Greece.

In the light of this ambition to involve a heterogeneous audience of users and stakeholders, it is evident how delicate the issue of engagement is. Ensuring that individuals are on board and stimulated in the co-creation and co-definition processes for new CCAM models and solutions hides several pitfalls that need to be addressed for effective data collection. Furthermore, another difficulty is posed by the diversity of territories in which the engagement methodologies will be carried out. In order to be able to coherently analyze the collected information, it is crucial that the data be comparable and computable, therefore it is necessary for researchers to agree on a common ground on which to build the engagement and data collection strategies.

For the purposes of the project, the concept of User Engagement here refers to the ability of researchers and project managers to meet and maintain the attention and interest of the individuals involved throughout the entire duration of the activities, so to achieve reliable data collection. To increase user engagement in the context of autonomous mobility, some strategies are going to be considered and integrated with the results obtained in previous projects and research.

First of all, the technologies applied and adopted in all the activities will have to be user-friendly and intuitive. This aspect will ensure that the autonomous vehicle technology will be easy to use and understandable for a wide range of users. The contribution of social sciences and human factors experts in the research will be crucial, in this sense. Adapting the technological tools and instruments to the capabilities of the audience can help to increase user engagement and reduce anxiety about using the technology. At the same time, regular collection of comments, user feedback and concerns about the autonomous vehicles will give the possibility to improve the engagement methodologies adopted and increase user engagement.

Finally, to ensure the soundness of the methodology, the research activities will be carried out through an iterative approach. The refined strategies will be revisited in three rounds based on the feedback received from the participants and any shortcomings identified by the users. This will allow a final strategy to be optimally tailored to meet research needs.

One of the cross-cutting objectives that will be pursued by these activities will be the nurturing of a sense of trust with users, by being transparent about the technology's capabilities and limitations, and by demonstrating its safety and reliability also through the personalization of the experience of users by providing them with options for customization, such as preferred routes, entertainment, and in-vehicle features, or creating an engaging environment inside the autonomous vehicle by the usage of interactive displays and games, and by offering a comfortable and relaxing atmosphere.

All these research objectives will be achieved through different engagement strategies which will be selected on the basis of the research groups to which they will be applied. In particular, the interesting challenge of this study consist in the identification of the most suitable strategy for the specific type of user to which it will be addressed.

Specific questions oriented to highlight the characteristics of the users to be involved, their strengths and weaknesses, will make it possible to identify the most suitable engagement strategy to maintain their interest and involvement for all the phases of the project.

5 Conclusions

The opinion of people and their point of view are important contributions that must be taken into consideration by researchers and by those who have the goal of producing and promoting products that are oriented to people. Their opinions, their needs are the essential basis for starting any research activity. It is therefore in charge of the researchers to involve users and maintain their active involvement during all phases of the research process, to collect their opinions and to translate their opinions into requirements and design indications. But the challenge for researchers is not only to translate the opinions and needs of citizens in requirements for the development, but also to find the best way to collect this information, finding the most suitable methodology to enable to the entire population to express its voice, thus adapting the methodologies based on the characteristics of the people that are important to reach and involve. As shown, there is not a single methodology, but multiple methodologies with different facets that must be deepened according to the needs and research objectives to be achieved.

References

1. Zrari, C., Balbo, F., Ghedira, K.: Multi-Agent based platform dedicated to C-ITS. Proc. Comput. Sci. **134**, 243–250 (2018)
2. Kousaridas, A., et al.: 5G cross-border operation for connected and automated mobility: Challenges and solutions. Future Internet **12**(1), 5 (2019)
3. Raposo, M.A., Grosso, M., Mourtzouchou, A., Krause, J., Duboz, A., Ciuffo, B.: Economic implications of a connected and automated mobility in Europe. Res. Transp. Econ. **92**, 101072 (2022)
4. Jing, P., Xu, G., Chen, Y., Shi, Y., Zhan, F.: The determinants behind the acceptance of autonomous vehicles: a systematic review. Sustainability **12**(5), 1719 (2020)
5. Grippenkoven, J., Fassina, Z., König, A., Dreßler, A.: Perceived safety: a necessary precondition for successful autonomous mobility services. In: Proceedings of the Human Factors and Ergonomics Society Europe (2018)
6. Löcken, A., et al.: WeCARe: workshop on inclusive Communication between Automated Vehicles and Vulnerable Road Users. In: 22nd International Conference on Human-Computer Interaction with Mobile Devices and Services, pp. 1–5 (October 2020)
7. Holländer, K., Colley, M., Rukzio, E., Butz, A.: A taxonomy of vulnerable road users for hci based on a systematic literature review. In: Proceedings of the 2021 CHI Conference on Human Factors in Computing Systems, pp. 1–13 (May 2021)
8. Owens, J.M., et al.: Automated vehicles & vulnerable road users: representing the underrepresented. In: Road Vehicle Automation, vol. 7(6), pp. 97–107. Springer International Publishing (2020). https://doi.org/10.1007/978-3-030-52840-9_10
9. Löcken, A., et al.: Accessible automated automotive workshop series (a3ws): international perspective on inclusive external human-machine interfaces. In: Adjunct Proceedings of the 14th International Conference on Automotive User Interfaces and Interactive Vehicular Applications, pp. 192–195 (September 2022)

10. Meesmann, U., et al.: ESRA2–Road Safety Culture. Synthesis from the ESRA2 survey in, 48 (2022)
11. Kassens-Noor, E., Cai, M., Kotval-Karamchandani, Z., Decaminada, T.: Autonomous vehicles and mobility for people with special needs. Trans. Res. Part A: Policy Pract. **150**, 385–397 (2021)
12. Lee, Y.C., Mirman, J.H.: Parents' perspectives on using autonomous vehicles to enhance children's mobility. Trans. Res. Part C: Emerging Technol. **96**, 415–431 (2018)
13. Ayala, A., Lee, Y.C.: Autonomous vehicles, children's mobility, and family perspective. In: Proceedings of the Human Factors and Ergonomics Society Annual Meeting, vol. 65(1), pp. 747–751. SAGE Publications, Sage CA (2021)
14. Bagnoli, A., Clark, A.: Focus groups with young people: a participatory approach to research planning. J. Youth Stud. **13**(1), 101–119 (2010)
15. Fuller, D., Kitchin, R.: Radical theory/critical praxis: academic geography beyond the academy? (2004)
16. PytlikZillig, L.M., Tomkins, A.J.: Public engagement for informing science and technology policy: What do we know, what do we need to know, and how will we get there? Rev. Policy Res. **28**(2), 197–217 (2011)
17. Ray, S., Kim, S.S., Morris, J.G.: The central role of engagement in online communities. Inf. Syst. Res. **25**(3), 528–546 (2014)
18. Fung, A.: Empowered participation. Princeton University Press, In Empowered Participation (2009)
19. Guijt, I.: Participatory approaches. Methodol. Briefs: Impact Evaluat. **5**(5) (2014)
20. Quick, K.S., Feldman, M.S.: Distinguishing participation and inclusion. J. Plan. Educ. Res. **31**(3), 272–290 (2011)
21. Quick, K.S., Feldman, M.S.: Boundaries as junctures: Collaborative boundary work for building efficient resilience. J. Public Administration Res. Theory **24**(3), 673–695 (2014)
22. Lindenau, M., Böhler-Baedeker, S.: Citizen and stakeholder involvement: a precondition for sustainable urban mobility. Trans. Res. Proc. **4**, 347–360 (2014)
23. Fredricks, J.A., Blumenfeld, P.C., Paris, A.H.: School engagement: potential of the concept, state of the evidence. Rev. Educ. Res. **74**(1), 59–109 (2004)
24. Gastil, J., Levine, P.: The deliberative democracy handbook: Strategies for effective civic engagement in the twenty-first century. Jossey-Bass (2005)
25. Davies, T., Chandler, R.: Online deliberation design: choices, criteria, and evidence. arXiv preprint arXiv:1302.5177 (2013)
26. Nabatchi, T., Amsler, L.B.: Direct public engagement in local government. Am. Review Public Administ. **44**(4_suppl), 63S–88S (2014)
27. Waddington, H., Sonnenfeld, A., Finetti, J., Gaarder, M., John, D., Stevenson, J.: Citizen engagement in public services in low-and middle-income countries: A mixed-methods systematic review of participation, inclusion, transparency and accountability (PITA) initiatives. Campbell Syst. Rev. **15**(1–2), e1025 (2019)
28. Cornet, H., Stadler, S., Kong, P., Marinkovic, G., Frenkler, F., Sathikh, P.M.: User-centred design of autonomous mobility for public transportation in Singapore. Trans. Res. Proc. **41**, 191–203 (2019)
29. Distler, V., Lallemand, C., Bellet, T.: Acceptability and acceptance of autonomous mobility on demand: the impact of an immersive experience. In: Proceedings of the 2018 CHI Conference on Human Factors in Computing Systems, pp. 1–10 (April 2018)
30. Niitamo, V.P., Kulkki, S., Eriksson, M., Hribernik, K.A.: State-of-the-art and good practice in the field of living labs. In: 2006 IEEE International Technology Management Conference (ICE), pp. 1–8. IEEE (June 2006)

31. Bergvall-Kareborn, B.H.M.S.A., Hoist, M., Stahlbrost, A.: Concept design with a living lab approach. In: 2009 42nd Hawaii International Conference on System Sciences, pp. 1–10. IEEE (January 2009)
32. Bucchiarone, A., Battisti, S., Marconi, A., Maldacea, R., Ponce, D.C.: Autonomous shuttle-as-a-service (ASaaS): Challenges, opportunities, and social implications. IEEE Trans. Intell. Transp. Syst.Intell. Transp. Syst. **22**(6), 3790–3799 (2020)
33. Cravero, S.: Methods, strategies and tools to improve citizens' engagement in the smart cities' context: a Serious Game classification. Valori e Valutazioni (24) (2020)
34. Alonso Raposo, M., et al.: An analysis of possible socio-economic effects of a Cooperative, Connected and Automated Mobility (CCAM) in Europe: effects of automated driving on the economy, employment and skills (2018)

Review and Reappraisal of Safety Pertaining to Battery Electric Vehicles

Claudia Escribens[✉] and Vincent G. Duffy

Purdue University, West Lafayette, IN 47906, USA
cescribe@purdue.edu

Abstract. This paper takes performs a review and reappraisal discussion on safety pertaining to battery electric vehicles. This is in response to the various pressures to advance the technology used to power battery electric vehicles to a safe state. A variety of bibliometric and co-citation tools are used to source references and relevant sources. Other tools are used to understand how the topic is trending and growing, and how it compares to other well-established and safety-related topics. These tools and their results are discussed. Graphs of leading authors and leading countries are presented, to show who is doing this work and where. The topic is tied back into the course, emphasizing the safety aspects, and getting a base level understanding of what the hazards created are. This leads to the future work section, where the National Science Foundation website is explored to see if there are grants being awarded to further this research.

Keywords: Electric vehicle · battery · lithium-ion

1 Introduction and Academic Justification

1.1 Introduction

In response to environmental and regulatory concerns, the automotive (and overall transportation) industry is moving towards full electrification. These technologies, while not brand new, are still lacking with regards to usability, and safety, and present a myriad of issues and hazards, especially at the scale needed to meet demands and expectations. This topic encapsulates safety, economics, statistics, and manufacturing, all falling within the scope of Industrial Engineering. Engineers with more in-depth technical backgrounds, like mechanical and chemical engineers, are working on finding and addressing the root cause of the battery safety issues. The scope of the selected topic does not deal with human factors and ergonomics or human-computer interaction.

In addition to environmental and regulatory pressures, there are market pressures on the automotive industry to advance the technology to a usable and safe state. There have been headlines about safety issues caused by electric vehicle batteries to the point where the National Transit Safety Board has had to issue a statement about their dangers (National Traffic Safety Board 2020). The urgency is clear, and so this paper seeks to gain a better understanding of the safety issues caused by electric vehicle batteries.

© The Author(s), under exclusive license to Springer Nature Switzerland AG 2023
V. G. Duffy et al. (Eds.): HCII 2023, LNCS 14057, pp. 277–293, 2023.
https://doi.org/10.1007/978-3-031-48047-8_18

1.2 Academic Justification and Purpose

As will be shown and discussed in depth in the forthcoming review and reappraisal, every search and every database show a sharp and steep increase in interest and research in the area of electric vehicle battery safety. Given the specificity of the topic (electric vehicle battery safety), the sprawl across and into other subjects is not very wide, and the pool of researchers is close, but the sheer increase in the volume of work on the topic year over year is clear. Figure 1 below, taken from the Web of Science database with search terms "electric vehicle" & "battery" & "safety," shows a rapid increase in the volume of topical documentation, with the documents more than doubling from 2019 (227) to 2022 (504).

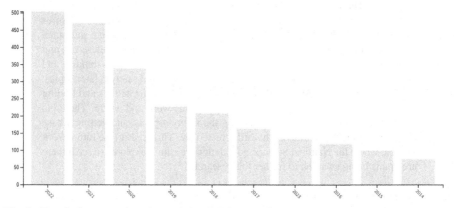

Fig. 1. Trend diagram taken from Web of Science with search terms "electric vehicle" & "battery" & safety.

The search popularity and relevancy of the topic are skyrocketing. The market and political pressures are present and only increasing. There are outstanding safety and usability issues with the technology, leading to a perfect storm in justification. The automotive industry is wanting to scale up the production of electric vehicles but knows it would not be prudent to do so without a more robust grasp of the safety issues with the batteries, and how to contain these issues prior to a more massive launch. The purpose of this research is to understand who is doing the work in this space, where are they doing this work, when has this work been done, how is this type of research trending, and what general conclusions being reached. Providing a personal anecdote, amid company-wide layoffs my employer expanded a dedicated group to solving these problems, which I will be joining. The issue is pressing.

2 Review

Table 1 below shows the databases used for sourcing articles, the search terms used for each database, and the number of articles each database yielded. All the articles sourced for this paper come from scholarly databases, with access to these databases granted by Purdue Libraries. Additional sources or definitions come from either government (.gov), organizations (.org), or university (.edu) websites.

Table 1. Search terms by database and associated result quantity

Database	Search Terms	Number of Articles
Scopus	**"electric vehicle" & "battery" & "safety"**	4,417
Web of Science: Core Collection	**"electric vehicle" "battery" "safety"**	1,159
Google Scholar	**"electric vehicle" & "battery" & "safety"**	About 121,000

Various trend and bibliometric tools were used for the ensuing analysis. The following sections outline the procedures for each tool. Sameeran Kanade's "Use of Virtual Reality for Safety Training: A Systematic Review" employs a similar methodology (Kanade 2022).

2.1 Vicinitas

Vicinitas is a tool that enables analytics of tweets. Unfortunately, the usefulness of this tool has severely decreased since the management change at Twitter, where a decision was made to no longer make historical tweets accessible. Nevertheless, Vicinitas allows for a slice-of-time type analysis.

On April 27th, 2023, a Vicinitas search was conducted using the search terms "electric vehicle safety." The word "battery" was excluded, given Vicinitas' newly limited scope, and the nature of tweets; tweets are very concise by nature. It was figured that the addition of the "battery" term would greatly limit the search results, and it would have been interesting and notable to see if the term "battery" appeared in the search organically.

Figures 2, 3 and 4 below show engagement measures from Vicinitas.

192	199	520	2.8M
Users	Posts	Engagement	Influence

Fig. 2. Engagement numbers from Vicinitas for search term "electric vehicle safety" on 4/27/23

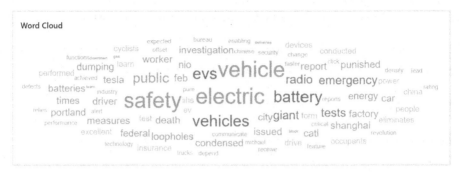

Fig. 3. Word cloud from Vicinitas for search term "electric vehicle safety" on 4/27/23

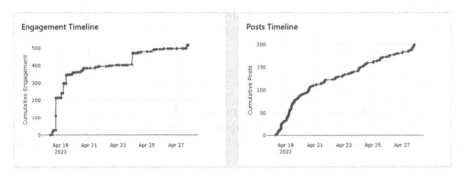

Fig. 4. Engagement and posts timelines from Vicinitas for search term "electric vehicle safety" on 4/27/23

2.2 Trend Diagrams

To go forward with the topic of electric vehicle battery safety, in order to academically justify it, it was important to see how the topic is trending in scholarly databases. In doing these analyses, an upward trend in the volume of articles was sought.

Scopus was accessed through Purdue Libraries and was used for analysis purposes. Figure 5 below shows a trend chart from Scopus for search terms "electric vehicle" & "battery" & "safety."

With the clear upward trend found in the Scopus database, it was important to put these numbers into context. Figure 6 below shows a Google nGram, comparing the topical search terms to other terms that have been relevant in class, "ergonomics" and "digital human modeling," with the years being limited to 1980–2019.

Documents by year

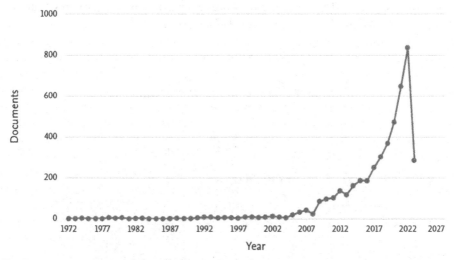

Fig. 5. Documents by year taken from the Scopus database with search terms "electric vehicle" & "battery" & "safety"

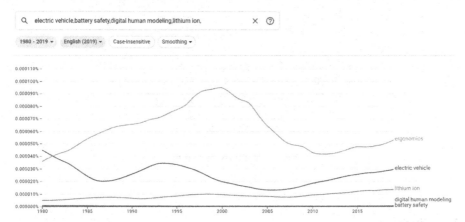

Fig. 6. Google nGram of search terms "electric vehicle," "battery safety," digital human modeling," "ergonomics," and "lithium ion

2.3 VOSviewer

VOSviewer is a software tool used to depict bibliometric networks. This tool has been used by other researchers in their bibliometric analyses, such as Sameeran Kanade (Kanade 2022).

Figure 7 below shows the results of an analysis performed in VOSviewer for battery electric vehicle safety. This was generated from a Scopus search using the terms "battery," "electric vehicle," and "safety," yielding 4417 results.

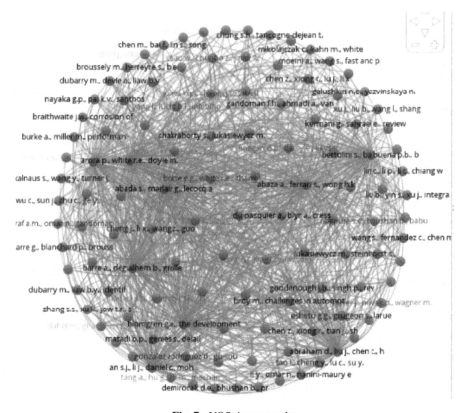

Fig. 7. VOSviewer results

2.4   CiteSpace

CiteSpace is another software tool that enables the visualization of trends and patterns in scientific literature. The CiteSpace software required a search in the Web of Science database as input, with search terms "electric vehicle lithium-ion battery safety" (lithium-ion batteries are the ones used to power electric vehicles, more in the reappraisal section), yielding 2530 results. Figure 8 below shows the set-up screen for CiteSpace.

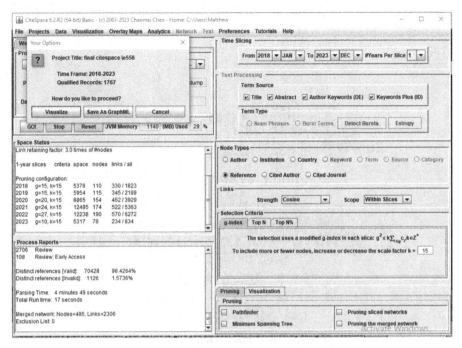

Fig. 8. Set up screen for CiteSpace software

The accessible version of CiteSpace has significant limitations that warranted a significant adjustment of the inputs. The year span covered had to be lowered to 2018–2023 and the k-value had to be lowered from 25 to 15.

Figure 9 below shows the cluster analysis results derived from CiteSpace.

In addition to the cluster analysis shown in Fig. 9, the CiteSpace software shows a citation burst, showing active areas of research and what pieces of work are getting attention from peers. Figures 10 and 11 below show snips from the results of the citation burst from CiteSpace.

Figure 10 is a screen capture taken from the top of the list. Figure 11 is a screen capture taken from the bottom of the list. The results from the middle of the list were omitted for brevity. Note that there is a constraint on the years for this analysis, as noted earlier in this section.

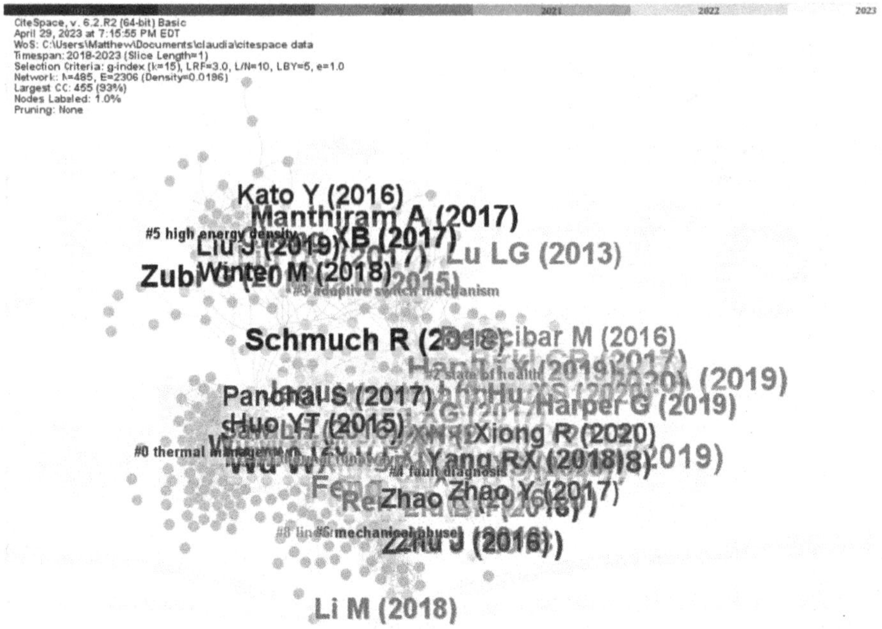

Fig. 9. Cluster analysis from CiteSpace

Top 97 References with the Strongest Citation Bursts

References	Year	Strength	Begin	End	2018 - 2023
Feng XN, 2014, J POWER SOURCES, V255, P294, DOI 10.1016/j.jpowsour.2014.01.005, DOI	2014	16.11	2018	2019	
Nitta N, 2015, MATER TODAY, V18, P252, DOI 10.1016/j.mattod.2014.10.040, DOI	2015	11.4	2018	2020	
Waag W, 2014, J POWER SOURCES, V258, P321, DOI 10.1016/j.jpowsour.2014.02.064, DOI	2014	11.21	2018	2019	
Abada S, 2016, J POWER SOURCES, V306, P178, DOI 10.1016/j.jpowsour.2015.11.100, DOI	2016	8.81	2018	2020	
Xu K, 2014, CHEM REV, V114, P11503, DOI 10.1021/cr500003w, DOI	2014	8.77	2018	2019	
Huo YT, 2015, ENERG CONVERS MANAGE, V89, P387, DOI 10.1016/j.enconman.2014.10.015, DOI	2015	8.75	2018	2020	
Han XB, 2014, J POWER SOURCES, V251, P38, DOI 10.1016/j.jpowsour.2013.11.029, DOI	2014	8.28	2018	2019	
Sahraei E, 2014, J POWER SOURCES, V247, P503, DOI 10.1016/j.jpowsour.2013.08.056, DOI	2014	7.79	2018	2019	
Zou Y, 2015, J POWER SOURCES, V273, P793, DOI 10.1016/j.jpowsour.2014.09.146, DOI	2015	7.79	2018	2019	
Feng XN, 2015, J POWER SOURCES, V275, P261, DOI 10.1016/j.jpowsour.2014.11.017, DOI	2015	7.58	2018	2020	
Feng XN, 2015, APPL ENERG, V154, P74, DOI 10.1016/j.apenergy.2015.04.118, DOI	2015	6.99	2018	2020	
Nykvist B, 2015, NAT CLIM CHANGE, V5, P329, DOI 10.1038/nclimate2564, DOI	2015	6.81	2018	2019	
Berecibar M, 2016, RENEW SUST ENERG REV, V56, P572, DOI 10.1016/j.rser.2015.11.042, DOI	2016	6.77	2018	2019	
Zhao R, 2015, J POWER SOURCES, V273, P1089, DOI 10.1016/j.jpowsour.2014.10.007, DOI	2015	6.7	2018	2020	
Jaguemont J, 2016, APPL ENERG, V164, P99, DOI 10.1016/j.apenergy.2015.11.034, DOI	2016	6.58	2018	2020	
Farmann A, 2015, J POWER SOURCES, V281, P114, DOI 10.1016/j.jpowsour.2015.01.129, DOI	2015	6.33	2018	2019	
Finegan DP, 2015, NAT COMMUN, V6, P0, DOI 10.1038/ncomms7924, DOI	2015	5.53	2018	2020	
Wang T, 2014, APPL ENERG, V134, P229, DOI 10.1016/j.apenergy.2014.08.013, DOI	2014	5.35	2018	2019	
Panchal S, 2016, INT J HEAT MASS TRAN, V101, P1093, DOI 10.1016/j.ijheatmasstransfer.2016.05.126, DOI	2016	5.35	2018	2019	
Sahraei E, 2015, RSC ADV, V5, P80369, DOI 10.1039/c5ra17865g, DOI	2015	4.95	2018	2020	
Chen ZY, 2016, APPL ENERG, V184, P365, DOI 10.1016/j.apenergy.2016.10.026, DOI	2016	4.36	2018	2020	

Fig. 10. Citation burst from CiteSpace, part 1

Xiong R, 2020, RENEW SUST ENERG REV, V131, P0, DOI 10.1016/j.rser.2020.110048, DOI	2020	4.38 **2021** 2023	
Wang YJ, 2020, RENEW SUST ENERG REV, V131, P0, DOI 10.1016/j.rser.2020.110015, DOI	2020	4.25 **2021** 2023	
Lipu MSH, 2018, J CLEAN PROD, V205, P115, DOI 10.1016/j.jclepro.2018.09.065, DOI	2018	4.24 **2021** 2023	
Lyu PZ, 2020, ENERGY STORAGE MATER, V31, P195, DOI 10.1016/j.ensm.2020.06.042, DOI	2020	3.94 **2021** 2023	
Xiong R, 2020, ISCIENCE, V23, P0, DOI 10.1016/j.isci.2020.101010, DOI	2020	3.65 **2021** 2023	
Harper G, 2019, NATURE, V575, P75, DOI 10.1038/s41586-019-1682-5, DOI	2019	3.38 **2021** 2023	
Zhu XQ, 2019, ENERGY, V169, P868, DOI 10.1016/j.energy.2018.12.041, DOI	2019	3.36 **2021** 2023	
Fan YQ, 2019, APPL THERM ENG, V155, P96, DOI 10.1016/j.applthermaleng.2019.03.157, DOI	2019	3.21 **2021** 2023	
Chaoui H, 2017, IEEE T VEH TECHNOL, V66, P8773, DOI 10.1109/TVT.2017.2715333, DOI	2017	3.06 **2021** 2023	
Chung Y, 2019, ENERG CONVERS MANAGE, V196, P105, DOI 10.1016/j.enconman.2019.05.083, DOI	2019	3.06 **2021** 2023	
Liu KL, 2019, FRONT MECH ENG-PRC, V14, P47, DOI 10.1007/s11465-018-0516-8, DOI	2019	2.92 **2021** 2023	
Jiang ZY, 2019, APPL ENERG, V242, P378, DOI 10.1016/j.apenergy.2019.03.043, DOI	2019	2.92 **2021** 2023	
Hu XS, 2018, IEEE T VEH TECHNOL, V67, P10319, DOI 10.1109/TVT.2018.2865664, DOI	2018	2.92 **2021** 2023	
Li PH, 2020, J POWER SOURCES, V459, P0, DOI 10.1016/j.jpowsour.2020.228069, DOI	2020	2.92 **2021** 2023	
Liu KL, 2021, IEEE T IND ELECTRON, V68, P3170, DOI 10.1109/TIE.2020.2973876, DOI	2021	2.77 **2021** 2023	
Li WD, 2020, NAT ENERGY, V5, P26, DOI 10.1038/s41560-019-0513-0, DOI	2020	2.63 **2021** 2023	
Tian HX, 2020, J CLEAN PROD, V261, P0, DOI 10.1016/j.jclepro.2020.120813, DOI	2020	2.63 **2021** 2023	
Chemali E, 2018, J POWER SOURCES, V400, P242, DOI 10.1016/j.jpowsour.2018.06.104, DOI	2018	2.63 **2021** 2023	
Wang ZP, 2017, APPL ENERG, V196, P289, DOI 10.1016/j.apenergy.2016.12.143, DOI	2017	2.63 **2021** 2023	
Richardson RR, 2017, J POWER SOURCES, V357, P209, DOI 10.1016/j.jpowsour.2017.05.004, DOI	2017	2.63 **2021** 2023	
Choudhari VG, 2020, INT J HEAT MASS TRAN, V163, P0, DOI 10.1016/j.ijheatmasstransfer.2020.120434, DOI	2020	2.48 **2021** 2023	
Pastor-Fernandez C, 2017, J POWER SOURCES, V360, P301, DOI 10.1016/j.jpowsour.2017.03.042, DOI	2017	2.33 **2021** 2023	
Wang AP, 2018, NPJ COMPUT MATER, V4, P0, DOI 10.1038/s41524-018-0064-0, DOI	2018	2.33 **2021** 2023	
Li YL, 2019, ACS APPL MATER INTER, V11, P46839, DOI 10.1021/acsami.9b16589, DOI	2019	2.31 **2021** 2023	
Feng F, 2020, J POWER SOURCES, V455, P0, DOI 10.1016/j.jpowsour.2020.227935, DOI	2020	2.22 **2021** 2023	
Akinlabi AH, 2020, RENEW SUST ENERG REV, V125, P0, DOI 10.1016/j.rser.2020.109815, DOI	2020	2.12 **2021** 2023	

Fig. 11. Citation burst from CiteSpace, part 2

2.5 BibExcel

BibExcel is another bibliographical tool that allows for export into the Microsoft Excel application. For this analysis, a Google Scholar search was performed in Harzing, another bibliometric analysis and literature review enabling software. The terms "battery" & "electric vehicle" & "safety" were input. With some setting configuration, BibExcel was able to yield a list of authors and the number of associated relevant publications by author. These results were exported to Excel, sorted into a pivot table, and graphed, as shown in Fig. 12 below.

2.6 MAXQDA

MAXQDA is yet another software used to gain insights from a large number of documents or articles. Five articles were taken from the Scopus database, with the usual search terms of "electric vehicle" & "battery" & "safety," sorted by relevance (Bisschop 2020) (Omariba 2018) (Rangarajan 2022) (Shao 2022) (Xinghui 2022); the first five files that were readily available in PDF format were chosen, for ease of use with the MAXQDA software.

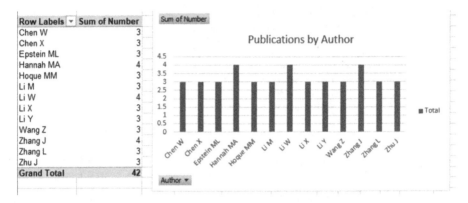

Fig. 12. BibExcel output exported to Excel, arranged in a pivot table, and graphed

From the five articles input into MAXQDA, the software generated a word cloud and then an extended lexical search based on the term "safe". The term "safe" was chosen as the search word for relevance, to tie in with course themes, and because MAXQDA would not take more than one word in the search bar ("safe," "safety," and "unsafe" were tried together to no avail). Figures 13 and 14 below show these.

Fig. 13. Word cloud generated from MAXQDA

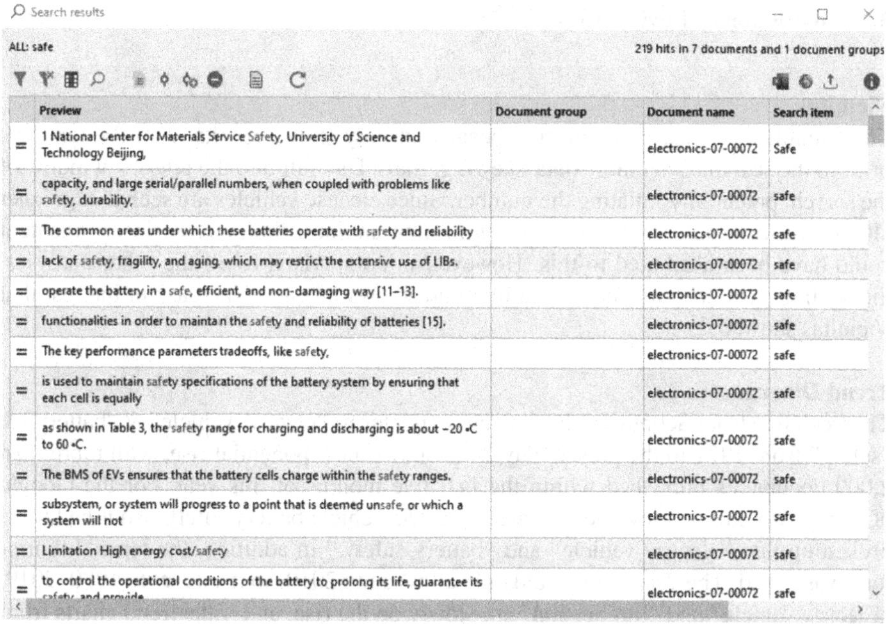

Fig. 14. Lexical search results from MAXQDA with "safe" search term

3 Discussion and Reappraisal

This discussion and reappraisal will analyze the results from the review and seek to gain insights.

3.1 Key Definitions

Battery Electric Vehicle (EV)
An EV is defined as a vehicle that can be powered by an electric motor that draws electricity from a battery and is capable of being charged from an external source. An EV includes both a vehicle that can only be powered by an electric motor that draws electricity from a battery (all-electric vehicle) and a vehicle that can be powered by an electric motor that draws electricity from a battery and by an internal combustion engine (plug-in hybrid electric vehicle) (Alternative Fuels Data Center n.d.).

Lithium-Ion Battery
A lithium-ion (Li-ion) battery is an advanced battery technology that uses lithium ions as a key component of its electrochemistry (Clean Energy Institute University of Washington 2020).

Electrode/Electrolyte Interface
The electrode-electrolyte interface sets the stage for a wide range of fundamental processes in chemical physics [facilitating] the interconversion of chemical and electrical energy [playing] a central role in a wide range of existing and emerging technologies [such as LI batteries] (The Chemical Physics of the Electrode-Electrolyte Interface 2021).

3.2   Discussion of Review Results

Vicinitas

The Vicinitas free search is limiting because it only shows results from the ten days prior to the search. Even more data-skewing, Earth Day fell into the ten-day window of the search, potentially inflating the number. Since electric vehicles are seen as a greener alternative to vehicles with internal combustion engines, the increase in engagement could have been attributed to this. However, in comparison to all the other analyses, the Vicinitas results coincide, as the literature shows the same increase in interest that Vicinitas showed.

Trend Diagrams

The trend line from Scopus in Fig. 5 using search terms "electric vehicle" & "battery" & "safety" from 1971 to the present day 2023 shows an exponential rise, with more than 2,000 documents published within the first five months of this year. For the Google nGram, it would not allow me to search "electric vehicle battery safety," so it had to be broken up into "electric vehicle" and "battery safety." In addition, the term "lithium-ion" was added. The year span would only allow up to 2019, so it was set to 1980–2019. "Electric vehicle" and "lithium-ion" are slowly on the rise, and if the trend charts from the other databases are any indication, I believe the upward slope has only gotten steeper in the past four years. "Battery safety" is low on the chart, but I believe that this term will also show an upward trend since 2019.

Regarding the trend line graphs, especially when put into context via the Google nGram, the term "electric vehicle battery safety" is highly specific. Compared to "ergonomics," a well-established and studied field, the term "electric vehicle battery safety" almost did not register on the graph. By breaking up the terms into "electric vehicle" and "battery safety" the Google nGram becomes more meaningful. Having made this decision to set up the nGram analysis as such emphasizes the fact that the topic of battery safety in electric vehicles is rising, but still up and coming.

VOSviewer

With all the connections shown in Fig. 7, it is clear to see that all of the people doing research in this area are tight-knit and reference each other frequently, building on each other's work. This also speaks to the uniqueness of the topic, as everyone relies on each other and furthers the research, as will be explored further down in this report.

CiteSpace

With the clusters in Fig. 9 being so close together, this indicates that the search term that was used is very specific and unique. The specificity of the term "electric vehicle lithium-ion battery safety" does not allow for much deviation into the research of other topics; the results remain topical and clustered together.

Figures 10 and 11 of the citation bursts show that the lower down the list you get, the more it is evident that newer articles are getting cited. This shows how fast the technology is developing and building on itself.

Topic Uniqueness

The results from VOSviewer and CiteSpace really show the uniqueness of the topic. Both results show how focused the topic is, and how the output of both software packages provides highly relevant articles and co-citations.

For example, VOSviewer's co-citation analysis yielded a 2016 article that discussed modeling work focusing on lithium-ion battery thermal runaway hazards (Abada 2016). This same article was cited and built upon two years later by Dongsheng Ren, where Ren looks to develop a "reliable battery [thermal runaway] model from kinetics analysis of cell components" to mitigate the "major safety concern in lithium-ion batteries" (Ren 2018). These researchers are really getting into the physics of lithium-ion batteries and are looking to gain a deeper understanding of their hazards through modeling.

Another example from VOSviewer has George Blomgren in 2016 talking about how lithium-ion batteries were invented in 1991, how they have progressed, and how he sees them as a robust product (Blomgren 2016). Paolo Cicconi goes on to cite Blomberg, also building on his work but, relevant to this topic, applies it to electric vehicles, specifically lightweight commercial EVs (Cicconi 2017).

Amirhossein Moeini presented his research at the 2018 IEEE Energy Conversion Congress and Exposition. His paper on short circuit detection on lithium-ion batteries (Moeini 2018) is linked to Blomgren's and Abada's works in VOSviewer. It is also linked to DP Abraham's 2003 work on high-power lithium-ion cells (Abraham 2003), which paved the way for hybrid electric vehicles, and in turn battery electric vehicles. Following the links, one arrives at Dr. Valadoula Deimede's work looking in depth at lithium-ion battery separators in hopes of facilitating ionic conduction (Deimede 2015). Lastly (for the purposes of this section, there are many more links), Deimede's work links to Seong An's 2016 work looking at the solid electrolyte interphase within lithium-ion batteries, specifically pertaining to electric vehicles (An 2016). An's work also ties back to Abada's.

Again, all of these ties speak to how closely the researchers in this space work together. They feed off each other and continue to progress the science.

BibExcel

BibExcel enabled some analysis that the Scopus database performs as well, but for the Web of Science database. I acknowledge the output retrieved from BibExcel, but given the difference yielded in Fig. 12 as far as quantity per author, it is vastly different than the results from Scopus, which will be discussed later.

MAXQDA

MAXQDA yielded two outputs. Beginning with the word cloud in Fig. 13, and comparing it to the word cloud derived from the Twitter Vicinitas search in Fig. 3, it is interesting to do a comparison and contrast. On a high level, both word clouds show similar results, such as "battery," "electric," and "vehicle," but the MAXQDA word cloud is much more technical and provides much greater insights into the terminology and relevant issues going on with the search topic. The MAXQDA word cloud shows terms like "position," "orientation," "capacity," "thermal," and "temperature" that are much too technical for anything you would find on a high-level platform such as Twitter.

For the lexical search terms in MAXQDA, I elected to keep it simple and topical, so the search term "safe" was chosen. This was in the hopes that related words such as "safety" and "unsafe" would also appear in the results, which they did. This helps direct the focus to the most relevant sections of more general papers, especially when a large quantity of papers is input for analysis.

Leading Tables

Figures 15 and 16 below are graphs showing the leading authors and leading countries in this research. The data was taken from Scopus (BibExcel was having issues) with the usual search terms "electric vehicle" & "battery" & "safety."

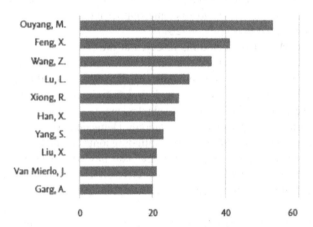

Fig. 15. Leading authors chart from Scopus

It is extremely clear that China is the leading country in this research space, having published around 200% more than the United States. Like it has been mentioned, there is a substantial amount of pressure to have a robust resolution to this issue, and the potential power and economic gain is great motivation to be first. Work is certainly being done on the subject, and the authors and countries listed are clearly dedicated.

In comparing to the leading authors table produced by BibExcel shown in Fig. 12, there does not appear to be much overlap. Note that the articles for each table came from different databases: Scopus for Figs. 15 and 16, and Google Scholar for Fig. 12.

Insights Gained

There is a clear consensus on thermal runaway being a cause of lithium-ion batteries. The following section discusses resources from class where more insight and basic knowledge of electric and fire hazards can be gained. A substantial amount of work is being done internationally, and the research results will be coveted.

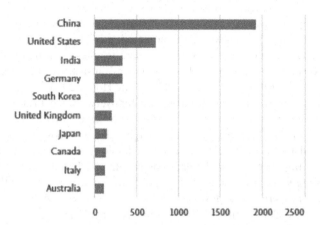

Fig. 16. Leading country/territory chart from Scopus

Course Text Relevancy

While the course text I have primarily used, Roger Brauer's *Safety and Health for Engineers*, did not have a section specific to electric vehicle battery safety, there were several chapters that were relevant to the topic.

Chapter 12 "Electrical Safety" in Brauer's book has s specific section about battery charging, shipping, and storage (Brauer, Safety and Health for Engineers 2016). In this section, Brauer discusses the gases produced during a charging operation that can be ignited by a spark coming from the physical manipulation of charging cables and ports, or from anywhere else. He also discusses safe storage of battery-powered vehicles, and best practices while charging. He includes a relevant case study about a battery fire on an empty aircraft. He lastly notes the need for additional study in case of performance issues, as the automotive industry is seeing.

Chapter 16 "Fire Protection and Prevention" (Brauer, Safety and Health for Engineers 2016) talks about exactly that, preventing and protecting against fires. It talks about the physics and chemistry of how fires get started, which is important to understand for those studying this topic of battery electric vehicle safety.

Future Work

From my professional perspective, there is a substantial amount of future work to be done in this space, pertaining to this topic. The automotive industry is highly incentivized and motivated to reach a solution to this issue. I have been brought into a group that was specifically expanded (amidst company-wide layoffs) to address these battery safety and usability issues. Ford Motor Company, my employer, has invested a huge amount of money in this technology, and sees this to be the future (Greene 2023). Ford cannot afford a misstep in this space. There are high expectations for this technology, and at its current state it does not meet those expectations.

In addition to internal research and work taking place in the corporate world, there is significant activity in this space in the National Science Foundation (NSF). A search of the NSF website for electric vehicle battery safety makes it very evident that there is ongoing research in this area, as millions of dollars are being awarded for this research. As every metric found has shown, the topic is rising in popularity, gaining more and more traction. Grants are being awarded, as there is substantial political pressure to make advancements. There is a nearly $23B federal infrastructural investment in the advancement of battery electric vehicles (The White House 2023).

Breakthroughs in this area have been ongoing for over a decade. In 2009, the advancements were sufficient to know confidently that batteries could solely power vehicles (Improved Lithium Ion Battery Could Fast-charge Vehicles, Boost Acceleration 2009). The current and future work relevant to the technology deals with the safety issues unknown at the time of the initial breakthroughs. Olivier Mathieu of Texas A&M University is leading some research recently funded by the NSF, looking at the chemistry and combustion properties of explosions in lithium-ion batteries (Mathieu, Experimental Investigation of the Combustion Properties of an Average Thermal Runaway Gas Mixture from Li-Ion Batteries 2022), and explosive gas formation (Mathieu, Experimental study of the formation of CO during ethanol pyrolysis and dry reforming with CO_2. 2022).

References

Abada, S.: Safety focused modeling of lithium-ion batteries: a review. J. Power. Sources **306**, 178–192 (2016)

Abraham, D.P.: Diagnosis of power fade mechanisms in high-power lithium-ion cells. J. Power. Sources **119**, 511–516 (2003)

Alternative Fuels Data Center (n.d.). https://afdc.energy.gov/laws/12660. Accessed 27 Apr 2023

An, S.: The state of understanding of the lithium-ion-battery graphite solid electrolyte interphase (SEI) and its relationship to formation cycling. Carbon **105**, 52–76 (2016)

Bisschop, R.: Handling lithium-ion batteries in electric vehicles: preventing and recovering from hazardous events. Fire Technol. **56**, 2671–2694 (2020). https://doi.org/10.1007/s10694-020-10138-1

Blomgren, G.E.: The development and future of lithium ion batteries. J. Electrochem. Soc. **164**(1), A5019 (2016)

Brauer, R.: Safety and Health for Engineers. Chap. 16 Fire Protection and Prevention, 14–16d. Wiley, Hoboken (2016a)

Brauer, R.: Safety and Health for Engineers. Chap. 12 Electrical Safety, pp. 167–168. Wiley, Hoboken (2016b)

Cicconi, P.: Thermal analysis and simulation of a Li-ion battery pack for a lightweight commercial EV. Appl. Energy **192**, 159–177 (2017)

Clean Energy Institute University of Washington (2020). https://www.cei.washington.edu/education/science-of-solar/battery-technology/. Accessed 27 Apr 2023

Deimede, V.: Separators for lithium-ion batteries: a review on the production processes and recent developments. Energy Technol. **3**, 453–468 (2015)

Greene, D.: Fox 13 Memphis (2023). https://www.fox13memphis.com/news/fox13-investigates-the-price-of-progress-and-the-land-leading-to-fords-blueoval-city/article_5abd7d98-e831-11ed-9336-6f540c77d24d.html. Accessed 3 May 2023

Improved Lithium Ion Battery Could Fast-charge Vehicles, Boost Acceleration. National Science Foundation (2009). https://new.nsf.gov/news/improved-lithium-ion-battery-technology-could-fast

Kanade, S.G., Duffy, V.G.: Use of virtual reality for safety training: a systematic review. In: Duffy, V.G. (ed.) Digital Human Modeling and Applications in Health, Safety, Ergonomics and Risk Management. LNCS, vol. 13320, pp. 364–375. Springer, Cham (2022). https://doi.org/10.1007/978-3-031-06018-2_25

Mathieu, O.: Experimental investigation of the combustion properties of an average thermal runaway gas mixture from li-ion batteries. Energy Fuels **36**, 3247–3258 (2022)

Mathieu, O.: Experimental study of the formation of CO during ethanol pyrolysis and dry reforming with CO2. Appl. Energy Combust. Sci. **11**, 100076 (2022)

Mathiew, O.: Experimental investigation of the combustion properties of an average thermal runaway gas mixture from li-ion batteries. Energy Fuels **36**, 3247–3258 (2022)

Moeini, A.: Fast and precise detection of internal short circuit on li-ion battery. In: 2018 IEEE Energy Conversion Congress and Exposition (ECCE) (2018)

National Traffic Safety Board (2020). https://www.ntsb.gov/safety/safety-studies/Pages/HWY19S P002.aspx. Accessed Apr 2023

Omariba, Z.B.: Review on health management system for lithium-ion batteries of electric vehicles. Electronics (2018). https://doi.org/10.3390/electronics7050072

Rangarajan, S.S.: Lithium-ion batteries—the crux of electric vehicles with opportunities and challenges. Clean Technol. **4**, 908–930 (2022). https://doi.org/10.3390/cleantechnol4040056

Ren, D.: Model-based thermal runaway prediction of lithium-ion batteries from kinetics analysis of cell components. Appl. Energy **228**, 633–644 (2018)

Shao, L.: Safety characteristics of lithium-ion batteries under dynamic impact conditions. Energies (2022). https://doi.org/10.3390/en15239148

The Chemical Physics of the Electrode-Electrolyte Interface (2021). https://publishing.aip.org/publications/journals/special-topics/jcp/the-chemical-physics-of-the-electrode-electrolyte-interface/. Accessed 27 Apr 2023

The White House. February 15 (2023). https://www.whitehouse.gov/briefing-room/statements-releases/2023/02/15/fact-sheet-biden-harris-administration-announces-new-standards-and-major-progress-for-a-made-in-america-national-network-of-electric-vehicle-chargers/#:~: text=President%20Biden%E2%80%99s%20Bi. Accessed 1 May 2023

Xinghui, Z.: A review on thermal management of lithium-ion batteries for electric vehicles. Energy (2022). https://doi.org/10.1016/j.energy.2021.121652

Evaluating the Potential of Interactivity in Explanations for User-Adaptive In-Vehicle Systems – Insights from a Real-World Driving Study

Julia Graefe[1]([⊠]) [iD], Lena Rittger[2], Gabriele Carollo[3], Doreen Engelhardt[2], and Klaus Bengler[1]

[1] Technical University of Munich, Boltzmannstr. 15, 85747 Garching, Germany
`{julia.graefe,bengler}@tum.de`
[2] Audi AG, Auto-Union-Str. 1, 85057 Ingolstadt, Germany
`{lena.rittger,doreen.engelhardt}@audi.de`
[3] Politecnico di Milano, Piazza Leonardo da Vinci 32, 20133 Milan, Italy
`gabriele.carollo@mail.polimi.it`

Abstract. Due to advances in artificial intelligence (AI), humans are increasingly facing algorithm-generated content in everyday applications. To avoid threads to the system's transparency and trustworthiness, the approach of explainable AI (XAI) will play an important role when designing these systems tied to the needs and characteristics of their end-users. Our work investigates explanation strategies for AI-based adaptive in-vehicle systems from a human-centered point of view. We present two explanation concepts: one interactive and one text-based approach. The concepts were evaluated and compared in a real-world driving study with 36 participants. The aim is to assess whether interactive engagement with explanations fosters the system's understandability and the user's mental model. Our results did not show significant differences between the concepts. Both groups performed well when assessing their mental model after experiencing the explanation concept. However, we found significant decreases in the mental model when measuring it again after participants experienced the prototypical adaptations of the system during the test drive.

Keywords: Human-AI Interaction · Human-Centered Explainable AI · User-Adaptive Systems · Automotive User Interfaces · Real-World Driving Study

1 Introduction

Artificial intelligence (AI) based user-adaptivity changes the way how people interact with digital systems and simultaneously entails chances and opportunities for human-computer interaction. For example, adaptivity can support efficiency [2, 26], effectiveness [26], and satisfaction [21] of the interaction. Research across various fields of HCI and human factors has shown an increasing interest in this topic over the past years

© The Author(s), under exclusive license to Springer Nature Switzerland AG 2023
V. G. Duffy et al. (Eds.): HCII 2023, LNCS 14057, pp. 294–312, 2023.
https://doi.org/10.1007/978-3-031-48047-8_19

[37]. User-adaptive systems are defined by their ability to change their behavior and outputs based on individual user preferences and characteristics [8, 12]. These systems utilize AI to perceive, interpret, and learn from data to make self-reliant decisions and automatically adapt to learned parameters [8, 10, 12]. Due to the rapid advantages of AI, humans are now facing challenges when interacting with learning systems and handling algorithm-generated content in everyday applications [10]. A frequently discussed challenge of human-AI interaction is the black-box effect of AI systems and the resulting threads to transparency, trust, and predictability on the part of the human user [5, 18, 29, 36]. The approach of *explainable AI* addresses this issue. However, an open question is how explanations should be integrated into the user interface (UI) from a user-centered point of view. Previous studies found that users only spend a short time looking at explanations [23] and react negatively to long, text-based explanations [17]. Furthermore, the system's acceptance significantly decreases if explanations do not match the user's expectations [17]. One approach to better integrate explainability into the UI would be interactive explanations that allow users to explore the system functioning through interactions with the algorithm and see how that affects the system behavior [1, 10].

This paper introduces a human-machine interface (HMI) concept for an interactive explanation approach for user-adaptive in-vehicle comfort and infotainment systems. Furthermore, the results of a real-world driving study comparing the interactive explanation concept to standard text-based explanations are presented. Our work contributes to the research gap on how explanations should be designed to add value for the human user by making the system more transparent and understandable. We do so by evaluating whether the presented interactive explanation concept contributes to an improved understandability and mental model of the system. The following research question will be answered within the paper: Does the understandability of the system's adaptations differ for the text-based and interactive explanation concepts?

2 Related Work

2.1 Human-AI Interaction

Through the increasing use of artificial intelligence (AI) in technical systems, people are exposed to algorithm-generated content in everyday applications. Algorithms are utilized in various domains, from smartphone applications and smart home systems to automotive domains [16]. Unlike traditional systems, AI-based systems are often user-adaptive and present different outputs or behavior to the user based on their characteristics, the current situation, or the system state [8, 12]. One of the main goals of implementing AI into systems is to assist the user in accomplishing their tasks [37]. However, this also raises new challenges to human-computer interaction that have not yet been completely addressed by research [10, 15].

These challenges include methodological issues like prototyping and testing AI systems [37]. Directly affecting human-computer interaction are threats to understandability and the mental model caused by AI systems' opaque and adapting character [18, 29] and the question of user control and feedback [10, 18]. Further challenges concern ethical issues caused by a lack of transparency and bias in AI models [19, 20] or data privacy

[18]. Similar to the development process of traditional systems, AI systems' developers should focus on the human to ensure that the systems are usable, controllable, and trustworthy [34]. Various design and usability guidelines have been developed and established for human-computer interaction, for example, the usability heuristics by Nielsen [30]. However, these guidelines need to be questioned in the context of AI, as they may have to be adjusted or extended for these kinds of systems. Thus, researchers address this topic by proposing new guidelines for human-AI interaction [3, 4, 14].

2.2 Explainable AI

When interacting with AI, humans are often confronted with black-box systems. Molnar [29] defines a black-box model as one that "does not reveal its internal mechanisms" and "cannot be understood by looking at their parameters". Opaque AI systems can lead to a lack of algorithmic awareness [11, 31], insufficient knowledge of system limits [20], or unfair and biased outputs [19]. Furthermore, an insufficient mental model of the AI system can lead to diminished efficiency of the interaction or an inappropriate level of trust [36]. The approach of explainable AI (XAI) addresses these issues. According to the definition by Markus et al. [25], a system is explainable "if the task model is intrinsically interpretable (here the AI system is the task model) or if the non-interpretable task model is complemented with an interpretable and faithful explanation". Consequently, explainability aims to present the inner mechanisms of the AI systems in a way that is understandable to a human and thereby fosters trust, transparency, effectiveness, efficiency, and satisfaction [9, 13, 33, 35].

Three groups of potential XAI stakeholders can be defined: developers and researchers, domain experts, and lay users [28, 32]. Explanations should be tailored to the different characteristics and needs of the user groups. While model debugging, identification of system bias, and understanding the system on a technical basis are important to developers and machine learning experts [5, 28], explainability becomes relevant to end users in terms of trust [33], informed decision-making [28], and perceived transparency and understandability [17]. Explanations can be differentiated between a global approach, explaining the system's overall functionality in a generic way, and a local approach, explaining specific individual outputs [25, 32]. Lim and Dey [24] propose five questions to consider when explaining system behavior: *what, why, why not, what if,* and *how to.* Conducting an empirical study, the authors found that both *why* and *why not* explanations can improve users' understanding, trust, and task performance. The greatest effects have been found for *why* explanations, while *how to* and *what if* explanations did not show a benefit. Miller [27] reviews human explanation strategies and derives implications for explainable AI. The author presents four major findings: explanations are contrastive, selected in a biased way, they are social, and probabilities are less effective than causalities.

Within the guidelines for human-AI interaction proposed by Amershi et al. [3], several points can be found that refer to explaining the AI system to end-users:

- Guideline 1: Make clear what the system can do.
- Guideline 2: Make clear how well the system can do what it can do.
- Guideline 11: Make clear why the system did what it did.
- Guideline 16: Convey the consequences of user actions.

3 Explanation Concepts

3.1 Explanation Categories

To develop the explanation concepts for our study, we build up on the guidelines for human-AI interaction by Amershi et al. [3], as they present well-funded guidelines to design human-centered AI systems. Derived from these, we identified three relevant explanation categories for end-users when interacting with an AI-based user-adaptive system. The three categories served as a basis for developing the tested explanation concepts.

The explanation category *reasons for output* is derived from the guidelines G1 – "Make clear what the system can do" and G11 – "Make clear why the system did what it did". The goal is to communicate which factors caused an adaptation by the system to establish a better understanding of how the system functions and an awareness of the algorithm's impact on the system's behavior.

The second explanation category, *consequences of user actions*, is based on guideline G16 – "Convey the consequences of user actions". The explanation aims to communicate how the system learns from user actions and how user behavior influences the system's future behavior and adaptations.

The third explanation type, *uncertainty*, follows guideline G2 – "Make clear how well the system can do what it can do" by communicating that the system's adaptations are based on probabilities and might be mismatching. The goal is to clarify how well the algorithm functions and when system outputs might be wrong.

3.2 Use Cases

We addressed three different use cases within the study with explanations tied to each: adaptive navigation, adaptive driving modes, and adaptive well-being modes. In each use case, the system proposes routes, drive modes, or well-being modes based on learned user preferences, the current situation, and the system state. Table 1 presents an overview of the system behavior in each use case. Details of how the system behaves during the study are given in Table 2 in the study design section.

Table 1. Overview of the use cases included in the study.

Use Case	Description
Navigation	The system recommends routes based on learned user preferences, the system state, and the current situation
Drive mode	The system selects and activates a suitable driving mode based on learned user preferences, the system state, and the current situation
Well-being	The system selects and activates a suitable well-being mode based on learned user preferences, the system state, and the current situation. The well-being mode adjusts the car's comfort setting according to the mode's parameters

3.3 HMI Prototype

After defining the explanation categories and the use cases that should be tested within the study, we conducted a prototyping workshop with three HCI researchers (first and third author and one independent) to develop ideas on how the explanations can be presented in a car's HMI in an interactive way. We decided on a generic and introductory explanation concept comparable to an onboarding process. The explanations are presented to the user in the standing vehicle when using the adaptive system for the first time. Consequently, the user has not yet experienced the respective adaptations when receiving the explanations. An introductory approach is beneficial for the in-vehicle context as it reduces the information load while driving.

Both explanation concepts consist of five screens the user can navigate by clicking "continue". Figure 1 shows how the screens are arranged. The first screen presents a welcome message briefly explaining the system's purpose. Three screens follow the introductory screen, each presenting one explanation category. The last screen shows a short statement that the introduction is finished and the window can be closed.

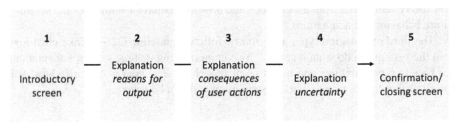

Fig. 1. Interaction flow of the HMI prototypes.

Interactive Explanation Concept

The goal of the interactive concept was to provide users the possibility to closely engage with the system and the explanation through interactively taking part in the system's initial setup. Following a question-answering approach, the interactive explanations ask questions about the user characteristics and preferences, thereby explaining how the system functions and will use the answers. Below the informative text, pre-defined possibilities to answer the questions are presented to the user. The figures below are examples from the prototype to show how the interactive concept was implemented. The study was conducted in Germany, and the prototype language was German.

Figure 2 shows how the screens for the explanation categories reasons for output and consequences of user actions are structured. The interaction was provided through buttons that presented the answer options. Only one selection was possible, and the prototype did not allow multiple selections.

For the explanation category uncertainty, the interaction was provided through a slider allowing users to adjust how conservatively the system's adaptations are executed, ranging from relaxed to conservative (see Fig. 3).

Fig. 2. Example screen from the interactive prototype demonstrating the screen setup for the explanation categories *reasons for output* and *consequences of user actions*.

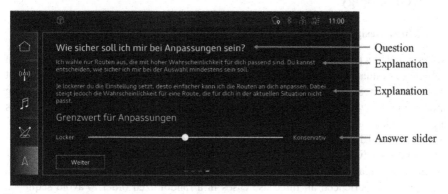

Fig. 3. Example screen from the interactive prototype demonstrating the screen setup for the explanation category *uncertainty*.

Text-Based Explanation Concept

The text-based explanation concept served as a baseline for the comparison with the interactive concept. The screen setup was similar for all three explanation categories. Figure 4 shows an example screen from the prototype to demonstrate how the screens are structured.

Fig. 4. Example screen from the text-based prototype demonstrating the screen setup.

4 Methodology

4.1 Study Design

We conducted a user study in a real-world driving scenario utilizing a wizard-of-oz test vehicle to evaluate the explanation concepts. The real driving setting was selected as it provides the most appropriate method to simulate the use case of the adaptive driving modes and the well-being features in a realistic way. The study's independent variables are the explanation concepts (text-based or interactive) and the use cases (navigation, well-being, and drive select). We implemented a mixed study design with the explanation concepts as a between-subjects factor and the use case as a within-subjects factor. Consequently, participants were split into two experimental groups: interactive and text-based. Participants experienced all three use cases in a randomized order to avoid sequence effects. Three use cases allowed six possible orders that were used during the study (see Table 3).

Test Vehicle
An Audi Q8 e-tron served as the test vehicle for the study. The car had an external computer connected to the CAN bus system. Through a remote connection between the computer and an experimenter tablet, it was possible to manually manipulate the car's comfort features and driving modes via an experimenter interface. This allowed us to simulate the adaptations during the study. The experimenter acted as the wizard from the car's backseat and manually triggered the adaptations at pre-defined trigger points during the drive. The trigger points for the adaptations are described in the chapter below.

Route and Test Drive
For the study's test drive, we selected a route along public roads in the area of the Audi facility in Ingolstadt, Germany. A visualization of the route is given in Fig. 5. The drive took place on a 6 km long route between the two checkpoints P1 and P2. Participants drove four times between the two points, two times in each direction. One drive took between 7 and 10 min. A parking lot was available at each checkpoint. The road conditions differed from country roads between P1 and T1, a highway between T1

and T3, and urban roads between T3 and P2. During the test drive, participants were asked not to drive faster than the speed limit and generally at a maximum of 80 km/h. They were also instructed to keep their primary attention on the road and other road users and to drive with a generally careful driving style (e.g., no overtaking).

Adaptations were carried out at three different pre-defined trigger points that are visualized as T1, T2, and T3 in Fig. 5. For navigation and well-being use cases, a trigger point on a straight road section (T2) was selected to avoid distraction in a critical driving situation. For the drive mode use case, trigger points were selected according to reasonable scenarios to change from efficient to dynamic and back to efficient. The first change from efficient to dynamic was done when entering the highway from the country road (T1). The second change from dynamic back to efficient was done when leaving the highway to urban roads (T3). Table 2 provides an overview of the system behavior that was triggered at the different points along the route. Due to the prototypical implementation of the adaptive system, we were not able to actually personalize the adaptations to the study participants. Thus, the system behavior was similar for each participant.

Table 2. Overview of the system behavior during the study in each use case.

Use Case	System behavior during the study
Navigation	The driver enters a destination. The system proposes three possible routes and highlights the recommended energy-efficient route (P1/P2). While driving, the system proposes an improved route for the driver to save more energy (T2)
Drive mode	The system activates the dynamic driving mode when entering the highway (T1). When leaving the highway and entering the urban roads, the system switches back to the efficient driving mode (T3)
Well-being	The system activates the well-being mode "activating" (T2)

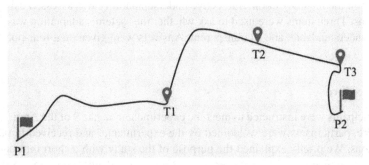

Fig. 5. Visualization of the route of the experimental drive between two checkpoints (P1 and P2) with the trigger points for the drive mode (T1 and T3) and navigation/well-being use cases (T2).

This use case was always conducted in the direction from P1 to P2 to ensure comparable conditions for the drive mode changes. Therefore, one of the four drives was conducted as an "empty" drive without an adaptation. To avoid confusion or an impact on the participants' mental models because of an empty drive between the use cases, this one was included either as part of the familiarization drive at the beginning of the study or as part of the drive back to the Audi facility. Table 3 shows how the use cases were distributed across the test drives depending on the permutation order.

Table 3. Distribution of the use cases across the four test drives between the two checkpoints of the route.

Order	P1 → P2	P2 → P1	P1 → P2	P2 → P1
1	Empty	Navigation	Drive mode	Well-being
2	Empty	Well-being	Drive mode	Navigation
3	Drive mode	Well-being	Navigation	Empty
4	Drive mode	Navigation	Well-being	Empty
5	Navigation	Well-being	Drive mode	Empty
6	Well-being	Navigation	Drive mode	Empty

4.2 Dependent Variables

To answer the research question, the system's understandability was measured subjectively and objectively. For an objective assessment of the participant's understanding of the system, six true/false statements were formulated. Participants were asked to rate whether they agreed or disagreed with the statement and also estimate their answer's certainty in percent. The rating was done two times during the study: after interacting with the explanation concept and a second time after the test drive to analyze how the mental model changes after experiencing the adaptation. The statements can be seen in Fig. 13 in the results section. Subjective understandability was assessed using Likert scale items. Three items were used to ask whether the system's adaptation was 1) relatable, 2) understandable, and 3) transparent. Answers were given on a four-point Likert scale.

4.3 Procedure

The Participants were instructed to meet the experimenter at gate 9 of the Audi company area. Here, participants were welcomed by the experimenter and received initial study instructions. We briefly explained the purpose of the study with a short introduction to the topic of explainable AI. However, we did not reveal details about the explanation concepts to avoid the initial biasing of the participant's mental model. After receiving initial instructions, participants completed the questionnaire on demographics and pre-knowledge of adaptive systems. Afterwards, they received instructions about the car and what to expect during the experimental drive. After finishing the instructions and clarifying upcoming questions, the study was started with the familiarization drive to P1 or P2, depending on the randomized use case order. Arriving at the parking lot of the first checkpoint, instructions on the first use case were given, followed by the presentation of the respective explanation concept. Participants read and interacted with the explanations followed by the first questionnaire, including the first round of true/false statements. Next, participants drove the standardized test route and experienced the simulated adaptations according to the use case at the defined trigger points. The test drive was finished at the parking lot of the next checkpoint, where the second questionnaire was filled out, including subjective understandability and the second part of true/false statements. The procedure was repeated two times until all three use cases were tested. The study was finished with the drive back from the last checkpoint to the starting point at Audi gate 9. The study procedure is visualized in Fig. 6.

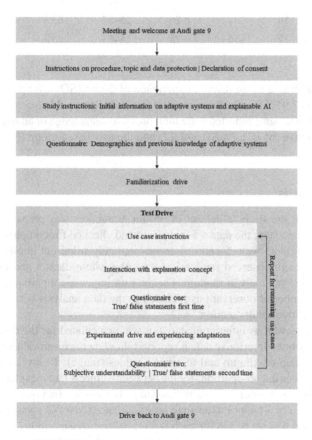

Fig. 6. Visualization of the experimental procedure.

4.4 Sample

In total, datasets of 36 participants were included for the data analysis. Nineteen participants tested the explanation concept of the interactive group and 17 the concept of the text-based group. An overview of the demographic data for both groups is presented in Table 4. As driving the test vehicle required a specific driving license issued by the AUDI AG, participants were recruited among the company's employees. For the recruiting procedure, we used designated groups for study participation within the company's internal social networks. Participating in the study was considered as working hours. Therefore, we did not pay incentives to the participants.

Table 4. Demographic data.

	N	Age			Gender	
		M	SD	Range	Male	Female
Interactive	19	38	8.76	25–57	63%	37%
Text-based	17	36	9.72	25–53	65%	35%

Participants had a mean driving experience of 20.84 (SD = 8.85) years in group interactive and 17.94 (SD = 9.38) years in the text-based group. Measured on a four-point Likert-scale, participants reported a medium previous knowledge of adaptive systems in both the interactive (M = 1.79, SD = 1.27) and the text-based group (M = 1.82, SD = 1.01).

4.5 Data Analysis

After completing the study, a dataset of 36 questionnaires was prepared for the data analysis. In the first step, the data was reviewed and checked for completeness. Several points of missing data were found due to incompletely filled-out questionnaires. The missing values were observed randomly across the whole dataset and therefore considered missing completely at random. For the missing cases, a pairwise deletion was applied. The number of observations included in the data analysis is reported for each test in the respective results section.

Descriptive as well as inferential statistics were calculated for the data analysis. In the following section, descriptive data is reported showing the mean values (*M*), standard deviation (*SD*), and maximum and minimum values (range). To investigate statistical differences between the observations for the between-subjects factor explanation concept (interactive and text-based) and the within-subjects use case (navigation, drive mode, and well-being), a two-factor mixed analysis of variance (ANOVA) was conducted. The significance level was set to 5% for each inferential test. Assumptions for the ANOVA were tested using the Levene's test for equality of variances and the Mauchly's test of sphericity. In case of violation of the assumptions, the required corrections will be applied.

5   Results

5.1   Understandability – Subjective

The understandability of the system was measured subjectively after participants experienced the explanation and the adaptation during the test drive. For the analysis, averages were calculated across the three items to create one score for each participant. The results of the descriptive analysis are visualized in Fig. 7. Due to missing values, the sample size of the text-based group was reduced to n = 15. The descriptive analysis shows that the average ratings lie closely together in both groups. The highest average rating of understandability can be observed for the navigation use case in both the interactive (M = 3.33, SD = 0.53, n = 19) and the text-based group (M = 3.38, SD = 0.62, n = 15). Lower ratings of subjective understandability can be observed for the other use cases. The average rating for the drive mode use case for the interactive concept was M = 2.72 (SD = 0.7, n = 19), and for the text-based concept, an average rating of M = 2.69 (SD = 0.72, n = 15) was given. For the well-being use case, an average rating of M = 2.67 (SD = 0.83, n = 19) was found for the interactive group, and M = 2.83 (SD = 0.59, n = 15) for the text-based group.

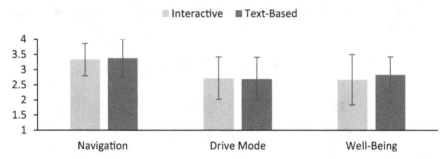

Fig. 7. Descriptive analysis of the subjective rating of understandability on a scale ranging from 1 (low) to 4 (high). The diagram shows the average rating ±1 SD.

A two-factor mixed ANOVA was calculated to test the data regarding statistically significant differences. Results can be found in Table 5. No significant interaction effect was found for the data. A significant main effect was found for the factor use case with a large effect size, according to Cohen [7].

Table 5. Two-factor mixed ANOVA on subjective assessment of understandability.

Factor	F	df	p	η^2_p
Use Case X Explanation Concept	0.24	2 | 64	.240	.007
Use Case	12.59	2 | 64	<.001	.282
Explanation Concept	0.14	2 | 32	.712	.004

Post Hoc comparisons were calculated to investigate further which groups of the factor use case differ from each other. Significant differences were found between the use cases navigation and drive mode (p < .001) as well as between the use cases navigation and well-being (p < .001). No significance was found for comparing drive mode and well-being (p = .756). Consequently, the test shows that averaged over both groups, the understandability was rated significantly lower for the use cases drive mode and well-being compared to the navigation use case.

5.2 Understandability – Objective

To evaluate the participants' mental models, six statements about the system were presented (three true and three false) and rated with agreement or disagreement. The statements were presented twice, the first time directly after receiving the explanation and a second time after experiencing the adaptation while driving.

In the first step, the results from the answers given directly after the explanation was presented were analyzed. Therefore, the number of correctly answered statements was calculated for each participant in each use case, resulting in a score from zero to six. The results of the descriptive analysis are visualized in Fig. 8. Participants performed comparably in both groups, achieving on average more than five correct answers for each use case. The results of a two-factor mixed ANOVA did not show significant interactions or main effects.

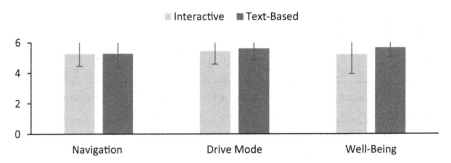

Fig. 8. Average number of correct answers within six true/false statements. The diagram shows the average ±1 SD.

For each statement, participants were asked to estimate the certainty of their answer ranging from 0% (not at all) to 100% (totally). Descriptive results can be seen in Fig. 9. On average, participants reported high confidence above 80% in both groups and for each use case. From the descriptive data, only small differences can be seen between the groups. A two-factor mixed ANOVA was calculated and did not show significant differences between the groups.

Participants were asked to answer the statements a second time after experiencing the system behavior during the experimental drive to see how the mental model changes after experiencing the adaptations. Figures 10, 11 and 12 show how the average number of correct answers changes after the adaptation was experienced. A decrease can

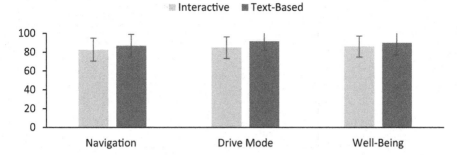

Fig. 9. Average rating of certainty for the answers within the true/false statements. The diagram shows the average ±1 SD.

be observed in both experimental groups and for each use case. A three-factor mixed ANOVA shows a significant main effect for the factor time of measurement (before/after) $(F(1, 32) = 12.5, p = .001, \eta^2p = .067)$ with a medium effect size according to Cohen [7]. Thus, the number of correct answers decreased significantly, averaged over both use cases and experimental groups.

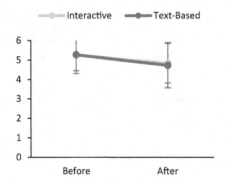

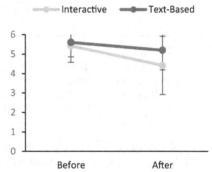

Fig. 10. Use case navigation. Average number (±1 SD) of correct answers for the true/false statements before and after experiencing the adaptation.

Fig. 11. Use case drive mode. Average number (±1 SD) of correct answers for the true/false statements before and after experiencing the adaptation.

To better understand for which statements participants showed a diminished performance, we compared the number of correct answers across all use cases for each statement. Figure 13 shows the results of the descriptive data analysis. In both groups, the greatest decrease of correct answers can be observed for the first statement, "The system adapts to personal preferences". The number of correct answers decreased by 21% for the interactive and 20% for the text-based group. The interactive group also shows larger deviations for statements three (9%), five (11%), and six (9%). For the text-based groups, larger differences can be seen for statements three (20%) and six (11%).

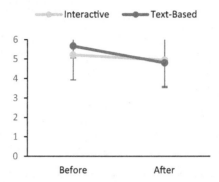

Fig. 12. Use case well-being. Average number (±1 SD) of correct answers for the true/false statements before and after experiencing the adaptation.

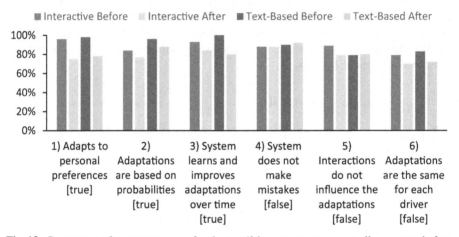

Fig. 13. Percentage of correct answers for the true/false statements across all use cases before and after the adaptation was experienced during the test drive.

6   Discussion

The presented study aimed to investigate the effect of the user's interactive engagement with explanations for AI-based in-vehicle systems on the understandability of the system. Two explanation concepts, an interactive and a text-based approach, were developed based on literature research and an expert workshop. The explanation concepts were tested in a real-world driving study, evaluating the users' mental models of the adaptive systems and the subjectively perceived understandability of the adaptations.

Based on recommendations found in the literature [22], we based the assumption that interactions can lead to a more interactive user engagement with the explanations and, thus, to an improved understandability of the AI-based system.

Results from the subjective assessment of understandability did not show significant differences between the group experiencing the interactive concept and the group experiencing the text-based concept. Concluding from that, our work did not find indications that interactive elements in the tested explanations contribute to an improved perceived understandability of the system. However, our data show a significant effect of the factor use case on the rating of understandability. In both groups, ratings are significantly higher for the use case "navigation" compared to "drive mode" and "well-being". While the perceived understandability of the use case navigation was rather high, only medium average ratings were observed for the other use cases. This difference might be due to the familiarity with adaptive routing proposals using applications such as Google Maps. As the drive mode and well-being system are not yet existing in current vehicles, these functionalities were new to the participants. Therefore, our results indicate that familiarity with a system might positively influence perceived understandability. Regarding the drive mode and well-being use case, both explanation concepts seem insufficient to establish a feeling of understandability. Our study did not investigate the reasons for rating the system as understandable. However, a possible reason might be that the explanations were given through an introductory approach before experiencing the adaptations. Perhaps it was difficult for users to connect the information in the explanation concept before experiencing the actual system behavior. Therefore, investigating a local explanation approach, as recommended by Laato et al. [22], would be beneficial in future studies.

The investigation of the participants' mental models through the true/false statements showed that both experimental groups performed well estimating the correctness of the statements directly after receiving the explanations and showed high confidence in giving the answers. This is contradictory to the low subjective ratings of understandability. The interactive explanation concept did not contribute to an improved mental model. Both explanation concepts seem sufficient to establish a correct initial mental model for the system users. However, we did not compare the explanation concepts to a baseline without explanations to see how participants perform without any introductory information on the systems. Therefore, it might be that the participants' mental model regarding AI-based adaptive systems was generally good due to previous knowledge. This has also been observed in other studies [6].

A significant decrease in correctly answered true/false statements was observed after the adaptation was experienced during the test drive. Consequently, the adaptations seem to have had a negative impact on the mental model. This is a possible reason for the low subjective ratings of understandability, as these have also been measured after experiencing the adaptations. As the greatest decrease of correct answers can be observed for the statement referring to the personalization of the adaptations (one, three, and six), a possible reason for the diminished performance could be that the adaptations did not match the participant's expectations. As a limitation of the prototypical adaptive system, we could not simulate real personalization within the study. Each participant experienced the same adaptations, regardless of individual preferences. From a methodological point of view, this also provides more standardization and comparability between the participants. Therefore, our results indicate that inappropriate adaptations made by the AI-system might negatively impact the user's mental model. The generic and introductory explanations presented to the participants before experiencing the adaptations were insufficient to avoid the deterioration of the mental model by possibly inappropriate adaptations.

However, we did not investigate the reasons for the diminished performance after experiencing the adaptations. The results should therefore be seen as a first indicator and require further research.

7 Conclusion

Explainable AI in the user interface of AI-based everyday systems becomes increasingly important to end-users regarding transparency and trust [13, 33]. Therefore, researchers should put the human into focus when developing explainable interfaces to avoid negative effects and ensure that explanations bring value to the human [17, 27]. Previous work suggested using interactive approaches to better include explanations into the interaction and foster user engagement with the explanation [1, 10]. Our work aimed to compare an interactive with a text-based explanation approach to investigate how interactivity can contribute to an improved understandability of the system and better support of the human mental model. We developed two explainability concepts in an expert workshop incorporating three explanation categories derived from literature [3]. The concepts were tested in a real-world driving study with a wizard-of-oz vehicle simulating adaptivity in the use cases navigation, drive mode, and well-being. Our results of both groups showed good performance and confidence of the participants when assessing their mental model of the system. We did not find significant differences between the interactive and the text-based concept. However, a significant decrease in the mental model after experiencing the simulated adaptations during the test drive could be observed. This indicates that unsuitable adaptations might have negatively affected the mental model and understandability of the system. The generic, introductory explanations tested in this study have not been sufficient to avoid this decrease, neither with the interactive nor the text-based approach. In future work, we suggest to further investigate how inappropriate system behavior affects the mental model and which kind of explainability works best to support these situations.

Acknowledgements. The authors would like to thank the AUDI AG for funding this work.

References

1. Abdul, A., Vermeulen, J., Wang, D., et al.: Trends and trajectories for explainable, accountable and intelligible systems. In: Mandryk, R., Hancock, M., Perry, M., et al. (eds.) Proceedings of the 2018 CHI Conference on Human Factors in Computing Systems, pp. 1–18. ACM, New York (2018)
2. Aizenberg, E., van den Hoven, J.: Designing for human rights in AI. Big Data Soc. **7** (2020). https://doi.org/10.1177/2053951720949566
3. Amershi, S., Weld, D., Vorvoreanu, M., et al.: Guidelines for human-AI interaction. In: Brewster, S., Fitzpatrick, G., Cox, A., et al. (eds.) Proceedings of the 2019 CHI Conference on Human Factors in Computing Systems, pp. 1–13. ACM, New York (2019)
4. Apple Inc. Human Interface Guidelines - Machine Learning (2021). https://developer.apple.com/design/human-interface-guidelines/machine-learning/overview/introduction/. Accessed 18 June 2021

5. Brennen, A.: What do people really want when they say they want "explainable AI?" We Asked 60 Stakeholders. In: Bernhaupt, R., Mueller, F., Verweij, D., et al. (eds.) Extended Abstracts of the 2020 CHI Conference on Human Factors in Computing Systems, pp. 1–7. ACM, New York (2020)
6. Bunt, A., Lount, M., Lauzon, C.: Are explanations always important? In: Duarte, C., Carriço, L., Jorge, J., et al. (eds.) Proceedings of the 2012 ACM International Conference on Intelligent User Interfaces, pp. 169–178. ACM, New York (2012)
7. Cohen, J.: Statistical power analysis for the behavioral sciences, Rev. ed., 4. [Dr.]. Academic Pr, New York, NY [u.a.] (1980)
8. Dorneich, M.C., McGrath, K.A., Dudley, R.F., et al.: Analysis of the characteristics of adaptive systems. In: IEEE International Conference on Systems, Man, and Cybernetics, pp. 888–893 (2013)
9. Eiband, M., Völkel, S.T., Buschek, D., et al.: When people and algorithms meet. In: Fu, W.-T., Pan, S., Brdiczka, O., et al. (eds.) Proceedings of the 24th International Conference on Intelligent User Interfaces, pp. 96–106. ACM, New York (2019)
10. Eslami, M., Rickman, A., Vaccaro, K., et al.: I always assumed that I wasn't really that close to [her]. In: Begole, B., Kim, J., Inkpen, K., et al. (eds.) Proceedings of the 33rd Annual ACM Conference on Human Factors in Computing Systems, pp. 153–162. ACM, New York (2015)
11. Feigh, K.M., Dorneich, M.C., Hayes, C.C.: Toward a characterization of adaptive systems: a framework for researchers and system designers. Hum. Factors **54**, 1008–1024 (2012). https://doi.org/10.1177/0018720812443983
12. Gedikli, F., Jannach, D., Ge, M.: How should I explain? A comparison of different explanation types for recommender systems. Int. J. Hum. Comput. Stud. **72**, 367–382 (2014). https://doi.org/10.1016/j.ijhcs.2013.12.007
13. Google PAIR: People + AI Guidebook (2019). https://pair.withgoogle.com/guidebook/
14. Graefe, J., Engelhardt, D., Bengler, K.: What does well-designed adaptivity mean for drivers? A research approach to develop recommendations for adaptive in-vehicle user interfaces that are understandable, transparent and controllable. In: 13th International Conference on Automotive User Interfaces and Interactive Vehicular Applications, pp. 43–46. ACM, New York (2021)
15. Graefe, J., Engelhardt, D., Rittger, L., et al.: How well does the algorithm know me? In: Soares, M.M., Rosenzweig, E., Marcus, A. (eds.) Design, User Experience, and Usability: Design Thinking and Practice in Contemporary and Emerging Technologies, vol. 13323, pp. 311–336. Springer, Cham (2022). https://doi.org/10.1007/978-3-031-05906-3_24
16. Graefe, J., Paden, S., Engelhardt, D., et al.: Human centered explainability for intelligent vehicles – a user study. In: Ji, Y.G., Jeon, M. (eds.) Proceedings of the 14th International Conference on Automotive User Interfaces and Interactive Vehicular Applications, pp. 297–306. ACM, New York (2022)
17. Jameson, A., Gajos, K.Z.: Systems that adapt to their users. In: Jacko, J.A. (ed.) The Human-Computer Interaction Handbook. Fundamentals, Evolving Technologies, and Emerging Applications, 3rd edn, pp. 431–455. Taylor & Francis, Boca Raton (2012)
18. Kayser-Bril, N.: Dutch city uses algorithm to assess home value, but has no idea how it works (2020). https://algorithmwatch.org/en/woz-castricum-gdpr-art-22/. Accessed 02 May 2022
19. Kayser-Bril, N.: Female historians and male nurses do not exist, Google Translate tells its European users (2020). https://algorithmwatch.org/en/google-translate-gender-bias/. Accessed 02 May 2022
20. Kussmann, H., Modler, H., Engstrom, J., et al.: Requirements for AIDE HMI and safety functions (2004). http://www.aide-eu.org/res_sp3.html. Accessed 10 Feb 2022
21. Laato, S., Tiainen, M., Najmul Islam, A., et al.: How to explain AI systems to end users: a systematic literature review and research agenda. INTR **32**, 1–31 (2022). https://doi.org/10.1108/INTR-08-2021-0600

22. Lim, B.Y., Dey, A.K.: Evaluating intelligibility usage and usefulness in a context-aware application. In: Kurosu, M. (ed.) HCI 2013. LNCS, vol. 8008, pp. 92–101. Springer, Heidelberg (2013). https://doi.org/10.1007/978-3-642-39342-6_11

23. Lim, B.Y., Dey, A.K., Avrahami, D.: Why and why not explanations improve the intelligibility of context-aware intelligent systems. In: Olsen, D.R., Arthur, R.B., Hinckley, K., et al. (eds.) Proceedings of the SIGCHI Conference on Human Factors in Computing Systems, pp. 2119–2128. ACM, New York (2009)

24. Markus, A.F., Kors, J.A., Rijnbeek, P.R.: The role of explainability in creating trustworthy artificial intelligence for health care: a comprehensive survey of the terminology, design choices, and evaluation strategies. J. Biomed. Inform. 113, 103655 (2021). https://doi.org/10.1016/j.jbi.2020.103655

25. Maybury, M.: Intelligent user interfaces. In: Maybury, M., Szekely, P., Thomas, C.G. (eds.) Proceedings of the 4th International Conference on Intelligent User Interfaces - IUI 1999, pp. 3–4. ACM Press, New York (1999)

26. Miller, T.: Explanation in artificial intelligence: insights from the social sciences. Artif. Intell. 267, 1–38 (2019). https://doi.org/10.1016/j.artint.2018.07.007

27. Mohseni, S., Zarei, N., Ragan, E.D.: A multidisciplinary survey and framework for design and evaluation of explainable AI systems. ACM Trans. Interact. Intell. Syst. 11, 1–45 (2021). https://doi.org/10.1145/3387166

28. Molnar, C.: Interpretable machine learning. A Guide for Making Black Box Models Explainable (2019)

29. Nielsen, J.: 10 Usability Heuristics for User Interface Design (2020). https://www.nngroup.com/articles/ten-usability-heuristics/. Accessed 10 Feb 2022

30. Rader, E., Cotter, K., Cho, J.: Explanations as mechanisms for supporting algorithmic transparency. In: Mandryk, R., Hancock, M., Perry, M., et al. (eds.) Proceedings of the 2018 CHI Conference on Human Factors in Computing Systems, pp. 1–13. ACM, New York (2018)

31. Ribera, M., Lapedriza, A.: Can we do better explanations? A proposal of user-centered explainable AI. In: Joint Proceedings of the ACM IUI 2019 Workshops, New York, NY, USA, 7 p. (2019)

32. Shin, D.: User perceptions of algorithmic decisions in the personalized AI system: perceptual evaluation of fairness, accountability, transparency, and explainability. J. Broadcast. Electron. Media 64, 541–565 (2020). https://doi.org/10.1080/08838151.2020.1843357

33. Shneiderman, B.: Human-centered artificial intelligence: reliable, safe & trustworthy. Int. J. Hum.-Comput. Interact. 36, 495–504 (2020). https://doi.org/10.1080/10447318.2020.1741118

34. Tintarev, N., Masthoff, J.: Evaluating the effectiveness of explanations for recommender systems. User Model. User-Adap. Inter. 22, 399–439 (2012). https://doi.org/10.1007/s11257-011-9117-5

35. Tomsett, R., Preece, A., Braines, D., et al.: Rapid trust calibration through interpretable and uncertainty-aware. AI Patterns 1, 100049 (2020). https://doi.org/10.1016/j.patter.2020.100049

36. Völkel, S.T., Schneegass, C., Eiband, M., et al.: What is "intelligent" in intelligent user interfaces? In: Paternò, F., Oliver, N., Conati, C., et al. (eds.) Proceedings of the 25th International Conference on Intelligent User Interfaces, pp. 477–487. ACM, New York (2020)

37. Yang, Q., Steinfeld, A., Rosé, C., et al.: Re-examining whether, why, and how Human-AI interaction is uniquely difficult to design. In: Bernhaupt, R., Mueller, F., Verweij, D., et al. (eds.) Proceedings of the 2020 CHI Conference on Human Factors in Computing Systems, pp. 1–13. ACM, New York, NY, USA (2020)

Covid-19 in Transportation: A Comprehensive Bibliometric Analysis and Systematic Review with a Reappraisal

Marziyah Husain[(✉)], Maria Nasab, and Vincent G. Duffy

Purdue University, West Lafayette, IN 47907, USA
{husain14,mnasab}@purdue.com, duffy@purdue.edu

Abstract. This paper explores the impact of COVID-19 on public transportation systems through a bibliometric analysis, systematic review, and reappraisal. A systematic review analyzes literature, identifies trends, and provides comprehensive insights. Metadata from Harzing's Publish or Perish via Scopus is utilized, with analysis conducted using tools like MAXQDA's Wordcloud, VOS Viewer for visualization, BibExcel, Citespace, and Mendeley for referencing. The study aims to comprehensively assess the existing literature, including publishing trends, research areas, and identifying knowledge gaps. It evaluates the quality of research and offers suggestions for future studies. The analysis reveals a significant increase in COVID-19 and transportation research since the pandemic's start, particularly in 2020 and 2021. Key themes identified include the pandemic's impact on public transportation, the effectiveness of health and safety measures, and the role of technology in mitigating the spread of the virus. The assessment also highlights research gaps, such as the need for studies on the long-term effects of the pandemic on transportation systems and its implications for social equity. This bibliometric study, systematic review, and reassessment provide valuable insights for current transportation research. The findings can guide future projects and assist policymakers in developing effective strategies to minimize the pandemic's impact on transportation infrastructures.

Keywords: 2020 · COVID-19 · Transport · Public · Pandemic · MAXQDA · BibExcel · VosViewer · Citespace

1 Introduction and Background

COVID-19's impact on transportation is a significant issue due to its effects on health and safety, the economy, social equality, and the environment. It is crucial to implement measures to protect individuals using public transportation, address existing disparities in transportation, promote sustainable transportation systems, and minimize the economic repercussions of the pandemic. By doing so, we can ensure that transportation continues to serve as a safe, accessible, and sustainable service for everyone (Tirachini et al. 2020). Factors like public health concerns, changes in travel habits due to the pandemic, the economic impact of decreased demand for transportation services, and

© The Author(s), under exclusive license to Springer Nature Switzerland AG 2023
V. G. Duffy et al. (Eds.): HCII 2023, LNCS 14057, pp. 313–329, 2023.
https://doi.org/10.1007/978-3-031-48047-8_20

environmental considerations drive the importance of research on COVID-19 in transportation (Abdullah et al. 2020). The relevance of COVID-19 in transportation to the field of industrial engineering (IE) lies in its potential to enhance and improve processes and systems, manage risks, address supply chain disruptions, and gain insights into the impact of human behavior and perception on transportation systems (Murata et al. 2020).

To address the challenges posed by COVID-19 in transportation, various measures are being implemented beyond the scope of industrial engineering. Examples of such initiatives include implementing public health measures, adapting transportation networks to evolving needs, leveraging technology solutions to minimize physical contact, and offering financial support to transportation providers. By combining these actions, we can effectively mitigate the risk of COVID-19 transmission in public transit, enhance safety measures, and ensure the sustainability of transportation systems during the pandemic (Jacobzone 2020).

Utilizing the Scopus database tools, a comprehensive analysis of publications was performed to ascertain the distribution of research articles by country. The outcomes of this analysis are presented in Fig. 1. Notably, the United States, China, and Australia emerged as countries with a substantial number of research articles on COVID-19, attributed to several factors. Firstly, these nations boast sizable populations and well-established research institutions capable of conducting and publishing research across diverse domains. Additionally, being among the early countries affected by COVID-19, there existed a pressing demand for research to comprehend the virus, its impact on public health, and various sectors, including transportation.

Documents by country or territory

Compare the document counts for up to 15 countries/territories.

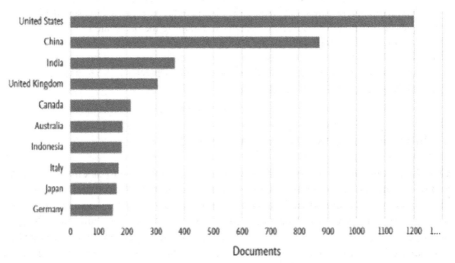

Fig. 1. Research articles on the topic "Covid in Transportation" based on country pulled fromScopus Database

2 Purpose of Study

The purpose of this paper is to conduct a systematic review of the topic of COVID-19 in transportation. The success of various strategies and regulations put in place to lessen the impact of COVID-19 on transportation networks could be revealed by a systematic evaluation of this subject. It could also point to areas that require additional study. To conduct this review, different applications, including VOSviewer, CiteSpace, BibExcel, and MAXQDA, which can analyze metadata, will conduct this systematic literature review.

2.1 Relation to Safety Engineering

The COVID-19 pandemic has brought significant disruptions to the transportation industry, highlighting the importance of safety engineering in ensuring the health and well-being of workers and passengers. Safety engineering principles play a crucial role in managing and mitigating the spread of the virus in transportation systems. For example, implementing physical distancing measures, mandating the use of face masks, providing personal protective equipment, improving ventilation systems, and increasing sanitation and cleaning protocols are all safety engineering measures that have been employed to reduce the risk of transmission. As such, the COVID-19 pandemic has emphasized the importance of safety engineering in transportation and has underscored the need for ongoing research and innovation in this field to help better prepare for future pandemics or other health crises (Zhang et al. 2020).

3 Research Methodology

3.1 Data Collection

By gathering metadata from multiple databases and subsequently analyzing it, a systematic literature review was conducted. Table 1 shows the number of works yielded. Scopus offered the highest number of results. Scopus data was extracted as a CSV file. WoS data, which included author, source title, source, abstract, and references, was extracted as a Txt file. Harzing's Publish or Perish data was extracted in the format called WoS and was specified to a limit of 200.

Table 1. Topic search in different databases

Search Term	Database	Citation
"Covid "AND "Transportation"	Scopus	5166
Using Harzing Software "Covid in Transportation"	Google Scholar	200
"Covid and Transportation"	Web of Science	5071

Table 1 shows the results obtained when the search terms "Covid" and "Transportation" were used. The results indicate there are a large number of publications and databases that have results on this search criterion.

3.2 Engagement Measure

Vicinitas is a tool that enables the monitoring and analysis of Twitter activity for social media campaigns and brands, both in real-time and historically. In this case, the tool was employed to assess the engagement of Twitter users in the realm of COVID-19 in transportation. To achieve this, a search using the keyword "COVID-19 in transportation" was conducted on tweets containing hashtags or keywords, and the findings are presented in Fig. 2.

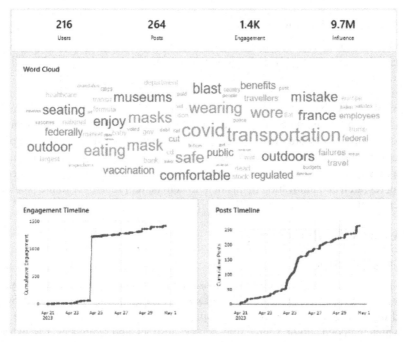

Fig. 2. The analysis carried out by Vicinitas was based on Twitter activity related to the key-the word "COVID-19 in transportation for the last ten days"

The timelines show that the term "COVID-19" has a steep incline which is realistic given the sudden appearance of the disease in human lives. The Word Cloud generated by Vicinitas points out the keywords that are associated with the disease.

3.3 Trend Analysis

Trend analysis allows for the detection of trends and variations in data over time. Trend analysis can be used to show how specific factors, such as infection rates or economic indicators, are changing over time as the pandemic affects many facets of our life. Researchers, decision-makers, and other stakeholders can acquire insight into the efficacy of various treatments or policies and make well-informed decisions for the future

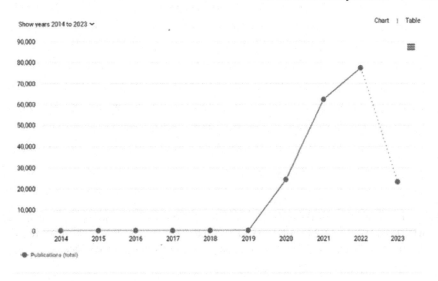

Show years 2014 to 2023 ˅

Chart ¦ Table

The visualization shows the number of publications published in each year.

Fig. 3. This graph from Dimensions.ai illustrates the annual publication count for the keyword "Covid and Transportation" from 2014 to 2023. The steady increase in publications reflects the growing interest and urgency in understanding the impacts of the Covid-19 pandemic on transportation systems.

by examining these trends. Figure 3 shows the trend analysis gathered from the various metadata collected from the Dimentions.ai application.

Trend analysis for COVID-19 can only begin from the year 2019 and after because the first case of COVID-19 was identified in December 2019 in Wuhan, China. This means that data related to the pandemic did not exist prior to this time. Figure 3 displays this fact and provides a visual of how steeply and quickly researchers started researching this disease.

Figure 4 shows the generated trend analysis from Google NGram. Google NGram Viewer is a web-based tool developed by Google that allows users to search and analyze word frequency in a vast collection of books and other texts that Google has digitized. The tool is based on the Google Books corpus, which contains millions of books published in many languages over several centuries.

Figure 5 shows the articles extracted from Scopus by the subject area. The biggest subject area is the Social Sciences subject followed by Engineering and Medicine (Figs. 6 and 7).

3.4   Relevant Book Chapters on the Topic

Chapter 20, "Industrial Hygiene and Confined Spaces," in David Goetsch's book, discusses the hazards associated with working in confined spaces, such as toxic gases, lack of oxygen, and physical hazards. The author emphasizes the importance of implementing a comprehensive industrial hygiene program that includes regular monitoring and

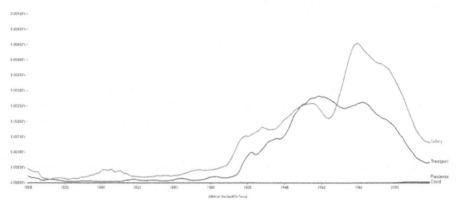

Fig. 4. Our analysis of the frequency usage of keywords "Safety," "Transport," "Pandemic," and "Covid" from 1800 to 2023 reveals that "Safety" and "Transport" have been the most frequently used terms, with "Pandemic" and "Covid" making a relatively minor impression.

Subject area ↓	Documents ↓
Social Sciences	1583
Engineering	1365
Medicine	1267
Environmental Science	1107
Computer Science	853
Business, Management and Accounting	531
Decision Sciences	412
Energy	404
Mathematics	318
Earth and Planetary Sciences	275

Fig. 5. Documents by subject area from the Scopus Database reveal that Social Sciences, Engineering, and Medicine are the top categories for research on this topic.

assessment of workplace hazards, as well as ongoing training and education for workers (Goetsch 2011, 440–482).

Chapter 14 of "Safety and Health for Engineers" by Roger L. Brauer covers the topic of transportation safety. The chapter provides an overview of transportation safety management, including identifying and assessing risks, safety regulations, and standards. The author discusses different modes of transportation, including road, rail, air, and water transportation, and highlights the safety challenges specific to each mode. The chapter also covers safety management systems, safety audits, and the use of safety technology in transportation. The chapter emphasizes the importance of safety management in transportation and guides engineers and safety professionals to enhance safety in transportation operations (Brauer 2016, 220–255).

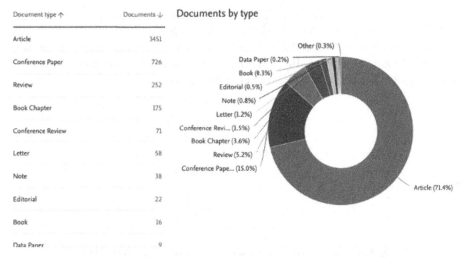

Fig. 6. Our analysis of "Covid and Transportation" publications reveals that more than 70% of the documents are articles, with 15% being conference papers.

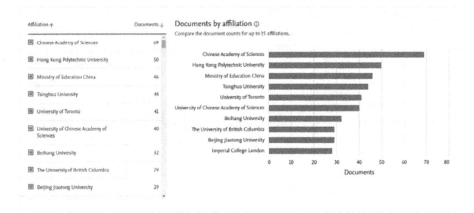

Fig. 7. The horizontal bar graph identifies the Chinese Academy of Sciences and Hong Kong Polytechnic University are the top institutes by affiliation.

4 Results

4.1 Co-citation Analysis

Co-citation analysis is a technique that entails looking for situations where many documents are cited in tandem with other documents to examine the connections between scholarly publications, journals, and authors. Insights into the intellectual structure of an area can be gained by locating networks or clusters of similar works. In disciplines like science and technology studies, information science, and bibliometrics, co-citation analysis is frequently employed to pinpoint significant authors, journals, and study areas and to chart the development of research trends over time.

A co-citation analysis was done through VOS viewer with the data extracted from Scopus. The articles shown in Fig. 8 are those that satisfied the criterion of being cited twice or more. The cluster can be seen in Fig. 8 (Fig. 9).

Fig. 8. Co-citation analysis extracted from Scopus using VOS viewer

Create Map   ✕

Verify selected authors

Selected	Author	Documents	Citations	Total link strength ⌄
✓	abdullah, m	4	754	9
✓	ali, n	3	203	8
✓	javid, ma	3	203	8
✓	zhang, j	7	714	8
✓	beck, mj	4	384	7
✓	dias, c	3	635	7
✓	hensher, da	4	384	7
✓	sun, x	4	432	7
✓	wandelt, s	4	432	7
✓	barbieri, dm	2	226	6
✓	brozen, m	2	57	6
✓	chen, kl	2	57	6
✓	hui, c	2	226	6
✓	li, s	3	72	6
✓	lou, b	2	226	6
✓	passavanti, m	2	226	6
✓	rollman, je	2	57	6
✓	ward, t	2	57	6
✓	wei, e	3	345	6

[< Back]   [Next >]   [Finish]   [Cancel]

Fig. 9. The co-citation table mentions the authors that have published articles on this discipline.

The articles identified in the cluster were deemed interesting and relevant for further examination and were therefore selected for more in-depth review.

4.2 Content Analysis

An analysis was done using Harzings' Perish to extract a "CSV" file with the keywords "Covid" and "Transportation." Then VOS viewer was used to create a cluster of keywords. Of the 595 terms, a threshold value of 4 was selected. The results are shown below in Fig. 10.

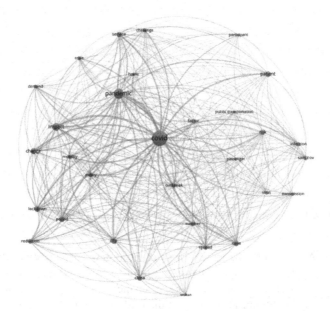

Fig. 10. Results from Harzing using the metadata

Figure 10 points out the keywords that are frequently repeated in the articles extracted from Harzing. It is shown that the words Covid, Pandemic, Outbreak, and Infection are the most common words detected. Figure 11 shows the words that occurred the most.

4.3 Pivot Table

In addition to using VOS viewer to analyze keywords for the Hazing extraction, the metadata was also analyzed in BibExcel. BibExcel has a number of tools for data cleaning, network analysis, and co-citation analysis. It may be used to examine citation data from bibliographic databases. It is beneficial for studying sizable citation databases and for displaying the connections among various writers, papers, and journals on a specific topic.

BibExcel was explicitly used to analyze the leading authors within a given topic. Using BibExcel to analyze the top authors in a field can offer many insights regarding the field's academic and emerging research trends. Researchers can better understand the fundamental ideas and arguments within the subject as well as the most crucial research issues and methodologies by recognizing the most significant writers and their

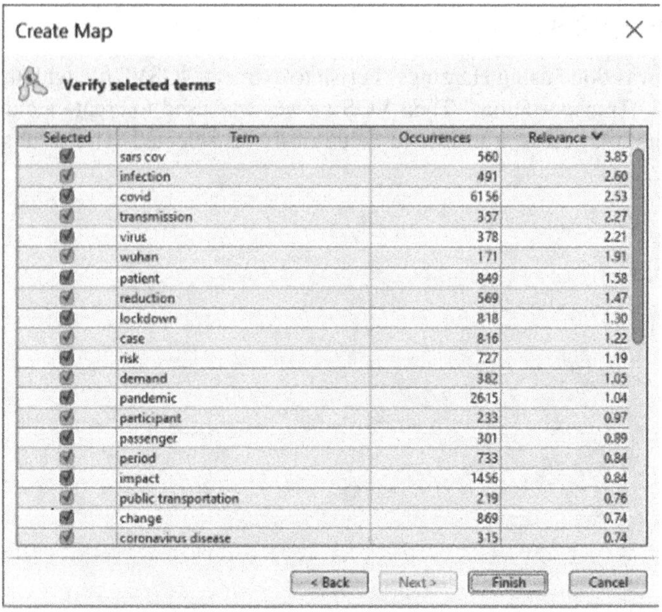

Selected	Term	Occurrences	Relevance ∨
☑	sars cov	560	3.85
☑	infection	491	2.60
☑	covid	6156	2.53
☑	transmission	357	2.27
☑	virus	378	2.21
☑	wuhan	171	1.91
☑	patient	849	1.58
☑	reduction	569	1.47
☑	lockdown	818	1.30
☑	case	816	1.22
☑	risk	727	1.19
☑	demand	382	1.05
☑	pandemic	2615	1.04
☑	participant	233	0.97
☑	passenger	301	0.89
☑	period	733	0.84
☑	impact	1456	0.84
☑	public transportation	219	0.76
☑	change	869	0.74
☑	coronavirus disease	315	0.74

Fig. 11. Keyword Co-Occurrence Network Generated by VOS viewer

contributions. Additionally, the analysis can point to new areas of study and research directions for the future. Additionally, being familiar with the top authors in a field can help researchers find potential coworkers or mentors and can help them create a professional network. Figure 12 is showing the leading authors from the data extracted from Harzings' publish.

Author Juanjaun Zhang is the leading author on the topic of Covid-19 in transportation which can be seen in Fig. 12. The author is from the School of Public Health at Fudan University, Shanghai, China.

4.4 Cluster Analysis

Another co-citation analysis was done using the Cite Space software. Cite Space is bibliometric analysis software that may be used to find and display patterns and trends in scientific literature. It provides a variety of tools for examining citation networks, co-citation networks, bibliographic coupling, and other bibliometric indicators and is especially helpful for locating important subjects, ideas, and research frontiers within a discipline.

Researchers can use Cite Space to find the most significant papers, writers, and journals on a topic and to follow the development of research trends through time. This data can be used to find new areas of research, potential partners or rivals, and to understand the intellectual hierarchy of a field. Additionally, Cite Space gives users the ability to spot groups of related studies, which can help them come up with fresh research questions.

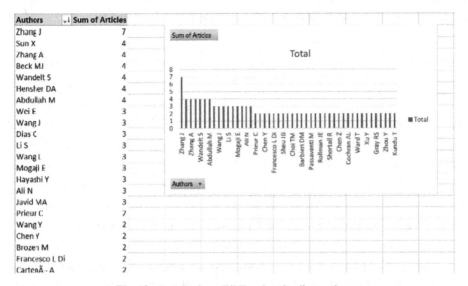

Fig. 12. Results from BibExcel on leading authors

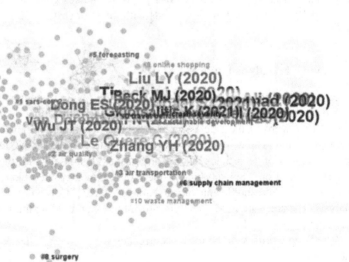

Fig. 13. Visualization of clusters in the field of transportation research using CiteSpace

Top 12 References with the Strongest Citation Bursts

References	Year	Strength	Begin	End	2020 - 2023
Bauwens M, 2020, GEOPHYS RES LETT, V47, P0, DOI 10.1029/2020GL087978, DOI	2020	3.64	2020	2021	
Wilder-Smith A, 2020, J TRAVEL MED, V27, P0, DOI 10.1093/jtm/taaa020, DOI	2020	3.64	2020	2021	
Sharma S, 2020, SCI TOTAL ENVIRON, V728, P0, DOI 10.1016/j.scitotenv.2020.138878, DOI	2020	2.91	2020	2021	
Nakada LYK, 2020, SCI TOTAL ENVIRON, V730, P0, DOI 10.1016/j.scitotenv.2020.139087, DOI	2020	2.72	2020	2021	
Shi XQ, 2020, GEOPHYS RES LETT, V47, P0, DOI 10.1029/2020GL088070, DOI	2020	2.36	2020	2021	
Wang PF, 2020, RESOUR CONSERV RECY, V158, P0, DOI 10.1016/j.resconrec.2020.104814, DOI	2020	2.36	2020	2021	
Zhou P, 2020, NATURE, V579, P270, DOI 10.1038/s41586-020-2012-7, DOI	2020	2.36	2020	2021	
Anderson RM, 2020, LANCET, V395, P931, DOI 10.1016/S0140-6736(20)30567-5, DOI	2020	2.18	2020	2021	
Baldasano JM, 2020, SCI TOTAL ENVIRON, V741, P0, DOI 10.1016/j.scitotenv.2020.140353, DOI	2020	2.18	2020	2021	
Li RY, 2020, SCIENCE, V368, P489, DOI 10.1126/science.abb3221, 10.1101/2020.02.14.20023127, DOI	2020	1.81	2020	2021	
Chen SM, 2020, LANCET, V395, P764, DOI 10.1016/S0140-6736(20)30421-9, DOI	2020	1.81	2020	2021	
Liu F, 2020, SCI ADV, V6, P0, DOI 10.1126/sciadv.abc2992, DOI	2020	1.63	2020	2021	

Fig. 14. Citation Bursts with the Top 12 References generated from CiteSpace

Figures 13 and 14 show a burst of citations and articles on the topic of "Covid in Transportation". These bursts can be used to represent a sudden increase in the number of citations of a particular publication or author within a relatively short period of time. Figure 13 shows the sub-topics that could be related to the topic of "Covid in Transportation". The number 1 burst sub-topic is the "SARS-COVID-19" keyword. Almost all clusters are from articles published in 2020 which makes sense as the pandemic started in late 2019. Figure 14 shows the bursts with the strongest top 12 references related to them.

4.5   Content Analysis Using MAXQDA

After downloading all the articles selected for the review, a content analysis was conducted on their text. This involved generating a word cloud that displays the most frequently used words in the articles, which can be used to identify relevant keywords for the literature review. The word cloud was generated through the MAXQDA software, based on the analysis of 18 articles taken from various databases, with the keyword "Covid and Transportation." Seventy-five of the most frequently cited words were chosen for analysis, with a threshold value of 8 and above. MAXQDA is helpful for qualitative data analysis. The software has a great visualization tool, including the word cloud tool that was used to generate Fig. 15.

The 5 top words with the most occurrences are 2020, COVID-19, transport, public, and pandemic.

Fig. 15. Word cloud generated using the MAXQDA software.

5 Discussion

The COVID-19 epidemic has significantly impacted the transportation industry, causing a decline in passengers and a loss of revenue for operators. Even though post-pandemic demand for public transportation has risen, it is unlikely to reach pre-pandemic levels, especially for commuting and business travel purposes. This will cause problems for operators as they may have to increase the frequency of services to provide sufficient capacity while maintaining social distancing. The short-term interventions used to maintain transport services during the pandemic, such as additional payments to operators are not sustainable in the long term, particularly for the mixed economy of public transport in the UK (Vickerman 2021).

In the UK, users have typically paid for higher public transportation fares rather than the taxpayers, which has resulted in more excellent farebox ratios globally. Governments experiencing deficits due to the pandemic are unlikely to continue supporting the transportation industry financially at the same level as before. All public and private methods of transportation have been adversely affected by the COVID-19 pandemic. This has wholly disrupted numerous business models. The UK government has contributed money to keep services running throughout the pandemic, but the length of the emergency and the delayed recovery raise questions about whether this can be done until demand reaches pre-pandemic levels (Vickerman 2021).

Covid-19 has not only affected the transportation of humans, but it has also affected the transportation of various goods and commodities across the globe. The pandemic has caused disruptions in supply chains, leading to shortages and delays in the delivery of critical items such as medical supplies, food, and other essential items. The restrictions on international travel have also had a significant impact on the movement of goods, particularly for countries that rely heavily on imports and exports. Additionally, the closure of borders and the quarantine measures imposed by various countries have disrupted the movement of people and goods, leading to a significant economic impact on the transportation industry (Shamshiripour et al. 2020).

COVID-19 has highlighted the vulnerabilities of the global food system, revealing its dependence on complex and fragile supply chains. The crisis has led to disruptions in the food supply chains, affecting food security and the livelihoods of millions of people, especially the most vulnerable populations. Building more resilient, diversified, and decentralized food systems could enhance the resilience of the global food system to future shocks and increase the capacity to meet the needs of all people while preserving the environment. Future policies and strategies should promote the diversification of food systems, support small-scale and local food production, and foster international cooperation to address the challenges of the global food system (Shamshiripour et al. 2020).

Efforts to address the issue of COVID-19 in transportation have been made by the human factors and ergonomics (HFE) and human-computer interaction (HCI) communities, as well as the safety-related community. These initiatives include the development of guidelines and standards to promote public health measures, designing and testing new technologies and systems, researching, and providing training and support to transportation workers. These efforts have improved transportation system safety and efficiency, promoted public health measures, and supported transportation workers during the pandemic (Wooldridge et al. 2022).

6 Conclusion

To respond to COVID-19 in transportation more effectively, society must take efforts in the areas of funding, mitigation, adaptation, education, and partnership. Governments can provide additional financing to promote research and development of new technology and procedures to improve transportation system safety and sustainability during the pandemic. Increased cleaning and disinfection, physical separation, and requiring face masks on public transit are all possible mitigation methods. Promoting active transportation, expanding bike-sharing and car-sharing programs, and establishing flexible work arrangements can all help to adapt transportation systems to changing needs. Education activities can assist enhance public understanding of COVID-19 dangers and how to avoid those risks when utilizing public transit, while collaboration among many stakeholders can help guarantee transportation systems remain safe, efficient, and successful (Karner et al. 2023).

7 Future Work

The study comprehensively addressed the wide range of limitations imposed by COVID-19 on various aspects of the world, including public transportation. Extensive research efforts were dedicated to understanding the necessary guidelines for taking precautions while using public transportation. However, there remains a noticeable scarcity of research on the long-term effects of COVID-19 on public transportation and the potential impact it may have on the overall concept of public transportation.

Fig. 16. Award shown from the NSF website dedicated to the research of Transportation of Workforce managers under COVID-19 conditions

As of 2023, the United States has discontinued the mask mandate, and people have resumed their usual way of life. This situation presents an opportunity for further investigation into whether the public transportation system has implemented new technologies to enhance the "self-cleaning" processes of public transportation. Examining this aspect would shed light on any advancements made in the industry to improve hygiene and ensure passenger safety.

The National Science Foundation (NSF) award grants researchers and institutions to support scientific research and discovery. These awards are given to individuals and teams who submit successful proposals for their research projects, which are then evaluated based on scientific merit and potential broader impact. The primary purpose of these awards is to advance scientific knowledge and promote innovation. Figure 16 shows an award given to program manager Daan Liang, from the University of Texas at Arlington.

The objective of a Rapid Response Research (RAPID) project is to understand the challenges and factors affecting workforce decision-making processes in the transportation construction industry during the COVID-19 pandemic. The transportation infrastructure construction industry has never had to adapt to such a nationwide threat to their workforce and changing public health guidelines and constraints. Workforce de-decision-makers are facing the daunting task of operating, maintaining, and constructing lifeline transportation infrastructure projects while ensuring the safety and health of their workers, operators, engineers, fabricators, and project managers. The public expects no disruptions in receiving critical infrastructure services and limited risk of virus infection while using these infrastructures. The research aims to collect time-bound data on the workforce managers' thought processes during the COVID-19 pandemic to provide critical information for the transportation construction industry on best practices during a pandemic and effective strategies for adapting to the uncertainties emerging and evolving from this unprecedented event.

References

Abdullah, M., Dias, C., Muley, D.: Exploring the impacts of covid-19 on travel behavior and mode preferences. Transp. Res. Interdisc. Perspect. (2020). https://www.sciencedirect.com/science/article/pii/S259019822030166

Borkowski, P., Jażdżewska-Gutta, M., Szmelter, A.: Lockdowned: everyday mobility changes in response to COVID-19. J. Transport Geogr. **90**, 102906 (2021). https://doi.org/10.1016/j.jtrangeo.2020.102906

Brauer, R.L.: Safety and Health for Engineers, 3rd edn. Wiley (2016). McFarland & Company, Inc., Jefferson (2016)

Bucsky, P.: Modal share changes due to COVID-19: the case of budapest. Transp. Res. Interdiscip. Perspect. (2020). https://www.sciencedirect.com/science/article/pii/S259019822030052X

Buehler, R., Pucher, J.: COVID-19 impacts on cycling, 2019–2020. Transp. Rev. **41**(4), 393–400 (2021)

Chinazzi, M.: The Effect of Travel Restrictions on the Spread of the 2019 Novel Coronavirus (COVID-19) Outbreak. Science.org (2020). https://www.science.org/doi/10.1126/science.aba9757

Das, S., Boruah, A., Banerjee, A., Raoniar, R., Nama, S., Maurya, A.K.: Impact of COVID-19: a radical modal shift from public to private transport mode. Transp. Policy **109**, 1–11 (2021). https://doi.org/10.1016/j.tranpol.2021.05.005

Du, Z., et al.: Risk for transportation of coronavirus disease from Wuhan to other cities in China. Emerg. Infect. Dis. **26**(5), 1049–1052 (2020). https://doi.org/10.3201/eid2605.200146

Dzisi, E.K.J., Dei, O.A.: Adherence to social distancing and wearing of masks within public transportation during the COVID 19 pandemic. Transp. Res. Interdisc. Perspect. **7**, 100191 (2020). https://doi.org/10.1016/j.trip.2020.100191

Galvani, A., Lew, A.A., Pérez, M.: COVID-19 is expanding global consciousness and the sustainability of travel and tourism. Tour. Geogr. **22**(3), 567–576 (2020). https://doi.org/10.1080/14616688.2020.1760924

Goetsch, D.L.: Industrial Hygiene and Confined Spaces. Essay. In Occupational Safety and Health for Technologists, pp. 440–482. Prentice Hall, Upper Saddle River (2011). https://www.ncbi.nlm.nih.gov/pmc/articles/PMC9468467/

Hu, M., et al.: Risk of coronavirus disease 2019 transmission in train passengers: an epidemiological and modeling study. Clin. Infect. Dis. **72**(4), 604–610 (2021). https://doi.org/10.1093/cid/ciaa1057. Int. J. Energy Res. **44**(13), 10953–10961 (2020). https://doi.org/10.1002/er.5706

Jacobzone, S.: OECD Policy Responses to Coronavirus (COVID-19). Building resilience to the Covid-19 pandemic: the role of centres of government (2020). https://www.oecd.org/coronavirus/en/policy-responses

Jenelius, E., Cebecauer, M.: Impacts of covid-19 on public transport ridership in Sweden: analysis of ticket validations, sales and passenger counts. Transp. Res. Interdisc. Perspect. (2020). https://www.sciencedi-rect.com/science/article/pii/S2590198220301536

Karner, A., LaRue, S., Klumpenhouwer, W., Rowangould, D.: Evaluating public transit agency responses to the COVID-19 pandemic in seven US regions. Case studies on transport policy. US National Library of Medicine (2023). https://www.ncbi.nlm.nih.gov/pmc/articles/PMC9987603/

Manzira, C.K., Charly, A., Caulfield, B.: Assessing the impact of mobility on the incidence of COVID-19 in Dublin City. Sustain. Cities Soc. **80**, 103770 (2022). https://doi.org/10.1016/j.scs.2022.103770

Murata, K.: On the Role of Industrial Engineering in the Covid 19 ERA - Researchgate. Research Gate (2020). https://www.researchgate.net/publication/346413665_On_the_Role_of_Industrial_Engineering_in_the_COVID-19_Era

Nižetić, S.: Impact of Coronavirus (COVID-19) Pandemic on Air Transport Mobility, Energy, and Environment: A Case Study (2020)

Shamshiripour, A., Rahimi, E., Shabanpour, R., Mohammadian, A.: How is COVID-19 reshaping activity-travel behavior? Evidence from a comprehensive survey in Chicago. Transp. Res. Interdisc. Perspect. **7**, 100216 (2020). https://doi.org/10.1016/j.trip.2020.100216

Shen, J., et al.: Prevention and control of COVID-19 in public transportation: experience from China. Environ. Pollut. **266**, 115291 (2020). https://doi.org/10.1016/j.en-vpol.2020.115291

Suau-Sanchez, P., Voltes-Dorta, A., Cugueró-Escofet, N.: An early assessment of the impact of COVID-19 on air transport: just another crisis or the end of aviation as we know it? J. Transp. Geogr. **86**, 102749 (2020)

Sun, C., Zhai, Z.: The efficacy of social distance and ventilation effectiveness in preventing COVID-19 transmission. Sustain. Cities Soc. **62**, 102390 (2020)

Tirachini, A., Cats, O.: Covid-19 and public transportation: current assessment, prospects, and research needs. J. Public Transp. (2020). US National Library of Medicine

Venter, Z.S., Aunan, K., Chowdhury, S., Lelieveld, J.: COVID-19 lockdowns cause global air pollution declines. Proc. Natl. Acad. Sci. **117**(32), 18984–18990 (2020). https://doi.org/10.1073/pnas.2006853117

Vickerman, R.: Will Covid-19 put the public back in public transport? A UK perspective. Transp. Policy **103**, 95–102 (2021)

Wooldridge, A.R., Carman, E.-M., Xie, A.: Human factors and ergonomics (HFE) applications in responses to the COVID-19 pandemic: lessons learned and considerations for methods. Appl. Ergon. (2022). US National Library of Medicine. https://www.ncbi.nlm.nih.gov/pmc/articles/PMC8898678/

Zhang, J., Hayashi, Y.: Covid-19 and transport: findings from a world-wide expert survey. Transp. Policy (2021). https://www.sciencedirect.com/science/arti-cle/pii/S0967070X21000172

Zhang, Y., Zhang, A., Wang, J.: Exploring the roles of high-speed train, air and coach services in the spread of COVID-19 in China. Transp. Policy **94**, 34–42 (2020). https://doi.org/10.1016/j.tranpol.2020.05.012

Zheng, R., Xu, Y., Wang, W., Ning, G., Bi, Y.: Spatial transmission of COVID-19 via public and private transportation in China. Travel Med. Infect. Dis. **34**, 101626 (2020). https://doi.org/10.1016/j.tmaid.2020.101626

NSF. NSF AWARD SEARCH: Award # 1400224 - Collaborative Research: Characterization, modeling and uncertainty analysis of Tornado Wind and its effects on buildings. https://www.nsf.gov/awardsearch/sho-Award?AWD_ID=1400224&HistoricalAwards=false.102. https://www.ncbi.nlm.nih.gov/pmc/articles/PMC7857701/. Accessed 4 May 2023

Evaluation of the Effect of Emotion on Lane-Keeping Performance Using Physiological Indexes

Narumon Jadram[✉], Tipporn Laohakangvalvit, and Midori Sugaya

Shibaura Institute of Technology, 3-7-5 Toyosu, Koto-Ku, Tokyo 135-8548, Japan
{nb23107,tipporn,doly}@shibaura-it.ac.jp

Abstract. Emotion is a significant factor that affects driving performance. To prevent accidents caused by drivers' emotions, it is important to understand the effect of emotion on driving performance. Many studies have used subjective evaluation methods to evaluate the effects of emotions on driving performance. However, these methods require direct questioning of the subject, which can be difficult to evaluate during driving. Furthermore, it is still unclear how positive emotions affect driving performance, especially on lane-keeping performance. Therefore, this study aims to objectively examine the effect of positive emotions on driving performance using physiological indexes. In the experiment, participants were asked to drive both with and without induced positive emotions via music stimuli. We collected electroencephalograph (EEG) and heart rate variability (HRV) data and offset from the lane position during driving. We used EEG and HRV indexes to evaluate arousal and comfort levels and compared how different positive emotions affect lane-keeping performance. Sixteen students participated in the experiment. The results showed higher RMSSD, lower β/α, and smaller the standard deviation of lateral position (SDLP) in the music condition. These results suggest that music induces a more relaxed emotional state. Furthermore, positive emotions, such as relaxation, can lead to better driving performance. However, future studies should focus more on how to induce emotions and the difficulty of driving tasks.

Keywords: positive emotion · lane-keeping performance · physiological indexes

1 Introduction

Human factors play a more important role in causing traffic accidents than other factors such as vehicles and roads. According to the National Highway Traffic Safety Administration's (NHTSA) report in 2015, nearly 94% of accidents are caused by human factors [1]. Distracted driving is the most common cause of human factors involved in traffic accidents, accounting for 41% of all accidents [1]. During driving, drivers have to pay significant attention in order to operate and make decisions safely. However, various emotional stimuli have the potential effect to capture attention, and pose a higher risk of producing driver distraction [2]. Emotion is an important factor involved in the process of thought and performing an action. It has been classified by the NHTSA as a source

V. G. Duffy et al. (Eds.): HCII 2023, LNCS 14057, pp. 330–339, 2023.
https://doi.org/10.1007/978-3-031-48047-8_21

of distraction [3]. Thus, it is likely that driving performance is also affected by emotion. Therefore, to decrease accidents involved by driver distraction, it is necessary to monitor drivers' emotions and understand how their emotions affect on driving performance.

The classification of emotions has been studied from two perspectives: the basic emotion model and the dimensional model of emotion. Ekman et al. classified emotions into six basic emotions: anger, happiness, surprise, disgust, sadness, and fear [4]. Russell et al. proposed a circumplex model that classifies emotions distributed in a two-dimensions: arousal and valence [5] (Fig. 1). Arousal refers to how stimulating the stimulus is, divided into arousing and sleepy. Valence refers to whether the stimulus is positive or negative, divided into pleasant and unpleasant. Different emotions are associated with different combinations of arousal and valence. For example, "Happy" is associated with high arousal and positive valence. "Relaxed" is associated with low arousal and positive valence. "Angry" is associated with high arousal and negative valence. "Sad" is associated with low arousal and negative valence. In this study, we define valence as a comfort level. Higher comfort levels led to positive valence.

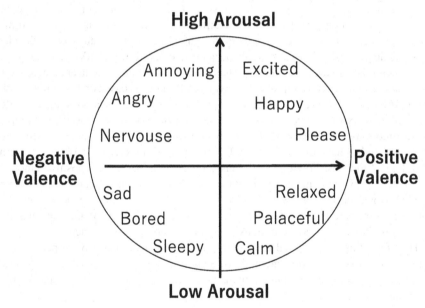

Fig. 1. Russell's circumplex model [5]

Previous studies have investigated the effects of various emotions on driving performance, including anger [6–8], anxiety [9], fear [10], sadness [11], and happiness [12]. Jeon et al. found that drivers in an induced angry state had degraded situation awareness and driving performance compared to a neutral state [6]. Cai et al. reported that drivers had poorer lane control ability in angry and excited states than in neutral state [7]. Kadoya et al. indicated that angry and sad emotions are related to an increase in driving speed [8]. Drivers with higher driving anxiety experience more anxiety about road rage and lower feelings of safety while driving [9]. Jallais et al. compared sadness and anger and found that sadness increased the localization error rate, while anger slowed down localization times [11]. Zimasa et al. studied the effect of different moods (sad, neutral, and happy) on driving safety using hazard perception videos and an eye tracker[12]. The study found that a sad mood had the greatest effect on drivers, resulting in the longest hazard response times, while the effects of a happy mood were less clear. Moreover, some studies have also investigated the effect of emotion in the different valence or arousal [13–15]. Pêcher et al. found that listening to happy music (positive valence) distracted drivers more than sad music (negative valence) [13]. The drivers' average speed unexpectedly decreased, and their lateral control deteriorated when they listened to happy music. Meanwhile, Ünal et al. indicated that listening to music may improve reaction time and lateral control in drivers due to increased arousal [14]. Several studies indicates that negative emotions can have a negative impact on driving performance. However, due to their limitations, it is still unclear how positive emotions may affect driving performance.

Most studies examine the effects of emotion on driving performance using subjective evaluation methods, such as questionnaires. These methods are convenient for collecting large amounts of data. However, subjective evaluation methods require direct questioning of participants, which can be difficult to evaluate during driving and may include respondent bias. Recently, a method using physiological data, such as the electroencephalogram (EEG), eye movement, heart rate variability (HRV), and heartbeat, has been proposed to evaluate emotion objectively. For instance, Ikeda et al. proposed a method for evaluating emotions using EEG and HRV indexes based on Russell's circular model [16]. This method plots the EEG index on the Y-axis (arousal axis) and the HRV index on the X-axis (valence axis) to evaluate emotions based on Russell's circumplex model. Emotions can be evaluated objectively using physiological indexes. However, only a few studies have examined the effect of emotions on driving performance using physiological indexes. Previous study has shown that experiencing positive emotions while listening to happy music can lead to a decrease in average speed and lateral control [13]. However, they did not use physiological indexes to evaluate emotions [13]. Moreover, some studies indicated that negative emotions also affect lane control ability [7], but it is also unclear how emotions affect lane-keeping performance.

Therefore, this study aimed to examine how emotions affect driving performance by using objective evaluation method. To achieve our goal, we used EEG and HRV indexes to evaluate emotion and compare how different emotions affect lane-keeping performance.

2   Experiment

2.1   Experimental Design

This experiment was designed to examine the effects of positive emotion on lane-keeping performance. Sixteen students (12 males and 4 females) in their 20s participated in the experiment. Participants were asked to drive under two conditions, with and without induced positive emotions through music stimuli. The study compared the arousal, comfort, and driving performance of the two conditions to evaluate how positive emotions (high arousal and high comfort) affect lane-keeping performance. Our first hypothesis is that driving while listening to music induces more positive emotions such as happy as the higher arousal and higher comfort levels than driving without music. The second hypothesis is that positive emotion led to better lane-keeping performance.

2.2 Emotion Stimuli

To ensure high validity in inducing positive emotions through music, participants were asked to choose their own music as emotion stimuli instead of selecting from a music database. Specifically, participants chose one favorite music that makes them feel comfortable and alert when listening. During the driving with the music listening condition, participants repeatedly listened to the same music to prevent different emotional effects that may be evoked by different musics.

2.3 Apparatus and Scenarios

The experiment was conducted using a fixed driving simulator. We used a UC-win/Road (FORUM8 Inc.) driving simulator software to create driving environment, driving scenario, and record driving information. To prevent distraction due to traffic environment, we constructed a low-complexity traffic environment and a monotonous two-lane highways road as shown in Fig. 2.

To operate the vehicle, we employed a Logitech G29 steering wheel and pedals. In addition, speakers were used to play engine sounds and music.

Fig. 2. Driving simulator

Figure 3 illustrates the driving scene in the experiment. We ask participants to drive with maintaining the center of the lane and press the button on the steering wheel immediately after seeing a warning sign displayed on the screen, which was used to ensure that the participants are focused while driving. During the experiment, warning

Fig. 3. Driving scene (left), driving scene when warning sign display (right)

signs were displayed six times. As shown in Fig. 4 the display timing of each warning sign was randomized between 60 and 90 s to prevent participants from predicting its appearance. The same timing was used for all participants. We defined the interval between displaying warning signs as drive1 to drive6.

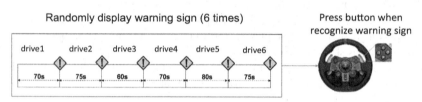

Fig. 4. Driving scenario

2.4 Evaluation Indexes

HRV Indexes

Heart rate variability (HRV) consists of changes in the time intervals between consecutive heartbeats called inter-beat intervals (IBIs) [17]. HRV is generally used to comprehend the autonomic nervous system. In this study, we used a pulse wave sensor (Switch Science) to collected HRV data. We employed the root of the mean of the sum of the squares of differences between adjacent IBIs (RMSSD) as comfort indexes. RMSSD is a HRV index that reflects the parasympathetic activity [17]. In this study, we interpreted a higher RMSSD as a higher comfort level.

EEG Indexes

We collected EEG data using Mindwave Mobile 2 (NeuroSky Inc.), which measures and transfers the power spectrum of EEG, as shown in Table 1, via Bluetooth. EEG signal is classified into several bands based on the frequency, including δ, θ, α, β, and γ. θ is related to drowsiness, α represents relaxation, and β corresponds to alertness [18]. β/α is one EEG index used to evaluate drowsiness while driving [19]. In this study, we employed β/α as arousal index interpreted as a higher β/α indicates a higher arousal level. Power spectrum of α wave was calculated by the sum of low α and high α. Power spectrum of β wave was calculated by the sum of low β and high β.

Table 1. The power spectrum of EEG output from Mindwave Mobile 2 [20].

Type	Frequency Band	Meaning
δ	1–3	Deep sleep without dreaming, unconscious
θ	4–7	Fantasy, imaginary, dream
Low α	8–9	Relaxed, peaceful, conscious
High α	10–12	Relaxed but focus
Low β	13–17	Thinking, aware of self & surroundings
High β	18–30	Alertness, agitation, irritability
Low γ	31–40	Memory, higher mental activity
Mid γ	41–50	Visual information processing

Questionnaires

We used the Self-Assessment Manikin (SAM) scale [21] for the questionnaire. SAM is a nonverbal method that uses avatars with different facial expressions to represent a user's level of arousal and valence (Fig. 5). The avatars have nine possible expressions, ranging from 1 (lowest) to 9 (highest).

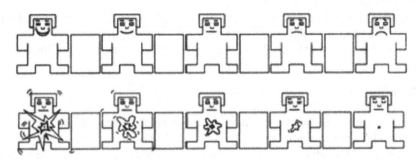

Fig. 5. SAM (self-assessment manikin) scale [21]

Driving Performance Indexes

To assess lane-keeping performance on the road, the standard deviation of lateral position (SDLP, measured in meters) is an index that has been used to evaluate the lane-keeping ability during secondary task driving [22]. We employed this index as the index for lane-keeping performance. In this study, the offset from the center of the vehicle to the center of the road data was automatically logged in the driving simulator. We calculated the standard deviation offset from the lane center as SDLP. Lower SDLP scores indicate better lane-keeping performance.

2.5 Experiment Procedure

Before the experiment, we asked participants to select their favorite music. Then, the participants wear brainwave sensor and pulse sensor. The experiment was performed by the following procedure.

1. Participants practice the operation of driving simulator until they feel familiar.
2. Participants rest for 1 min.
3. Participants drive according to the given scenario without listening to music.
4. After finish driving, participants answer questionnaires.
5. Participants rest for 3 min.
6. Repeat Step 3 and 4 with listening to the pre-selected music repeatedly.

Note that this paper only presents EEG and HRV results. The questionnaire result will be used for our further analysis.

2.6 Analysis Procedure

To evaluate the effect of positive emotions on lane-keeping performance, the analysis procedure is as follows:

1. Divide the data of each condition into six intervals (drive1 to drive6) based on the driving scenario. Each interval includes data between the display of two warning signs (Fig. 4).
2. Remove noise from the acquired EEG and HRV data and calculate the EEG index (β/α) and HRV index (RMSSD).
3. Calculate the mean values of the physiological indexes, and the driving performance. Index (SDLP) for each interval.
4. Compare the physiological and driving performance indexes in each interval with and without music conditions.
5. Perform a paired sample t-test to compare the difference in means of the indexes between with and without music conditions.

3 Results

A paired samples t-test was performed to compare the physiological indexes between with and without music conditions. As a result of RMSSD as a HRV index (Fig. 6), there was no significant difference between the two conditions. For all intervals, the mean of the RMSSD was higher in the with music condition than without music condition.

As a result of β/α as an EEG index (Fig. 7), there was a significant difference in the second interval of β/α ($t(15) = -2.94$, $p < 0.05$) between the two conditions. The β/α was higher without music conditions compared to with music conditions for all intervals. Moreover, there is a tendency that β/α decreased from the first (drive1) to the last (drive6) intervals.

In addition, the results of SDLP as an index for lane deviation are shown in Fig. 8. There was a significant difference in SDLP of the first interval (drive1) ($t(15) = -2.94$, $p < 0.05$) and the 4th interval (drive4) ($t(15) = -2.84$, $p < 0.01$) between driving with music and without music conditions. Moreover, SDLPs with music condition tend to be higher than those without music conditions for all intervals.

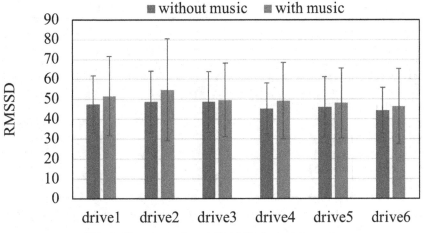

Fig. 6. The mean values of RMSSD for each interval.

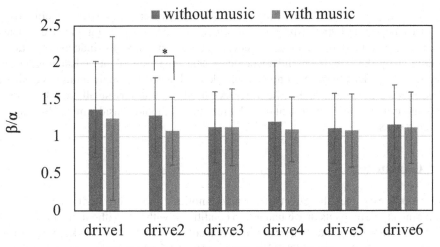

Fig. 7. The mean values of β/α for each interval

4   Discussion

The results showed higher RMSSD and lower β/α in the music condition for all analysis intervals. These results indicate that drivers had higher comfort and lower arousal levels in the music condition. Moreover, according to Russell's circumplex model, higher comfort and lower arousal could be interpreted as a more relaxed emotional state. Therefore, driving with music condition induced more relaxed emotion than driving without music condition. For driving performance, driving with music condition led to smaller SDLP for all intervals, indicating better lane-keeping performance than driving without music conditions. These results suggest that positive emotions such as relaxation led to better lane-keeping performance.

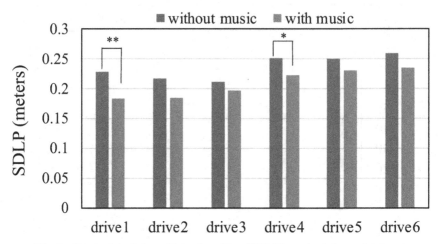

Fig. 8. Standard deviation of lateral position (SDLP in meters) for each interval

This study has several limitations. First, using music as a stimulus did not effectively induce emotions as hypothesized. As a result of lower β/α, the driver might be distracted by music. Future studies should consider alternative methods for inducing emotions. Additionally, the experiment did not counterbalance the order of music listening, meaning that the order effect could not be considered. Finally, the study aimed to evaluate lane-keeping performance, but the difference in SDLP was very small, possibly due to the easy driving task on a straight road. Future studies should consider more challenging driving tasks.

5 Conclusion

This study examines the effect of positive emotions on driving performance. In the experiment, participants drove under two conditions: with and without music. We used EEG and HRV indexes to evaluate arousal and comfort levels. The lane-keeping performance was evaluated using SDLP. We compared the EEG, HRV, and driving performance indexes between the two driving conditions. The results showed that driving with music induced a more relaxed emotional state and led to better lane-keeping performance. However, the study has limitations, such as the use of music as a stimulus and the easy driving task. Future studies should consider alternative methods for inducing emotions and more challenging driving tasks.

References

1. Singh, S.: Critical reasons for crashes investigated in the national motor vehicle crash causation survey (No. DOT HS 812 115). NHTSA's National Center for Statistics and Analysis
2. Cunningham, M., Regan, M.: Are Happy Drivers Better Drivers? The Impact of Emotion, Life Stress and Mental Health Issues on Driving Performance and Safety (2017)

3. National Highway Traffic Safety Administration: Overview of results from the international traffic safety data and analysis group survey on distracted driving data collection and reporting. Traffic Safety Facts
4. Ekman, P.: An argument for basic emotions. Cogn. Emot. **6**, 169–200 (1992)
5. Russell, J.A.: A circumplex model of affect. J. Pers. Soc. Psychol. **39**, 1161–1178 (1980)
6. Jeon, M., Walker, B.N., Gable, T.M.: Anger effects on driver situation awareness and driving performance. Presence **23**, 71–89 (2014)
7. Cai, H., Lin, Y., Mourant, R.R.: Study on driver emotion in driver-vehicle-environment systems using multiple networked driving simulators. In: Proceedings of the Driving Simulation Conference North America (DSC 2007) (2007)
8. Kadoya, Y., Watanapongvanich, S., Khan, M.S.R.: How is emotion associated with driving speed? A study on taxi drivers in Japan. Transp. Res. Part F Traffic Psychol. Behav. **79**, 205–216 (2021)
9. Taylor, J.E.: The extent and characteristics of driving anxiety. Transp. Res. Part F Traffic Psychol. Behav. **58**, 70–79 (2018)
10. Barnard, M.P., Chapman, P.: Are anxiety and fear separable emotions in driving? A laboratory study of behavioural and physiological responses to different driving environments. Accid. Anal. Prev. **86**, 99–107 (2016)
11. Jallais, C., Gabaude, C., Paire-ficout, L.: When emotions disturb the localization of road elements: effects of anger and sadness. Transp. Res. Part F Traffic Psychol. Behav. **23**, 125–132 (2014)
12. Zimasa, T., Jamson, S., Henson, B.: Are happy drivers safer drivers? Evidence from hazard response times and eye tracking data. Transp. Res. Part F Traffic Psychol. Behav. **46**, 14–23 (2017)
13. Pêcher, C., Lemercier, C., Cellier, J.-M.: Emotions drive attention: effects on driver's behaviour. Saf. Sci. **47**, 1254–1259 (2009)
14. Ünal, A.B., de Waard, D., Epstude, K., Steg, L.: Driving with music: effects on arousal and performance. Transp. Res. Part F Traffic Psychol. Behav. **21**, 52–65 (2013)
15. Du, N., et al.: Examining the effects of emotional valence and arousal on takeover performance in conditionally automated driving. Transp. Res. Part C: Emerg. Technol. **112**, 78–87 (2020)
16. Ikeda, Y., Horie, R., Sugaya, M.: Estimating emotion with biological information for robot interaction. Procedia Comput. Sci. **112**, 1589–1600 (2017)
17. Shaffer, F., Ginsberg, J.P.: An overview of heart rate variability metrics and norms. Front. Public Health **5**, 258 (2017)
18. Colic, A., Marques, O., Furht, B.: Driver Drowsiness Detection: Systems and Solutions. Springer, Cham (2014). https://doi.org/10.1007/978-3-319-11535-1
19. Eoh, H.J., Chung, M.K., Kim, S.-H.: Electroencephalographic study of drowsiness in simulated driving with sleep deprivation. Int. J. Ind. Ergon. **35**, 307–320 (2005)
20. Morshad, S., Mazumder, M.R., Ahmed, F.: Analysis of brain wave data using Neurosky Mindwave mobile II. In: Proceedings of the International Conference on Computing Advancements, pp. 1–4. Association for Computing Machinery, New York (2020)
21. Bradley, M.M., Lang, P.J.: Measuring emotion: the self-assessment manikin and the semantic differential. J. Behav. Ther. Exp. Psychiatry **25**, 49–59 (1994)
22. Hua, Q., Jin, L., Jiang, Y., Guo, B., Xie, X.: Effect of cognitive distraction on physiological measures and driving performance in traditional and mixed traffic environments. J. Adv. Transp. **2021**, 1–17 (2021)

The Evolution of Public Perceptions of Automated Vehicles in China: A Text Mining Approach Based Dynamic Topic Modeling

Jun Ma[1], Xuejing Feng[2(✉)], and Qinrui Yang[1]

[1] Tongji University, Shanghai, China
[2] College of Design and Innovation, Tongji University, Shanghai, China
fengxuejing@tongji.edu.cn

Abstract. Public attitudes and intentions are crucial for successful technological innovation, such as automated vehicles (AVs). To effectively advance the development and future evolution of AVs, it is crucial to comprehensively understand individuals' perceptions of autonomous driving. However, traditional survey methods using structured questionnaires may limit respondents' ability to express themselves freely. To address this limitation, we employ Natural Language Processing (NLP) techniques to analyze consumers' opinions and attitudes towards AVs as shared on social media platforms. Through Python programming, we collected and analyzed consumer comments from leading Chinese social media platforms (Sina Weibo, TikTok) and automotive social media platforms (Autohome Inc.) between June 2020 and April 2023, totaling 120,486 comments. Leveraging advanced text mining techniques such as Dynamic topic models (DTM), sentiment analysis, and semantic network analysis based on Pointwise mutual information (PMI) algorithms, we investigate the evolution of public perception regarding AVs over the past three years. Our findings unveil a predominant negative sentiment towards AVs, with discernible shifts in sentiment coinciding with major AV-related social events. Furthermore, we explore the reasons behind users' negative attitudes and identify potential factors contributing to the distrust of autonomous driving. These findings provide valuable guidance to public agencies, automobile manufacturers, and technology companies, enhancing their understanding of the adoption of AVs.

Keywords: Automated vehicles · Social media comments · Dynamic topic models · Semantic network Analysis · Sentiment analysis · Public perception

1 Introduction

Automated vehicles (AVs) are a disruptive innovation with the potential to enhance road safety, alleviate congestion, and provide convenience to the disabled and aged [1, 2]. However, widespread availability of fully autonomous driving for consumers is still a significant challenge that will require considerable time and effort to overcome [3]. Notably, there is a growing public skepticism surrounding AVs [4]. For instance, according to the American Automobile Association (AAA), only 10% of U.S. drivers would trust riding in a fully self-driving vehicle, with an additional 28% remaining uncertain [5]. Realizing the potential societal benefits of AVs hinges upon their extensive adoption [6]. The perception of the public significantly influences the pace of implementing new technologies [7]. Therefore, public attitudes and intentions play a crucial role in the successful technological innovation of AVs [8–10].

It is imperative to have a comprehensive understanding of individuals' perceptions toward autonomous driving to significantly advance the success and future evolution of AVs in the market [11]. While controlled laboratory research and questionnaires have been commonly used to analyze user preferences and acceptance of AVs [5], it has been observed that people's trust in autonomous driving and their future use of AVs are primarily influenced by their experiential and emotional connection with cars in their everyday lives, which may not always follow a rational or evaluative process [12]. Relying solely on surveys can also present certain limitations, including high costs and time requirements [13], relatively small sample sizes (typically ranging from 300 to 5,000 respondents) [14], and challenges in data collection and processing. Moreover, questionnaire designs often reflect the researchers' knowledge or biases, making it difficult to fully capture public perception [15].

In contrast, an open social platform can restore consumers' thoughts and opinions, freeing information transmission from time and geographical constraints. Previous studies have utilized social media data to understand the public perception of AVs [16, 17]. However, it is important to note that public views and readiness for automated vehicles can vary across countries and cultures [18]. Most previous research has predominantly focused on English tweets, limiting its applicability to the Chinese context due to cultural and language disparities. According to a report from global management consulting firm McKinsey & Co [19], the industry of autonomous driving in China has experienced significant disruption, resulting in ongoing debates and a wide range of opinions from consumers closely following this trend. While previous Chinese studies on AVs have primarily centered on keyword clustering or frequency analysis, failing to capture the evolving public attitudes and thematic developments surrounding AVs.

Moreover, although numerous studies have examined how demographic characteristics, including gender [16], influence public perceptions of AVs, the current body of literature on understanding these perceptions through social media data seldom considers regional variations. Even in experimental studies, the majority of participants are typically recruited from the same geographical area, leaving the question of divergent perceptions of AVs among users with distinct geographical attributes largely unanswered. This understanding is crucial for developing user-friendly AVs and formulating targeted policies for specific groups.

Therefore, this study employs innovative Natural Language Processing (NLP) techniques to survey consumers' opinions posted on social media and analyze their attitudes and perceptions towards AVs. We aim to address the aforementioned gaps by answering the following research questions:

1. Which topics are more sensitive to the public over the past three years, and how have these topics evolved over time?

2. What are the evolution sentiments of the Chinese public towards autonomous driving, and how do perceptions differ among users with different geographical characteristics?
3. What are the potential factors contributing to public distrust of AVs?

The rest of this paper is organized as follows: Sect. 2 outlines the analysis methods. Section 3 presents the results and findings. Finally, Sect. 4 provides the conclusion of the research.

2 Methodology and Data

2.1 Data Collection and Filtering

The study used Python programming to collect consumer comments on autonomous driving from mainstream Chinese social media platforms (Sina Weibo, TikTok) and automotive social media platforms (Autohome Inc.). Keywords such as "Automated vehicles", "Driving assistant" were searched. The sample data period was from June 2020 to April 2023. Our study collected 120,486 comments, 5,154 from Weibo, 3673 from Autohome Inc., and 111,659 from TikTok.

The cleaning process involved three essential steps to filter out the irrelevant data. Firstly, duplicated data was removed. Secondly, unrelated web links, symbols, and pictures within the text content were filtered out. Thirdly, the text was converted to simplified Chinese. Once the cleaning process was completed, user IDs, comments, dates, geographical information, and data sources were filtered out, resulting in a final set of 80,216 comments.

2.2 Analytical Methods

These filtered comments were applied advanced text mining techniques: Dynamic topic models (DTM), sentiment analysis, and semantic network analysis based on Pointwise mutual information (PMI) algorithms to understand how public perception of AV has changed over the past three years. The research framework is shown in Fig. 1.

Dynamic Topic Models. This study performed the DTM model to identify the most sensitive topics of user concerns about AVs and visualized the evolution of the topics over time. The DTM model is an inheritance and development of the Latent Dirichlet Allocation (LDA) topic model. Li et al. experimentally verified that the DTM model can identify and track the dynamic themes of a dataset by dynamically processing a sequentially organized text corpus [20]. The DTM model represents the evolution of topics as a discrete Markov process with gradual changes over time, generating doc-topic and topic-term matrices at each time point. The doc-topic matrix depicts documents as mixtures of multiple topics, enabling the computation of topic metrics and the representation of topic strength evolution based on timestamp links [21]. Equation (1) illustrates the theme evolution model of the identified continuous dataset:

$$\beta_{t+1,k} \mid \beta_{t,k} \sim N\left(\beta_{t,k}, \sigma^2 I\right) \tag{1}$$

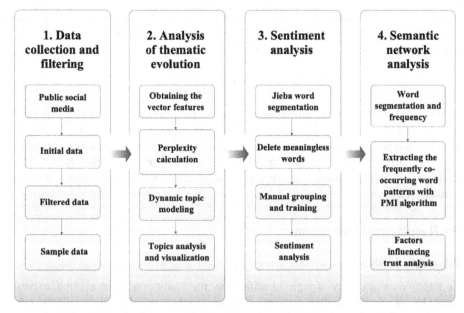

Fig. 1. Research framework of public perceptions of automated vehicles.

Perplexity serves as an important evaluation metric for determining the optimal number of topics in a topic model. A lower perplexity value indicates better generalization ability and an improved number of current topics. Perplexity is calculated using Eq. (2):

$$\text{perplexity(D)} = \exp\left\{ -\frac{\sum_{d=1}^{D}\log_2 p(w_d)}{\sum_{d=1}^{D}N_d} \right\} \tag{2}$$

Sentiment Analysis. Sentiment analysis, also known as opinion mining, involves extracting and analyzing people's opinions, sentiments, attitudes, and perceptions toward various entities such as topics, products, and services. It is a valuable tool for businesses, governments, and researchers to gain insights, make informed decisions, and understand public moods and viewpoints. In this study, each comment's sentiment analysis was performed using NLP technology. Sentiment values greater than 0.3 were positive attitudes, less than 0.3 were negative, and equal to 0.3-0.6 were neutral [22]. To optimize the quality of sentiment analysis, we manually grouped 6,000 comments and trained the model to improve the sentiment analysis with an accuracy rate of over 90%. Finally, the sentiment indices of consumer attitudes were calculated, and the evolution characteristics of consumers' attitudes were visualized. Furthermore, we analyzed the consumer sentiment of different regional economies based on the geographical information of the comments.

Semantic Network Analysis. Semantic network analysis focuses on understanding the semantic relationships between concepts. The Point mutual information (PMI) algorithm, a statistical measure, quantifies the associations between words or concepts. PMI can be employed in semantic network analysis to determine the strength of associations between concepts and construct a semantic network based on these associations. Equation (3) presents the calculation formula for PMI:

$$PMI(w_1, w_2) = log_2 \frac{p(w_1, w_2)}{p(w_1)p(w_2)} \tag{3}$$

In this study, the PMI algorithm was used to extract the frequently co-occurring word patterns in the negative attitudes with the keyword 'trust.' The relationships between factors influencing trust were revealed through the co-occurrence of text feature words and generated the social network graph. Visualizations are created in Gephi, where closeness vitality also indicates the degree to which each node contributes to the cohesive network [22].

3 Results and Discussion

3.1 Topic Modeling

To improve the accuracy of topic identification, this study conducted multiple experiments by varying the number of topics and assessing the level of perplexity. The experimental results revealed that a stable and optimal fit, characterized by a low redundancy and high representativeness, was achieved when the number of topics was set at 10. Accordingly, the DTM model in this study was configured with 10 topics as the threshold.

Next, relevant words that were both popular and reflective of the study's content were selected through modeling. The DTM model was used to determine the words' contribution to the topics, specifically the total probability of a word's distribution across all time segments. Based on this information, the words were ranked according to their contribution, and the final determination of the study's topics was made through manual assessment.

By modeling the hotness of research topics, this study generated a time-series-based matrix that enabled the analysis of the evolutionary trends in ten categories of research topics. To provide a visual representation of the changing heat levels of user-relevant topics in autonomous driving over time, a time-series-based heat graph depicting the ten main topics of was created. This graph serves to clearly illustrate the evolution of topics of user concerns about AVs over time (see Fig. 2).

The ten main topics could be divided into three categories: the first related to individual differences (Attitudes Toward Technology, Social Trust, Desire to Exert Control, Perceived Risk, Openness to Shared Use), the second related to automated driving systems (Performance Expectancy, Hedonic Motivation, Perceived Usefulness, Branding), and the third was social influence (Subjective Norms). As shown in Fig. 2, perceived risk, subjective norms and hedonic motivation about autonomous driving were the main topics of ongoing public concern. Consequently, ensuring safety and utility become a crucial challenge for consumers. Notably, following crashes involving vehicles with L2 driving automation, significant public opinion issues centered around social trust, branding, and perceived risk. Its topic intensity values were 0.33, 0.13, and 0.11, respectively. Additionally, there was a notable surge in the desire for control following these incidents. Furthermore, with the introduction of shared self-driving taxis in certain cities,

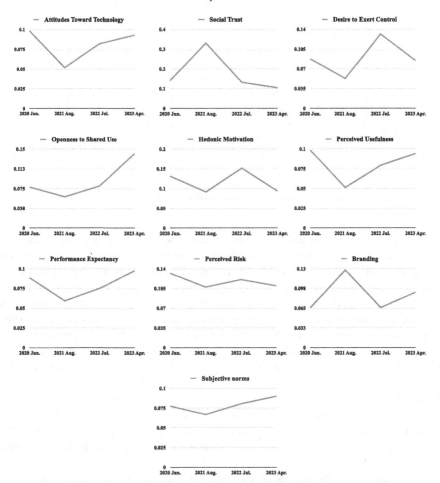

Fig. 2. The evolution of ten main topics of user concerns about automated vehicles.

discussions regarding the openness of shared use have witnessed a continuous rise in user engagement.

3.2 Evolution Characteristics of Public Sentiment

Sentiment analysis was conducted to track the evolving sentiments of the Chinese public towards autonomous driving during four distinct periods. As shown in Fig. 3, the analysis revealed a predominance of negative attitudes among users. Initially, in the first period (August 2020), positive public attitudes towards autonomous driving accounted for 27.21%. However, as time progressed, negative attitudes towards autonomous driving increased by 12.78%, reaching a peak of 59.28% during the most negative period. Subsequently, negative attitudes began to stabilize and gradually declined to 48.68% in the fourth period (April 2023).

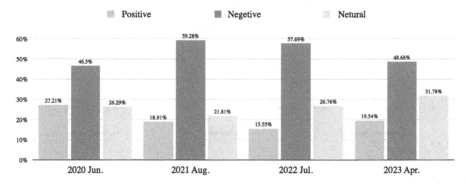

Fig. 3. Evolution trends of public sentiment towards autonomous driving.

Negative consumer attitudes towards autonomous driving can be attributed to several key themes of consumer concern. Firstly, driving safety stands out as a prominent factor. Incidents such as the NIO crash and the Tesla braking accident have significantly impacted public perception, leading to a prevailing negative sentiment. Despite the passage of time, the impact of these accidents on public opinion remains significant.

Secondly, the impact of brand perception is significant. Following the AV crashes, users' attitudes were more evident in their comments, specifically highlighting and evaluating both domestic and international AV brands. It is important for car companies to not only enhance the safety of autonomous driving but also proactively build a positive brand image, not just in response to accidents.

Thirdly, the transition from being a driver to a safety officer has raised concerns about unemployment, with some individuals questioning the value of their driver's licenses. The current understanding of the technology is incomplete, emphasizing the need for accurate and unbiased information from the media regarding the technology's current state, laws, and regulations.

In summary, addressing concerns related to driving safety, branding, and the role switching will be vital in improving consumer attitudes towards autonomous driving. Additionally, promoting accurate information and building public trust in the technology are crucial steps towards wider acceptance and adoption.

As shown in Fig. 4, it was also found that consumers at different regions had different sentiment indices toward AVs. The more developed the city, the lower the percentage of negative sentiment compared to less developed areas.

The Eastern region demonstrated a slightly higher proportion of positive attitudes compared to the Western and Central regions. Conversely, the Western and Central regions tended to have a more negative outlook. The Western region, characterized by relatively lower levels of economic development, displayed a greater prevalence of negative attitudes towards autonomous driving technology. This negative perception could be attributed to economic constraints that hindered people's acceptance and trust in new technologies. Insufficient access to information and educational resources may have contributed to a more conservative and negative stance among the public regarding autonomous driving.

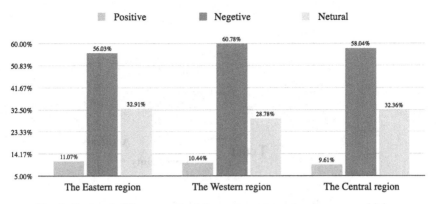

Fig. 4. Regional differences of public sentiment towards autonomous driving.

These insights can serve as valuable references for stakeholders involved in the development of rollout and communication strategies. It is crucial to consider regional variations, economic conditions, and cultural backgrounds in order to effectively address public concerns and promote widespread acceptance of autonomous driving technology. By taking these factors into account, stakeholders can tailor their approaches to better meet the needs and preferences of different regions and ensure successful implementation of autonomous driving initiatives.

3.3 Semantic Network Analysis

After analyzing the evolution of public sentiment, this study investigates the factors contributing to public distrust of AVs. By screening ninety-six negative comments using the keyword 'trust,' the results of the semantic network analysis reveal four potential reasons for consumer distrust towards AVs (see Fig. 5).

Firstly, there is technological anxiety, where users express concerns about the effectiveness and accuracy of different companies' technical solutions. They are hesitant to entrust their lives to autonomous driving systems that they believe are prone to errors.

Secondly, privacy concerns arise as drivers hesitate to embrace AVs due to increased connectivity and potential information system vulnerabilities. They worry about their location being exposed at any given time [23].

Thirdly, anxiety about not being in control is prevalent. Drivers, especially those with less experience with advanced driver assistance systems, have negative perceptions regarding the loss of control [24].

Lastly, the study identifies human-vehicle interaction as a source of anxiety. Drivers expect autonomous driving to replicate their preferred driving style, and sudden braking or acceleration often causes discomfort. They desire a customized driving experience to achieve seamless human-vehicle integration.

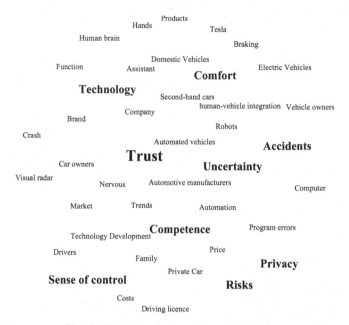

Fig. 5. The semantic network analysis results.

4 Conclusions

This research offers valuable insights into Chinese social media comments on AVs, addressing three key research questions. The first question explores the sensitive topics among the public over a three-year period and their evolution. Through the DTM, we identified three main categories of public concern: individual differences (Attitudes Toward Technology, Social Trust, Desire to Exert Control, Perceived Risk, Openness to Shared Use), automated driving systems (Performance Expectancy, Hedonic Motivation, Perceived Usefulness, Branding), and social influence (Subjective Norms). The results indicate that public interest in autonomous driving is heavily influenced by social events. Initially, there was a positive perception of the benefits of autonomous driving. However, this perception gradually shifted towards distrust in the technology's capabilities and brands, accompanied by a desire for control and the belief that electronic products will always have bugs, making them unpredictable. As the public discourse cooled down, there was a shift towards a more rational evaluation, with increasing attention to the human-vehicle interaction experience.

The second question investigates the changing sentiments of the Chinese public towards autonomous driving. Our sentiment analysis revealed a prevailing negative attitude, with an increase of 12.78% in negative sentiment after the crash incidents. Additionally, sentiment indices varied among different city levels, with more developed cities exhibiting lower percentages of negative sentiment compared to less developed areas.

The third research question explores the potential factors for public distrust of AVs. To facilitate public acceptance of autonomous driving, it is crucial for the government, car companies, and the media to collaborate. Their joint efforts should focus on effectively promoting autonomous driving knowledge, alleviating technological concerns, enhancing human-vehicle interaction design, and ultimately delivering an enhanced autonomous driving experience.

The novelty of this study lies in several aspects. Firstly, we collected and analyzed internet data, specifically consumer comments on AVs, rather than relying on traditional questionnaire data. Secondly, we employed various text-mining techniques to gain insights into the evolution of public attitudes and themes surrounding AVs. Thirdly, we conducted a comprehensive exploration of the potential factors contributing to consumer distrust, incorporating semantic network analysis into our study. By analyzing social media data from China and utilizing the latest available data, this research contributes to understanding public perceptions of AVs, promoting their healthy development, dissemination, and design optimization.

References

1. Fagnant, D.J., Kockelman, K.: Preparing a nation for autonomous vehicles: opportunities, barriers and policy recommendations. Transp. Res. Part A Policy Pract. **77**, 167–181 (2015)
2. Tan, H., Zhao, X., Yang, J.: Exploring the influence of anxiety, pleasure and subjective knowledge on public acceptance of fully autonomous vehicles. Comput. Hum. Behav. **131**, 107187 (2022)
3. Seter, H., Hansen, L., Arnesen, P.: Comparing user acceptance of integrated and retrofit driver assistance systems–a real-traffic study. Transp. Res. Part F Traffic Psychol. Behav. **79**, 139–156 (2021)
4. Hengstler, M., Enkel, E., Duelli, S.: Applied artificial intelligence and trust—the case of autonomous vehicles and medical assistance devices. Technol. Forecast. Soc. Change **105**, 105–120 (2016)
5. Raats, K., Fors, V., Pink, S.: Trusting autonomous vehicles: an interdisciplinary approach. Transp. Res. Interdisc. Perspect. **7**, 100201 (2020)
6. Zhang, T., et al.: The roles of initial trust and perceived risk in public's acceptance of automated vehicles. Transp. Res. Part C Emerg. Technol. **98**, 207–220 (2019)
7. Liljamo, T., Liimatainen, H., Pöllänen, M.: Attitudes and concerns on automated vehicles. Transp. Res. Part F Traffic Psychol. Behav. **59**, 24–44 (2018)
8. Choi, J.K., Ji, Y.G.: Investigating the importance of trust on adopting an autonomous vehicle. Int. J. Hum.-Comput. Interact. **31**(10), 692–702 (2015)
9. Xu, Z., et al.: What drives people to accept automated vehicles? Findings from a field experiment. Transp. Res. Part C Emerg. Technol. **95**, 320–334 (2018)
10. Nordhoff, S., van Arem, B., Happee, R.: Conceptual model to explain, predict, and improve user acceptance of driverless podlike vehicles. Transp. Res. Rec. **2602**(1), 60–67 (2016)
11. Nastjuk, I., et al.: What drives the acceptance of autonomous driving? An investigation of acceptance factors from an end-user's perspective. Technol. Forecast. Soc. Chang. **161**, 120319 (2020)
12. Pink, S., et al.: Design anthropology for emerging technologies: trust and sharing in autonomous driving futures. Des. Stud. **69**, 100942 (2020)
13. Das, S., et al.: Extracting patterns from Twitter to promote biking. IATSS Res. **43**(1), 51–59 (2019)
14. Gkartzonikas, C., Gkritza, K.: What have we learned? A review of stated preference and choice studies on autonomous vehicles. Transp. Res. Part C Emerg. Technol. **98**, 323–337 (2019)

15. Guo, Y., Barnes, S.J., Jia, Q.: Mining meaning from online ratings and reviews: tourist satisfaction analysis using latent dirichlet allocation. Tour. Manage. **59**, 467–483 (2017)
16. Jing, P., et al.: Listen to social media users: mining Chinese public perception of automated vehicles after crashes. Transport. Res. F Traffic Psychol. Behav. **93**, 248–265 (2023)
17. Ding, Y., et al.: How are sentiments on autonomous vehicles influenced? An analysis using Twitter feeds. Transp. Res. Part C Emerg. Technol. **131**, 103356 (2021)
18. Sauer, V., et al.: Designing automated vehicle interiors for different cultures: evidence from China, Germany, and the United States. Ergon. Des. **30**(3), 16–22 (2022)
19. Co, M.: From sci-fi to reality: autonomous driving in China (2023)
20. Li, D., et al.: Adding community and dynamic to topic models. J. Informet. **6**(2), 237–253 (2012)
21. Lafferty, J., Blei, D.: Correlated topic models. In: Advances in Neural Information Processing Systems, vol. 18 (2005)
22. Featherstone, J.D., et al.: Exploring childhood vaccination themes and public opinions on Twitter: a semantic network analysis. Telemat. Inform. **54**, 101474 (2020)
23. Mahoney, W.P., O'Sullivan, J.M.: Realizing the potential of vehicle-based observations. Bull. Am. Meteor. Soc. **94**(7), 1007–1018 (2013)
24. Planing, P.: Innovation Acceptance: The Case of Advanced Driver-Assistance Systems. Springer, Heidelberg (2014). https://doi.org/10.1007/978-3-658-05005-4

Colorful Commuting Journey: Non-driving Related Tasks that Drivers Willing to Perform Across Vehicles of Various Automation Levels and the Reasons

Jingyu Pang and Xingchen Zhou[✉]

Faculty of Psychology, Beijing Normal University, Beijing 100875, China
pjy@mail.bnu.edu.cn, zhouxc@bnu.edu.cn

Abstract. Automated vehicles relieve drivers' physical and cognitive load from driving and enable them to freely perform non-driving related tasks (NDRTs), which is promising to free modern citizens from the cost of the daily car-driving commute. Today, what NDRTs drivers are willing to perform and the reasons why they are willing to perform remain unclear, hindering the design of in-vehicle services. To fill this gap, we interviewed 15 drivers with driving experience in L2 automated cars to explore their preferred NDRTs during commutes in various levels of automation and why these tasks were performed. We classified four typical groups of NDRTs that can be performed during a commute, and the results indicated that drivers' preferred NDRTs change with the automation level of cars and the digital devices they use. We further revealed 11 reasons why drivers are willing to perform certain NDRTs, and these reasons were categorized into the drivers' needs and habits, the NDRT features, and the driving conditions. The findings of this study extend the understanding of user behaviors when commuting in automated cars, which will guide the design of non-driving related services for autonomous driving.

Keywords: Non-driving Related Tasks · Automated Vehicles · Commuting · Interview study

1 Introduction

SAE International [1] classified driving automation into six levels (i.e., L0-L5). Many manufacturers have launched L2 (Partial Driving Automation) vehicles, and L3 (Conditional Driving Automation) vehicles are in fast development. A market analysis report from McKinsey predicts that L3 vehicles will gradually take over the market in the next decade [2]. While L2 vehicles require the driver to be fully aware of the driving task and monitor the driving environment [3–5], automated vehicles of L3 and above relieve the drivers' physical and cognitive load, enabling them to perform more complicated non-driving related tasks (NDRTs), which will redefine the driving experience.

For urban inhabitants, one of the most frequent uses of cars is commuting. Autonomous driving will change the commuting experience by enriching the NDRTs.

© The Author(s), under exclusive license to Springer Nature Switzerland AG 2023
V. G. Duffy et al. (Eds.): HCII 2023, LNCS 14057, pp. 351–367, 2023.
https://doi.org/10.1007/978-3-031-48047-8_23

As commuting is a routine part of daily life, it will finally influence the life experience. Thus, this study focuses on autonomous driving for commuting purposes. We interviewed drivers who need to commute by car and who have driving experience with L2 cars. To guide the design of in-vehicle non-driving services and improve the commuting experience, this study investigated what NDRTs drivers are willing to perform in cars with higher-level automation and explored the reasons.

1.1 Non-driving Related Tasks

The affordance of performing NDRTs is important for the design of future automated cars [6]. In previous studies, NDRTs can be classified as standard and natural tasks [7]. Standard tasks are easy to be controlled and widely used for lab experiments, but they are hardly performed in real contexts. Natural tasks are those performed in real driving situations, such as sending messages, listening to music, watching videos, etc. This study focuses on NDRTs that could be performed in natural settings.

Previous research showed that region, type of journey, and level of automation all influence drivers' willingness to engage in NDRTs [6, 8]. For example, Schoettle and Sivak [8] surveyed people in the United States, the United Kingdom, and Australia and found that attitudes toward NDRTs varied by country. People in the United States and the United Kingdom were most likely to read, while Australians were more likely to communicate with friends/family or send messages. In addition, they found significant effects of demographic variables (i.e., gender, age, education, and employment). Other studies also found that NDRTs performed in autonomous driving are influenced by the journal types [6, 9]. For example, Wilson et al. [6] classified journey types as the daily commute, one-day tour, and longer domestic holiday and found that performed NDRTs varied with trip type: productive activities, such as work and meetings, were frequently performed in daily commute contexts but were hardly present in the other two contexts. As for the automation level, Kyriakidis et al. [10] found that from L3 to L5, the number of people planning to make phone calls, send emails, watch movies, or read increased dramatically.

The methods used to study NDRTs varied in previous research. In addition to surveys, many studies chose field observations of passenger activities on current public transportation, as the role of the driver in highly automated vehicles will be closer to that of the passenger [11–14]. Other observations were conducted by using simulators [15, 16]. Semi-structured interviews were also commonly used to dig deeper into drivers' opinions of future automated vehicles [6, 17].

Previous studies on NDRTs have some limitations. First, these studies mainly focused on highly automated driving (i.e., L4 and L5 automation). As we are still far from reaching fully automated driving, understanding NDRTs in L3 automation (conditional automatic driving) will have more practical values. Second, few participants have real experience with automated driving, so the validity of the results will be challenged. Third, most research only revealed the NDRTs but did not examine why people would perform these NDRTs. Understanding the reasons behind drivers' choices will help understand what is the real need of drivers in automated driving and guide the design of in-vehicle services.

1.2 NDRTs During the Commute

Commuting, a transportation behavior that arises due to the spatial separation of the workplace and the residence, is a crucial journey type due to its frequency in daily life. In major cities around the world, commuting generally costs more than one hour per day [18, 19]. More than 14 million people currently endure extreme commutes, and extreme commutes have increased in 70% of major cities [20]. In China, traffic congestion during commuting is one of the major challenges due to accelerated urbanization and rapid growth in vehicle ownership. The annual congestion time per capita in 50 major congested cities in 2022 was 104 h, and in mega-cities such as Beijing, this number was even as high as 174 h [21].

Long commuting distances and great congestion increase time spent commuting, and people have less time to engage in other activities, which has led to problems. A previous study showed that people with longer commutes are less productive, more tired, and have lower job satisfaction [22]. As autonomous driving allows commuters to engage in NDRTs, it seems promising to solve the problems caused by daily long commutes in big cities. Although the commuting distance is not changed, the time spent driving can be decreased, so people can engage in more fulfilling and productive tasks.

When commuting in vehicles with low automation, people already conduct NDRTs with low cognitive demands, such as listening to music. Teodorovicz et al. [23] suggested that commuters in highly automated vehicles would like to engage in more visual and cognitive resource-demanding activities, such as emailing, programming, analyzing data, etc. To better support the design of in-vehicle operation systems used for NDRTs, it is necessary to understand commuters' behavioral intentions in automated cars.

The trip type (i.e., inbound or outbound) during commuting can influence the NDRTs that drivers would like to engage in. For example, Wadud and Huda [9] found that the same activities were currently conducted differently on outbound and inbound trips when commuting. On the return trip, the number of commuters who would like to work/study, eat, and drink decreases, while the number of commuters who would like to sleep/snooze rises. These findings are based on user behavior in cars with low automation, and how people's behaviors in commuting with highly automated cars will be affected by the direction of commuting remain unclear.

1.3 Research Questions

Autonomous driving is in fast development and cars with conditional automation (L3) is predicted to become a mainstream product of the market in the near future, which will change our daily life. For people who live in big cities and should take a long trip for work, autonomous driving is promising to influence their commuting experience by allowing them to freely engage in NDRTs. To date, a few studies have already investigated NDRTs in automated driving, but they did not pay a closer look at the commuting journey and did not reveal why people chose to do different NDRTs. These limitations hindered the design of in-vehicle services, because only after understanding users' behaviors and their needs can we provide good services. In this study, we focused on the commuting journey in automated cars and aimed to figure out how to improve the in-vehicle services for daily commuters. To arrive at this aim, we proposed two research questions: (1) what

NDRTs people would like to perform during commuting in autonomous cars? and (2) why would they perform different NDRTs? As previous research figured out that the automation level influenced drivers' behaviors, we also considered this factor in our study.

2   Methods

2.1   Participants

Our study recruited participants through online advertisement (7) and snowballing (8). In total, 15 vehicle owners participated in our study, including six females and nine males. Seven participants lived in Chengdu, and eight lived in Beijing. Both cities are famous for their traffic congestion. The age of participants ranged from 25 to 45 years (mean = 33), and they all had no less than five years of driving experience and live in their cities for more than 5 years. All participants were required to (1) drive a vehicle with L2 or higher-level automation, (2) have usage experience of autonomous driving functions, and (3) commute by driving a car. The demographic information of the participants is presented in Table 1.

2.2   Procedures

We conducted a semi-structured interview. Before the interview, we collected demo-graphic information of the participants. Participants were asked questions about (a) their experience of daily commuting, (b) current experience with driving in L2 automation, (3) NDRTs that they did during a commute, (4) NDRTs that they were willing to do during commuting in automated driving (L3 and above), and (5) why they would like to do these NDRTs.

The interviews were conducted through WeChat voice call and face-to-face meetings. The interview was audio recorded with the participants' consent. Interviews lasted from 50 to 90 min. All interviews were conducted in Mandarin. After the interviews were completed, participants were compensated with 80 Chinese yuan for their time. All interview recordings were transcribed intelligent verbatim.

2.3   Data Analysis

We used Nvivo 11.0 for data analysis. According to the Grounded Theory [24], we first conducted open coding. We read all the interview manuscripts repeatedly, labeled them using sentence-by-sentence coding, and determined a list of first-level nodes. In the axial coding phase, two researchers merged, extracted, and named the results of the open coding independently and proposed different clustering methods. After comparison and discussion, we reached an agreement and get a coding book. Finally, we identified ways to classify NDRTs and the reasons for doing them, and our findings are detailed in the next section.

Table 1. Overview of Participants

#	Gender	Age	Occupation	Vehicle Information	PAS usage frequency	Commuting Distance
P1*	F	32	Individual Investor	Tesla Model Y	Sometimes	Not fixed
P2*	M	35	Travel Blogger	Tesla Model Y	Frequently	Not fixed
P3	M	38	Company Staff	Tesla Model Y	Almost always	8 km
P4	M	27	Doctor	Tesla Model 3	Frequently	10 km
P5	F	36	Designer	Tesla Model 3	Sometimes	12 km
P6	M	30	Project Manager	Huawei AITO M5	Sometimes	20 km
P7	F	27	Civilian Staff	Tesla Model 3	Sometimes	15 km
P8*	M	36	Private Business Owner	Tesla Model 3	Almost always	12 km
P9	M	37	Textile Businessman	XPeng P7	Frequently	20 km
P10	M	45	Financial Analyst	NIO ES8	Frequently	25 km
P11*	M	40	Accountant	XPeng P7	Frequently	20 km
P12	M	25	Travel Agent	XPeng P5	Frequently	20 km
P13	F	32	Business Manager	XPeng P7	Frequently	50 km
P14	F	25	Teacher	BYD Song PLUS EV	Frequently	10 km
P15	F	30	Bank Teller	Tesla Model 3	Frequently	15 km

Note: P1-P7 are vehicle owners living in Chengdu; P8-P15 are vehicle owners living in Beijing
Frequency of use: never - rarely - sometimes - often - almost always.
*Owners who pay additional fees for automated driving functions beyond the standard.

3   Results

The interview results showed that under L2 automation drivers already engaged in a wide variety of NDRTs during their daily commute. As the automation level increased, drivers would like to perform more diverse and complex non-driving activities. Some NDRTs were performed at all automation levels, while some NDRTs would only be performed at high automation levels. We categorized all these NDRTs into four types: work, entertainment, basic needs, and social activities (see Table 2). In the analysis, we also found that the digital devices drivers used to perform some NDRTs changed with the automation level of cars. Thus, we further distinguished four types of NDRTs based on how they would be influenced by the automation level of cars. They are (1) NDRTs that will be performed at different digital devices as the automation level increases, (2)

NDRTs whose complexity increases as the automation level increases, (3) NDRTs that will only be performed at high automation, and (4) NDRTs that will not be influenced by the automation level of cars.

After determining the possible NDRTs, we further explored the reasons why drivers want to do these NDRTs. Through open coding, we first obtained a total of 32 reasons. Through axial coding, we summarized these 32 reasons into 11 aspects. We then clustered these 11 aspects into 3 groups: drivers' needs and habits, NDRTs' features, and driving conditions. They will be introduced in detail in Sect. 3.2.

3.1 NDRTs in Autonomous Driving

NDRTs that will be Performed at Different Digital Devices as Automation Level Increases

Table 3 showed the NDRTs reported by the participants and the digital devices they used to perform them. The results illustrated that at L2, cell phones are the primary device used for NDRTs, whether for work or entertainment. For work, participants used cell phones to read, join voice/video conferences, and view and forward emails. For entertainment, participants used cell phones to play mini games, browse static content, and sing songs.

Today, many manufacturers have developed intelligent in-vehicle systems, especially in electric vehicles. Many participants reported that, when driving L2 cars, they were also willing to use in-vehicle systems for NDRTs. They used in-vehicle systems because they had bigger displays and were easier to operate than cell phones. For example, P9 told us, *"I'll use the in-vehicle system for WPS because the font can be enlarged."* Meanwhile, he also used the Karaoke application through the in-vehicle system with his daughter on the way home, *"We like to use the in-vehicle Karaoke application. The MV will be exhibited on the screen, and you can watch the lyrics."* P14 highlighted the flexibility of her in-vehicle system, *"The screen can be rotated horizontally and vertically. When you use applications like TikTok, it can automatically turn to vertical."* P6 used the in-vehicle system rather than his cell phone because the in-vehicle system is easier to operate. He liked photography and often took pictures when driving, *"I usually use the in-vehicle camera to record the landscape inside and outside the car. Using my phone to do so is kind of dangerous."*

When the drivers were required to imagine their behaviors in L3 cars, many of them wished for improvement of in-vehicle systems, and they regarded the in-vehicle systems as the primary platform to conduct NDRTs in this automation stage, especially drivers who now rarely use it while driving. P4 loved playing games, and he suggested introducing a game handle to the in-vehicle system, *"Mini games can have more fun if you play them with external handles."* P13 expected to use in-vehicle systems to more conveniently handle instant messages, *"I wish that it will prompt me. When somebody sends messages, it will ask me whether to reply. If I agree to reply, it can edit and send the texts."* In addition, P9 and P14 wished to use in-vehicle systems for more complex editorial work at L3, *"The in-vehicle system should be connected with an external keyboard so that typing will be much more convenient."*

Table 2. Comparison of NDRTs performed at different automation levels

	L2	L3	L4/L5
Work	Instant messages (cell phone)	Instant messages (cell phone / in-vehicle system)	Instant messages (multiple devices)
	Instant messages (voice)	Instant messages (typing/voice)	Instant messages (typing/voice)
	Reading (mobile)	Reading (phone/in-vehicle system)	Reading (multiple devices)
	Phone calls	Phone calls	Phone calls
	Voice conference	Voice conference	Voice conference
	Video conference	Video conference	Video/face-to-face conference
	Emails (View/Forward)	Emails (View/Forward/Edit)	Emails (View/Forward/Edit)
		Editing	Editing
		Creative work	Creative work
			Study
Entertainment	Songs/podcasts/audiobooks/crosstalk	Songs/podcasts/audiobooks/crosstalk	Songs/podcasts/audiobooks/crosstalk
	Videos (long-form)	Videos (long-form)	Videos (long-form)
	Videos (short-form)	Videos (short-form)	Videos (short-form)
	Browsing static content	Browsing static content	Browsing static content
	Pictures taking (in-vehicle camera)	Pictures taking (cell phone)	Pictures taking (multiple devices)
	Simple Games	Complex Games	Multiplayer online games
	Singing	Singing	Singing
			Playing cards (face to face)
Basic Needs	Simple foods	More complex foods	DIY some food
	Drinking	Drinking	DIY some drinks
	Smoking	Smoking	Smoking
	Shaving	Shaving	Shaving
	Simple makeup / partial makeup	More sophisticated makeup	Full makeup
	Rest/Nap	Light sleep	Deep sleep
	Placing things	Placing things	Placing things
	Reservations	Reservations	Reservations
		Shopping	Shopping
			Clothes changing
			Brushing teeth/Washing face
			Sports/Exercise
Social activities	Talk with passengers	Talk with passengers	Talk with passengers
	Online Social	Online Social	Online Social
	Check on children	Interaction with children	Childcare

Note:

Orange – NDRTs that will be performed on different digital devices as the automation level increases

Blue – NDRTs of which complexity increases as automation level increases

Purple – NDRTs that will only be performed at high automation

Red – NDRTs that will not be influenced by the automation level of cars

Table 3. NDRTs performed by different digital devices

	Cell phone	In-vehicle system	Laptop / Tablet
Work	Instant messages	Instant messages	Instant messages
	Reading	Reading	Reading
	Phone calls	Phone calls	Phone calls
		Editing	Editing
	Voice conference	Voice conference	Voice conference
	Video conference	Video conference	Video conference
	Emails (View/Forward)	Emails (View/Forward/Edit)	Emails (View/Forward/Edit)
	Study	Study	Study
		Creative work	Creative work
Entertainment	Watch the video	Watch the video	Watch the video
	Complex games	Complex games	Complex games
	Simple games	Simple games	
	Static content	Static content	
	Singing	Singing	
	Pictures taking	Pictures taking	
	Songs/podcasts/audiobooks/crosstalk	Songs/podcasts/audiobooks/crosstalk	
Social activities	Online Social activities	Online Social activities	Online Social activities
Basic needs	Reservations	Reservations	
	Shopping		

Note: Orange – mainly at L2, Blue – mainly at L3, Purple – mainly at L4/L5, Red – across all automation levels.

Many participants contended that they would only use external devices like laptops and tablets in high-level autonomous driving (i.e., L4 or L5). P6, a frequent telecommuter, expressed that his desire for the future commute was to "*use the laptop anywhere and anytime.*" Participants also wished to have a more comfortable environment to use external devices. For example, P7 reported, "*Even now sometimes I will stop the car to use the laptop, but I feel uncomfortable and inconvenient because the space is too small.*" Some drivers believed that a basic need in high-level automation cars is to design a table in the car. When asked why external devices like the laptop were to be used at L4/L5, P10 gave the following reasons, "*The in-vehicle system can be used more for entertaining activities, and work can be better finished on the laptop. Of course, using the laptop for entertainment is also possible.*"

NDRTs of which Complexity Increases as Automation Level Increases
As the automation level increases, the cognitive and physical load of driving will be relieved. Thus, drivers can get more immersed and finish more complex NDRTs. For example, most drivers reported that they mainly used voice interaction while commuting at L2. P10 told us, "*Generally I use voice messaging when I drive because it won't distract too much attention. Typing is quite complicated, unsafe, and time-consuming.*" A problem is that many participants thought for work-related communication, voice messaging seemed impolite. P11 and P12 suggested, "*It's OK to use voice messages when chatting with friends or family. But when communicating with leaders or customers,*

typing words is more acceptable." P4 believed that in L3 automation, the problem of typing can be solved, "*I usually type for communication. But after finishing typing, I must hurry to shift my eyes back to the road for safety concerns. At L3 and above, there will be nothing to worry about.*"

When commuting in L2 automation cars, drivers choose to join voice-only meetings. "*I join in the conference and just listen.*" (P14) When a video conference cannot be refused, P11 told us that he would "*stop the car and find a quiet place for the conference.*" P15 avoided this problem by scheduling meetings in advance, "*I will schedule the meetings to stagger the driving time. Meetings I join when driving are usually not important, so I can just put my phone aside and don't have to listen to it.*" As one of the few who attended video conferences in the car, P1 shared with us her solution, "*I bought a phone holder and put my phone on it. I can use it for video meetings, but it's not very convenient.*" P8 argued, "*The video conference can only be realized when the road conditions are good.*" In a word, most participants thought video conferences at L2 is heavily restricted. They wished this problem can be solved in L3 cars.

During the commute, drivers also conducted NDRTs for entertainment. But they would not devote their full attention to the entertainment in L2 cars. For example, P11 described, "*I like browsing TikTok (while driving), but it won't last too long. Maybe just 5 min. You still have to keep your eyes on the road. That is to say, you can only have 30% of the attention distracted. But you cannot completely release your hands or get completely distracted.*" P14 had similar opinions. She told us that she often watched TV series during her commute, but she would choose those which will not attract her attention too much. "*The series I watch in the car are those I watch casually, just to kill time. I will not watch TV series that I love in the car. I will stay at home and enjoy them.*" Participants also reported that they only play mini games when commuting in L2 automation, but they can easily get bored with these mini games, so they wished to play more complex games as the automation of cars increased. For example, P12 told us, "*When I got my car at first, there was a sense of novelty, so I would play the in-vehicle mini games. But the game is too simple, after a few times, I don't want to play it anymore.*" Drivers nominated some games that they would like to play at higher levels of automation. P13 had to commute up to 50 km each way and was a big fan of *Battlegrounds*. She said: "*A round of the game will last about half an hour. If the way is not long, you may arrive at the destination before the game ends. But if you are driving long distances, or commute as long as I do, it's okay to play such games.*" Yet P8 had different opinions, he thought "*Those highly immersing games are only suitable for L4/L5 automated driving.*" For commuting with full automation, P12 and P13 even imagined the scene of playing games with other people, "*PC can be equipped (in that situation), and you can play online multiplayer video games.*"

Participants also mentioned routine activities during their commute. Almost everyone told us that they ate food or drank something during their commute, especially in the morning when they hurried to work. "*I get up so early every day that I can't eat at home. I have to eat during the commute.*" (P13) The food they eat was also very limited, as P13 argued, "*You can only eat something simple, like fast food, just to fill your stomach.*" Participants were not satisfied with this lifestyle, for example, P14 complained that "*every morning, I can't enjoy a decent meal, and it's not nutritious to eat bread for breakfast all the time.*" Participants wished commuting with higher automation can improve this situation. P12, who often missed dinner because of the evening rush hour, wished to be able to have meals when commuting in L3 cars. However, most drivers still thought if they wanted to have decent meals during their commute, they had to wait for fully automated cars.

Besides eating and drinking, some drivers shared their experience of accidentally falling asleep during the commute. *"Autopilot (AP) makes driving much easier. But after turning on it, sometimes I ended up falling asleep and woke up scared."* (P4) P15 had a similar experience and said: *"It's true that many people accidentally fall asleep while driving after turning on the AP...Sleeping while driving is very dangerous. Even at L3, I only dare to take a nap."* All drivers believed that they can sleep in the car only when full automation was achieved, correspondingly, the vehicles' internal layout would change. *"The interior layout, including seats, will be changed. Just like the high-speed rail or airplane, you can do everything, including sleeping."* (P2).

Some female drivers also reported strong demand for makeup. P13 talked about her makeup strategy on weekday mornings: *"First, I'll finish the most complicated part at home, leaving the easy parts to be completed when driving."* They all thought makeup for eye-related parts was most complicated because *"The car forwards and stops alternately."* P14 explained that *"to finish a good makeup, the problem of road bumps needs to be solved."* As a result, even at L3, no female drivers believed they could finish a full makeup, they wished that they could realize the dream when full automation was achieved.

As the automation increased, drivers also thought the quality of in-vehicle social activities can be improved. For example, P3 and P9 had to drop off and pick up their children during their daily commute. For them, commuting time is precious parent-child time and they wanted to make good use of it. Now, they could only keep an eye on their children while driving. But when driving *cars with* L3 automation, they wished to have more interactions with their children. For example, P3 imagined a situation and told us: *"(in L3 automation) if your kid is crying, you can hug your kid and soothe them."*

NDRTs that will only be Performed at High Automation
Although drivers already engaged in a wide variety of NDRTs at L2, some NDRTs cannot be realized at present. Participants reported many NDRTs that they thought can only be performed at high automation.

In terms of work, L3 or higher levels of automation make editorial work possible. P14 told us: *"Making course slides or writing a teaching plan can all be achieved in the car at L3 and above."* P11 also thought *"editing emails is possible at L3, and you don't have to put your full attention into driving your car."* However, P7 was more cautious about driving and believed that *"activities at L3 should still mainly be visual, such as reading reports, PDFs, and images. It will still be inconvenient if typing is involved."* P5, who is an architect, thought she still couldn't complete work at L3: *"Architectural design demands high computing performance. We must operate on more powerful desktops to finish our work, which can only be achieved at L4 or L5."* P1 thought studying in L3 cars was limited: *"I can simply study for a little while (in L3 cars), and I cannot get fully concentrated on the study. The performance can't be so good."* Therefore, she wished that after L4/L5 was realized, she could devote her full attention to studying.

Besides work, participants also reported many other activities that they wanted to do only when full automation was achieved. For example, P14 wished the car was equipped with a *refrigerator* so she could DIY some food. P11 even wanted to wash up in the car, especially in a hurry on a weekday morning.

NDRTs that will not be Influenced by the Automation Level of Cars

There were also activities that participants thought would not be influenced by the automation level of cars, such as phone calls which already can be well conducted in L2 cars. Other NDRTs of this type reported by the participants included listening to songs/podcasts/audiobooks/crosstalk, smoking, and shaving. The common nature of these NDRTs is that they do not require many cognitive or physical resources, so they won't be influenced as more resources are freed by automated driving.

3.2 Reasons for Doing NDRTs

Drivers' Needs and Habits

In the group named Drivers' Needs and Habits, we identified five reasons to conduct an NDRT (see Fig. 1). They are necessary routine, utilitarian purposes, hedonic purposes, social purposes, and improvement of personal conditions.

Necessary routine. As commute is an essential part of daily life and occupies a period, drivers have to finish a few necessary routines during the commute. For example, P15 told us that *when she was too late to make up at home, she would finish it in the car.* After practice, now she could handle it very well. P13 and P14 also reported that they had to eat breakfast during the commute.

Utilitarian purposes. Besides necessary routines, many drivers also said to conduct work-related NDRTs during the commute, especially when the automation of cars increased. P12 told us: "*I think a higher level of automation will allow me to make better use of my time. (during the commute) I can handle most of the work that I used to deal with in the office.*" Automated vehicles cannot shorten distances, but they can allow drivers to make use of the time which used to be cost by driving the car.

Hedonic purposes. Drivers also conduct NDRTs for hedonic purposes. P13 complained about the current commute: "*After I get home,* I have to eat and take a shower. When I can finally lie in bed, it's already late, but I can't help using my phone for entertainment, which makes me sleep late every night. Even so, I still feel that I need some entertaining time anyway." Thus, she wished to satisfy her needs for entertainment during the commute when automated driving can be used: "At L3 and above, I can use cell phones freely on my way back home. It will improve my happiness a lot." Some drivers contended that the important thing is "to have control over time" but not "*have to do* specific things." (P1) P5 also agreed with this idea: "Although the length of commute may remain the same in the future. Five hours of free time will be different from five hours of driving. Whether you use it for entertainment or work, you will gain a lot from it, because it is your own time."

Social purposes. As mentioned above, drivers also conducted NDRTs for social purposes. They had online communication with friends and families or talked with other passengers in the car.

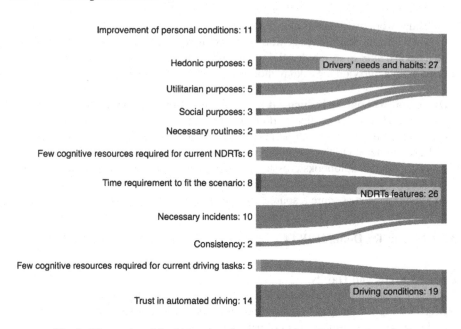

Fig. 1. The results of the 11 aspects of reasons and how they are categorized

Improvement of personal conditions. Drivers also conducted NDRTs to regulate themselves when they were in a bad state of mind during the commute. For example, P15 told us: *"When driving in Beijing, it's inevitable to suffer from road rage. When you've been stuck in traffic congestion for a long time, you can easily lose your temper. To relieve the negative feelings, I will use my cell phone for entertainment, then I feel the congestion lasts short."* In another case, P7 conducted NDRTs to deal with sleepiness. She said: *"When you only focus on driving, you might get sleepy, so that's why drivers like to smoke or listen to songs when driving, just to make themselves awake."* P12 chose to chat with passengers, and he thought it had two effects: *"On the one hand, it makes me not so sleepy. On the other hand, if no one talks, I will feel a little awkward, so I'll liven up the atmosphere."* Another negative feeling of driving is boredom. Many participants reported to perform NDRTs to deal with boredom. P10 stated that *"watching videos and playing games is common because you have nothing else to do when the car drive automatically, so it's the only way to make yourself feel slightly better."* (P10).

NDRT Features

Limited by the automation level, drivers cannot perform all NDRTs as they wish until full automation is achieved. As a result, they showed a tendency to choose NDRTs based on tasks' features.

Necessary incidents. *Dealing with necessary tasks* was most commonly reported by participants, and most of the necessary incidents were work-related. For instance, P4 told us: *"I drive quite carefully, so I only deal with something urgent, such as sending messages and communicating. Other unrelated things won't be considered."* P6's work required him to keep in communication with others all the time, so he had to *"hold the* *phone to frequently check it while driving."* P8 thought it was especially urgent when the message was from the boss: "If *leaders sent something to you, or ask you some questions when you are driving, you cannot reply 'wait for a moment, I'm driving, and I'll get you back later'. You must answer it immediately."*

Few cognitive resources required for current NDRTs. Many drivers claimed that they tended to reserve as few cognitive resources as possible for NDRTs by choosing simple events or simplifying them. P14, who killed time during the commute by watching TV series, said: *"I would choose TV series that I know very well, and I can take it as a background sound."* P15, who loved to listen to crosstalk, also told us: *"If you listen to crosstalk that you aren't familiar with, you may need to clearly understand every word. But when you are driving, you cannot completely concentrate on it. Thus, I prefer to listen to music, because you don't have to recite the words or something."* When talking about L3, although drivers reported a wider variety of NDRTs, they continued to show this tendency to take up as few cognitive resources as possible. P11 told us that *"even at L3, it's okay to be a little more focused, but not so immersed."*

Time requirement to fit the scenario. We also found that drivers considered the time factor. If one task lasted for a short time, drivers tended to conduct it; but if it lasted too long, they would consider the length of the commuting journey. P10 said: *"If a meeting lasts for a long time, usually I will find a place to stop my car and then attend it. If it lasts for a relatively short period, joining it will not be a problem. It mainly depends on the duration."* Similarly, P7 thought *reading a message, a post, or an article, can be very quick, but watching a video lasted too long, so she will not choose to watch videos.* Moreover, drivers also consider the match between the duration of the commute and that of the NDRTs. For example, P11 argued, *"The period for commute is not that long. You don't have the opportunity to do too many things."* P7 also commented: *"Making a report may take ten minutes, but the commute might last only twenty minutes. Will you spend your entire commute sitting there and concentrating on a report? That's a little bit ridiculous."* In addition, considering the takeover scenarios in L3, many participants tended to conduct NDRTs that could be interrupted. *"Watching a movie, browsing TikTok, reading novels, and editing Excel or slides can all be paused when you have to take over the control of the car."* (P8) But some drivers did not like the feeling of being interrupted. *"I prefer to watch short videos. Long videos will require coherence. For example, if you get interrupted by takeover requests when watching a movie, it's surely uncomfortable."* (P11).

Consistency. Some drivers believed that the coherence between different tasks was also an important factor. For example, P6 said: *"After replying to WeChat messages, incidentally, I will turn to Moments to see new updates."*

Driving Conditions

Few cognitive resources required for current driving tasks. At the low automation level, drivers considered the cognitive demand of the driving task to determine whether or not to conduct an NDRT. We found that drivers would engage in NDRTs when they were familiar with the road. P7 said: *"I am familiar with the route to work, so I listen to songs to relieve my boredom, and I'm not worried."* Low speed and good traffic conditions were also reasons for NDRTs. P3 shared his experience: "When *driving slowly, you can have one hand off the steering wheel for almost twenty seconds, during which you can do* *a lot of things, such as peeling an orange, eating something, drinking water, or having physical touch with your children."*

Trust in automated driving. We also found that drivers' willingness to conduct NDRTs essentially depended on their trust in automated driving technology. When it came to L3 automated driving, some participants showed a wait-and-see attitude. *"This kind of technology still needs to be iterated further. I won't try it immediately once it's launched."* P6 had similar opinions: *"Unless manufacturers have introduced something revolutionary, or it has become a core selling point for costumers... Only when it makes me feel that this technology has become mature, I will do what I want to do (i.e., NDRTs)."*

The Reasons for Doing NDRTs Change with Automation Levels

Figure 2 showed the reasons reported by participants when targeting different levels of automation. The results illustrated that the improvement of personal conditions, the cognitive resources required for driving conditions, the necessity of NDRTs, and the cognitive resources required for NDRTs were the main considerations when commuting in L2 cars. However, for higher levels of automation, the cognitive resources required for driving and NDRTs were not key factors. Drivers' trust in the automated driving technology, the necessity of the NDRTs, and whether the NDRTs meet drivers' utilitarian or hedonic needs were key determinants.

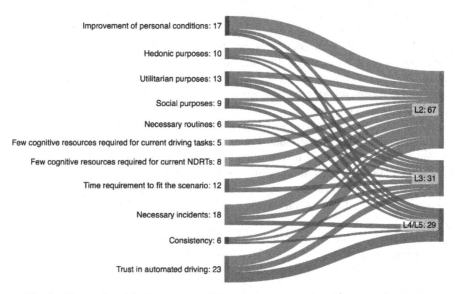

Fig. 2. The results of the 11 aspects and how they correspond to the automation levels

4 Discussion

This study focused on the use of automated driving in daily commuting and how the technology shaped drivers' non-driving behaviors. We interviewed 15 participants who had to drive for work and had experience of driving cars with L2 automation. Through the interview, we revealed drivers' preferred NDRTs during commuting at various automation levels and also summarized the reasons behind them.

First, we discovered the NDRTs that people are willing to conduct across different levels of driving automation. We classified these NDRTs from two perspectives. In terms of the characteristics of the tasks, we classified NDRTs as work, entertainment, basic needs, and social activities. This is similar to the typology proposed by Wilson et al. [6]. In addition, we proposed to classify NDRTs from the devices, which can be classified as being conducted through a cell phone, an in-vehicle system, a laptop/tablet, or no electronic devices required. We further found that NDRTs and the devices used to conduct NDRTs changed as the automation of cars increased.

In-vehicle systems are commonly equipped in cars on the market. These in-vehicle systems still have many limitations. For example, for many in-vehicle systems, during driving the display only exhibit the navigation map, and the embedded applications in the in-vehicle systems had poor adaption and copyright restrictions. Therefore, we found that cell phones were still the primary device to engage in NDRTs. But for L3 cars, participants in our study showed a strong willingness to engage in NDRTs through in-vehicle systems. At higher levels of automation, drivers showed a tendency to use their laptops or tablet directly. In addition, we also found that drivers tended to perform more complex NDRTs as the automation level increased because their cognitive and physical resources would be relieved by the automated driving system.

Second, we explored the reasons for performing NDRTs. We further clustered these reasons into three groups: drivers' needs and habits, NDRT features, and driving conditions. Among these reasons, improvement of personal condition, necessary incidents, and trust in automated driving was mentioned most frequently. During commuting, drivers can easily get in negative states, such as fatigue, anger, boredom, etc. Drivers conducted NDRTs to improve their mental state. Drivers also emphasized the necessity and urgency of some NDRTs, and usually, these tasks were related to their work. Trust in automated driving mainly influenced drivers' behaviors in automated driving.

We further found that the reasons why drivers performed certain NDRTs would be influenced by the automation level. At L2, drivers would consider the cognitive loading of the current driving task and the NDRT. Drivers tended to engage in NDRTs when road conditions were good, when speeds were slow, when they were familiar with the road, and when the NDRT demanded few cognitive or physical resources. As the automation level increased, the load of driving decreased, and drivers were less likely to consider the constraints. They would consider the reliability of the automated driving technology, the necessity of the NDRTs, and whether the NDRTs meet their utilitarian or hedonic needs.

Compared with previous research, our study has some key contributions. First, we recruited drivers who had rich usage experience with L2 automated cars. They had a deeper understanding of autonomous driving than normal drivers, which improved the validity of our findings. Second, we focused on the daily commute in automated driving, which is a crucial part of many citizens' daily life. But in automated driving literature, few studies have examined drivers' NDRTs in this situation. Third, we revealed reasons why drivers would like to perform certain NDRTs. In addition, we considered the influence of automation level. The results can deepen our understanding of how and why drivers' non-driving behaviors would change as the automation of cars increased.

This study has some practical implications. First, we found that in commute, work- or entertainment-related NDRTs were most frequently performed. The commute, as an extension of the office and home, is a place for both work and leisure. Service design that meets these two needs will have a big market. Second, the requirement for in-vehicle services changes with the automation level. In cars with low automation, drivers emphasized the efficiency of conducting an NDRT. While in high-level automation, drivers emphasized the safety of automated driving. Third, drivers' needs for the interior environment of the car changed with automation. At L3, drivers emphasized the use of in-vehicle displays. While in full automation cars, they wished for bigger changes in the interior space, such as a table for more complex work tasks and a refrigerator.

The present research also has some limitations. First, we did not identify the direction of the commute. Previous studies showed that people had different behaviors when they went to work and came home [9]. Second, the sample size of this study is small, which may limit the representation. We tried to relieve the concern of this limitation by recruiting people who were from different cities and had different occupations.

Acknowledgments. This study was supported by the Fundamental Research Funds for the Central Universities (Grant No. 2022NTSS13).

References

1. Committee, C.D.: Taxonomy and Definitions for Terms Related to Cooperative Driving Automation for On-Road Motor Vehicles (2021)
2. Deichmann, J., Ebel, E., Heineke, K., Heuss, R., Kellner, M., & Steiner, F.: Autonomous Driving's Future: Convenient and Connected. McKinsey & Company (2023)
3. Gasser, T.M., Westhoff, D. BASt-study: definitions of automation and legal issues in Germany[R]. Bergisch Gladbach: Federal Highway Research Institute (2012)
4. Schartmüller, C., Weigl, K., Löcken, A., Wintersberger, P., Steinhauser, M., Riener, A.: Displays for Productive Non-Driving Related Tasks: Visual Behavior and Its Impact in Conditionally Automated Driving. Multimodal Technologies and Interaction. **5**, 21 (2021). https://doi.org/10.3390/mti5040021
5. Organization, W.H.: Global Status Report on Road Safety 2015. World Health Organization (2015)
6. Wilson, C.D., Gyi, D.E., Morris, A.P., Bateman, R.C., Tanaka, H.: Non-Driving Related tasks and journey types for future automated vehicle owners. Transportation Research Part F-traffic Psychology and Behaviour. **85**, 150–160 (2022). https://doi.org/10.1016/j.trf.2022.01.004
7. Guo, L., Xu, L.L., Qin, Z.K., Wang, X.: Analysis and Overview of Influencing Factors on Automated Driving Takeover. J. Transp. Syst. Eng. Inf. Technol. **22**(2), 72–90 (2022). (in Chinese)
8. Schoettle, B., Sivak, M.: A Survey of Public Opinion about Automated and Self-driving Vehicles in the U.S., the U.K., and Australia. Ann Arbor: University of Michigan Transportation Research Institute (2014)

9. Wadud Z., Huda, F.Y.: Fully automated vehicles: the use of travel time and its association with intention to use. Proceedings of the Institution of Civil Engineers. 1–15 (2019). https://doi.org/10.1680/jtran.18.00134

10. Kyriakidis, M., Happee, R., De Winter, J.C.F.: Public opinion on automated driving: Results of an international questionnaire among 5000 respondents. Transportation Research Part F-traffic Psychology and Behaviour. **32**, 127–140 (2015). https://doi.org/10.1016/j.trf.2015.04.014

11. Kamp, I., Kilincsoy, Ü., Vink, P.: Chosen postures during specific sitting activities. Ergonomics **54**, 1029–1042 (2011). https://doi.org/10.1080/00140139.2011.618230

12. Hecht, T., Darlagiannis, E., Bengler, K.: Non-driving Related Activities in Automated Driving – An Online Survey Investigating User Needs. In: Advances in intelligent systems and computing. pp. 182–188. Springer Nature (2019)

13. Gripsrud, M., Hjorthol, R.: Working on the train: from 'dead time' to productive and vital time. Transportation **39**, 941–956 (2012). https://doi.org/10.1007/s11116-012-9396-7

14. Susilo, Y.O., Lyons, G., Jain, J., Atkins, S.: Rail Passengers' Time Use and Utility Assessment. Transp. Res. Rec. **2323**, 99–109 (2012). https://doi.org/10.3141/2323-12

15. Large, D.R., Burnett, G., Morris, A., Muthumani, A., Matthias, R.: A Longitudinal Simulator Study to Explore Drivers' Behaviour During Highly-Automated Driving. In: Stanton, N.A. (ed.) AHFE 2017. AISC, vol. 597, pp. 583–594. Springer, Cham (2018). https://doi.org/10.1007/978-3-319-60441-1_57

16. Hecht, T., Feldhütter, A., Draeger, K., Bengler, K.: What do you do? an analysis of non-driving related activities during a 60 minutes conditionally automated highway drive. In: Ahram, T., Taiar, R., Colson, S., Choplin, A. (eds.) Human Interaction and Emerging Technologies: Proceedings of the 1st International Conference on Human Interaction and Emerging Technologies (IHIET 2019), August 22-24, 2019, Nice, France, pp. 28–34. Springer International Publishing, Cham (2020). https://doi.org/10.1007/978-3-030-25629-6_5

17. Pfleging, B., Rang, M., Broy, N.: Investigating user needs for non-driving-related activities during automated driving. In: Proceedings of the 15th International Conference on Mobile and Ubiquitous Multimedia, pp. 91–99. Association for Computing Machinery, New York, NY, USA (2016). https://doi.org/10.1145/3012709.3012735

18. Kalia, A.: The Daily Commute: Travel Times to Cities Around the World Mapped. The Guardian (2018)

19. Lyons, G., Chatterjee, K.: A human perspective on the daily commute: costs benefits and trade-offs. Transp. Rev. **28**, 181–198 (2008). https://doi.org/10.1080/01441640701559484

20. 2022 annual commuting monitoring report for major cities in China. Urban Rural Dev. **653**(02), 56–65 (2023). (in Chinese)

21. 2022 Annual Traffic Analysis Report for Major Cities in China. https://report.amap.com/download_city.do. Accessed 18 Jan 2023. (in Chinese)

22. Gino, F., Staats, B., Jachimowicz, J.M., Menges, J.I.: Reclaim your commute. Harvard Business Review. May-June, 149–153 (2017)

23. Teodorovicz, T., Kun, A.L., Sadun, R., Shaer, O.: Multitasking while driving: a time use study of commuting knowledge workers to assess current and future uses. Int. J. Hum. Comput. Stud. **162**, 102789 (2022). https://doi.org/10.1016/j.ijhcs.2022.102789

24. Glaser, B.G., Strauss, A.L.: Discovery of Grounded Theory: Strategies for Qualitative Research. Routledge (2017)

The Design of Smart Product-Service Systems (PSSs) with Autonomous Vehicles as the Service Medium Based on User Activity and Behavior Data

Bei Ran[1] and Jingyan Qin[2(✉)]

[1] South China University of Technology, Guangzhou 510006, China
ranbei@scut.edu.com
[2] University of Science and Technology Beijing, Beijing 100083, China
20443530@qq.com

Abstract. Each individual has become a mobile smart sensor under the supporting conditions of Artificial Intelligence, Big Data, Internet of Everything, Location Based Services and other technologies, which provide technical support for the research on user activity and behavior at a fine scale. Meanwhile, traditional product design methods are no longer applicable to the Smart Product-Service System Design with autonomous vehicles as the medium. Changes have occurred from product design to service system design of smart products and their composition, from intuition-based design to data-driven design, from human-machine design to relational design between service participants and smart bodies and smart service systems, and from styling design to experience design. It is required to integrate design thinking and smart mobility so as to explore methods and tools for terminal smart design, network smart design and cloud smart design.

Keywords: Smart Product-Service Systems (PSSs) · Autonomous Vehicles · Activity and behavior data · Smart Service Design

1 Research Background

1.1 Autonomous Vehicles——Smart Mobile Service Space

The germination of autonomous driving technology dates back to the 1920s. In 1925, Francis Houdina, a U.S. Army electrical engineer, and his team developed a vehicle called American Miracle. With the remarkable development of smart hardware and information and communication technologies (ICT), academic exploration and industrial development of autonomous vehicles have been accelerated accordingly [1]. In 2012, the Model S launched by Tesla created the concept of software defined vehicles with regular updates and upgrades of software including driving range, braking performance, user interface and infotainment as well as constant improvement of user experience, which overturned the entire automotive industry and driving scenarios. Tesla Motors are equipped with hardware such as sensors and computer systems sufficient to meet the requirements of future Level 4 autonomous driving technology, which gradually approach the autonomous vehicles. In 2016, Volvo announced a partnership with Netflix to provide live streaming services for commuters in their vehicles, while Ford obtained a patent for autonomous vehicles entertainment system in which the entire windshield becomes an entertainment display for content presentation. In the future, autonomous vehicles will become the smart link of the three value streams of urban passenger flow, logistics and service flow. On the basis of the platform and the integrated architecture of vehicle and cloud, new value scenarios will be quickly customized such as new services, new commuting and new logistics, thus cutting into the existing and potential emerging markets of billions of dollars in different fields such as smart city, home-based care, maternal and child growth and O2O experience marketing.

1.2 Autonomous Vehicles——Smart Mobile Service Medium

Artificial intelligence technology is driving human society to build a symbiotic, all-win Mobility Ecosystem of the future. Three cross-industry megatrends including electric vehicles (EVs), smart connected autonomous vehicles (CAVs) and Mobility as a service (MaaS) are fundamentally reshaping the mobility for consumers and enterprises. Autonomous vehicles playing a role in value creation develop efficient, sustainable mobile service strategies for users, create an outstanding mobile service experience, and build a collaborative and all-win mobile service model for the network society. Autonomous vehicles, which can move independently and are smartly connected, have overturned the traditional way of human mobility. Car-sharing, bike-sharing and other travel sharing business models are emerging, while the number and market share of new energy vehicles are gradually increasing. Autonomous vehicles that are capable of automated mobility, networked mobility and electric mobility will build for human beings a faster, cleaner and safer mobile service ecosystem with more convenience, efficiency and personalization.

1.3 Autonomous Vehicles——Smart Mobile Data Mining

In human social life scenarios, the smart mobile terminals of autonomous vehicles are applied to mine an enormous amount of user activity and behavior data with significant commercial value. On this basis, barrier-free, automated and personalized on-demand mobile service mechanisms and infrastructures are planned, a human-vehicle-environment smart ecosystem created that integrates capabilities, technologies, data and services, the restructuring of industrial chain, the transformation of value realization and the innovation of business models driven, thus gradually forming a new social life and economic growth model.

Smart connected autonomous vehicles are the collection terminal and interaction platform for individual and group user activity and behavior data, as well as the intermediate hub and core link of the smart mobile service system, which will transform the concept of vehicle as transportation tool to as mobile living space and information service platform. In addition to the purposeful acquisition of user activity and behavior data, another significant feature of the era of intelligence is that everything can be quantified, which is also the core of data technology. The value of data lies in innovation, that is, how to achieve the calculation and analysis, reorganization and expansion, and innovation and application of these user activity and behavior data. The source of user activity and behavior data is mainly based on the conscious or unconscious behavior of human beings in social life. In other words, it is a quantitative reflection of the objective existence of perceptual object activity of human social life. In the era of intelligence, each individual is a mobile sensor, as well as the producer, recorder and beneficiary of user activity and behavior data. Autonomous vehicles quantify human spatio-temporal mobility behavior comprehensively and profoundly, and these data can reflect the characteristics of human mobility in time, space and social attributes.

2   Transformation Mechanism of User Activity and Behavior in Smart Service Design

2.1   Transformation Pattern of User Activity and Behavior Data

The user activity and behavior data is mined to explore the profound semantic knowledge such as purpose intention, travel pattern, living habit, social attributes and social relationship, and realize the transformation from user activity and behavior data and information to knowledge (Fig. 1), which provides unlimited potential for design innovation and practical application in social service field. The externalized user activity and behavior data needs to be explored and internalized into human mobility knowledge for application in the design process through the mining of human activity information, evolving into the value embodiment that drives social innovation. Perceptual intelligence uses interconnectable sensors and hardware to connect objects and sense themselves and their environment, collects user activity and behavior data in real time, and focuses on real scenarios where user activity and behavior data occurs [2]. Decision intelligence uses perceived user activity and behavior data to identify and smartly analyze information, explore explicit and implicit user needs, and make decisions to meet individual user needs [3]. Empathic intelligence incorporates emotion as a major factor in the construction of knowledge discovery to realize emotion recognition based on experience in the process of knowledge application, infers and understands users' internal states from empathy, and features the ability to respond appropriately in emotion and influence users' emotions. The fundamental role of emotion in human cognition and perception suggests that empathic intelligence can not only provide better service quality, but also enhance the perceptual ability and decision-making ability of the service system.

Acquisition, analysis and application of user activity and behavior data are three elements of user activity and behavior transformation, corresponding to data acquisition, information identification and knowledge discovery of user activity and behavior respectively. Firstly and foremost, through collecting electronic footprint data such as GPS track data of floating cars, smartphone usage data, mobile smart terminal usage data, social network check-in data and public service facility usage data, technologies including sensor network, mobile positioning, wireless communication and mobile Internet are applied to acquire enormous individual and group mobile big data with high spatial and temporal fineness. Then, the raw data are pre-processed by mobile track processing technology as well as spatio-temporal data expression and mining technology to extract

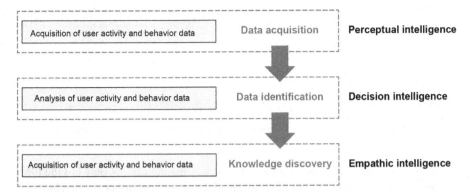

Fig. 1. Transformation mechanism of user activity and behavior

the tracks and itineraries that directly or indirectly reflect human movement. And the analysis and research of tracks and itineraries contribute to revealing human activity patterns and laws, such as the discovery of characteristics of periodicity, sociality and spatio-temporal distribution. Finally, the patterns, laws and formation mechanisms of individual and group human activity and behavior are recognized, and future user activity and behavior are predicted, which helps to carry out applications in the fields of smart transportation service, social public service, public health and health service, etc.

2.2 Access to User Activity and Behavior Data

With the remarkable development of smart sensing technology and smart network technology, as well as the popularity and application of location-aware mobile devices, a large amount of big data in digital space reflecting the trajectory of human movement in physical space, namely electronic footprint data, has been accumulated, and these electronic footprint big data are the mapping of the real spatio-temporal footprint of human society in the digital world. With an increasing number of people start to leave personal spatio-temporal activity information actively or passively on location-based sensing services, the activities and behaviors at different times, places and scenes are recorded in detail, which can reflect not only the movement trajectories of human individuals and groups, but also people's social relationships and lifestyles. Smart sensing technology, location-based service technology and smart network connect technology are used to collect user activity and behavior data represented by smartphone usage data, social network check-in data, floating car data, public service facility usage data, and smart mobile device usage data. (Fig. 2)

Floating Car Data. Cabs and buses in many large cities are equipped with global positioning system (GPS) and wireless communication devices. These floating cars driving in the cities accumulate a large amount of human movement data with high positional accuracy and fine temporal granularity, which contain rich information about individual and group human mobility [4]. Each track in the floating car trajectory data corresponds to a car, and each trip in the track to a trip of a passenger. These passengers are usually not the same person, and the data center accumulates numerous vehicle trajectories and

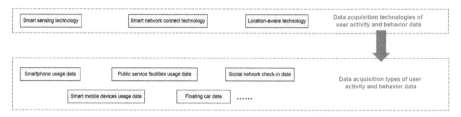

Fig. 2. Acquisition technologies and types of user activity and behavior

trips everyday. The autonomous vehicle, as an smart floating car, not only has the function of autonomous mobility, but also has the ability to collect in-person synchronous, in-person asynchronous, remote synchronous and remote asynchronous user activity and behavior data in physical and digital space in the form of co-presence, remote presence and presence. A network system for sustainable production of user activity and behavior data is formed between the human, vehicle, environment and cloud system.

Smartphone Usage Data. Smartphone is also the main medium for collecting large amounts of individual mobile big data. Cell phone call data records the call time and location. A complete and continuous spatio-temporal mobility trajectory of the owner can be obtained through analyzing the call records of a cell phone over a period of time. A trajectory generated by the same individual consists of a sequence of points with spatio-temporal location information. The trajectory usually contains some stopping points which correspond to the individual's activity information, such as work, dining, entertainment, etc. A sub-trajectory between two consecutive stopping points is called a trip which corresponds to a single movement of an individual. Zuguang Wang used cell phone data to identify users' stopping points, occupation and residence points, and origin destination (OD). Then, algorithms were designed to identify medical origin destination, while the gender and age structure of medical travelers as well as the travel time, arrival time and travel distance of medical travelers were analyzed, thus obtaining the relevant laws of medical travel to optimize the layout of medical public service facilities [5]. In 2007, Microsoft Asia Research Institute sent 128 volunteers cell phones with GeoLife, a positioning application, to record their spatial and temporal trajectories for four years, and used them for research on location prediction, transportation mode determination and lifestyle habit mining [6].

Smart Mobile Devices Usage Data. Smart mobile devices are developed on the basis of traditional mobile devices, typically cell phones. Yet cell phones are limited by the operating system and processor computing power so as to lack the ability to calculate and process multi-tasking and complex tasks. Wireless network technology provides higher bandwidth, faster access and more convenient access, which makes it possible to connect smart mobile devices to each other and to the system platform in the form of cloud [7]. Smart mobile devices constantly on the move realize the connection of user activity and behavior data with other smart mobile devices and cloud systems through wireless networks. The application of embedded technology of smart mobile devices makes the processing performance greatly improved, and the hardware function and software function significantly enriched. Dayin Yu proposed to apply smart mobile terminals such as smart wearable devices to vehiclediac rehabilitation patients after PCI surgery to achieve data collection, transmission and analysis between doctors and patients, so that doctors can monitor and supervise patients' conditions through mobile big data and improve patients' compliance [8].

Social Network Check-in Data. Check-in is the behavior that users actively submit their current location and spatio-temporal data via mobile terminals in location-based social networking services (e.g., WeChat, Sina Weibo, Xiaohongshu, Tik Tok, etc.). The resulting data with Geo-tag is called check-in data which is widely used in human mobile behavior analysis [9]. Users actively record and share their location, usually accompanied by semantic information such as text images that reflect the user's activity content and interests. Taking bicycle sharing and shared power bank as examples, their rental records can reflect the activity information of individuals and groups, as well as the dynamic change characteristics of urban travel behavior in space.

Public Service Facilities Usage Data. The rental systems of public service facilities such as public bicycles, electric bicycles and shared power bank also record the location information of users' usage. The rental system can automatically record the check-in/check-out time and location of all items, while its rental records can roughly reflect the activity information of a part of the urban population. However, the amount of information is small and the coverage of the population is limited. Therefore, the study cannot target individual travel but only generally make a time-series analysis of the use of each rental point at the group level to reflect the dynamic changes of urban travel behavior in space [10]. For example, bicycle sharing services such as Mobike and Hellobike have recorded the usage and circulation of bicycles in the city through check-in to provide users with favorable experience of using bicycles.

2.3 Information Identification of User Activity and Behavior Data

With the development and advancement of mobile communication technology in modern society, people's movement trajectories in the real world are recorded actively and passively for a long time through the usage of smart devices such as smart floating cars, smart phones, smart mobile terminals and public service facilities, which are digitized into electronic footprint data. Researchers use these digitized human mobility data to analyze the spatio-temporal structure and pattern in human trajectories, model human activity characteristics and quantitatively study the activity and behavior patterns of human individuals and groups [11]. Similar and correlated features exist in human spatial activity and behavior patterns that reflect the universal mechanisms governing human spatio-temporal activity behavior. Describing human spatio-temporal activity and behavior through building models contribute to revealing the underlying mechanisms of various phenomena and statistical law formation. Autonomous vehicle as agent has the ability to collect, compute and analyze user activity and behavior in real time while moving, which expands the analysis platform for human mobility. Autonomous vehicle can extract meaningful models from sporadic and scattered user activity and behavior data through data analysis methods, and use them as the basis for defining functional specifications of autonomous vehicles [12].

2.4   Knowledge Discovery of User Activity and Behavior Data

The concept of Mobility as a Service (MaaS) was proposed at the EU ITS Conference in 2014 based on the discussion of future smart transport systems [12]. Nowadays, Mobility as a Service is mostly translated as travelling service just in time in Chinese literature, but it is still a concept to be defined in academic circles. In 2016, the EU Mobility as a Service Consortium considered MaaS as an on-demand travel service integrating multiple forms of transportation, which meets the individual travel needs of passengers through a set of customized mobility products based on the combination of mobility services [13]. In 2018, Mobility as a Service Lab at the University College London identified MaaS as an user-centric smart travel management and assignment system that integrates multi-modal and sustainable mobility services, which lays emphasis on the personalization and diversification of travel modes and services for users, and provides a seamless one-stop travel experience with the crowdsourcing service model [14]. MaaS system is an integrated service platform that provides a one-stop travel experience for users in a crowdsourcing service model, reducing the use of private vehicles and promoting public transportation as a new solution to travel problems. MaaS system is an integrated service system providing decentralized transportation services which mainly uses big data to make decisions and deploys optimal resources to meet users' travel needs. The system requires coordination of single or composite travel modes, travel services, innovative products, pricing models, and real-time on-demand service planning. The complexity and immediacy of the coordinated content coexist and multiple stakeholders are involved, while the information and data need to be interoperable among stakeholders. The UK's National Innovation Agency has constructed the MaaS system architecture (Fig. 3), which expresses the relationship between four stakeholders including MaaS users, service providers, transport operators and data providers, and refines the service providers into service providers, operators and data providers. The traffic operator hands over the acquired user activity and behavior data to the data provider for analysis and insight into user needs, and then the service provider implements services to meet user needs, a process that also transforms from data needs to information needs and service needs.

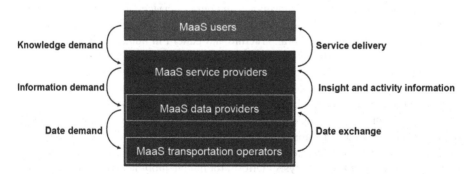

Fig. 3. MaaS system architecture by The UK's National Innovation Agency

3 Research on Smart Product-Service System Design Based on User Activity and Behavior

3.1 Smart Product-Service System Design Processes Based on User Activity and Behavior

Smart sensor technology improves the autonomous vehicle's ability to integrate resources with user activity and behavior data. Smart network technology enhances the ability of autonomous vehicles to jointly store human activity information. Smart computing technology promotes the autonomous vehicle's ability to predict and perceive human mobility knowledge in context. Smart algorithmic platform supporting autonomous vehicles for decision making, evaluation and execution is the realization of human mobility wisdom. The acquisition scope of user activity and behavior data includes the mobility of human individuals or groups in physical and digital space, while the content scope incorporates the transportation field and social service field, which is a complex information system covering the interaction information between vehicle and vehicle, vehicle and individual, vehicle and information carriers, and vehicle and system [15].

Smart products such as floating cars, smartphones, shared service facilities and smart mobile devices with smart sensing and location-aware technologies generate massive amounts of big data that reflects users' activity behavior when interacting with users and the environment, which is the objective quantification and mapping in the virtual world of human activity and behavior in the real world. Through integrating data thinking and design thinking, big data-driven user experience design changes from user definition, demand mining and function development by a single quantitative or qualitative method to the combination of quantitative and qualitative research based on user group big data and individual user small numbers that transforms user activity and behavior data into information and knowledge, which can be used to guide the development of autonomous vehicles and smart mobile service system concept design.

The author proposes the design processes and element model based on user activity and behavior from the perspective of user experience, which are oriented to smart product and smart service system design. (Fig. 4) For the strategy layer, it is necessary to build and identify the stakeholders relationship and inspire the demands of recipients. For the scope layer, it is necessary to build service relationship based on the strategy layer and clarify the service content. For the structure layer, it is necessary to refine the service content into information relationship structure and information content based on the structure layer. For the framework layer, it is necessary to plan the service media such as products and software that participate in the service on the basis of the structure layer, and clarify the media functions. For the presentation layer, the visual representation design of service media is required on the basis of the framework layer. User experience subjective and dynamic in nature describes the feelings and thoughts of individual users, which will change over time and with changes in the environment.

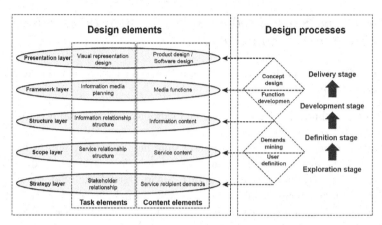

Fig. 4. Smart product-service system design processes and element model based on user activity and behavior

3.2 Smart Product-Service System Design Tools Based on User Activity and Behavior

Exploration Stage——User Definition. As is shown in Fig. 5, user activity and behavior data is obtained by using floating cars, smart phones, smart mobile terminals, public service facilities, etc. The massive heterogeneous big data is structured to propose individual user attributes and characteristics and to define user profile dimensions. On this basis, semantic analysis is performed to obtain individual user attribute tag and user group tag systems, which are matched and categorized through classifying and aggregating the user group to generate the user profile. The whole process involves data acquisition, data processing, data mining and knowledge discovery. The use of big data technology to describe and model to build user profile helps designers to accurately and efficiently analyze the attributes and characteristics of individual and group users, and to deeply understand the needs of users so as to implement accurate services. Yuan Kong collected and stored user activity and behavior data through the original GPS data of floating cars and Internet information, extracted features and semantic annotations for spatio-temporal features and social network POI points, measured the similarity of trajectories and performed clustering analysis to mine spatio-temporal patterns, eventually constructing the motorist profile including motorist travel characteristics sub-profile, trajectory characteristics sub-profile, shopping behavior sub-profile and deep semantic sub-profile. The model of parking place + area of interest + charging service is proposed to provide decision support for urban traffic, personal travel planning, information recommendation and other services [16]. On the basis of the data of express logistics blog posts in a period of time, Jiling Li et al. conducted the user behavior profile of express physical services in the context of the epidemic, abstracted five behaviors and twenty-two thematic dimensions, and generated corresponding user profiles which provide reference for express logistics enterprises to formulate service strategies and improve service experience [17].

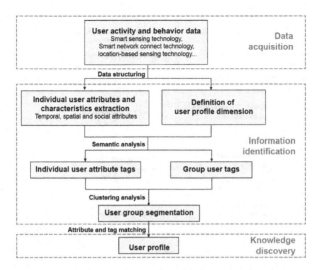

Fig. 5. Framework of user profile based on user activity and behavior

Definition Stage——Demand Mining. The big data of user behavior is used to figure out user behavior rules and provide insight into the real demands of users, which guide designers to develop and design products and services with outstanding user experience. In a broad sense, the concept of big data using for insight into user needs refers to the process of analyzing users' explicit and implicit demands based on a large amount of user data through using data mining and other technologies [18]. The author develops a framework of user demand insight based on user activity and behavior data (Fig. 6). User activity and behavior data is obtained through floating cars, smart phones, smart mobile devices, shared service facilities, etc. On the basis of this, user activity and behavior data is analyzed through attributes, features, clusters, etc. to obtain user subgroup characteristics and user profiles, while user interest and preference characteristics are obtained through semantic analysis. Traditional research methods and mining tools such as in-depth questionnaires, scenario interviews and scenario simulations are used to obtain user behavior data, and journey-type research tools with time sequence are applied to express user data and perform slicing analysis through scenario analysis, thus obtaining information touch points, logistics resource touch points and social touch points that rely on user behavior content. The causality and correlation of user behavior in user interest preference characteristics as well as touch point content are analyzed to acquire user demands including user explicit and implicit demands. Guangsheng Cheng divided the massive user behavior data of smart library into small data and big data, used small data to build individual user profiles and big data to build group user profiles, and accurately excavated users' implicit and explicit demands to precisely adapt user demands and knowledge resources [19].

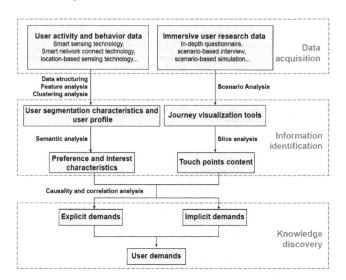

Fig. 6. Framework of user demands insight based on user activity and behavior data

Development Stage——Function Development. It is supposed to integrate data thinking and design thinking, and take the user mental model as a goal to guide designers
in developing products and services. In terms of classical product design, the construction of user mental models is based on user researchers' second-order understanding
of users' cognitive and perceptual abilities through interviews, questionnaires and other
means. Data can more truly reflect the user's original cognition, perception ability and
experience. The author constructs a personalized product function and service content
framework based on user activity and behavior data. The motivation guide and ability
guide for users are formed through mining user attribute prediction model, user behavior prediction model, user interest preference prediction model, user demand prediction
model, etc., so as to provide personalized product functions or service content for individual or group users. (Fig. 7). User activity and behavior data has penetrated into every
aspect of people's lives. Based on quantitative thinking, user activity and behavior data
can reproduce the real life of human beings with the advantages of objectivity, efficiency
and predictability. The design research needs to integrate data technology and design
thinking, along with quantitative and qualitative methodological tools, to restore the
real life scenario where the data occurs. Moreover, the technology could provide accurate insight into and response to users' demands by using human mobility knowledge
and design tools, while personalized services are supposed to meet users' diversified
demands. Qiuli Zhou analyzed the data information generated by users' location-based
social networks, studies the location prediction of users in social networks, considers the
endogenous and exogenous factors that influence users' check-in behavior, and predicts
the check-in location of users in new locations [20].

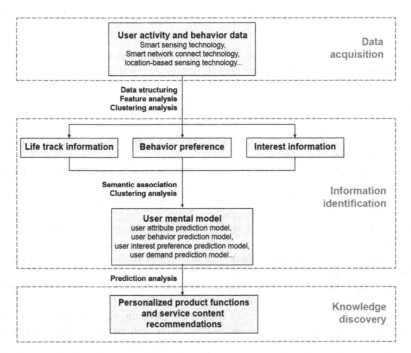

Fig. 7. Personalized product functions and service content recommendation framework based on user activity and behavior data

4　Conclusion

With the wide application of devices equipped with smart sensing technology, smart network technology and location-aware technology, a large amount of human activity and behavior data with individual granularity of spatio-temporal markers is generated as the quantification and mapping of human in real life, which is represented by cell phone usage data, social networking site check-in data, shared facility usage data, floating car trajectory data, etc. The author explores the design methods of smart product-service system with autonomous vehicles as the medium which are based on user activity and behavior. A framework for user profiles based on user activity and behavior data is constructed in the exploration stage. The definition stage proposes a framework for user demand insight based on user activity and behavior data. In the development stage, a framework for personalized product functions and service content recommendation based on user activity and behavior data is developed. In doing so, the deficiency is improved that traditional user experience design is mainly based on a single qualitative or quantitative research tool, which makes it difficult to obtain a large number of samples with fine granularity of user behavior for a long time and efficiently. Integrating data thinking and design thinking, data technology enriches user-centered design paths and methods, realizes complementary advantages in user-centered design processes and methods, and enhances the user experience value of design results.

References

1. Pendleton, S., Andersen, H., Du, X., et al.: Perception, planning, control and coordination for autonomous vehicles. Machines **5**, 6 (2017)
2. Dreyer, S., Olivotti, D., Lebek, B., et al.: Focusing the customer through smart services: a literature review. Electron. Mark. **29**(1), 55–78 (2019)
3. Marquardt, K.: Smart services - characteristics, challenges, opportunities and business models (2020)
4. Liu, Y., Kang, C., Gao, S., et al.: Understanding intraurban trip patterns from taxi trajectory data. J. Geograph. Syst. **14**(4), 463–483 (2012)
5. Wang, Z.G.: Study on the Layout Optimization of Urban Medical Public Service Facilities Based on Cell Phone Data. Southeast University, Nanjing (2020)
6. Liao, D.L.: Human Mobility Prediction Based on Semantic Spatio-Temporal Data. University of Science and Technology of China, Beijing (2019)
7. Geng, Q., et al.: GIS services for smart mobile devices. Geospat. Inf. 10(03), 64–66+69+3 (2012)
8. Yu, D.Y.: The role of smart mobile devices in post-PCI cardiac rehabilitation of coronary patients. Clin. Stud. **29**(09), 54–55 (2021)
9. Noulas, A., Scellato, S., Mascolo, C., et al.: An empirical study of geographic user activity patterns in Foursquare. In: ICWSM11, pp. 70–573 (2011)
10. Froehlich, J., Neumann, J., Oliver, N.: Sensing and predicting the pulse of the city through shared bicycling. In: International Joint Conferences on Artificial Intelligence, pp. 1420–1426 (2009)
11. Liu, Y., et al.: Study of big data-driven human mobility patterns and models. Geomatics Inf. Sci. Wuhan Univ. **39**(006), 660–666 (2014)
12. Qin, J.Y., Hao, Z.Y.: Interaction design of human mobility in multiple spaces for autonomous vehicles. Packa. Eng. **39**(14), 70–76 (2018)
13. Karjalainen, P.: White Paper: Guidelines & Recommendations to Create the Foundations for a Thriving MaaS Ecosystem. MaaS Alliance (2017)
14. Kamargianni, M., Matyas, M., Li, W., et al.: The MaaS Dictionary. MaaSLab, Energy Institute, University College London, London (2018)
15. Schmidt, A., Spiessl, W., Kern, D.: Driving automotive user interface research. IEEE Perv. Comput. **9**, 85–88 (2010)
16. Kong, Y.: Spatio-Temporal Trajectory Mining Based on Massive Floating Vehicle Data and Social Network Interest Points. Tsinghua University, Beijing (2017)
17. Li, J.L., et al." Research on user behavior profile and theme mining of express logistics service in the context of epidemic. J. East China Normal Univ. (Nat. Sci.) **05**, 100–114 (2022)
18. Li, W.C., Jia, Y.W., Zhao, H.X.: Research on user demand mining based on big data analysis. Innov. Technol. **11**, 72–74 (2016)
19. Cheng, G.S.: Construction of an accurate user profile model for smart libraries based on big data and small data. Libr. Theory Pract. **05**, 90–95+104 (2022)
20. Zhou, Q.L.: Location Prediction Research Based on LBSN Users' Mobile Behavior. Chongqing University of Posts and Telecommunications, Chongqing (2020)

I Also Care in Manual Driving - Influence of Type, Position and Quantity of Oncoming Vehicles on Manual Driving Behaviour on Straights on Rural Roads

Patrick Rossner[✉], Marty Friedrich, Konstantin Felbel, André Dettmann, and Angelika C. Bullinger

Chair for Ergonomics and Innovation, Chemnitz University of Technology, Chemnitz, Germany
patrick.rossner@mb.tu-chemnitz.de

Abstract. There is not yet sufficient knowledge on how people want to be driven in a highly automated vehicle. Many studies suggest that automated vehicles should drive like a human driver, e.g. moving to the right edge of the lane when meeting oncoming traffic. To generate naturally looking trajectory behaviour, more detailed studies on manual driving are necessary. The authors report on a driving simulator study investigating twelve different oncoming traffic scenarios. 46 subjects experienced scenarios with variations in type of vehicle (trucks, cars), quantity (one, two) and position (with/without lateral offset) – each on a lane 3.00 m or on 2.75 m wide respectively. Results show that subjects react to oncoming traffic by veering to the right edge of the lane. We also found that quantity, type, and position of oncoming vehicles influence manual driving behaviour. Trucks and vehicles with lateral offset to the road centre lead to greater reactions and hence to more lateral distance between the ego and the oncoming vehicle. From this study on manual driving, we recommend an adaptive autonomous driving style which adjusts its trajectory behaviour on type and position of oncoming vehicles. Thus, our results help to design an accepted and trusted trajectory behaviour for highly automated vehicles.

Keywords: Automated driving · Manual driving · Trajectory behaviour · Rural roads · Straights

1 State of Knowledge

Sensory and algorithmic developments enable an increasing implementation of automation in the automotive sector. Ergonomic studies on highly automated driving are essential aspects for later acceptance and use of highly automated vehicles [1, 2]. In addition to studies on driving task transfer or out-of-the-loop issues, there is not yet sufficient knowledge on how people want to be driven in a highly automated vehicle [3, 4].

First insights show that preferences regarding the perception and rating of driving styles are widely spread. Many prefer their own or a very similar driving style and reject

© The Author(s), under exclusive license to Springer Nature Switzerland AG 2023
V. G. Duffy et al. (Eds.): HCII 2023, LNCS 14057, pp. 381–389, 2023.
https://doi.org/10.1007/978-3-031-48047-8_25

other driving styles that include e.g. very high acceleration and deceleration rates or small longitudinal and lateral distances to other road users [5–7]. Studies show that swift, anticipatory, safe and seemingly natural driving styles are prioritized [7–9]. In literature, trajectory behaviour as one part of the driving style is mostly implemented as a lane-centric position of the vehicle in the lane. From a technical point of view this is a justifiable and logical conclusion, but drivers show quite different preferences, especially in curves and in case of oncoming traffic [10, 11].

In manual driving situations without oncoming traffic, participants drive close to the centre of the lane on straights [12, 13]. In curves, participants show a different driving behaviour and move closer to the road centre in left turns and closer to the roadside in right turns [14]. Several studies report a tendency to cut the curve by hitting the apex, especially for left turns [15–17]. When meeting oncoming traffic in manual driving, participants increase their lateral safety distance by moving to the right edge of the lane, both on straights [12, 13, 18] as well as in left and right curves [11, 12]. When meeting heavy traffic, participants' reactions are even greater [12, 13, 17, 19–21]. With the appearance of oncoming traffic in left curves, two manual driving strategies overlay: to hit the apex and to avoid short lateral distances to the oncoming traffic.

In summary, the implementation of this natural driving behaviour into an automated driving style includes high potential to improve the driving experience in an automated car. Previous studies [14, 22–25] show that reactive trajectory behaviour in highly automated driving leads to significantly higher acceptance, trust and subjectively experienced driving performance on straights and in curves. In order to implement adaptive trajectories that modify trajectory behaviour on different lane widths and adjust their behaviour on type and position of oncoming vehicles, it seems most relevant to investigate manual trajectory behaviour in more detail.

The aim of this study is to gain more knowledge on manual driving to implement better reactive trajectories that include less negative side effects and lead to a better driving experience. The results of the study will help to design an accepted and trustfully trajectory behaviour for highly automated vehicles.

2 Method and Variables

Fig. 1. Driving simulator with instructor centre (left) and an exemplary subject (right)

A fixed-based driving simulator (Fig. 1) was used to conduct a mixed-design experiment. Forty-six participants experienced twelve different oncoming traffic scenarios that varied in type (trucks and cars), quantity (one or two in a row) position (cars in the middle of the oncoming lane and cars with lateral offset to the road centre) in balanced order to minimize sequence and habituation effects – see Fig. 2 – either on a 3.00 m or on a 2.75 m lane width in manual driving.

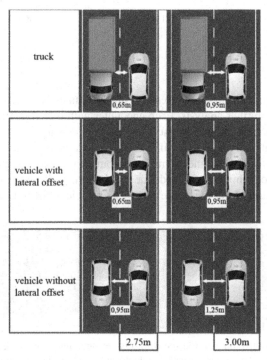

Fig. 2. Variations of oncoming traffic and theoretical lateral distances to the oncoming traffic from a central ego vehicle position

The speed of the oncoming traffic was set at 80 km/h. Participants were instructed to drive 100 km/h, but should feel free to reduce speed. Higher speeds of the ego vehicle were excluded by an activated limiter function at 100 km/h within the driving simulation. Driving data, e.g. velocity or lateral position, was recorded throughout the whole experiment. All subjects were at least 25 years old and had a minimum driving experience of 2.000 km last year and 10.000 km over the last five years (see Table 1 for details).

Table 1. Subjects characteristics

	Number	Age		Driver's license holding [years]		Mileage last five years [km]	
		M	SD	M	SD	M	SD
female	13	35.2	6.9	17.3	6.9	60,300	57,000
male	33	33.9	7.7	15.7	7.8	98,300	69,900
total	46	34.3	7.4	16.2	7.5	87,500	68,100

3   Results

Script-based data monitoring discovered zero invalid data recording cases, which needed to be excluded for further analysis. Each encounter with oncoming traffic was divided into 10 equal parts of 40 m, which results in 400 m of driving data – 250 m before and 150 m after meeting the oncoming traffic. Driving data were averaged for each section (S). The analysis focused on the lateral behaviour of the ego vehicle in each section in dependence of oncoming traffic and lane width. Lateral distance as main dependent variable was measured form the centre of the ego vehicle to the roadside (Fig. 3).

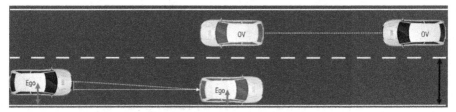

Fig. 3. Measures in oncoming traffic scenario. OV = Oncoming vehicle, Ego = Ego vehicle, black double arrow = lane width, green double arrow = lateral distance measured as distance between centre of the ego vehicle and the roadside

Figure 4 and 5 show mean values of lateral distances to the roadside for each section for lane widths 2.75 m and 3.00 m. Dashed lines represent a theoretical central ego vehicle position.

In the absence of oncoming traffic, participants tended to favour a slightly off-centred position of the ego vehicle by about 0.25 m. When approaching oncoming traffic at the end of Sect. 6, similar driving behaviour can be observed on both lane widths. Starting earliest at section two, a relocation of the trajectory in reaction to the oncoming traffic is executed. At Sect. 8 respectively Sect. 9, the initial position of the ego vehicle is regained. Participants reduce their lateral distance to the roadside and simultaneously increase their lateral distance to oncoming traffic by 0.10 to 0.15 m, depending on the width of the lane and the type, position and number of oncoming vehicles. Participants show greater reactions to cars with lateral offset and trucks compared to cars in the middle of the lane, especially on a lane width of 2.75 m. In addition, two oncoming vehicles cause a larger and longer relocation of the ego vehicle's trajectory compared to one oncoming vehicle. In summary, the trajectory behavior on the narrower lane are slightly less harmonious due to the generally higher stress on lane keeping.

Mean values of lateral distance to the roadside were compared performing ANOVAs with repeated measurements including lane width, section and oncoming traffic. The factors oncoming traffic (F(3.80, 155.72) = 8.64, p < .001, ηp^2 = .17) and section (F(2.13, 87.50) = 30.22, p < .001, ηp^2 = .42) were identified as significant main effects. Lane width also led to significantly different lateral distances (F (1, 44) = 12.79, p < .001, ηp^2 = .24).

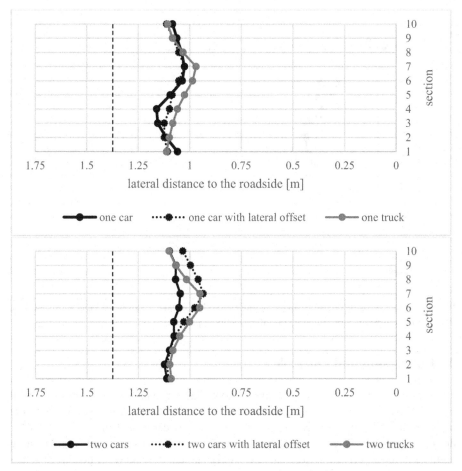

Fig. 4. Mean values of lateral distance to the roadside for each section for lane width 2.75 m, dashed line represents a theoretical central ego vehicle position

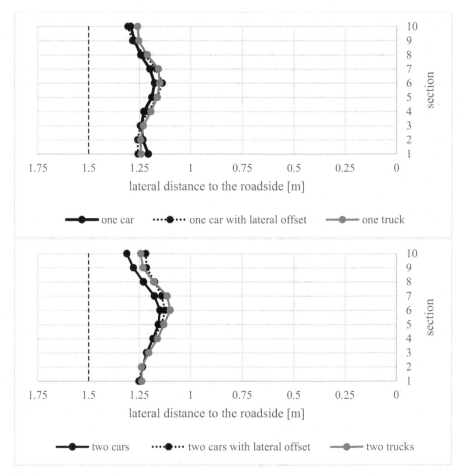

Fig. 5. Mean values of lateral distance to the roadside for each section for lane width 3.00 m, dashed line represents a theoretical central ego vehicle position

4   Conclusion and Outlook

The aim of this study was to gain more knowledge on manual driving to implement better reactive trajectories that include less negative side effects, e.g. passing oncoming traffic with too small distances to the OV or to the roadside, and that lead to a better driving experience. The use of manual drivers' trajectories as basis for implementing highly automated driving trajectories shows high potential to increase perceived safety on straights and curves [22–25].

Results of the study show that without oncoming traffic, participants tended to favour a slightly off-centred position of the ego vehicle by about 0.25 m. When considering the oncoming traffic situations, a distinction can be made with regard to the type of oncoming traffic. On both lane widths, differences in lateral position are found comparing none oncoming traffic, oncoming cars, oncoming cars with lateral offset and oncoming trucks.

When meeting oncoming vehicles, the lateral safety distance should be increased by moving about 0.10 m to 0.15 m to the roadside based on the trajectory without oncoming traffic. The results show less trajectory reactions than shown by studies in curves [15, 17].

These results amplify the need of adaptive trajectories for highly automated vehicles to generate a positive driving experience and, therefore, higher acceptance rates of highly automated vehicles [9, 26]. In all use cases, a safe driving performance has to be guaranteed. Finally, the limitations of studies in fixed-based driving simulators depict the transfer of the results to real world driving situations. Specific use cases can be researched and various parameters (e.g. speed, lateral distance, angle of the brake pedal) can be recorded in driving simulator studies [27]. Of course, no movement forces are perceptible, but the visual impression has a great influence on the perception of oncoming traffic situations and perceived lateral distances. The study focused on straights on rural roads with minimal longitudinal and lateral accelerations, so that the absence of movement forces is not that important. Nevertheless, it is very much recommended to conduct a similar study in a real-world driving environment. The results also cover only a small part of existing use cases. Other factors, such as straights with additional horizontal course or the influence of additional traffic on the ego vehicle's lane, are further topics to be investigated.

Acknowledgements. This research was partially supported by the German Federal Ministry for Economic Affairs and Climate Action (research project: STADT:up, funding code: 19A22006R). The sponsor had no role in the study design, the collection, analysis and interpretation of data, the writing of the report, or the submission of the paper for publication. We are very grateful to Maximilian Hentschel for his assistance in driving simulation programming and to Samuel Pollmer for data collection and analysis.

References

1. Banks, V.A., Stanton, N.A.: Keep the driver in control: automating automobiles of the future. Appl. Ergon. **53**, 389–395 (2015)
2. Elbanhawi, M., Simic, M., Jazar, R.: In the passenger seat: investigating ride comfort measures in autonomous cars. IEEE Intell. Transport. Syst. Maga. **7**(3), 4–17 (2015). https://doi.org/10.1109/MITS.2015.2405571
3. Gasser, T.M.: Herausforderung automatischen Fahrens und Forschungsschwer-punkte. 6. Tagung Fahrerassistenz, München (2013)
4. Radlmayr, J., Bengler, K.: Literaturanalyse und Methodenauswahl zur Gestaltung von Systemen zum hochautomatisierten Fahren. In: FAT-Schriftenreihe, vol. 276. VDA, Berlin (2015)
5. Festner, M., Baumann, H., Schramm, D.: Der Einfluss fahrfremder Tätigkeiten und Manöverlängsdynamik auf die Komfort- und Sicherheitswahrnehmung beim hochautomatisier-ten Fahren. In: 32nd VDI/VW- Gemeinschaftstagung Fahrerassistenz und automatisiertes Fahren, Wolfsburg (2016)

6. Griesche, S., Nicolay, E., Assmann, D., Dotzauer, M., Käthner, D.: Should my car drive as I do? What kind of driving style do drivers prefer for the design of automated driving functions? In: Contribution to 17th Braunschweiger Symposium Automatisierungssysteme, Assistenzsysteme und eingebettete Systeme für Transportmittel (AAET), ITS automotive nord e.V., pp. 185–204 (2016). ISBN 978-3-937655-37-6

7. Dettmann, A., et al.: Comfort or not? automated driving style and user characteristics causing human discomfort in automated driving. Int. J. Human-Comput. Interact. 37, 331–339 (2021). https://doi.org/10.1080/10447318.2020.1860518

8. Bellem, H., Schönenberg, T., Krems, J.F., Schrauf, M.: Objective metrics of comfort: developing a driving style for highly automated vehicles. Transport. Res. F: Traffic Psychol. Behav. 41, 45–54 (2016)

9. Hartwich, F., Beggiato, M., Dettmann, A., Krems, J.F.: Drive me comfortable: Customized automated driving styles for younger and older drivers. VDI-Tagung Der Fahrer im 21. Jahrhundert (2015)

10. Bellem, H., Klüver, M., Schrauf, M., Schöner, H.-P., Hecht, H., Krems, J.F.: Can we study autonomous driving comfort in moving-base driving simulators? a validation study. Human Fact. 59(3), 442–456 (2017). https://doi.org/10.1177/0018720816682647

11. Lex, C., et al.: Objektive Erfassung und subjektive Bewertung menschlicher Trajek-toriewahl in einer Naturalistic Driving Study. VDI-Berichte Nr. 2311, 177–192 (2017)

12. Schlag, B., Voigt, J.: Auswirkungen von Querschnittsgestaltung und längsgerichteten Markierungen auf das Fahrverhalten auf Landstrassen. Berichte der Bundesanstalt für Stra-ßenwesen. Unterreihe Verkehrstechnik, 249 (2015)

13. Rosey, F., Auberlet, J.-M., Moisan, O., Dupré, G.: Impact of narrower lane width: comparison between fixed-base simulator and real data. Transport. Res. Rec. J. Transport. Res. Board 2138(1), 112–119 (2009). https://doi.org/10.3141/2138-15

14. Rossner, P., Bullinger, A.C.: Drive me naturally: design and evaluation of trajectories for highly automated driving manoeuvres on rural roads. In: Technology for an Ageing Society, Postersession Human Factors and Ergonomics Society Europe Chapter 2018 Annual Conference, Berlin (2018)

15. Bella, F.: Speeds and lateral placements on two-lane rural roads: analysis at the driving simulator. In: 13th International Conference "Road Safety on Four Continents" (2005)

16. Bella, F.: Driver perception of roadside configurations on two-lane rural roads: effects on speed and lateral placement. Accid. Anal. Prev. 50, 251–262 (2013). https://doi.org/10.1016/j.aap.2012.04.015

17. Spacek, P.: Track behavior in curve areas: attempt at typology. J. Transport. Eng. 131(9), 669–676 (2005). https://doi.org/10.1061/(ASCE)0733-947X(2005)131:9(669)

18. Triggs, T.J.: The effect of approaching vehicles on the lateral position of cars travelling on a twolane rural road. Aust. Psychol. 32(3), 159–163 (1997). https://doi.org/10.1080/000500 69708257375

19. Dijksterhuis, C., Stuiver, A., Mulder, B., Brookhuis, K.A., de Waard, D.: An adaptive driver support system: user experiences and driving performance in a simulator. Human Fact. 54(5), 772–785 (2012). https://doi.org/10.1177/0018720811430502

20. Mecheri, S., Rosey, F., Lobjois, R.: The effects of lane width, shoulder width, and road cross-sectional reallocation on drivers' behavioral adaptations. Accid. Anal. Prevent. 104, 65–73 (2017). https://doi.org/10.1016/j.aap.2017.04.019

21. Räsänen, M.: Effects of a rumble strip barrier line on lane keeping in a curve. Accid. Anal. Prev. 37(3), 575–581 (2005). https://doi.org/10.1016/j.aap.2005.02.001

22. Rossner, P., Bullinger, A.C.: Do you shift or not? influence of trajectory behaviour on perceived safety during automated driving on rural roads. In: Krömker, H. (ed.) HCII 2019. LNCS, vol. 11596, pp. 245–254. Springer, Cham (2019). https://doi.org/10.1007/978-3-030-22666-4_18

23. Rossner P., Bullinger A.C.: Does driving experience matter? Influence of trajectory behaviour on drivers' trust, acceptance and perceived safety in automated driving: under-standing human behaviour in complex systems. In: de Waard, D., et al. (eds.) (2020). Proceedings of the Human Factors and Ergonomics Society Europe Chapter 2019 Annual Conference (2020). ISSN 2333–4959

24. Rossner, P., Bullinger, A.C.: I care who and where you are – influence of type, position and quantity of oncoming vehicles on perceived safety during automated driving on rural roads. In: Krömker, H. (ed.) HCII 2020. LNCS, vol. 12213, pp. 61–71. Springer, Cham (2020). https://doi.org/10.1007/978-3-030-50537-0_6

25. Rossner, P., Friedrich, M., Bullinger, A.C.: Hitting the apex highly automated? – influence of trajectory behaviour on perceived safety in curves. In: Stephanidis, C., Duffy, V.G., Krömker, H., Nah, F.F.-H., Siau, K., Salvendy, G., Wei, J. (eds.) HCI International 2021 - Late Breaking Papers: HCI Applications in Health, Transport, and Industry: 23rd HCI International Conference, HCII 2021, Virtual Event, July 24–29, 2021 Proceedings, pp. 322–331. Springer International Publishing, Cham (2021). https://doi.org/10.1007/978-3-030-90966-6_23

26. Siebert, F., Oehl, M., Höger, R., Pfister, H.R.: Discomfort in automated driving – the disco-scale. In: Proceedings of HCI International 2013, Communications in Computer and Information Science, Las Vegas, USA, vol. 374, pp. 337–341 (2013)

27. Bella, F.: Can driving simulators contribute to solving critical issues in geometric design? Transport. Res. Rec. J. Transport. Res. Board **2138**(1), 120–126 (2009). https://doi.org/10.3141/2138-16

Maneuver and Parameter Interventions in Automated Driving to Enhance User Satisfaction: A Kano Method Application

Lorenz Steckhan[1]([✉]) [iD], Wolfgang Spiessl[2] [iD], and Klaus Bengler[1] [iD]

[1] Chair of Ergonomics, Technical University of Munich, Garching, Germany
lorenz.steckhan@tum.de
[2] BMW Group, Munich, Germany

Abstract. This paper investigates participants' perceptions and preferences regarding different cooperative intervention features for automated driving with level 2 driving automation. The experiment conducted involved 40 participants. A Kano questionnaire and a semi-standardized interview were employed to collect participants' feedback on features for interventions in different maneuvers (e.g., initiating a lane change) and parameter settings (e.g., changing target speed). The results revealed a positive influence of most features on user satisfaction. Certain features were rated as essential requirements, while others were perceived as exciting additions. The response distributions show a high variance, indicating the existence of multiple user groups with different needs. The interviews conducted subsequently to the experiment provide qualitative insights, emphasizing the significance of implementation and the varying relevance between different maneuver and parameter interventions regarding satisfaction. The findings contribute to the design of experience-oriented human-machine interfaces (HMIs) in automated driving, highlighting the importance of cooperative features. The results can be used to prioritize the integration of distinct features. Future research should consider larger and more diverse samples to further enhance generalizability.

Keywords: automated driving · driver vehicle cooperation · user preference · user satisfaction · user experience · maneuver control · parameter control · kano model

1 Introduction

Automated driving functions are becoming increasingly common in modern vehicles. These functions are responsible for making their own motion-planning decisions. According to SAE (Society of Automotive Engineers International) J3016 [1], low-level automation systems may not consistently make accurate decisions in every possible scenario. As a result, level 2 systems, according to SAE J3026, require continuous monitoring by a human driver [1, 2]. To address resulting problems and failures, cooperation between the driver and the automated system can be established. While failures may not always imply mandatory intervention scenarios, they can still have a negative impact on user experience (UX) [2]. Therefore, non-critical optional interventions by users into the automated driving task can be used to adapt the automated driving behavior to individual user needs and thus improve user satisfaction.

The literature provides various human-machine interface (HMI) concepts that allow for driver-vehicle cooperation [3–5]. Cooperation can be achieved through shared guidance, enabling joint decision-making on the maneuver selection level [3]. Furthermore, parameters such as distances, speeds, and accelerations in reference to other objects and vehicles may be varied to adapt the respective maneuver under execution [2]. Existing HMI concepts focus on mandatory interventions, either based on functional requirements or limited to exemplary maneuvers. Providing a separate optional intervention feature for every maneuver and parameter may not be practical, considering that manual driving can still be utilized in certain situations to ensure a good UX. In addition to technical feasibility, users' perceptions of specific maneuver and parameter interventions should be considered in order to choose which features to integrate in future HMIs.

This paper aims to provide insights into users' perspectives on adjusting maneuvers and parameter settings within the optional action space as a feature for automated vehicles equipped with level 2 driving automation. To achieve this, we conducted a questionnaire based on the Kano model, which enabled us to draw conclusions regarding various maneuver and parameter interventions as potential features.

2   Related Work

This section provides a brief overview of relevant literature on maneuvers and parameters, as well as the Kano model.

2.1   Maneuvers and Parameters

The driving task can be divided into navigation, guidance, and stabilization level [6]. Maneuvers refer to abstract sequences of vehicle movement at the level of guidance. Particular maneuvers are optional in certain scenarios, such as overtaking a vehicle to reach the destination faster [2]. Various parameters, such as speeds, accelerations, or distances, need to be defined to specify a maneuver. Defining these parameters creates an additional optional action space within the driving task [2].

The literature provides numerous interaction concepts for (partly) automated vehicles that enable cooperative interactions at the level of guidance [3]. A maneuver control system that delegates the guidance task entirely to the user while automating the stabilization task has been implemented through the Conduct-by-Wire (CbW) system [7]. The CbW system uses a functional maneuver catalog that consists of the following maneuvers [7–9]:

- starting up
- braking
- standing still
- following the road
- turning left/right
- overtaking

- changing lanes left/right.

The catalog includes explicit (e.g., lane change) and implicit (e.g., following road) maneuvers and is applicable to both, highway and urban driving [9]. The CbW system allows users to intervene in explicit maneuvers using a touchscreen-based HMI [3, 7]. A separate intervention for overtaking was not included [7] as it may lead to misunderstandings because it can also be executed by performing two subsequent lane change maneuvers [9]. Users can also intervene in the following parameters: desired speed, time gap towards vehicles in front, and eccentricity between lane markings [7].

Another HMI concept, introduced by Walch et al. [10], focuses on cooperative interventions specific to the overtaking maneuver. This concept distinguishes between two discrete states for maneuver interventions: approval and cancellation. There are no additional parameter or maneuver interventions included.

2.2 Kano Model

The Kano Model, initially proposed by Kano et al. [11], is a framework that categorizes product features based on their relationship to customer satisfaction. It helps identify customer needs and prioritize product development efforts. The Kano method utilizes a questionnaire with two questions per feature: a functional and a dysfunctional one [12]. The functional question asks participants, "How would you feel if you had this feature?" while the dysfunctional question explores the absence of features, asking, "How would you feel if you did not have this feature?". Participants respond to each question using a scale equal to the following one [13]:

- I like it
- I expect it
- I am neutral
- I can tolerate it
- I dislike it.

Based on the responses users provide, features can be categorized into one of the following categories [14, 15]:

- **Must-be (basic) features:** The absence of these features is dissatisfying, and their presence is expected as a baseline requirement. Their presence does not provide any additional advantage in terms of satisfaction.
- **One-dimensional (performance) features:** These features directly correlate with satisfaction. Their absence leads to dissatisfaction, while their presence contributes to satisfaction.
- **Attractive (exciting) features:** These features surpass users' expectations and increase satisfaction when present. They often elicit emotions and experiences. The absence of these features does not result in dissatisfaction.
- **Indifferent features:** Features in this category are deemed unimportant by users. Neither their presence nor their absence has an impact on customer satisfaction.
- **Reverse features:** A presence of these features negatively affects satisfaction. Their absence is preferred. This can occur, for example, as a feature may make a product overly complex without providing any benefits for users.

- **Questionable:** The participant gave contradicting answers for both questions of one feature.

Several critiques and enhancements of the Kano model and method have been discussed [12, 14, 16]. For example, additional questions can be used to establish various subcategories within the original categories based on perceived relevance [15]. Madzik [17] proposes an optimized categorization to enhance accuracy. In addition to the original Kano method, alternative approaches exist for classifying features into the five categories of the Kano model. Current studies predominantly rely on the original method, presumably due to critical assessments of the validity and reliability of newer approaches [16].

The kano method has been widely used in various industries, e.g., in healthcare [18], marketing [19], and the tourism industry [20]. It has been applied to evaluate different transportation services for large events [21], intelligent car features [22], and various emerging technologies in passenger cars [23]. In the context of automated driving, Albers et al. [24] analyzed different scenarios involving speech output in vehicles with level 3 driving automation. The results indicate that users prefer the existence of speech outputs in critical scenarios, while preferences are mixed in non-critical scenarios [24]. Shin et al. [25] investigated 21 elements associated with the acceptance of automated driving to identify features that hinder future sustainability and commercialization of automated driving. The results show the varying influence of different features on satisfaction and therefore also on acceptance.

3 Methods

In this section, the applied experimental design, as well as the data recording and analysis, are described. Informed consent was obtained from individual participants. The Technical University of Munich Ethics Committee reviewed and approved the experiment under reference number 2022-501-S-KH.

3.1 Experimental Design

This study was conducted as part of a larger experiment in which users experienced and evaluated different interaction concepts that allowed for cooperative interventions. All participants experienced identical scenarios in a vehicle with level 2 driving automation to assess potential use cases more realistically. Within this section, only information relevant to this paper is reported. We briefly describe the experimental procedure, experienced HMIs, and experienced scenarios of the larger study and focus on the parts of the Kano survey in more detail. A detailed description of the larger experiment and the concept evaluation is given in [26].

Experimental Procedure. At the beginning of the larger experiment, each user experienced and evaluated two HMI concepts for manipulating maneuvers and parameters in a realistic driving simulator. Each user experienced a baseline concept and one of two newly developed concepts. Both concepts were experienced in identical scenarios, with the order permuted among participants. After evaluating the concepts, participants were informed that the evaluation phase was completed and that a second overarching part of the study started.

The second part of the experiment forms the data basis for the investigation of this paper. Participants were instructed that the implementation of the features is open-ended, and the HMIs experienced earlier were only prototypical examples to showcase use case scenarios. It was emphasized that the vehicle being assessed for its features possesses a similar level of automation as the one previously experienced. Furthermore, it was mentioned that the functions would always be optional alongside manual driving. Using the Kano method, participants were required to evaluate different maneuver and parameter interventions as separate features. Subsequently, a short semi-standardized interview was conducted to gather individual needs and comments regarding the features.

HMIs & Experienced Features. As part of the larger experiment, each participant experienced two HMIs that enabled cooperation with the level 2 driving automation. The baseline concept experienced by all users consists of control elements located on and around the steering wheel. It is based on the current state of the art of production vehicles. The other HMI was one of two newly developed concepts: one implemented using a touchscreen with multiple sliders and buttons, and the other one implemented using a joystick with force feedback. The specific implementation details of these concepts are disregarded for the research of this paper and can be found in [15]. The newly developed HMIs allowed participants to experience the following features, while the baseline concept solely supported the subset marked with an asterisk (*):

- reduce target speed*
- increase target speed*
- reduce dynamic of speed changes
- increase dynamic of speed changes
- reduce distance to the vehicle in front*
- increase distance to the vehicle in front*
- shift position between lane markings to the left
- shift position between lane markings to the right
- initiate lane change to the right*
- initiate lane change to the left*
- abort lane change
- initiate overtaking.

Scenarios. In each drive of the larger experiment participants encountered each feature three times, following instructions from the experimenter within different scenarios. Adjustment of acceleration and deceleration was the only feature that was not explicitly instructed. During instructed interventions into the target speed, participants could independently adjust and customize it according to their preferences.

Scenarios were formulated based on the objectives of "anticipatory actions for more efficient time management" and "anticipatory actions for enhanced control in potentially critical situations". These scenarios allowed users to experience the functionalities in possible use cases. For the time-efficiency theme, scenarios that required users to overtake slower vehicles or switch to faster lanes were designed. In individual scenarios, the lane position or the distance to vehicles in front had to be modified to gain a more beneficial position for monitoring the overtaking situation. To address the objective of improved control experience, scenarios involving non-critical roadside vehicles, wildlife, side barriers in construction sites, or slightly reduced visibility due to fog were included. Participants were asked to reduce the speed or change the distance to vehicles in front or the position between lane markings. Given that the main emphasis of this study revolves around optional interventions, the destination was reached without encountering any accidents, even in cases where no interventions were applied.

3.2 Data Recording and Analysis

The Kano questionnaire was constructed using the original Kano method, following [13]. The survey was conducted in German, and the questions' wording as well as response options aligned with existing German publications [27, 28]. LimeSurvey was used to administer the questionnaire on a notebook, and responses were analyzed post-survey. The questionnaire covered the following features:

- change target speed
- change distance to the vehicles in front
- change acceleration/deceleration
- change position between lane markings
- initiate a lane change
- abort current lane change
- initiate an overtaking
- initiate a stand-still maneuver.

First, results were analyzed using a discrete analysis [20]. Statistical significance was tested using the Fong test [29, as cited in 30]. The discrete analysis focuses on categorizing responses from individual participants and examining the distribution of responses across categories. The most frequently assigned category is considered the overall category. The Fong test determines statistical significance by comparing the distribution of responses across the remaining categories with the overall category [30]. Second, a continuous analysis [13] was conducted. In contrast to the discrete one, the continuous analysis considers individual responses from all participants. It uses the means and standard deviations of all participants for both questions of the Kano method to conclude the overall category of each feature [13]. For this analysis, all responses are transformed into an asymmetrical scale (-2, -1, 0, 2, and 4) because the categories "must-be" and "performance" are considered stronger responses than "reverse" or "questionable" [13]. Outliers have a greater impact on this analysis than on the discrete one.

After the Kano survey, participants were interviewed in a semi-standardized manner to gather their comments on the features. Topics included preferences for separate overtaking features versus changing lanes features and the subjective relevance of the features compared to one another. The interviews were recorded and analyzed post-interview.

4 Results

Participants were randomly assigned to one of the experimental groups of the larger experiment. The groups experienced different HMIs though identical scenarios and features prior to completing the survey of this paper. The survey asked about the features' outcome rather than about the implementation. Therefore, no distinction is made among the experimental groups of the larger experiment within this section.

4.1 Sample

The experiment involved 40 persons (mean: M = 36.9 years, standard deviation: SD = 11.3 years). 16 identified as female and 24 as male. All participants had a valid German driver's license. The average duration of possession was 20.1 years (SD = 11.2 years) at the time of the investigation. Figure 1 shows the average driving mileage per year, and Table 1 shows participants' prior experience with driver assistance systems.

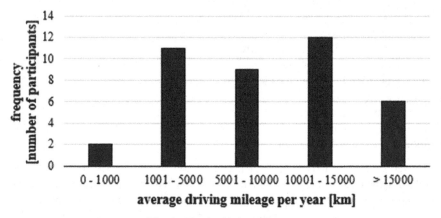

Fig. 1. Yearly driving mileage

Table 1. Prior experience with different driver assistance systems

Driver assistance system	Percentage of participants with prior experience
Cruise control	92.5%
Adaptive cruise control	70.0%
Lane-keeping system	62.5%
Automated driving (combined lateral and longitudinal control)	60.0%

4.2 Kano Method

Results of the Kano questionnaire are presented separately for the discrete and the continuous evaluation since differences appear for some features.

Discrete Analysis. Based on the discrete analysis, the feature of initiating a stand-still maneuver is categorized as "indifferent". All other features are assigned to the "must-be" or the "attractive" category. Not all assignments reach statistical significance. The distribution of participants across the categories shows considerable variance, as depicted in Table 2. This variance was particularly evident for features without significant overall categorization. None of the participants responded in the "questionable" category.

Table 2. Discrete analysis of the Kano method: Proportions of responses within the categories of must-be (M), performance (P), attractive (A), indifferent (I), reverse (R), and questionable (Q), with indicated statistical significance (*) based on the Fong test

Feature	M [%]	P [%]	A [%]	I [%]	R [%]	Q [%]	Overall category
Initiate lane change	**37.5**	5	32.5	20	5	0	M
Abort lane change	**62.5**	20	7.5	10	0	0	M *
Initiate overtaking	22.5	10	**45**	22.5	0	0	A *
Initiate stand-still	22.5	7.5	20	**50**	0	0	I *
Change target speed	**62.5**	20	7.5	10	0	0	M *
Change distance to vehicles in front	**42.5**	7.5	20	30	0	0	M
Change acceleration/ deceleration	27.5	20	**32.5**	20	0	0	A
Change position between lane markings	7.5	12.5	**47.5**	32.5	0	0	A

Continuous Analysis. Figure 2 presents the results of the continuous analysis graphically. In accordance with [13], the axes are limited to positive values of the transformed scale. To enhance readability, standard deviations are visualized one-sidedly only. Similar to the discrete analysis, the results of all features show a high degree of variance, see Table 3. Based on this analysis, most features' mean values are positioned within the performance quadrant. The mean of "change position between lane markings" lies within the quadrant associated with attractive features, while the feature "initiate stand-still" is categorized as indifferent. The standard deviations of all features extend into other quadrants due to their large magnitude. Furthermore, all features are located near the boundaries of adjacent quadrants. In particular, the feature "initiate stand-still" is close to one of these boundaries.

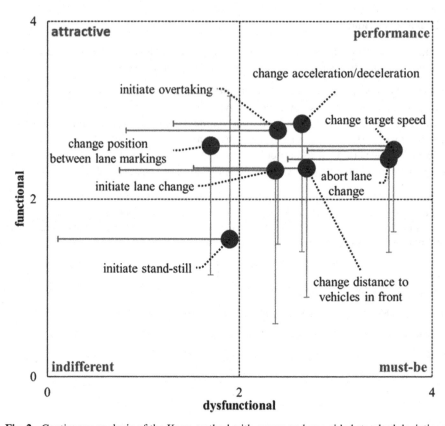

Fig. 2. Continuous analysis of the Kano method with means and one-sided standard deviations

Table 3. Means and standard deviations of the continuous analysis of the functional and dysfunctional question of the Kano method

Feature	Functional question		Dysfunctional question	
	M	SD	M	SD
Initiate lane change	2.33	1.73	2.38	1.62
Abort lane change	2.45	1.05	3.55	1.05
Initiate overtaking	2.78	1.28	2.40	1.57
Initiate stand-still	1.55	1.61	1.90	1.79
Change target speed	2.55	0.92	3.60	0.89
Change distance to vehicles in front	2.35	1.45	2.70	1.17
Change acceleration/deceleration	2.85	1.44	2.65	1.33
Change position between lane markings	2.60	1.45	1.70	1.84

4.3   Interview

During the interviews, participants had the opportunity to provide comments on all features. Six participants referred to the "initiate a stand-still" function as "unnecessary" and "preferred to perform this action manually". Four participants stated that the feature "change position between lane markings" benefited them in particular in "driving further away from lateral barriers in tight construction zones". They considered it a "positive experience" that they had "not anticipated beforehand".

14 participants mentioned that the implementation of the functions is crucial in determining whether they contribute positively or negatively to the experience. Regarding the design of interventions in the "position between lane markings" parameter, three participants commented that "having settings for left, right, and center would be sufficient, and a more finely graded intervention is not needed". Concerning the design of target speed interventions, two participants suggested that there should be possible settings beyond the speed limit, while one participant requested that such interventions should be restricted.

All participants stated perceived relevance varies among the features. Certain features, such as "acceleration and deceleration interventions", were considered more like "gimmicks" (n = 3) or "would only need to be set once per user" (n = 4). On the other hand, features such as "initiate a lane change" and "abort a lane change" were deemed essential for particular users (n = 4) and therefore considered more important than other features. Two participants justified a higher relevance of acceleration interventions based on their preferred driving style, which they described as "fast" or "dynamic".

77.5% of the participants preferred using an additional function for initiating an overtaking maneuver compared to independently executing it through two lane changes. Eleven participants commented it would be "more comfortable" for them, and seven considered it "easier". One participant considered it "safer" because "less time is spent on initiating the maneuver, allowing more time to be used for monitoring". Additionally, two participants argued it was safer because "they could not forget the return lane change at the end of the maneuver". In total, seven participants stated despite the availability of an overtaking feature, they would prefer to perform lane changes individually in several situations as this would provide a higher degree of control. Participants who did not require this feature referred to it as an "unnecessary add-on feature with no significant advantage".

5   Discussion

The results of the Kano questionnaire, analyzed using both discrete and continuous approaches, reveal distinct patterns for the tested features. With both methods, the "initiate a stand-still" feature is categorized as "indifferent", suggesting that participants do not consider it a significant addition to the driving experience. This indifference could be attributed to user trust in the automation system's ability to handle stand-still situations effectively or a perception that manual control is still preferred in such scenarios. In addition, this feature was the only one that did not occur in the larger experiment, and therefore the evaluation of use cases might have been difficult for the participants. Further research is needed to interpret the reasons behind this classification and explore ways to enhance the value proposition of stand-still maneuver interventions. The feature "change position between lane markings" is categorized as "attractive" with both methods, indicating participants find it valuable even though they did not expect it. These feature categorizations align with the statements provided by participants during the interviews.

In the discrete analysis, most features are categorized as "must-be" or "attractive", highlighting their functional importance to participants. On the other hand, within the continuous analysis these features are mostly categorized as "performance" features. The differences between both analyses can be attributed to the variance of the responses. It suggests the existence of different user groups with varying needs, possibly influenced by personal driving styles and prior experience with such systems. Participants' diverse opinions influence the categorization of the continuous analysis and are not entirely captured with the overall category assignment of the discrete analysis. Therefore, it is essential to examine the distribution of responses. The findings show that the "performance" category is rarely selected by individual participants for any features. Following this, the discrete analysis might fit better for this data set. However, all classifications show a neutral or positive relationship between satisfaction and the presence of these features, indicating their potential to enhance UX.

The discrete analysis categorizes the features "initiate lane change", "change target speed", and "change distance to vehicles in front" as "must-be" features. This can be explained by the widespread availability of these features in modern vehicles, leading users to consider them standard functionalities already. The "abort lane change" feature is also categorized as a "must-be" feature by many participants, indicating its essentiality for a satisfactory automated driving experience. These must-be features are crucial for users to maintain a sense of control and adaptability while the vehicle operates automated.

The features "initiate overtaking" and "adjust acceleration/ deceleration" are categorized as "attractive" features according to the discrete analysis. These features enhance overall UX but may not be necessary for basic functionality. Nonetheless, they contribute to a more personalized and enjoyable driving experience by offering additional customization options and flexibility.

The interviews conducted with the participants provided qualitative feedback on the features. Participants highlighted the importance of the implementation of functions, suggesting that the respective design of cooperative interventions greatly influences their perceived value. Feedback regarding interventions in the "position between lane markings" parameter emphasized the need for simplicity and ease of use, with participants expressing a preference for a limited set of settings. The relevance of the features varied among participants, with certain features perceived as more essential than others. The function for initiating an overtaking maneuver received positive feedback, as participants considered it more comfortable and easier to use than independently executing the maneuver through two lane changes. However, individual participants regarded it as an unnecessary add-on feature, highlighting the diversity of opinions within the sample.

These findings underscore the importance of prioritizing essential features that align with users' expectations and preferences. They emphasize the significance of considering individual preferences, implementation details, and functionality range when designing HMIs for cooperative interventions in automated driving scenarios.

6 Limitations

The findings of this study provide valuable insights. However, it is essential to acknowledge and consider the following limitations. The study was conducted exclusively with participants from Germany, which may limit the generalizability of the results to other cultural contexts. E.g., cultural aspects have been shown to influence manual driving behavior [30] and the level of mistrust regarding automated driving functions [31].

This study was conducted as part of a larger study, with partially overlapping topics, to enable participants to carry out a realistic assessment of the functions and potential use cases. Consequently, the results should be interpreted within the specific context of this study and should only be directly extrapolated to other use cases or automation levels with further investigations. The subjective ratings of individual participants may have been influenced by the HMIs they experienced, even though they were exposed to two different HMIs and instructed to view them as prototypical examples to demonstrate usage scenarios.

The results suggest the existence of different user groups. The distribution of these user groups within the sample may distort the results. Therefore, the results should be interpreted while considering the reported user characteristics. Results may differ when applied to different samples.

7 Conclusion and Future Work

This paper shows how users classify various maneuver and parameter intervention features during automated driving into satisfaction-based categories. The study's findings provide broader implications for the design and development of automated vehicles. The integration of these functionalities into vehicle HMIs can be prioritized by identifying the "must-be", "performance", and "attractive" features. Offering users a comprehensive set of intervention features tailored to their preferences can improve the user experience and acceptance of automated vehicles.

As this study suggests the existence of various user groups with varying intervention needs and preferences, a detailed analysis of these user groups should be included in future work to better structure the user-centered development process. HMIs with an adaptable or adaptive range of intervention features may result in optimized UX for all user groups. Furthermore, the findings highlight the potential for vehicle segment differentiation based on the range of intervention features. Manufacturers could target specific user groups with their product offerings by emphasizing certain features as key selling points.

Furthermore, it is essential to conduct further investigations of the relationship between user satisfaction and interventions in maneuvers and parameters. Future studies should address the limitations of this study to strengthen the validity and generalizability of the findings. In particular, future experiments should consider cultural effects.

In conclusion, this study provides valuable insights into preferences for intervention features during automated driving and their impact on user satisfaction. The findings pave the way for future research to improve design and implementation of HMIs of automated vehicles, ultimately enhancing overall UX and acceptance of this emerging technology.

Acknowledgments. We thank all those involved in the implementation of the experiment for their support.

Funding. This work was funded by the BMW Group.

References

1. SAE International: Taxonomy and Definitions for Terms Related to On-Road Motor Vehicle Automated Driving Systems. J3016. SAE International, USA (2021)
2. Steckhan, L., Spiessl, W., Quetschlich, N., Bengler, K.: Beyond SAE J3016: new design spaces for human-centered driving automation. In: Krömker, H. (ed.) HCI in Mobility, Transport, and Automotive Systems. 4th International Conference, MobiTAS 2022, Held as Part of the 24th HCI International Conference, HCII, 2022, vol. 13335, pp. 416–434. Springer, Heidelberg (2022). https://doi.org/10.1007/978-3-031-04987-3_28
3. Flemisch, F.O., Bengler, K., Bubb, H., Winner, H., Bruder, R.: Towards cooperative guidance and control of highly automated vehicles: H-mode and conduct-by-wire. Ergonomics (2014). https://doi.org/10.1080/00140139.2013.869355
4. Franz, B., Kauer, M., Bruder, R., Geyer, S.: pieDrive - a new driver-vehicle interaction concept for maneuver-based driving. In: 2012 IEEE Intelligent Vehicles Symposium Workshops (2012)
5. Walch, M., Sieber, T., Hock, P., Baumann, M., Weber, M.: Towards cooperative driving. In: Green, P., Boll, S., Burnett, G., Gabbard, J., Osswald, S. (eds.) Proceedings of the 8th International Conference on Automotive User Interfaces and Interactive Vehicular Applications, USA, pp. 261–268. ACM Press (2016). https://doi.org/10.1145/3003715.3005458
6. Donges, E.: Driver behavior models. In: Winner, H., Hakuli, S., Lotz, F., Singer, C. (eds.) Handbook of driver assistance systems, pp. 19–33. Springer, Cham (2016). https://doi.org/10.1007/978-3-319-12352-3_2
7. Franz, B., Kauer, M., Geyer, S., Hakuli, S.: Conduct-by-Wire. In: Winner, H., Hakuli, S., Lotz, F., Singer, C. (eds.) Handbuch Fahrerassistenzsysteme. A, pp. 1111–1121. Springer, Wiesbaden (2015). https://doi.org/10.1007/978-3-658-05734-3_59
8. Schreiber, M., Kauer, M., Bruder, R.: Conduct by wire - maneuver catalog for semi-autonomous vehicle guidance. In: IEEE Intelligent Vehicles Symposium 2009, China, pp. 1279–1284. IEEE (2009). https://doi.org/10.1109/IVS.2009.5164468
9. Schreiber, M., Kauer, M., Schlesinger, D., Hakuli, S., Bruder, R.: Verification of a maneuver catalog for a maneuver-based vehicle guidance system. In: 2010 IEEE International Conference on Systems, Man and Cybernetics, Turkey, pp. 3683–3689. IEEE (2010). https://doi.org/10.1109/ICSMC.2010.5641862
10. Walch, M., Woide, M., Mühl, K., Baumann, M., Weber, M.: Cooperative overtaking. In: Proceedings, 11th International ACM Conference on Automotive User Interfaces and Interactive Vehicular Applications, Netherlands, pp. 144–155. ACM Press (2019). https://doi.org/10.1145/3342197.3344531
11. Kano, N., Seraku, N., Takahashi, F., Tsuji, S.-I.: Attractive quality and must-be quality. J. Jpn. Soc. Qual. Control (1984). https://doi.org/10.20684/quality.14.2_147
12. Löfgren, M., Witell, L.: Two decades of using kano's theory of attractive quality: a literature review. Qual. Manag. J. (2008). https://doi.org/10.1080/10686967.2008.11918056
13. Berger, C., et al.: Kano's methods for understanding customer-defined quality, vol. 2, pp. 3–36 (1993)

14. Shahin, A., Pourhamidi, M., Antony, J., Hyun Park, S.: Typology of Kano models: a critical review of literature and proposition of a revised model. Int. J. Qual. Reliabil. Manag. (2013). https://doi.org/10.1108/02656711311299863
15. Yang, C.-C.: The refined Kano's model and its application. Total Qual. Manag. Bus. Excell. (2005). https://doi.org/10.1080/14783360500235850
16. Mikulić, J., Prebežac, D.: A critical review of techniques for classifying quality attributes in the Kano model. Manag. Serv. Qual. Int. J. (2011). https://doi.org/10.1108/096045211111 00243
17. Madzík, P.: Increasing accuracy of the Kano model – a case study. Total Qual. Manag. Bus. Excell. (2018). https://doi.org/10.1080/14783363.2016.1194197
18. Materla, T., Cudney, E.A., Antony, J.: The application of Kano model in the healthcare industry: a systematic literature review. Total Qual. Manag. Bus. Excell. (2019). https://doi.org/10.1080/14783363.2017.1328980
19. Mikulić, J.: The Kano model–a review of its application in marketing research from 1984 to 2006. In: Proceedings of the 1st International Conference Marketing Theory Challenges in Transitional Societies, pp. 87–96 (2007)
20. Pandey, A., Sahu, R., Joshi, Y.: Kano model application in the tourism industry: a systematic literature review. J. Qual. Assur. Hosp. Tour. (2022). https://doi.org/10.1080/1528008X.2020. 1839995
21. Chen, M.-C., Hsu, C.-L., Huang, C.-H.: Applying the Kano model to investigate the quality of transportation services at mega events. J. Retail. Cons. Serv. (2021). https://doi.org/10.1016/ j.jretconser.2021.102442
22. Dominici, G., Roblek, V., Abbate, T., Tani, M.: Click and drive. Bus. Process. Manag. J. (2016). https://doi.org/10.1108/BPMJ-05-2015-0076
23. Kohli, A., Singh, R.: An assessment of customers' satisfaction for emerging technologies in passenger cars using Kano model. XJM (2021). https://doi.org/10.1108/XJM-08-2020-0103
24. Albers, D., Grabbe, N., Forster, Y., Naujoks, F., Keinath, A., Bengler, K.: (Don't) talk to me! application of the kano method for speech outputs in conditionally automated driving. in: human factors in transportation. In: 13th International Conference on Applied Human Factors and Ergonomics (AHFE 2022). AHFE International (2022). https://doi.org/10.54941/ahfe10 02484
25. Shin, J.-G., Heo, I.-S., Yae, J.-H., Kim, S.-H.: Kano model of autonomous driving user acceptance according to driver characteristics: a survey study. Transport. Res. F: Traffic Psychol. Behav. (2022). https://doi.org/10.1016/j.trf.2022.10.002
26. Steckhan, L., Spiessl, W., Bengler, K.: Evaluation of user interfaces for cooperation between driver and automated driving system. In: 2023 IEEE International Conference on Systems, Man and Cybernetics (2023). (in press)
27. Hölzing, J.A.: Die Kano-Theorie der Kundenzufriedenheitsmessung. Eine theoretische und empirische Überprüfung. Gabler (2008)
28. Sauerwein, E.: Das Kano-Modell der Kundenzufriedenheit. Reliabilität und Validität einer Methode zur Klassifizierung von Produkteigenschaften. Springer Fachmedien Wiesbaden GmbH (2020)
29. Fong, D.: Using the self-stated importance questionnaire to interpret Kano questionnaire results. Center Qual. Manag. J. 5, 21–24 (1996)

30. Özkan, T., Lajunen, T., Chliaoutakis, J.E., Parker, D., Summala, H.: Cross-cultural differences in driving behaviours: a comparison of six countries. Transport. Res. Part F: Traff. Psychol. Behav. (2006). https://doi.org/10.1016/j.trf.2006.01.002
31. Hergeth, S., Lorenz, L., Krems, J.F., Toenert, L.: Effects of take-over requests and cultural background on automation trust in highly automated driving. In: Proceedings of the 8th International Driving Symposium on Human Factors in Driver Assessment, Training, and Vehicle Design: Driving Assessment 2015, pp. 331–337 (2015). https://doi.org/10.17077/drivingassessment.1591

Standardization of User Experience Evaluation: Theory, Method and Promotion of High-Quality Development of Chinese Intelligent Vehicle Industry

Shiyan Tang, Ruilin Ouyang, and Hao Tan[(✉)] [ID]

Hunan University, Changsha 410006, Hunan, China
htan@hnu.edu.cn

Abstract. User experience (UX) evaluation can improve product quality, which has been confirmed in many studies. In recent years, the Chinese government has continued to promote the digitalization, intelligence and standardization of automobiles and the high-quality development of the intelligent automobile industry. However, there is still space for progress in production standardization and quality standardization, and mechanisms have not yet been designed to comprehensively measure the UX of intelligent vehicles. Therefore, the purpose of this paper is to develop a comprehensive framework for the evaluation of UX in intelligent vehicle human-machine interface (HMI) from the perspective of literature research and industry research. The framework was determined after a review of related literatures to analysis and summary existing evaluation approaches and was analyzed and organized according to the following components: UX evaluation object, the type of evaluation performer, HMI UX metrics, the most frequently applied evaluation methods, and UX influence factors. Through this method, it is possible for developers to obtain the theoretical knowledge and practical experience required for the evaluation of UX of HMI of intelligent vehicles, to carry out the evaluation to ensure the consistency of product quality, and then promote the high-quality development of the intelligent vehicle industry.

Keywords: Intelligent Vehicle · Human-Machine Interaction · User Experience Evaluation

1 Introduction

The world is experiencing a great change. The last wave of technological revolution and industrial change has not yet ended, and Intelligent vehicle have become an inevitable trend in the global automotive industry. Intelligent vehicle is a vehicle with automatic driving function by carrying advanced sensors and other devices, using new technologies such as artificial intelligence, and gradually becoming an intelligent mobile space and application terminal. The recognized classification standard for automatic driving was developed by SAE (society of Automotive Engineers) in 2014, which defined 6 levels of driving automation ranging from 0 (fully manual) to 5 (fully autonomous).

© The Author(s), under exclusive license to Springer Nature Switzerland AG 2023
V. G. Duffy et al. (Eds.): HCII 2023, LNCS 14057, pp. 405–420, 2023.
https://doi.org/10.1007/978-3-031-48047-8_27

In order to guide enterprises to participate in the wave of Intelligent vehicle development standardized, China has introduced a few policies to promote the development of road traffic autonomous driving. At present, the governments of several regions in China, such as Beijing, Shanghai and Guangzhou, have also introduced Policies related to the development of the Intelligent vehicle industry to help the rapid development of it in China. In December 2020, the Shanghai Government released the Special Plan for the Intelligent Connected Vehicle Industry (2020–2025), which focus on promoting the cluster development of intelligent vehicle industry, technology innovation, etc.

Close to the development trend of automobile technology and the actual needs of the industry, improve the top-level design of standards and the technical standard system of intelligent vehicle to promote automobile standardization thus providing powerful support for the high-quality development of the intelligent vehicle [1]. Currently, Intelligent vehicle is in the exploration stage of rapid development. Intelligent vehicles differ significantly from traditional vehicles in terms of product structure and other aspects, and vehicle-related parameters are constantly changing. The auto industry should take the initiative to carry out standardization work and promote the development of the standard system of the auto industry, which requires ensuring product quality and production consistency, and emphasizes that updating the self-driving function of vehicles requires approval before implementation [2].

Automobile human-machine interface (HMI) is one of the important roles in the field of intelligent vehicle design, which has a significant impact on the development of the automobile industry. Although the formulation of industrial standards have aroused widespread concern among national policies, domestic and foreign automobile related enterprises and manufacturers, there is still a lack of formulation of HMI quality standards for intelligent vehicles, and a mechanism to comprehensively evaluate user experience (UX) of intelligent vehicles.

As the medium of communication between the driver and the vehicle, HMI will affect the driver's ability to control the vehicle, receive information and monitor the system. The HMI of the intelligent vehicle must correctly display the running status of the auto drive system. When the driver is required to perform dynamic driving tasks under specific conditions, it has the function of recognizing the ability of the driver to perform dynamic driving tasks and can reasonably interact with the road users outside the vehicle [2]. HMI design of intelligent vehicles has become the focus of domestic and foreign industries. Ensuring product functions, improving product experience and continuous and stable production are issues that need to be considered in product research and development. Therefore, it is necessary to evaluate the relevant characteristics of HMI of intelligent vehicles. The design of HMI of Intelligent Vehicle is the key factor to attract users and provide differentiated services [3]. The feedback of the evaluation aids with the automobile developers to design and improve products [4–7].

Based on this, the main goal of this study is to build a UX evaluation system to measure the quality of HMI in a standardized and systematic way. This paper reviewed the relevant research on UX evaluation of HMI of intelligent vehicles, summarized and combed the evaluation methods and technologies that have been proposed or used to evaluate HMI. Selected basic articles according to content relevance and cited frequency after retrieval, and extracted basic information such as research title, author, abstract, as well as the key information such as experimental settings and data analysis. Finally, summarized the information according to the following parts: UX influence factors, evaluation metrics and evaluation methods. The construction of the UX evaluation system provides intelligent vehicle manufacturers, researchers and developers with a comprehensive and useful evaluation tool, enabling them to identify and select UX evaluation methods, technologies and tools that are most suitable for their evaluation needs and available resources.

2   Evaluation of HMI from the Perspective of UX

2.1   Human-Machine Interface of Intelligent Vehicle

User interfaces are an essential part of any complex system that requires communication with the user. A user interface is composed, in turn, of a human–machine interface (HMI), which is responsible for establishing physical communication between user and system. Users can observe the status of the system but also act on it, modifying the parameters of its operation [8]. In a broad sense, all fields involved in the processing of information, material and energy between human and machine can be considered as HMI. From this point of view, HMI can be divided into three categories: control system HMI, tool HMI and environment HMI [9]. This paper only discusses the first one. Automotive HMI consist mainly of output channels that provide information about the system state to the driver (e.g., via displays and auditory signals), input channels to receive the driver's input (e.g., via buttons, steering wheel, and pedals), and a dialog logic to specify the relationships among input, output, and context parameters [10].

   With networking and intellectualization evolution of vehicles, a new relationship between humans and cars emerged, creating opportunities and prospects for the innovative development of HMI [11]. A previous study reviewed the latest display technology and the layout of HMI in the vehicle and discussed the impact of the location of display on driver performance [12]. The study focused on the interaction between the vehicle and the passengers, which only involves one aspect of the interaction of intelligent vehicles. From a macroscopic perspective, there is also a need for interaction between intelligent vehicles and other road users. Some studies [13–15] have been carried out on the technology of external human-machine interface (eHMI). Recent research has begun to focus on cross-device connectivity in mobile environments (such as smartphones and computers) [16].

2.2   User Experience

In the 1970s, the fourth generation of electronic computers appeared with the invention of personal microcomputers, setting off a wave of computer popularization. The complexity of early computer use made the population for which it was intended more limited, and as more and more use was demanded, the public began to demand a better experience. In the field of computer science, the slogan of "user friendly" has been translated into the concept of "usability" of human-computer interface. Usability, as a practical part of user experience, is described as the extent to which a system, product or service can be used by specified users to achieve specified goals with effectiveness, efficiency and satisfaction in a specified context of use [17], so as to ensure efficient human-computer interaction.

The design field of interaction is expanding, and the tendency of quality in product evaluation criteria is expanded to more important UX from the overall perspective of human-machine interaction. UX emphasizes the non-utilitarian aspects of interaction, shifting the focus to the user's emotions and feelings. It is widely believed that the concept of "user experience" was pioneered by Don Norman and is well known in the industry [18]. According to the latest definition of ISO 9241–11: 2018 proposed by the International Organization for Standardization (ISO), UX refers to the feeling users experience when using a product, application, system, or service [17].

2.3 The Influence Factors of UX

UX factors are used to identify the reasons behind a certain experience. It is difficult to distinguish UX factors from key components by definition, thus, many scholars described these key components as influence factors while attempting to define the UX concept [19]. ISO 9241–11 mentions some components related to the influencing factors of UX, but the UX is complex, and the experience of using the product is not only determined by the user and the use process. Hassenzahl et al. introduced three aspects of UX: a user's internal state (predispositions, expectations, needs, motivation, mood, etc.), the characteristics of the designed system (e.g. complexity, purpose, usability, functionality, etc.) and the context (or the environment) within which the interaction occurs (e.g. organizational/social setting, meaningfulness of the activity, voluntariness of use, etc.) [20]. The element of machine is the center of attention in design. Jodi Forlizzi et al. believed that each product told a story of use through its form language, its features, its aesthetic qualities, and its accessibility [21]. Virpi Roto et al. gave a more detailed description of the environment and outlined four kinds of situations in the user experience field: social context, physical context, task context, technical and information context [22].

Based on the above discussion, Fig. 1 shows the influencing factors and relationships of UX.

2.4 UX Evaluation Metrics

The evaluation metrics describe the content of UX measurement. There may be multiple measures for one evaluation metric. In other words, for a given evaluation metric, there may be multiple measured values through different evaluation methods. The system usability scale (SUS) gives three evaluation metrics of effectiveness, efficiency and satisfaction to measure the usability results, which are adopted in many studies [23, 24]. It is likely that the SUS will continue to be a popular measurement of perceived usability for the foreseeable future [25].

Albert et al. divided the dependent variables in the study into observational data and subjective data [26]. In the specific research, a certain type of evaluation index is selected to be used alone or in combination according to the research purpose. Subjective data depends on the user's subjective feelings in the test, such as trust [27], use attitude

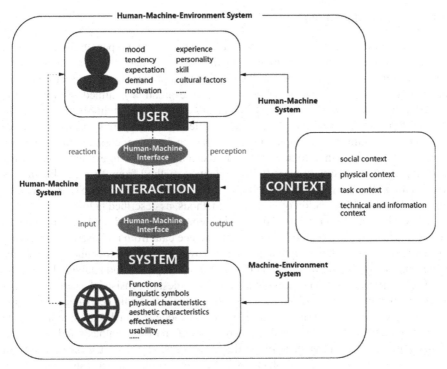

Fig. 1. UX influence factors.

[28], workload [29], preference [30], etc. The direct or indirect data reflecting the user's performance in the task (such as task completion time [31], error rate [29], Sight switch [32], etc.) can be obtained from the evaluator's observation of the user's behavior, which belongs to observation data.

Driving is a highly complex task. Although the automobile continues to develop towards intelligence and automation, the driver needs to maintain a high degree of attention before fully automatic driving is realized. The evaluation of driving safety takes priority in the evaluation of the HMI of the automobile. In order to quantify drive distraction, drive workload and situational awareness more accurately, scholars mostly use quantitative research based on driving simulator in addition to the field research which is generally qualitative research. The advantage of simulator research is that it can make up for the data that cannot be obtained by observation research. For the physiological measurement system, metrics such as fixation count [33], electrocardiogram (ECG) [31], and heart rate (HR) [31] can be developed. These data are more accurate and reflect the system performance from more aspects.

The UX of HMI can be evaluated by various metrics. In the evaluation, it is not enough to use only the traditional usability metrics. It is necessary to subdivide the metrics and establish two-level or multi-level metrics.

2.5   UX Evaluation Methods

According to the goal of UX evaluation, there are usually two types of UX evaluation: formative evaluation and summative evaluation [34]. Formative evaluation is used to collect and improve UX problems in the development process, with the focus on facilitating the formation of design, while summative evaluation is aimed to evaluate the usage of the product in the real environment and evaluate the quality of the design. In the development and design of UX of automobile HMI, it is popular to use formative evaluation and summative evaluation together in each design process. In order to choose a better evaluation method to answer "what to evaluate", "how to evaluate" and "what to obtain", it is necessary to classify the evaluation method from different dimensions and obtain multiple types of combined data for researchers to choose. Some literatures have studied the classification of evaluation methods, as described below.

UX evaluation methods can be divided into empirical methods and analytical methods [35]. The empirical method obtains performance data from real users by observing the use process, while the analytical method is carried out around the inherent attributes of design. In fact, some evaluation methods are both empirical and analytical.

The complete evolution process of an interaction design consists of a series of stages and corresponding activities, and each stage in the process should be evaluated by some methods. Summarize a variety of design process models, which can summarize the process of interaction design as a three-step model of analysis, synthesis and evaluation [36]. Analysis is the initial stage of the design process. At this stage, the design team usually has to define design problems by collecting design requirements. Synthesis is the place where ideas are generated. Demand and other user data are transformed into design ideas through the creative process. Evaluation is to use the requirements of the analysis stage to evaluate the potential design solutions and select the final concept.

At different stages of progress, it is necessary to consider who will participate. Nielson believes that UX experts are the best evaluators. In the early stage of design, professional design walk-through and heuristic evaluation can obtain higher benefits at lower cost. From the perspective of the whole process, evaluators may be design teams, UX experts, user representatives and potential users. Experts and users should be regarded as people with different professional abilities. In the evaluation process, corresponding methods must be considered according to actual needs and objectives.

The evaluation method can be faster, cheaper and smarter, such as design walk-through. The flexibility of this kind of evaluation method can meet the needs of various situations. The evaluation method can also be based on the laboratory or in the real use environment. Because it is closer to the actual usage of users, the data obtained has the characteristics of more thorough, more effective and more controllable. Arnold et al. carried out analysis according to the context of use and divided the evaluation methods into laboratory-based evaluation, field selected by researchers, user's own context of use, and online on the web [37].

Christian Rohrer [38] identified two dimensions based on the research object, namely, attitudinal and behavioral. Attitudes and behaviors can be summarized by comparing "what people say" and "what people do". The purpose of attitude research is usually to understand or measure people's stated beliefs, which is why attitude research is widely used in marketing departments. The main focus on behavior is to understand what people do with relevant products or services.

From the perspective of data attributes, the data obtained by UX evaluation has qualitative or quantitative attributes and subjective or objective attributes. The research methods of social science are roughly divided into qualitative research methods and quantitative research methods, which are used to describe the problems observed or experienced in the process of use, as well as the motivation, needs, pain points and views of user behavior, or quantify the user experience to obtain numerical quantitative data and measure and analyze it. Because the UX research objects have attitudes and behaviors, the evaluation of attitudes can obtain subjective data that represent the views, judgments and other subjective user feedback on user experience and interaction design satisfaction. Objective data can be obtained through observation or experiment by the evaluator or participant according to the user's behavior.

Only using a single evaluation method is not comprehensive. Researchers usually combine multiple evaluation methods to obtain more comprehensive and accurate results [39]. Build a multi-dimensional evaluation method model to provide researchers with reference for method selection from different perspectives, as shown in Fig. 2.

3 Framework for UX Evaluation in HMI of Intelligent Vehicle

Based on the UX factors, evaluation metrics and evaluation methods obtained in the literature review process in the previous chapter, the framework for UX evaluation in HMI of intelligent vehicle is conceptualized and constructed, which is composed of the following components:

Evaluation objects, evaluation performer type (user/expert), evaluation metrics, common evaluation methods, UX influence factors (user, interaction, product, situation). Figure 3 shows the design of the UX evaluation framework.

3.1 Component of Evaluation Objects

The evaluation object of the framework for UX evaluation in HMI of intelligent vehicle is the control system HMI. The progress of various technologies has made the evaluation object diversified. Traditional HMI such as central control interface and dashboard are applied to almost all vehicles. New-type HMI such as head-up display (HUD) and passenger entertainment system bring more possibilities for the design and evaluation of HMI.

3.2 Component of Evaluation Performer

The subject of evaluation in UX research can be anyone who wants to complete some tasks through the system. The evaluation subject is regarded as a person with different levels of professional knowledge, and can be divided into novice users, intermediate users, expert users and experts with strong design knowledge. Experts play an important role in the early stage of design, such as exploration, definition and development. In the

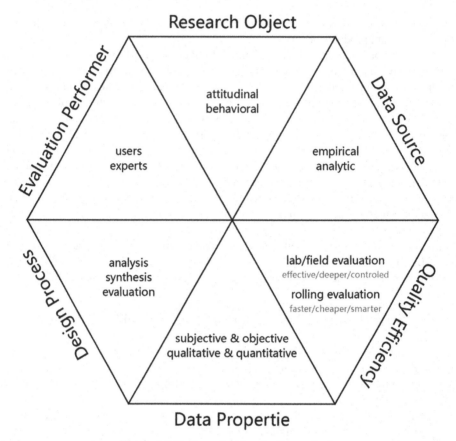

Fig. 2. Multi-dimensional evaluation method.

process of testing, it is highly effective to let real users use the system to best reflect users' needs.

In fact, in practice, users can also participate in the evaluation by experts, who are users with strong professional capabilities.

3.3 Component of UX Metrics

Based on the performance of participants in the UX evaluation, some UX evaluation metrics are summarized, as shown in Fig. 4.

John Whiteside et al. proposed a usability specification table, which lists the content information used by the UX metric such as measurement attributes, measurement concepts, measurement methods, and data information such as the worst performance, target performance, best performance, and current performance [40]. Rex Hartson et al. optimized the usability specification table and formed a UX metric table. Each row in the table is called a "UX metric" [41]. The first three columns are about the work role used by the user experience indicator, the relevant user type, the relevant user experience goal, and the user experience measurement, followed by the measurement content,

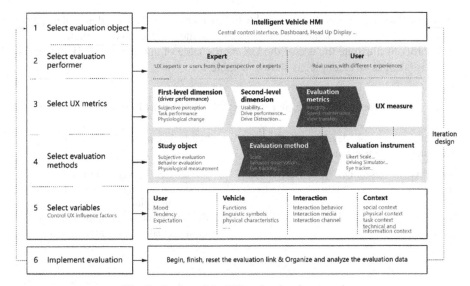

Fig. 3. Design of the UX evaluation framework.

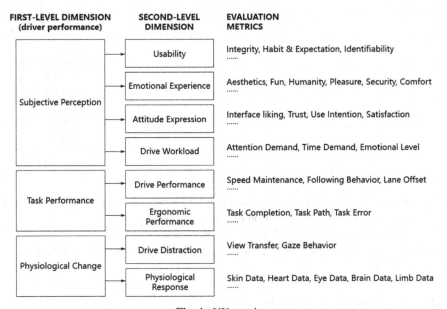

Fig. 4. UX metrics.

method, and the obtained value. In order to make the UX metric table applicable to the evaluation of automobile HMI, the UX metric table in the automobile field is constructed based on the dimension division of the UX metrics for automobile HMI in Sect. 2.3. An evaluation metric can obtain multiple data through different measurement methods. These data can be seen as the content of measurement methods in operation, which is called operation definition. In the actual test, it is appropriate to consider which type of evaluation measure and method are appropriate for the given evaluation metric.

In order to illustrate the use of the UX metric table of automobile HMI, "identifiability" is taken as an example, as shown in Table 1.

Table 1. UX metric table (taking "identifiability" as an example).

First-level dimension	Second-level dimension	Evaluation metric	Metric definition	Operation definition
Subjective perception	Usability	identifiability	The degree to which the system output is easy for users to view and identify during actual operation	During the task, do you think the relevant information or functions you need are easy to find?
				Can users quickly find common key information (such as air conditioning information, time, etc.)?
				Is there enough contrast between interactive content and non-interactive content?
				...

First-level dimension: the performance of participants in different aspects of the test.
Second-level dimension: definition of participant performance.
Evaluation metric: general UX characteristics related to use.
Operation definition: the value obtained from the UX evaluation that represents the content to be tested.

3.4 Component of Evaluation Methods

According to the difference in the research object, evaluation methods can be divided into attitudes and behaviors [38]. In the study of human engineering, it includes both human behavior and psychology, as well as their physiological state. Psychophysiological methods are a way of characterizing mental states by measuring physiological changes through electrophysiological measurement indices. From this, three types of evaluation methods can be determined: subjective evaluation, behavior evaluation, and psychophysiology measurement.

Subjective evaluation: subjective user feedback of fact-based, opinion-based, and attitude-based. This includes evaluation methods such as design walk-through and self-report.

Behavior evaluation: Observation and recording of user activities during the entire use period. This includes evaluation methods such as vehicle monitoring and behavior observation.

Psychophysiology measurement: Measurement of the intrinsic physiological mechanisms of mental activity. This includes means such as electroencephalography, eye tracking, and facial recognition.

Figure 5 lists commonly used evaluation methods in the industry, both inside and outside, and in the literature.

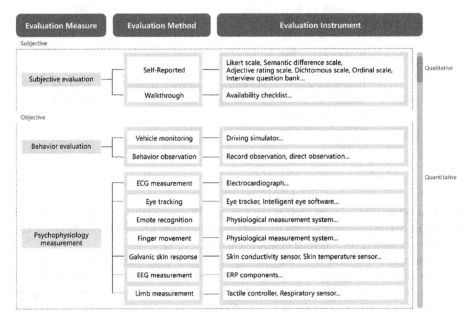

Fig. 5. Common methods for user experience evaluation.

For each metric in the UX metric table, one or more evaluation methods can be employed to obtain evaluation data. Taking " identifiability " as an example, the relationship between evaluation metrics and evaluation method selection is demonstrated, as shown in Table 2.

3.5 Component of UX Influence Factors

The expertise of the evaluator directly affects the accuracy of the evaluation results in a fast-paced design walkthrough. Whether it be laboratory-based or field-based evaluations, it is necessary to determine issues such as the evaluation team, participants, the evaluated prototype, test environment, test tasks, etc. prior to conducting a more stringent

Table 2. The selection of user experience evaluation indicators and methods (with "identifiability" as an example).

Evaluation metric	Operation definition	Evaluation measure	Evaluation method	Evaluation instrument
identifiability	During the task, do you think the relevant information or functions you need are easy to find?	Subjective evaluation	Self-Reported	Likert scale
	Can users quickly find common key information (such as air conditioning information, time, etc.)?	Subjective evaluation	Walkthrough	Availability checklist
	Is there enough contrast between interactive content and non-interactive content?	Subjective evaluation	Walkthrough	Availability checklist
	…	…	…	…

UX evaluation. The relevant factors influencing UX, as identified in Sect. 2.3, should be considered and controlled prior to conducting the evaluation. Figure 6 illustrates the variables impacting the outcome of UX evaluation.

Human. In the human-machine system, the human component is described as the "subject that interacts with the system or product" in the majority of literature and referred to as the "user" from a market perspective. Within a vehicle, users encompass not only drivers who undertake the task of driving, but also passengers who engage in non-driving related tasks. As the intelligence and automation of vehicles advances, drivers are gradually freed from their driving tasks and begin to shift towards a passenger identity. Furthermore, human-machine interactions outside the vehicle impact the behavior intentions of other road users, such as pedestrians, cyclists, and other vehicles, and these other road users are also considered as constituents of the user population [42]. The human factor encompasses aspects such as human-factors hierarchy (i.e., safety, efficiency, and experience), sensory organs (size, movement), and social-cultural factors [43] (e.g., demographics, personality, situational factors).

Interaction. The interaction between human and machine is a process in which information is processed and acted upon. According to the human information processing model, the human perceives stimuli through a perception system, processes the information through a cognition system, and reacts through a response system. Machines receive control commands from users through input systems, process and store information, and deliver the result to users through an output system that can be perceived by the

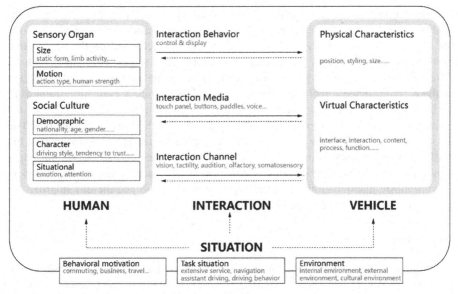

Fig. 6. The Characteristics of UX influence factors.

human. The control behavior of the human and the display behavior of the machine are mediated through a human-machine interface and realized through multiple channels. In researching the factors affecting interaction, it is indexed according to behavior layer, performance layer, and channel layer, based on the different perspectives of human and machine.

Vehicle. The experiences and evaluations of different users for different types of products are diverse. In the design process, not only must the product type be considered, but also the constituent elements of the product. These elements can be differentiated into physical and virtual elements. In physical elements, size, position, and shape all contribute to the hardware of the human-machine interface. In virtual elements, the interface, interaction, flow, and functionality of the software can be evaluated, as well as the overall experience.

Situation. The impact of context on human-machine interactions must consider various factors, including behavior motivation (such as driving vs. parked), task scenario (e.g., general service, navigation, assistance, and driving behavior), and environment (internal, external, and cultural). In evaluating intelligent vehicles, it is also important to consider the effect of automation levels on the user experience.

4   Conclusions and Limitations

The Chinese intelligent vehicle industry has embraced a rare historical opportunity and a golden era of prosperity. The policy environment continues to be optimized, presenting institutional advantages that are not present in many other countries. Standardization of the Chinese intelligent vehicle industry is of great significance, however, the existing

UX evaluation frameworks in and out of the industry cannot meet the needs of high-quality development of intelligent vehicles. On the one hand, UX standards outside the industry cannot be fully applied to the automotive field, and on the other hand, China's automotive industry UX standards are in the initial stages. This paper conducts a literature review, analyzes the factors affecting UX, evaluation metrics, and evaluation methods, and provides theoretical support for establishing a UX evaluation framework for the automobile HMI. This paper also builds an evaluation framework to highlight the relationships among these components. The evaluation method can be applied based on the user type performing the evaluation and the evaluation requirements to evaluate the HMI attributes (evaluation metrics). By applying this evaluation framework, this paper provides a reference for the practical application of UX research, allowing researchers to consciously manipulate them in the experimental process and thereby improve the quality of the intelligent vehicle HMI.

References

1. Key points of automobile standardization in 2022. http://www.springer.com/lncs https://www.miit.gov.cn/jgsj/zbys/qcgy/art/2022/art_b703341da41a49c682a7c878c868dcbb.html Accessed 06 Feb 2023
2. Opinions on Strengthening Management of Intelligent Connected Vehicle Manufacturers and Product Access. https://www.miit.gov.cn/zwgk/zcwj/wjfb/yj/art/2021/art_bf9a399907d94b8c9ac9f79f2045fe14.html. Accessed 06 Feb 2023
3. Yang, Z., Zeng, J., Huang, X., Lu, Y.: Research on man-machine interface design based on intelligent vehicle. In: Rau, PL.P. (eds) HCII 2022, LNCS, vol. 13314, pp. 276–285. Springer, Cham (2022). https://doi.org/10.1007/978-3-031-06053-3_19
4. Maurer, S., Erbach, R., Kraiem, I., Kuhnert, S., Grimm, P., Rukzio, E.: Designing a guardian angel: giving an automated vehicle the possibility to override its driver. In: Proceedings of the 10th International Conference on Automotive User Interfaces and Interactive Vehicular Applications, pp. 341–350. Association for Computing Machinery, New York (2018)
5. Rezvani, T., Driggs-Campbell, K., Sadigh, D., Sastry, S.S., Seshia, S.A., Bajcsy, R.: Towards trustworthy automation: user interfaces that convey internal and external awareness. In: 2016 IEEE 19th International Conference on Intelligent Transportation Systems (ITSC), pp. 682–688. IEEE, New York (2016)
6. Tran, C., Bark, K., Ng-Thow-Hing, V.: A left-turn driving aid using projected oncoming vehicle paths with augmented reality. In: Proceedings of the 5th international conference on automotive user interfaces and interactive vehicular applications, pp. 300–307. Association for Computing Machinery, New York (2013)
7. Politis, I., Brewster, S., & Pollick, F.: Language-based multimodal displays for the handover of control in autonomous cars. In: Proceedings of the 7th international conference on automotive user interfaces and interactive vehicular applications, pp. 3–10. Association for Computing Machinery, New York (2015)
8. Carmona, J., Guindel, C., Garcia, F., de la Escalera, A.: EHMI: review and guidelines for deployment on autonomous vehicles. Sensors 21(9), 1–21 (2021)
9. Wang, L., Zhong, L.: Human Engineering, 1st edn. Hunan University Publisher, Hunan (2011)
10. Bengler, K., Rettenmaier, M., Fritz, N., Feierle, A.: From HMI to HMIs: towards an HMI framework for automated driving. Information 11(2), 1–17 (2020)
11. Tan, Z., et al.: Human–machine interaction in intelligent and connected vehicles: a review of status quo, issues, and opportunities. IEEE Trans. Intell. Transp. Syst. 23(9), 13954–13975 (2021)

12. Olaverri-Monreal, C., Hasan, A.E., Bulut, J., Körber, M., Bengler, K.: Impact of in-vehicle displays location preferences on drivers' performance and gaze. IEEE Trans. Intell. Transp. Syst. **15**(4), 1770–1780 (2014)

13. Lau, M., Jipp, M., Oehl, M.: One solution fits all? Evaluating different communication strategies of a light-based external human-machine interface for differently sized automated vehicles from a pedestrian's perspective. Accid. Anal. Prev. **171**, 106641 (2022)

14. Dey, D., et al.: Taming the eHMI jungle: A classification taxonomy to guide, compare, and assess the design principles of automated vehicles' external human-machine interfaces. Transp. Res. Interdisc. Perspect. **7**, 100174 (2020)

15. Deb, S., Strawderman, L.J., Carruth, D.W.: Investigating pedestrian suggestions for external features on fully autonomous vehicles: a virtual reality experiment. Transport. Res. F: Traffic Psychol. Behav. **59**, 135–149 (2018)

16. Chang, H., Li, L.: Smart and seamless: investigating user needs and recognition for smartphone-automobile interactive features. In: Krömker, H. (ed.) HCII 2020. LNCS, vol. 12212, pp. 217–229. Springer, Cham (2020). https://doi.org/10.1007/978-3-030-50523-3_15

17. ISO 9241–11:2018(en) Ergonomics of human-system interaction — Part 11: Usability: Definitions and concepts. https://www.iso.org/obp/ui/#iso:std:iso:9241:-11:ed-2:v1:en. Accessed 06 Feb 2023

18. Norman, D., Miller, J., Henderson, A.: What you see, some of what's in the future, and how we go about doing it: HI at Apple Computer. In: Conference companion on Human factors in computing systems, p. 155. ACM Press, New York (1995)

19. Berni, A., Borgianni, Y.: Making order in user experience research to support its application in design and beyond. Appl. Sci. **11**(15), 6981 (2021)

20. Hassenzahl, M., Tractinsky, N.: User experience-a research agenda. Behav. Inf. Technol. **25**(2), 91–97 (2006)

21. Forlizzi, J., Ford, S.: The building blocks of experience: an early framework for interaction designers. In: Proceedings of the 3rd conference on Designing interactive systems: processes, practices, methods, and techniques, pp. 419–423. Association for Computing Machinery, New York (2000)

22. Roto, V., Law, E.L.C., Vermeeren, A., Hoonhout, J.: 10373 Abstracts Collection--Demarcating User eXperience. In: Dagstuhl Seminar Proceedings. Taylor & Francis, London (2011)

23. Voinescu, A., Morgan, P.L., Alford, C., Caleb-Solly, P.: The utility of psychological measures in evaluating perceived usability of automated vehicle interfaces–a study with older adults. Transport. Res. F: Traffic Psychol. Behav. **72**, 244–263 (2020)

24. García-Díaz, J.M., García-Ruiz, M.A., Aquino-Santos, R., Edwards-Block, A.: Evaluation of a driving simulator with a visual and auditory interface. In: Collazos, C., Liborio, A., Rusu, C. (eds.) Human Computer Interaction, LNCS, vol. 8278, pp. 131–139. Springer, Cham (2013)

25. Lewis, J.R.: The system usability scale: past, present, and future. Int. J. Hum. Comput. Inter. **34**(7), 577–590 (2018)

26. Albers, D., et al.: Usability evaluation—advances in experimental design in the context of automated driving human–machine interfaces. Information **15**(5), 240 (2020)

27. Detjen, H., Salini, M., Kronenberger, J., Geisler, S., Schneegass, S.: Towards transparent behavior of automated vehicles: design and evaluation of HUD concepts to support system predictability through motion intent communication. In: Proceedings of the 23rd International Conference on Mobile Human-Computer Interaction, pp. 1–12. Association for Computing Machinery, New York (2021)

28. Holländer, K., Colley, A., Mai, C., Häkkilä, J., Alt, F., Pfleging, B.: Investigating the influence of external car displays on pedestrians' crossing behavior in virtual reality. In: Proceedings of the 21st International Conference on Human-Computer Interaction with Mobile Devices and Services, pp. 1–11. Association for Computing Machinery, New York (2019)

29. Riegler, A., Aksoy, B., Riener, A., Holzmann, C.: Gaze-based interaction with windshield displays for automated driving: impact of dwell time and feedback design on task performance and subjective workload. In: 12th International Conference on Automotive User Interfaces and Interactive Vehicular Applications, pp. 151–160. Association for Computing Machinery, New York (2020)
30. Xu, J., Chen, J., Liu, Z.: Research on active interaction and user experience of community intelligent vehicle system. In: 2021 International Symposium on Artificial Intelligence and its Application on Media (ISAIAM), pp. 43–50. IEEE (2021)
31. Su, Y., Tan, Z., Dai, N.: Changes in usability evaluation of human-machine interfaces from the perspective of automated vehicles. In: Ahram, T.Z., Falcão, C.S. (eds.) AHFE 2021, LNCS, vol. 275, pp. 886–893. Springer, Cham (2021)
32. Xie, Y., Murphey, Y.L., Kochhar, D.S.: Personalized driver workload estimation using deep neural network learning from physiological and vehicle signals. IEEE Trans. Intell. Veh. 5(3), 439–448 (2019)
33. Weidner, F., Broll, W.: Smart S3D TOR: intelligent warnings on large stereoscopic 3D dashboards during take-overs. In: Proceedings of the 8th ACM International Symposium on Pervasive Displays, pp. 1–7. Associa-tion for Computing Machinery, New York (2019)
34. Sauro, J., Lewis, J.R.: Quantifying the User Experience: Practical Statistics for User Research. Morgan Kaufmann, Massachusetts (2016)
35. Hartson, H.R., Andre, T.S., Williges, R.C.: Criteria for evaluating usability evaluation methods. Int. J. Hum. Comput. Inter. 13(4), 373–410 (2001)
36. Chen, F., Terken, J.: Automotive Interaction Design: From Theory to Practice, 1st edn. China machine press, Beijing (2022)
37. Vermeeren, A.P., Law, E.L.C., Roto, V., Obrist, M., Hoonhout, J., Väänänen-Vainio-Mattila, K.: User experience evaluation methods: current state and development needs. In: Proceedings of the 6th Nordic conference on human-computer interaction: Extending boundaries, NordiCHI 2010, pp. 521–530. Association for Computing Machinery, New York (2020)
38. Rohrer, C.: When to use which user-experience research methods. Nielsen Norman Group (2014)
39. Naujoks, F., Forster, Y., Wiedemann, K., & Neukum, A.: A human-machine interface for cooperative highly automated driving. In: Stanton, N., Landry, S., Di Bucchianico, G., Vallicelli, A. (eds) Advances in Human Aspects of Transportation, Advances in Intelligent Systems and Computing, vol. 484, pp. 585–595. Springer, Cham. (2017). https://doi.org/10.1007/978-3-319-41682-3_49
40. Helander, M.G.: Handbook of Human-Computer Interaction. Hunan University Publisher, Elsevier (2014)
41. Hartson, R., Pyla, P.S.: The UX Book: Process and guidelines for ensuring a quality user experience, Elsevier (2012)
42. Cœugnet, S., Cahour, B., Kraïem, S.: A psycho-ergonomic approach of the street-crossing decision-making: toward pedestrians' interactions with automated vehicles. In: Bagnara, S., Tartaglia, R., Albolino, S., Alexander, T., Fujita, Y. (eds.) IEA 2018. AISC, vol. 823, pp. 132–141. Springer, Cham (2019). https://doi.org/10.1007/978-3-319-96074-6_14
43. Hock, P., Kraus, J., Babel, F., Walch, M., Rukzio, E., Baumann, M.: How to design valid simulator studies for investigating user experience in automated driving: review and hands-on considerations. In: Proceedings of the 10th International Conference on Automotive User Interfaces and Interactive Vehicular Applications, pp. 105–117. Association for Computing Machinery, New York (2019)

Crowdsourcing Data to Improve Transportation Safety and Efficiency: A Systematic Review

Daniel J. Tillinghast[✉] and Vincent G. Duffy

Purdue University, West Lafayette, IN 47907, USA
`{dtilling,duffy}@purdue.edu`

Abstract. To understand how crowdsourced data is being used to boost transportation safety and efficiency, this study uses bibliometric analysis and data mining tools to draw insights from the body of academic literature regarding prominent authors and sub-topics, while identifying key articles that provide foundational knowledge. Results are shown in the form of descriptive figures created in software tools useful for bibliometric analysis. Insights from these figures and articles found related to the topic present an opportunity for review and reappraisal of the use of crowdsourced data in transportation. A review of recent and well-established literature shows that crowdsourced data represents an emerging opportunity for designers and policymakers interested in improving the safety of transportation systems where technology can be leveraged to uncover data continuously being collected by everyday users through popular apps like Strava and Waze.

Keywords: Transportation · safety · crowdsourcing · bibliometric analysis · Strava · Waze

1 Introduction

As the developed world moves toward initiatives and dreams such as smart cities and connected, safe transportation experiences for all, designers and policymakers are confronted with the pivotal question of how to create and maintain reliable data to promote visibility on emerging systems of transportation. In 2016, over 7 million crashes were reported by police in the United States, causing 2.17 million injuries and nearly 35,000 deaths (Li et al. 2020, 1). Such high statistics demand constant evaluation of ways to improve safety along with other priorities such as increased roadway throughput.

One relatively new method to gain better visibility on the transportation landscape is known as crowdsourcing, which "refers to obtaining data from a group of users who contribute their information via smartphones, social media, or the internet" (Hoseinzadeh et al. 2021, 1). This method represents an opportunity to collect real-time, detailed data in a cost-effective manner that requires no improvements to the built environment or harm to the user. Popular smartphone apps like Strava and Waze offer users valuable services while also providing a way for thousands of individuals to contribute information at once. Data provided by these services can potentially be leveraged to gain insight into any number of issues in transportation today.

© The Author(s), under exclusive license to Springer Nature Switzerland AG 2023
V. G. Duffy et al. (Eds.): HCII 2023, LNCS 14057, pp. 421–435, 2023.
https://doi.org/10.1007/978-3-031-48047-8_28

2   Purpose of Study

This study makes use of data mining and bibliometric analysis tools to identify how the topic of crowdsourced data in transportation is emerging and garnering interest in the general body of academic literature. Using popular academic databases like Web of Science, Google Scholar, Scopus, ResearchGate, and SpringerLink, data is collected for analysis. Tools including VOSviewer, Vicinitas.io, CiteSpace, and MAXQDA will be utilized to visualize trends qualitatively.

3   Procedure

To assess the topic of crowdsourcing in transportation, multiple bibliometric analysis and data mining tools are useful for drawing insights from the current body of literature. Co-author analysis, trend analysis, categorization of leading authors, co-citation analysis, and content analysis will be discussed.

3.1 Assessing Emergence

To begin to understand what is being written about the topic in the literature, searches in SpringerLink's database and Clarivate's Web of Science were conducted to uncover any articles of cursory interest. Without applying restrictions on a keyword search for "crowdsourcing transportation", 349 documents were found, including one from the Stevens Institute of Technology in New Jersey explaining how "mobile and embedded technology provides unique opportunities for crowdsourcing platforms to gather more user data for making data-driven decisions" for transportation systems, with applications such as "infrastructure health, navigation pathways, and congestion management" (Lucic et al. 2020, 1). This article is helpful for understanding how crowdsourced data in general is used, but it lacks a focus on safety engineering. Narrowing down the search to using the keywords "transportation crowdsourced data safety" is helpful for boosting that cursory understanding, though this search reveals just 57 documents from Web of Science. The first result shows a document from Texas A&M University titled "Rethinking Highway Safety Analysis by Leveraging Crowdsourced Waze Data", which discusses the limitations of using police crash reports to understand traffic crash data, proposing that data be supplemented with user reports from the popular mapping app, Waze, (Li et al. 2020, 1). The article discusses the challenges of using data from a wide base of users, especially when it comes to managing redundancy.

Using ResearchGate, it was discovered that one of the authors of this publication, Bahar Dadashova, has been active in the area of transportation safety. In 2021, she helped author a study with colleague Xiao Li aimed at leveraging "crowdsourcing solution[s] to identify high-risk highway segments by analyzing driving jerks," which "represent abrupt changes of acceleration, which have been shown to be closely related to traffic risks" (Li et al. 2021, 1). This work begins to cover the applications of crowdsourced data in pinpointing areas of greatest risk on American highways, offering decision makers reliable data as they consider best practices for reducing crash risk.

In general, the fact that these articles are recent suggests that the use of crowd-sourced data to improve transportation safety is an emerging area in the fields of computer science and human factors and ergonomics. However, the challenge of gathering transportation data for transportation accident investigation is by no means a new one. In Patrick Dempsey's chapter on that very topic in the *Handbook of Human Factors and Ergonomics, Fourth Edition*, he notes that "Although administrative data can provide insights into accidents, the data can be of variable quality, particularly narratives" (2012, 1087). As Li, et al. note, issues like underreporting of crashes that cause minimal property damage tend not to be reported, skewing the data in a significant manner (2020, 1).

3.2 Data Collection

From the outset, direct searches on the topic of crowdsourcing and transportation safety garner very few results from Web of Science and the Scopus database from Elsevier, which will both be used for further analysis in this report. Searching "transportation crowdsourced data safety" yields just 57 results in Web of Science and 36 in Scopus. Such a low number of results would not normally be expected to describe a topic that is increasing in relevance and significance, but the articles already mentioned to seem to indicate that the use of crowdsourced data is a topic of interest and relevance even if the academic literature may not yet be expansive in the topic.

One potential reason for this dissonance is the fact that the use of crowdsourced data is a very specific method. Kankanamge et al. reference crowdsourcing as "a type of participative online activity in which an individual, institution or company proposes to a group of individuals of varying knowledge, heterogeneity and number, via a flexible open call voluntary undertaking of a task" (2019, 3). The task outsources data collection to the crowd, which for the specific application of safety in transportation, seems to be a relatively new concept.

Regardless, a relative dearth of articles need not invalidate the emergence of the topic at large. In fact, the low yet generally increasing number of articles would befit an emerging area in the literature.

In the end, a variety of databases were used to reduce the negative effects of any one database's breadth limitations. In both Web of Science and Scopus, both the searches aforementioned and more general searches using variations of the words "transportation" and "crowdsourcing" yielded more general results but still offered articles that were helpful for understanding the topic. Using Harzing's Publish or Perish software to search the Google Scholar database, it was easy to find 500 articles, and SpringerLink returned over 3,000 documents (n.d.). Each of these database searches lends credibility to the topic where the Scopus and Web of Science searches may have indicated low academic interest in the topic (Table 1).

Table 1. Summary of keyword searches conducted to extract data in support of analyses presented in this study.

Database	Search Keywords	Search Settings	Number of Articles
SpringerLink	"crowdsourcing transportation safety"	Year > 2010	3,217
Web of Science	"crowdsourcing transportation"	None	349
Web of Science	"transportation crowdsourced data safety"	None	57
Scopus	"transportation crowdsourced"	None	294
Scopus	"transportation crowdsourced data safety"	None	36
Harzing Google Scholar Search	"human automation control transportation"	None	500
National Science Foundation Award Search	"crowdsourcing transportation safety"	None	3,000

4   Results and Discussion

4.1   Identification of Emergence

Before digging into more detailed bibliometric analysis, trends of authorship and measures of engagement with the public can offer helpful context for understanding the topic.

While the analysis of crowdsourced data is not an activity that many individuals will engage with, thousands already provide the data to make these analyses possible, and the concept of crowdsourcing is not limited to simple data collection. It is common knowledge that transportation services like Uber rely on the contributions of many for their sustained success. Using the Twitter data mining service from Vicinitas.io, it is possible to understand the popularity of a topic with the general public, as detailed in Fig. 1. Using a Twitter search, Vicinitas scrapes the site for text and rich content, showing key measures of engagement (Vicinitas n.d.). Figure 1 shows Vicinitas engagement measures extracted from a search for the keywords "crowdsourcing data".

The word cloud in Fig. 2 shows expected terms like "crowdsourcing" and "data", but also shows "analytics", "ai", and "model" as common as well. "Participation" also underlies the fact that crowdsourcing is a voluntary activity for users involved.

Though just 139 posts were found from the 7 days prior to the search, they reached nearly 600,000 users. Over one year, the impact of these posts could prove enormous.

138	139	223	578.5K
Users	Posts	Engagement	Influence

Fig. 1. Twitter engagement measures for the keyword search "crowdsourcing data" obtained via Vicinitas.

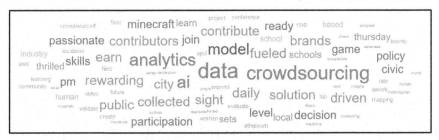

Fig. 2. Word cloud from Vicinitas revealing top keywords discovered in Twitter posts related to the keyword search "crowdsourcing data".

4.2 Trend Analysis

In the Web of Science, Scopus, and Harzing database queries, an observable upward trend in article count exists (Fig. 3). Both Web of Science and Scopus see a drastic increase in article count after 2015 for the more general "transportation crowdsourced" search. Fig. 4 shows the trend by publication year for articles found through Web of Science, peaking in 2021 with 13 articles. In Fig. 5 and 6, a similar trend is seen for Scopus. The more general search peaks with 42 articles in 2021 (Fig. 5), while the more specific search peaks with 11 articles in the same year (Fig. 6).

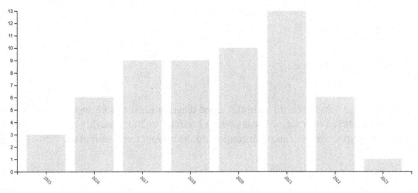

Fig. 3. Web of Science trend by year starting in 2015 for articles found in topic search "transportation crowdsourced data safety. The trend peaks with 13 articles in 2021, but the overall topic in the literature shows relatively increased interest since 2015, suggesting the topic is an emerging area despite the lack of articles published in the past year and a half. This trend covers articles found in the Web of Science Core Collection.

Documents by year

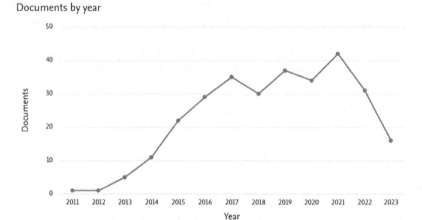

Fig. 4. Article count by year for the search "transportation crowdsourced" in the Scopus database. This search peaks in 2021 with 42 documents, confirming the trend seen in the Web of Science trend diagram.

Documents by year

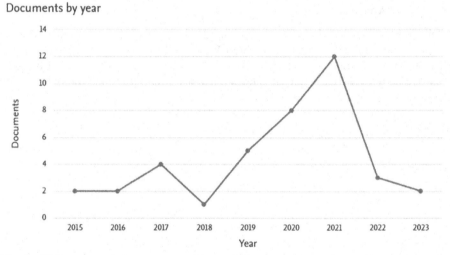

Fig. 5. While more varied year to year, this trend diagram for the more specific search "transportation crowdsourced data safety" peaks with 11 articles in 2021, roughly mirroring the trend from the general Scopus search and also confirming the upward trend seen in the Web of Science trend diagram.

Figure 6 illustrates how the number of authors active in the topic has risen since 2011, when the topic first started to draw attention. The trend moves upward then dips after the peak of 72 authors in 2021, but the general increase in authors continues to support the idea that this topic is an emerging one in the field.

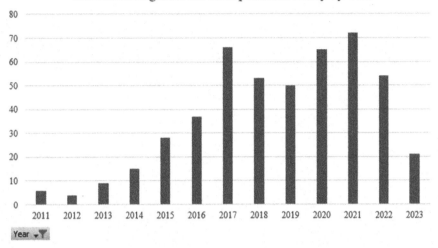

Count of Authors

Number of Authors Publishing Articles Related to Crowdsourcing Data for Transportation Safety by Year

Year

Fig. 6. A PivotChart created in Microsoft Excel to summarize Google Scholar data generated from Harzing's Publish or Perish software. An upward trend in the number of authors publishing articles related to the topic can be noted, with a peak of 72 in 2021.

4.3 Co-author Analysis

Co-author analysis examines how often authors within a certain topic collaborate to publish articles. With the metadata from the Web of Science query, VOSviewer was used to conduct a co-author analysis (n.d.). Setting the threshold minimum number of occurrences (the number of articles on which any two authors collaborate) to four, the result is Fig. 7. Meghan Winters appears with the highest link strength, publishing multiple articles concerning bicycling safety and promoting it using crowdsourced data (Fischer et al. 2022, 556). Her team aimed to "quantify factors that influence the spatial variation in unsafe bicycling across a city" with crowdsourced data as official reports "capture only about 20% of crashes and often lack coordinates, injury outcomes, and narratives needed for understanding where and why incidents occurred" (Fischer et al. 2022, 556).

It is possible to examine authors in the topic by analyzing Scopus search results. In Table 2, one can see the ten authors with the most articles available in the Scopus database according to the query of the topic. This table also features keywords to describe their work in brief detail.

Using the Scopus feature for analyzing search results, authors can be observed in greater detail. Table 2 shows the top ten leading authors by article count from the Scopus query. Their publications' top keywords are also featured. Four of five authors discovered in the VOSviewer co-author analysis also show up in this table.

These authors' work shows a specific interest in bicycle traffic, a popular mode of transportation around the world. Some articles discuss the simple use of apps like Waze

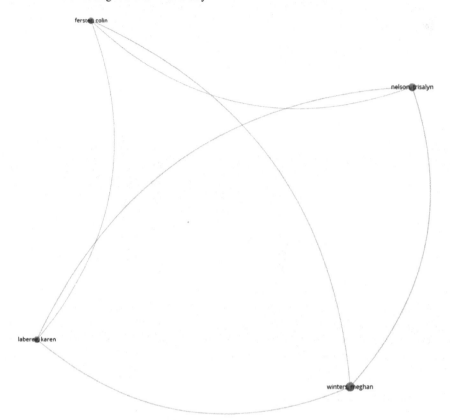

Fig. 7. VOSviewer co-author analysis, which shows the most well-connected authors in the topic and with whom they collaborate.

to discover insights on traffic speed and the level of service on freeways (Hoseinzadeh et al. 2021; Zhang et al. 2022).

At particular institutions, the topic is of particular interest. Multiple American institutions as well as one in Canada and one in the United Kingdom publish articles related to the Scopus topic search (Table 3).

4.4 Co-citation Analysis

The data from the Web of Science search was also used to create a co-citation analysis. The process of co-citation analysis uses bibliometric metadata from the search to examine if two articles might be found as references on the same third article. In Fig. 8 and 9, it can be seen that Ben Jestico's work in the Transportation Geography is a core work that others have been citing. It uses GPS data from the Strava app to collect ridership data (Jestico et al. 2016).

Figure 9 shows Jestico's article at the center of the co-citation analysis, with others featured in the aforementioned "Leading" table, including Griffin and Winters. The latter happens to be a co-author on Jestico's 2016 article.

Table 2. Ten leading authors, sorted by article count from among 294 documents returned from Scopus search. Each one features three top keywords related to their work.

Author	Years Active	Leading Keywords	Article Count
Nelson, T	2016–2022	Cycle transport, spatial analysis, transportation safety	7
Hong, J	2019–2022	Cycling, crowdsourced data, cycle transport	6
Griffin, G.P	2015–2020	Crowdsourcing, bicycles, nonmotorized transportation	4
Han, L.D	2020–2022	Crowdsourced data, speed, transportation agencies	4
Liu, J	2016–2019	Real time traffics, complementary services, deep penetration	4
Sun, Y	2017	Air pollution, crowdsourced geographic information, cycling	4
Winters, M	2016–2019	Crowdsource, cycling, accident prevention	4
Zhou, Z	2016–2022	Crowdsourcing, localization services, contextual feature	4
Cheng, G	2019	Public transportation systems, resource consumption, traffic congestion	3
Dadashova, B	2020	Crowdsourcing, bicycles, crowdsourced data	3

Table 3. Top five leading institutions from topic search as identified by Scopus among 294 documents.

Institution	Country	Article Count
Simon Fraser University	United States	5
Texas Transportation Institute	United States	5
University of Victoria	Canada	4
University of Glasgow	Scotland, UK	3
Arizona State University	United States	3

4.5 Cluster Analysis

With the analysis of authors and citation strength complete, showing the relevance of the topics, the use of content analysis cannot be forgotten. This process helps to identify which particular sub-topics are of interest for the use of crowdsourced data for transportation safety. A cluster analysis, shown in Fig. 10, is conducted using a program

Create Map   ✕

🔧   **Verify selected cited references**

Selected	Cited reference	Citations	Total link strength ⌄
☑	jestico b, 2016, j transp geogr, v52, p90, doi 10.101...	15	33
☑	griffin gp, 2015, j transp health, v2, p238, doi 10.10...	12	30
☑	hochmair hh, 2019, j transp geogr, v75, p58, doi 10...	8	27
☑	boss d, 2018, j transp health, v9, p226, doi 10.1016/...	8	23
☑	conrow l, 2018, appl geogr, v92, p21, doi 10.1016/j....	8	23
☑	broach j, 2012, transport res a-pol, v46, p1730, doi ...	8	12

Fig. 8. The references that will be featured in the co-citation analysis in VOSviewer. This type of analysis pinpoints articles with the most citations by other articles and determines the strength of the link between those articles and others in the search data.

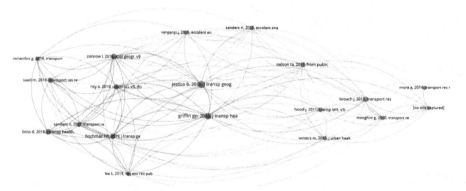

Fig. 9. VOSviewer co-citation analysis, showing the strength and frequency of citations between certain articles found via the same Web of Science search.

called CiteSpace, which creates clusters based on specific sub-topics from the Web of Science bibliometric dataset. The cluster analysis features articles from the entire range of dates as the topic is relatively new.

4.6 Content Analysis from MAXQDA

Having completed the measures already shown, one last analysis was conducted using MAXQDA to create a word cloud to show in a visualize the most impactful keywords from top articles on crowdsourcing in transportation. To complete this task, MAXQDA requires that PDF copies of the articles be imported into the program. Included in the list were the articles already discussed. The summary of a recent NSF grant, which will be explained in Future Work, was also included. One article from the SpringerLink

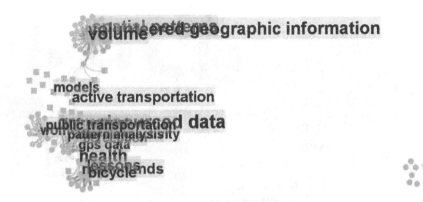

Fig. 10. Keyword clusters found via CiteSpace. Keywords like "active transportation" and "geographic information" suggest that crowdsourcing data functions as more of a system-based approach. The word "bicycle" nods to the many articles that concern cyclist safety.

search was included to show an overview of how crowdsourcing is being used in smart cities. This article shows how mobile crowdsourcing can be used to help citizens find parking spaces, track public transport, view road defects, see gas prices, and even receive location-based recommendations for music to play in the car (Vahdat-Nejad et al. 2022). Lucic et al.'s article was also featured for its discussion of using smart vehicles to better manage city traffic congestion. As suggested by the CiteSpace analysis and Leading Authors table, cycling is an important transportation mode to be improved and analyzed via crowdsourcing methods, so multiple articles surrounding this topic are included. For insight regarding the way that accident data is used, Dempsey's chapter from the *Handbook of Human Factors and Ergonomics, Fourth Edition* was included as it speaks to well-established methods of actually making use of accident data, no matter the method utilized to gather it. Lastly, Guo et al.'s article discussing bibliometric methods was added to emphasize the very tools that are used to complete the analyses in this paper (2020). Using a stop list, unimportant words like definite articles and random numbers were manually taken out of the word list for the word cloud (Fig. 11).

5   Discussion

Going through the analysis of this systematic review, several important themes worth discussing came to the forefront. Examining the top keywords from the MAXQDA analysis, certain terms like "system" were pervasive in all articles, suggesting that a system-based approach is necessary to use crowdsourced data appropriately. This makes sense as crowdsourcing by nature can only exist within a system as the data must come from a broad base of people. Cycling, safety, and traffic and congestion appeared to be of particular interest to authors in the field, so each topic will be addressed briefly in this discussion.

Fig. 11. MAXQDA word cloud output from the articles mentioned in the previous paragraph. Larger words represent more frequent usage in the set of articles imported into MAXQDA. Unsurprisingly, "crowdsourcing" is shown as the most frequent word used, followed by "system" and "use". Words like "traffic", "report", and "information" hint at the applications of crowdsourced data.

5.1 Subtopics of Interest

Cycling. Multiple articles mention cycling as a specific application of crowdsourcing data. According to Daraei et al., "Bicycles offer a promising transportation alternative to private vehicles, especially in areas with congestion, poor air quality, and high fuel prices" and promoting cycling safety is critical to the development of future cities that include a variety of transportation options that are accessible and safe (2021, 1). However, cycling-related accident data can be rather hard to come by, which is where crowdsourced data can earn its keep. Fischer et al. use this kind of data from the popular fitness app Strava paired with injury data from a website for the cycling community to "highlight incident characteristics, road conditions, and infrastructure that impact variation in bicycling incidents and injury" (2022, 566). It can also be used to "improve infrastructure for cyclists and pedestrians" (Sun et al. 2017, 1). Crowdsourced data makes the process of analyzing this transportation niche for safety insights easier for researchers.

Safety. Reports of crashes represent a key source of data for boosting safety on roadways. Crowdsourced data can help boost transportation safety as it "has the potential to fill in gaps in reports to official collision sources" and allows users to transmit data in real time (Branion-Calles, et al. 2017, 1). In an environment where "police crash reports (PCR) have been used as the primary source of crash data in safety studies", underreporting and limitations on the data abound (Li et al. 2020, 1). With very high adoption of apps like Waze, it becomes possible to create visibility on the incidence of accidents in more road segments where they could occur. The data can also be used to direct police officers to areas of greatest need (Flynn et al. 2022, 1). However, studies that use popular apps like Waze to crowdsource data still struggle to integrate this new kind of data into traditional safety analyses. Nonetheless, crowdsourced data has great potential to make a difference in improving safety on the road.

Traffic and Congestion. Perhaps a more traditional approach to crowdsourcing data deals with its use to assess congestion on freeways and within cities. Using "traditional fixed location sensors and cameras is expensive and otherwise unrealistic", and "Traditional intelligent transportation system facilities are typically limited to major urban areas in different states", making crowdsourced data a potential "low-cost solution" for boosting traffic flow and safety. With machine learning available to analyze level-of-service information garnered from crowdsourced data, it is possible to make real headway on understanding traffic flow on stretches of road that would be otherwise overlooked.

6 Conclusion and Future Work

6.1 Conclusion

As a relatively new concept brought on by the advent of widespread personal technology like smartphones, crowdsourcing has created a new and potentially very impactful source of data for decision makers concerned with safety and optimization of transportation networks. From cycling to automotive travel, researchers have increasingly become interested in the topic since 2011, publishing the most related articles in the year 2021. The relatively small number of articles published on the topic suggest that this topic is still in the early stages of emergence in academic literature. However, researchers have already identified areas of great promise for the use of crowdsourced data. Popular apps like Strava and Waze make it possible for academics to study and propose solutions to macro- and micro-level transportation challenges. A system-based approach was discovered to be a very important element of crowdsourcing transportation data as a broad base of users must be able to submit their inputs by sharing the same digital systems. As the field develops, the possibilities and potential impact of using crowdsourced data will likely only grow.

6.2 Future Work

As crowdsourcing for transportation data still represents an emerging area, the National Science Foundation offers new opportunities for funding to study its applications (n.d.). The NSF website offers a search tool to give the public an opportunity to discover research projects that receive NSF grants for their potential to create helpful research. One such grant funded an opportunity for Chunming Qiao of SUNY Buffalo to improve the ability to "collect and disseminate road/traffic condition information accurately, efficiently, and timely" (2017). The project aimed to create a "road sensing system" fed by data from multiple sources such as smartphones, social media, or even connected vehicles of the future. Its impact could prove rather helpful in an array of dimensions. Traveslers, policy makers, and vehicle manufacturers could benefit from "seamlessly integrating the technological and social dimensions" of road information. As such, this project may create core knowledge in the pursuit of quality crowdsourced data collection and dissemination methods.

References

Branion-Calles, M., Nelson, T., Winters, M.: Comparing crowdsourced near-miss and collision cycling data and official bike safety reporting. Transp. Res. Rec. **2662**(1), 1–11 (2017). https://doi.org/10.3141/2662-01

Brauer, R.L.: Chapter 14: transportation. Essay. In: Safety and Health for Engineers. 3rd edn., pp. 375–409. Wiley, New York (2016). ProQuest Ebook Central

Brauer, R.L.: Chapter 3: Fundamental concepts and terms. Essay. In: Safety and Health for Engineers. 3rd edn., pp. 375–409. Wiley, New York (2016). ProQuest Ebook Central

CiteSpace © 2003-2020 Chaomei Chen. CiteSpace: visualizing patterns and trends in scientific literature (n.d.). http://cluster.cis.drexel.edu/~cchen/citespace/. Accessed 2 May 2023

Daraei, S., Pelechrinis, K., Quercia, D.: A data-driven approach for assessing biking safety in cities. EPJ Data Sci. **10**(1), 1–16 (2021). https://doi.org/10.1140/EPJDS/S13688-021-00265-Y

Dempsey, P.: Accident and incident investigation. In: Salvendy, G. (ed.) Handbook of Human Factors and Ergonomics. Wiley, Hoboken (2012)

Fischer, J., et al.: Spatial Variation in bicycling risk based on crowdsourced safety data. Can. Geogr. (Le Géographe Can) **66**(3), 556–568 (2022). https://doi.org/10.1111/CAG.12756

Flynn, D.F.B., Gilmore, M.M., Patrick Dolan, J., Teicher, P., Sudderth, E.A.: Using crowdsourced data to improve models of traffic crash propensity: Tennessee highway patrol case study. Transp. Res. Rec. **2676**(8), 267–278 (2022). https://doi.org/10.1177/03611981221083305

Guo, F., Li, F., Lv, W., Liu, L., Duffy, V.G.: Bibliometric analysis of affective computing researches during 1999–2018. Int. J. Hum. Comput. Interact. **36**(9), 801–814 (2020). https://doi.org/10.1080/10447318.2019.1688985

Harzing, A.W.: Publish or Perish. Harzing.com (n.d.). https://harzing.com/. Accessed 2 May 2023

Hoseinzadeh, N., Gu, Y., Han, L.D., Brakewood, C., Freeze, P.B.: Estimating freeway level-of-service using crowdsourced data. Informatics **8**(1), 17 (2021). https://doi.org/10.3390/INFORMATICS8010017

Jestico, B., Nelson, T., Winters, M.: Mapping ridership using crowdsourced cycling data. J. Transp. Geogr. **52**, 90–97 (2016). https://doi.org/10.1016/J.JTRANGEO.2016.03.006

Kankanamge, N., Yigitcanlar, T., Goonetilleke, A., Kamruzzaman, M.: Can volunteer crowdsourcing reduce disaster risk? A systematic review of the literature. Int. J. Disaster Risk Reduction **35**, 101097 (2019). https://doi.org/10.1016/J.IJDRR.2019.101097

Li, X., Dadashova, B., Yu, S., Zhang, Z.: Rethinking highway safety analysis by leveraging crowdsourced Waze data. Sustainability **12**(23), 10127 (2020). https://doi.org/10.3390/SU122310127

Li, X., Mousavi, S.M., Dadashova, B., Lord, D., Wolshon, B.: Toward a crowdsourcing solution to identify high-risk highway segments through mining driving jerks. Accid. Anal. Prev. **155**, 106101 (2021). https://doi.org/10.1016/J.AAP.2021.106101

Lucic, M.C., Wan, X., Ghazzai, H., Massoud, Y.: Leveraging intelligent transportation systems and smart vehicles using crowdsourcing: an overview. Smart Cities **3**(2), 341–361 (2020). https://doi.org/10.3390/SMARTCITIES3020018

MAXQDA. (n.d.). https://www.maxqda.com/. Accessed 2 May 2023

National Science Foundation (n.d.). https://www.nsf.gov/awardsearch/simpleSearch.jsp. Accessed 2 May 2023

Sun, Y., Mobasheri, A.: Utilizing crowdsourced data for studies of cycling and air pollution exposure: a case study using Strava data. Int. J. Environ. Res. Public Health **14**(3), 274 (2017). https://doi.org/10.3390/IJERPH14030274

Qiao, C.: NSF Award Search: Award # 1737590 - SCC-IRG Track 2: Towards Quality Aware Crowdsourced Road Sensing for Smart Cities (2017). https://www.nsf.gov/awardsearch/showAward?AWD_ID=1737590&HistoricalAwards=false

Vahdat-Nejad, H., Tamadon, T., Salmani, F., Kiani-Zadegan, Z., Abbasi, S., Seyyedi, F.S.: A survey on crowdsourcing applications in smart cities. Stud. Comput. Intell. **1061**, 239–253 (2022). https://doi.org/10.1007/978-3-031-14748-7_14/TABLES/1

Vicinitas. (n.d.). https://www.vicinitas.io/free-tools/download-search-tweets. Accessed 2 May 2023

Visualizing Scientific Landscapes. VOSviewer (n.d.). https://www.vosviewer.com/. Accessed 2 May 2023

Web of Science. (n.d.). https://apps.webofknowledge.com/WOS_GeneralSearch_input.do?product=WOS&search_mode=GeneralSearch&SID=6Fq7F5HAcvLG6mNPgG2&preferencesSaved=. Accessed 2 May 2023

Zhang, Z., Han, L.D., Liu, Y.: Exploration and evaluation of crowdsourced probe-based Waze traffic speed. Transp. Lett. **14**(5), 546–554 (2022). https://doi.org/10.1080/19427867.2021.1906477

The Design of a Community New Energy Vehicle Shared Charging Service System Based on the KJ-AHP Method

Wenjing Wei$^{(\boxtimes)}$ ⓘ, Shihan Tang ⓘ, and RuiSi Huang

Nanjing University of Science and Technology, Nanjing, China
122109223162@njust.edu.cn

Abstract. Based on the review of research methods in the design field, it can be found that the KJ method is heavily used in the information induction stage of user research, but the KJ method has the disadvantage of subjectivity in the clustering process. Quantitative research characteristics of the AHP method through weight calculation can effectively overcome the subjectivity of the KJ method, so the KJ method is combined with the AHP method to form a bottom-up exogenous innovation integration method. In this paper, the method is applied to the research on the topic of community new energy vehicle charging service designs in line with the current era, and outputs a set of service design for community new energy vehicle charging based on user needs research.

Keywords: User research · KJ-AHP method · community charging post · service design

1 Introduction

China's energy structure has been dominated by coal for a long time, and there is an urgent need for a clean and low-carbon energy transition, with "carbon peaking and carbon neutrality" as our goal to meet the changing times. At the same time, the epidemic has accelerated the process of new infrastructure. As one of the important areas of energy transition and new infrastructure, new energy vehicles and vehicle charging stations are facing huge challenges while booming. The location of fast charging stations is an important factor. The charging process requires a long stay of the vehicle, and the fact that the parking space is not in the same place as the charging facility will reduce the user experience; at the same time, charging stations in busy areas will affect the public transportation of the location, and in serious cases will lead to traffic jams [1]. Therefore, it is more reasonable to establish parking spaces with public charging service capability in residential communities and commercial centers, shopping markets, cultural and sports service centers, etc., which is also the development direction of charging pile system construction.

© The Author(s), under exclusive license to Springer Nature Switzerland AG 2023
V. G. Duffy et al. (Eds.): HCII 2023, LNCS 14057, pp. 436–449, 2023.
https://doi.org/10.1007/978-3-031-48047-8_29

2   Methodological Overview and Integration of Innovation

2.1   Overview of Research Methods

In domestic and international research, the KJ method is mostly used in the design field (see Fig. 1), but its application is limited to the combing and summarizing of information and extraction, and other methods are needed for follow-up research to ensure the rigor of the study [2]. The AHP method is mostly used in information evaluation (see Fig. 2), and can also be combined with various methods to improve the accuracy of user requirements research [3]. The AHP method is used in information assessment as shown in Fig. 2, and can also be combined with multiple methods to improve the accuracy of user needs research [4].

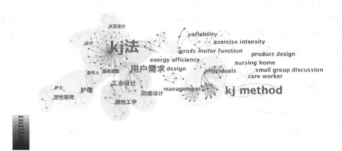

Fig. 1. Visual analysis of KJ method literature review

Fig. 2. Visual analysis of literature review by AHP method

2.2   Integration of Innovation

There has been no research that combines the KJ method with the AHP method in the design of community charging services. This study extends the scope of application of the theory while providing innovative design ideas for community charging service design. The KJ method is used to integrate a list of user needs, and then the AHP hierarchical analysis method is used to quantify the user needs, obtain a ranking of the weight of the needs, and determine the key factors affecting the charging experience of community tram users. We propose an innovative design method for a community charging app that integrates KJ and AHP methods with user needs as the starting point (see Fig. 3). The integrated innovation design method is divided into three main steps:

Target User Research and Demand Summary. This phase identifies the target users, obtains the original needs of users through questionnaire research and focus interviews, then analyzes the target users' behavior by combining the results of user research, and summarizes the needs of users by using the KJ method after deep excavation, and hierarchizes the needs [5].

User Needs Analysis. In this stage, the hierarchical analysis method will be used to quantify the summarized user requirements, construct a recursive hierarchical model and requirement judgment matrix according to the requirement hierarchy obtained by the KJ method, and then carry out weight calculation and ranking to establish a user requirement unfolding table to lay the foundation for the community charging stake APP design practice [6].

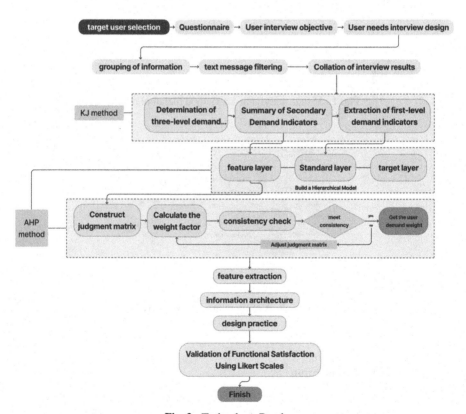

Fig. 3. Technology Roadmap

Design Analysis of Important Demand Indicators. From the perspective of user needs, we explore the community charging post service and ensure the one-to-one correspondence between needs and functions by adding and deleting functions. Finally, the first seven high-weighted demand points derived from the AHP method are used as the evaluation dimensions of the APP, and users are invited to try it and fill in the experience perception questionnaire, and a 5-graded LIKERT scale is used for statistical scoring, with -2 ("unsatisfactory") to $+2$ ("satisfactory") to measure whether the users are satisfied with the final effect of the charging post APP design.

3 Research on the Design of a Community New Energy Vehicle Shared Charging Service System Based on the KJ-APH Method

3.1 User Requirements Acquisition and Analysis

To understand the real scenes and processes of tram users' charging and to uncover potential problems hidden under the questionnaire data, this study adopted the real-world interview method and conducted in-depth interviews with the target user group to provide the basis for the subsequent charging process and user behavior analysis [7]. The interview outline is divided into three parts: the first part is the basic background information of users, the second part is the attitude towards trams and charging APP, and the third part is the charging needs of users in a community scenarios to understand the real scenarios and specific behaviors of users in the community charging process [8]. In this interview, to ensure the accuracy of the data, the identity of the interviewees was restricted, and the interviewees were 10 deep tram users. At the end of the interviews, the data information from the user feedback was summarized and organized based on the interview transcripts and conversation recordings.

Based on the results of the preliminary user research and analysis, the KJ method was used to organize the user requirements and make a detailed division. First, the user requirements were initially organized into efficient and simple processes, clear charging information, and complete maintenance services. Then, based on the user requirement data, the required items are converted into user requirement descriptions by combining the preliminary research and analysis to express them in a more specific way [9]. Finally, the user requirement hierarchy was organized into a summary table (see Fig. 4).

3.2 Quantification and Importance Analysis of User Needs

To make the results more objective, 15 users with in-depth experience in trolley charging and 5 designers were selected as decision makers in this study, and the indicators of each demand pain point were compared between two, and each element in the hierarchy was assigned a value, and a judgment matrix was constructed concerning the scale values

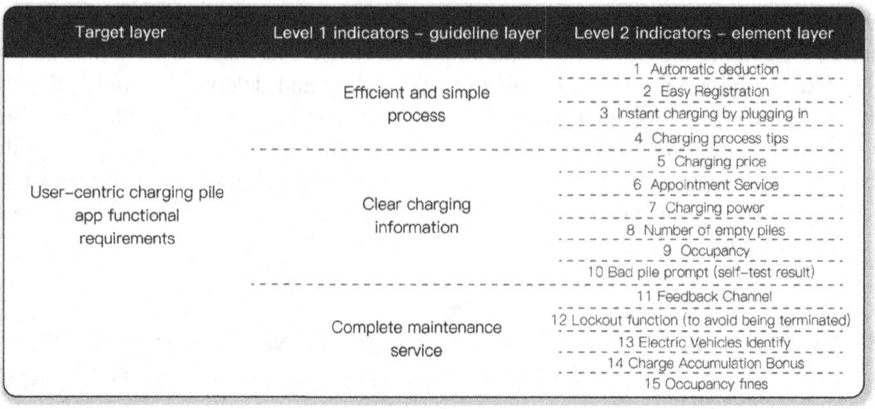

Target layer	Level 1 indicators – guideline layer	Level 2 indicators – element layer
User–centric charging pile app functional requirements	Efficient and simple process	1 Automatic deduction
		2 Easy Registration
		3 Instant charging by plugging in
		4 Charging process tips
	Clear charging information	5 Charging price
		6 Appointment Service
		7 Charging power
		8 Number of empty piles
		9 Occupancy
		10 Bad pile prompt (self–test result)
	Complete maintenance service	11 Feedback Channel
		12 Lockout function (to avoid being terminated)
		13 Electric Vehicles Identify
		14 Charge Accumulation Bonus
		15 Occupancy fines

Fig. 4. User Needs Hierarchy

of 1–9 [10]. After obtaining the comparison results of each expert, the geometric mean was taken to obtain the total relative importance of the comparison results [11]. To avoid scoring experts from having cognitive errors about the same thing to the extent that the scoring of the judgment matrix appears self-contradictory, it is necessary to conduct consistency tests on the judgment matrix, and the final calculation results show that the CR value of the criterion layer is 0.034 less than 0.1, which indicates that the matrix of the judgment criterion layer is consistent. The weights of each index in the criterion layer are reasonable and valid (see Table 1).

Table 1. Weights of each indicator in the target layer

Indicator	Efficient and simple process	Clear charging information	Complete maintenance services
weight	0.353	0.330	0.317

According to the calculation process of the AHP method to calculate the weights of each index of the element layer and consistency test, according to the calculated process efficient and simple, charging information clear and maintenance services complete under the element layer index consistency CR values are 0.002, 0.005, 0.006, these CR values are less than 0.1, proving that the judgment matrix has consistency.

According to the results of weight calculation, the ranking of user demand priority in the design process of the community's new energy vehicle shared charging service system (see Fig. 5).

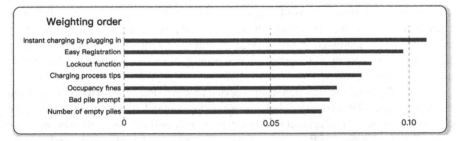

Fig. 5. User Needs Hierarchy

4 Design Practice of Community New Energy Vehicle Shared Charging Service System

4.1 Service System Construction

The service system diagram shows the interconnection of the components of the service system and the internal flow of information, money, services, and materials [12]. The diagram can sort out the key information about the purpose, rights, and interests, and demand nodes among users, public charging piles, charging operators, charging providers, and community properties (see Fig. 6).

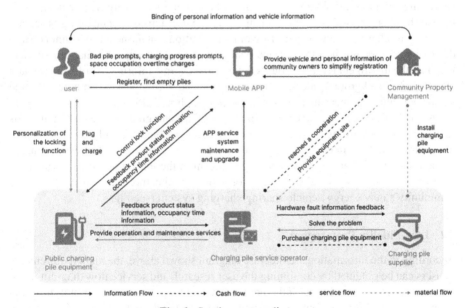

Fig. 6. Service system diagram

Among the user requirements studied in the previous section, the top seven items in the weighting order are taken as the requirement solution objects in this study, so the seven service requirements of plug-and-charge, simple registration, lock function, charging process prompt, occupancy charge, bad pile prompt, and the number of empty piles need to be addressed in this service system. The following section will mainly elaborate on the system relationship of each primary service stakeholder in the line of user usage process.

Before charging, the first step of the service process, users put forward the demand for a simple registration account. In response to this demand, in this service system, the community property management provides the vehicle and personal information of the owner for the charging APP, replacing the user's steps of entering complicated identity information, thus simplifying the registration. Secondly, users need to know the status information of community shared charging piles, such as the number of empty piles and bad pile alert information, therefore, the intelligent terminal of charging pile equipment will be directly connected to the cell phone APP for information interconnection [13]. Meanwhile, to ensure the subsequent use of the charging pile service, for the bad pile problem, the information will be uploaded to the webpage of the charging service operator side synchronously, and the background will confirm the fault information and equip maintenance personnel to provide operation and maintenance services.

In charging, to meet the user's plug-in charging function, the charging post equipment built-in induction function, while with the binding of personal information, to achieve the plug-in is automatically charged, pull the charging gun is to stop charging function. Based on this, the personalized selection service of the locking function is provided to prevent others from unplugging the charging gun even when the user is not around the car during charging. In addition, the intelligent terminal of the charging pile device will upload the charging status in real-time and give the user taps on the charging process.

After the charging service ends, to avoid the situation that the next user cannot charge due to overtime occupancy, this service system proposes an occupancy charging service, in which the intelligent terminal counts the occupancy time information of vehicles, and the operation background calculates the occupancy charging fee and communicates the occupancy charging measures to users through cell phone APP.

After clarifying and classifying the functions of this charging service system, it needs to be organized according to the priority of user needs in a hierarchically manner to make the goals of the later interface development more clear. Combining the design concept of the more popular new energy charging platform in the market and the prioritization of users' needs finally results in the information architecture diagram of the Home community's new energy vehicle sharing charging system (see Fig. 7).

4.2 Low-Fidelity Prototyping

According to the information architecture diagram shown above, the main requirements of users can be obtained by combining the user research and service flow diagram in the previous section. Using Figma and other prototyping tools to create the prototype of the Home user-side APP and back-end related interfaces, the designed "Home Community new energy car-sharing charging mobile application interface is based on the latest Ios 16 system for interface design, with the screen size of iPhone 14 as the base size. This is because the current iPhone 14 has better visual effects, a wide range of users, high market retention of a single model, and high visibility of the cell phone manufacturer,

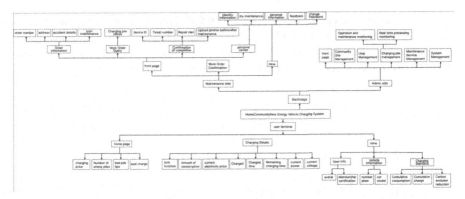

Fig. 7. HOME Community Shared Charging System Information Architecture

based on which the iPhone 14 interface meets the visualization experience of mainstream users [14].

The user's mobile terminal mainly includes four modules: login and registration, the home page, charging details, and my. Meanwhile, the lock screen page can display the charging process in real time, and the app will make a pre-prompt of occupying and moving the car through a pop-up window five minutes before the end of the charging process (see Fig. 8).

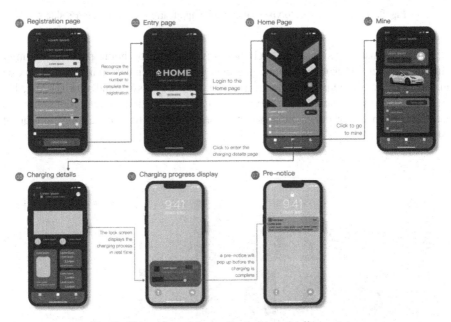

Fig. 8. User-side mobile application low-fidelity prototype

The mobile terminal of the repairer is divided into three modules: home page (charging stake repair management), work order confirmation (repair reply management), and personal me, in which the home page contains order information and work order query entrance, and the corresponding page is accessed by clicking on it (see Fig. 9).

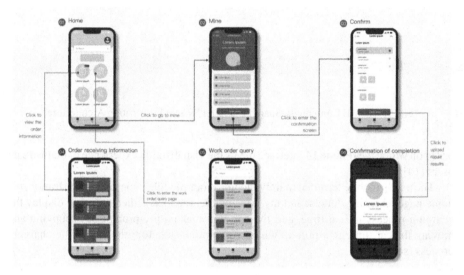

Fig. 9. Low-fidelity prototype of the mobile application on the repairer's side

The administrator side is the web side, divided into the home page, community site management, user management, charging pile management, maintenance service management, and system management, according to the user's demand priority order, this study only shows the maintenance service management function module, containing two interfaces of operation and maintenance monitoring and real-time processing monitoring (see Fig. 10).

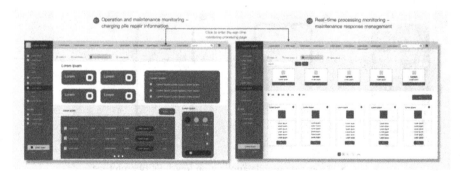

Fig. 10. Low-fidelity prototype of the administrator-side web interface

4.3 High-Fidelity Prototyping

User-Side High-Fidelity Interface. Home Community New Energy Vehicle Shared Charging User App has four basic modules: registration/login, home page (find empty piles), charging details, and personal center in the bottom column of the interface. The interface adopts the current mainstream flat and minimalist design style, and the main color of all sectors is unified, with a bright green color scheme, which is a typical color scheme of calm, innovative, and technological. The monochromatic color scheme is slightly monotonous in the interface design, so the same color gradient and shape modifications are added to it. The gradient blue is at the top of the interface and white dominates the interface, as it is easy for users to distinguish information and highlight important information in the interface. The blue color as the main color at the top of the interface highlights the concept of "environmental protection" and "technology" conveyed by the "Electric Car Sharing Charging Post" app designed in this paper, which can keep the users The blue color at the top of the interface emphasizes the concept of "environmental protection" and "technology" conveyed by the app, which can keep the user's visual effect clear during use and enhance the user's adaptability to the interface.

The theme pictures are interspersed in all walks of life, with the current popular electric car models as the main background pictures. The design of each function module adopts common icons, each icon has its inherent color, and the neighboring icons try to use the color with a large color difference to represent so that the user can remember the system function in color and reduce the user's misoperation when selecting the function operation [15]. The icons of the function modules are colored in light tones to highlight the characteristics of lightness, and create a relaxing experience for users in terms of visual effects (see Fig. 11).

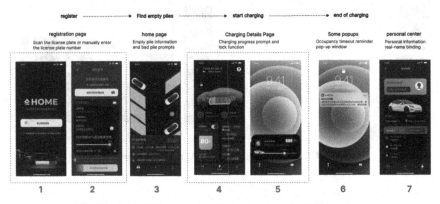

Fig. 11. HOME Community Charging user-side APP interface

High-Fidelity Interface on the Repairer's Side. The mobile terminal of Home Community New Energy Vehicle Shared Charging Repairer is divided into three modules: Home (charging stake repair management), Work Order Confirmation (repair response management) and, Personal My. The specific high-fidelity interface design is shown below (see Fig. 12).

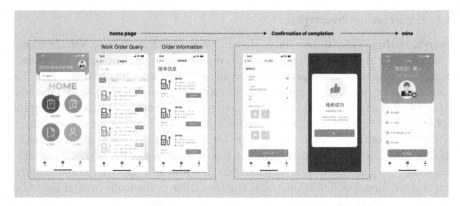

Fig. 12. HOME Community Charging user-side APP interface

High-Fidelity Interface for Administrator-Side Focus Functions. Home community new energy vehicle shared charging administrator side is a web end, divided into home page, community site management, user management, charging stake management, maintenance service management and system management, according to the user's demand priority ranking, this study only shows the maintenance service management function interface. The specific high-fidelity interface design is shown below (see Fig. 13).

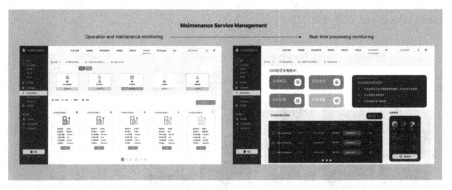

Fig. 13. HOME Community Charge Administrator web interface

4.4 Design Verification and Optimization

The results of the design practice were evaluated for user satisfaction and effectiveness. Since the current service cannot be operated online, this study designed a corresponding questionnaire with interface design, textual narrative, and other elements to explain, and the questionnaire feedback was given to the users of electric vehicles in Xuanwu District, Nanjing [16]. The questionnaire was designed to solicit feedback from users in terms of whether the visual design meets public aesthetics and whether the functional framework meets user needs so that users can give a more intuitive evaluation. The questionnaire was scored on a 5-point LIKERT scale, ranging from -2 ("dissatisfied") to $+2$ ("satisfied"), to measure user satisfaction with the charging pile app (see Table 2).

Table 2. User satisfaction test questionnaire settings

Satisfaction question	Answer options
Is the APP's registration process easy to learn? (Scan to recognize the license plate number or manually enter the number of vehicles to complete the registration)	-2 (very dissatisfied), -1 (not satisfied), 0 (fair), 1 (satisfied), 2 (very satisfied)
Is the number and location of empty piles prominent and clear when searching for empty piles with the help of the APP?	-2 (very dissatisfied), -1 (not satisfied), 0 (fair), 1 (satisfied), 2 (very satisfied)
When looking for empty piles with the help of the APP, is the bad pile prompt clear and prominent?	-2 (very dissatisfied), -1 (not satisfied), 0 (fair), 1 (satisfied), 2 (very satisfied)
Are you satisfied with binding your real personal information and vehicle information to your APP account to achieve "plug in and charge"?	-2 (very dissatisfied), -1 (not satisfied), 0 (fair), 1 (satisfied), 2 (very satisfied)
After charging, is the charging process prompt interface of the APP clear and simple, and key information can be found quickly?	-2 (very dissatisfied), -1 (not satisfied), 0 (fair), 1 (satisfied), 2 (very satisfied)
After charging is completed, does the placeholder charging process provided by the APP help you improve your charging experience?	-2 (very dissatisfied), -1 (not satisfied), 0 (fair), 1 (satisfied), 2 (very satisfied))
Is the APP interface aesthetically pleasing?	-2 (very dissatisfied), -1 (not satisfied), 0 (fair), 1 (satisfied), 2 (very satisfied)

This questionnaire survey received 15 responses, and the score of each question was calculated based on the statistical data, and the average score of each question score was used as the final score of this question, to draw the user satisfaction diagram of this questionnaire survey(see Fig. 14). According to the validation results, the seven key functions and aesthetics of the service system scored in the range of 1.0–2.0, and there were no cases of 1 or less, indicating that most users were satisfied with the design practice of this APP.

Among the eight questions, the lowest score is the occupancy deduction function. After communicating with users who hold low satisfaction on this question, this study proposes optimization measures: extending the user's moving time to 10 min and adopting a phase-time charging standard, where no charge is made during the time provided for moving, and beyond that time, the charge is calculated at RMB2/minute for up to one

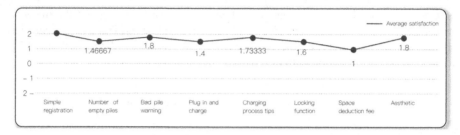

Fig. 14. User satisfaction feedback scores (Self-drawn by the author)

hour, RMB4/minute for more than one hour but not more than two hours, and so on. The maximum charge for occupancy is 6 yuan/minute to ensure that users have sufficient time to move their cars, and also to ensure more efficient charging services for the next user.

5 Summary and Outlook

5.1 Summary

This paper conducts in-depth research on user requirements based on the KJ-AHP method, constructs the functional architecture and visual interface of the community new energy vehicle shared charging service system, and obtains a community charging service system that serves electric vehicle users by satisfying procedural coherence, logical fluency, functional integrity, and user stability. The service system is divided into two parts, the foreground is the user side of the charging APP, the background is divided into the maintenance staff side and the management staff side, and the three parts together constitute the HOME community new energy vehicle sharing charging service system to enhance the user experience.

5.2 Outlook

Due to space and conditions, the paper is deficient in some aspects:

The Data is Limited. Due to the small number of users who use electric vehicles and the limited number of users who participated in this paper's questionnaire and field research, future research can increase the scope of data and the number of research on this basis to ensure a more universal sample.

Low System Integrity. The design practice in this paper is developed based on the first seven items of the weighting of the current user requirement analysis results, and only the key functions in the service system are shown in detail, failing to show the interfaces corresponding to other user requirements. Future researchers can extend more user requirement indicators as research elements to explore more service improvement methods and make the user interaction experience more complete.

References

1. Li, X.: Research on the Design of Charging Pile APP Based on Context-Awareness. Nanjing University of Science and Technology (2020)
2. Tan, X.: Research on Collaborative Governance of Community Car Charging Piles. Shandong University (2022)
3. Chen, L.M., Zhao, C.: Update of service model of Shixing vegetable market based on KJ method. Packag. Eng. **43**(08), 348–357 (2022)
4. Zhu, Y.W.: Design of Ankle Rehabilitation Robot Based on KJ/AHP/QFD. Yanshan University (2019)
5. Yan, Y., Kun, C.: Research on the design of modular construction toys based on mortise and tenon. Design **33**(23), 135–137 (2020)
6. Wang, Y., Yu, S.-H., Lu, L.-S., et al.: Research on user requirement acquisition method of product based on persona. Comput. Eng. Appl. **51**(14), 247–252 (2015)
7. Pang, Y.: Research on Smart TV Interaction Based on Hierarchical Analysis and Task Analysis. Tianjin University (2012)
8. Bin, W.: An expert system for automobile design knowledge evaluation based on AHP. J. Adv. Manuf. Syst. **12**(1), 69–84 (2013)
9. Zhao, Y.: A comparative study on the influencing factors of customer satisfaction between courier locker and courier post based on AHP. Comput. Age **368**(02), 84–86+91 (2023). https://doi.org/10.16644/j.cnki.cn33-1094/tp.2023.02.019
10. Wu, J., Li, T.: Research on the appearance design proposal of dual-use sweeper combined with KJ-AHP-QFD. Packag. Eng. **37**(16), 77–82 (2016). 19554/j.cnki.1001-3563.2016.16.020
11. Yin, L., He, R., Hao, S.: User requirements research based on big data user portrait and KJ-AHP method. Design **35**(01), 82–85 (2022)
12. Wu, M., Song, D., He, Q.: Design and application of reservation charging based on new energy vehicles. Automot. Manuf. **678**(02), 14–15+18 (2022)
13. Sun, X., Wang, Z., Xu, Z.: Design and implementation of new energy vehicle charging service APP. Softw. Eng. **21**(04), 36–38 (2018). https://doi.org/10.19644/j.cnki. ISSN 2096-1472.2018.04.010
14. Zhou, Y.: Research and Design of Android-Based Electric Vehicle Charging Stake APP. Qingdao University (2018)
15. Hemavathi, S., Shinisha, A.: A study on trends and developments in electric vehicle charging technologies. J. Energy Storage **52**, Part C, 105013 (2022). ISSN 2352-152X
16. Glitman, K., Farnsworth, D., Hildermeier, J.: The role of electric vehicles in a decarbonized economy: supporting a reliable, affordable and efficient electric system. The role of electric vehicles in a decarbonized economy: supporting a reliable, affordable and efficient electric system

Artificial Intelligence and Transportations on Road Safety: A Bibliometric Review

Seung Ho Woo, Min Soo Choi[(✉)], and Vincent G. Duffy

School of Industrial Engineering, Purdue University, West Lafayette, IN 47906, USA
{woo44,choi502,duffy}@purdue.edu

Abstract. The topic of road safety modeling by applying artificial intelligence has been aroused in the research field. The purpose of this study was to explore artificial intelligence enhancing road safety using bibliometric analyses. The data sources were collected from three databases: Scopus, ProQuest, and Web of Science. Numerous analysis tools were applied to visualize the trends and get meaningful outcomes, such as MaxQDA, Vicinitas, Scopus, etc. The measures of analysis were shown in five individual analysis results which include content, co-citation, keyword, trend, and statistical analysis. Statistical analysis was performed by ANOVA to distinguish the significant predictors in publication yields with interpretation. The recent trend in artificial intelligence and road safety has increased in the field of research. All analysis and findings are shown in the analysis section. We briefly mention the future work area ideas in various aspects of the study.

Keywords: Artificial Intelligence · machine learning · road safety · transportation · human-computer interaction

1 Introduction and Background

Road safety and human factors are of utmost importance because of the wide-ranging impact that road accidents have on society. Road accidents are responsible for not only the loss of human lives but also for leaving many individuals with permanent disabilities. The economic costs of these accidents are also staggering. The World Health Organization (WHO) has reported that road traffic accidents cause about 1.35 million deaths globally each year, ranking them as the eighth leading cause of death [21]. Furthermore, the economic burden of road accidents is significant. The estimated cost of road traffic crashes is approximately 3% of the Gross Domestic Product (GDP) of high-income countries, and up to 5% in low- and middle-income countries [22]. This significant economic impact makes it essential to develop effective measures to reduce the number and severity of road accidents, considering the role of human factors, such as driver behavior and perception, in road safety. Therefore, it is essential to carry out research in road safety and human factors to ensure that effective measures are developed and implemented to enhance road safety, reducing the number of accidents and saving lives.

S. H. Woo and M. S. Choi—Equally contributed the work.

© The Author(s), under exclusive license to Springer Nature Switzerland AG 2023
V. G. Duffy et al. (Eds.): HCII 2023, LNCS 14057, pp. 450–464, 2023.
https://doi.org/10.1007/978-3-031-48047-8_30

One of the key applications of AI in road safety is through advanced driver assistance systems (ADAS). ADAS uses sensors, cameras, and machine learning algorithms to analyze data from the environment around a vehicle and provide drivers with real-time information about potential hazards on the road. For example, a forward-facing camera and radar sensor can detect the distance between the vehicle and the one ahead, and if the vehicle gets too close, the system can automatically apply the brakes to prevent a collision. [24] Other ADAS features include adaptive cruise control, which automatically adjusts the speed of the vehicle to maintain a safe distance from the vehicle ahead, and lane departure warning, which alerts drivers if they start to drift out of their lane. [25].

Furthermore, AI is also being used to analyze data from infrastructure such as traffic lights and road signs. One of the applications of the AI, Computer vision algorithms can detect pedestrians, cyclists, and other hazards on the road, and provide real-time warnings to drivers. If a pedestrian is detected crossing the road ahead, the system can alert the driver with a visual or audio warning. [23] The other area where AI is being used in road safety is in predictive maintenance systems. These systems use data from sensors and vehicle diagnostics to detect potential issues with a vehicle before they become serious safety concerns [26]. In addition to these applications, AI is also being used to analyze data from cameras and sensors in vehicles to provide insights into driver behavior. This data can be used to identify patterns of behavior that are associated with increased risk, such as distracted driving [28, 29]. By identifying these patterns, safety officials can develop targeted interventions to reduce the risk of accidents caused by these behaviors. Overall, the use of AI in road safety is a rapidly evolving field with many potential applications, as we can see from the publication increases in Fig. 1.

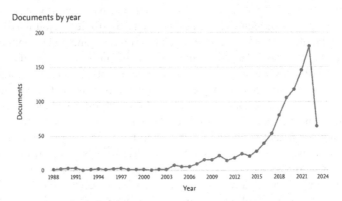

Fig. 1. The number of published papers per year from the SCOPUS search result.

Consequently, there have been many review papers on AI and Road Safety as well. Bhattacharya et al. [12] reviews the techniques adopted for implementing an intelligent road safety system, with emphasis on the behavior of drivers, vehicle condition, road and bridge health, and theft-related issues using RFID, highlighting the role of IoT and AI. Sagberg et al. [14] This study outlines a conceptual framework for understanding driving styles and conducts a systematic literature search to review the state-of-the-art research on driving styles in relation to road safety. Wang et al. [14] examines China's traffic problems, focusing on pedestrian and bicyclist safety and aggressive driving, through a review of 43 Chinese journal articles on road safety. Torbaghan et al. [15] provides a systematic review of the potential of digital technologies, such as AI, Machine-Learning, and IoT, in improving road safety, and highlights a key gap in their effectiveness in real-world environments. Olugbade et al. [16] discusses the potential use of artificial intelligence and machine learning in establishing an automatic incident detection system to decrease road accidents, with a systematic review, focusing on the application of these technologies in road management and safety, as well as the challenges and potential solutions associated with their use. Zheng et al. [17] reviews the use of traffic conflicts as an alternative measure of road safety and identifies conceptual and methodological issues associated with the modeling of traffic conflicts, indicating that more research is needed to address these challenges. Vecino-Ortiz and Hyder [18] reviews the available literature on the links between Bus Rapid Transit (BRT) systems and road safety and calls for more research to strengthen the evidence on the effect of BRT systems on road safety in low- and middle-income countries. Tselentis and Papadimitriou [19] reviews the AI and ML approaches developed for driver profile and driving pattern recognition, identifying efficient methodologies, and proposing a new framework for combining microscopic and macroscopic driving behavior analysis to improve traffic risk models and the development of applications that monitor drivers in real-time to enhance road safety. However, most of the review papers on AI and Road Safety depend on authors' selections of articles, and focus on one or a few aspects of factors that affect road safety.

In our study, utilizing computer-aided software, we conducted a *bibliometric* literature review in AI and Road Safety., and provided insights on the history and the trends of the previous research. At the best of the authors' knowledge, this is the first *bibliometric* literature review in this research area. The use of bibliometric analysis for various purposes, such as identifying emerging trends in article and journal performance, exploring collaboration patterns and research constituents, and understanding the intellectual structure of a particular field in the existing literature. This type of analysis deals with large and objective data sets, such as the number of citations and publications or the occurrences of keywords and topics. Interpretations of the data often involve both objective and subjective evaluations established through informed techniques and procedures. Bibliometric analysis is useful for deciphering and mapping the accumulated scientific knowledge and nuances of established fields, making sense of unstructured data in rigorous ways. Well-conducted bibliometric studies can provide a solid foundation for advancing a field by helping scholars gain an overview, identify knowledge gaps, derive novel ideas for investigation, and position their intended contributions to the field. The tools of the bibliometric analysis we have used were Scopus, Web of Science (WoS), ProQuest, Harzing software [27], VOSViewer co-citation software [30], MAXQDA [31], and further.

The rest of this paper is organized in the following manner: Sect. 2 of this paper elaborates on the details of our literature review methodology, which involves the use of several software tools to extract, analyze, and organize relevant research papers from a vast database. We will discuss the advantages of using these tools and how they helped us streamline the literature review process. In Sect. 3, we present the results of our analysis, highlighting the most commonly used methodologies and techniques in the field of road safety research, as well as identifying research gaps and areas for further investigation. Lastly, in Sect. 4, we summarize our findings, provide insights into the current state of research on AI and road safety, and offer concluding remarks on the importance of continued research in this area.

2 Procedures

2.1 Data Collection

Initial data sources were acquired from multiple resource databases, including Web of Science, Scopus, and ProQuest. The search process was conducted by Harzing's Publish or Perish software and direct search from the databases. The aimed timeline of the search was 20 years of publications; we set up the timeline as 2004 to 2023, which sums to 20 years. The investigation was done by whole publication counts and publication counts of each year. 20 years of the timeline was set up to visualize and track the trend of publications in the Artificial Intelligence and Road Safety area. The initial search of three databases were shown in the Table 1 below, and the annual publication trends were visualized in the Fig. 2. Furthermore, after collecting the publication counts from each database, significant reference research articles were extracted from the database. In each database, four relevant articles were extracted from the original source to conduct the analysis overall.

Table 1. Keywords search result from three databases

Database	Search keywords	# publications	Time period
SCOPUS	"Artificial Intelligence" AND "Road Safety"	290	2004–2023
Web of Science	"Artificial Intelligence" AND "Road Safety"	1143	2004–2023
ProQuest	"Artificial Intelligence" AND "Road Safety"	505	2004–2023

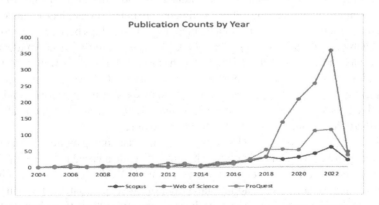

Fig. 2. Publication trends per database per year, from 2004 to 2023.

2.2   Content Analysis

By the initial search, four research articles of each database were collected. Total 12 research articles were applied to perform the content analysis. The content analysis was conducted by the MAXQDA software. The irrelevant words including preposition, article, and pronouns were removed before conducting the analysis. By utilizing MAXQDA software, the word cloud was generated with the most relevant terminologies regarding artificial intelligence and road safety as Fig. 3 shown below.

After generating the word cloud, MAXQDA software was applied to find the most frequent terminologies in the searched articles. Figure 3 below describes the top 10 frequent words from the contents. The most frequent words were vehicles, drivers, systems, detection, etc., in the field of the topic.

Rank	Word	Frequency
1	vehicle(s)	1143
2	driver(s)	831
3	system(s)	913
4	detection	637
5	driving	609
6	road	390
7	image	389
8	data	355
9	traffic	294
10	safety	273

Fig. 3. Word cloud visualization (left) and the 10 most frequent words (right) after removing stop words (e.g. and, is, then).

2.3   Co-citation Analysis

Co-citation analysis is a bibliometric technique used to identify the frequency of citation of two or more documents by other documents. It helps researchers to uncover the intellectual structure of a research area by mapping relationships between the most cited articles, authors, or journals in a given field. Co-citation analysis is used to identify the key concepts and themes that are frequently discussed in a field, as well as to identify the most influential works and authors in that field. In this study, we used two softwares, VOS Viewer and Citespace, for a co-citation analysis. Furthermore, we conducted a keyword analysis on the same list of articles using VOS Viewer. For the analysis, we used 290 articles sourced from SCOPUS search results.

VOS Viewer is a software tool for constructing and visualizing bibliometric networks. It uses various clustering and mapping techniques to create a visual representation of the co-citation network. In our co-citation analysis using VOS Veiwer, we set the minimum citation count parameter as 2, and in total 87 out of 290 papers satisfied this threshold. However, most of the 87 are singleton clusters, and only 23 of them belong to non-singleton clusters (i.e. connected to one or more articles). Figure 4 shows results of the co-citation analysis in the form of the network visualization and the density visualization.

There are in total four clusters detected: namely, cluster 1 for reds, cluster 2 for greens, cluster 3 for blues, and cluster 4 for yellows. The two-to-three articles of the most link strengths from each cluster are provided in the Table 2.

Cluster 1 is characterized as spatial analysis in accident hotspot identification using data-driven methodology. Both of the articles are published in the journal called Accident Analysis & Prevention. Cluster 2 is characterized as the fundamentals of neural networks. Both of the papers provide a theoretical foundation of deep learning that is the most popularly used methods in AI applications. Cluster 3 is characterized as road artifact detections (e.g. traffic signs) using computer vision-based AI. Lastly, Cluster 4 is characterized as the fundamentals of modern deep learning in computer visions. Both articles in this cluster discuss convolutional neural networks and are highly cited over many AI application domains.

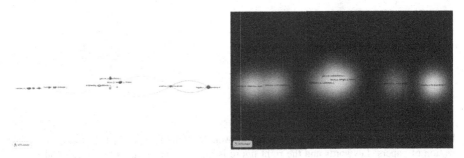

Fig. 4. Co-citation analysis result using VOS Viewer. The left figure is a network visualization of co-cited papers and the right figure is a density visualization of the network.

Table 2. The highest link counts nodes from each cluster (VOS Viewer co-citation analysis).

Cluster	Article	Links count	Link strength
Cluster 1	Anderson. [33]	9	9
	Yu et al. [34]	6	11
Cluster 2	Hochreiter and Schmidhuber. [35]	3	4
	McCulloch, and Pitts. [36]	3	3
Cluster 3	LeCun et al. [37]	6	7
	Gao et al. [38]	4	6
	Mogelmose et al. [39]	4	6
Custer 4	Krizhevsky et al. [40]	9	11
	Szegedy et al. [41]	5	6

2.4 Keyword Analysis

Furthermore, we conducted keyword analysis in VOS Viewer with the same dataset. The results are presented in Fig. 5. Especially, Fig. 5-a shows the result of the clusters analysis, and Fig. 5-b shows the temporal analysis on the keywords network. From Fig. 5-a, we can observe that there are four prominent clusters of risks involved in the road hazards (red), specifications of methodologies used in AI and road safety (yellow), broader categories of various methodologies (blue), and qualitative and systemic point of views (purple and cyan). Looking at the temporal analysis result, we also find interesting evolutions of research topics. In the 2010s, the major keywords are the road safety related risks, and, as it goes to the current time, keywords related to advanced AI methodologies become more prominent. Furthermore, in the very recent keywords (light yellow colors), we can also view the emerging interests in viewing road safety in a bigger context (i.e., the systems); as keywords such as communication, traffic management, vehicular networks, traffic sign detection implies.

Fig. 5. Keyword analysis result using VOS Viewer. The left figure is the basic network visualization of papers' keywords and the right figure is the same network with the temporal feature overlaid. (Color figure online)

Moreover, in Fig. 6, the keyword analysis using CiteSpace is presented. In this case, we sourced the raw data from Web of Science which consists of about 1300 articles, and among them we analyzed the papers from 2014 to 2023. There are three major categories on machine learning methodologies (cluster 3 and 6), on systems (cluster 0, 1, 2, and 8), non-ML human factors research (cluster 7). Interestingly, unlike the keywords research from VOS Viewer, there are no prominent clusters with keywords related to the risks of road conditions itself. However, there are also overlapping areas on AI/ML methodology, and road systems. We believe this is attributed to the years included in the analysis. Due to the technical limitation, we used articles published since 2014 only in CiteSpace, and they includes more AI and system-based analysis, as we can view from Fig. 5, the temporal feature graph.

2.5   Trend Analysis

In the Fig. 7. Below shows the brief trend of the three terms related to the topic which are "Artificial Intelligence", "Road Safety", and "Safety Management System". The analysis was conducted by the Google Ngram Viewer. The Google Ngram Viewer is a tool that exhibits a graph representing the frequency of user-selected words or phrases(ngrams) in a corpus of scanned books available in Google Books. The graph is generated with the publication year in the X axis with the frequency of the ngrams throughout the corpus

Fig. 6. Keyword analysis result using CiteSpace. Clusters are color-coded and titled.

in the Y axis. Researchers can enter the terms in ngrams and modify the case sensitivity, language, date range, and smoothing. [32] Our designated timeline for search was 1960 to current that the trend of the publications were easily visualized.

Using the Scopus database, various trend analyses were conducted. Figure 7 below shows the publication trends of the area of the journal. The top 6 highest appearances in the journal area were Computer Science (29.4%), Engineering (26.7%), Social Sciences (8.5%), Mathematics (8.0%), Physics and Astronomy (4.6%), and Decision Science (4.2%).

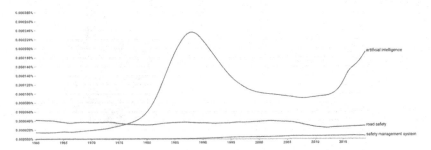

Fig. 7. Bigrams for artificial intelligence, road safety, and safety management system.

The annual trend of publications in three databases (Scopus, Web of Science, ProQuest) is described in Table 3. The highest publication count year was 2022 in all three databases. Furthermore, the lowest publication count year was 2004–2007 in Scopus, 2008 in Web of Science, and 2004 in ProQuest. The annual trend of the number of publications in all databases is growing recently. The annual publication trends in the area of "Artificial Intelligence" and "Road Safety" tracked from the year 1988 to 2023. The yearly publication trends of the research area have been arousing from 2014 to 2022, which is shown in Fig. 1, It can be interpreted as the topic has emerged. As shown in Fig. 8, the most frequent academic journal author of the publications in this area are Zhang J., Taddeo M., Qi D., Szolovits P., Xu W., Yudkowsky E., and Bostrom N using Bibexcel and Harzing software. The top 10 countries in the most frequent publications presented in this field were China (182), the United States (138), India (129), Germany (55), the United Kingdom (51), Italy (47), Canada (36), Spain (35), France (31), and Australia (27) as in Fig. 8. Furthermore, the highest publication count affiliations were Tongji University, Wuhan University of Technology, Southeast University, etc.

Table 3. Annual trend of publications from 2010 to 2023 per database.

Database	Year (20xx)													
	10	11	12	13	14	15	16	17	18	19	20	21	22	23
SCOPUS	6	7	3	6	4	10	13	19	31	24	31	41	61	22
Web of Science	7	7	13	7	6	14	16	23	32	137	208	256	357	47
ProQuest	3	4	1	13	1	7	10	26	53	54	52	110	114	37

To track the hashtags and keywords in social media, the Vicinitas free software was applied. The keyword that we investigated was artificial intelligence and transportation which includes the topic of road safety. The analysis conducted shows word cloud, engagement timeline, posts timeline, types of posts, and the types of rich media in the social media as in Fig. 9.

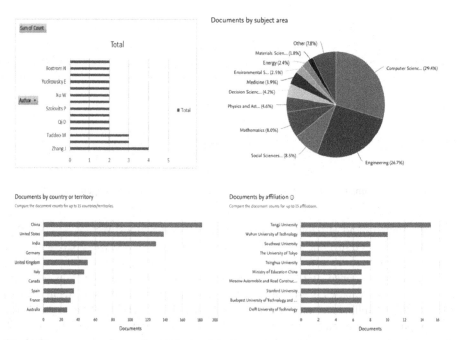

Fig. 8. Frequency analyses of published articles by authors, subject area, country/territory, and affiliation, respectively.

Fig. 9. Vicinitas social media trend analysis

2.6 Statistical Analysis

Statistical analysis was performed by the Minitab software. The analysis was based on the linear regression model. To figure out which predictors are working as a key feature affecting response predictor, the number of articles. The method of the statistical analysis conducted was categorical predictor coding. The linear regression equation of the model is as the following:

$$(\#articles) = 5.4 + 0.0 * DB_{PQ} - 29.3 * DB_{SCOPUS} + 44.0 * DB_{WoS} + 0.0 * Y_{15} \\ + 28.3 * Y_{18} + 125.3 * Y_{21}$$

where DB stands for database and subscripts PQ, SCOPUS and WoS stands for the three databases respectively; Y stands for year and each subscript is for each year.

According to the coefficient table, which is shown in Fig. 10, the year 2021 is the most significant predictor among others by the p-value in the analysis of the coefficients. The p-value is used to determine the significance of the predictors; if the p-value is less than or close to 0.1, the predictor is relatively significant. Additionally, the R-squared value of the linear regression model shown in Fig. 10 is 67.71%, which could interpret the amount of the observed variables in the model. Since the R-squared value is relatively high in this model, it can be defined that the linear regression model did fit well.

Furthermore, the analysis of variance (ANOVA) result also reveals the analysis of the linear regression model, which is shown in Fig. 11. According to the p-value of the ANOVA table, the only significance feature is the Year, whose p-value is 0.149, which is relatively low compared to other features. The four residual plots for the number of

Coefficients

Term	Coef	SE Coef	T-Value	P-Value	VIF
Constant	5.4	47.5	0.11	0.914	
Database					
Scopus	-29.3	52.1	-0.56	0.603	1.33
WoS	44.0	52.1	0.85	0.446	1.33
Year					
2018	28.3	52.1	0.54	0.615	1.33
2021	125.3	52.1	2.41	0.074	1.33

Model Summary

S	R-sq	R-sq(adj)	R-sq(pred)
63.7569	67.71%	35.42%	0.00%

Fig. 10. Summaries of the regression analysis result.

Analysis of Variance

Source	DF	Adj SS	Adj MS	F-Value	P-Value
Regression	4	34094	8524	2.10	0.245
Database	2	8174	4087	1.01	0.443
Year	2	25920	12960	3.19	0.149
Error	4	16260	4065		
Total	8	50354			

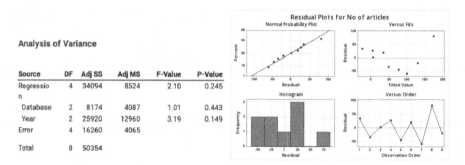

Fig. 11. The summary table of the ANOVA result.

articles are shown in Fig. 11. In a normal probability plot, the data points are aligned with the fitted linear line, which means that the residual number of articles fits well in the probability plot. The versus fits and versus order plot show that those data points are randomly scattered. Lastly, the histogram of the residual is skewed left, and most of the frequency is concentrated on 25 residuals.

3   Discussion

Transportation is an important factor in our daily life everywhere on earth. This, however, also means that we are exposed to the risk of accidents on the roads every day. Due to the expansion of the population on the globe, more vehicles are produced and driven by humans. It directly increases the rate of road accidents and the rate of mortality by accident. Furthermore, when the system of transportation infrastructure grows and becomes more complex, more regulation rules needs to be added to control the transportation system. Thus, it is important for modern society to run the best practices to keep the road safe from fatal accidents. Utilizing Artificial Intelligence technologies that have advanced dramatically over recent decades, we can keep individuals safe on the roads from critical accidents more effectively since the AI is able to model complex non-linear systems such as road transportation infrastructure networks and conditions.

Related to artificial intelligence and road safety, there are various research works conducted in the field. We emphasize the trend of the publications in the area by the bibliometric analysis in multiple resources. Before performing the analysis, we derived the data sources from three databases; Scopus, ProQuest, and Web of Science. We set up the timeline as 2004 to 2023, which includes the recent 20 years period. By comparing the acquired publication counts, the highest number of articles appeared in the Web of Science, followed by ProQuest and Scopus. The publication trends are aroused from the year 2016 to recent years.

The content analysis was performed by the MaxQDA software by word cloud and frequent term search. The word cloud was utilized to visualize relevant words used in the research articles on the topic of the research area. And the top 10 frequent content terminologies are also queried. The most frequent terms in the area were vehicles, drivers, systems, detection, driving, road, image, data, traffic, and safety.

To track the publication trends in various areas, we conducted a trend analysis. Google Ngram Viewer was used to compare the trends of our topic with related topics; "Artificial Intelligence", "Road Safety", and "Safety Management Systems". The artificial intelligence topic has been aroused recently in the research field. Furthermore, we also tracked the leading factors in publication, such as subject areas, authors, countries, and affiliations. Social media hashtags and keywords were also investigated by the Vicinitas software to analyze the trend in public.

Moreover, we analyzed the relationships between articles, using co-citation analysis and co-occurrence analysis of keywords through VOS Viewer and CiteSpace. Through those cross relational analyses we could find the clusters and temporal patterns in publications on AI and Road Safety. The major clusters are related to road environments evaluation/prediction, road artifacts (e.g. traffic signs), transportation systems analysis (e.g. vehicles network), and machine learning and artificial intelligence methodologies frequently used in the field (e.g. computer vision related). We also found that the field of AI and Road Safety is moving toward tackling the problem from a systemic point of view from focusing on smaller tasks, such as road sign detection or accident hotspot detection, which was more popular a decade ago.

Lastly, we conducted statistical analyses using Minitab software to identify the important predictors in the publication trend and to understand the relationships between the predictor(s) and the dependent variable. As a result, the year predictor is the only significant factor among the variables in the search for publications.

4 Conclusion

Artificial intelligence is rapidly grown in the field of research and industry to solve current social problems. Transportation area is also evolving due to expansion of population and vehicles. Specifically, safety issue has been arouse concurrently with the transportation field of study. By utilizing the co-citation analysis results, artificial intelligence and road safety area of research shares the common idea. Furthermore, the trend of both research area continually grows since the leading researchers are publishing research articles actively.

As the research grows in this field, there are several funded works from the National Science Foundation grant research on-going. One research award is titled as "Acquisition of Connected Autonomous Vehicles(CAV) Infrastructure to Support Cooperative Human-Robot Driving and Pedestrian Safety". The research grant #2216489 was awarded to Deepankar Medhi of UNLV Computer and Network Systems department. This project aims to create a "living laboratory" at the UNLV to facilitate research on connected and autonomous vehicles (CAVs) by deploying advanced sensors and vehicle-to-everything(V2X) communication equipment at three intersections adjacent to campus. The project seeks to investigate the cooperative and collaborative aspects of V2X connectivity and to develop AI algorithms that can adapt to different driving scenarios.

In this paper, we employed computer-aided software to systematically analyze the vast amount of academic publications in the field of AI and Road Safety. By utilizing various software tools – MaxQDA, VOS Viewer, CiteSpace, and Minitab –, we were able to identify the research history and trends in this field. Our study provides researchers interested in the field of AI and Road Safety with a comprehensive understanding of the research landscape as well as valuable insights into the future direction of this field.

References

1. Silva, P.B., Andrade, M., Ferreira, S.: Machine learning applied to road safety modeling: a systematic literature review. J. Traffic Transp. Eng. **7**(6), 775–790 (2020)
2. Halim, Z., Kalsoom, R., Bashir, S., et al.: Artificial intelligence techniques for driving safety and vehicle crash prediction. Artif. Intell. Rev. **46**, 351–387 (2016)
3. Barodi, A., Bajit, A., Harrouti, T.E., Tamtaoui, A., Benbrahim, M.: An enhanced artificial intelligence-based approach applied to vehicular traffic signs detection and road safety enhancement. Adv. Sci. Technol. Eng. Syst. J. **6**(1), 672–683 (2021)
4. Taib, R., Tederry, J., Itzstein, B.: Quantifying driver frustration to improve road safety. In: CHI 2014 Extended Abstracts on Human Factors in Computing Systems (CHI EA 2014), pp. 1777–1782. Association for Computing Machinery, New York, NY (2014)
5. Panda, C., Mishra, A.K., Dash, A.K., Nawab, H.: Predicting and explaining severity of road accident using artificial intelligence techniques, SHAP and feature analysis. Int. J. Crashworthiness **28**(2), 186–201 (2023)
6. Abduljabbar, R., Dia, H., Liyanage, S., Bagloee, S.: Applications of artificial intelligence in transport: an overview. Sustainability **11**(1), 189 (2019)
7. Laurell, C., Sandström, C.: The sharing economy in social media: analyzing tensions between market and non-market logics. Technol. Forecast. Soc. Chang. **125**, 58–65 (2017)
8. Rai, A., et al.: Emerging concepts in bacterial taxonomy. In: Satyanarayana, T., Johri, B., Das, S. (eds.) Microbial Diversity in Ecosystem Sustainability and Biotechnological Applications. Springer, Singapore (2019). https://doi.org/10.1007/978-981-13-8315-1_1
9. Carroll, J.M.: Human-computer interaction: psychology as a science of design. Annu. Rev. Psychol. **48**(1), 61–83 (1997)
10. Goerlandt, F., Li, J., Reniers, G.: The landscape of safety management systems research: a scientometric analysis. J. Saf. Sci. Resilience **3**(3), 189–208 (2022). ISSN: 2666–4496. https://doi.org/10.1016/j.jnlssr.2022.02.003
11. Stanton, N.A., Chambers, P.R., Piggott, J.: Situational awareness and safety. Saf. Sci. **39**(3), 189–204 (2001)

12. Bhattacharya, S., Jha, H., Nanda, R.P.: Application of IoT and artificial intelligence in road safety. In: 2022 Interdisciplinary Research in Technology and Management (IRTM), pp. 1–6 (2022)
13. Sagberg, F., Selpi, Bianchi Piccinini, G.F., Engström, J.: A review of research on driving styles and road safety. Hum. Fact. **57**(7), 1248–1275 (2015)
14. Wang, P., Rau, P.L.P., Salvendy, G.: Road safety research in China: review and appraisal. Traffic Inj. Prevent. **11**(4), 425–432 (2010)
15. Torbaghan, M.E., Sasidharan, M., Reardon, L., Muchanga-Hvelplund, L.C.: Understanding the potential of emerging digital technologies for improving road safety. Acc. Anal. Prevent. **166**, 106543 (2022)
16. Olugbade, S., Ojo, S., Imoize, A.L., Isabona, J., Alaba, M.O.: A review of artificial intelligence and machine learning for incident detectors in road transport systems. Math. Comput. Appl. **27**(5), 77 (2022)
17. Zheng, L., Sayed, T., Mannering, F.: Modeling traffic conflicts for use in road safety analysis: a review of analytic methods and future directions. Anal. Methods Acc. Res. **29**, 100142 (2021)
18. Vecino-Ortiz, A.I., Hyder, A.A.: Road safety effects of bus rapid transit (BRT) systems: a call for evidence. J. Urban Health **92**, 940–946 (2015)
19. selentis, D.I., Papadimitriou, E.: Driver profile and driving pattern recognition for road safety assessment: main challenges and future directions. IEEE Open J. Intell. Transp. Syst. (2023)
20. Donthu, N., Kumar, S., Mukherjee, D., Pandey, N., Lim, W.M.: How to conduct a bibliometric analysis: an overview and guidelines. J. Bus. Res. **133**, 285–296 (2021). ISSN: 0148–2963
21. World Health Organization. Global status report on road safety 2018. World Health Organization (2018)
22. Gostin, L.: Traffic injuries and deaths: a public health problem we can solve. JAMA Forum Archive (2018). https://doi.org/10.1001/jamahealthforum.2018.0009
23. Mandal, V., Mussah, A.R., Jin, P., Adu-Gyamfi, Y.: Artificial intelligence-enabled traffic monitoring system. Sustainability **12**(21), 9177 (2020)
24. Kala, R.: 4 - advanced driver assistance systems. On-Road Intelligent Vehicles, Butterworth-Heinemann, pp. 59–82 (2016). ISBN: 9780128037294.https://doi.org/10.1016/B978-0-12-803729-4.00004-0
25. Woo, H., Madokoro, H., Sato, K., Tamura, Y., Yamashita, A., Asama, H.: Advanced adaptive cruise control based on operation characteristic estimation and trajectory prediction. Appl. Sci. **9**(22), 4875 (2019)
26. Katreddi, S., Kasani, S., Thiruvengadam, A.: A review of applications of artificial intelligence in heavy duty trucks. Energies **15**(20), 7457 (2022)
27. Harzing, A.W.: Publish or Perish (2007). https://harzing.com/resources/publish-or-perish
28. Vural, E., Çetin, M., Erçil, A., Littlewort, G., Bartlett, M., Movellan, J.: Automated drowsiness detection for improved driving safety (2008)
29. Arbabzadeh, N., Jafari, M.: A data-driven approach for driving safety risk prediction using driver behavior and roadway information data. IEEE Trans. Intell. Transp. Syst. **19**(2), 446–460 (2017)
30. van Eck, N.J., Waltman, L.: Software survey: VOSviewer, a computer program for bibliometric mapping. Scientometrics **84**, 523–538 (2010)
31. VERBI Software. "Online Manual." maxqda.com/help-max22/welcome
32. Michel, J.B., et al.: Quantitative analysis of culture using millions of digitized books. Science **331**, 176–182 (2010)
33. Anderson, T.K.: Kernel density estimation and K-means clustering to profile road accident hotspots. Accid. Anal. Prev. **41**(3), 359–364 (2009)
34. Yu, H., Liu, P., Chen, J., Wang, H.: Comparative analysis of the spatial analysis methods for hotspot identification. Accid. Anal. Prev. **66**, 80–88 (2014)

35. Hochreiter, S., Schmidhuber, J.: Long short-term memory. Neural Comput. **9**(8), 1735–1780 (1997)
36. McCulloch, W.S., Pitts, W.: A logical calculus of the ideas immanent in nervous activity. Bull. Math. Biophys. **5**, 115–133 (1943)
37. LeCun, Y., Bengio, Y., Hinton, G.: Deep learning. Nature **521**(7553), 436–444 (2015)
38. Gao, X.W., Podladchikova, L., Shaposhnikov, D., Hong, K., Shevtsova, N.: Recognition of traffic signs based on their colour and shape features extracted using human vision models. J. Vis. Commun. Image Represent. **17**(4), 675–685 (2006)
39. Mogelmose, A., Trivedi, M.M., Moeslund, T.B.: Vision-based traffic sign detection and analysis for intelligent driver assistance systems: perspectives and survey. IEEE Trans. Intell. Transp. Syst. **13**(4), 1484–1497 (2012)
40. Krizhevsky, A., Sutskever, I., Hinton, G.E.: Imagenet classification with deep convolutional neural networks. Commun. ACM **60**(6), 84–90 (2017)
41. Szegedy, C., et al.: Going deeper with convolutions. In: Proceedings of the IEEE Conference on Computer Vision and Pattern Recognition, pp. 1–9 (2015)

Sustainable Green Smart Cities and Smart Industry

Smart Cities as Future Internet-Based Developments that Adapt to Climate Change and Which Green the Intellectual Capital of Urban and Regional Innovation Systems

Mark Deakin and Alasdair Reid(⊠)

School of Computing, Engineering and the Built Environment, Edinburgh Napier University, Edinburgh, Scotland
al.reid@napier.ac.uk

Abstract. Many in the academic community find claims made about the virtuous nature of smart cities dumbfounding. In that sense left not only bewildered by the claims which academics make about the virtues of smart cities, but the audacious nature of the expectations advocates of them as developments based on the future internet also harbour. In surveying the foundations of smart cities as developments based on the future internet, this paper shall address the bewilderment over the claims made about the virtues of smart cities by academics and audacious nature of the expectations the IEA, IRENA, UN, WB and WHO now also harbour of them as developments based on the future internet. In rendering both the virtues of smart cities and audacious nature of them as future internet-based developments, the paper shall reveal how cities can be smart in developing the future internet as a basis to meet the social challenge adapting to climate change poses. This shall go some way to close a gap that has opened in the past decade over the foundations of smart cities by reporting on the results of a case-study into the metrics of future internet-based developments. Those metrics that provide smart cities with a system of measurements which link the informatics of digital technologies to data management platforms and connect the infrastructures of future internet-based developments to the management of natural resources. To the management of natural resources as environments that in turn relate the energetic of climate change adaptation strategies to a metabolic which serves to green the intellectual capital of urban and regional innovation systems. Green the intellectual capital of urban and regional innovation systems and qualify whether in meeting the social challenge SDG7 poses this keeps 1.5 alive.

Keywords: Smart cities · Metrics · Future internet-based developments · Social challenges · Climate change adaptation strategies · Intellectual capital · Greening intellectual capital · Urban and regional innovation systems

1 Introduction

Papers on smart city development have proven contentious and left critics of the movement nothing less than dumbfounded as to the claims they make. This paper addresses the polemic on smart cities and responds to the call for an alternative to the corporate

V. G. Duffy et al. (Eds.): HCII 2023, LNCS 14057, pp. 467–480, 2023.
https://doi.org/10.1007/978-3-031-48047-8_31

model of the developments high-tech companies champion. It does this by uncovering the genealogy of smart cities and revealing the evolving body of work which this founds as the basis of the development.

As a critical reflection on the foundations of smart cities, this paper serves to double down on the insights Giffinger *et al.* [1], Schaffers *et al.* [2], Calagilu *et al.* [3], Batty *et al.* [4], Leydesdorff and Deakin [5] and Lazaroiu and Roscia [6] offer into smart cities and what they say about them as future internet-based developments. This turns attention to the stage the future internet sets for the management of natural resources as environments that are wise in meeting the social challenge which the joint 2022 statement from the International Energy Agency (IEA), International Renewable Energy Agency (IRENA), United Nations (UN), World Bank (WB), and World Health Organisation (WHO), make on Sustainable Development Goal (SDG) 7. That goal which targets affordable and clean energy and serves to highlight SDGs 8–13. Highlight SDGs 8–13 in terms of the relationship which affordable and clean energy have to economic growth and the urban and regional innovation system which is needed to service the infrastructures that not only sustain cities, but which also allow the communities inhabiting them to become sites of responsible consumption and production. Sites of responsible consumption and production whose climate actions in turn adapt to sustain development.

Drawing on the Tripel Helix Model (THM) of smart cities advanced by Hirst *et al.* [7] and Kourtic *et al.* [8], the paper begins to close the gap in the metrics of future internet-based developments left by the IEA, IRENA, UN, WB and WHO. This is achieved by drawing on the lesson smart cities such as Manchester, Amsterdam, Malmo, Barcelona and London teach us about the metrics of future internet-based developments (also see, Deakin [9, 10]). Those lessons smart cities teach us about the modulation of the future internet into the informatics of the digital technologies underpinning the developments and data management platforms they in turn support (Hirst *et al.* [7]; Kourtic *et al.* [8]; Deakin, [9, 10]). This modulation of the future internet also serves to highlight the top-level issues surfacing as a basis for the development. With computer science, the top-level issues relate to the digital technologies underpinning the data management platforms and as infrastructures supporting the management of natural resources. The management of natural resources that bottom-out as environments for the engineering of intelligent energy systems which the construction sector installs into the fabric of buildings.

The paper goes on to suggest this is how future internet-based developments ground these digital technologies as data management platforms. Ground them as infrastructures relating to the management of natural resources and environments of climate change adaptation strategies. Climate change adaptation strategies that green the intellectual capital of urban and regional innovation systems. Urban and regional innovation systems which in turn serve to verify whether the informatics, energetic and metabolic this accounts for, qualify the status of future internet-based developments as intelligent energy systems that construct buildings clean enough for the net zero growth strategies SDG7 champions to keep1.5 alive.

2 Claims Made About Smart Cities

Smart city development has proven contentious. Hollands [11], Kitchin [12], Söderström [13] and Vanolo [14], are all dumbfounded by the claims the likes of IBM and Cisco make about them. In assembling what they refer to as a polemic on the entrepreneurial legacy of smart cities that high-tech companies promote, this group of academics refer to the development as something which is more symbolic than real. In that sense, the imaginary of a utopian future, univocal in the singularity of the computer science, digital technologies and data management platforms which the storylines of these corporations champion in the name of progress. In seeking to get beyond this polemic and offer something more than a critical insight into the nature of smart city developments, this group of academics go on to call for an alternative to the corporate model of smart cities high-tech companies champion, by uncovering the genealogy of the developments and revealing the evolving body of work which they found as the basis of smart city developments.

As Hollands [15, 16] acknowledges, what such critiques uncover about this genealogy of smart cities is limited to revelations about the social divisions and inequalities of the computer science and digital technology these developments are founded on. In seeking to break with these limitations and found an alternative model of smart cities on that science and technology which is not socially divisive, but instead provides equal access to goods and services (in this instance clean and affordable energy), Hollands [15, 16] calls for a body of work that is not locked into the symbolic imaginaries of entrepreneurial legacies. Not in that sense locked into the symbolic imaginaries of entrepreneurial legacies, or any free-floating utopian future, univocal in the singularity of the science and technologies they offer storylines for, but something more progressive.

3 The Foundations of Smart Cities

What the call for smart city development to be more progressive means is not easy to discern. The tone the statement strikes is clearly neither structurally opposed to nor antagonistic towards smart cities. Not so much calling for a radical departure from the entrepreneurial legacy, as disruption of the corporate storylines high-tech companies found smart city development on. For in going on to assemble a model that reaches beyond the symbolic imaginary and captures the realities of a future in which smart cities do stand as a real alternative, what these critical insights do is set out the foundations for a body of work that double down on the insights which Giffinger et al. [1], Schaffers et al. [2], Calagilu et al. [3], Batty et al. [4], Leydesdorff and Deakin [5] and Lazaroiu and Roscia [6] offer as the basis for such a development. That body of work, which is less polemic in nature and serves to offer a series of more constructive insights into the entrepreneurial legacy Hollands [11, 15] and [16], Greenfield [17], Kitchin [12], Söderström et al. [13] and Vanolo [14] are all critical of. They are critical of, but also all equally quick to acknowledge, does nevertheless provide the raw material for a new body of work. For a new body of work that is not predominately scientific nor technological, but instead progressively sociological in nature, offering a synthesis of the computer science, digital technologies and data management platforms which uncover the genealogy of smart cities and in turn reveal the foundations of a future internet able to make sense of these developments.

In capturing the evolutionary dynamics of this smart city development programme, Deakin and Leydesdorff [18] and Deakin [9] note it serves to:

- highlight the types of ranking systems that Giffinger *et al.* [1] provides as a tool for cities to be smart in marketing the innovative qualities which they offer;
- throw light on how this marketing tool modifies standard ranking systems by pre-fixing the word smart to cities and by going on to measure the performance of smart cities against rival cities who lack the innovative qualities needed to be smart;
- draw attention to Schaffers *et al.* [2], who claim smart cities do not lie with the marketing of some ill-defined innovative qualities: for example; entrepreneurialism, economic image and trademarks, creativity, cosmopolitism and open mindedness, but instead rest on the cybernetic qualities of that experimental logic which computer science is founded and the digital technologies of the data management platforms that underpin them as a set of metrics which support future internet-based developments;
- show how for Schaffers *et al.* [2], the future internet is based on developments that relate to computer science and the digital technologies of data management platforms which surround a broadband of services. That broadband of services which orientate towards wireless technologies and centre on the use of cloud computing. That orientate towards wireless technologies which centre on the use of cloud computing and whose operation configure the Internet of Things (IoT) as national innovation systems. Those technologies, services and uses, Hernández-Muñoz *et al.* [19] and Álvarez *et al.* [20], also draw attention to the significance of.

4   Advocates of Future Internet-Based Developments

When comparing what the research on smart cities conducted by Giffinger *et al.* [1] and Schaffers *et al.* [2] say about the metrics of these future internet-based developments, with the statement Calagilu *et al.* [3] and Lazaroiu and Roscia [6] also make, the problem both encounter in modelling them as the underlying attributes of an experimental logic quickly begin to surface. For when conducting such a comparison, it soon becomes clear the attribute-based account of them offered by Giffinger *et al.* [1] is too free-floating, leaving the relationship between smart cities, computer science and digital technologies of data management platforms open and while Schaffers *et al.* [2] do offer the programme that society needs for the metrics of future internet-based developments to begin closing this gap, it is Calagilu *et al.* [3], Leydesdorff and Deakin [5], along with Lazaroui and Roscia [6], whose approximation of the distance between them which provides the basis to meet this requirement. What the discussion from Calagilu *et al.* [3], Leydesdorff and Deakin [5] and Lazaroiu and Roscia [6] on the metrics of the future internet serves to do is give the development that status which both Giffinger *et al.* [1] and Schaffers *et al.* [12] ask of it. They achieve this by founding smart cities as the basis of future internet-based developments and in terms of the computer science these relate to as the digital technologies of data management platforms. Those which in turn relate wireless services to the cloud computing of an IoT as infrastructures that approximate these in terms of the national innovation systems they go on to study the significance of.

The Triple Helix (TH) model of smart cities that Leydesdorff and Deakin [5] and Hirst *et al.* [7] offer advances this line of reasoning. This is achieved by approximating the role of smart cities in the computer science, digital technologies and data management platforms of those national innovation systems both Calagilu *et al.* [3] and Lazaroui and Roscian [6] draw attention to the significance of and by showing how these evolve as the intellectual capital Leydesdorff and Deakin [5] and Hirst *et al.* [7] suggest is turnkey. They suggest is turnkey and as a consequence, should lie at the heart of any measurement system compiled to account for the metrics of future internet-based developments.

Leydesdorff and Deakin [5], Hirst *et al.* [7] and Deakin [9] achieve this by drawing attention to the informatics of computer science as the basis for the development of a future internet that is founded on the digital technologies underpinning the data management platforms which support the broadband of services they deliver. Future internet-based developments that underpin the digital technologies of these infrastructures and which support the data management platforms this broadband of services stand alongside. The infrastructures which this platform of services stand alongside and they in turn suggest set out a stage for the management of natural resources as environments that are wise.

As Deakin *et al.* [21] indicate, this resource-based account of smart cities in turn suggests that any attempt made by the TH model to uncover the multi-scalar (not just sectoral, or national, but also urban and regional) nature of this intellectual capital means doing something novel. In that sense, searching for the metrics of future internet-based developments, not in national innovation systems. Not in national innovation systems but instead in the infrastructures and platforms these assemble and set out as a stage for managing the exploitation of natural resources as environments which are wise. Which are wise because they meet the social challenge that greening the intellectual capital of the urban and regional innovations systems these are embedded in poses and achieves this by way of and through a material stock and flow analysis. That stock and flow analysis which Deakin and Reid [22] indicate offers the means for any such greening of the intellectual capital found embedded in an urban and regional innovation system to scope out, draw in on and qualify whether the energetic of the renewables installed into the fabric of buildings are not only clean but if the metabolic of the resource consumption is also able to keep 1.5 alive [23].

5 Climate Change Adaptation

The case for future internet-based developments that set the stage for the management of natural resources as environments which are wise, is that social challenge which the IEA, IRENA, UN, WB and WHO lay down for Sustainable Development Goal (SDG) 7 [24]. That SDG which they review the prospect of meeting in terms of the UNs commitment to affordable and clean energy for all by 2030. That goal which also draws on developments in SDG 8–13 in terms of the relationship between affordability and clean energy, economic growth, industry and the innovation needed to service the infrastructures required for cities to sustain communities as sites of responsible consumption and production. In that sense, sites of responsible consumption and consumption which can sustain communities because they do not either degrade the environment or destroy ecosystems. Do not either degrade the environment or destroy ecosystems but instead are just in restoring them and providing everyone equal access to the infrastructures of that industrial innovation which member states deploy. Which member states deploy to green the intellectual capital of urban and regional innovation as systems overseeing the installation of renewable energies into the fabric of buildings driving the transition to net zero by 2050.

This is a matter the IEA [25], WEF [26] and IRENA [27] report on. They identify the following:

- the installation of renewables offers immediate improvements in the energy efficiency of buildings, mainly from large-scale retrofit programmes;
- currently only about 1% of buildings are retrofitted each year;
- to meet the net zero target, the rate of building retrofit shall have to increase to 2% per annum;
- by 2050, the vast majority of existing residential buildings shall need retrofitting to net zero standards;
- currently about 10% of water and space heating is sourced from renewable energies, by 2050 this shall need to be 43%, with an additional 38% powered by electricity sourced from renewables and district heating plants. The remainder from hydrocarbon fuels;
- about three-quarters of this increase in renewable energies shall be sourced from solar and wind power, the rest from geothermal reserves;
- any energy sourced from fossil fuels shall be subject and carbon capture, utilisation and storage;
- smart grids, artificial intelligence, IoTs and the development of them as the future energy internet, will be key to the integration of renewables into buildings and the operation of this renewable-driven future for energy shall account for approximately 10% of the energy saving carbon reduction needed to achieve net zero by 2050;
- where access to the national grid is remote, smart micro grids shall drive the development of this future energy internet as an urban and regional innovation;
- within these innovation systems net zero installations shall develop as smart buildings and smart homes. As installations, the operation and use of them shall be automated by way of the IoT and through machine-based learning drawing on big data analytics. This in turn shall offer a demand responsive control of appliance-related energy consumption and the related carbon emission by way of chatbots and through blockchain.

Together the IEA [25], WEF [26] and IRENA [27] suggest the digitisation of this process shall be key to any such ecological modernisation and whether-or-not the transformation of the built environment this is the harbinger of will be sufficiently inclusive in terms of the growth it relates to. However, as IRENA [27] go onto acknowledge:

> *"To date, the principal focus has been on gathering data on inputs into th[is] innovation process. There has been substantially less activity trying to define meaningful metrics to track the outputs and outcomes from clean energy technology innovation. Such metrics would allow for a more rigorous comparative analysis of the relative performance of innovation support for different technologies."*

In short, they suggest the existence of these metrics would provide future internet-based developments with that system of measurements needed to meet the social challenge the greening of any intellectual capital embedded in the urban and regional innovation system poses in terms of scoping out, drawing in on and confirming whether the energetic of the renewables installed into the fabric of buildings are not only clean but have the metabolic required to keep 1.5 alive.

Unfortunately, the metrics IRENA [27, 28] offer to map out the "innovation landscape for a renewable-powered future", does not provide such a system of measurement. They are instead typically mode 2 in nature, focussing on the "perfect storm" of rising generation capacity, falling costs and increasing job opportunities within the nation states driving these innovations, not as the computer science which they highlight to be the key amplifier of the intellectual capital greening them.

As a result, the digital technologies and infrastructures servicing the data management platforms that support this management of natural resources and as environments which are wise in meeting this social challenge, vis-a-vis greening the intellectual capital of the urban and regional innovation system this future calls for are ignored. The significance of this omission should not be underestimated, because it leaves the smart cities championing the future internet-based developments singled out by the IEA, IRENA, UN, WB and WHO, without the means to meet the social challenge set for SDG7. In that sense without the means to meet the social challenge SDG7 set by confirming whether the greening of the intellectual capital found to be embedded in the urban and regional innovation system administered by nation states, indicates 75% of the estimated 50 billion square meters of floor space built before 1945 and up to 1969 i.e., that share of the stock which is deemed to perform below standard and therefore needing to be retrofitted, shall be renovated at the rate of 2% per annum. That rate which is needed to achieve the circa 90% energy saving and carbon emission reduction required to achieve net zero by 2050.

6   The Metrics of Future Internet-Based Developments

Drawn from the THM of smart cities advanced by Hirst *et al.* [7] and Kourtic *et al.* [8], what follows begins closing the gap in the metrics of future internet-based developments left by the IEA, IRENA, UN, WB and WHO. Focussing on London as a smart city key to the UK nation state, the rest of this paper shall report on the metrics of that future internet-based development which is greening the intellectual capital of an urban and regional innovation system in the Borough of Sutton and known as the Hackbridge project.

The policy leadership for this project has already been reported on by Day *et al.* [29], Hodson and Marvin [30] and Bulkeley *et al.* [31]. Set within the guidelines laid down by OECD [32] and WB [33], it is the ECs Smart, Sustainable and Inclusive Growth Strategy [34] and this commitment to research and innovation in the computer science, engineering and construction sectors, Bulkeley *et al.* [31] note the UK has sought to participate in the development of by sourcing funding from Horizon 2020 and the European Regional Development Fund (ERDF). They also go on to indicate how the UKs national innovation system has sought to supplement the resources available to fund such future internet-based developments. Funding Bulkeley *et al.* [31] suggest has been secured from the Technology Strategy Board's championing of digital technologies as data management platforms able to support London's commitment to the management of natural resources. That management of natural resources as environments which are wise in greening the intellectual capital of urban and regional innovations as a decentralised energy system, that no longer centres on fossil fuels, but which is sufficiently distributed to concentrate on the renewables of CHP networks, solar and wind power. That development which in the London Borough of Sutton is overseen by Bio-regional and presents itself as the environment of an intelligent energy system capable of installing renewables into the fabric of buildings across Hackbridge.

The case study also serves to reveal the significance of these developments in morphological terms. This is achieved by augmenting the post-building physics modelled by Ratti *et al.* [35] as the computer science found in the informatics of the Digital Elevation Model (DEM) and those digital technologies which Salat [36], Bourdic and Salat [37] and Bourdic *et al.* [38] expand on the status of as data management platforms. Those technologies and platforms Kourtit *et al.* [8], Deakin [9], Deakin *et al.* [21], Brandt *et al.* [39], Mosannenzadeh *et al.* [40–42] and both Deakin [43] and Deakin and Reid [22] also go on to extend. Initially as the informatics of the digital technologies servicing data management platforms found in the London Borough of Sutton and subsequently by way of, and through the Hackbridge project.

The metrics this case study captures are threefold. The first relates to the computer science found in the informatics of the digital technologies serving the data management platforms of Sutton as a Borough of London. The second, the management of natural resources by society and as environments for the engineering of intelligent energy systems which are energetic and relate to the construction sector's installation of renewables into the fabric of buildings in Hackbridge. The third to the metabolic of this ecological modernisation as a circular growth economy wherein energy is conserved, not wasted but consumed responsibly from renewable sources restored by nature. These are sustainable developments that in turn allow the community to participate in the adaptations to climate change which green the intellectual capital of the urban and regional innovation system. Green the intellectual capital of the urban and regional innovation system as an ecological modernisation which decarbonises the built environment of Sutton and that sustains the city-district as neighbourhoods in Hackbridge which develop the status of energy efficient-low carbon zones.

Set within the Borough's vision of Hackbridge as a sustainable suburb, the Master Plan and Energy Options Appraisal conducted for the project, maps out the footprint of the mass retrofit (covering 1.7 km^2, involving 6,000 people and extending to 2,500 properties) they promote for the city-district and draws upon data sourced as that which provides information on the energy savings and reduction in the carbon emissions resulting from this management of natural resources in the neighbourhoods (Hackbridge [44, 45]; London Borough of Sutton [46, 47]).

The Energy Options Appraisal conducted offers a fourfold classification for the management of natural resources. The first baselines the current situation in terms of energy consumption and carbon emissions. The second is the thermal option, whereby the existing buildings are subject to a retrofit comprised of thermal improvements. The third is referred to as the thermal-plus option. This cuts deeper into the heating and lighting of buildings by extending the retrofit to cover such components and the installation of renewables into the fabric of buildings. The fourth augments these with that CHP, solar and wind option which manages these natural resources as the environments of an intelligent energy system. The fifth escalates the intelligent energy system into the AI of an IoT for the real-time management of this energetic and as the renewables of that metabolic which the ecological modernisation draws on to decarbonise the built environment.

The technologies of these options are in turn clustered as stages 1, 2 & 3. The first cluster focusing of the fabric of the buildings (options 1, 2 and 3), with the second (option 4) centring on the exploitation of natural resources out with the building envelope and as the environment of the renewables this intelligent energy system orientates towards as option 5. These options in turn form the basis of a measurement system able to do what Batty [48, 49] and Kandt and Batty [50] call for. That is, overcome the current impasse which exists in qualifying the informatics of these developments as merely technical and achieve such a computation by not only quantifying what the renewables of the intelligent energy system contribute to the energetic of the mass retrofit, but how the metabolic of this ecological modernisation also serves to decarbonise the built environment.

The analytic and calculus adopted for this material stock and flow analysis offer standard measures of energy consumption and carbon emissions by proprietary unit and in relation to the savings and reductions the retrofit achieve. With an average of 21,116 kWh and 6.7 tons of CO_2 emissions per annum attributed to each building, this ecological modernisation decarbonises the built environment to the extent it produces:

- a 3-ton reduction in CO_2 emissions, sourced from stage 1. With 2.76 tons of the reduction coming from energy savings related to the buildings and 0.24 tons to the instillation of renewables;
- a further 1.7-ton reduction in CO_2 emissions from the servicing of stage 2, generated from the biogas and CHP and supplemented with the solar and wind power installed as natural resources into the environment of an intelligent energy system able to exploit the potential these renewables have as an ecological modernisation;
- a 70% overall reduction in CO_2 emissions from stages 1 & 2 as an ecological modernisation which decarbonises the built environment. Which decarbonises the built environment and greens the intellectual capital of this urban and regional innovation system to the extent that it sustains the suburb as a city-district with neighbourhoods which take on the status of an energy efficient-low carbon zone;
- a position whereby the micro-grids, peak load management and dynamic pricing business model of cloud computing developed for the IoT, also has the potential to further consolidate the levels of energy savings and carbon reductions from the renewables. In this instance, by an extra 5%, which is critical in the sense that it places the full potential of the energy savings and carbon reductions into the 75% bracket, which the Intergovernmental Panel on Climate Change [51] suggest puts the retrofit on track to be neutral. To be neutral in the sense which this greening of the intellectual capital is clean enough for the urban and regional innovation system not to add anything more to the current level of global warming. Put in slightly different terms, keeps it within 1.5% of the pre-industrial era. However, as at the time

of writing, the retrofit does not yet have the ESCO in place for the city-district to capture the full potential of the savings and reductions available under stage 3, they are left out of the ecological modernisation due to the experimental status of them as the neighbourhoods of energy efficient-low carbon zones;

- situation whereby 28% of this reduction in CO2 emission is attributable to the instil- lation of renewables, with a relatively small proportion of this coming by way of the buildings (stage 1), the majority through the distributed energy of the CHP, solar and wind power servicing the heating and cooling systems (stage 2) and a smaller proportion from the business model the cloud computing and IoT these environments relate to (stage 3).

As a landing stage for the 2030 milestone in the transition to net zero, this retrofit can be seen to meet the targets set by IRENA [27, 28] and the World Economic Forum (WEF) for the heating of buildings [26, 52]. For in meeting the 25% renewables threshold and procuring electricity drawn from solar and wind power and procured offsite, these direct and indirect thresholds are met, along with the 58% limit placed on fossil fuel as a source of energy. The savings and reductions tied up with this energetic also allow the savings and reductions sourced from these infrastructures to future proof the retrofit and act as a platform for furthering this transition to net zero in 2050. Here it is anticipated that future innovations in biofuels, geothermal energy, hydrocarbons and carbon capture technologies shall account for up to 85% of the energetic needed from renewables (direct and indirect) over the next 25 years to progress the transition. The enhanced efficiencies derived from this energetic also allow for the anticipated growth in electrical appliances to be factored into the calculus and accounted for in the metabolic of this transition to net zero.

International comparisons can be drawn by referring to the retrofit components of the ECs Strategic Energy Plans (SEP) for 2030 and 2050. The first relates to "From Nearly-Zero Energy to Net-Zero Energy Districts", the second refers to "Positive Energy Districts". The results of the former are reported on by Saheb *et al.* [53]. The metrics for the Net-Zero Energy Districts capture the informatics for the management of natural resources as environments covering the instillation of renewables into the fabric of build- ings but not as an intelligent energy system. The range of case studies for the Net-Zero Energy Districts show energy savings and carbon emission reductions of approximately 40%. Lindholm *et al.* [54] draw attention to the "Positive Energy District" case studies, especially the intelligent energy systems they highlight as the energetic of the renewables and metabolic of that ecological modernisation which the deep retrofit of this renovation wave relates to. That ecological modernisation, deep retrofit and renovation wave which in Amsterdam, Groningen, Oulu, Bilbao and Trondheim, is forecast to produce a 70% reduction in energy consumption and decarbonisation of the built environment by 2030. Target forecasts that are in line with the climate change adaptation measures which the EC lay down for such renovations to be neutral.

Deakin and Reid [22] and Deakin *et al.* [23] develop these metrics to confirm whether such adaptations to climate change not only sustain any such transformation of the built environment, but in a manner which is sufficiently inclusive. The results of this analysis provide evidence to suggest the cost and benefits of retrofits are socially divided, with the upper and middle income groups benefitting at the cost of the low-income groups being excluded from the renovations due to the status of them as a social group that are environmentally benign, occupying buildings which perform at the upper limit of what is technically possible in terms of energy efficiency and carbon emissions. This leaves several SDG 7 questions over universal access to and the affordability of the modernisation, along with the inclusiveness of the transformation hanging.

7 Greening the Intellectual Capital of Urban and Regional Innovation Systems

Unlike the IEA, IRENA, UN, WB, WHO and WEF reports on the sustainability of such developments, the results of this case study do tend to indicate how retrofits are not just high priorities of the climate change adaptation agenda, but escalations of what might be referred to as strategies for the greening of the intellectual capital the urban and regional innovation system is embedded in. In that sense, a strategy for the greening of the intellectual capital urban and regional innovation systems gives rise to as the basis of an ecological modernisation which transforms the built environment. This also serves to demonstrate how it is the digital that cuts across this and as the data of an analytic for engineering and construction to deploy in calculating the energetic of this. The initial deployment of the DEM as the key enabling technology and translation of it into a data management platform with the metrics, vis-à-vis, informatics, energetic and metabolic future internet-based developments need for any such greening of the urban and regional innovation system to account for the ecology of such a transformation serves to demonstrate this. As too do the synergies they also offer in the calibration of this against the 2030 and 2050 milestones set for the transition to net zero.

8 Conclusion

The findings of this investigation into smart cities, indicate that critiques of them have been blind-sided by a tendency to qualify future internet-based developments as little more than corporate storylines, while ignoring the cybernetic qualities of that evolving body of research which works to uncover computer science as the foundation of an alternative model. That alternative model which makes smart city development intelligible. In that sense, a development which we should no longer be dumbfounded by, or left bewildered about the audacious nature of the claims they make, but on the contrary get behind and stand alongside. Get behind and stand alongside as the foundation of a programme which uncovers that evolutionary dynamic which is genial in the sense the analytic this offers and calculus that it lays down, rests on the metrics of future Internet-based developments able to make sense of the progress they sign-post.

As such, the knowledge this paper on smart cities produces goes someway to fill the void the polemic Hollands [11, 15, 16] articulates, leaves in its wake and serves to not so much close the gap between this and the body of work that has developed in the interim, but structural hole which is otherwise left behind. Not in this instance as an emergent landscape that either excavates the past, nor recycles imaginary futures as symbols from another era and whose stories provide corporations with powerful straplines, but by founding smart cities instead on a critical synthesis of the scientific and technological prospect which the development of them offer to meet social challenges. In that respect on a critical synthesis of the computer science, engineering and construction technologies underlying the metrics of those future internet-based developments which support the climate change adaptation strategies they contribute towards the analysis of and calculations the case study reported on in this paper serves to demonstrate, not only begin to green the intellectual capital of the urban and regional innovation systems they rest but ecological modernisation this also turns. In that sense, they not only rest on but which the transformation of the built environment also turns as that transition to a net zero growth strategy which generates wealth, secures prosperity and safeguards health and wellbeing by keeping 1.5 alive.

These are links and connections that have hitherto been too tenuous to make, but investigations into the genealogy of smart from the likes of Batty [48, 49] and Kandt and Batty [50] call for as the evolving structures of a city science that study the computation, engineering and construction of futures in which the power of the internet can be deployed as the technology to achieve the SDGs headlined by the IEA, IRENA, UN, WB, IRENA and WEF. This paper offers a demonstration of how to ground this. How to ground this science of smart cities in the technologies of future internet-based developments and what is more, do so by greening the intellectual capital of that urban and regional innovation system which the metrics account for. The metrics account for as an ecological modernisation that transforms the built environment, wealth which this generates, prosperity it secures and health and wellbeing the transition to net zero also delivers on.

References

1. Giffinger, R., Kramar, H., Haindl, G.: The role of rankings in growing city competition. In: 11th European Urban Research Association (EURA) Conference, Milan, Italy, October, pp. 9–11 (2008)
2. Schaffers, H., Komninos, N., Pallot, M., Trousse, B., Nilsson, M., Oliveira, A.: Smart cities and the future internet: towards cooperation frameworks for open innovation. In: Domingue, J., et al. (eds.) FIA 2011. LNCS, vol. 6656, pp. 431–446. Springer, Heidelberg (2011). https://doi.org/10.1007/978-3-642-20898-0_31
3. Caragliu, A., Del Bo, C., Nijkamp, P.: Smart cities in Europe. J. Urban Technol. 18(2), 65–82 (2011)
4. Batty, M., et al.: Smart cities of the future. Eur. Phys. J. Spec. Top. 214, 481–518 (2012)
5. Leydesdorff, L., Deakin, M.: The triple-helix model of smart cities: a neo-evolutionary perspective. J. Urban Technol. 18(2), 53–63 (2011)
6. Lazaroiu, G.C., Roscia, M.: Definition methodology for the smart cities model. Energy 47(1), 326–332 (2012)
7. Hirst, P., et al.: JESSICA for Smart and Sustainable Cities. Retrieved from the European Commission website (2012): http://ec.europa.eu/regional_policy/sources/thefunds/instruments/doc/jessica/jessica_horizontal_study_smart_and_sustainable_cities_en.pdf
8. Kourtit, K., et al.: An advanced triple-helix network framework for smart cities performance. In: Deakin, M. (ed.) Smart Cities: Governing, Modelling and Analysing the Transition, pp. 196–216. Routledge, New York (2013)

9. Deakin, M.: Smart cities: the state-of-the-art and governance challenge. Triple Helix 1(1), 1–16 (2014). https://doi.org/10.1186/s40604-014-0007-9

10. Deakin, M.: Smart cities and the internet: from mode 2 to triple helix accounts of their evolution. In: Handbook of Research on Social, Economic, and Environmental Sustainability in the Development of Smart Cities, pp. 26–43. IGI Global (2015)

11. Hollands, R.G.: Will the real smart city please stand up? City 12(3), 303–320 (2008)

12. Kitchin, R.: The real-time city? Big data and smart urbanism. GeoJournal 79, 1 (2014)

13. Söderström, O., Paasche, T., Klauser, F.: Smart cities as corporate storytelling. City 18(3), 307–320 (2014)

14. Vanolo, A.: Smartmentality: the smart city as disciplinary strategy. Urban Stud. 51(5), 883–898 (2014)

15. Hollands, R.: Critical interventions into the corporate smart city. Camb. J. Reg. Econ. Soc. (2015)

16. Hollands, R.G.: Beyond the corporate smart city?: glimpses of other possibilities of smartness. In: Smart Urbanism, pp. 168–184. Routledge (2015)

17. Greenfield, A.: Against the Smart City: A Pamphlet. This is Part I of "The City is Here to Use". Do projects (2013)

18. Deakin, M., Leydesdorff, L.: The triple helix model of smart cities: a neo-evolutionary perspective. In: Smart Cities, pp. 146–161. Routledge (2013)

19. Hernández-Muñoz, J.M., et al.: Smart cities at the forefront of the future internet. In: Future Internet Assembly, pp. 447–462, May 2011

20. Álvarez, F., et al.: The Future Internet: Future Internet Assembly 2012: From Promises to Reality. Springer, Heidelberg (2012). https://doi.org/10.1007/978-3-642-30241-1

21. Deakin, M., Campbell, F., Reid, A., Orsinger, J.: The Mass Retrofitting of an Energy Efficient–Low Carbon Zone. Springer, London. (2014). https://doi.org/10.1007/978-1-4471-6621-4

22. Deakin, M., Reid, A.: Smart cities: Under-gridding the sustainability of city-districts as energy efficient-low carbon zones. J. Clean. Prod. 173, 39–48 (2018)

23. Deakin, M., Reid, A., Mora, L.: Smart cities: the metrics of future internet-based developments and renewable energies of urban and regional innovation. J. Urban Technol. 27(4), 59–78 (2020)

24. IEA, IRENA, UN, World Bank and WHO: Tracking SDG7 progress across targets: indicators and data, World Bank, Washington DC (2022)

25. International Energy Agency: World Energy Outlook (2019)

26. World Economic Forum: Green Building Principles: The Action Plan for Net-Zero Carbon Buildings (2021)

27. IRENA: Renewable Technology Innovation Indicators: Mapping progress in Costs, Patents and Standards. International Renewable Energy Agency, Abu Dhabi (2022)

28. IRENA: Innovation Landscape Brief: Internet of Things. International Renewable Energy Agency, Abu Dhabi (2019)

29. Day, A.R., Ogumka, P., Jones, P.G., Dunsdon, A.: The use of the planning system to encourage low carbon energy technologies in buildings. Renew. Energy 34(9), 2016–2021 (2009)

30. Hodson, M., Marvin, S.: Low Carbon Nation? Routledge (2013)

31. Bulkeley, H., Castán Broto, V., Maassen, A.: Low-carbon transitions and the reconfiguration of urban infrastructure. Urban Stud. 51(7), 1471–1486 (2014)

32. OECD: The Future of the Internet Economy: A statistical profile. Statistical profile prepared for the OECD Ministerial meeting on the Future of the Internet Economy taking place in Seoul on 17–18 June

33. World Bank: World development report 2010: development and climate change. The World Bank (2009)

34. EC–European Commission: Europe 2020: A strategy for smart, sustainable and inclusive growth. European Commission Communication, 3 (2010)

35. Ratti, C., Baker, N., Steemers, K.: Energy consumption and urban texture. Energy Build. **37**(7), 762–776 (2005)
36. Salat, S.: Energy loads, CO2 emissions and building stocks: morphologies, typologies, energy systems and behaviour. Build. Res. Inf. **37**(5–6), 598–609 (2009)
37. Bourdic, L., Salat, S.: Building energy models and assessment systems at the district and city scales: a review. Build. Res. Inf. **40**(4), 518–526 (2012)
38. Bourdic, L., Salat, S., Nowacki, C.: Assessing cities: a new system of cross-scale spatial indicators. Build. Res. Inf. **40**(5), 592–605 (2012)
39. Brandt, N., et al.: Technical Report: European Cities Moving Towards Climate Neutrality Participation, Indicators and Benchmarking. KTH, Stockholm (2014)
40. Mosannenzadeh, F., Bisello, A., Vaccaro, R., D'Alonzo, V., Hunter, G.W., Vettorato, D.: Smart energy city development: a story told by urban planners. Cities **64**, 54–65 (2017)
41. Mosannenzadeh, F., Bisello, A., Diamantini, C., Stellin, G., Vettorato, D.: A case-based learning methodology to predict barriers to implementation of smart and sustainable urban energy projects. Cities **60**, 28–36 (2017)
42. Mosannenzadeh, F., Di Nucci, M.R., Vettorato, D.: Identifying and prioritizing barriers to implementation of smart energy city projects in Europe: an empirical approach. Energy Policy **105**, 191–201 (2017)
43. Deakin, M.: Smart cities, metrics and the future internet-based governance of urban and regional innovations. Scienze Regionali **17**(1), 39–56 (2018)
44. Hackbridge Masterplan (2008). https://www.sutton.gov.uk/index.aspx?articleid=3990
45. Hackbridge Sustainable Suburb, Draft Sustainability Action Plan (2008). http://www.sutton.gov.uk/CHttpHandler.ashx?id=5175&p=0
46. London Borough of Sutton: Energy Options Appraisal for Domestic Buildings in Hackbridge. Parity Projects (2008)
47. London Borough of Sutton and Bioregional: Hackbridge – a Zero Carbon Suburb (2012)
48. Batty, M.: Urban informatics and big data. A Report to the ESRC Cities Expert Group, pp. 1–36 (2013)
49. Batty, M.: On the confusion of terminologies. Environ. Plan. B Urban Anal. City Sci. **46**(6), 997–999 (2019)
50. Kandt, J., Batty, M.: Smart cities, big data and urban policy: towards urban analytics for the long run. Cities **109**, 102992 (2021)
51. Intergovernmental Panel on Climate Change, Climate Change 2014: Mitigation of Climate Change, vol. 3. Cambridge University Press, Cambridge (2015)
52. World Economic Forum: Accelerating the Decarbonization of Buildings: The Net-Zero Carbon Cities Building Value Framework (2022)
53. Saheb, Y., Shnapp, S., Paci, D.: From Nearly-Zero Energy Buildings to Net-Zero Energy Districts. Publications Office of the European Union, Luxembourg (2019)
54. Lindholm, O., Rehman, H.U., Reda, F.: Positioning positive energy districts in European cities. Buildings **11**(1), 19 (2021)

Architectural and Emotional Reactions: Proposal of a Framework

Bárbara Formiga[1]([✉]), Francisco Rebelo[1,2], Jorge Cruz Pinto[1], and Ana Vasconcelos[1]

[1] CIAUD, Research Center for Architecture, Urbanism and Design, Lisbon. School of Architecutre, Universidade de Lisboa, 1349-055 Lisbon, Portugal
barbaranevesf@gmail.com
[2] ITI/LARSys Universidade de Lisboa, Lisbon, Portugal

Abstract. When architects design a space and want to provoke reactions of surprise, relaxation, sadness, or excitement in users, how they combine the architectural characteristics of form, materials or light will influence these emotional reactions. The possibility of combining architectural elements is so vast and complex that it requires constant study and testing by the architect to achieve the reaction, sensation, or emotion he is trying to produce. This article results from preambular research that aims to create a methodological working framework that allows the development of a continuous study of the systematic relationship between different architectural features and emotional responses. As a main result, the proposed framework allows for obtaining emotional reactions related to architectural spaces, obtained through biosensors or self-report surveys, which feed the inference engine developed through the Kansei method. It is expected that the compilation of future studies based on this framework can be consulted as a guide or as an inspiration to read the built/designed spaces and/or open new possibilities and perspectives of spaces and architectural forms in the relationship with the human being. In the end, a comic narrative synthesizes the content of this article visually, having Le Corbusier as the main character.

Keywords: Architecture · Neuroscience · Emotional Reactions · Multisensory Perception · Architecture Comics

1 Introduction

The complexity of combining architectural elements requires continuous research and experimentation by the architect to evoke the sensation or desired emotional response. In addition, the limited time for designing a project, added to the profession's demands, doesn't always allow for a more in-depth study between the imagined space and the possible users. This question constitutes an opportunity for continuous research demonstrating and systematizing the relationship between the combinations of architectural features and emotional reactions through a scientific basis and method. Establishing these relationships, such as the effect of steel and concrete, concave and convex shapes, or the dimensions and proportions of space with users' emotional reactions, can be valuable for architectural design, expanding awareness of new ways of equating space.

Neuroarchitecture is a field that combines neuroscience and architecture to understand how the built environment affects human behavior, health, and well-being [1]. By applying principles of neuroscience to architectural spaces, architects can create buildings and spaces that are optimized for human experience and performance. There are different ways in which neuroarchitecture can improve the architect's performance: improving user productivity; enhancing user creativity; improving user experience, and reducing stress and anxiety.

Architects can create spaces optimized for the human experience by incorporating neuroscience principles into architectural projects. For example, creating spaces with optimal acoustics, lighting, geometry, and ventilation can help to promote concentration, leading to better user performance. Architects can project spaces that stimulate creativity and user inspiration by understanding how the brain processes information and perceives the environment. For example, incorporating natural light, views of nature, and biophilic elements can help reduce stress and increase cognitive performance, enhancing creativity. Understanding how the brain processes spatial information can also help architects design buildings and spaces that are easy to navigate and understand. Stress and anxiety are known to impact cognitive performance and overall well-being negatively. Architects can help improve the building occupants' performance and well-being by designing spaces that promote relaxation and reduce stress. For example, incorporating nature-based elements, providing access to natural light, and incorporating calming colors, can help to reduce stress and anxiety.

In this context, the main objective is to propose a framework to provide architects with a tool to incorporate the emotional aspects and preferences of the users into the project process. By understanding the emotional reactions of the users provoked by architectural space, architects can create spaces and environments that include and engage the users emotionally. Also, other researchers can use this framework in future studies that relate architectural space with emotional reactions.

For the constitution of this work, this research was developed in three phases: First, identify and discuss methods and instruments that can be used to measure users' emotional reactions to space. Second, identify the space's characteristics and the emotional responses that can be measured and worked on. Finally, propose and explain the framework.

It is important to clarify that the results of applying this framework in future research do not intend to replace the architect's unique conception. On the contrary, it can help his creative process and possibly add other aims that were not in the architect's conscious.

As a synthesis of this work, we have developed a small comic book, presented in the end, which briefly describes the scope and purpose of the research we propose. This way, there will be two readings, one through a traditional text and another through an illustrated narrative comic book. The storyboard makes fiction through the character of Le Corbusier, who proposes an innovative design method, establishing relationships between architectural characteristics and emotional reactions. As Le Corbusier said, architecture is the mystery of "l'espace indicible" he is trying to decipher in our short story, looking for the emotions that space can invisibly provide.

2 Architecture and Neuroscience

2.1 Measures of Emotional Reactions Inside Architectural Spaces

According to Guopeng Li [2], people constantly absorb information from their environment, whether they are aware of it or not, which can affect their actions, feelings, and thoughts. This ability is valid for any space context, from homes, offices, schools, or recreational areas.

The imperceptible way the brain reacts to the built environment has been the subject of significant study in neuroscience, presenting concepts and a set of techniques that best translate the sensory, cognitive, and behavioral stimuli of the human being to a particular environment [3]. Thus, a new interdisciplinary field emerged in 2003 by the ANFA academy in the United States, entitled Neuro-architecture, to investigate architecture's influence on human perception and behavior. As mentioned by António Damásio, the organism formed by the body and the brain interacts just as intensely with its external environment as it does with itself [4]. This coincides with Fred Gage, explaining that changes in the environment cause changes in the brain, which alter behavior [5]. The characteristics/variables of shape, scale, or light are properties of the environment that stimulate and interact intimately with the subject. They can change users' way of thinking, living, and interacting since humans spend about 80% of their lives inside buildings. The same principles can be applied to conceiving and qualifying architecture, urban spaces, and landscapes considered artificial and natural environments.

Measuring emotional user responses to architectural spaces requires careful planning and execution to avoid bias. Several methods and tools are available for measuring emotional responses to architectural spaces. The choice of method and tool depends on the research question, the characteristics of the architectural spaces, the target population, and the activity inside the buildings.

2.1.1 Subjective Measures – Self-report Surveys

One commonly used method for measuring emotional responses to architectural spaces is self-reported surveys [6–9]. These surveys typically ask participants to rate their emotional reactions to architectural space stimuli, such as geometry, shape, light, color, and materials. Self-reported surveys can be used in different formats, including paper-based questionnaires, online surveys, and in-person interviews. Self-reported surveys can capture a range of emotional responses, such as pleasure, arousal, dominance, relaxation, and engagement. Participants can rate their emotional responses on different scales, such as Likert scales, semantic differential scales, or visual analog scales.

Herzog et al. [10] used a self-report survey to measure the restorative components of natural and built environments. In this study, participants rated their emotional responses to different environments on dimensions such as pleasantness, calmness, and fascination. In the context of urban spaces, Qiao et al. [11] used a self-report survey to measure participants' emotional responses to urban spaces. Participants rated their emotional responses to the spaces on dimensions such as beauty, excitement, and relaxation. An essential aspect of the previous studies is the validity and reliability of surveys. It is very important to pay attention to several factors, such as the clarity and specificity of the survey items, the representativeness and diversity of the respondent sample, and the consistency and stability of the survey results over time [12, 13]. Another essential aspect to consider is to avoid potential biases and confounding factors that may influence respondents' emotional responses, such as social desirability bias, cognitive load, and situational context [14].

In case we want to mediate the emotional reactions and feelings that derive from the external environment, we have to deal with the fact that emotions are not always easy to identify and describe by people unequivocally. As Plutchik [15] said, many struggle to distinguish between fear and anxiety, guilt and shame, or envy and jealousy. To explain these emotions, we often rely on metaphors. This condition shows that using questionnaires to measure emotional reactions as a subjective method may not be sufficiently enlightening and reliable.

One of the methods used in this type of investigation is the Self-Assessment Manikin (SAM). The SAM is a non-verbal pictorial assessment technique that directly measures the pleasure, arousal, and dominance associated with a person's affective reaction to a wide variety of stimuli [16], with each "Manekin" pictorially representing a different level of a particular emotional state [17]. This method allows it to be combined with objective methods since it can measure the same variables from the point of view of the participant's conscious perception.

The Geneva Emotional Wheel is an innovative tool for understanding emotions. Developed by Geneva Emotion Research Labs, it visually represents the various states and intensities of human emotion. The inner wheel is divided into eight sectors, each representing a different emotional state, such as joy, sadness, fear, and anger. The outer wheel is divided into four sectors, each representing an intensity of an emotional state, such as low, medium, high, and very high. This tool allows researchers to quantitatively measure the intensity of a person's emotional reaction and compare the intensity of different emotions across different individuals and situations. The Geneva Emotional Wheel is an invaluable tool for gaining insight into the human emotional experience.

2.1.2   Objective Measures – Biosensors

In addition to self-reported surveys, other methods for measuring emotional responses to environments include biosensors to measure the physiological user reactions, such as heart rate variability, skin conductance, electroencephalography, and behavioral measures, such as approach-avoidance behavior, exploration behavior, and attention allocation. These methods can provide complementary information to self-reported surveys and help to validate and refine the survey results.

In recent years, some important research reviews have been developed to prove that biosensors can be successfully used to measure the user's emotional reaction in architectural spaces [18–21]. The findings of hundreds of studies using biosensors have proven biosensors' potential to establish a relationship between architectural spaces' characteristics and users' emotional reactions. However, there are problems in the use of biosensors linked to technological limitations and incorrect methodological setups. From a technological point of view, it is challenging to develop experimental protocols with the acquisition of data involving the movement of the human body, making it difficult to carry out field studies. Also, the need for high control of the experimental conditions during data collection makes it difficult for architects and designers to use biosensors. In this context, using biosensors in virtual environments for data collection can solve these problems. Architects and designers easily create three-dimensional environments that, integrated into virtual reality, allow for high levels of experimental control. Another major challenge is integrating subjective information obtained with biosensors with objective information measured with biosensors in a single system [22]. Integrating this information in a virtual environment will allow a collection of data that provides more robust evidence of the relationships between the characteristics of the architectural space and the emotional reactions that occur. In addition, Rinella et al., 2022 [17] state that before carrying out experiments in the architectural space, it is crucial to measure the psychological condition of the participant, like the level of anxiety/stress and state of mind/mood of the participant. It is relevant not only to have the same basis of comparison when the data are analyzed but also to understand whether the architectural space could positively or negatively change the participants during the experience, given their initial internal state.

2.2 Multisensory Virtual Experience

Virtual Reality is a technology that creates a simulated environment that a user can interact with, giving the feeling of being in a place that is not physically present [23]. It can be a fully immersive experience, using sensory stimuli such as visual, auditory, and tactile feedback to create a realistic and interactive virtual world. Users can explore, manipulate, and interact in the virtual world through headsets, controllers, and other hardware.

When applying VR in architecture and urbanism, the objective is to simulate an environment that immerses users in a particular spatial reality. The greater the number of senses stimulated within a virtual environment, the greater the sensation and immersion experienced [24]. Riva et al. [25] refer that virtual environments establish an affective and effective means of communication in inducing emotional, behavioral, and physiological responses consistent with the content of the recreated environment, constituting a good method to assess the dynamic changes of these same responses in context experimental [26]. Loomis et al. [27] refer to the same when he states that this technology offers a range of benefits to experimental research. It includes more precise control over experimental conditions, more realistic simulations, the ability to control variables easily, a simplified setup of experiments, access to new data sources, and the capacity to perform experiments that would otherwise be impossible.

Usually, the studies found that measure emotional reactions of environments/architectural spaces use the sense of vision as their main focus. Currently, this sense is considered dominant, corroborated by several authors. Paallasmaa [28] and Nudds [29] state that the human experience of the world is not limited to using one sense at a time but uses many simultaneously, interacting, integrating, and influencing each other. Sarah Robinson [30] further adds that sight priority creates and maintains a limited, oversimplified perception of our physical selves and our environment. By contrast, our reactions to sound and touch broaden our usual conception of the body and our traditional notion of space. In the virtual environment, the same principles must maintain, stimulating the same senses that are active during everyday life. Ciccarelli et al. [31] say that visuals, sound, tactile feedback, and other sensory modalities like temperature (thermoception) and the senses of movement and position (kinesthesia and proprioception) must be incorporated to create a realistic and engaging experience.

3 Architectural Space Features and Emotions

3.1 Multisensory Virtual Experience

The characteristics of architecture are the visible and invisible attributes that construct and compose space. The geometry, the shape, the light, the color, and the materials, are examples of these characteristics that, when transforming the elements of architecture such as the walls, the floor, the roof, the doors, the windows, the stairs, etc., alter the quality space and the way it is perceived.

Francis Ching, in his work "Architecture: Form, Space and Order" [32], names six spatial qualities: form, proportion, scale, texture, color, light, and sound. Rob Krier in "Elements of Architecture" [33] points to the different interior spatialities that depart from shape/geometry variables as square interior spaces, distorted geometries, rhythmic series of spaces, rectangular interior spaces, octagonal interior spaces, cross-shaped interior spaces, and circular spaces. In "Analysing Architecture" [34], Simon Unwin recognizes that the modifying elements of architecture are light, temperature, ventilation, sound, odor, scale, texture, and touch. Ernst Neufert, in "Art of Projecting in Architecture" [35] presents a series of ergonomic references and dimensioning of architectural space, referring to color, scale, proportion, shape, light, materials, openings, among other elements that make it up.

3.2 Emotional Reactions and Feelings

An emotional reaction is a psychological state characterized by a physiological, cognitive, and behavioral response to an internal or external stimulus. Feelings are thoughts and attitudes resulting from interpreting and evaluating the emotional experience [4].

Several authors have focused on the study of emotions. Paul Ekman found six basic universal emotions based on observing and analyzing facial expressions: anger, fear, disgust, surprise, happiness, and sadness [36]. On the other hand, Plutchik [37] proposed a psycho-evolutionary classification approach for general emotional responses. He created an emotion wheel to illustrate different emotions and first proposed his cone-shaped (3D) model, or wheel model (2D), in 1980 to describe how emotions were related. The middle of the emotion wheel reflects the maximal levels of arousal of each emotion: Grief, Loathing, Terror, Vigilance, Rage, Admiration, Amusement, and Ecstasy. These emotions are associated with eight primary bipolar emotions: joy versus sadness; anger versus fear; trust versus disgust; and surprise versus anticipation. The model links the concept of emotions to a color wheel. Just as various shades of color can be created by combining primary colors, so too can different emotions be produced by combining primary emotions [17].

In recent decades (1980s) a new circumplex model of emotions called Russell's model emerged. This model argues that affective states are attributable to two main neurophysiological systems, which can be translated through the linear combination of the two dimensions, varying in valence (positive or negative) and arousal/activation (high or low). The first explains the value of the emotion (along a pleasant-unpleasant continuum), and the other describes the corresponding level of physiological activation [6]. Russell's model turned out to be very appropriate and widely used, particularly in studies applied to environmental psychology and/or architecture.

Gerald Franz [38] is one of the authors who use the models above to measure the affective responses of architectural space. It presents the "dimensions of architectural experience" represented through pairs of opposing adjectives, such as pleasingness (pleasant/beautiful vs. unpleasant/ugly), arousingness (arousing/interesting vs. calming/boring), and dominance (formal/strict/tensed/ controlled vs. unformal/loose/relaxed/in control).

4 Framework Proposal: Affective Relationship with Space

We started with the methods that we used to create this framework. Next, in the results, we presented the framework evolving into three main parts: the characteristics of the space, the emotional reactions, and the instruments and methods to be used.

4.1 Methods

To determine the characteristics of the architectural space used for this framework, we first surveyed the characteristics presented by each author in the referred works [32–35]. As a criterion, we chose to identify the characteristics repeated in different authors, such as light, shape, color, and texture. We then held work meetings to evaluate and hierarchically organize these variables. This evaluation resulted in a table of variables and sub-variables with several levels of representation.

Considering the set of variables identified by the various authors mentioned above [32–35], we established a hierarchy between the most subjective, intermediate and most objective variables. The subjective variables are related to form, mainly linked to cultural and individual value systems (aesthetic taste and sensitivity, education linked to visual form). The intermediate variables are related to materials and light and have a double condition. These variables are linked to the formal appearance (brightness, light/dark, color, texture, patterns) and establish a bridge with the more objective variables, through the relationship with touch (hot/cold sensations, rough/soft, etc.) and through the relationship with vision, in the case of light. Finally, the objective variables refer to those that gather the better consensus on the part of the users. The latter, defined by the technical parameters of light (lumens), smell, temperature, and sound, are more consensual for users as they are physically felt, positively or negatively affecting sensory terms, regardless of aesthetic and cultural value systems.

We used the Kansei method to determine the emotional reactions we can measure. Kansei is a method that can also use subjective and/or objective methods. The method was developed in the 1950s by Mitsuo Nagamachi and can gather information from potential users and make emotional reactions to a specific environment/architectural space. Each Kansei word expresses a quality or characteristic that must be included in the future architectural space, activating an emotional feeling in the user's cognitive perception. The variety of these Kansei words extends from the physical and visible description of form, color, texture, touch, sound, smell, to the description of immaterial and invisible characteristics such as comfortable, calming, exciting, stressful, distressing, among others. Kansei is commonly applied in engineering and design. According to a literature review, few studies of its application in architecture or architectural design have been found, some of which are methodological proposals [39]. In 2021, a study was carried out that applied Kansei to measure the affective responses of the architectural space to a hospital entrance [40].

To find Kansei's words that represent the emotional reactions measured, we looked for models of various authors [36–38] to choose the one that could work with subjective methods (based on self-report surveys) and objective methods (based on of biosensors). Considering the bibliographical review, Russell's model suggests a better facility to combine and synchronize the data obtained with objective and subjective methods. In this way, we can consider that the "unit of measurement" for the objective methods (biosensors) will be the arousal (high or low) and the valence (positive or negative). For the subjective method (self-reports), we can consider the corresponding emotional reactions to the four quadrants of the circumplex model (anxious/tense vs. calm/relaxed and depressed/annoyed vs. excited/energetic). We designed a table to organize the variables presented.

To integrate the tables created for architectural characteristics and emotional reactions with the instruments and methods, we designed a diagram to organize and show the chaining of each work phase that represents the framework proposal.

4.2 Framework, Proposal of Research

Regarding the characteristics of the space, after studying and organizing the variables, we obtained a table (Table 1), as a result, which facilitates the choice and combination of variables to be worked on in the following studies. From this table, it will be possible to create any type of space derived from one or more combinations of architectural features.

In the first column, we have the generic variables of shape, material, light, and other sensory stimuli, each representing a group of sub-variables. For example, configuration, regularity, symmetry, scale, and proportion are the sub-variables of form, which acquire various levels of expression. Each sub-variable can have up to three levels of variation. Although there are many more variable variations than those presented, as is the case with the quality of the material (stone, wood, metal), we chose to select a maximum of three to simplify and orientate the universe of future studies. This table does not represent the totality of variables that constitute the characteristics of the space. However, it serves as a matrix for the investigation we intend to conduct.

Concerning emotional reactions, we obtained a table based on Russell's model as a result. This table (Table 2) shows on the left side the data obtained with the biosensors (Arousal and Valence) and on the right side the data obtained with the self-report surveys (e.g., excited, tense, bored, relaxed).

Considering the various methods and variables studied by the authors presented, as well as our experience in previous studies, we aim to present a methodology that will serve as a basis for future studies in the field of architecture and emotions.

Table 1. Table of considered architectural space characteristics

	VARIABLES		LEVEL I	LEVEL II	LEVEL III
ARCHITECTURAL SPACE / FORM	shape configuration		rectilinear	curvilinear	
	shape regularity		regular	irregular	
	shape simmetry		symmetric	asymmetric	
	scale		small	medium	large
	proportion	high-foot	low	medium	high
		depth	small	medium	large
		width	small	medium	large
MATERIAL	material quality		stone	wood	metal
	texture		smooth	rough	
	color		cold colors	warm colors	
LIGHT	opening configuration		rectilinear	curvilinear	
	opening dimension		small	medium	large
	opening position	surface	walls	ceiling	
		simmetry	symmetric	asymmetric	
OTHER SENSORIAL STIMULI	temperature		cold	warm	
	sound		noisy	silent	
	smell		sour	fragrant	

The integration of the previous tables for the creation of this framework's method is explained through the diagram in Fig. 1. Firstly, we look at the characteristics of the space presented in Table 1. Second, we select the characteristics of the space we want to evaluate in the same study (it is recommended to start with fewer variables and then increase). Within the variation of the chosen variables, we design distinct architectural spaces to be tested by a sample of participants. Each space is modeled and rendered in Virtual Reality to create an immersive multisensory experience that participants will evaluate.

Using Kansei Method, an inference engine is created that systematically relates the space's characteristics to users' emotional reactions. The emotional reactions (Table 2) will be measured by data obtained through biosensors (physiological responses of the autonomic nervous system) and self-reports (responses from the participants' conscious perception).

Table 2. Table of Emotional reactions based on Russell's model.

EMOTIONAL REACTIONS	BIOSENSORS	SELF-REPORTS
	HIGH AROUSAL + HIGH VALENCE	alert
		excited
		elated
		happy
	LOW AROUSAL + LOW VALENCE	tense
		nervous
		stressed
		upset
	LOW AROUSAL + LOW VALENCE	sad
		depressed
		bored
		tired
	LOW AROUSAL + HIGH VALENCE	content
		serene
		relaxed
		calm

5   Final Considerations

The main objective is to propose a framework to provide architects with a tool to incorporate the emotional needs and preferences of the users into the architectural design process, and this objective was successfully achieved. In previous studies [14] we applied a less developed version of this framework, without VR and biosensors, using the Kansei method. We also tested biosensors with VR in another study [10] to measure emotional reactions related to curved and rectilinear forms in a housing context.

Although we had already developed previous studies with the partial application of the presented framework, we still need proof that it works in an integrated way with all the proposed instruments.

The proposal of this framework aims, in the long term, to show architects the possibilities of formal and spatial combinations that can be designed to invoke or approximate certain states of mind, allowing to open the conscience to a new focus and a field of architectural exploration more directed towards human beings and their well-being. With the hope that, in the future, the application of the results of this research, and other researches like this, in the various types of project, will start to become an intrinsic knowledge of the architect. By knowing how to evoke different emotional responses in the experience of the architectural space, the architect has the possibility of adding to

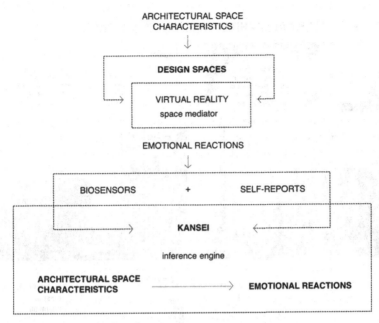

Fig. 1. Framework diagram.

the developed model the knowledge that comes from his practical experience. By understanding users' emotional reactions related to architectural space, architects can create spaces and environments inspired by how people will engage and feel in the space.

Applying this framework in architectural design process may enable a critical awareness of the relation between emotions, space, and form. The expansion of the architect's consciousness, through the relationship between the perception and emotions of the human being with space and form, with which architects can operate to find better or other possible architectural solutions.

In the end, the illustrated story in comics comes as an effective way to summarize the idea of this article, as it allows the reader to visualize the subject concisely and creatively.

Acknowledgement. National funds finance this work through FCT – Fundação para a Ciência e a Tecnologia, I.P., under the Strategic Project with the references UIDB/04008/2020 and UIDP/04008/2020 and ITI-LARSyS FCT Pluriannual fundings 2020–2023 (UIDB/50009/2020).

A FRAMEWORK STORY IN ARCHITECTURE TO "ÉMOUVOIR"

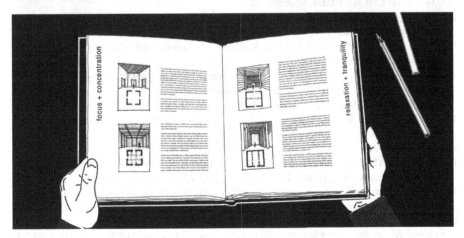

References

1. Trujillo, H., Luis, J., Llinares, C., Macagno, E.: The cognitive-emotional design and study of architectural space: a scoping review of neuroarchitecture and its precursor approaches. Sensors **21**, 2193 (2021). https://doi.org/10.3390/s21062193
2. Li, G.: The dynamics of architectural form: space, emotion and memory. Art Des. Rev. **7**, 187–205, 194 (2019)
3. Higera-Trujillo, J.L., Llinares, C., Macagno, E.: The cognitive-emotional design and study of architectural space: a scoping review of neuroarchitecture and its precursor approaches. Sensors **21** (2021)
4. Damásio, A.: Descartes' Error – Emotion, Reason, and the Human Brain, Penguin, New York (1994)
5. Bager, E.: Corridors of the Mind: Could neuroscientists be the next great architects? Pacific Standard. http://www.psmag.com/culture/corridors-of-the-mind-49051/. Accessed 12 June 2022
6. Nasar, J.L.: Urban design aesthetics: the evaluative qualities of building exteriors. Environ. Behav. **26**(3), 377–401 (1994). https://doi.org/10.1177/001391659402600305
7. Lohr, V.I., Pearson-Mims, C.H., Goodwin, G.K.: Interior plants may improve worker productivity and reduce stress in a windowless environment. J. Environ. Hortic. **14**(2), 97–100 (1996)
8. Dazkir, S.S., Read, M.A.: Furniture forms and their influence on our emotional responses toward interior environments. Environ. Behav. **44**(5), 722–732 (2012). https://doi.org/10.1177/0013916511402063
9. Küller, R., Ballal, S., Laike, T., Mikellides, B., Tonello, G.: The impact of light and colour on psychological mood: a cross-cultural study of indoor work environments. Ergonomics **49**(14), 1496–1507 (2006). https://doi.org/10.1080/00140130600858142
10. Herzog, T.R., Maguire, C.P., Nebel, M.B.: Assessing the restorative components of environments. J. Environ. Psychol. **23**(2), 159–170 (2003)
11. Qiao, L., Zhuang, J., Zhang, X., Su, Y., Xia, Y.: Assessing emotional responses to the spatial quality of urban green spaces through self-report and face recognition measures. Int. J. Environ. Res. Public Health **18**(16), 8526 (2021). https://doi.org/10.3390/ijerph18168526. PMID: 34444282; PMCID: PMC8393696
12. Tourangeau, R., Rips, L., Rasinski, K.: The Psychology of Survey Response. Cambridge University Press, Cambridge (2000). https://doi.org/10.1017/CBO9780511819322
13. Oral, E.: Surveying sensitive topics with indirect questioning. Stat. Methodol. (2020). https://doi.org/10.5772/intechopen.84524
14. Tan, H.C., Ho, J.A., Kumarusamy, R., Sambasivan, M.: Measuring social desirability bias: do the full and short versions of the Marlowe-Crowne social desirability scale matter? J. Empir. Res. Hum. Res. Ethics **17**(3), 382–400 (2022). https://doi.org/10.1177/15562646211046091
15. Plutchik, R.: The Nature of Emotions: Human emotions have deep evolutionary roots, a fact that may explain their complexity and provide tools for clinical practice. Am. Sci. **89**(4), 344–350 (2001)
16. Bradley, M.M., Peter, J., Lang, J.P.: Measuring emotion: the self-assessment manikin and the semantic differential. J. Behav. Ther. Exp. Psychiatry **25**(1), 49–59 (1994)
17. Rinella, S., et al.: Emotion recognition: photoplethysmography and electrocardiography in comparison. Biosensors **12**, 811 (2022). https://doi.org/10.3390/bios12100811
18. Mostafavi, A.: Architecture, biometrics, and virtual environments triangulation: a research review. Archit. Sci. Rev. **65**(6), 504–521 (2022). https://doi.org/10.1080/00038628.2021.2008300

19. Kim, J., Kim, N.: Quantifying emotions in architectural environments using biometrics. Appl. Sci. **12**(19), 9998 (2022). https://doi.org/10.3390/app12199998

20. Higuera-Trujillo, J.L., Llinares, C., Macagno, E.: The cognitive-emotional design and study of architectural space: a scoping review of neuroarchitecture and its precursor approaches. Sensors **21**(6), 2193 (2021). https://doi.org/10.3390/s21062193

21. Shaffer, F., Ginsberg, J.P.: An overview of heart rate variability metrics and norms. Front. Public Health **5** (2017). https://www.frontiersin.org/articles/10.3389/fpubh.2017.00258

22. Bower, I. Tucker, R., Enticott, P.G.: Impact of built environment design on emotion measured via neurophysiological correlates and subjective indicators: a systematic review. J. Environ. Psychol. **66**, 101344 (2019). https://doi.org/10.1016/j.jenvp.2019.101344

23. Rebelo, F., Noriega, P., Soares, E.: Using virtual reality to assess user experience. J. Hum. Factors Ergon. Soc. (2012)

24. Rebelo, I.B.: Realidade Virtual Aplicada à Arquitetura e Urbanismo: Representação, Simulação e Avaliação de Projetos. Disseratation in Universidade Federal de Santa Catarina - UFSC, Florianópolis (1999)

25. Riva, G., et al.: Affective interactions using virtual reality: the link between presence and emotions. CyberPsychol. Behav. **10**(1), 45–56 (2007)

26. Ribeiro, A., Monteiro, L.: Induction affective scenarios virtual reality: assessment of the sensation of presence. Psicol. Clin. **27**(1), 139–160 (2015)

27. Loomis, J.M., Blascovich, J.J., Beall, A.C.: Immersive virtual environments as a basic research tool in psychology. Behav. Res. Methods Instrum. Comput. **31**, 557–564 (1999)

28. Pallasmaa, J.: The Eyes of the Skin, 3rd edn. Wiley, New York (2012)

29. Nudds, M.: Is audio-visual perception 'Amodal' or 'Crossmodal'? In: Perception and Its Modalities. s.l.: Oxford Scholarship (2014)

30. Ritchie, I.: Neuroarchitecture: Designing with the Mind in Mind. 06, vol. 90. Wiley, Oxford (2020)

31. Ciccarelli, S., White, J.: Â Psychology. Harlow, Essex, Pearson (2018)

32. Ching, F.D.K.: Architecture: Form, Space & Order, 3rd edn. Wiley, Hoboken (2007)

33. Krier, R.: Elements of Architecture, vol. 9. AD Publications (1983)

34. Unwin, S.: A análise da Arquitetura, 3rd edn. Bookman (2013)

35. Neufert, E.: Arte de Projetar em Arquitetura, 13 edn. Editorial Gustavo Gili, San Adrián de Besos (1998)

36. Ekman, P.: Emotions Revealed: Recognizing Faces and Feelings to Improve Communication and Emotional Life. Times Books, New York (2003)

37. Plutchik, R.: The nature of emotions: human emotions have deep evolutionary roots, a fact that may explain their complexity and provide tools for clinical practice. Am. Sci. **89**, 344–350 (2001)

38. Franz, G.: An empirical approach to the experience of architectural space. Dissertation at the Max Planck Institute for Biological Cybernetics, Tübingen and the Bauhaus University, Weimar (2005)

39. Castilla, N., Llinares, C., Blanca, V.: Ingeniería Kansei aplicada al diseño lumínico de espacios emocionales Kansei engineering in the lighting design of emotional spaces. Anales de Edificación **2**(1), 7–11 (2016)

40. Formiga, B., Rebelo, F., da Cruz Pinto, J., Noriega, P.: Hospital lobby and user's perceptions architectural Kansei method. In: Rebelo, F. (ed.) AHFE 2021. LNNS, vol. 261, pp. 159–166. Springer, Cham (2021). https://doi.org/10.1007/978-3-030-79760-7_20

High Performance Control and Extended Kalman Filter Based Estimation of Sensorless Permanent Magnet Synchronous Motor Drive for Robotic Applications

Gopinath G. R.$^{(\boxtimes)}$ and Mahesh Bharath Pudutha

School of Engineering Sciences, Mahindra University, Hyderabad, India
{gopinath.gr,bharath21meee010}@mahindrauniversity.edu.in

Abstract. Owing to high efficiency and high performance controllability, permanent magnet synchronous motors (PMSM) are being considered for various robotic applications including the Articulated Robots. PMSM drive includes a position/speed sensor for self synchronous control. Sensorless operation refers to the possibility of removing the afore-mentioned position/speed sensor to increase the robustness of the system and improve the reliability against sensor failures. This requires speed/position estimation for closed loop control. Extended Kalman filter (EKF) is a viable option as an observer owing to its noise rejection characteristics, ease in tuning the observer and the recursive algebraic nature of the algorithm which translates to real time hardware implementability. This paper proposes sensorless PMSM drive for robotic applications, with the dual perspective of improving the control and estimation aspects of the drive. A modification to the speed controller of Proportional+Integral (PI controller) type is proposed, wherein the overshoot in speed is drastically reduced without the necessity of including the Differential control. Likewise, a Proportional+Differential (PD) type is proposed for position control, with a suggestion to reduce the peak overshoot in position response. An adaptive Kalman filter is proposed to improve the estimation of speed/position, to achieve a high performance closed loop controlled PMSM drive.

Keywords: Position control · Speed control · Adaptive EKF · PMSM drive · Sesnsorless control

1 Introduction

High performance control of the PMSM drives can be achieved with the field oriented control (FOC) and the direct torque control (DTC) techniques. DTC offers the following advantages: absence of coordinate transformations, absence of voltage modulation and decoupling circuits, and a simple control structure [1, 2]. DTC is limited due to possible problems during starting, high torque ripples, variable switching frequency and poor low speed performance [2]. FOC controls the motor with decoupled torque and flux control in the rotor dq reference frame, which demands continuous rotor position feedback. The advantages of the DTC cannot be availed in the FOC; nevertheless a high accuracy and reduced torque ripple can be achieved at almost all speeds using the FOC.

In this paper, we propose a high-bandwidth control strategy for position and speed control of PMSM drives using a closed-loop field-oriented control (FOC) approach. The proposed strategy employs a nested control loop, with proportional-integral (PI) controller for inner current control and a proportional-integral (PI) controller for outer speed, proportional-derivative (PD) controller for outer position control. To reduce the overshoot of the controllers without compromising on performance, this paper proposes a new compensation technique. An additional compensation block is added before the PI and PD controllers to reduce the overshoot of the speed and current controllers. The outer control loop consists of a speed/position controller which generates the reference currents tracked by the inner current control loop. Bandwidth of the inner loop is set high enough for fast tracking of the currents, thereby presenting unity gain for the outer speed/position control loop of a relatively lower bandwidth. The control of permanent magnet synchronous motor (PMSM) drives is essential for their efficient operation in various industrial applications.

Accurate speed and position information is a prerequisite for high performance control of PM synchronous machines. Speed and position sensors require regular maintenance, while sensor faults reduce the reliability of the permanent magnet synchronous motor (PMSM) drive. Improvement in system reliability can be eventuated with the estimation of speed and position in lieu of these sensors. An obvious advantage of mechanical robustness can also thereby be achieved. A vast range of estimators have been employed to facilitate speed and position estimation from standstill, extending to the field weakening region of operation. Those used in standstill and low speed range may not be suitable at medium to high speeds. Likewise, the ones suitable for medium to high speeds may fail to operate in the extremely low speeds with arbitrary initial rotor position. The concerns regarding noise rejection are addressed exclusively by the paradigm of stochastic estimation. Based on whether the noise characteristics are being addressed, the observers used for sensorless control can be conveniently categorized into deterministic and stochastic.

The *analytical approximation* of the general Bayesian estimation equations forms the basis of the various Extended Kalman filter (EKF) observers used for state and parameter estimation of nonlinear systems. They have provided promising results for the sensorless PMSM drive [3–5], occasionally being associated with combined load torque estimation as well. The possibility of joint parameter and state estimation with the EKF has been reported in the literature [6, 7]. Most applications of the EKF for sensorless PMSM drives concern with the estimation of speed, position and load torque. This paper proposes an adaptive EKF for position and speed estimation, wherein improvements are achieved in steady state noise rejection as well as decrease in the settling time of transient response in position and speed estimation.

2   Permanent Magnet Synchronous Motor

Permanent magnet synchronous machines (PMSMs) replace the rotor electromagnets of the synchronous machines with permanent magnets to generate the required air gap flux, so that the slip rings and brush assembly are eliminated. The copper losses in the rotor are hence absent in a PMSM, which increases its efficiency. Advancements of high energy density permanent magnets further make the PMSMs viable for a wide range of applications. PMSMs are being increasingly used in robotic applications [8], wind energy systems, electric vehicles, paper mills, elevators, ship propulsion and other medium and high power applications [9]. The wave shape of the induced emf differentiates the PMSM into trapezoidal and the sinusoidal types [9]. Trapezoidal types are commonly referred to as brushless DC (BLDC) machines and the sinusoidal ones by the more generic term PMSM. The sinusoidal type PMSM exhibits smooth torque production, and requires accurate speed and position information for all rotor angles and speed. Closed-loop control of the PMSM drive requires a minimum of two current sensors, and a voltage sensor to measure the DC voltage. The rotor position is usually sensed using an optical encoder or an electromagnetic resolver for high performance control of the drive. Speed is estimated from the sensed position, the speed resolution being limited by the resolution of the position sensor and also by the sampling time.

2.1   Modeling of PMSM

Dynamic model of PMSMs is preferably derived using a two-phase motor model in direct and quadrature axes. The mathematical model derived in the rotating dq reference frame aligned with the rotor magnets has a simple form and is suitable for the design of current controllers. The PMSM model in stationary $\alpha\beta$ reference frame has time varying inductances which makes the model complicated for controller design. Formulation of observers for speed and position sensorless control demands minimum nonlinearity in the output equation. The currents in stationary reference frame being the measurement outputs are linear functions in the $\alpha\beta$ reference frame, and are sinusoidal functions of rotor angle θ_r in the dq reference frame. Linearity of the output equation makes the motor model in $\alpha\beta$ reference frame suitable for Kalman filter based observer design. Dynamic modeling of PMSMs in both dq and $\alpha\beta$ reference frames hence presents complementary advantages.

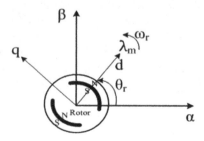

Fig. 1. Stationary $\alpha\beta$ and dq rotor reference frames

Coordinate Transformations

Figure 1 shows the relation between stationary and rotating reference frames. dq rotor reference frame is aligned with the rotor magnetic axis. Equation 1 defines the transformation from 3-phase abc to stationary $\alpha\beta$ quantities. x_α, x_β represents currents, voltages and flux linkages in the $\alpha\beta$ stationary frame. In space vector notation, quantities in $\alpha\beta$ and dq frames are defined by Eq. 2. The transformations of quantities between the reference frames are given by Eq. 3.

$$\begin{bmatrix} x_\alpha \\ x_\beta \end{bmatrix} = \frac{2}{3} \begin{bmatrix} 1 & -\frac{1}{2} & -\frac{1}{2} \\ 0 & \frac{\sqrt{3}}{2} & -\frac{\sqrt{3}}{2} \end{bmatrix} \begin{bmatrix} x_a \\ x_b \\ x_c \end{bmatrix} \tag{1}$$

$$x_{dq} = x_d + jx_q \tag{2a}$$

$$x_{\alpha\beta} = x_\alpha + jx_\beta \tag{2b}$$

$$x_{\alpha\beta} = \frac{2}{3}\left(x_a + x_b e^{j2\pi/3} + x_c e^{-j2\pi/3}\right)$$

$$x_{\alpha\beta} = x_{dq} e^{j\theta_r} \tag{3a}$$

$$x_{dq} = x_{\alpha\beta} e^{-j\theta_r} \tag{3b}$$

Coordinate transformations are represented in the matrix form as given by Eq. 4.

$$\begin{bmatrix} x_d \\ x_q \end{bmatrix} = \begin{bmatrix} \cos\theta_r & \sin\theta_r \\ -\sin\theta_r & \cos\theta_r \end{bmatrix} \begin{bmatrix} x_\alpha \\ x_\beta \end{bmatrix} \tag{4a}$$

$$\begin{bmatrix} x_\alpha \\ x_\beta \end{bmatrix} = \begin{bmatrix} \cos\theta_r & -\sin\theta_r \\ \sin\theta_r & \cos\theta_r \end{bmatrix} \begin{bmatrix} x_d \\ x_q \end{bmatrix} \tag{4b}$$

Modeling in dq Rotor Reference Frame

The power non-invariant transformation between dq and abc quantities is given in Eq. 5. x_d, x_q denote dq rotating reference frame quantities which may be currents, voltages or flux linkages. x_a, x_b, x_c similarly denote the 3-phase abc quantities [9].

$$\begin{bmatrix} x_d \\ x_q \end{bmatrix} = \frac{2}{3} \begin{bmatrix} \cos\theta_r & \cos(\theta_r - 2\pi/3) & \cos(\theta_r + 2\pi/3) \\ -\sin\theta_r & -\sin(\theta_r - 2\pi/3) & -\sin(\theta_r + 2\pi/3) \end{bmatrix} \begin{bmatrix} x_a \\ x_b \\ x_c \end{bmatrix} \tag{5}$$

Voltages in dq frame v_d, v_q are related to the currents i_d, i_q and fluxes λ_d, λ_q as given in Eqs. 6 and 7, where $\omega_r\lambda_q$ and $\omega_r\lambda_d$ denote the rotationally induced emfs [3].

$$\begin{aligned} v_d &= R_s i_d + \frac{d}{dt}\lambda_d - \omega_r\lambda_q \\ v_q &= R_s i_q + \frac{d}{dt}\lambda_q + \omega_r\lambda_d \end{aligned} \tag{6}$$

$$\lambda_d = L_d i_d + \lambda_m$$
$$\lambda_q = L_q i_q$$
(7)

L_d, L_q are the dq axes inductances which take constant values in the dq rotating reference frame. R_s is the per phase resistance of the stator winding. λ_m represents the flux linkage of the permanent magnet. ω_r is the electrical angular frequency in rad/sec, which is related to the mechanical rotational speed ω_m by Eq. 8; where P is the number of poles of the PMSM. The same relation relates the mechanical and electrical rotor positions θ_m and θ_r respectively.

$$\omega_r = \omega_m \frac{P}{2}; \theta_r = \theta_m \frac{P}{2}$$
(8)

$$v_d = R_s i_d + L_d \frac{d}{dt} i_d - \omega_r L_q i_q$$
$$v_q = R_s i_q + L_q \frac{d}{dt} i_q + \omega_r (L_d i_d + \lambda_m)$$
(9)

Equation 10 gives the matrix form of the PMSM model in dq frame. Due to the absence of saliency in SPMSM, d and q axis inductances have the same value $L_d = L_q$.

$$\begin{bmatrix} v_d \\ v_q \end{bmatrix} = \begin{bmatrix} R_s & -\omega_r L_q \\ \omega_r L_d & R_s \end{bmatrix} \begin{bmatrix} i_d \\ i_q \end{bmatrix} + \begin{bmatrix} L_d & 0 \\ 0 & L_q \end{bmatrix} \frac{d}{dt} \begin{bmatrix} i_d \\ i_q \end{bmatrix} + \begin{bmatrix} 0 \\ \omega_r \lambda_m \end{bmatrix}$$
(10)

abc quantities are transformed to dq using the power non-invariant transformation. Hence, the generated motor torque is given by Eq. 11.

$$T_m = \frac{3}{2} \frac{P}{2} [\lambda_m + (L_d - L_q) i_d] i_q$$
(11)

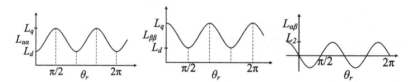

Fig. 2. Variation of inductances in $\alpha\beta$ frame as a function of rotor electrical angle

Modeling in αβ Stationary Reference Frame

Stationary $\alpha\beta$ reference frame inductances have a second harmonic variation as a function of the rotor electrical angle θ_r. The variations of self inductances $L_{\alpha\alpha}$, $L_{\beta\beta}$ and the mutual inductance $L_{\alpha\beta}$ are shown in Fig. 2. Equation 13 gives the relevant mathematical expressions [9].

$$L_{\alpha\alpha} = \frac{L_d + L_q}{2} - \frac{L_q - L_d}{2} \cos 2\theta_r$$
(13a)

$$L_{\beta\beta} = \frac{L_d + L_q}{2} + \frac{L_q - L_d}{2} \cos 2\theta_r$$
(13b)

$$L_{\alpha\beta} = -L_2 \sin 2\theta_r \tag{13c}$$

$$L_1 = \frac{L_d + L_q}{2}; L_2 = \frac{L_q - L_d}{2} \tag{13d}$$

Electrical angle of the rotor is defined with respect to the α-axis, with counter clockwise direction increase in θ_r. Self inductances have the maximum value of L_q with the alignment of q-axis and a minimum value of L_d with the alignment of d-axis. Mutual inductance has a maximum value when q or d axis is midway between the $\alpha\beta$ axes. Equations 14 and 15a, b relate the voltages, currents and flux linkages.

$$\begin{aligned} v_\alpha &= R_s i_\alpha + \frac{d}{dt}\lambda_\alpha \\ v_\beta &= R_s i_\beta + \frac{d}{dt}\lambda_\beta \end{aligned} \tag{14}$$

$$\lambda_\alpha = L_{\alpha\alpha} i_\alpha + L_{\alpha\beta} i_\beta + \lambda_m \cos\theta_r \tag{15a}$$

$$\lambda_\beta = L_{\beta\beta} i_\beta + L_{\beta\alpha} i_\alpha + \lambda_m \sin\theta_r \tag{15b}$$

The flux linkages in Eq. 15 can be represented in the matrix form of Eq. 16.

$$\begin{bmatrix} \lambda_\alpha \\ \lambda_\beta \end{bmatrix} = \begin{bmatrix} L_{\alpha\alpha} & L_{\alpha\beta} \\ L_{\alpha\beta} & L_{\beta\beta} \end{bmatrix} \begin{bmatrix} i_\alpha \\ i_\beta \end{bmatrix} + \lambda_m \begin{bmatrix} \cos\theta_r \\ \sin\theta_r \end{bmatrix} \tag{16}$$

A compact matrix form of the model after simplification is given in Eq. 17.

$$\begin{aligned} \begin{bmatrix} v_\alpha \\ v_\beta \end{bmatrix} &= R_s \begin{bmatrix} i_\alpha \\ i_\beta \end{bmatrix} + \begin{bmatrix} L_1 - L_2 \cos 2\theta_r & -L_2 \sin 2\theta_r \\ -L_2 \sin 2\theta_r & L_1 + L_2 \cos 2\theta_r \end{bmatrix} \frac{d}{dt} \begin{bmatrix} i_\alpha \\ i_\beta \end{bmatrix} \\ &+ 2\omega_r L_2 \begin{bmatrix} \sin 2\theta_r & -\cos 2\theta_r \\ -\cos 2\theta_r & -\sin 2\theta_r \end{bmatrix} \begin{bmatrix} i_\alpha \\ i_\beta \end{bmatrix} + \lambda_m \omega_r \begin{bmatrix} -\sin\theta_r \\ \cos\theta_r \end{bmatrix} \end{aligned} \tag{17}$$

All L_2 terms which depend on saliency will equate to zero for a SPMSM, with the model simplified to Eq. 18.

$$\begin{bmatrix} v_\alpha \\ v_\beta \end{bmatrix} = R_s \begin{bmatrix} i_\alpha \\ i_\beta \end{bmatrix} + \begin{bmatrix} L_s & 0 \\ 0 & L_s \end{bmatrix} \frac{d}{dt} \begin{bmatrix} i_\alpha \\ i_\beta \end{bmatrix} + \lambda_m \omega_r \begin{bmatrix} -\sin\theta_r \\ \cos\theta_r \end{bmatrix} \tag{18}$$

Torque expression is given by Eq. 19.

$$T_m = \frac{3}{2}\frac{P}{2}[\lambda_m + (L_d - L_q)(i_\alpha \cos\theta_r + i_\beta \sin\theta_r)](i_\beta \cos\theta_r - i_\alpha \sin\theta_r) \tag{19}$$

Mechanical model of the PMSM is given in Eq. 20. J, B and T_L are moment of inertia, coefficient of friction and load torque respectively.

$$T_m = T_L + J\frac{d\omega_m}{dt} + B\omega_m \tag{20a}$$

$$T_m = T_L + J\frac{2}{P}\frac{d\omega_r}{dt} + B\frac{2}{P}\omega_r \tag{20b}$$

3   Control of PMSM

The purpose of Field Oriented Control is to regulate the current i_d and i_q in the direct and quadrature axes respectively to generate the desired torque. The control of speed/position and current is taken care by two separate control loops, one for the inner current control loop and the other is the outer speed/position control loop.

3.1   Current Control Loop

Current controllers are designed in the dq rotor reference frame, in which the electrical quantities take DC values in steady state operation. The cross coupling terms between the dq axes make the system nonlinear, which is otherwise linear with a series combination of Resistance and Inductance. i_d and i_q do not depend only on v_d and v_q respectively. i_d depends on i_q through the term $\omega_r L_q i_q$, whereas i_q depends on i_d through $\omega_r(L_d i_d + \lambda_m)$. The above cross coupling can be removed by the feed forward method wherein the back emf terms are added to the PI control outputs [9]. The plant transfer function for current control is obtained as:

$$G_{pd}(s) = \frac{i_d(s)}{v_{ds}(s)} = \frac{1}{sL_d + R_s} \tag{21}$$

$$G_{pq}(s) = \frac{i_q(s)}{v_{qs}(s)} = \frac{1}{sL_q + R_s} \tag{22}$$

The controller is designed for a target open-loop gain cross-over frequency ω_{cq} of 3750 rad/s and a phase margin PM_q of 75^0. The values of K_{pq} and K_{iq} are derived from the following angle and magnitude conditions at the gain cross-over frequency [10].

$$\omega_{cq}\frac{K_{pq}}{K_{iq}} = \tan\left(PM_q - \frac{\pi}{2} + \tan^{-1}\left(\frac{\omega_{cq}L_q}{R_s}\right) + \tan^{-1}\left(\omega_{cq}T_i\right)\right) \tag{23}$$

$$K_{iq} = \omega_{cq}\frac{\sqrt{R_s^2 + \left(\omega_{cq}L_q\right)^2}\sqrt{1 + \left(\omega_{cq}T_i\right)^2}}{\sqrt{1 + \left(\omega_{cq}\frac{K_{pq}}{K_{iq}}\right)^2}} \tag{24}$$

3.2   Proposed Speed Controller

Figure 3 shows the closed loop PMSM drive with PI controllers for speed and currents. The proposed modification for the PI controller for speed is shown in Fig. 4. This achieves a drastic reduction in the speed and torque overshoots, which eventually improves position control for robotic applications.

The overshoot in speed is associated with an overshoot in torque, reduction of which decreases the momentary overloading of the machine when operated especially near rated conditions. Limiting the.overshoot in torque by placing a saturation block after the controller sacrifices the linearity of the controller. A smooth starting of the machine with a reduction in speed overshoot without sacrificing the transient response to step changes in load torque, can be achieved by the proposed controller shown in Fig. 4.

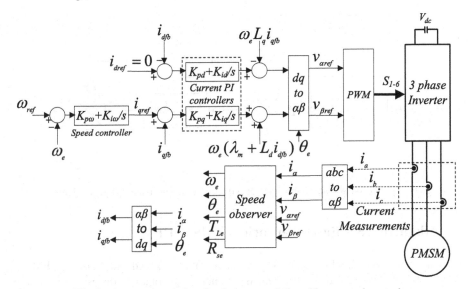

Fig. 3. System description for the proposed closed loop speed control

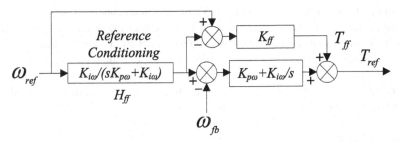

Fig. 4. Proposed speed controller for reduction in speed and torque overshoots

3.3 Proposed Position Controller

Plant transfer function for position control is given in Eq. 25. It consists of a pole at the origin, and hence a PI controller might tend the closed loop system more unstable as it adds one more pole at the origin. A PD controller is proposed in this paper, which inherently has the problems related to overshoot akin to closed loop speed control using the PI controller. Hence, a modification similar to that proposed for speed control loop is suggested for position control, which introduces a compensating term as shown in Fig. 5.

$$G_\theta(s) = \frac{1}{s(sJ + B)} \tag{25}$$

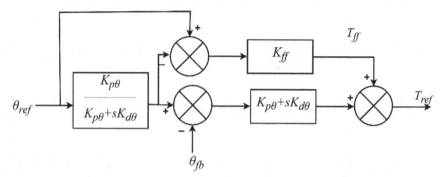

Fig. 5. Proposed position controller for reduction in position and torque overshoots

4 Adaptive EKF Based Sensorless PMSM Drive

EKF has found wide application for the estimation of rotor speed and position of PMSM drives [3–7, 11]. Variations in mechanical parameters do not affect the estimation accuracy of the EKF, given the EKF is tuned for convergence. The modeling of disturbances is of concern, as the following conditions have to be met for the derivation of the EKF as an optimal estimator: (i) zero mean, (ii) temporal independence (uncorrelated), (iii) a fixed or a varying known covariance. Fixed covariances imply the constant tuning of the EKF. Varying covariances demand the application of adaptive techniques to tune the EKF with relation to the known noise characteristics. The tuning of the EKF involves a heuristic procedure, which accounts to proper selection of the model and measurement noise covariance matrices Q and R respectively. The various steps involved in the recursive EKF algorithm is given below.

Prediction Step:

1) The predicted mean is computed from the time-discretized state model.

$$x_{p,k|k-1} = x_{e,k-1|k-1} + F_k x_{e,k-1|k-1} T_s + B u_{k-1} T_s \tag{26}$$

2) The corresponding estimation error covariance is given as:

$$P_{p,k|k-1} = P_{k-1|k-1} + (F_k P_{k-1|k-1} + P_{k-1|k-1} F_k^T) T_s + Q \tag{27}$$

Innovation Step:

3) The Jacobian of the output model with respect to the predicted states $x_{p,k|k-1}$ is given as:

$$H_k = \left. \frac{\partial h_k}{\partial x} \right|_{x=x_{p,k|k-1}} \tag{28}$$

The *observation model* predicts the output as given in Eq. 29.

$$y_{pk} = h_k\left(x_{p,k|k-1}\right) \tag{29}$$

4) The Kalman gain is calculated using Eq. 30.

$$K_k = P_{p,k|k-1}H_k^T \left(H_k P_{p,k|k-1}H_k^T + R\right)^{-1} \tag{30}$$

5) The state and error covariances are updated

$$x_{e,k|k} = x_{p,k|k-1} + K_k\left(y_{mk} - y_{pk}\right) \tag{31}$$

$$P_{e,k|k} = (I - K_k H_k)P_{p,k|k-1} \tag{32}$$

$$P_{e,k|k} = (I - K_k H_k)P_{p,k|k-1}(I - K_k H_k)^T + K_k R K_k^T \tag{33}$$

Improvisations over the basic EKF algorithm are achieved through the adaptive and iterative techniques. The performance of the filter can be attempted to be improved by using an Adaptive EKF in, wherein the system noise covariance matrix Q is online updated based on the stochastic model of the machine. This paper proposes a simple adaptive tuning of EKF wherein the model covariance matrix Q is adaptively tuned so as to reduce steady state noise in speed and position estimation and also achieving faster transient speed and position tracking. The former requires relatively lower values of Q matrix, whereas the latter requires a very high value of Q. A smooth transition from higher values of Q to relatively low values is achieved by setting it as a function of the feedback speed.

5 Simulation Results

Figure 6 and Fig. 7 show the reduction in speed and position overshoots respectively, with the inclusion of the proposed modification to the PI controller for speed and the proposed modification for the PD controller for position Fig. 8 shows the reduction in torque response.

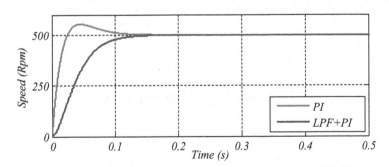

Fig. 6. Speed response for step speed reference

Figure 9 and Fig. 10 show the speed and position tracking respectively, with the proposed adaptive EKF.

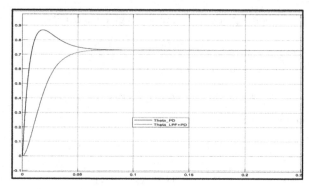

Fig. 7. Position response for step position reference

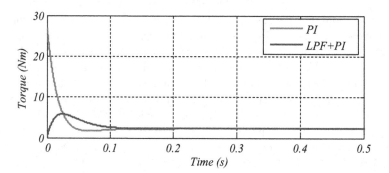

Fig. 8. Torque response for step speed reference

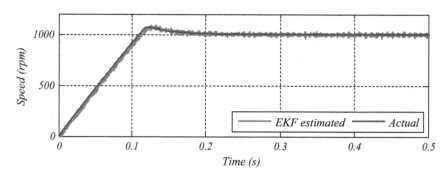

Fig. 9. Speed response with adaptive EKF

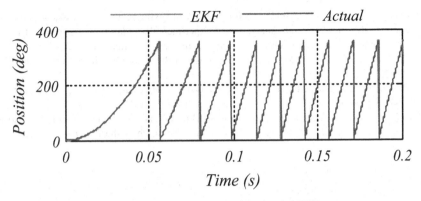

Fig. 10. Position response with adaptive EKF

6 Conclusion

A detailing of current, speed and position controllers for vector control of PMSM drives is presented in this paper. A speed controller is subsequently proposed to obtain reduced overshoots in speed and torque, and the performance thereof compared with that of the conventional PI controller. Similarly, a position controller is proposed on similar lines with a PD controller and its modification to obtain reduced overshoots in position. Simulation results show a considerable improvement as compared to conventional PI and PD controllers for speed and position respectively. An Adaptive EKF is proposed to achieve sensorless control, wherein the speed and position tracking is shown to be substantial in terms of noise rejection as well as transient tracking. The complete closed loop drive with combined improvements in control and estimation is shown to seamlessly integrate without any interference in the bandwidths of controller and observer, thereby achieving a high performance sensorless closed loop drive for PMSM.

References

1. Dwivedi, S., Singh, B.: Vector control vs direct torque control comparative evaluation for PMSM drive. In: 2010 Joint International Conference on Power Electronics, Drives and Energy Systems & 2010 Power India, New Delhi, pp. 1–8 (2010)
2. Foo, G.: Sensorless direct torque and flux control of interior permanent magnet synchronous motors at very low speeds including standstill, Ph.D. thesis, The University of New South Wales, Sydney, August 2010
3. Bolognani, S., Tubiana, L., Zigliotto, M.: Extended Kalman filter tuning in sensorless PMSM drives. IEEE Trans. Ind. Appl. **39**(6), 1741–1747 (2003)
4. Smidl, V., Peroutka, Z.: Advantages of square-root extended Kalman filter for sensorless control of AC drives. IEEE Trans. Ind. Electron. **59**(11), 4189–4196 (2012)
5. Idkhajine, L., Monmasson, E., Maalouf, A.: Extended Kalman filter for AC drive sensorless speed controller - FPGA-based solution or DSP-based solution. In: 2010 IEEE International Symposium on Industrial Electronics, Bari, pp. 2759–2764 (2010)
6. Du, T., Vas, P., Stronach, F.: Design and application of extended observers for joint state and parameter estimation in high-performance AC drives. IEE Proc. Electr. Power Appl. **142**(2), 71–78 (1995)

7. Vas, P.: Sensorless Vector and Direct Torque Control. Oxford University Press, Oxford (1998)
8. Hong, D.-K., et al.: Design, analysis, and experimental validation of a permanent magnet synchronous motor for articulated robot applications. IEEE Trans. Mag. (2017)
9. Krishnan, R.: Permanent Magnet Synchronous and Brushless DC Motor Drives. CRC Press (2009)
10. Mohan, N.: Advanced Electric Drives Analysis, Control and Modeling using Simulink. MNPERE (2001)
11. Gopinath, G.R.: Nonlinear Kalman filter based observers for speed and position sensorless control of permanent magnet synchronous motor drives, Ph.D. thesis, IIT Kanpur (2018)

Towards Designing Smart Public Spaces: A Framework for Designers to Leverage AI and IoT Technologies

Shuran Li[1] , Chengwei Wang[2] , Liying Rong[3], Yuwei Wu[1] ,
and Zhiqiang Wu[1]([✉])

[1] Tongji University, Shanghai 200000, China
sl2935@cornell.edu
[2] Tongji Architectural Design and Research Institute (Group) Co., Ltd., Shanghai 200000, China
[3] Future City (Shanghai) Design Consulting Co., Ltd., Shanghai 200000, China

Abstract. Artificial Intelligent (AI) and Internet of Things (IoT) will provide novel solutions in the area of public spaces design if the designers could understand how these technologies can be best utilized. This study aims to address the question, "How can practitioners be supported in applying AI and IoT technologies in the early design process of smart public spaces?" In order to answer the question, the author developed a framework includes three categories and 48 technologies that can be utilized in smart public spaces design. A focus group was run to evaluate the feasibility. The evaluation suggests that the framework can be used as design stimuli in the concept design phase. At the end, the paper discusses the usage and iteration direction for the framework.

Keywords: Artificial Intelligent · Public Spaces · Design Tools · Internet of Things

1 Introduction

Public space refers to the unfenced areas situated between architectural entities in urban settings, serving as a forum for public interaction and diverse activities among urban residents. The public nature of urban public space renders it a crucial enabler of civic social life, while simultaneously offering a pivotal platform for showcasing a city's appearance and spirit. Along with the technological advancements, people's demand for public spaces have been shaped as well. With the daily activities and life style were reshaped by information and communication technologies, the usage of public spaces is undergoing transformation, which presents new challenges for public space designers.

In recent years, with the proliferation of sensing networks and the development of smart cities, public space has acquired interactive and responsive attributes [1]. Artificial intelligence (AI) and the Internet of Things (IoT) present numerous possibilities for the design of public spaces [8]. Designers can utilize these technologies to perceive the usage patterns of users and enable the environment to respond promptly. By meeting the needs of different user groups, designers can offer various application scenarios and personalized experiences for users. Numerous practical examples of smart public space implementation have been successfully completed. Smart public spaces comprise interactive facades, augment reality, smart urban furniture [2, 3], smart transportation [4] and data management platform [5], transforming the public space from purely physical spaces into smart public space with the ability to sensing, decision make, and respond.

There is no doubt that AI is a fundamental technology that can enhance competitiveness, increase productivity, and bring new perspectives to address traditional challenges in public space design [9]. However, several researchers have suggested that practitioners face challenges in comprehending AI capabilities and applying AI as a design material in their design process [7]. For example, some researchers point out that user experience designers struggle to understand the capabilities and limitations of machine learning [6]. Other scientists indicates that designers often unable to identify obvious questions can be optimized by machine learning [10].

In recent years, leverage AI into the design process became a popular research topic. To support designer practitioners to apply AI in their design, various tools, methods and aids [11, 12] have been developed. Saleema Amershi et al. have developed a list contain 18 guidelines for Human-AI interaction [13]. Qian yang et al. demonstrate how to work with Machine Learning by series of interview [14]. Zhibin Zhou et al. developed a ML-Process Canvas, which is a design tool to support the UX design of machine learning-empowered products [15]. The majority of design tools are primarily focused on user experience and product design, with limited exploration in the field of urban public space design. Most design tools lacking a comprehensive consideration of potential technologies for designers. This lack of overview puts designers at a disadvantage because smart public space design often requires a combination of multiple technologies to address specific problems. Therefore, it becomes crucial for designers to have a comprehensive understanding of potential technologies. With a holistic perspective, designers can selectively combine and integrate technologies based on specific design problems and requirements, thus formulating design solutions for intelligent public spaces.

Therefore, this study aims to address the question, "How can practitioners be supported in applying AI and IoT technologies in the early design process of smart public spaces?" This paper focus on developing a framework with potential technologies that can be used in designing smart public spaces. The framework aims to facilitate designers in building a comprehensive understanding of the potential technologies available and generated more creative ideas during the design process.

The first part of the paper reports the development process of the framework. Second, the framework is described by sections. Third, a focus group session was run to test the feasibility of the framework. Last, the implications and limitations of the framework are discussed and future research steps are proposed.

2 Development the Framework of Potential AI and IoT Technologies

This part describes the framework development procedure. The first stage was collecting a long list of AI and IoT technologies from existing literature and practice. For the second stage, all technologies were clustered into three categories.

2.1 Development the Framework of Potential AI and IoT Technologies

The first step in our study was to create an overview of related technologies reported in the literature. To conduct the literature review, we utilized Google Scholar due to its comprehensive coverage. In the initial exploration, searching keywords "smart public space", "AI technology" and "Interaction design" were used. After a forward and backward search, keyword "sensing" and "smart cities"was added. According to the relevance of the content, a list included 131 papers was created. Besides literature, this work also tried to learn from existing design practice. This study collected 119 completed cases of smart public space practices, in which the IoT and AI technologies employed were categorized.

2.2 Cluster the Technologies

In the second stage, one researcher from IoT background and two experienced AI engineer were invited. All collected technologies was discussed during this stage. The technologies that have the similar purpose with different terms were merged. Technologies have that have similar object were clustered together. A list includes 48 potential technologies were created. The 48 technologies were subsequently clustered into three categories: sensing, decision, and reaction.

3   Three Categories of Potential Technologies

To help designers understand these technologies as design materials, we further clustered the technologies in three categories based on their purpose. Figure 1 demonstrates the framework of the clustered technologies, which include sensing, decision and reaction. Designers can combine technologies from different categories in their design process.

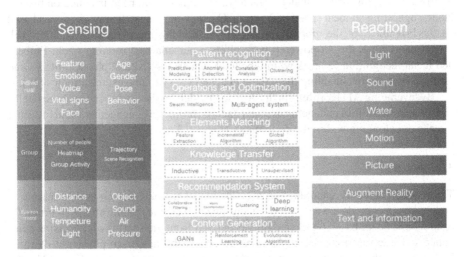

Fig. 1. Framework of clustered technologies.

3.1 Sensing

Sensing technology has revolutionized public space design by providing designers with a wealth of individual and group information as well as environmental data. With IoT-enabled sensors, designers can gather valuable insights about individuals in public spaces, such as their voice [18], facial features [19, 20], and even emotions [21, 22]. This allows for personalized and adaptive interactions, tailoring experiences to meet the specific needs and preferences of individuals. By analyzing group information such as number of people [23], heat maps [24, 25] and group activities [26, 27], designers can gain a deeper understanding of collective behaviors and dynamics within public spaces. This knowledge enables the creation of inclusive and engaging environments that promote social interactions and foster a sense of community. Furthermore, sensing technology allows designers to monitor environmental conditions such as temperature [28], humidity [29], and light [30], enabling them to optimize the design of public spaces for comfort and safety. Overall, the sensing category provides technologies that can assist designers in gathering in-time information about the user and the public space environment.

3.2 Decision

The decision category suggests the potential algorithms that can be embedded during the public spaces design. Based on the information collected through sensing stage, decision technologies empower public spaces to make informed and adaptive decisions. Numerous applications of decision-making enabled public spaces have already been implemented. In order to further enhance urban traffic efficiency, Copenhagen has invested 60 million kroner in the creation of 380 "smart traffic signals." These new signals are equipped to gather real-time traffic information and adjust signal timings accordingly to improve traffic flow. Additionally, "green wave" signals have been installed on bicycle lanes, suggesting an ideal speed of 20 km/h. Cyclists can adjust their riding speed based on the brightness of the green light, thereby improving the overall throughput [16]. In Beijing, China, the AI-powered park offers a personalized running track. Embedded facial recognition cameras within the track can assess visitors' physical fitness and exercise completion, enabling them to be matched with suitable exercise routes [18].

By leveraging AI algorithms in the decision model, public spaces can become intelligent entities capable of enhancing user satisfaction, promoting engagement, and fostering a sense of belonging within the community (Figs. 2, 3 and 4).

3.3 Reaction

The reaction category encompasses a collection of actionable responses that can be undertaken in accordance with the decisions made. It enables public spaces to promptly respond and adapt based on the judgments derived from the sensing and decision components. These reactions encompass a range of possibilities, from physical to virtual. For example, the reaction can by the adjustment of environmental lighting [31], the playback of carefully selected audio and music [32], and the provision of relevant visual information [33].

Fig. 2. The Green Wave at Copenhagen. Source: https://www.swarco.com/stories/bike-friendly-cities

Fig. 3. The Intelligent track at Haidian AI park Source: https://language.chinadaily.com.cn/a/201811/06/WS5be12540a310eff303286db1.html, http://travel.people.com.cn/n1/2018/1104/c41570-30380593.html.

The timeliness of responses in smart public space design can vary. It can involve immediate reactions based on specific circumstances, such as adjusting lighting based on the proximity of individuals. Additionally, it can entail long-term optimization achieved through continuous learning from the collected information.

By harnessing the insights garnered through sensing and the subsequent decision-making process, the reaction category facilitates instantaneous and contextually tailored responses, thereby elevating the overall user experience within public spaces.

4   Case Study

To evaluate the feasibility of the framework, the first author conducted a focus group with three experienced designers in the fields of urban planning and landscape architecture. During the workshop, the author provided a 10-min presentation to introduce the framework and the existing design practices that applied the technologies in the framework to the participants. A design site was demonstrated afterward (a riverside park in Shanghai, China). All participants were invited to generated as many concepts as possible in 20 min by utilizing the framework. Each designer was given five minutes to present their outcomes. Afterward, all participants were asked to discuss their feedback and experiences of designing using the framework. The entire focus group was audio recorded. All data were translated and iteratively reviewed to cluster similar responses using thematic analysis [34] and meaning make techniques such as affinity diagramming [35].

Table 1. ...

#	Design Description	Participant Number	Sensing	Decision	Reaction
1	A range of devices responded to the ambient temperature and humidity to create a comfortable visiting environment for tourists, such as adjustable pavilions and cooling mist sprays	#1	Temperature, Humidity, Light, Air,Sound	N/A	Motion, Water
2	Optimizing tourists the touring route based on crowd density. Utilizing lighting and sound cues along pathways to guide the flow of people	#1	Heat map	Operations and Optimization	Light, Information, Sound, AR/VR
3	Tailoring to the preferences and physical abilities of different individuals, provides personalized recommendations of fitness dance music and exercise guidance that suit their needs	#1	Pose, Emotion,Vital Sign	Element Matching, Recommendation System	Sound, Image

(*continued*)

Table 1. (*continued*)

#	Design Description	Participant Number	Sensing	Decision	Reaction
4	Provide visitors with different tour atmospheres and interactions based on their relationships	#1	Face, Age, Gender, Group Activity	Element Matching	Sound, Water,Light,AR/VR
5	Collect the long-term usage data of the park and provide suggestions for its planning, design, and operation	#1	Heat Map, Trajectory	Pattern Recognition	Information
6	Offer personalized tour routes based on the preferences of the visitors	#2	Heat map, Trajectory, Feature	Pattern Recognition	Information
7	Illuminate special warning lights when a large dog passes by in the vicinity	#2	Pressure,object	Element Matching	Light、Sound
8	Provide energy-efficient and secure lighting during nighttime solo walks in the park for everyone's comfort and safety	#2	Distance	N/A	Light

(*continued*)

Table 1. (*continued*)

#	Design Description	Participant Number	Sensing	Decision	Reaction
9	Predict the crowd flow in the park to assist visitors in avoiding peak visiting times	#3	Number of People	Pattern Recognition	Information
10	A photo taking installation that allow visitor take a photo with virtual reality environment	#3	Gender, Temperature,Age 、 Feature	Element Matching	Image

During the focus group session, the three participants employed a variety of design elements provided by the framework, encompassing sensing, decision-making, and reaction. Table 1 provides a comprehensive overview of the design outputs and applied design strategies for each participant.

Fig. 4. Participants designed smart public spaces with the framework during the focus group

5 Discussion

10 concept design ideas were generated during the 20 min session. The high usage rate of the technologies from the framework suggests its feasibility. In this part, the key insights from the focus group were discussed.

The design that emerges from the focus group is characterized by its diversity. It encompasses various aspects such as enhancing visitors' sense of security, improving the aesthetics of the park, fostering social interactions among individuals, providing enriched functional services, and assisting in park management. Designers can seamlessly integrate their designs with ongoing projects, as participant 1 eloquently stated, "I have recently been assisting a park in optimizing its operations and management. I believe that analyzing and utilizing crowd relationships can be highly beneficial."

The framework provides the designers with an overview of the potential technologies. All three participants expressed their previous understanding and attempts at employing similar intelligent techniques in public space design. However, due to a lack of comprehensive awareness about intelligent technologies, their designs often remained limited to replicating existing cases or applying isolated technological solutions. This framework, on the other hand, enables them to swiftly grasp the potential technological means and facilitates the generation of original design proposals.

The participants acknowledged that understanding technologies in the sensing and reaction category is relatively straightforward. However, they expressed difficulties in distinguishing between the various technologies in the decision category. Throughout the design process, the participants sought clarification from the organizers regarding the meaning of certain aspects within the decision section. The organizers attempted to provide a simple explanation of the algorithms in the decision section, covering both fundamental principles and application examples. During the discuss session, the designers' outcomes demonstrated a correct understanding of the decision section and applied decision strategies in their design. Their feedback once again confirmed the challenges of treating AI as a design material. The highly specialized terminology of algorithms hindered the designers' comprehension of what the technology can accomplish. In the course of the discussions, the author observed that, compared to the principles of algorithms, designers were more interested in the application cases and practical capabilities of algorithms. Participant 2 remarked, "The mathematics makes me feel confused as well. However, when you explain the algorithms with examples, I can immediately visualize them in my mind." The decision section not only features the main decision algorithms but also includes subtitles for each category. However, the participants expressed confusion about the purpose of the subtitles, finding it challenging to differentiate between the sub-techniques and determine when to apply each technology. One participant mentioned that they were not concerned about the specific branches within the technologies since addressing those issues falls under the purview of algorithm engineers. As designers, their focus is on providing design solutions rather than delving into the algorithmic implementation process.

The participants have raised questions regarding the next steps for implementing the design. In the realm of traditional public space construction, designers readily acquaint themselves with an array of prospective collaborators, spanning the realms of architectural, construction, and electrical and plumbing teams. However, in the design of smart public spaces, they are uncertain about which teams they will be cooperating with. They vaguely mention the involvement of teams such as software development and hardware design, but they lack specific understanding of their precise engagement timeline, responsibilities, and collaboration models. The participants express their desire for more guidance to help them comprehend how to collaborate with multiple teams during the design process and ensure the feasibility of the design.

6 Conclusion

6.1 General Discussion and Conclusion

This research significantly contributes to the realm of public space design and human-computer interaction through the development of a comprehensive framework comprising potential AI and IoT technologies for the design of intelligent public spaces. By conducting an extensive analysis of relevant literature and real-world practice examples, a total of 48 technologies were meticulously extracted and categorized into three categories: sensing, decision, and reaction. To assess the efficacy of the framework, a evaluation was conducted utilizing a focus group approach. In a specific case study involving the design of a riverside park, three designers generated ten distinct concept designs. Notably, the implementation of the framework yielded a remarkable utilization rate, with 20 out of 22 sensing strategies, 4 out of 6 decision-making strategies, and all 7 reaction strategies being effectively employed. The pronounced utilization of the framework underscores its inherent comprehensibility and applicability. Additionally, the ensuing discussion session underscored the immense potential of employing the framework as a potent design stimulus tool during the nascent conceptual design phase, effectively harnessing the capabilities of AI and IoT technologies in the design process.

6.2 Limitation and Future Work

The participants' frequent utilization of strategies provided by the framework serves as a validation of its utility while also indicating the requirements for its further development. Building upon the designers' unique cognitive approach to technology, the author aims to expound on the technologies within the decision category using designerly language in the upcoming phase. Concrete design cases and visual aids will be employed to facilitate designers' comprehension of these technologies. Equally important are the application guidelines for the framework.

Considering diverse design objectives, such as environmental beautification, social facilitation, and enhancing security, the author will furnish designers with practical guidance on applying the framework. This will prove invaluable in aiding designers unfamiliar with AI and IoT in swiftly acquainting themselves with these technologies.

References

1. Suurenbroek, F., Nio, I., de Waal, M.: Responsive public spaces: exploring the use of interactive technology in the design of public spaces (2019)
2. Premier, A., GhaffarianHoseini, A.: Solar-powered smart urban furniture: preliminary investigation on limits and potentials of current designs. Smart Sustainable Built Environ. (2022)
3. Ciaramella, A., et al.: Smart furniture and smart city. IOP Conf. Ser. Mater. Sci. Eng. **365**(2), 022012 (2018)
4. Oberheitmann, A.: The Development of Smart Cities in China. Smart Urban Regeneration, pp. 201–213 (2017)
5. Burange, A.W., Misalkar, H.D.: Review of Internet of Things in development of smart cities with data management & privacy. In: 2015 International Conference on Advances in Computer Engineering and Applications, pp. 189–195. IEEE (2015)
6. Dove, G., Halskov, K., Forlizzi, J., Zimmerman, J.: UX design innovation: Challenges for working with machine learning as a design material. In: Proceedings of the 2017 Chi Conference on Human Factors in Computing Systems, pp. 278–288 (2017)
7. Yang, Q., Steinfeld, A., Rosé, C., Zimmerman, J.: Re-examining whether, why, and how human-AI interaction is uniquely difficult to design. In: Proceedings of the 2020 Chi Conference on Human Factors in Computing Systems, pp. 1–13 (2020)
8. Townsend, A.M.: Smart Cities: Big Data, Civic Hackers, And The Quest For A New Utopia. W.W. Norton & Company, New York (2013)
9. Yang, Q.: Machine learning as a UX design material: how can we imagine beyond automation, recommenders, and reminders?. In: AAAI Spring Symposia, vol. 1(2.1), pp. 2–6 (2018)
10. Yang, Q., Zimmerman, J., Steinfeld, A., Tomasic, A.: Planning adaptive mobile experiences when wireframing. In: Proceedings of the 2016 ACM Conference on Designing Interactive Systems, pp. 565–576 (2016)
11. Bond, R.R., et al.: Human centered artificial intelligence: weaving UX into algorithmic decision making. In: RoCHI, pp. 2–9 (2019)
12. Xu, W.: Toward human-centered AI: a perspective from human-computer interaction. Interactions **26**(4), 42–46 (2019)
13. Amershi, S., et al.: Guidelines for human-AI interaction. In: Proceedings of the 2019 Chi Conference on Human Factors in Computing Systems, pp. 1–13 (2019)
14. Yang, Q., Scuito, A., Zimmerman, J., Forlizzi, J., Steinfeld, A.: Investigating how experienced UX designers effectively work with machine learning. In: Proceedings of the 2018 Designing Interactive Systems Conference, pp. 585–596 (2018)
15. Zhou, Z., Sun, L., Zhang, Y., Liu, X., Gong, Q.: ML lifecycle canvas: designing machine learning-empowered UX with material lifecycle thinking. Hum.-Comput. Interact. **35**(5–6), 362–386 (2020)
16. Cardwell, D.: Copenhagen lighting the way to greener, more efficient cities, New York Times, p. 8 (2014)
17. Pk, J., Sen, A., Chen, X., Murali, A.: Inside Haidian Park: A stroll through the world's first "ai-park" (2018). https://archive.factordaily.com/inside-haidian-park-the-worlds-first-artificial-intelligence-park/
18. Arriany, A.A., Musbah, M.S.: Applying voice recognition technology for smart home networks. In: 2016 International Conference on Engineering & MIS (ICEMIS), pp. 1–6. IEEE (2016)
19. Li, L., Mu, X., Li, S., Peng, H.: A review of face recognition technology. IEEE access **8**, 139110–139120 (2020)

20. Praveen, G.B., Dakala, J.: Face recognition: challenges and issues in smart city/environments. In 2020 International Conference on Communication Systems & NetworkS (COMSNETS, pp. 791–793. IEEE (2020)

21. Pujol, F.A., Mora, H., Martínez, A.: Emotion recognition to improve e-healthcare systems in smart cities. In: Research & Innovation Forum 2019: Technology, Innovation, Education, and their Social Impact 1, pp. 245–254. Springer International Publishing (2019). https://doi. org/10.1007/978-3-030-30809-4_23

22. Hossain, M.S., Muhammad, G.: Emotion recognition using deep learning approach from audio–visual emotional big data. Informat. Fusion **49**, 69–78 (2019)

23. Marsden, M., McGuinness, K., Little, S., O'Connor, N.E.: Resnetcrowd: a residual deep learning architecture for crowd counting, violent behaviour detection and crowd density level classification. In: 2017 14th IEEE International Conference on Advanced Video and Signal based Surveillance (AVSS), pp. 1–7. IEEE (2017)

24. Jarvis, N., Hata, J., Wayne, N., Raychoudhury, V., Gani, M.O.: Miamimapper: crowd analysis using active and passive indoor localization through wi-fi probe monitoring. In: Proceedings of the 15th ACM International Symposium on QoS and Security for Wireless and Mobile Networks, pp. 1–10 (2019)

25. Atta, S., Sadiq, B., Ahmad, A., Saeed, S.N., Felemban, E.: Spatial-crowd: a big data framework for efficient data visualization. In: 2016 IEEE International Conference on Big Data (Big Data), pp. 2130–2138. IEEE (2016)

26. Yan, R., Tang, J., Shu, X., Li, Z., Tian, Q.: Participation-contributed temporal dynamic model for group activity recognition. In: Proceedings of the 26th ACM international conference on Multimedia, pp. 1292–1300 (2018)

27. Deng, Z., Vahdat, A., Hu, H., Mori, G.: Structure inference machines: Recurrent neural networks for analyzing relations in group activity recognition. In: Proceedings of the IEEE Conference on Computer Vision and Pattern Recognition, pp. 4772–4781 (2016)

28. Channi, H. K., Kumar, R.: The role of smart sensors in smart city. In: Smart Sensor Networks: Analytics, Sharing and Control, pp. 27–48. Springer International Publishing, Cham (2021). https://doi.org/10.1007/978-3-030-77214-7_2

29. Siregar, B., Nasution, A.B.A., Fahmi, F.: Integrated pollution monitoring system for smart city. In: 2016 International Conference on ICT For Smart Society (ICISS), pp. 49–52. IEEE (2016)

30. Hancke, G.P., de Carvalho e Silva, B., Hancke Jr., G.P.: The role of advanced sensing in smart cities. Sensors **13**(1), 393–425 (2012)

31. Dheena, P.F., Raj, G.S., Dutt, G., Jinny, S.V.: IOT based smart street light management system. In: 2017 IEEE International Conference on Circuits and Systems (ICCS), pp. 368–371. IEEE (2017)

32. Sarmento, P., Holmqvist, O., Barthet, M.: Musical Smart City: Perspectives on Ubiquitous Sonification. arXiv preprint arXiv:2006.12305. (2020)

33. Murshed, S.M., Al-Hyari, A.M., Wendel, J., Ansart, L.: Design and implementation of a 4D web application for analytical visualization of smart city applications. ISPRS Int. J. Geo Inf. **7**(7), 276 (2018)

34. Clarke, V., Braun, V., Hayfield, N.: Thematic analysis. Qualitative Psychol. Pract. Guide Res. Methods **3**, 222–248 (2015)

Affordance and User Behavior: Implication for Inclusive Public Facilities to Promote User Experience

Xin Yi Liang[1], Jia Xin Xiao[1,2](✉), Ming Jun Luo[3,4], Zhi Han Liu[1], Xi Nan Teng[1], and Yang Zhong Cao[1]

[1] School of Art and Design, Guangdong University of Technology, 729 Dongfengdong Rd., Guangzhou 510000, China
cynthia.xiao@gdut.edu.cn
[2] Guangdong International Center of Advanced Design, Guangdong University of Technology, Guangzhou 510000, China
[3] Guangdong Industry Polytechnic, Guangzhou 510000, China
[4] City University of Macau, Macau, China

Abstract. Public facilities are necessary to our daily lives, but not everyone will have a positive experience using them in open spaces, particularly those with different abilities. Affordance theory has brought more attention to people with different disabilities. The interaction between persons with different disabilities and public facilities in open spaces is observed and analyzed as part of this paper's investigation of the connection between affordance and user behavior. This paper presents a user experience framework based on affordance that reveals the interaction between users and artifacts from the perspective of affordance and makes recommendations for inclusive public design to promote user experience in open spaces, drawing on the literature on affordance and user experience.

Keywords: Affordance · Inclusive design · Open space · Public design · User experience

1 Introduction

Everyday life depends significantly on open space. It not only provides access to leisure and sporting activities but also increases municipal vibrancy. In recent decades, people have paid increasing attention to the experience of open space, especially the user experience of public facilities. The needs of people in public facilities are also changing due to the aging social situation, and these needs differ based on individual cognitive, perceptual, and physical abilities (Wu & Song, 2017). Different needs lead to different desired experiences. User experience is subjective. People with different abilities may have different experiences, and even the same individual can have different experiences at different times.

Hassenzahl (2005, 2010) considers interaction a goal-directed action, and both hedonic and pragmatic product qualities can potentially improve the user experience. Pucill

(2014) summarizes and maps out Hassenzahl's user experience theory, and this paper builds on that foundation. Affordance theory shows the interaction between humans and artifacts—focusing on the link between people and technology, particularly people with different cognitive, perceptual, and physical abilities (Davis, 2020).

Gibson created the term "affordance," and according to his explanation, affordance refers to some of the possibilities that the environment or object offers to a person or animal (Gibson, 2014). Norman (1988) introduced affordance to the design community. Since then, many academics have utilized affordance theory to investigate the interactions between subjects, objects, and the environment. Hartson (2003) proposes four types of affordances—cognitive, sensory, functional, and physical—and combines them with Norman's (1988) seven stages of action. The mechanisms and conditions framework of affordances, presented by Jenny L. Davis (2020), describes the relationship between subjects and objects. Mechanisms of affordance represent an object's response to a subject, including request, demand, encouragement, discouragement, refusal, and allowance. Conditions of affordance include perception, dexterity, and cultural and institutional legitimacy—which separately cover how subjects perceive things, as well as their functioning, obstacles, possibilities, and limits; the skill with which subjects can interact with objects; and the extent to which normative standards and official codifications sanction the subject-object connection. Affordance theory may inspire inclusive public facility design and a better open-space user experience.

Public facilities should be welcoming, accommodating, and conducive to a positive user experience. User behavior and how individuals engage with public facilities in open spaces are directly tied to the user experience. Making public facilities more inclusive and optimizing the user experience with public facilities can improve lives. An in-depth study of the relationship between affordance theory and user behavior is valuable in promoting an inclusive user experience in open spaces for more individuals.

2   Method

The study lasted 60 days from April 2023 to May 2023, and was conducted in Guangzhou, China. The approach utilized in this research is direct nonparticipant observation, in which the research team took photos in public facilities from 8 a.m. to 6 p.m. to capture users' interactions with the facilities in the most realistic way possible. Eleven parks were the subject of the research team's study of public facilities, which included four different categories of parks: comprehensive parks, special parks, community parks, and "youyuan" (游园 in Chinese, a green space with independent land use, at a small scale or with diverse shapes, convenient for residents to enter nearby and with certain recreational functions). This research covers ramps, public restrooms, sinks, pavilions, checkerboard tables, railings, benches, rain shelters, and other public facilities. Older adults, children, persons with different disabilities, and other vulnerable populations make up the research population.

Drawing on the literature on affordance and user experience, the research team observed and documented the interactions between persons with varied abilities and public facilities in parks. Lastly, an in-depth analysis of user behavior gave insights into the user's psychological process and experience.

3   Results

According to the observations, most people interact with public facilities as expected; for example, seats are a kind of facility to sit and rest, but beyond that, some users have a unique understanding of the facility according to their requirements, such as lying down on a seat as if it were a bed. In other words, facilities afford some possible actions that might not have expected. Following observation and research, it was discovered that the park's three most frequently used and abundant facilities are seats, fences, and pavilions, so this paper will focus on these three types of facilities. ·

Seats are the most common public facilities in open spaces, affording support and providing the function of sitting down and resting for the user. Sometimes, seats are used as tables, as exemplified in Fig. 1. A man sat on a small stool he had brought with him, placing a notebook and tablet on the "table". People can also use a seat as a table and chair at the same time. There was a scene photographed in a park on an overcast afternoon; the two men in the scene may have had mobility problems because they both had a wheelchair next to them. They sat opposite each other on a long stone seat, with a chess board between them. Their physical posture of curling their legs and bending sideways to face each other to play chess did not appear comfortable. Despite this, they still played chess in the same place for at least four hours.

Fig. 1. A middle-aged man using a seat as a table

What is unexpected is that seats may be an exercise facility. Figure 2 depicts one such scene: a young man discovered new possibilities for a seat. He wanted to do push-ups but not get his hands dirty, so he used the seat as a support tool. The man supported his hands with the seat and tilted his body, but he gave up after only three to five push-ups. Under normal circumstances, people would first get down and support their bodies with both hands, but in this scenario, the user needed to rely only on his hands to support his tilted body at the beginning, which required more strength; hence, he gave up. Due to the acceptable seat height, vigorous and energetic old individuals, such as the man in Fig. 3, may use it to help rest their legs after some activity. Figure 4 shows how a seat may also be utilized as a footpad.

Some of the seating designs are unique. Figure 5 clearly shows a steep slope in front of the seat. The architectural objective of this slope may be for aesthetics or to hold people's legs for those who need to sit down and rest. Nevertheless, it also serves as a playground for children. Children may utilize the slope as a slide or climbing area (Fig. 5).

Fig. 2. A man using a seat to train with push-ups

Fig. 3. A vigorous and energetic elderly man using a seat to relax his leg muscles

Fig. 4. Two people relaxing their legs on a seat

Fig. 5. A little boy climbing up the slope

The second typical facility is a pavilion. Park visitors shielded from heat and rain by the pavilions and shelters there. Almost all pavilions and shelters are spacious and ventilated; most are furnished with chairs. Interestingly, pavilions and shelters have been transformed into public activity rooms for chess, singing, dancing, and so on. One of them is the pavilion seen in Fig. 6. Thanks to the Chinese chess tradition, chess has developed into a national sport in China, especially among the senior population. Small tables and chairs are frequently brought to the pavilion, and some even purchase massive chess sets to position in strategic areas for visitors' use. An older adult watched while a middle-aged man and another older man played chess (Fig. 7), and Fig. 8 shows Go self-taking points.

Fig. 6. The pavilion becomes a chess room.

Fig. 7. An older adult watching while a middle-aged man and another man play chess

The last one is an observation about fences. Fences in parks prevent people from entering specific areas, such as lakes, flower beds, and lawns. Different kinds of fences also have different functions for people. Usually, the low fences around flower beds or lawns may serve as seating or props for children to play with, but some relatively high fences around lakes only allow leaning when people are tired. Figure 9 shows a woman sitting on a spherical stone fence and four children playing with water. The small spherical stone fence around the lake warns and discourages people from entering. However, the small lake is not deep enough to put children in danger; hence, the fence is used as a seat. For kids, this object can support their bodies and prevent them from

Fig. 8. Different kinds of chess and cards, benches, and small tables at self-taking points

falling into the water. Unlike these spherical fences, some one-meter-high continuous stone fences do not allow people to sit on them. Still, such a fence is not only a resting facility that can be leaned on but also an exercise/stretching facility. In Fig. 10, a man stretches his leg on the fence after a run.

Fig. 9. A woman sitting on a stone fence and four children playing with water

Fig. 10. A man puts his leg on a fence to stretch after a run

In observing the behavior of older adults who use wheelchairs, the research team found that wheelchair users have less need for park facilities than normal or healthy older adults. Wheelchair users do not need sitting facilities to rest and cannot use any sports or recreational facilities. On the contrary, they focus more on accessibility due to ground that is not flat or has been changed for aesthetic reasons. Pavement conditions are just as important for the elderly as quality rest facilities (Xu, 2020). In addition to concrete fences, some invisible fences do not have a strong sense of warning but can hinder people's actions to a certain extent. Figure 11 presents a park divided into sports areas. Some people fix themselves inside this area to play ball sports, such as tennis and badminton. This area is surrounded by ornamental vegetation and has two entrances. The ground at these two entrances is not flat—with the grass intersecting with the marble floor to form the pavement, which invariably dissuades wheelchair users from entering because there is a certain chance that the wheels of the wheelchair will get stuck in the grass. Wheelchair users are allowed to enter, although it is not quite convenient. Figure 12 shows a small entrance to the park; this steel fence denies access to wheelchair users. Only one person is allowed through.

Fig. 11. A sports area with two invisible fences discouraging wheelchair users from entering

Fig. 12. A steel fence that denies access to wheelchair users

In conclusion, some of the facilities commonly found in parks, such as seats, fences, and pavilions, offer users different functions and other new possibilities of action to meet their needs. The park's most common facility, seats, allows users to sit, lie, write, play chess, exercise, stretch, etc. The pavilion is a reasonably significant part of the park, continually attracting several people and giving birth to certain agreed-upon community activities. Fence styles vary based on the surrounding location: plant kinds, common spherical stone types, taller continuous ones, etc. There are even some invisible barriers. Altogether, these fences encourage diverse user behaviors and experiences.

4 Discussions

Varying user experiences result from various behaviors of individuals with different cognitive, perceptual, and physical capacities toward public facilities. Based on user behavior, this paper analyzed various behavioral possibilities of seats. According to the observations, a seat satisfied the demand of two wheelchair users for enjoyment purposes (i.e., playing chess), and their bodies could complete the act. In fact, they had a more straightforward approach to playing chess by sitting in their wheelchairs. They do not require an extra seat; they only require a tall enough table or seat to support the chessboard. However, there are no such facilities, so the only other option is to get out of their wheelchairs and sit on the sitting device to play chess. They may prefer the current way of playing chess, but if there were a higher table with no seats, they would have a more suitable choice.

Another behavioral possibility of the seat is doing exercises such as push-ups. However, the man in Fig. 2 did not have a good attempt because his requirement was not satisfied. It can be presumed that first, he wanted to exercise. He realized the seat provides the possibility of such behavior. However, the man's physical flexibility and fitness were insufficient to support him to complete such action because doing exercise in this way requires more strength and body balance, so he gave up in less than one minute.

From the perspective of the conditions of affordance theory, cultural and institutional legitimacy are the reasons for the transformation of pavilions into open chessboard rooms. The culture of a particular group or region is intangible, but it can reflect through user behavior, activities, and even language (Siu, 2005). In other words, culture influences user needs and somewhat dominates user behavior. Of course, user behavior must conform to institutional legitimacy. In the case of the pavilion, Chinese chess culture produced such a new need for entertainment that it encouraged people to play chess. People needed a free, accessible, and ventilated area to play, and they realized that the park pavilion had ample space, was shielded from the heat and rain, and did not violate any laws or regulations. The pavilion eventually became the agreed-upon outdoor chess room.

Next, the mechanism of affordance theory will be analyzed with the example of fences. Different fences have different degrees of warning against the degree of entry, while each fence may bring different behavioral possibilities, leading to different user behaviors. From the point of view of affordance theory, the spherical stone fence is low and spaced, indicating that it has a particular dissuasive effect on the user but does not refuse entry; children are still allowed but discouraged from playing delightfully with water. The invisible fence between the lawn and the marble indicates a dissuasive effect but is more targeted at wheelchair users. The stainless steel fence clearly rejects wheelchair users, as the gap between the two fences is not large enough for wheelchairs to pass through. For wheelchair users, this route is not feasible, which means they need to take a longer detour to enter the park, which may put them in a bad mood. The taller continuous stone fence is a stronger statement of rejection for all and indicates that the area is more dangerous for people. In addition to entry, other actions, such as stretching and relaxing the legs, are permitted, as long as the user can recognize the feasibility and legality of the action and their physical condition allows them to achieve it.

Considering prior research, this paper proposes a framework of user experience based on affordance, which can reflect the interaction between humans and artifacts (Fig. 13).

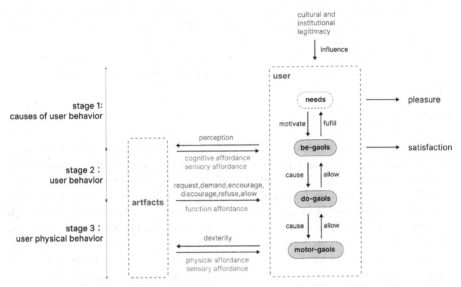

Fig. 13. A user experience framework based on affordance theory

The framework is divided into three stages. Stage 1 is the cause of the behavior. Under the influence of cultural and institutional legitimacy, user demands stimulate the psychological expectations of user behavior (be-goals). Users must perceive artifacts at this stage and understand whether they can meet their demands. At the same time, cognitive and sensory affordances are needed here to convey information to users. For example, the shape of the spherical stone fence in Fig. 9 conveys to the woman who wants to rest that the sphere is round and of appropriate height and size and that the lake is shallow and not hazardous, implying that the sphere may be used for sitting. Before sitting down, the woman must perceive the information concerning the potential of sitting on the sphere. Furthermore, this information is obtained through the user's senses and cognition.

Stage 2 is the user's behavior (do-goals). The user learns that their needs may be addressed by the activity perceived in stage 1, and then they take action. Artifacts respond to users through demanding, requesting, discouraging, encouraging, refusing, and allowing. As mentioned in the above example, the invisible fence in Fig. 12 discourages but allows wheelchair users, while the stainless steel fence explicitly denies access to wheelchair users. At this stage, functional affordance is needed to afford different features for different users and meet different needs, just like different fences offer different possibilities for users, with spherical fences to sit on and high continuous stone fences for leg stretching but disallowing sitting.

Stage 3 is how the user performs the behavior. To satisfy the user's demands, the user must have the physical flexibility to do the action (motor-goals). Both physical and sensory affordances are at work here, assisting the user with physical activity. Regarding the need to stretch the leg muscles, the older adults in Fig. 3 and the young people in Fig. 10 make different choices. Unable to put the legs as high, the older adult's legs may not be as flexible as the young person's. Hence, for the older adult, the low seat as a stretching tool is appropriate, and for the young man, the height of the seat is not enough to meet his needs, so he chooses a higher fence.

Suppose the user's physical condition and the artificial object's behavioral possibility can meet the user's psychological needs. In that case, they will get a satisfactory user experience.

5 Conclusion

This paper provides some insights and suggestions for improving the user experience in open spaces by observing the interactions of children, the elderly, and people with disabilities with public facilities. First, pay attention to the influence of park culture on user behavior. Cultures may be regional or classified by group. In the observation, chess culture prevails in some parks, while visitors to other parks prefer other activities, such as fishing, painting, and dancing. Only by understanding the preferences of the visitors of a particular park can the facilities these people need be increased, improving their park experience. In the case of the pavilion above, users are brought together by chess culture. There are not enough facilities in this area, so users must bring their small stools to the park daily, which may affect the user experience. Second, the government should not only emphasize park development and completion but also focus on the conduct of the users who utilize it long after it is finished. Because users' cognition and experiences of park facilities may differ, it is more vital to analyze user behaviors in the park, and relevant management departments should maintain park facilities to improve user satisfaction (Au-Yong, 2023; Siu, 2013). The park is available to everyone and should cater to everyone's needs. Designers can only achieve some of the requirements from the beginning of construction, though this is the ideal condition all people should all pursue. For example, the placement of fences in Fig. 12 reflects that the park only considers the needs of ordinary people and that the needs of wheelchair users are not taken into account. Some parks are often visited by wheelchair users and others may not be visited by disabled people, but it may be popular with young children. Measuring park use is one of the most important factors that may influence park usefulness, and space consumption measurements are critical for preserving and enhancing park space (Abdelhamid, 2020). As actual usage may not match expectations, the government should optimize the park experience based on its current use.

From the perspective of user experience, designing more inclusive public facilities, and enhancing user experience in open spaces, the proposed framework enables designers and relevant management departments to understand the relationship between public facilities and user behavior so that individuals may make beautiful memories at the park and increase their happiness.

Acknowledgments. The authors would like to acknowledge the National Natural Science Foundation of China (Grant No. 52008114), Philosophy and Social Sciences Fund of Guangdong Province (GD22XYS17), Undergraduate Teaching and Learning Project of Guangdong University of Technology (GDUT[2022]No.59), Student Innovation Training Project of Guangdong University of Technology (xj2023118450788) for the data collection and the preparation of the paper. The authors thank Ministry of Housing and Urban-Rural Development, China Disabled Persons' Federation, Office of Guangzhou Municipal Commission on Aging, China Association for the Blind, China Disabled Persons' Federation, Guangzhou Disabled Persons' Federation and Guangzhou Volunteer Association for providing support for the research. The authors also acknowledge Prof. Siu, the Chair professor of Public Design Lab of The Hong Kong Polytechnic University for providing a lot of useful information.

References

Abdelhamid, M.M., Elfakharany, M.M.: Improving urban park usability in developing countries: case study of Al-Shalalat Park in Alexandria. Alex. Eng. J. **59**(1), 311–321 (2020)

Au-Yong, C.P., Gan, X.N., Azmi, N.F., Zainol, R Radzuan, I.S.M.: Maintenance priority towards the features and facilities in Malaysian public parks: visitors' perspective versus actual experience. Ain Shams Eng. J., 102133 (2023)

Davis, J.L.: How artifacts afford: the power and politics of everyday things. MIT Press (2020)

Gibson, J.J.: The ecological approach to visual perception: classic edition. Psychology press (2014)

Hartson, R.: Cognitive, physical, sensory, and functional affordances in interaction design. Behav. Inform. Technol. **22**(5), 315–338 (2003)

Hassenzahl, M.: The Thing and I: Understanding the Relationship Between User and Product. Funology (2005)

Hassenzahl, M.: Experience design: technology for all the right reasons. Synthesis Lect. Hum.-Centered Inform. **3**(1), 1–95 (2010)

Norman, D.A.: The psychology of everyday things. Basic books (1988)

Pucillo, F., Cascini, G.: A framework for user experience, needs and affordances. Des. Stud. **35**(2), 160–179 (2014)

Siu, K.W.M.: Pleasurable products: public space furniture with userfitness. J. Eng. Des. **16**(6), 545–555 (2005)

Siu, K.W.M.: Accessible park environments and facilities for the visually impaired. Facilities **31**(13/14), 590–609 (2013)

Wu, K.C., Song, L.Y.: A case for inclusive design: Analyzing the needs of those who frequent Taiwan's urban parks. Appl. Ergon. **58**, 254–264 (2017)

Xu, T., Nordin, N.A., Aini, A.M.: Urban green space and subjective well-being of older people: a systematic literature review. Int. J. Environ. Res. Public Health **19**(21), 14227 (2022)

Research on the Idea of Realizing "Low-Carbon Economy and Zero-Carbon City" by Electric Power and Transportation System in Smart Cities

Yanlin Liu[1][✉], Shuiyong Li[1], Peng Yue[1], and Tingwei Zhao[2]

[1] University of Jinan, No. 336, West Road of Nan Xinzhuang, Jinan, Shandong, China
liuyanlin269@163.com
[2] CDI College, 3D Modeling and Animation Design, Brampton, Canada

Abstract. Low-carbon economy and zero-carbon cities are a systematic social transformation that is taking place worldwide. As we all know, the key to the generation and reduction of carbon is to change the production mode. In urban development, we should take the path of green development. For each of us, the carbon dioxide produced by eating, wearing and living will leave "footprints" on the earth. Although "low carbon" is no longer a new concept for many people, we still need to make more efforts from recognition to action. Internationally, Singapore first proposed the "Smart City 2015" plan in 2006, followed by IBM's new concept of "Smart Earth" in 2008, which set off a boom in the construction of global smart cities at that time. Japan, which followed closely, put forward the "I-Japan" smart city plan, and South Korea also put forward the "U-City" smart city outline. In this situation, the United States, the European Union and other countries also quickly put forward corresponding smart city construction concepts for pilot. Therefore, smart city construction has become a new round of global development direction, and its strategic and cutting-edge nature is self-evident. It can be said that whoever takes the lead in planning and building smart cities in the future can lead a new round of development.

Keywords: low- carbon economy · zero-carbon city · intelligent transportation · electric energy · city planning

1 Introduction

The development of traditional urban planning has brought about serious urban population expansion, frequent occurrence of vicious public security incidents, traffic congestion, deterioration of public health, destruction of ecological environment, and waste of resources. Historical experience shows that only expanding the number of infrastructure in cities or improving the local operation system of cities cannot fundamentally solve these problems. To build a future city is to deepen the application of Internet/Internet of Things/cloud computing services by adopting the new generation of information and communication technology, and make informatization and intelligence penetrate into all industries and fields of the city. Urban planning should be able to enhance the use efficiency of urban infrastructure, improve the level of urban operation management and public services, accelerate the transformation of economic development mode, adjust the urban industrial structure, and make people live and work better (Fig. 1).

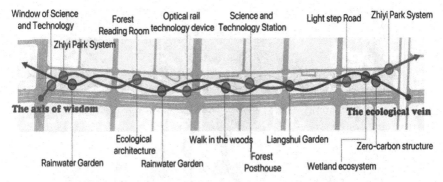

Fig. 1. Smart city planning system

2   "Low-Carbon Economy and Zero-Carbon City" is an Ongoing Global Systematic Social Transformation

August 25 is China's Low-Carbon Day. "Low-CarGreen Building the Future" is the theme of this year. As we all know, the key to carbon peak and carbon neutrality in the "low-carbon economy" is to transform the production mode of enterprises and take the path of green development. But for each of us, the carbon dioxide produced by eating, wearing, living and walking will also leave the "footprint" of the earth. Although "low carbon" is no longer a new concept for many people, we still need to make more efforts from recognition to action.

2.1   Science Helps Advance the Development of "Low Carbon Economy" and Gains Time and Confidence for Realizing "Zero Carbon City"

Low-carbon economy is an economic way to reduce carbon emissions and energy consumption advocated by the world today. In order to make low-carbon economy become a reality and enter a higher level, science has played an important role. On the one hand, scientific research enables us to use more clean energy. More and more countries have successfully developed clean energy, including solar energy, wind energy, etc., which has greatly reduced the emissions of traditional energy such as coal, natural gas and oil. This not only helps to reduce carbon emissions, but also makes a great contribution to environmental protection. On the other hand, scientific research has provided us with more effective low-carbon transportation modes. For example, in recent years, due to the progress of science and technology, electric vehicles, hydrogen vehicles and other vehicles have been widely welcomed by the public. In addition, new energy vehicles equipped with new technologies can help promote the development of low-carbon economy. In short, science plays an indispensable role in achieving a low-carbon economy. Only with continuous progress and breakthroughs in science and technology can we win time and build confidence in building a zero-carbon city (Fig. 2).

Fig. 2. Smart city planning

2.2 We Will Comprehensively Promote Low-Carbon Transformation and the Two-Wheel Drive of Carbon Fixation Layout, and Steadily Promote the Realization of "Zero Carbon City"

In recent years, global warming has become more and more serious, and air pollution is occurring all over the world, which has attracted the attention of all countries. In order to reduce carbon emissions, building a "zero carbon city" without carbon dioxide emissions has become an urgent need of the times. In order to achieve this goal, it is necessary to implement the joint promotion of "low-carbon transformation and carbon fixation layout two-wheel drive". On the one hand, we need to vigorously promote low-carbon transformation and innovate low-carbon technologies. We can use renewable energy such as solar energy, wind energy and hydropower to replace fossil fuels, which can not only reduce carbon dioxide emissions, but also improve the quality of life. On the other hand, we need to carry out scientific and technological research on carbon sequestration and carry out relevant pilot experiments. Through these measures, the amount of carbon dioxide in the atmosphere will be reduced, and cities will benefit from it. Therefore, by vigorously promoting low-carbon transformation and carrying out carbon fixation pilot experiments, we can move towards a "zero carbon city". Only in this way can we effectively reduce carbon emissions and make cities more sustainable and livable (Figs. 3 and 4).

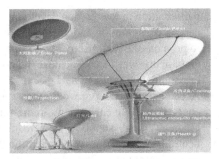

Fig. 3. Urban planning system   **Fig. 4.** Energy acquisition and conversion

2.3 Vigorously Consolidate the Development Foundation of Low-Carbon Economy and "Zero-Carbon City" and Promote the High-Quality Development of Smart City Planning

1) Establish the status of low-carbon development in national laws and regulations and major decisions and arrangements. Strengthen comprehensive and coordinated decision-making, promote high-quality economic development and achieve the goal of "zero carbon". Accelerate the legislative process to deal with climate change, and confirm the total carbon emission control system and carbon emission trading system in legal form;

Reflect the legal status of addressing climate change in the revision process of existing laws and regulations, and strengthen the concept of low-carbon or even zero-carbon development. Adhere to the system view, further improve the macro top-level design, take the implementation of "low-carbon economy" and "zero-carbon city" as the important content of the national economy and urban development planning and design, and make overall efforts to integrate low-carbon development and economic system optimization and upgrading, energy system cleaning, low-carbon security and efficient transformation, scientific and technological innovation, ecological environment protection, land space optimization, national security maintenance and other related work.

2) Improve the incentive mechanism for low-carbon development. Low-carbon development has become an important part of the global response to climate change. In response to the call of the Secretary-General of the United Nations, Ban Ki-moon, all countries in the world are accelerating the construction of a low-carbon economy. In order to achieve this goal, it is necessary to establish a set of incentives to encourage low-carbon development. First, we must continue to invest in basic research and development, such as clean energy technology and environmental protection technology, to improve energy efficiency and reduce emissions. Second, the government should provide financial subsidies and tax incentives, encourage low-carbon projects, and accelerate the realization of the popularization and application of clean energy. Third, we should adopt a stricter evaluation system to evaluate the role of enterprises in low-carbon development. Fourth, we should establish a sound monitoring and evaluation system. All enterprises should be required to regularly report their green practices and make corresponding adjustments. Finally, we need to promote public

participation in low-carbon development. People should be actively inspired by low-carbon consumption and green life. In short, we must continue to strengthen efforts to promote the establishment of a fully functional low-carbon incentive mechanism. Only in this way can we achieve the goals of green growth, low-carbon economy and environmental protection.

3) Accelerate the energy revolution towards "zero carbon cities". The focus of China's energy development strategy in the future is to build a clean, low-carbon, safe and efficient energy supply system to meet the energy demand of achieving "carbon neutrality". It is necessary to scientifically assess the energy resource potential of each region, combine the resource endowment and adjust measures to local conditions, and formulate a long-term strategy of multi-energy complementary energy for each region to achieve the goal of "carbon neutral", which is based on coal and is also the control of total energy consumption. We will deepen the institutional reform in the energy sector, give play to the decisive role of the market in the allocation of energy resources, straighten out the relationship between the price of different energy resources and the relationship between the price of coal and electricity, and take into account carbon emissions to promote the development and utilization of renewable and new energy (Fig. 5).

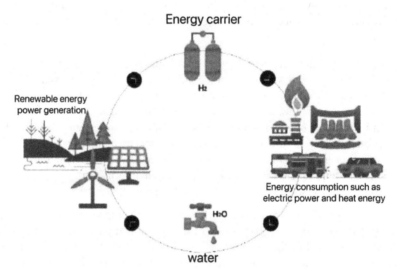

Fig. 5. Green hydrogen energy

4) Innovation in deep-seated energy storage and CCUS technologies is essential towar achieving a low-carbon energy transition. As energy consumption will increase and the desire for longer-lasting and affordable batteries escalates, breakthroughs in this field can have profound impacts in society. Deep-seated energy storage, such as batteries and ultracaps, provides increased energy density compared to traditional chemical storage. This allows us to store more energy for use at a later time. This allows us to become more flexible and efficient in how we use energy and reduces the

demand for new energy infrastructure. On top of that, advancements in this technology could lead to large cost savings for power providers and consumers alike. The other big breakthrough is CCUS, which stands for Carbon Capture, Utilization, and Storage. It involves capturing carbon dioxide from power plants and other industrial activities and storing it underground. This technology could reduce emissions that are damaging for both the environment and public health. It could also be used to develop new technologies that could further reduce emissions in the future. Innovation in deep-seated energy storage and CCUS technologies could be a major step towards a low-carbon energy transition. It will require continued research and development, as well as collaboration between the public and private sectors. We must continue to invest in this technology, so that we can achieve our long-term environmental goals (Fig. 6).

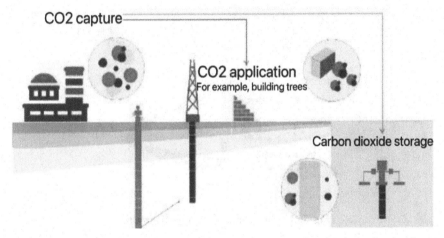

Fig. 6. Media capture, utilization and market CCCUS in the low-level wooden decision

5) Improve the carbon fixation capacity of the ecosystem. In the past few decades, climate change has been the main concern of the world. Deforestation, desertification and other harmful activities caused by human beings have worsened the environment and caused great damage to the global ecosystem. Therefore, the carbon capacity of ecosystems must be strengthened to offset the impact of global climate change. The key to strengthen the carbon sequestration of ecosystems is to reduce human damage to the ecological environment and protect forest resources. Deforestation must be stopped. Governments around the world should formulate clear and effective decrees and laws to further support the protection of forest resources and strengthen the supervision of relevant personnel. Secondly, increase financial support for scientific research of ecological protection projects, accelerate the pace of technological innovation in this field, and improve the information feedback and management level of ecological protection projects. In addition, ecological restoration projects should be carried out in time, such as desert restoration, grass planting and tree planting. All countries should form a global alliance, coordinate their resources, cooperate and take action to deepen ecological protection and mineral protection. In short, to

strengthen the carbon sequestration of ecosystems, effective actions must be taken in legislation, scientific research, ecological restoration and international coordination. Only in this way can we effectively mitigate the impact of climate change and promote the sustainable development of human society. Pay attention to maintaining the carbon sink function of the existing terrestrial ecosystem for a long time, encourage relevant industries and regions to develop, apply and promote various technologies to enhance the carbon sink of the ecosystem, such as artificial afforestation, forest vegetation protection and management, conservation tillage and soil management, grassland grazing management, wetland restoration management, and take measures such as policy support and investment guidance to improve the carbon fixation capacity of the regional and national terrestrial ecosystems (Fig. 7).

Fig. 7. Carbon fixation capacity of ecosystem

6) Guide the whole society to actively participate in the social governance process of low-carbon development. Low carbon has now become one of the important indicators leading the overall development direction of society. In recent years, serious environmental problems have occurred frequently and global warming has become increasingly serious, which has aroused people's high attention to low-carbon life. Therefore, it is necessary for the society to actively participate in the process of low-carbon development. On the one hand, the concept of low-carbon development should be popularized. At present, the public still lacks awareness of the need for a low-carbon life. Therefore, it is necessary for relevant government departments to take the lead in promoting low-carbon knowledge so that everyone can understand and accept this concept. On the other hand, incentives should be provided to encourage people to actively participate in the process of low-carbon development. The government can set up relevant incentives, subsidies and other incentive policies to promote people to develop low-carbon habits rationally, while also enjoying certain benefits and rewards. In addition, it is also important to formulate some environmental policies and regulations to promote and regulate the low-carbon process. Some restrictions and punishment measures should be formulated to ensure the implementation and integrity of the whole process. In short, all of us should take the

initiative to join this low-carbon development process and make the world a better place. Popularize low-carbon knowledge and policies in the smart city planning and design system through information disclosure, hearing, product carbon standard, policy propaganda and other channels, improve the national low-carbon awareness, and advocate low-carbon production and lifestyle. To play the role of media supervision, form a low-carbon development atmosphere in the whole society, achieve carbon peak and carbon neutrality, and thus mitigate climate change, it is also necessary for the general public to start from small things, practice a simple and moderate lifestyle, and make the green life of "low-carbon economy and zero-carbon city" a new fashion. For example, actively participate in voluntary tree planting activities, select low-carbon products such as energy-saving appliances and new energy vehicles, participate in the Clean Your Plate Campaign, and avoid wasting food and beverage (Fig. 8 and 9).

Fig. 8. Zero carbon urban social governance

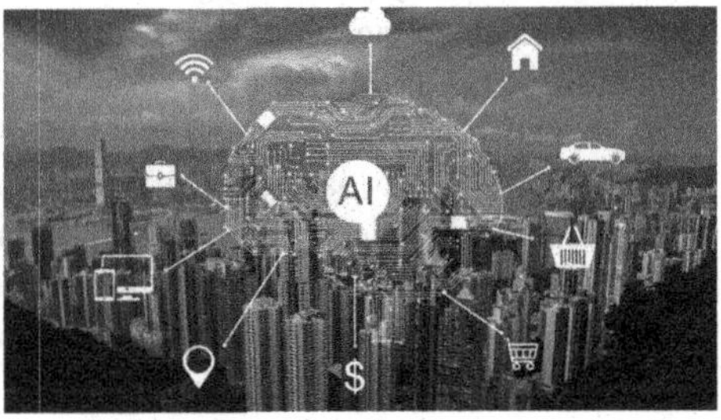

Fig. 9 .

3   Urban Power: Scheme Discussion in the Planning of "Low Carbon Economy and Zero Carbon City"

Energy is an important material base for economic and social development. Since the reform and opening up, China's energy industry has developed rapidly and has become the world's largest energy producer and consumer country, which has strongly supported the economic and social development. However, China's energy structure has been dominated by coal for a long time, and its dependence on oil and gas is relatively high. It is currently the largest country in the world in terms of carbon emissions, and the requirements for clean and low-carbon energy transformation are urgent. The new energy security strategy points out the direction for China's energy development and opens a new path for the development of characteristic energy. Continue to promote carbon emission reduction and take the lead in the world in governance actions. Promote the energy and power industry to achieve low peak and peak at an early date; We will guide green and low-carbon production and lifestyle, and promote the early realization of "zero carbon city" in the whole society.

3.1 Promote the Upgrading of Power Grid to Energy Internet, and Strive to Build a Clean Energy Optimization Platform

In the context of the rapid development of new energy and the market demand for clean energy, the upgrade of power grid to energy interconnection has become an important part of promoting energy revolution. In this way, clean energy can be efficiently utilized, energy security and sustainable development can be realized, and energy usage can be optimized. In terms of power grid upgrade, it is necessary to further strengthen the network management capabilities, enhance the accuracy and effectiveness of collecting and processing data, prediction and analysis, and integrate the various aspects of the data. In addition, intelligent energy management systems, information and communication technology and other monitoring and control equipment should also be introduced to optimize energy distribution, optimize energy efficiency and optimize energy consumption. Simultaneously, the smart grid will combine with the internet of things and build an optimized clean energy platform, giving full play to the functions of intelligent monitoring, real-time optimization, load balancing, big data tracking and analysis. By keeping accurate, real-time and all-round records of the energy data in the grid, the device can accurately predict the load curve, efficiently allocate the energy sources, and recommend the best energy production and consumption plan. In conclusion, the upgrade of power grid to energy interconnection and the construction of clean energy optimization platform are of great significance for implementation of energy revolution, ensuring energy security and promoting energy efficiency.

3.2 Promote the Coordinated Development of Network Sources and the Optimization of Dispatching and Trading Mechanism, and Strive to do a Good Job in the Consumption of Clean Energy Well Networks

Now our living standard is getting better and better with the technological development in recent years. As we all know, with the source of electricity from conventional sources getting gradually depleted, it has become the focus of the public to establish clean power grid to ensure the long-term development and practicality of sustainable energy sources. To this end, I suggest that we should increase the coordination, development and efficient optimization of power supply and dispatch. Firstly, we should expand the availability of clean energy sources. On the one hand, policy and financial rewards are needed to prompt them to enter the clean energy industry, on the other hand, we should also relieve their cost pressure by providing them with sufficient financial assistance. Secondly, we should strengthen related regulations and standards, so as to ensure the safety of electricity consumption and to strengthen the control on net transmission. Last but not least, it is necessary to improve the friendly interconnection between different clean energy sources, to build supply and demand docking, and to make timely and effective dispatching and negotiation, so as to realize efficient use and conversion of clean energy and effectively promote the development and optimization of the clean energy network. In a word, to make full and effective use of clean energy sources, it is important to coordinately develop the power grid and optimize the scheduling and trading mechanisms.

3.3 Promote Energy Conservation and Efficiency Improvement in the Whole Society, and Strive to Improve the Electrification Level of Terminal Consumption

Nowadays, people pay more attention to the environmental protection, and reducing energy consumption is an important part to protect the environment. Therefore, it is necessary to promote energy saving and efficiency improvement among the whole society. The first step is to increase our awareness of energy conservation and environmental protection, so that people can form the concept of protecting environment, reduce unnecessary energy consumption and increase efficiency in the daily life. The second step is to strengthen the construction of energy-saving equipment. From the government side to vigorously promote energy-saving products, continuously improve its energy efficiency, reduce energy consumption, so as to make product energy-saving performance more obvious. The third step is to increase investment in energy-saving research and development on a regular basis to promote the development of energy-saving technology, so as to achieve the purpose of energy saving and efficiency improvement. In conclusion, the whole society should be aware of energy conservation and environmental protection, strengthen the energy-saving construction and increase investment in energy-saving research and development in order to promote energy saving and efficiency improvement.

3.4 Promote the Implementation of Energy Conservation and Emission Reduction of "Low Carbon Economy", and Strive to Reduce its Own Carbon Emission Level

As we all know, global warming is one of the most serious issues we are now facing. In order to protect our planet and make the climate better, we must promote the implementation of "Low-Carbon Economy" and reduce carbon emission. First of all, we should vigorously develop clean energy. For example, we can promote renewable energy, such as hydropower, nuclear power and solar energy, which are environmentaly friendly and can significantly reduce carbon emissions. Besides, we should also seek out ways to use energy efficiently, for example, reducing energy waste in industrial production and transportation. Second, we should take active measures to reduce the emission of greenhouse gases. We should plant more trees and other plants to absorb carbon dioxide from the atmosphere. We can also encourage people to use public transportation instead of cars and bicycles instead of motor vehicles. Finally, we can make more people aware of the importance of saving energy and reducing carbon emissions by increasing education and public communication. We should also encourage people to choose products with low energy consumption and set up regulations, policies and incentive systems to further reduce our carbon emissions. In conclusion, the implementation of "Low-Carbon Economy" is an important measure to reduce carbon emissions and protect our planet. All of us have a responsibility to promote this important work. Let's work together to build a better world (Fig. 10).

Fig. 10. Compound project development mode

3.5 Promote Energy and Power Technology Innovation, and Focus on Improving Operation Safety and Efficiency

Nowadays, with the acceleration of urbanization, the increasing demand for energy and the increasingly serious environmental problems, the development of energy and power technology innovation has become an important issue. First of all, it is necessary to promote technological innovation in the field of energy and power. With the development of technology, intelligent sensing, intelligent decision and intelligent control systems are now forming, which greatly increase the level of safety and efficiency of energy production. In addition, the development of new energy sources should be supported and encouraged. New energy technologies, such as solar energy, wind energy and biomass energy, are sustainable and green ways that can reduce environmental pollution. At the same time, the development of renewable energy policy should be supported, and the access to renewable energy sources should be streamlined. This can not only save the cost of building renewable energy sources, but also speed up the implementation of renewable energy plans and promote the acceptance of the public. In conclusion, promoting energy and power technology innovation and upgrading the level of safety and efficiency are essential, and it relies on the joint efforts of all related units. Only by making good use of advanced technology and providing necessary support can we achieve better energy efficiency, environmental protection and economic development.

3.6 Promote the Deepening of International Exchange and Cooperation, and Focus on Gathering the Largest Combined Force of Energy Green Transformation

With rapid development of globalization, an immense amount of exchange of information and goods has been established, making communication and collaboration between countries become essential in peace, security and sustainable development. In this regard, deeper international communication and cooperation should be promoted to amplify our collective strength to ensure the successful transition to a green and sustainable future. First and foremost, it is important to improve the knowledge exchange between countries regarding green and sustainable development. Relevant as well as authoritative data and scientific information could be shared between countries to jointly explore solutions to tackle challenges impeding the green and sustainable transformation. Also, governments should increase financial support to research institutions so that they can produce more innovative plans and technologies which can advance the green and sustainable transformation. Secondly, international collaboration between countries should be further promoted. For instance, investing more in the renewable energy sector could be projects jointly participated by countries. This kind of joint investment can reduce the burden of each party to invest in the green energy sector and consequently relaxes the pressure of innovation and sustainability. Last but not least, global partnerships and organizations are also essential in promoting deeper international collaboration. For example, the UN has launched many initiatives to encourage countries to engage in more international cooperation in order to implement a green transformation in the fields of energy, resources and the environment. Moreover, international organizations could also set global standards on green development and governance, helping to ensure the sustainability of green transformation. In conclusion, international collaboration and cooperation plays an important role in ensuring the success of green transformation. More efforts should be devoted to improve the existing collaborations, including data and knowledge exchange, joint investments and global organizations and partnerships, thus mobilizing the greatest collective strength of all countries in advancing the green transformation.

3.7 People in The Whole Society Take Voluntary Actions to form a Green and Low-Carbon Production and Lifestyle

With the development of human society, the climate change gradually shows up, and global warming is increasing constantly. To defend our homeland and keep the earth green and sustainable, we need to take action to form a green low-carbon production and lifestyle. First of all, it is necessary to give up the traditional energy sources and utilize the new energy sources. Therefore, we can save the limited energy source in the world and help reduce CO_2 emissions. What's more, we should also encourage people to develop more efficient methods to reduce wastes. Meanwhile, people should stop throwing rubbish randomly. In this way, we can keep our environment clean and face up with less pollution. In addition, we should foster public's awareness in terms of green low-carbon lifestyle. We should promote the lifestyle in communities or schools, so as to enhance people's knowledge on energy-saving and environmental protection. We can hold special activities regularly, such as graffiti painting competition or lectures, so that people can learn more about this issue. On top of that, every citizen needs to be responsible for the future of our world. We should start with individuals and live with green low-carbon lifestyle. As long as we all join in this activity, we are able to make the society green and sustainable in the long run. In a nutshell, to relieve the environmental tension, we must take fast and effective measures and carry out green low-carbon lifestyle for the sustainability of our home.

4   Urban Transportation: Scheme Discussion in the Planning of "Low Carbon Economy and Zero Carbon City"

In the face of the challenge of "low-carbon economy and zero-carbon city", the urban transportation system will be the top priority. In the smart city planning project, it is urgent to coordinate the transformation of transportation mode, optimize the structure mode of goods transportation, and use technology to improve efficiency to achieve emission reduction, so as to promote the planning of smart cities to achieve carbon peak as soon as possible, and finally move towards the strategic goal of carbon neutrality (Fig. 11).

Fig. 11. New energy vehicles help the planning and development of smart cities

4.1   Problems and Challenges

Greenhouse gas emissions caused by urban transport activities have brought enormous pressure on the earth's ecology. As a major source of emissions, it has become the focus of many countries. Countries have formulated low-carbon economic development plans, put forward the goal of achieving a zero-carbon city, and put it into practice step by step in the field of transportation, such as vigorously promoting public transport such as public transport and subway, replacing traditional fossil fuels with new energy such as electricity, and replacing private cars, etc., These measures are aimed at reducing greenhouse gas emissions caused by urban traffic and have achieved certain success. However, there are still many problems and challenges in the development of zero-carbon cities. First, it is necessary to establish new energy infrastructure and modify existing models and industries. For example, the subway and bus driven by new energy need to be supplemented, and other related industries such as automobile manufacturing and oil exploitation also need to be adjusted accordingly. Secondly, in order to solve the local air pollution caused by urban traffic, we must introduce advanced information technology and take comprehensive measures such as traffic information management and optimization. Last but not least, economic factors are also an important factor. We need to take full account of energy consumption and costs when implementing various anti-carbon measures to reduce the economic burden of the government and citizens. In short, the development of low-carbon economy and zero-carbon cities is a major trend. Solving the problems and challenges of urban transportation is of great significance to the protection of the earth's ecology. I believe that with the joint efforts of all parties, we can achieve the goals of low-carbon economic development, zero-carbon city and clean transportation.

4.2 Countermeasures and Suggestions

In the process of realizing the smart city planning of "low-carbon economy and zero-carbon city", it is urgent to promote the sustainable development of the transportation industry and find a sustainable urban transportation scheme that can reduce carbon emissions. First of all, cities should implement effective traffic management policies and implement the goal of reducing urban motor vehicles and commuting population. Improving the charging system and reasonable pricing and charging policies can effectively reduce the use frequency of urban motor vehicles. For large cities, road toll can be implemented to reduce urban traffic pressure and achieve low-carbon development. Secondly, urban traffic improvement technology can effectively improve urban traffic problems. For example, automatic driving technology can greatly reduce traffic accidents, thus improving urban traffic safety; Expanding public transport network coverage, optimizing its operation strategy, improving passenger travel efficiency and reducing the use of private cars will also help reduce urban carbon emissions. In addition, the use of clean energy, such as natural gas, wind energy, solar energy and other renewable energy, can effectively replace traditional fuels, reduce urban carbon emissions and save energy. Therefore, cities can build clean energy travel infrastructure, such as bus power stations and charging piles, to support clean energy travel. To sum up, in order to realize the plan of "low carbon economy and zero carbon city", effective measures must be taken in urban transportation, including improving the traffic management system, improving urban transportation technology and developing clean energy travel.

1) Promote the coordinated development of transportation and cities, and create a low-carbon lifestyle.

With the increasing population, transportation and cities are increasingly integrated to cope with important issues such as environmental pollution and climate change. Cities must change the traditional high-carbon consumption mode and adopt the low-carbon mode. Therefore, transportation and cities should establish a mutually coordinated development relationship and create a low-carbon lifestyle. First of all, it is necessary to implement effective transportation planning, incorporate public transport travel into the planning, encourage citizens to use low-carbon travel modes such as public transport, bicycle and walking, vigorously develop new energy vehicles, and accelerate the improvement of urban public transport network, such as social public transport, road network layout, etc. At the same time, control the number of cars, reduce the pollution of automobile exhaust emissions, strengthen environmental protection, and promote healthy urban development. Secondly, we should build a green transport development model. Build a humanized transportation system, improve the road system, design intelligent transportation solutions, implement energy conservation and emission reduction measures, establish an intelligent and sustainable transportation system, innovate the urban traffic management system, optimize the urban traffic center, and improve social and economic benefits, social development level and residents' happiness. Finally, strengthen traffic safety and ensure travel safety. Formulate and improve safe travel mechanism, improve traffic management, strengthen safety awareness, improve traffic accident handling mechanism, control traffic accidents, ensure driving safety, and improve traffic safety. Through the coordinated development of transportation and cities, it can effectively promote the formation of a green travel low-carbon life model, which not only improves the urban traffic conditions and environmental quality, but also strengthens the urban ecological sustainable development, providing residents with higher quality of life and more development opportunities.

2) Promote the transformation of transportation mode.

As a major transportation mode in our daily life, the efficiency and stability of traffic has become a concern of all. To this end, intelligent traffic has become the direction of technology development in recent years. The application of intelligent traffic not only improves the safety of transportation, but also greatly improves the transportation efficiency. For example, the establishment of the electronic toll collection system not only realizes the automatic collection of tolls, but also realize the electronic payment, greatly reduces the waiting time of vehicles, improves the efficiency of transportation. In addition, the traffic control system improves the real-time monitoring and control of traffic. Traffic lights and time loops control the flow of vehicles in an orderly manner, ensuring the smooth transit of vehicles. In general, intelligent traffic has brought great convenience to our daily traffic and improved the efficiency of transportation. However, intelligent traffic is only a solution at the current stage. We need to continue to improve it, making it really play its due role in our daily traffic (Fig. 12).

3) Accelerate the zero-carbon transformation of motor vehicle energy structure.

The transition of vehicle energy structure to zero carbon is an important measure to achieve the goal of greenhouse gas emission reduction and carbon neutrality. As an important part of daily travel, the acceleration of the transition of the energy structure of motor vehicles to zero carbon has increasingly become a research hotspot. On the one hand, the promotion of electric vehicles should begin with the idea of changing travel resources. Traditional models are constantly improving fuel efficiency, using cleaner transportation energy and energy technology, and vigorously developing new energy vehicles such as electric vehicles, which can reduce emissions and improve energy efficiency. On the other hand, it is urgent to establish a complete and convenient charging system. For new energy vehicles, it is necessary to build a complete charging system to effectively improve the utilization efficiency of new energy vehicles. At the same time, we should actively explore the application of intelligent charging technology, such as automatic charging and discharging scheduling, advanced charging and V2X energy internet technology, to ensure the demand of the grid and the convenience of users. At the same time, we should strengthen efforts to involve more stakeholders in

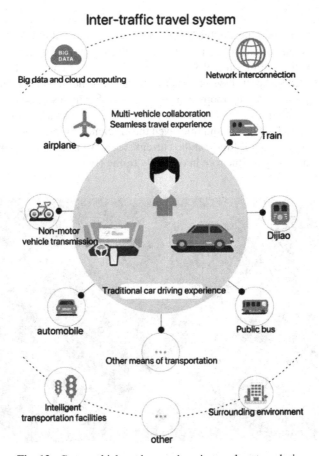

Fig. 12. Cross-vehicle and cross-domain travel system design

the development of new energy vehicles. For example, the government can introduce market-oriented incentives for enterprises to accelerate the development of new energy vehicle technology and reduce costs, so that more citizens can accept and use new energy vehicles. In short, the transition of motor vehicle energy structure to zero carbon requires joint efforts of all parties. The government should actively introduce relevant policies and measures to guide the society's demand for the transformation of the kinetic energy structure. Enterprises should assume the responsibility of upgrading new energy vehicle technology and reducing production costs, and individuals should also assume the main responsibility of reducing motor vehicle emissions. I believe that through joint efforts, we will build a sustainable future with zero emission of motor vehicles.

4) Intelligent transportation helps improve the efficiency of transportation operation.

As a major transportation mode in our daily life, the efficiency and stability of traffic has become a concern of all. To this end, intelligent traffic has become the direction of technology development in recent years. The application of intelligent traffic not only improves the safety of transportation, but also greatly improves the transportation efficiency. For example, the establishment of the electronic toll collection system not only realizes the automatic collection of tolls, but also realize the electronic payment, greatly reduces the waiting time of vehicles, improves the efficiency of transportation. In addition, the traffic control system improves the real-time monitoring and control of traffic. Traffic lights and time loops control the flow of vehicles in an orderly manner, ensuring the smooth transit of vehicles. In general, intelligent traffic has brought great convenience to our daily traffic and improved the efficiency of transportation. However, intelligent traffic is only a solution at the current stage. We need to continue to improve it, making it really play its due role in our daily traffic (Fig. 13).

Fig. 13. Distribution of smart transport base stations

5   Research Summary

In the current innovative development, the planning and design scheme of smart city adopts the principle of multi-platform cooperation, integrates and promotes digital technology, innovates energy development, and constantly deepens the transformation of cities at all levels into smart cities. The new smart city will continue to improve under the challenges and opportunities (Fig. 14).

Use digital technology to improve the efficiency of smart city planning and management as soon as possible. During the period when all sectors of society are more involved in urban smart transformation, take the ecological environment, circular development, low-carbon economy, zero-carbon city as the goal, fully integrate and utilize the natural land, mountains, rivers, all kinds of climate and energy, supplemented by cultural heritage, so that our living environment becomes a healthier and more beautiful town with regional characteristics A beautiful town with ethnic characteristics.

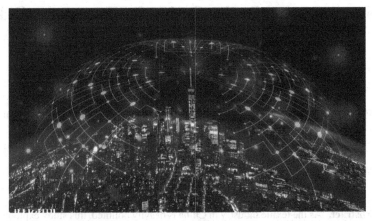

Fig. 14. Digital technology means to improve the efficiency of smart city planning and management

With the development of the new generation of information technology and the innovation of business models, the "low-carbon economy and zero-carbon city" will play an increasingly important role in promoting the planning and development of smart cities. We should vigorously promote the good opportunities of intelligence and informatization, improve the level of government service, improve the efficiency of urban operation, improve the ability of scientific and technological innovation, reduce energy consumption, maintain the green ecological environment, gradually achieve the goal of zero carbon, truly build a new system of large, medium and small supporting, high-quality smart cities, and create a harmonious, happy, zero-carbon and efficient beautiful city for the people.

References

1. Liuyuhao: Indoor scene reconstruction technology based on depth information. Qinhuangdao: Yanshan University (2016)
2. Luomingxuan: Talking about the Technology and Application of Motion Capture [EB/OL] (14 Mar 2013). http://blog.sina.com.cn/s/blog_6be92b950101bqtt.html
3. Jiangyajie: Human body gesture recognition and robot control based on Kinect. Shenzhen University, Shenzhen (2017)
4. Zhanqinchuan: Analysis of the application and development status of virtual reality technology. Industry Technol. Forum **7**, 75–76 (2014)

Smart Sewing Device Design for Transform Old Clothes Based on Multimodal Interaction

Yun Liu[1(✉)], Liya Dong[1], Jiayi Zhang[1], Dong Lee[1], and Han Ni[2]

[1] Fuzhou University, Xiamen Academy of Arts and Design College, Xiamen, China
liuyun525@fzu.edu.cn
[2] School of Fine and Applied Art, University of Illinois at Urbana Champaign, Champaign, USA

Abstract. As the textile industry in China is heavily polluted, this study explores the design of a smart sewing device for recycling used clothing based on multi-modal Interaction to create a fun way to collect used clothing, for users who have a need to recycle and a desire to transform used clothing. User needs for online and offline services are identified through the KANO model user needs analysis. With the analysis of the user's channel characteristics and the operating tasks of the smart sewing device, the quantitative requirements of the user VACP channel resources for different operating interfaces of the smart sewing device are obtained, and specific design strategies are proposed to guide the completion of the design practice. Furthermore, product iterations and optimizations are carried out based on the feedback results to initially validate the effectiveness of multi-modal Interaction mechanisms in VACP theory for the design of smart sewing devices.

Keywords: multi-modal interaction · used clothing transformation · sustainable development

1 Introduction

As the largest clothing producer and exporter, China's recycling rate of waste textiles is low. According to the data of China Recycling Economy Association, about 26 million tons of old clothes are thrown into waste container every year in China [1]. Problems of low recycling rate and single recycling form also exist. Under the background of circular economy, the public's attitude towards the recycling of old clothes has gradually changed, and most users are willing to realize the continuous utilization of their residual value by the means of old clothes transformation.

The survey found that the development of the field of old clothes recycling at the interactive level is sluggish, and there is no research in this field to promote the sustainable behavior of old clothes reconstruction from the perspective of user experience.

V. G. Duffy et al. (Eds.): HCII 2023, LNCS 14057, pp. 554–567, 2023.
https://doi.org/10.1007/978-3-031-48047-8_37

This research will be based on the VACP theory and above problems, using multi-modal prompt and multimodal presentation technology for information feedback through market research, demand analysis, user research and explore the design of intelligent sewing equipment for old clothes reconstruction based on multimodal interaction, and create an interesting way of old clothes recycling.

2 Conceptual Analysis

2.1 Multi-modal Interaction Theory

"Modality" is another neurophysiological category introduced by Wilhelm Helmholtz, the famous German philosopher, and refers to the various ways in which living organisms acquire the ability to receive information from the outside world through various sensory organoleptic and experiential sensations, such as the visual, auditory, tactile, gustatory and olfactory modalities that are part of the human nervous system. Multimodality involves the integration of multiple senses, whereas multi-modal interaction means that a person communicates with a computer through a variety of channels such as voice, body language, information carriers (text, pictures, audio, video) and the environment, in a way that fully simulates human interaction [2].

Multimodal interaction technology covers the interaction of various senses between the human senses of sight, hearing, smell, touch and taste, and is achieved through the use of the human eye, ear, nose, mouth and hand skin, whose application is also designed around these interactive senses in real-life scenarios.

2.2 Kano Model

Kano model is a useful tool for categorizing and prioritizing user needs, based on the analysis of the impact of user needs on user satisfaction, reflecting the non-linear relationship that exists between product characteristics and the satisfaction of product users. In the Kano model, all basic quality characteristics of goods and related service products are split into four basic categories: (1) required attributes; (2) expected attributes; (3) attractive attributes; and (4) undifferentiated attributes [3].

2.3 VACP Model

VACP theory was developed by MacCracken and Aldridge and others who summarized and developed the theory of multiple resources [4]. In the course of their research, VACP theory can be a task to analyse, involving defining a task process, analyzing each task, identifying the functions of individual meta-actions, and it is possible to analyze the four processes of visual, auditory, perceptual-motor and psychomotor responses of meta-actions to the needs of the user's mental resources on these four channels, in a data model constructed on the basis of people's visual, auditory, cognitive and psychomotor. Of these, each letter represents a different channel, with V representing is visual behavior, A representing auditory behaviour, C representing cognitive behavior and P representing psychomotor, with a score of 0–7 in each channel, and a higher score representing a higher active channel (refer to the Table 1) [5].

Table 1. VACP standard scale

Resource Requirements	Score	Behavior	Resource Requirements	Score	Behavior
Visual	0.0	No visual behavior	Cognitive	0.0	No cognitive behavior
	1.0	Visual registration and detection		1.0	The act of being unconscious
	3.7	Visual discrimination		1.2	Scheme selection
	4.0	Visual inspection and verification		3.7	Symbol and signal recognition
	5.0	Visual alignment and positioning		4.6	Evaluation and judgment (unilateral)
	5.4	Visual tracking and following		5.3	Encode, decode, recall
	5.9	Visual reading		6.8	Evaluation and judgment (Multifaceted)
	7.0	Scanning, searching, monitoring		7.0	Evaluation, calculation and conversion
Auditory	0.0	No auditory behavior	Psychomotor	0.0	No psychomotor movement
	1.0	Auditory registration and detection		1.0	Speak
	2.0	Determine the direction of the sound		2.2	Discrete behavior (button pressing, etc.)
	4.2	Locate the sound		2.6	Continuous adjustment
	4.3	Verify auditory feedback		4.6	Manual control
	4.9	Interpret semantic content		5.8	Discrete adjustment (turning buttons)
	6.6	Identify the characteristics of sound		6.5	Symbol generation (writing)
	7.0	Explain patterns of sound		7.0	Manual control of discrete sequence

3   Analysis on the Feasibility of Old Clothing Recycling Under Multiple Modal

The whole process of old clothing recycling DIY includes design, drawing, cutting, sewing, etc., which is a difficult task for most inexperienced people. Introducing interacted multiple modal simplification and designing intelligent sewing assistant can simplify this process, realize old clothing recycling and further promote sustainable development.

3.1   Interactive Requirements in Old Clothing Recycling Environment

The Necessity of Analysis on Old Clothing Recycling

In terms of environmental protection, recycling old clothes is of great significance for sustainable development. In today's society, people's demand for fashionable clothes is higher and higher, resulting in more and more old clothing being wasted. At present, the mainstream recycling methods for old clothes are landfill, incineration, etc., which will lead to increased pollution. The recycling of old clothes can not only enhance people's awareness of energy conservation and environmental protection but also save social resources, save energy and reduce emissions.

In terms of sentimental value, recycling old clothes can preserve the collection value of clothes. Many old clothes retain the precious memories of the wearer, such as the school uniform that represents youth, the first gift from a friend, etc. Although the use value of these old clothes is not that high, they have high spiritual value. Old clothes recycling can redesign and reuse some memorable old clothes, prolong the life of clothes while injecting new value, and turn it into a special emotional sustentation.

The Development Status of Old Clothing Recycling at the Interactive Level

At present, many communities in China have set up garbage recycling bins, but due to the lack of administration and other factors, the recycling result of these bins is not satisfactory. The current process of old clothes recycling is, on the one hand, to teach the public the skills of recycling old clothes. For example, on the website 'about.com' there are courses about famous designers guiding old clothing recycling DIY which attracted enthusiasts to learn. The website also provides lots of dyeing, embroidery as well as other makeover tips for enthusiasts to learn and develop in the recycling process [6]. On the other hand, the designers recycle old clothes to form a unique style brand. For instance, the Chinese brand "FAKENATOO", founded by Chinese designer Zhang Na, reorganizes old clothes into fashionable new clothes by means of reorganization and redesign.

In general, the development of old clothing recycling is relatively slow at the interactive level, and it is urgent to introduce new interactive ways to promote the development.

3.2 The Advantage of Old Clothing Recycling Under the Perspective of Multiple Modal

The primary feature of DIY personalized old clothes is individuation. Many personalized designs can be done according to the material, style, color, style and the story behind different clothes. Creators can deconstruct and reorganize old clothes or add new elements to produce unique designs. The content of DIY may be simple or complex. The process of participating in the production of new clothes can produce many new memories and bring the fun of designing and producing new clothes by themselves.

According to the questionnaire, most people, especially females, are interested in this kind of DIY, but only a few of them are willing to do it (refer to the Table 2). Further interviews show that there are three main factors affecting the enthusiasm of participants to complete DIY of old clothes: 1. Do not know how to carry out a new design for old clothes. 2. Do not know the basic clothing plate-making knowledge or how to make plate-type. 3. Do not have relevant tools to DIY.

Multiple modal interaction balancing mechanism can improve user experience in all directions, introducing the combination of multiple modal interaction mechanism can effectively solve the above problems. For question 1: Do not know how to redesign old clothes. We can analyze the data of old clothes uploaded by users on the software, match and combine the data uploaded by users from the database to generate a few personalized reconstruction schemes, and provide users choices. For problem 2: Not knowing basic plate-making knowledge, we introduced a multiple model gesture interaction system, connecting hardware to intelligent projection device, then project intelligent plate-type generated by the software onto the old clothes, and users can use gestures to interact with the projection to enhance user experience. For problem 3: there is no corresponding tool, we provide systematic intelligent sewing equipment including a full set of sewing tools, in order to attract customers using experiential marketing.

The introduction of multiple modal interactive leveling mechanism can simplify the design and sewing process of old clothing recycling in all directions, lower the threshold of old clothing recycling, and attract more people to join the group of environmental protection.

Table 2. Partial questionnaire survey

Your attitude towards old clothing recycling is?

No.	Option	Percentage	Number of participants
1	Very supportive	33.3%	52
2	Supportive	48.1%	75
3	Do not mind	9.6%	15
4	Unsupportive	5.7%	9
5	Very unsupportive	3.2%	5

Would you like to remake old clothes yourself?

No.	Option	Percentage	Number of participants
1	Often	8.3%	13
2	Occasionally	6.4%	10
3	Very few	16.0%	25
4	Hardly	54.5%	85
5	Never	14.7%	23

4 Need Analysis of Intelligent Sewing Equipment Under Multimodality

On the basis of in-depth user research, qualitative and quantitative analysis of needs, and analysis of environmental needs from a multimodal perspective, this study is conducted to establish an experience model more in line with human-computer interaction by means of integrating the real research data.

4.1 Analysis of User Needs

Qualitative Classification of Need for Intelligent Sewing Equipment
In the analysis of the user needs of those who have the intention to transform their used clothes, the research team headed to the residential area of Gulangyu Island in Xiamen to conduct focus groups and interviews with such users. In the meantime, an online questionnaire survey was released, with a total of 156 valid questionnaires received. According

to Bastable (2008), three broad categories of barriers need to be addressed in evaluation: lack of clarity, lack of ability, and fear of punishment or loss of self-esteem [7]. To address the lack of clarity, the operational logic of the sewing equipment needs to be clearly explained to the respondents when formulating the question. In order to address the lack of competency, the designer needs to have some professionalism and coaching skills. To address the last question, it should be clearly explained to the interviewees that there are no right and wrong answers, so they do not view the assessment as a Judgments of personal worth [8].

Fig. 1. Qualitative classification of requirements

In accordance with the real research results, while incorporating Maslow's Hierarchy of Needs Theory, the needs mentioned therein are categorized into four levels (refer to the Fig. 1), which are (1) Physiological needs: The sewing equipment is required to complete the basic interactive feedback and give a corresponding response to each step of the user's operation, while fulfilling the psychological needs and behavioral logic of the user regarding color, appearance and structure. (2) Safety needs: In terms of operational safety, the steps in the user's behavior that may involve operational risks were analyzed, while designing in structural functions and other aspects to deliver safety reminders, warnings and protective measures in a timely manner. (3) Belongingness needs: Given the high degree of DIY and personalization binding, the sewing equipment design is required to take into account the production needs of various users, thereby generating exclusive solutions. (4) Esteem needs: The designer is expected to make consideration of the objective guidance during the operation process of users and the completion effect of the finished product to boost user satisfaction and sense of accomplishment, whereby incentives such as voice images need to be available during the production process. (5) Self-actualization needs: The design is expected to demonstrate the significance of environmental protection of used clothes transformation, and the realization of self-worth by one's own hands, in addition to enhancing the participation of users through uploading to the online community or donating clothes.

In the light of the statistical data, the user needs were substituted into the Kano 2D high-quality model, (refer to the Table 3) which was analyzed to derive a qualitative classification of user needs for the design function of used clothes transformation under multimodality (refer to the Fig. 2).

Table 3. Statistical data

Function	O	I	M	A	Satisfaction Coefficient After Increase	Dissatisfaction Coefficient After Elimination
Zero-based hands-on	52	21	14	78	78.6%	42.3%
Generate personalized solutions	70	19	39	37	65.0%	66.2%
Novel appearance	48	35	16	65	68.4%	38.8%
Teaching mode	34	15	70	46	48.5%	63.0%
Gesture control	64	39	26	36	61.2%	52.1%
Voice prompt	89	31	19	26	69.5%	58.6%

The data from the table indicates the better-worse coefficients of the partial needs, while constructing the above quartile chart. The analysis reveals that product appearance and zero-based hands-on are charming factors; providing teaching is a necessary factor; the remaining multimodal functions such as vision, hearing and touch are desired factors. In addition, the provision of such multimodal interaction functions will increase user satisfaction, whereas the absence of such functions will decrease user satisfaction.

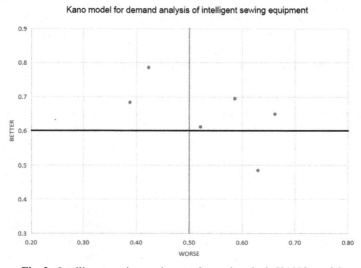

Fig. 2. Intelligent sewing equipment demand analysis KANO model

VACP Need Quantitative Analysis

The whole flow analysis of users utilizing intelligent sewing equipment is listed (refer to the Fig. 4), the qualitative classification of the need for intelligent sewing equipment under the multimodality is integrated, while incorporating the VACP standard scale (refer to the Table 1), the user need quantification table for intelligent sewing equipment is derived from the analysis (refer to the Tables 4 and 5).

Table 4. Intelligent sewing equipment operation process hierarchy diagram

4.2 Multimodal Environment Analysis

External Environment

The speedy advancement and in-depth application of a new generation of information technology such as artificial intelligence, big data and Internet of Things has introduced tremendous variations in all walks of life, which has also exerted a far-reaching effect on sewing products, thereby facilitating the development of sewing equipment in the multimodal field [9]. For the sake of delivering a more perfect psychological experience to users, designers are called upon to apply and select the design of products with the assistance of environmental scenes, to give full play to the dynamic role of products in the environment, in addition to delivering users with a situational experience that fits the products.

Hardware Environment

On the basis of establishing multi-modal interaction in the external environment, attention should be paid to the interaction needs between users and products: a) shares valuable information regarding the manufacturing process and hardware actions to the user, and b) allows user to effectively interact with the hardware without compromising operation productivity. Analyze the action logic of users when using smart sewing equipment, the

Table 5. Intelligent sewing equipment interface design VACP demand quantitative processing

Operand Layer	Vision	Hearing	Cognition	Spirit
Watch the video about production process	5.9	4.9	1.2	0.0
Pick the suitable used clothes	3.7	0.0	1.2	4.6
Select the target finished product	4.0	0.0	1.2	2.2
Determine the size of the finished product	4.0	0.0	4.6	2.2
Scan the used clothes	5.0	1.0	3.7	0.0
Select the color scheme of preset style	5.9	1.0	6.8	2.2
Operate with voice prompts	5.4	4.9	6.8	4.6
Plot cutting lines with projection	5.0	6.6	7.0	6.5
Tailor the clothes	5.0	4.3	7.0	4.6
Fabric markings after cutting	5.0	4.3	5.3	6.5
Sewing fabric following instruction	5.4	4.9	5.3	2.6
Add decoration or watermark	5.0	0.0	3.7	2.6
Check the effect against the target	7.0	4.9	6.8	4.6
Clean up the desktop	4.0	0.0	3.7	4.6
Take photos and upload to the community	5.4	0.0	1.2	2.2
Donate or take it away yourself	1.0	0.0	1.2	0.0
End of shutdown	1.0	1.0	1.2	2.2

system needs to be capable of providing useful information to operators allowing them to make the right decisions in the right way and the safest context [10].

5   Design Scheme and Practice of Intelligent Sewing Equipment

5.1   Software Interface Construction

Software Interface Analysis
According to the analysis of user VACP channel resources in the hardware layout interface of intelligent sewing equipment, it is found that it has the highest demand for user visual channel resources and the lowest demand for auditory channel resources (refer to the Table 6).

In the design process of software interface, the user's demands for hearing can be appropriately increased to compensate for the demand for other channel resources [9].

The Presentation of Design Strategy
Based on the data analysis, the following specific design strategy is proposed.

(1) Design strategy based on image recognition

Table 6. Intelligent sewing equipment software layout interface VACP analysis

Interface Type	Metaoperand	VACP Score	Visual(V)	Audio(A)	Cognition(C)	Spirit(P)
Software Interface Construction	7	56.6	19.9	5.9	17.4	13.4

The user imports the old clothes data in the form of images, and the software scans and analyze the old clothes image to extract the redesign elements, and presents the personalized scheme for the user to choose based on the background data. In this process, visual elements should be used to clearly guide users to pass in multi-directional images of old clothes and style intentions.

(2) Design strategy based on speech recognition

Users can provide multiple input methods to describe old clothes by voice input of old clothes features and elements they want to retain, so as to facilitate users to fully express their needs and enhance the user experience.

5.2 Hardware Build

Hardware Analysis
According to the analysis of the user's VACP pathway resource in the hardware layout interface of intelligent sewing machine, it's found that it has the highest demand for user's cognitive pathway resource and the lowest demand for the auditory modality resource (refer to the Table 7). Therefore, in the process of design, the user's demand for auditory and visual modality resources can be appropriately increased to compensate for the demand for cognitive channel resources. Meanwhile, the cognitive pathway can be enhanced to reduce the user's cognitive load and optimize the effect of man-machine interaction [9].

Table 7. Intelligent sewing equipment hardware layout interface VACP analysis

Interface type	A meta-operand	VACP Total Score	Visual(V)	Hearing(A)	Cognition(C)	Spirit(P)
Hardware layout interface	10	169	47.8	31.9	50.5	38.8

The Presentation of Design Strategy
Based on the data analysis, the following specific design strategy is proposed.

(1) Design strategy based on gesture interaction recognition

Provide cutting line interactive projection to guide users to complete the board, the board is the pain point of most users with the consciousness of old clothes transformation, by setting interactive projection to solve the problem of zero-based users' clothes boarding, users only need to put the old clothes on the desktop, and then log in to the system can project the shape line of the design scheme selected in advance, this process does not require the user to have a complex clothing board foundation, just use chalk to draw the projected version line on the clothing and cut it to complete the version part.

(2) Design strategy based on speech recognition

The introduction of intelligent voice prompts to guide zero-based users to operate. By introducing intelligent voice prompt in the interactive process of cutting clothes, stitching cloth, adding cloth, users can be guided to complete the operation, so as to reduce the operation burden of zero-base users (refer to the Fig. 3).

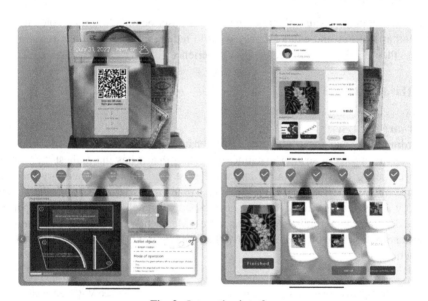

Fig. 3. Interactive interface

(3) Integrated and concise functional layout under cognitive channel intervention

Because most users prefer to operate on the basis of zero, the complex layout will increase the user's operation difficulty, so the use of comprehensive consideration of the use of scenarios, using a relatively simple retro-integrated design, blend simple wind, desktop more clean and practical.

The user first makes an appointment online, and then goes to the offline intelligent sewing equipment, which consists of a projection module, a line drawing area and a sewing area. First, in the standing condition, the following steps are completed: Logon device; scanning used clothes; operating according to voice prompts; projection drawing cutting line; cutting clothes; cutting cloth marking. Next, in order to complete the sitting condition: according to the teaching sewing cloth, add decoration or watermark, check against the target effect, clean the desktop. Finally, the entire operation process ended, shutdown and left.

The design strategy of intelligent sewing equipment under the intervention of auditory and visual channel compensation and cognitive channel enhancement was analyzed, and the practical scheme of the interface layout design of intelligent sewing equipment was effectively guided and completed (refer to the Fig. 4).

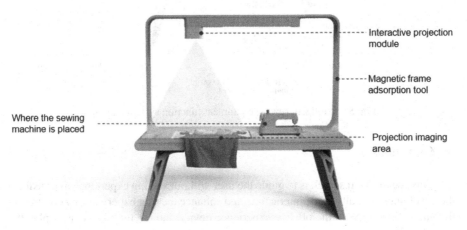

Fig. 4. Intelligent sewing equipment interface layout design

In addition, in order to improve the systematicness and integrality of the research, the design strategy of the software interactive interface and the hardware layout interface of the intelligent sewing equipment is analyzed comprehensively, and the systematic design of the intelligent sewing equipment is carried out, the function system design of intelligent sewing equipment is as follows (refer to the Fig. 5).

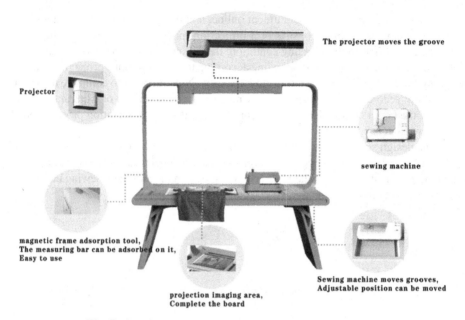

The projector moves the groove

Projector

sewing machine

magnetic frame adsorption tool,
The measuring bar can be adsorbed on it,
Easy to use

Sewing machine moves grooves,
Adjustable position can be moved

projection imaging area,
Complete the board

Fig. 5. Intelligent sewing equipment function system diagram

6 Conclusion

The purpose of this research is to guide the user without sewing experience to transform the old clothes by multi-mode interaction, and enhance the user experience by combining the interaction between the off-line experience device and the mobile, so as to play the role of multi-mode in the experience design, provide a new transformation of old clothes for users. It achieves the concepts of turning waste into treasure and sustainable use, and provides a new carrier of emotional transmission and commemorative significance. Besides, this kind of entry angle can also provide the theory reference for the design of other fields.

Acknowledgments. This work was financially supported by the 2022 Google China Education Cooperation Program Funding Program, student development program (China-US Young Maker Competition special channel) (PJ220080).

References

1. China Renewable Resources Recycling Association: Sharing the Green World. People's Posts and Telecommunications Press
2. Zhang, H., Yu, P.: Multimodal cross-sensory experience design of agents [EB/OL]. (2019–05–19) [2022–02–17]. https://mp.weixin.qq.com/s/DTW9tWBRTXxv2PNV2eMmVg
3. Lu, Chaoqun, S.: Research on age-appropriate design of healthy all-in-one machine under multimodal interactive balance. Des. Art Res. **04**, 61–66 (2022)

4. Wandi, J., Xufeng, C.: Moxibustion product design based on KANO model. Design **04**, 108–111 (2023). https://doi.org/10.20055/j.cnki.1003-0069.000425
5. Mccracken, J.H., Aldrich, T.B.: Analyses of selected LHX mission functions: Implications for operator workload and system automation goals. Fort Rucker: U.S. Army Research Institute (1984):1-H-37
6. Jianyi, G.: Application of DIY concept in clothing secondary design Decoration **06**, 92–93 (2009). https://doi.org/10.16272/j.cnki.cn11-1392/j.2009.06.002
7. Bastable, S.B., Gramet, P., Jacobs, K., Sopczyk, D.: Evaluation in healthcare education. Health Professional as Educator 541–573 (2011)
8. Fujs, D., Vrhovec, S., Žvanut, B., Vavpotič, D.: Improving the efficiency of remote conference tool use for distance learning in higher education: a kano based approach. Comput. Educ. **181**, 104448 (2022)
9. Qintai, H., Wenyan, W., Guang, F., Tingfeng, P., Kaixing, Q.: Research on interpretability analysis of multimodal learning behavior supported by deep learning. Educ. Res. **11**, 77–83 (2021). https://doi.org/10.13811/j.cnki.eer.2021.11.011
10. Andronas, D., Apostolopoulos, G., Fourtakas, N., Makris, S.: Multi-modal interfaces for natural Human-Robot Interaction. Procedia Manufacturing **54**, 197–202 (2021)

Inclusive Design and the User Experience in Green Spaces: A Case in Guangzhou, China

Yi Lan Long[1], Jia Xin Xiao[1,2(✉)], Ming Jun Luo[3,4], Yi Chen[1], and Wei Wei Huang[1]

[1] School of Art and Design, Guangdong University of Technology, 729 Dongfengdong Road, Guangzhou 510000, China
cynthia.xiao@gdut.edu.cn
[2] Guangdong International Center of Advanced Design, Guangdong University of Technology, Guangzhou 510000, China
[3] Guangdong Industry Polytechnic, Guangzhou 510000, China
[4] City University of Macau, Macau, China

Abstract. In recognition, high-quality green space can maintain the sustainable development of cities and promote health and well-being for the most significant possible people, regardless of age, ability, and circumstances. Improving the inclusiveness of urban parks can promote a positive user experience and social equity for different user groups, especially vulnerable people. Using green spaces in Guangzhou as a case study, this paper investigates human behavior in green spaces. It identifies barriers and opportunities for creating inclusive urban parks. A general integrated green space framework for inclusion and user experience is proposed. The result shows that the disparity in the quality of urban would lead to different experiences for users. The paper concludes by making some recommendations for researchers, urban planners, and policymakers to formulate specific planning and guidance for providing more inclusive green spaces and consider ways to improve the quality of green spaces that respond to the varying needs of different user groups.

Keywords: Green space · Inclusive design · User experience · Urban parks

1 Introduction

With Rapid urbanization, more than 4.3 billion people now live in urban areas (Ritchie and Roser, 2018). Across the globe, many governments are realizing the beneficial impact of green spaces on health outcomes and life (Siu et al. 2021). It has been widely suggested that green space exposure positively influences human health and well-being (Yang et al. 2020; Zhang et al. 2021). However, various people may experience green spaces quite differently (Siu 2013). Vulnerable groups—for example, women—only visit parks if they feel they are secure and inclusive spaces, and there are many parks where they may not judge that to be the case (Chenyang et al. 2022).

Building a high-quality and inclusive green space requires paying attention to vulnerable groups and satisfying their psychological, physical, and social needs. Accordingly, institutions have released various policies and plans to improve the quality of green spaces and reduce the proportion to which certain people feel excluded. For example, providing universal access to secure, inclusive, and accessible green and public spaces, particularly for women and children, older people, and people with disabilities, has been targeted by 2023 in Sustainable Development Goal (SDG) 11 Target 7 (UN Department of Economic and Social Affairs 2018). Achieving that goal requires adopting inclusive design principles. According to the UK Design Council, inclusive design is a general approach seeking to ensure that open spaces, products, and services are accessible to as many people as possible (Design Council 2008). As such, inclusive design aims to benefit all people.

Inclusive design proceeds in a top-down manner, first considering those at the top to be people with severe difficulties. Only when the needs of this group are met can the needs of other users also be accommodated. When applying that principle to design a safer, accessible, high-quality, and inclusive green space, we should first consider the needs and experiences of people with low socio-economic status. Designing the green space first and foremost to meet their needs can reduce exclusion and inequality and thus contribute to the health and well-being of the city.

This paper presents a case study, which was explored using both qualitative and quantitative research methods, on the conflict between various behavior of users, green space design, and the user experience of a park in Guangzhou, China. A framework is proposed that attends to the diverse needs of people of various ages, physical conditions, and cultural backgrounds, one that helps them to enjoy a high-quality green space equally. The aims are for the park to be inclusive and to promote the user experience in this green space. The findings provide a theoretical reference for future studies from researchers, urban planners, and policymakers on developing inclusive, open spaces.

2 Method

2.1 Case Study in Guangzhou

Guangzhou is a typical high-density city in Southern China. After investigating 11 parks in Guangzhou, the People's Park was chosen for this case study since it had recently undergone improvement works (Fig. 1). The information about the park before the update work was assessed from secondary information. By examining the environment and facilities and making a before-and-after comparison, this paper examines whether the development of the park has made it more inclusive for vulnerable groups. The People's Park is in Yuexiu, an old district of Guangzhou, the capital of Guangdong. Established in 1918 in the Western model, it was the first Comprehensive public park to be opened in the center of Guangzhou. The People's Park is rectangular, with an area of 6.1 ha and a symmetrical layout. It is close to the traditional administrative, cultural, and commercial center of Guangzhou, meaning it is a convenient park for many people to visit. Accordingly, the park receives diverse users.

The People's Park was made accessible to everyone in 1997 with the removal of its surrounding fence, and there has never been an entrance charge. Recently, a landscape optimization project was completed in 2020 to update the appearance of the park. Today, the park has a primary pathway that links the south gate, fountain, music pavilion, and north gate. Eight pathways branch off from that, with stone benches so users can rest and stay a while. Furthermore, on the eastern and western edges of the park are pavilions that provide shade so users can cool down on sunny days, and take cover on days when it rains. Additionally, several sculptures around the park complement one another and offer users a pleasant visual experience.

Fig. 1. Location of the People's Park and images of the park environment

In the context of the People's Park, by applying behavior mapping (BM) and taking a comparative approach, this paper examines whether the refurbishment of the park has impacted the behavior of different users and usage of the park. The aim is to identify how the update work has succeeded in creating an inclusive green space and improving the user experience, especially for vulnerable groups, while also noting which barriers remain to access the park for some groups of the population of Guangzhou.

2.2 Research Method and Procedures

BM is an observation technique developed by Ittelson, Rivlin, and Orohansky (1970) that helps researchers to collect data on environmental psychology, which they can use to analyze a place since those data capture people's behavior in a design setting. Implementing BM based on the individual-centered approach (Sommer and Sommer 2002), with the observer actively contributing to the data that are collected. The technique follows five steps:

1. Creating a base map identifying the physical features
2. Defining human behavioral categories and codes
3. Constructing an observation schedule
4. Developing a systematic observation process

5. Forming a counting and coding system

To apply BM, in this study, locations of individuals and behaviors were observed and recorded using photography and video. Based on observations on the day and later of those recordings, a base map (Fig. 2) was drawn using AutoCAD 2024, including physical elements that users seemed interested in, such as lawns, paths, benches, and built elements. The boundaries of the park itself were extracted from Baidu Map, and the park was divided into three zones.

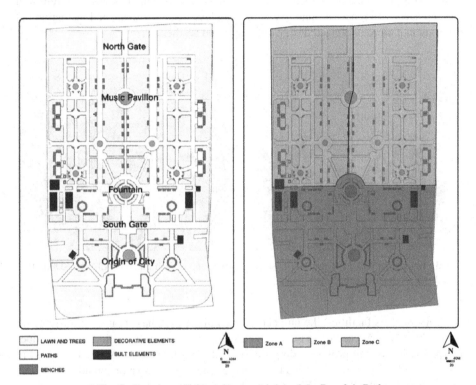

Fig. 2. Base map (left) and zones (right) of the People's Park

The data were collected in May 2023, when the weather was not too hot for outdoor activities. Observations were conducted under both sunny and cloudy weather conditions. Each of the three zones of the park was observed eight times, four on a weekday and four on the weekend. The observations were made at different times—morning (from 10 a.m. to 12 p.m.) and afternoon (from 12 p.m. to 2 p.m., 2 p.m. to 4 p.m., and 4 p.m. to 7 p.m.)—with each observation lasting 20 min. The researcher and five others were trained to use the same BM method. They were divided into three teams of two observers, and each team monitored one zone of the park. Before beginning to make observations, the date, time, and weather conditions were recorded by the observers.

3   Results

3.1   Refurbished Environment and Facilities in the People's Park

The People's Park refurbishment plan has used the architectural principle of revealing the axis, opening the interface, optimizing the space, and improving the quality to turn a previously underused green space into one better suited to activities and create a high-quality urban park (Fig. 3). The environment and facilities have been changed significantly in the process. A fundamental change is that many ancient trees have been removed and replaced with fences around lawns, leaving less space for shade and recreation but bringing in a more organized design and improved aesthetics.

Fig. 3. Images of the park pre- (left, source: https://mp.weixin.qq.com/s/dlAaKnSD0lpdt6T-Wbd3cA) and post-refurbishment (right)

Regarding its facilities, the number of seats in the park has significantly decreased from 800 to 188. According to field statistics and secondary information on the number pre-2020, the seating provision does not meet the needs of users. When the seats are taken up, elderly people are forced to sit on the fence by the lawn or spread out a picnic blanket to sit on the ground (Fig. 4), and there are security risks associated with those practices. Additionally, most benches in the park lack a backrest, meaning they offer little support to users, which cannot provide a positive experience for the elderly. The suboptimal seating has shortened the time people spent at the park. What is more, the drinking water fountains in the park are too high for children to use. Furthermore, while several streetlights are in the park, the light is too dim, which is they are ineffective at alleviating some people's security concerns.

Other groups of users we must consider are those with a physical disability requiring them to use an aid such as a wheelchair, along with users bringing a small child in a pushchair. The facilities and the park space were designed to meet accessibility standards; however, these groups of users still face barriers to accessing the park. For instance, ramps at various entrances now make it easier to enter on wheels. However, the management of the park had placed obstacles at some entrances that could only be passed by one person at a time. Those are placed there to bar the entry of electric vehicles, but they have the unintended effect of blocking wheelchairs and pushchairs. People who are affected must either divert to another entrance to the park or, in the case of pushchairs, can carry those up the steps. Then, once inside the park, it was noted that there are two toilets for users to use, located next to pavilions in the park, but only one is accessible at the ground level. The other was installed on upper platforms.

Fig. 4. An older person was forced to sit on the fence by the lawn

3.2 Data on the Park's Users

Table 1 presents the data collected on the two observation days in May 2023. One was a weekday when it was cloudy, and the temperature ranged from 21 to 29 °C, while the other was at the weekend, when it was sunny, and the temperature ranged from 25 to 34 °C. Data are shown for various user categories and their behaviors in the three zones of the People's Park at different times of the day. It was discovered that the weather was not as pleasant at the weekend. There were fewer people in the park than on the weekday. Most users were present between 10:00 a.m., and 4:00 p.m., but at 1:00 p.m. the number of users was observed to drastically decline due to a lack of shade provided by the trees and facilities. Most users were middle-aged or elderly, and most of them were men. Data on 3405 users were collected in total.

3.3 The Relationship Between User Behavior and Environments and Facilities

This paper concentrates on the interactions between user behavior, park facilities, and the environment to determine the successes of creating an inclusive urban park and the

Table 1. Behaviors of different user groups in the People's Park

No. of people involved in activity	Group				Gender		
	Children and teenagers	Adults	Elderly	Physically disabled	Male	Female	Total
Walking	43	827	135	12	566	451	1017
Laying	1	2	0	0	3	0	3
Laying on a bench	0	2	0	0	2	0	2
Pausing	0	3	4	0	5	3	7
Sitting and using their phone	9	259	24	0	219	73	292
Sitting on a bench	8	177	116	8	196	112	309
Siting and eating	0	3	6	0	8	1	9
Sitting and talking	18	208	118	2	193	153	346
Sitting with a child	30	31	4	0	26	39	65
Sitting and playing chess	1	25	24	4	49	5	54
Sitting and playing cards	0	90	51	0	110	31	141
Sitting and watching others play cards/chess	0	91	13	0	95	9	104
Standing	83	222	48	0	200	149	353
Standing and talking	8	93	20	0	53	68	121
Standing and watching others play cards/chess	1	49	5	0	47	6	55
Running	26	48	2	0	43	32	76
Pushing a pushchair	0	9	0	0	9	7	9
Pushing a pushchair + walking a child	24	30	6	1	28	33	61

(*continued*)

Table 1. (*continued*)

No. of people involved in activity	Group				Gender		
	Children and teenagers	Adults	Elderly	Physically disabled	Male	Female	Total
Singing	0	21	4	0	18	5	25
Dancing	0	65	7	0	8	66	72
Playing	5	33	0	0	29	9	38
Badminton	8	11	4	0	12	11	23
Cycling	4	5	0	0	7	2	9
Exercising	8	108	65	0	102	79	181
Roller-skating	26	7	0	0	16	17	33
All	303	2419	656	27	2044	1361	3405

remaining barriers to access that remain. Figures 5 and 6 show the number of users broken down by gender and user group, and the results show how different groups— particularly vulnerable groups—use the site differently. Most people choose to stroll, rest, use their phones, or converse in the park, primarily for recreation and fitness. Generally, the only group activity taking place in the morning is dancing; between 1:00 and 4:00 p.m., many people engage in dancing, singing, card games, and chess games. Children leave school throughout the week between 5 p.m. and 6 p.m., and parents or elderly relatives may take them to the park around then for walks and playtime. Nonetheless, fewer children are in the park than adults and the elderly. Now that the park has been updated, physically disabled people can often be seen. The observers noted about six wheelchair users in the park daily. Some pass the time watching other people engage in activities, while others choose to play chess.

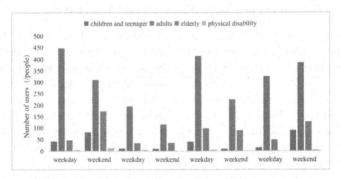

Fig. 5. Number of visits of different group types in the park on weekdays and on the weekend

The distribution of various groups in the park and their behavior patterns were discerned through behavior mapping. Despite being the smallest of the three zones, it was

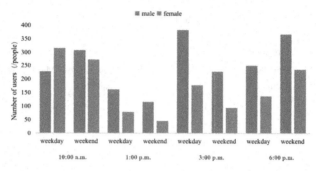

Fig. 6. Number of visits of different gender types in the park on weekdays and on the weekend

found that zone A had the most users, followed by zone B, with the least in zone C. Zone A has more activity space than the other two areas, and the main facilities and toilets are located in zone A. Many middle-aged and elderly people congregated at the entrance to zone A, the south gate, and front of the two pavilions in this zone to dance and sing. Others used pavilions and the circular seats next to the entrance, including some physically disabled people, to play chess. At the weekend, many children token skating lessons at the entrance at 10:00 a.m. and 6:00 p.m. Most people often gathered in areas with facilities, such as seats. Others spread out around those areas.

Zones B and C, symmetrical areas on either side of the main walkway, consist of lawns with pathways and benches. They offer less shade than zone A. Most users strolled, sat, or exercised in these zones. There are simple sports grounds within the two zones, but only some people use them for their exercise. Some middle-aged and elderly people in these zones often selected a space near the music pavilion to rest, play shuttlecock, or engage in other physical activities. There are additional simple sports grounds on the left and right sides of these two places, although only some people use them for exercise. See Figs. 7 and 8 for an example of behavior mapping of the park.

3.4 Factors Related to Park Inclusiveness and the User Experience

At the People's Park, the facilities, space, activities, social and cultural factors, and accessibility are all closely connected to park inclusiveness and the user experience. Some people have changed the functions of the facilities. For instance, middle-aged and elderly people use the benches as exercise tools, and children use a fence following the slope of the lawn as a play object due to the current facilities and activities of the park do not meet their needs. The park, in general, was observed to be friendly and comfortable to spend time in, the facilities were clean, and there was a pleasant atmosphere among users, who seemed to be enjoying their outing cleaner, which enhanced enjoyment of the space both hedonistically and pleasantly of users.

In China, middle-aged and older people enjoy dancing, singing, and playing chess in open spaces such as parks. It was noted that while the People's Park can accommodate them, there are no designated spaces for these activities, nor are chess tables provided. Many chess players gather at the pavilions on both sides of zone A, more to the right, and set up tables and chairs that they have brought in trolleys. Groups in the park can

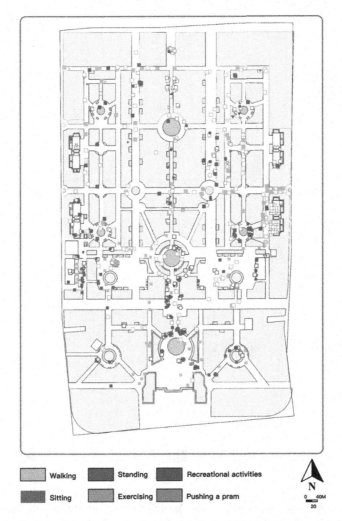

Fig. 7. Behavior mapping for the People's Park at 10:00 a.m. on a weekday

prevent other users from enjoying the space and facilities, leading to usage conflicts. In general, however, the park offers a setting for social activities where people may meet new acquaintances with the same interests, and it was noted that physically disabled people also gather with friends to chat or play chess in the park. The park may thus satisfy the social needs of people, especially the vulnerable, and improve their self-esteem, self-confidence, and mental health. Moreover, an added benefit of the park is that its volunteer station that offers unpaid volunteer work, which is something else people can get involved in.

It was noted that the accessibility of the park is not ideal. Even though there are numerous accessible routes, many are closed for management reasons, which is limiting

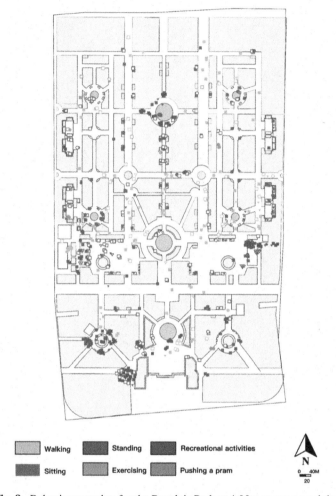

	Walking		Standing		Recreational activities
	Sitting		Exercising		Pushing a pram

N

0   40M
  20

Fig. 8. Behavior mapping for the People's Park at 4:00 p.m. on a weekday

for physically disabled people and decreases the overall accessibility of the park. Furthermore, various facilities, such as drinking water fountains in the park, do not cater to children's needs.

As many people walk in the park in the evening (e.g., 7:00 p.m.), the management implements measures, such as the supervision provided by the park security team, to help make users feel safe. However, these have the effect of making the park inaccessible to the homeless. It was discovered during the observation period that many staff works in the park to maintain both the environment and the facilities, which support the quality of the park and uphold its natural beauty, thus satisfying the need of users for green space.

4 Discussion

4.1 Factors Related to Park Inclusiveness and the User Experience

According to the observations and behavior mapping, this research identified the impact of park improvement work on user behavior and the user experience in an urban park, considering how those differ among various groups. This paper focuses on the inclusiveness of the park for vulnerable groups such as children, the elderly, and people with physical disabilities. The main findings are that park inclusiveness is related to the facilities, space, safety, activities, and social and cultural factors.

The quality and inclusive feel of the People's Park has been improved by the modernization work carried out, such as through the expansion of the accessible facilities, which potentially increases the opportunities for physically disabled and elderly people to visit. Meanwhile, the shortage of spaces for diverse activities and facilities, such as benches and spaces for exercise, leads to adverse user experience. Furthermore, facilities, such as activity sites (badminton courts, soccer fields, fitness equipment, chess tables) and service-Type facilities (seats, toilets, shade, and drinking water fountains), may encourage or discourage using the green park space. If such activity sites and facilities are well-planned, they may reduce park usage conflicts and enable the same space today to go further to meet the various needs of different groups. Elderly people typically prefer less demanding activities like playing chess. However, the park lacks chess tables and covered leisure areas. Children need specific areas or facilities for their activities, and other facilities must consider their needs. Even though the park has considered the needs of those who are physically unable, its accessibility facilities are insufficient, and the barriers at the park entrances may make it more difficult for them to go to parks.

After visiting 11 parks, the study discovered that middle-aged and elderly people who enjoy participating in group activities such as dancing, singing, and playing chess were influenced by Chinese culture. They can mingle, play, unwind, and interact through these social activities. Even though the People's Park is modest in size, several dance, singing, and chess clubs and the volunteer station in the park host various programs for children, among other events. Visiting the People's Park to meet up with others for activities can boost social support and social inclusion, which is essential for vulnerable people and improve their physical and emotional health. Additionally, from a visual standpoint, the park's upgrades have made it easier to see across the green space; this makes the park feel safer for people to visit, as does the supervision provided by the park security team.

4.2 An Integrated Green Space Framework

Akkar Ercan and Oya Memlük (2015) asserted that the three main factors affecting open space inclusivity are the physical environment, personal experience, and process & context. Similarly, the Gehl Institute and Robert Wood Johnson Foundation (2017) outlined the inclusive, healthy place framework, which comprises 16 drivers, 52 indicators, and four guiding concepts—context, process design, program, and sustain. Supported by those previous works and a literature review, along with the data collected during the research period, this study led to the development of an integrated green space framework for inclusivity and the user experience (see Fig. 9). The integrated green space framework comprises three guiding principles—physical environment, user experience, and the socio-cultural environment—and 13 factors influencing the inclusiveness of urban parks. Essentially, the proposal is that for researchers to understand park's inclusiveness, they should focus to spatial user experiences rather than accessibility (Heylighen et al. 2017). The framework prioritizes access to green spaces for the vulnerable, neglected, disadvantaged, and disenfranchised. All factors concerning a green space should be perceived by such users rather than by designers and experts.

The first guiding principle in this framework, the physical environment, which is planned and designed by urban planners, impacts health and well-being through user behavior within the space and its facilities. The physical environment contains five factors: access, accessibility, facilities, visuals and aesthetics, and safety. Then the second guiding principle, the user experience, concerns the connection between the planning and design of urban green areas and the experiences of those various user groups. It is considered that parks must be both practical and pleasant if they are to satisfy the demands of various user groups. Beyond that, though, people's interactions with and perceptions of green park spaces can also be influenced by the wider context, including their gender, age, and socio-economic status. Finally, the third guiding principle is the socio-cultural environment, comprising the social (including social inclusion and social support) and cultural factors that shape and influence user behavior. Factors such as park policies, management, and user control can also affect user behavior.

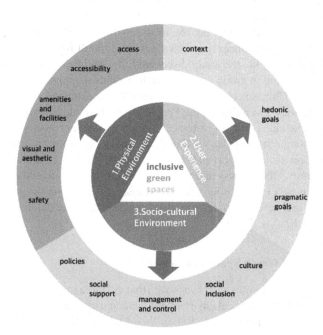

Fig. 9. Integrated green space framework for inclusion and the user experience

5 Conclusion

An inclusive green space offering a pleasant user experience can encourage vulnerable groups to participate in outdoor social activities and create more activity opportunities. The paper has investigated the relationship between the behavior of various groups visiting the People's Park in Guangzhou with BM, which has recently been improved. It has explored the park environment, broken down into the physical and socio-cultural environments, and the impact of these environmental factors on user experiences.

We have found that due to its modest size, the People's Park needs to be designed into a flexible space, the use of which can change to fit the needs of various groups on different days and at different times, thus providing unique experiences for each group. The modernization work carried out has helped to create an environment that focuses on the health and well-being of users. However, we recommend incorporating facilities based on local cultures, such as the chess tables, when future update work is carried out.

The findings of this study have offered lessons for researchers, urban planners, and policymakers who wish to provide high-quality green spaces and promote positive user experiences for a wide range of people. The most important takeaway is that they should be cognizant of the needs of different groups. Moreover, it is recommended that they utilize the presented framework of guiding principles and factors that can help them evaluate the current state of green space and identify areas where there are issues with its quality.

Acknowledgments. The authors would like to acknowledge the National Natural Science Foundation of China (Grant No. 52008114) , Philosophy and Social Sciences Fund of Guangdong Province (GD22XYS17), Undergraduate Teaching and Learning Project of Guangdong University of Technology (GDUT [2022] No.59), Student Innovation Training Project of Guangdong University of Technology (xj2023118450788) for the data collection and the preparation of the paper. The authors thank Ministry of Housing and Urban-Rural Development, China Disabled Persons' Federation, Office of Guangzhou Municipal Commission on Aging, China Association for the Blind, China Disabled Persons' Federation, Guangzhou Disabled Persons' Federation and Guangzhou Volunteer Association for providing support for the research. The authors also acknowledge Prof. Siu, the Chair professor of Public Design Lab of The Hong Kong Polytechnic University for providing a lot of useful information.

References

Akkar Ercan, M., Oya Memlük, N.: More inclusive than before?: the tale of a historic urban park in Ankara, Turkey. Urban Des. Int. **20**, 195–221 (2015)

Chenyang, D., Maruthaveeran, S., Shahidan, M.F.: The usage, constraints and preferences of green space at disadvantage neighbourhood: a review of empirical evidence. Urban Forestry Urban Greening **75**, 127696 (2022)

Design Council: Inclusive Design Education Resource (2008). http://www.designcouncil.info/inc lusivedesignresource/

Gehl Institute and Robert Wood Johnson Foundation: Inclusive Healthy Places (2017). http://ihp. gehlpeople.com/framework/

Heylighen, A., Van der Linden, V., Van Steenwinkel, I.: Ten questions concerning inclusive design of the built environment. Build. Environ. **114**, 507–551 (2017)

Ittelson, W. H.: The use of behavioral maps in environmental psychology (1970)

Ritchie, H., Roser, M.: Urbanization. Our world in data (2018)

Siu, K.W.M.: Accessible park environments and facilities for the visually impaired. Facilities **31**(13/14), 590–609 (2013)

Siu, K.W.M., Xiao, J.X., Wong, Y.L.: Quality open space experiences for the visually impaired. Appl. Res. Qual. Life **16**, 183–199 (2021)

Sommer, R., Sommer, B.: Mapping and trace measures. A practical guide to behavioural research: Tools and techniques, 63–79 (2002)

UN Department of Economic and Social Affairs: Disability. Sustainable Development Goals (SDGs) and Disability (2018). https://www.un.org/development/desa/disabilities/about-us/sustainable-development-goals-sdgs-and-disability.html

Yang, M., Dijst, M., Faber, J., Helbich, M.: Using structural equation modeling to examine pathways between perceived residential green space and mental health among internal migrants in China. Environ. Res. **183**, 109121 (2020)

Zhang, L., Tan, P.Y., Richards, D.: Relative importance of quantitative and qualitative aspects of urban green spaces in promoting health. Landsc. Urban Plan. **213**, 104131 (2021)

Wearable Devices for Communication and Problem-Solving in the Context of Industry 4.0

Ricardo Nunes[1]([envelope]) [iD], Rodrigo Pereira[1] [iD], Paulo Nogueira[3], João Barroso[1,2] [iD], Tânia Rocha[1,2] [iD], and Arsénio Reis[1,2] [iD]

[1] Universidade de Trás-os-Montes e Alto Douro, Vila Real, Portugal
{rrnunes,jbarroso,trocha,ars}@utad.pt, a168798@alunos.utad.pt
[2] Instituto de Engenharia de Sistemas e Computadores, Tecnologia e Ciência (INESC TEC), Porto, Portugal
[3] Continental Advanced Antenna, Vila Real, Portugal
paulo.nogueira@continental-corporation.com

Abstract. This research focuses on developing a wearable device that aims to enhance problem-solving and communication abilities within the context of Industry 4.0. The wearable is being developed in the Continental Advanced Antenna, and it allows operators to notify material shortages on the manufacturing line and helps minimize workflow disturbance. The wearable gives a list of missing materials using context-aware computing, allowing operators to identify and prioritize the missing item quickly. We used the Quick and Dirty usability testing approach to ensure the device's usability and efficacy, allowing quick feedback and iterative modifications throughout the development process. Experienced consultants of project participated initial tests on the device and found that it has the potential to improve efficiency and communication in an industrial setting. However, further testing involving end users is necessary to optimize the device for the unique demands of the production environment. This paper offers valuable insights into the lessons learned from the project and proposes potential future research directions.

Keywords: Wearable · Industry 4.0 · Usability Testing · Human-Machine Interaction

1 Introduction

Technological advances arising from the fourth industrial revolution, also known as Industry 4.0 (I4.0) substantially increased industrial production automation. This phenomenon, driven by international initiatives, promoted a significant transformation in the industrial environment [1].

From the perspective of Ambient Assisted Working concept [2], aligned with the I4.0 design principle of Technical Assistance [3], the I4.0 manufacturing environment assists the Operator 4.0 [4, 5] needs, enabling informed decisions based on data. In this context,

V. G. Duffy et al. (Eds.): HCII 2023, LNCS 14057, pp. 583–592, 2023.
https://doi.org/10.1007/978-3-031-48047-8_39

the worker is an essential part of these advances, highlighting the importance of human-machine interaction in the industrial sector [6, 7]. To boost productivity, efficiency, and safety, the fundamental goal in this field is to promote a more harmonic and synergistic integration of humans and machines [8].

Wearables like smartwatches, smart clothing and smart glasses offer great promise for enhancing development within the industrial sector. These technologies can help with ergonomics, communication, and mobility issues, e.g., allowing operators to monitor processes in real-time, helping to identify problems and suggesting improvements. In another hand, analysis of the use of these devices reveals consumer concerns about the security and privacy of the data gathered. Therefore, research should be done to thoroughly examine these limits, boost the confidence of users, and contribute to increasing industrial production [9].

In this context, this paper describes a wearable device that enables the operator to communicate with responsible parties to solve issues in the industrial environment without leaving the workstation or deviating from what must be done. Following this, we introduce an intelligent computer systems approach that integrates operators with cyber-physical assistance in the factory.

This work is being carried out in the context of Continental Advanced Antenna (AA), which studies and develops applications for the interaction between information systems and operators, aiming to increase the factory production capacity. In the factory, unexpected production stoppages and financial losses occur due to unpredictable material shortages in the production lines, such as the use cases we are going to deal with in this paper: (1) lack of labels and (2) lack of components - that are essential manufacturing elements.

In this research, the application of wearables is explored, providing contextual information, and improving communication between workers. In Sect. 2, investigations of some wearables applications in Industry 4.0 are presented. In Sect. 3, Continental AA context is presented. The wearable development in the context of this research is provided in Sect. 4. The evaluation method of the wearable is described in Sect. 5. Preliminary results are in Sect. 6 and in Sect. 7 are presented the conclusions and limitations of this research. Finally, Sect. 8 points directions for future research.

2 Background and Related Work

In response to changes in the external environment, such as technological advances, globalisation, changes in consumer demand, sustainability and regulations, the industrial sector has experienced a gradual revolution. Consequently, the advent of steam power, then moving to the division of labor, and finally reaching the era of digitalization, have marked the three significant industrial revolutions [10]. In the context of the fourth industrial revolution, or I4.0, the Internet of Things (IoT), a new paradigm that combines people and interconnected gadgets, results from recent digital technologies advancements [11]. Wearables have developed into electronic gadgets that incorporate the IoT and may be used in various contexts, including the industrial sector [12]. These gadgets are smart electronic devices placed close to the human body and have built-in sensors that enable continuous monitoring of human activity. These devices have the feature to communicate with external devices, applications, or cloud computing, and provide a wealth of data that can be used to improve connectivity and access to employee information.

This section reviews some of the recent studies on the use of wearables in I4.0. Due to their relevance and possible applicability to the Industrial 4.0 setting, the following studies were specially chosen. Each research study offers a distinct viewpoint on how wearables and IoT improve output, security, and well-being in the industrial setting. Additionally, these studies show innovative uses of these technologies in various contexts, including smart homes, industrial augmented reality, and wellness sensor networks, providing insightful data that might be used in the industrial sector.

For example, the research conducted by Ghayvat et al. [13] investigated the application of wellness sensor networks for smart home systems. This work utilized wireless networking-based heterogeneous sensors and actuator nodes in a domestic environment. These nodes produced real-time data about object usage and movement inside the home, generating predictions about a person's well-being. While the study was primarily focused on smart home systems, the principles and techniques applied, such as monitoring and predicting wellness based on sensor data, can also be relevant and beneficial in an industrial setting. In this context, it can be viewed as a subset of Industry 4.0 applications, due to its use of interconnected devices and real-time data for predictive purposes, even though the setting is not directly industrial.

Fraga-Lamas et al. [14] conducted a detailed examination of Industrial Augmented Reality (IAR) systems for industrial and shipbuilding applications. The research suggests a cloudlet and fog computing-based IAR system architecture that would speed up rendering processes and lower response latency while outsourcing compute-intensive jobs to the cloud. The support of physically dispersed and low-latency applications is made possible by this technology, which lowers network traffic and lowers the computational burden compared to conventional cloud computing systems. Additionally, because fog gateways often have limited processing capability, Cloudlets are required if an IAR system requires real-time rendering or other compute-intensive services.

The wearIT@work project [15], led by the University of Bremen, is a significant milestone in wearable computing for industrial applications. This project, which involved a consortium of partners, adopted a cyclical innovation and user-centred design approach to assess the impact of wearable computing on workforce productivity and quality of work in four application domains: emergency response, production, maintenance, and healthcare. In the production scenario, wearable computing was used to overcome the challenge of intelligent information integration and presentation by replacing a paper checklist with a wearable solution that allowed workers to handle all necessary tools with dynamic checklists. This innovation improved system interfaces and context recognition in addition reduced worker training time. Despite the advances, the project identified areas that still need research, such as the miniaturisation of wearable devices, battery life for multiple shifts, localisation in industrial settings and the lack of interoperability and reliable wireless communication at the user level [16].

Smailagic & Siewiorek [17] present four user interface models that map problem-solving capabilities to application requirements based on their experience developing wearable computers at Carnegie Mellon University. These models include pre-stored procedures, master-apprentice help desk, team collaboration, and context-aware collaboration with a proactive virtual assistant. The paper also presents examples of systems and evaluation methods to show how user tests can quantify wearable systems effectiveness. The authors conclude that addressing several significant challenges, such as developing social and cognitive application models, integrating input from multiple sensors, anticipating user needs, and interacting with users, is necessary to integrate wearable computers into ubiquitous computing environments effectively.

The RT-PROFASY [18] is a project that aims to enhance the workers well-being, safety, and productivity by using wearable sensors and Artificial Intelligence (AI). The project aims to monitor workers stress and fatigue levels in real time and integrate within a single platform data from production processes, the environment, and indoor localisation. This approach allows in-depth aggregated data analysis, positively impacting worker safety and productivity. The project goal is to help companies pursue product quality through sustainable processes for workers and appropriate working environments.

Despite challenges, the background highlights the growing importance of wearables in I4.0. This work could contribute to the study field by presenting a wearable device development that improves the communication and efficiency in the industrial environment. The following sections will present the project this research is part of and detail the wearable, exploring its design, implementation, and preliminary evaluation.

3   Context of Research

Continental AA aims to develop new technical-scientific knowledge to accelerate the creation of high-tech assets for the I4.0 environment. These assets combined will be addressing the challenging problems anticipated for the next generation of automotive parts production.

Developing solutions that improve the interface between operators and machines (Human-Machine) and between operators and the work environment (Human-Factory) is a significant focus area of the project. In the field of contextual interfaces and virtual assistants, the project proposes the creation of virtual assistants and new intelligent digital interfaces sensitive to the factory context, *e.g.*, wearables.

The wearables design aims to equip operators with all the necessary information for making informed, timely and appropriate decisions, thereby enhancing their production capacity. This strategy aligns with leveraging intelligent computer systems principles to assist operators, integrating them seamlessly into the factory cyber-physical systems and increasing the workers operational capabilities.

4   Wearable Device Solution

Continental AA plans to use I4.0 solutions to facilitate employee activities on the production environment and ease communication about production material request. The wearable device can be used in this context to increase efficiency. The device allows operators to report material shortages on the line without stopping the ongoing activities. By pressing a specific button, the operator can issue alerts about the specific material shortage and its priority level (see Fig. 1).

Fig. 1. The operator selects the priority request: High, Medium, or Low.

Since that, the warehouse manager in charge receives a list of materials requested containing the reference of the parts, the quantity required, the line that placed the request, and its priority. The warehouse is responsible for changing the status ("Handled" and "Call Robot"). In addition to these changes, the request can also be deleted ("Delete").

Upon receiving the request, the warehouse manager confirms that they will handle it (see Fig. 2.a). The Fig. 2.b, the manager in charge has already collected all the requested materials and can call a Automated guided vehicle (which we call 'robot') to gather the requested material and send it to the production line. Upon completing its designated role in retrieving materials, the robot concludes its next objective by ensuring a seamless delivery process by transporting them along a predetermined path leading directly to the production line.

The robot continuously transmits information regarding the request, alerting the warehouse to events that may occur along the path. The warehouse manager may follow the status and development of the request in real-time from to these updates. In this manner, warehouse manager is able to respond quickly to issues and, if required, stop ("Request stopped" - see Fig. 2.c) or cancel the request ("Request cancelled" - see Fig. 2.d). For the robot to pick and transport products in an effective and seamless manner, there must be this constant contact between it and the warehouse (Fig. 2).

The alerts are communicated to the material delivery robot operator, the warehouse manager, and the production supervisor simultaneously, facilitating the management of the material shortages on the production line.

The wearable device provides to the operator a list of possible missing materials based on the wearable device user location. The context determines the production line, the part produced, and the related materials. The operator can then select the missing material and its priority through wearable. This communication process helps avoid production downtime due to material shortages.

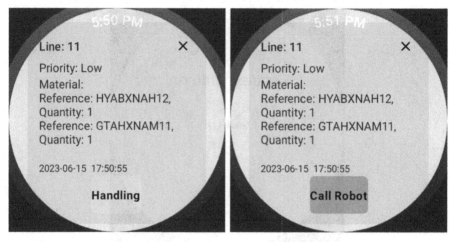

(a) New material request received.

(b) Request status changed to "Call Robot".

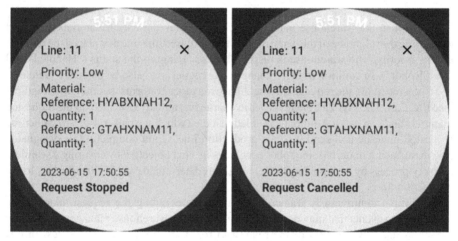

(c) Request status changed to "Request Stopped".

(d) Request status changed to "Request Cancelled".

Fig. 2. Warehouse manager wearable interface.

5   Quick and Dirty Usability Testing for Wearable Development

In developing the wearable device for the Industry 4.0 environment, usability testing is crucial. Specifically, the Quick and Dirty usability testing method [17, 18] provides rapid feedback over wearable design and functionality. This method, known for its flexibility and efficiency, allows for iterative improvements throughout development.

Quick and Dirty usability testing involves conducting informal tests at various stages of the development process [19]. The wearable end users are often represented by a limited group of volunteers in these testing. The participants are asked to perform a series of tasks using the device while the researchers observe and note any difficulties or issues. The evaluation entails casual meetings with industry experts, software engineers, product managers, or end users, to discuss new product ideas, test prospective icons, evaluate the aesthetic appeal of a graphic, or confirm the accurate categorization of content on a system. The data gathered, which is often informal and descriptive, is included in the design process as either verbal or written notes, drawings, and stories. In the context of this wearable device development, these tasks include issuing a material shortage alert, selecting the priority level of an alert, or navigating through the different pages available on the device. The objective is to find any usability problems that prevent users from doing these jobs successfully and efficiently.

In this research context, the tests were carried out in different stages using the consultants, who are Continental's consortium partners who have the role of project managers. With their experience and knowledge, these consultants provided valuable feedback that helped shape the wearable device development. Thus, the wearable has been consistently updated and enhanced thanks to this collaborative and iterative methodology, ensuring that it satisfies the demands of end users in the production environment. This iterative process allows continuous device refinement, intending to enhance its usability and overall user experience.

It is crucial to remember that while Quick and Dirty usability testing offers insightful information, it is not intended to substitute more thorough usability testing techniques. Instead, it is a complementary approach that allows for rapid improvements during development. To ensure that the wearable device satisfies the needs and expectations of its end users in the industrial setting, more formal and thorough usability testing techniques should be used after the wearable has reached a more advanced level of development.

6   Results and Discussion

The Quick and Dirty usability tests were conducted by Continental AA consultants with experience and skills in project management throughout the development of the wearable device. These experiments produced crucial findings that influenced the wearable layout and operation.

The consultants deemed the wearable user-friendly and intuitive, indicating that it might be successfully incorporated to enhance collaboration and productivity in the production environment. They assumed that wearable users could quickly issue warnings about material shortages, as well as the alert's priority level.

The consultants also well-liked the wearable capability to present a list of potential missing supplies depending on the user's precise position in the production environment. Such an illustration underscores how enhancing wearable usefulness can be achieved through contextualization.

Some difficulties were noted, such as doubts regarding the product toughness in a manufacturing setting. From these observations, it becomes apparent that additional efforts are necessary to ensure the wearable reliability under the rigorous conditions of a production environment.

The explanation of these findings emphasizes the significance of a user-centred, iterative development approach. The Quick and Dirty usability testing allowed changes to the wearable functioning and design fast in response to consultant comments. As a result, the wearable now is more closely matches of the end users' requirements and preferences.

The test results show that the wearable has the potential to enhance efficiency and communication in the industrial setting. Before it can be used in a production setting, the device functionality and design still need to be enhanced.

7 Conclusions and Limitations

The process of creating a wearable device for the Industry 4.0 environment has been instructive, demonstrating both the advantages and disadvantages of incorporating such technology into a manufacturing environment. In preliminary testing, the wearable, intended to improve productivity and communication in an I4.0 industrial environment, has shown promise. It has proven capable of streamlining the procedure for sending out alerts regarding material shortages and choosing the priority level of these signals, resulting in a potential decrease in downtime and an increase in productivity.

Conversely, the wearable durability in a rigorous production line environment is still an issue. The wearable possesses the ability to endure tough conditions, but the consultant's remarks suggest that its durability and reliability require further enhancement.

In addition, the testing procedure itself exposed a weakness in research strategy: instead of the actual end users, the consultants carried out the testing. The consultants' experience and knowledge were helpful in helping to develop the wearable, but in the future, testing should include the end users to make sure the product suits their unique requirements.

We acknowledge the value of an iterative, user-centred approach to development as we summarize these findings. The Quick and Dirty usability testing created a feedback loop that helped to improve the product. However, to ensure wearable efficiency and durability enough for the industrial setting, we must expand our testing methodology as we go forward.

In integrating I4.0 technology into the manufacturing environment, the wearable gadget represents a substantial advancement. However, the procedure still needs to be finished. The lessons learnt from this project will direct the future work as we move towards a synergetic coexistence of humans and robots in the I4.0 production environment.

8 Future Works

As we move forward, our main goal will be to carry out wearable device usability tests in the end-of-line, involving device operators, or end users: their practical experience and unique knowledge will be valuable in improving the device to better meet the demands and challenges of the I4.0 production environment. We hope that this direct involvement not only improves the functionality and use of the device but also fosters a sense of ownership and acceptance among the operators.

We will examine the information gathered from these on-site usability testing in the next phase, to find any recurring problems or obstructions that can reduce the effectiveness of the wearable in practical applications, altering the wearable functionalities and design as appropriate considering these findings. We will continue this iterative process of testing, receiving input, and refining until we have a wearable that is not only durable and dependable but also fits as seamlessly as possible into the I4.0 industrial production workflow.

Acknowledgements. The study was developed under the Mobilizing Agenda "A-MOVER - Development of Products & Systems towards an Intelligent and Green Mobility", supported by the PRR-Recovery and Resilience Plan and the European NextGeneration EU Funds.

References

1. Alcácer, V., Cruz-Machado, V.: Scanning the industry 4.0: a literature review on technologies for manufacturing systems. Eng. Sci. Technol. Int. J. **22**(3), 899–919 (2019). https://doi.org/10.1016/j.jestch.2019.01.006
2. Reis, A., Rocha, T., Barroso, J., Carvalho, D.: The ambient assisted working (AAW) concept: assistance according to I4.0 technical assistance design principle. In: Proceedings of the 15th International Conference on PErvasive Technologies Related to Assistive Environments, pp. 316–318 (2022). https://doi.org/10.1145/3529190.3534713
3. Hermann, M., Pentek, T., Otto, B.: Design principles for industrie 4.0 scenarios. In: 49th Hawaii International Conference on System Sciences (HICSS), pp. 3928–3937. Koloa, HI, USA (2016). https://doi.org/10.1109/HICSS.2016.488
4. Margherita, E.G., Bua, I.: The role of human resource practices for the development of operator 4.0 in industry 4.0 organisations: a literature review and a research agenda. Businesses **1**(1), 18–33 (2021). https://doi.org/10.3390/businesses1010002
5. Romero, D., et al.: Towards an operator 4.0 typology: a human-centric perspective on the fourth industrial revolution technologies. In: Proceedings of the International Conference on Computers and Industrial Engineering (CIE46), Tianjin, China, pp. 29–31 (2016)
6. Pereira, A.C., Romero, F.: A review of the meanings and the implications of the industry 4.0 concept. Procedia Manufact. **13**, 1206–1214 (2017). https://doi.org/10.1016/j.promfg.2017.09.032
7. Borisov, N., Weyers, B., Kluge, A.: Designing a human machine interface for quality assurance in car manufacturing: an attempt to address the "functionality versus user experience contradiction" in professional production environments. Adv. Hum. Comput. Interact. **2018**, 1–18 (2018). https://doi.org/10.1155/2018/9502692
8. Tofail, S.A., Koumoulos, E.P., Bandyopadhyay, A., Bose, S., O'Donoghue, L., Charitidis, C.: Additive manufacturing: scientific and technological challenges, market uptake and opportunities. Mater. Today **21**(1), 22–37 (2018). https://doi.org/10.1016/j.mattod.2017.07.001
9. Anes, H., Pinto, T., Lima, C., Nogueira, P., Reis, A.: Wearable devices in Industry 4.0: A systematic literature review. In: 20th International Conference on Distributed Computing and Artificial Intelligence (DCAI23), Guimarão, Portugal (2023). https://doi.org/10.1007/978-3-031-38318-2_33
10. Xu, M., David, J.M., Kim, S.H.: The fourth industrial revolution: opportunities and challenges. Int. J. Financ. Res. **9**(2), 90–95 (2018). https://doi.org/10.5430/ijfr.v9n2p90

11. Witkowski, K.: Internet of things, big data, industry 4.0 – innovative solutions in logistics and supply chains management. Procedia Eng. **182**, 763–769 (2017). https://doi.org/10.1016/j.proeng.2017.03.197

12. Ometov, A., et al.: A survey on wearable technology: history, state-of-the-art and current challenges. Comput. Netw. **193**, 108074 (2021). https://doi.org/10.1016/j.comnet.2021.108074

13. Ghayvat, H., Mukhopadhyay, S., Gui, X., Suryadevara, N.: WSN-and IOT-based smart homes and their extension to smart buildings. Sensors **15**(5), 10350–10379 (2015). https://doi.org/10.3390/s150510350

14. Fraga-Lamas, P., Fernandez-Carames, T.M., Blanco-Novoa, O., Vilar-Montesinos, M.A.: A review on industrial augmented reality systems for the industry 4.0 shipyard. IEEE Access **6**, 13358–13375 (2018). https://doi.org/10.1109/ACCESS.2018.2808326

15. Lawo, M., Herzog, O., Boronowsky, M., Knackfuss, P.: The open wearable computing group. IEEE Pervasive Comput. **10**(2), 78–81 (2011). https://doi.org/10.1109/MPRV.2011.34

16. Kong, X.T.R., Luo, H., Huang, G.Q., Yang, X.: Industrial wearable system: the human-centric empowering technology in Industry 4.0. J. Intell. Manufact. **30**(8), 2853–2869 (2019). https://doi.org/10.1007/s10845-018-1416-9

17. Smailagic, A., Siewiorek, D.: Application design for wearable and context-aware computers. IEEE Pervasive Comput. **1**(4), 20–29 (2002). https://doi.org/10.1109/MPRV.2002.1158275

18. Donati, M., Olivelli, M., Giovannini, R., Fanucci, L.: RT-PROFASY: enhancing the well-being, safety and productivity of workers by exploiting wearable sensors and artificial intelligence. In: IEEE International Workshop on Metrology for Industry 4.0 & IoT (MetroInd4.0&IoT), pp. 69–74. IEEE (2022). https://doi.org/10.1109/MetroInd4.0IoT54413.2022.9831499

19. Preece, J., Rogers, Y., Sharp, H.: Interaction Design: Beyond Human-Computer Interaction, 1st Edition. Wiley (2002)

20. Lim, D., Lee, M.: Quick and dirty prototyping and testing for UX design of future robotaxi. In: Yang, X.-S., Sherratt, S., Dey, N., Joshi, A. (eds.) Proceedings of Sixth International Congress on Information and Communication Technology. LNNS, vol. 236, pp. 345–356. Springer, Singapore (2022). https://doi.org/10.1007/978-981-16-2380-6_30

21. Thomas, B.: 'Quick and dirty' usability tests. In: Usability Evaluation in Industry, pp. 107–114. CRC Press (1996)

User-Centered Design of a Digital Citizen Inquiry Project on Plastic Circular Economy for Young People

Niwat Srisawasdi[(✉)] [ID] and Patcharin Panjaburee [ID]

Faculty of Education, Khon Kaen University, Khon Kaen 40000, Thailand
niwsri@kku.ac.th

Abstract. Digital citizen science projects have become globally popular in the last decade, with mobile platforms and devices engaging people in observing environmental phenomena. Youth participation in citizen science has been regarded as an opportunity to learn about science within the context of education, and they can better understand scientific processes and methods and gain self-efficacy, motivation, and responsible behavior by refining inquiry-based learning with the research paradigm of citizen science known as "citizen inquiry." This study investigates how user-centered design contributes to designing a digital citizen inquiry mobile application, Plastic Detectives, for young citizen inquirers to create an effective method of monitoring plastic, raising awareness about plastic pollution at the societal level. The Plastic Detectives mobile application was developed using the design life cycle model. One hundred twenty-eight participants, from elementary school to university students, contributed to the user-centered Plastic Detectives' app development in three research periods. The life cycle model application ensures that consumers are involved in the design and that the process is appropriately planned and tested. Semi-structured interviews, focus groups, and investigative record data have been used to identify the efficacy of the development. According to the findings, young participants positively accepted the digital citizen inquiry technology. They were satisfactory regarding contextual data sharing, task monitoring, expeditious selection, recording-to-sharing experience flow, positive social tasks, and visual affordance. The findings reveal successful mechanisms for the design of effective and sustainable citizen inquiry communities, as well as methods for their maintenance.

Keywords: HCI Theories and Methods · Interface for Children · Mobile HCI and Automobiles

1 Introduction

Since the late 20th century, "citizen science" has become a trendy term for many citizen-led participatory research activities in the sciences [1]. It has become increasingly prominent in science policy discourse in the United States, Europe, and Asia [2, 3] at the beginning of the twenty-first century. Citizen science broadly refers to initiatives that

© The Author(s), under exclusive license to Springer Nature Switzerland AG 2023
V. G. Duffy et al. (Eds.): HCII 2023, LNCS 14057, pp. 593–605, 2023.
https://doi.org/10.1007/978-3-031-48047-8_40

recruit members of the public that are becoming more ambitious and diverse and involve a vast array of field-based scientific investigations. Due to the widespread availability of smartphones and other Internet and communications technologies for accumulating and sharing observational data, the expression has gained significant traction in recent years.

As a result, digital citizen science projects have become globally popular in the last decade, with mobile platforms and devices engaging people in observing environmental, i.e., climate change, and social, i.e., COVID-19 pandemic phenomena, as mobile technology has become pervasive and autonomously capable of capturing, classifying, and transmitting location, image, voice, video, and other data. In addition, digital citizen science employs technology to assist individuals in conducting activities such as collecting, categorizing, transcribing, or analyzing scientific data on a phenomenon of interest. Furthermore, most digital citizen science platforms are designed to support user-generated data and collect empirical evidence via mobile devices. More research on human–computer interaction (HCI) focuses on designing, developing, and using digital citizen science tools due to their increasing popularity and technological integration. HCI studies could be used to promote social good and pursue global and local sustainability of digital citizen science projects.

Youth participation in citizen science has been regarded as an opportunity to learn about science within the context of education. Youth can better understand scientific processes and methods, have an interest in science and the environment, self-efficacy, motivation, knowledge of science's nature, scientific inquiry skills, and responsible behavior. A refinement of inquiry-based learning with the research paradigm of citizen science known as "citizen inquiry" has been proposed to reduce the complexity of and enhance active learning opportunities for young people. Citizen inquiry is an innovative way for non-professionals to engage in practical scientific activities in which they assume the role of self-regulated scientists in informal learning contexts. It begins with an explicit pedagogy of inquiry-based learning combined with a citizen science practice. This new pedagogy-based science practice is intended to facilitate both good scientific outcomes (from widespread participation in data collection and or/analysis) and good learning outcomes, such as learning about the scientific investigation process, the topic under investigation, and gaining digital literacy. As with digital citizen science projects, it is crucial to design citizen inquiry projects that will attract and engage members based on HCI to facilitate the success of young people in initiating and participating in long-term citizen-led investigations.

Designing and developing online citizen inquiry platforms where young people can interact with projects by submitting data online, classifying and interpreting sounds, videos, and images, or perusing large databases is difficult. In addition, the design, evaluation, and implementation of computing systems for human use to support the increasing quantities of co-collected data, as well as the increased accessibility of data and its visualization and readability, are essential for implementing digital citizen inquiry. This study proposes creating and evaluating a digital citizen inquiry project to monitor plastic waste and its circularity in the local environment with the active participation of juvenile citizens.

2   Literature Reviews

2.1   A Connection Between Citizen Science and Citizen Inquiry

Citizen Science (CS) typically involves the participation of the general public in various stages of the scientific process, frequently involving data collection or analysis within initiatives directed by scientists [4]. CS initiatives have been categorized as contributory, collaborative, and co-created depending on the level of collaboration between scientists and citizens. In contributory projects, participants are primarily involved in the data collection and analysis phases; in collaborative projects, they also assist in designing the study and interpreting or disseminating the data; and in co-created projects, participants collaborate with scientists at every stage of the project, including defining the research question, discussing results, and planning future work [5]. However, these initiatives may assume a high level of scientific expertise and a lack of explicit learning objectives to enhance citizens' comprehension of the scientific method and confidence in science and inquiry.

Citizen inquiry (CI) overcomes the dilemma of prioritizing learning in CS projects by emphasizing the active participation of the public in initiating and carrying out their own projects, and CI connects CS and inquiry-based science learning as an innovative way for engaging the public in learning with science participation [6]. In CI, public members establish their own agenda of personally meaningful scientific studies and produce recognizable learning results led by scientific inquiry models and co-investigators (Aristeidou, Scanlo, & Sharples, 2020). In addition, CI has several advantages over our previous method, including the fact that anyone (student, teacher, or member of the public) can initiate an investigation, it draws on the power of the crowd to provide data and commentary, and it can be applied to a wide range of topics in the physical, environmental, and social sciences [7].

2.2   Digital Citizen Inquiry Project and Its Impacts

The citizen inquiry approach prioritizes and facilitates learning and engages individuals in all phases of the scientific process by involving them in inquiry-based learning while participating in citizen science activities. A growing number of studies have documented the positive effects of digital citizen inquiry participation on science learning, including enhanced science knowledge, the development of scientific skills and scientific literacy, and increased awareness and personal change (e.g., [8–11]). To promote youth participation in citizen inquiry projects, networked technology facilitates the running of projects with geographically dispersed members and allows for broad public participation. Using integrated platforms that utilize additional data collection technology, such as cameras, sensors, and geo-positioning software, can improve participants' user experience in citizen science initiatives [12].

Several digital citizen inquiry initiatives have been developed to promote the growth of youth's scientific competence and comprehension. Herodotou et al. (2023) proposed an integrated learning framework for biodiversity monitoring and implemented the participation of young people in community-based citizen inquiry using the iNaturalist platform. This study found that the use of iNaturalist encouraged young people to participate, particularly those with less scientific expertise, and facilitated science learning to enhance their science comprehension and learning competency. In addition, Aristeidou, Scanlon, and Sharples (2020) investigated the influence of online citizen science communities designed for inquiry on the Rock Hunters and Weather-it projects by utilizing citizen inquiry technology, such as the nQuire-it platform. According to the study, participants gained content knowledge and practiced science skills, such as observation and identification, data collection and annotation, and developed transferable skills, such as digital literacy.

2.3 Interaction and User-Centered Design in Digital Citizen Inquiry for Youth

The design and development of digital inquiry-based citizen science platforms are challenging because each project has unique characteristics and constraints, and there is no singular tool or framework to guide these projects [13]. Human-Computer Interactions (HCI) is a field that studies the design, evaluation, and implementation of computing systems for human use, and it can aid in the development of interactive, complex citizen science communities and online inquiry-based platforms [14]. User-centered design (UCD) serves as a guiding framework within HCI, providing a systematic approach to designing and evaluating user interfaces, and UCD could enhance the citizen science and inquiry approaches by promoting participant engagement, tailoring the design to user needs, improving usability, ensuring data quality and reliability, fostering inclusivity, enabling iterative improvement, and empowering citizen scientists. User-centered design (UCD) refers to design approaches that advocate putting users' requirements, behavior, preferences, and dislikes at the center of design decision-making and practices [15]. UCD principles play a crucial role in designing and developing effective digital citizen science and inquiry platforms. User-centered interaction design could sustain a high level of engagement in citizen science or inquiry projects where citizen scientists and volunteers, like young people, collaborate at all stages of the scientific process.

A case of applying UCD to a digital citizen science project was presented by Golumbic, Fishbain, and Tsabari (2019), who aimed to create active involvement of users in improving the platform and conducting iterations of the design and evaluations for monitoring air quality in the local environment. They also investigated the outcomes of the use of UCD in a citizen science context. The findings of this study indicated that participants were interested in real-time, locally relevant, simple-to-understand, applicable, ready-to-use, and contextually presented information. As such, UCD principles, research, and practices would be a significant platform to empower the design and development of digital citizen inquiry projects for enhancing public engagement in science.

3 Materials and Methods

3.1 Setting: Plastic Detectives Mobile Application

Plastic pollution is a global societal concern due to its potential to create ecological and socioeconomic harm. Understanding its quantity, distribution, and composition in the environment is critical for informing, creating, and executing effective management measures aimed at lowering inputs and the associated consequences [16]. In an effort to limit the amount of plastic pollution in the environment, the prevalence of citizen science clean-up projects, such as plastic waste management, is growing globally.

Plastic Detectives is a citizen inquiry web and mobile application to train students to conduct a circular plastic economy investigation (Fig. 1). The application utilizes functions and features of digital citizen science to allow the learner a more pedagogic learning environment than a regular community science investigation, meaning that the user interacts with inquiry-based active science learning tasks to increase their inclusiveness of learning in a community environment. The Plastic Detectives app has a responsive interface so that it can be accessed on internet-connected smartphones and tablets as well as laptop or desktop devices. All user-collected data was accessible online via a data presentation platform for this project. Participants had access to all information gathered by the plastic detectives application. They could use the data for their own benefit, analyze it, discuss the results on social media, suggest additional investigations, and apply their newly acquired scientific information for learning community-building purposes.

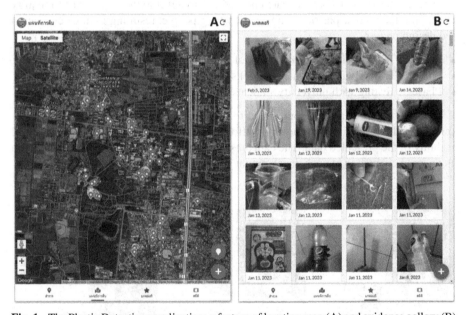

Fig. 1. The Plastic Detectives application: a feature of location map (A) and evidence gallery (B).

3.2 Approach: User-Centered Design

User-centered design (UCD) is a design methodology that places the end users' requirements, preferences, and behaviors at the forefront of development. It involves understanding the target users' objectives and context of use in order to design effective and enjoyable experiences. Typically, the UCD process consists of several iterative phases, beginning with collecting user requirements and user research. This study accomplished this using an integration of the life-cycle model proposed by Preece, Sharp, and Rogers (2015) and multi-user centered design (MCD) proposed by [17] for user-centered development (Fig. 2).

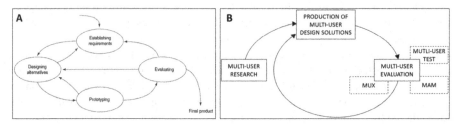

Fig. 2. Life-cycle model used for the user-centered design (A) and multi-user centered design (B) in the digital citizen inquiry project development.

The life-cycle model was repeated three times to develop the digital citizen inquiry project on the circular plastic economy for young people, resulting in three evaluation and design phases.

- Phase 1: Testing with elementary school students.
- Phase 2: Testing with secondary school students.
- Phase 3: Testing with university students.

Each of the three phases contributed to the improvement of the design and development of the digital citizen inquiry platform tool and added to the clarification and usability of the presented data. The data presentation tool was refined concurrently with its ongoing evaluation at each development stage (Fig. 3).

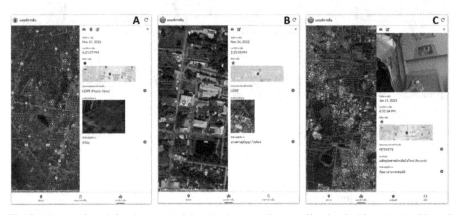

Fig. 3. The continued development of the Plastic Detectives application in Phase 1 (A), Phase 2 (B), and Phase 3 (C).

3.3 Participants and Data Collection

128 participants (14 elementary school students, 74 secondary school students, and 40 university students) participated in this study throughout the three research phases. They ranged in age from 10 to 19, and both males and women were equally represented. Data collection utilized quantitative and qualitative approaches, with semi-structured interviews, focus groups, and investigative record data as data collection instruments (Table 1).

Table 1. Methods of data collection employed in each of the three phases of design, with the number of participants at each stage indicated.

Phase	User	semi-structured interviews	focus groups	Log data of app usage
Phase 1	Elementary school students (N = 14)	N = 2	N = 3	N = 125
Phase 2	Secondary school students (N = 74)	N = 5	N = 5	N = 1154
Phase 3	University students (N = 40)	N = 5	N = 5	N = 338

Semi-Structured Interviews

During the three phases, participants' perspectives on plastic waste investigation data were investigated through interviews. Semi-structured interviews were chosen because they ask all interviewees the same open-ended questions. In general, interviewees were more active participants who participated very well in collecting plastic data using the Plastic Detectives app, and the interviews were conducted individually at school and via Zoom online platform and lasted approximately a half hour. Participants were shown plastic investigation data relevant to the platform design in use at the time of the interviews. The interviews were videotaped, transcribed, and evaluated qualitatively using thematic analysis to identify clusters of reoccurring concerns; the overarching themes that shed light on the participants' points of view were derived from these clusters.

Focus Groups

Three focus groups were organized throughout the study, and prospective participants interested in engaging in plastic investigation activities with the Plastic Detectives app joined the focus groups. Similar to the interview procedure, the latest version of the app's design was made available to the focus group participants. After evaluating the design, the clarity and utility of the data presentation format were discussed. The duration of the focus group was approximately one hour, and the discussions were recorded and transcribed. Emerging themes from focus group discussions were qualitatively analyzed.

Log Data

Throughout the study, log files were used to record and preserve the users' precise app-based plastics investigation actions. These files contained the time, date, and location of each investigation, as well as user login information and website activity (such as uploading photographs and reporting plastic debris). These files were accessed to ascertain engagement levels and types. The log data were analyzed based on the usernames of registered users.

4   Results of Formative Evaluation

For the analysis of participants' perceptions and experiences, the Technology Acceptance Model (TAM) was used as a theoretical framework. One female and one male doctoral-level researcher conducted the analysis: the first author, an assistant professor in science education with prior qualitative experience, and the second author, an associate professor in computer education unfamiliar with qualitative approaches. The preliminary results of how participants described their experiences of the digital citizen inquiry project on the circular plastic economy using TAM overarching theoretical framework could be summarized as follows.

4.1   Perceived Usefulness

The preliminary result around the perceived usefulness aspect of the TAM with respect to each of the three phases can be presented as shown in Table 2.

Throughout the semi-structured interviews and focus groups discussion, participants expressed their perceived usefulness with the digital citizen inquiry project on the circular plastic economy, as shown in Table 2, and the researchers developed two sub-themed from the obtained data; *Contextual Data Sharing* and *Task Monitoring*.

4.2   Perceived Ease of Use

Table 3 shows the interim results regarding the perceived ease of use aspect of the TAM for each of the three phases.

In summary, participants expressed their perceived ease of use with the digital citizen inquiry project during the semi-structured interviews and focus group discussions, as shown in Table 3, and the researchers created two sub-themes from the gathered data; *Prompt Selection* and *Flow of Recording-to-Sharing Experience*.

4.3   Attitude Toward Using and Behavioral Intention to Use

Initial findings about the TAM's attitude toward using during each of its three phases are reported in Table 4.

Participants' opinions on the digital citizen inquiry project and their responses on attitude toward using and behavioral intention to use are summarized in Table 4. The researchers used this information to build two sub-themes. *Positive Social Tasks* and *Visual Affordance*.

Table 2. Summary of design features and content on usefulness by participants in each of the three phases.

Main points	Phase		
	Phase 1	Phase 2	Phase 3
Most useful/usable features	Data sharing on a geographical map; class working statistics	Evidence collection by photo shooting; data sharing on a geographical map; working statistics	Evidence collection by photo shooting; data sharing on a geographical map; working statistics
Lease useful/usable features	Gallery of investigation	–	
Controversial among participants features	–	Gallery of investigation	Self-choice preference
Suggestions	Rewarding; gaming task	Individual data presentation; Automatic grading: level-up mechanism;	Automatic grading; Individual progress monitoring

Table 3. Summary of design features and content on ease of use by participants in each of the three phases.

Main points	Phase		
	Phase 1	Phase 2	Phase 3
Most ease-of-use features	Automatic list for selection; evidence collection by photo shooting	Automatic list for selection; recording of observational data	Automatic list for selection; recording of observational data; data sharing on a geographical map
Lease ease-of-use features	Date and time recording	Working statistics	–
Controversial among participants features	–	–	–
Suggestions	Rewarding; color of the investigative location	Automatic grading: level-up process; observational data deletion	Automatic grading; Individual progress monitoring

4.4 Actual System Use

As shown in Fig. 4, the platform's actual usage and the number of data collected by participants are reported. Log data from the digital citizen inquiry platform were accessed and analyzed to identify individual users. This allowed us to ascertain the number of

Table 4. Summary of design features and content on attitude toward using by participants in each of the three phases.

Main points	Phase		
	Phase 1	Phase 2	Phase 3
Most favorable features	Competitiveness of learning opportunities with friends; personal action for protecting the environment	Visual monitoring of investigation; personal action for protecting the environment	Visual monitoring of investigation
Lease favorable features	–	–	–
Controversial among participants features	–	–	Gallery of investigation
Suggestions	More outdoor science activities with app usage	More environmental investigation opportunities	More environmental investigation opportunities

visits and activities performed by each user, as well as their levels of engagement with regard to the prescribed requirements of learning tasks.

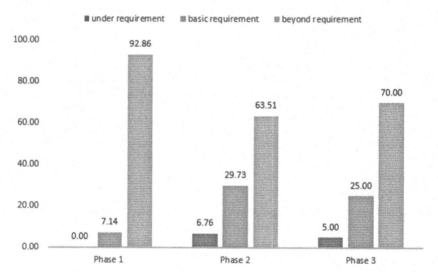

Fig. 4. The usage statistics of participants who interacted with the digital citizen inquiry project using the Plastic Detectives app.

With the Plastic Detectives app, 88 (68.75%) of 1,617 investigative records obtained from 128 users (see Table 1) exceeded the requirements of the citizen inquiry task. 33

(25.78%) and 7 (5.47%) of the users completed the learning assignments satisfactorily and inadequately, respectively.

5 Discussions

This study described the interaction design and development of a digital citizen inquiry platform called Plastic Detectives for the circular plastic economy using a UCD approach. In our case, the UCD was used to determine the requirements of a platform for the presentation of citizen inquiry data based on the active participation of multiple youth users. There are two contributions made by this paper. First, we propose a novel method for designing a citizen inquiry platform that accommodates the requirements and experiences of users. Second, we reflect on the development process of the circular plastic economy citizen inquiry project by highlighting the key elements that emerged from the development process. The three-phase design and evaluation process from multiple users used to develop the Plastic Detectives platform yielded numerous insights into the preferences and participation of young people that could not have been identified in any other way. Participants perceived the usefulness of the platform in terms of its *Contextual Data Sharing* and *Task Monitoring* features, which allow them to share their practical information on a geographical map via global positioning system (GPS) on a smartphone with their friends and to monitor the amount of work following citizen inquiry tasks. In terms of perceived ease-of-use features, *Prompt Selection* and *Flow of Recording-Sharing* emerged from the responses of the participants, indicating that an automatic list of selections has been provided to support their decision-making and that the recording and sharing of observational data on a geographical map could facilitate their investigation process [13, 18] found that simplifying information, avoiding the presentation of raw data, creating easy-to-use interfaces, and enhancing a simple concept presentation are effective means of enabling broader public participation. *Positive Social Tasks* and *Visual Affordance* are additional major findings of this study in terms of attitude toward and behavioral intention to use the platform as a result of interaction with the project supporting visual information of the investigation in the real context, and they enjoyed and were pleased to conduct the investigations in outdoor learning environments. The findings are consistent with prevalent science communication practices, which suggest that scientific topics are best communicated through visual representations and that communication messages should contain information the recipients need in a format they can understand [19, 20].

6 Conclusions

The design of the digital citizen inquiry project centered on the Plastic Detectives platform, which explores the circular plastic economy and incorporates specific phases of the inquiry-based scientific process, namely data collection and analysis via field observations. This initiative was developed using a User-centered Design (UCD) approach, which required the active participation of various user groups, including elementary school students, secondary school students, and university students. The objective was to comprehend the requirements of a data presentation platform for citizen inquiries.

Although the evaluation and design process discussed in this study is related to a specific scientific topic within a singular project, the underlying principles can be applied to other digital citizen inquiry projects.

This research focuses on an integrative framework that integrates the life-cycle model with the multi-user-centered design introduced in this study. The findings suggest that this strategy can result in a favorable reception of digital citizen inquiry technology among youth. As a tool utilized in the field, the Plastic Detectives mobile application was found to improve the perception of science learning and cultivate personal engagement within the learning community and environment. It also facilitated specific scientific learning processes. In addition, the scaffolding of learning enabled and developed by the interaction design of technology, guided by UCD principles, emerged as a crucial factor for obtaining a successful science learning experience. We propose that the emerging theme derived from the TAM can be extensively generalized and used as valuable recommendations for future citizen inquiry project designs.

Acknowledgement. The authors would like to thank Banjon Prasonsup and Tawinan Jan-in for generously sharing their teaching data and experiences with us.

References

1. Strasser, B.J., Baudry, J., Mahr, D., Sanchez, G., Tancoigne, E.: Citizen science"? rethinking science and public participation. Sci. Technol. Stud. **32**, 52–76 (2018)
2. Kera, D.: Open source hardware (OSHW) for open science in the global south: geek diplomacy? In: Albagli, S., Maciel, M.L., Abdo, A.H. (eds.) Open Science, Open Issues, pp. 133–156. Brasilia IBICT, Rio de Janeiro (2015)
3. Pham, N.Q, Tran, H.N., Thi, K.V.L., Nong, A.B., Rutten, M.M.: Ecosystem service monitoring using remote sensing, citizen science and other ground observations and current practices in Vietnam. http://resolver.tudelft.nl/uuid:031dab85-cd80-462d-9b7c-4a5da79a8c64
4. Bonney, R., et al.: A CAISE Inquiry Group Report, pp. 1–58 (2009)
5. Aristeidou, M., Scanlon, E., Sharples, M.: Learning outcomes in online citizen science communities designed for inquiry. Int. J. Sci. Educ. Part B Commun. Public Engagem. **10**(4), 277–294 (2020)
6. Herodotou, C., Sharples, M., Scanlon, E. (eds.): Citizen Inquiry: Synthesising Science and Inquiry Learning. Routledge (2017). https://doi.org/10.4324/9781315458618
7. Sharples, M., Aristeidou, M., Villasclaras-Fernández, E., Herodotou, C., Scanlon, E.: The sense-it app: a smartphone toolkit for citizen inquiry learning. Int. J. Mobile Blended Learn. **9**(2), 16–38 (2017)
8. Herodotou, C., et al.: Online community and citizen science supports environmental science learning by young people. Comput. Educ. **184**, 104515 (2022)
9. Herodotou, C., et al: Young people in iNaturalist: a blended learning framework for biodiversity monitoring. Int. J. Sci. Educ. Part B 1–28 (2023) https://doi.org/10.1080/21548455.2023.2217472
10. Aristeidou, M., Herodotou, C.: Online citizen science: a systematic review of effects on learning and scientific literacy. Citizen Sci. Theor. Pract. **5**(1), 1–12 (2020)
11. Jennett, C., et al.: Motivations, learning and creativity in online citizen science. J. Sci. Commun. **15**(3), 1–23 (2016)

12. Aristeidou, M., Scanlon, E., Sharples, M.: Profiles of engagement in online communities of citizen science participation. Comput. Hum. Behav. **74**, 246–256 (2017)
13. Yaela, N.G., Barak, F., Ayelet, B.T.: User centered design of a citizen science air-quality monitoring project. Int. J. Sci. Educ. Part B **9**(3), 195–213 (2019)
14. Preece, J.: Citizen science: new research challenges for human–computer interaction. Int. J. Hum. Comput. Interact. **32**(8), 585–612 (2016)
15. Preece, J., Rogers, Y., Sharp, H.: Interaction Design: Beyond Human—Computer Interaction. 4th ed. Wiley, Chichester, UK (2015)
16. Sarah, E.N., et al.: The role of citizen science in addressing plastic pollution: challenges and opportunities. Environ Sci Policy **128**, 14–23 (2022)
17. Fleury, S., Chaniaud, N.: Multi-user centered design: acceptance, user experience, user research and user testing. Theoretical Issues in Ergonomics Science (2023)
18. May, A., Ross, T.: The design of civic technology: factors that influence public participation and impact. Ergonomics **61**(2), 214–225 (2018)
19. Fischhoff, B.: The sciences of science communication. In: Proceedings of the National Academy of Sciences, pp. 14033–14039 (2013)
20. Lipkus, I.M., Hollands, J.G.: The visual communication of risk. JNCI Monogr. **1999**(25), 149–163 (1999)

IoT-Based User Interface for Remote Control
of a Mobile Robot

José Varela-Aldás[1]([✉]) [ID] and Guillermo Palacios-Navarro[2]

[1] Centro de Investigaciones de Ciencias Humanas y de La Educación - CICHE,
Universidad Indoamérica, Ambato 180103, Ecuador
josevarela@uti.edu.ec
[2] Department of Electronic Engineering and Communications, University of Zaragoza,
44003 Teruel, Spain
guillermo.palacios@unizar.es

Abstract. Recent advancements in mobile robot research have resulted in the development of precise robot control tools, while information technology research has focused on the Internet of Things (IoT) in the context of the fourth industrial revolution. This study evaluates a user interface designed for remote control of the Crowbot BOLT robot. This robot utilizes the ESP32 board and is controlled through the M5Stack Core2 kit with a touch screen. The user interface offers two modes of operation: touch-based buttons for movement control and gyroscope control based on the M5Stack's angular position. Communication between the robot and the user interface is established using the MQTT protocol through the ThingSpeak server, allowing control from any location with a line of sight and internet connectivity. Operation data is collected by recording control orders and measuring sending times, while user acceptance is evaluated using an IoT-based technology acceptance model. The results indicate the need for remote control response time improvement and reveal low scores in perceived usefulness and influence social. In conclusion, the study demonstrates the feasibility of remote control of a mobile robot using the MQTT protocol, providing valuable insights for similar applications and considering user recommendations for future enhancements and system expansion.

Keywords: Mobile robot · MQTT protocol · M5Stack Core2 · ESP32 board · remote control

1 Introduction

Robotics is a dynamic and rapidly evolving field with a wide range of applications, spanning from robot manipulators to mobile robots [1–3]. In [4], the authors highlight the key considerations that must be taken into account when designing robots in this class. They address the main control problems that arise in robotics and explore the corresponding solutions. Additionally, they provide a summary of the most significant approaches used to achieve autonomy in mobile robots. By understanding and addressing these considerations, control problems, and autonomy approaches, we can propel the development of mobile robots and unlock their potential in various industries and domains.

© The Author(s), under exclusive license to Springer Nature Switzerland AG 2023
V. G. Duffy et al. (Eds.): HCII 2023, LNCS 14057, pp. 606–617, 2023.
https://doi.org/10.1007/978-3-031-48047-8_41

Since late 2019, the COVID-19 pandemic has posed a significant global challenge, impacting the health and safety of individuals, medical personnel, and healthcare systems worldwide. In response to this crisis, there has been a global proposition to employ robots to enhance patient care and alleviate the burden on healthcare systems [5]. In [6], reviews and discusses the current advancements of robotic technologies in various categories, followed by an assessment of the technology readiness level of representative works. Furthermore, future research trends and essential technologies, such as artificial intelligence, 5G, big data, wireless sensor networks, and human-robot collaboration, are highlighted. On the other hand, the development of autonomous guided robots poses a significant challenge for the robotics industry, with far-reaching implications for both current research and future applications. Despite advancements in robotics technology, the progress in this specific area has been relatively limited due to a greater focus on other robotic fields. Unlike fixed robots commonly used in industrial settings, mobile robots require a different approach and have limited available resources. In [7], introduces a comprehensive platform designed to facilitate real-time control and monitoring of a mobile robot, referred to as an explorer. The platform aims to enable user-robot interaction from any location via the internet. Additionally, the solution incorporates embedded navigation algorithms to provide a certain level of autonomy for the robot, in addition to teleoperated mode.

The Internet of Things (IoT) has become a prominent topic in the field of Information Technology, representing a vision of the future where everyday objects are transformed into intelligent virtual entities [8, 9]. The IoT aims to create a unified infrastructure that connects and controls various objects, providing us with control and information about the world around us [10]. Specifically, [11] summarizes the potential of adopting IoT in education, including its applications in medical education and training, vocational education and training, Green IoT in education, and wearable technologies in education. The findings indicate that the adoption of IoT and its applications in developing countries is still in its early stages, emphasizing the need for further research and exploration in this area.

The ongoing revolution of the IoT has combined with the increasing presence of robots in our daily lives, leading to the emergence of tangible IoT-aided robotics applications in our future. This convergence has paved the way for advanced services that assist humans through the interplay between robots and connected "things" [12, 13]. However, the development of mature IoT-aided robotics applications requires the resolution of pivotal issues, the consolidation of design methodologies, and the exploration of strong architectural choices. In [14], addresses the technological implications, open challenges, and target applications within the domain of IoT-aided robotics. It provides a comprehensive state-of-the-art overview of communication networks, distributed and pervasive robotics applications, semantic-oriented consensus approaches, and network security. Additionally, the paper highlights the significant research challenges, explores available technological tools, and summarizes the lessons learned to encourage collaborative scientific investigation among research teams with complementary skills. In [15] offers a review of the automation potential in various agricultural practices, utilizing robotics, IoT, and AI. It discusses current and future perspectives, focusing on technological innovations such as smart farming, precision agriculture, vertical farming, modern greenhouse practices, autonomous workforce, drones, and connected farms. In the post-Covid-19 era, the automation of the agricultural industry has gained increased relevance due to labor migration and shortages, making it an essential consideration for adapting to the new norm.

In this research, a remote control for an educational robot is developed using the MQTT protocol on the ThingSpeak platform. The remote control is based on the M5Stack Core2 hardware platform. The proposed system is evaluated using a technology acceptance model for IoT. This paper has been organized into five sections: This Sect. 1 presents the introduction to the topic; Sect. 2 describes materials and methods; Sect. 3 illustrates the results; Sect. 4 describes the discussion; and Sect. 5 contains the conclusions obtained.

2   Materials and Methods

The objective of this study is to evaluate a user interface specifically designed for remote control of an educational mobile robot with a unicycle configuration. The research design is depicted in Fig. 1.

Fig. 1. Design of the research.

To control the robot, it needs to be programmed with a local code that responds to the received commands. These commands originate from an MQTT server or broker, allowing control from any location with line of sight and internet connectivity for both devices. The remote control interface is developed on an IoT hardware platform, and user acceptance of the proposed system is assessed using a technology acceptance model. Furthermore, the data managed by the broker is recorded in the cloud for subsequent analysis.

2.1 Mobile Robot

For this study, the Crowbot BOLT, a commercial robot designed for educational purposes, is utilized. Manufactured by Elecrow and depicted in Fig. 2, this robot serves as the primary subject of investigation. The ESP32 board forms the core component of the robot, enabling the development of IoT applications.

Fig. 2. Mobile robot.

The robot is programmed using the Arduino IDE software, as depicted in Fig. 3. The necessary libraries, such as WiFi.h (for network connectivity), PubSubClient.h (for MQTT services: publish and subscribe), WiFiClient.h (for MQTT Client), and analog-Write.h (for motor control in ESP32), are included. Additionally, the WiFi network connection details and the MQTT broker information are entered. The robot control orders are based on commands that execute specific movements, with all movements configured to operate at a speed of 25% of the robot's maximum speed.

2.2 M5tack Application

On the other hand, remote control is performed using the M5Stack Core2 kit with a touch screen interface, specifically designed for IoT projects [16]. The user interface features two modes of operation: the first mode employs touch-based buttons to direct the robot's movement, while the second mode utilizes the gyroscope to move the robot based on the angular position of the M5Stack. Figure 4 illustrates the developed user interface.

The second control mode utilizes the accelerometer data from the M5Stack Core2, as depicted in Fig. 5. The robot's rotations are controlled by Y-axis rotations, while X-axis rotations regulate the linear speed. Minimum control order activity ranges are defined to prevent undesired movements. The M5Stack program is developed in the UIFlow application using MQTT communication blocks.

Communication between the two endpoints is established using the MQTT protocol through the ThingSpeak server. This IoT platform is configured online through channels, where fields are declared. In this case, a channel named "MQTT" is created to

```
RemotoM5 §
#include <WiFi.h>
#include <PubSubClient.h>
#include <WiFiClient.h>
#include <analogWrite.h>

WiFiClient espClient;
PubSubClient client(espClient);

char ssid[] = "NET XYZ";
char pass[] = "***********";
const char* mqtt_server = "mqtt3.thingspeak.com";
const char* publishTopic ="channels/2106021/publish";
const char* subscribeTopicFor_Command="channels/2106021/subscribe/fields/field2";
```

Fig. 3. Code in Arduino IDE.

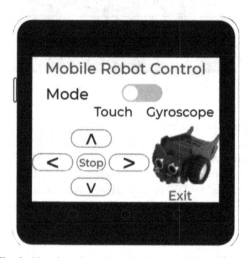

Fig. 4. User interface of application in M5Stack Core2.

handle the robot's control variable. Figure 6 illustrates the creation of MQTT devices: an M5Stack device for the remote control and a CrowBot BOLT device for the robot. The identification and password for subscription and publication access are generated automatically.

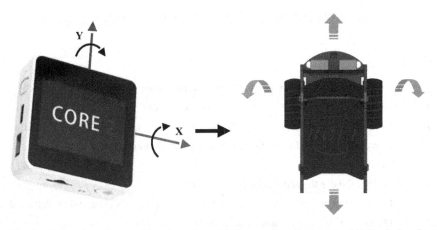

Fig. 5. Illustration of controlling the robot with the accelerometer of the M5Stack Core2.

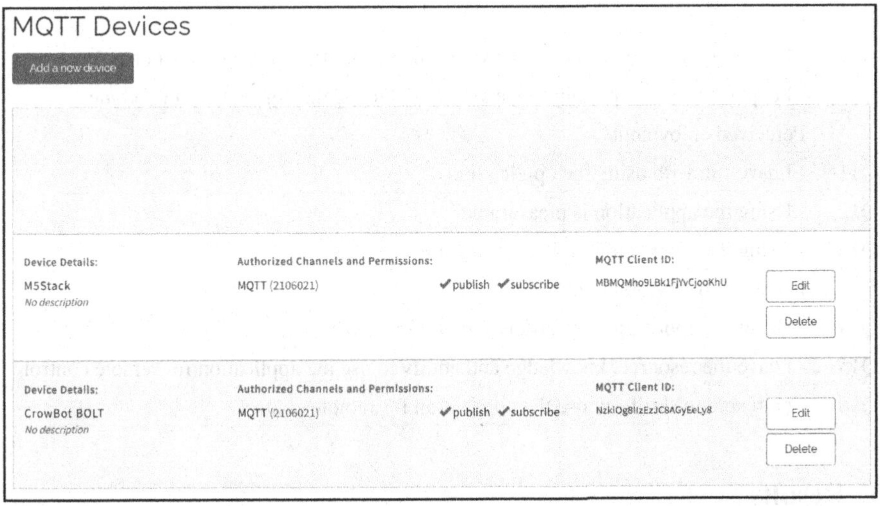

Fig. 6. Configuration of MQTT devices on the ThingSpeak platform.

2.3 Acceptance of IoT Technology

In the acceptance analysis, a technology acceptance model is utilized, specifically, the Consumer Acceptance of Internet of Things Technology [17]. The model encompasses components such as perceived usefulness, perceived ease of use, social influence, perceived enjoyment, and perceived behavioral control. All items of the acceptance model were measured using seven-point scales, ranging from strongly disagree (1) to strongly agree (5). Table 1 presents the items evaluated by the users to assess the acceptance of this proposal, comprising 16 components.

Table 1. Items of technology acceptance model.

ID	Item
	Perceived usefulness
Q1	- Using the application would enable me to remote control the robot more quickly
Q2	- Using the application would make it easier for me to remote control the robot
Q3	- Using the application would significantly increase the quality or output of my life
Q4	- Overall, I would find using the application to be advantageous
	Perceived ease of use
Q5	- Learning to use the application is easy for me
Q6	- I find my interaction with the application for remote control clear and understandable
Q7	- I think using the application for remote control is easy
	Social influence
Q8	- People who are important to me would recommend using the application for remote control
Q9	- People who are important to me would find using the application beneficial
Q10	- People who are important to me would find using the application a good idea
	Perceived enjoyment
Q11	- I have fun with using the application
Q12	- Using the application is pleasurable
Q13	- Using the application gives enjoyment to me
	Perceived behavioral control
Q14	- Using the application is entirely within my control
Q15	- I have the resource, knowledge and ability to use the application for remote control
Q16	- I am able to skillfully use the application for remote control

3   Results

Once the system is implemented, preliminary and final tests are conducted, incorporating necessary corrections. Figure 7 displays images of the robot in operation, being controlled through the two modes of operation: manual mode on the left and inertial mode on the right. The robot is operated by six computer engineering students, and their subsequent acceptance analysis is carried out.

3.1   Operation

Figure 8 illustrates the recorded operation orders for 100 samples. Initially, the robot starts with order 1 (forward movement) for several samples, and subsequently, various movements are executed to avoid obstacles throughout the process. Overall, the remote control of the robot exhibits good performance as it successfully executes all the sent orders.

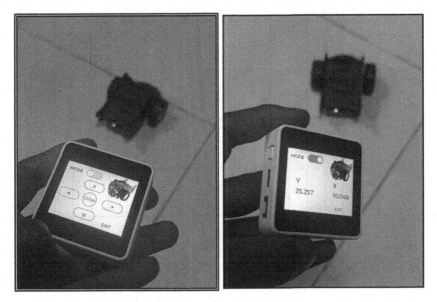

Fig. 7. Remote control in operation.

3.2 Sending Times

Figure 9 displays the sending times of robot movement orders. The graph shows multiple samples where the sending time is 1 s, which is a result of continuous order transmission in inertia mode, where movements are controlled based on the angular position of the M5Stack. The commercial service of ThingSpeak imposes a maximum speed of 1 s. In contrast, when the robot is controlled in manual mode, the sending times vary according to the operator's requirements, with a maximum of 45 s.

3.3 Acceptance

The results of the acceptance model are presented in Fig. 10, displaying the average scores assigned by the participants for each item of the model. Overall, an average score of 3.776/5 was obtained, indicating a 75.58% acceptance rate. The lowest scores were observed in perceived usefulness and social influence. Users expressed concerns about a delay affecting movement control and perceived a weakness in the system.

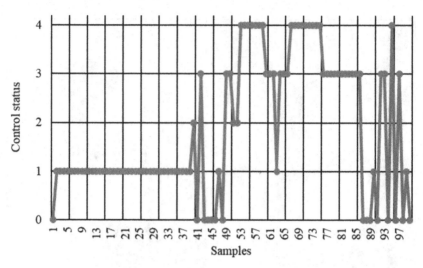

Fig. 8. Robot remote control status.

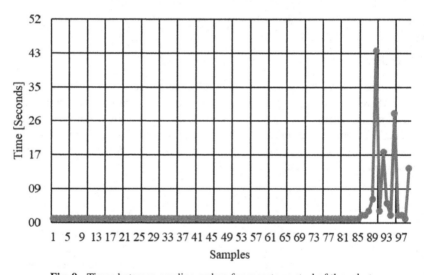

Fig. 9. Times between sending orders for remote control of the robot.

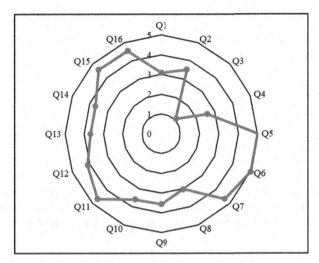

Fig. 10. Results of technology acceptance model.

4 Discussions

In [18] focus on developing remote control technology for robotic fingers using the MQTT protocol and the M5Stack board. It highlights the various activities that can be performed remotely using the robot fingers and explains the role of MQTT in providing string inputs and representing servo angles. In contrast, our work evaluates a user interface designed for remote control of the Crowbot BOLT robot. It discusses the collection of operation data, user acceptance evaluation, and the need for improvement in remote control response time. Both works discuss remote control of robots using MQTT and hardware platforms. However, the first work focuses on robotic finger control and activities, while this evaluates a user interface for controlling the Crowbot BOLT robot, addressing response time, user acceptance, and system expansion.

In [19] discuss Blockly programming as a way to represent programming code in a visual and easily understandable form. It explains how Blockly programming is used in this research to program the M5Stack board and run the motion sensor. The paper also mentions the use of various sensors on the M5Stack board using the MQTT protocol. It further explains the use of MQTT for representing commands and processes in real-time communication. Both papers mention the use of the M5Stack board, Blockly programming, and the MQTT protocol. However, [19] focus more on explaining Blockly programming and its application with the M5Stack board.

Finally, [20] discusses the advantages and disadvantages of MQTT and REST communication protocols for IoT devices. It demonstrates their integration in an experiment using the ESP32 S3 board and Node-Red flow, showcasing data acquisition, transfer, and storage in a relational database. The experiment verifies data transfer, records connections, and explores working with different data types. It also highlights the impact of communication protocols on device power consumption. This work emphasizes the advantages and disadvantages of MQTT and REST protocols, with a specific focus on data acquisition, transfer, and power consumption. It includes an experiment with the

ESP32 board and highlights working with different data types. In short, there are several applications with technologies related to our work but there are no works that carry out the combinations of instruments presented in this research.

5 Conclusion

The results indicate that the technology used needs improvement in the response time of the remote control, and the acceptance analysis shows a low score in the perceived usefulness and influence social. The results suggest that remote control of a mobile robot from a remote device is feasible using the MQTT protocol, despite not being entirely favorable. This proposal provides a perspective for similar applications that require remote control of robots through a single user interface. Lastly, user recommendations will be considered to enhance the proposal in the future and expand the system to include more devices.

References

1. Rubio, F., Valero, F., Llopis-Albert, C.: A review of mobile robots: concepts, methods, theoretical framework, and applications. Int. J. Adv. Robot. Syst. **16**, 172988141983959 (2019). https://doi.org/10.1177/1729881419839596
2. Herrera, D., Roberti, F., Carelli, R., Andaluz, V., Varela, J., Ortiz, J.: Modeling and path-following control of a wheelchair in human-shared environments. Int. J. Humanoid Rob. **15**, 1–33 (2018). https://doi.org/10.1142/S021984361850010X
3. Ortiz, J.S., Molina, M.F., Andaluz, V.H., Varela, J., Morales, V.: Coordinated control of a omnidirectional double mobile manipulator. In: Kim, K.J., Kim, H., Baek, N. (eds.) ICITS 2017. LNEE, vol. 449, pp. 278–286. Springer, Singapore (2018). https://doi.org/10.1007/978-981-10-6451-7_33
4. Silva Ortigoza, R., et al.: Wheeled mobile robots: a review. IEEE Lat. Am. Trans. **10**, 2209–2217 (2012). https://doi.org/10.1109/TLA.2012.6418124
5. Varela-Aldás, J., Buele, J., Guerrero-Núñez, S., Andaluz, V.H.: Mobile manipulator for hospital care using firebase presented at the (2022). https://doi.org/10.1007/978-3-031-17618-0_24
6. Wang, X.V., Wang, L.: A literature survey of the robotic technologies during the COVID-19 pandemic. J. Manuf. Syst. **60**, 823–836 (2021). https://doi.org/10.1016/j.jmsy.2021.02.005
7. Tompa, V., Hurgoiu, D., Neamtu, C., Popescu, D.: Remote control and monitoring of an autonomous mobile robot. In: Proceedings of 2012 IEEE International Conference on Automation, Quality and Testing, Robotics, pp. 438–442. IEEE (2012). https://doi.org/10.1109/AQTR.2012.6237750
8. Rawat, A.: Recent trends in IoT: a review. J. Manage. Serv. Sci. (JMSS) **2**(2), 1–12 (2022). https://doi.org/10.54060/jmss.v2i2.21
9. Salazar, M., Castillo, F., Andaluz, V.H., Palacios-Navarro, G., Varela-Aldás, J.: Monitoring system for plants based on a smart plant pot presented at the (2022). https://doi.org/10.1007/978-3-031-06388-6_47
10. Madakam, S., Ramaswamy, R., Tripathi, S.: Internet of Things (IoT): a literature review. J. Comput. Commun. **03**, 164–173 (2015). https://doi.org/10.4236/jcc.2015.35021

11. Al-Emran, M., Malik, S.I., Al-Kabi, M.N.: A survey of Internet of Things (IoT) in education: opportunities and challenges. In: Hassanien, A.E., Bhatnagar, R., Khalifa, N.E.M., Taha, M.H.N. (eds.) Toward social internet of things (SIoT): Enabling technologies, architectures and applications. SCI, vol. 846, pp. 197–209. Springer, Cham (2020). https://doi.org/10.1007/978-3-030-24513-9_12

12. Tzafestas, S.G.: Synergy of IoT and AI in modern society: the robotics and automation case. Robot. Autom. Eng. J. **3**, 5555621 (2018). https://doi.org/10.19080/RAEJ.2018.03.555621

13. Qadri, I., Muneer, A., Fati, S.M.: Automatic robotic scanning and inspection mechanism for mines using IoT. IOP Conf. Ser. Mater. Sci. Eng. **1045**, 012001 (2021). https://doi.org/10.1088/1757-899X/1045/1/012001

14. Grieco, L.A., et al.: IoT-aided robotics applications: technological implications, target domains and open issues. Comput. Commun. **54**, 32–47 (2014). https://doi.org/10.1016/j.comcom.2014.07.013

15. Krishnan, A., Swarna, S., Balasubramanya, H.S.: Robotics, IoT, and AI in the automation of agricultural industry: a review. In: 2020 IEEE Bangalore Humanitarian Technology Conference (B-HTC), pp. 1–6. IEEE (2020). https://doi.org/10.1109/B-HTC50970.2020.9297856

16. M5Stack: M5Core2. https://docs.m5stack.com/en/core/core2

17. Gao, L., Bai, X.: A unified perspective on the factors influencing consumer acceptance of internet of things technology. Asia Pacific J. Mark. Logist. **26**, 211–231 (2014). https://doi.org/10.1108/APJML-06-2013-0061

18. Adi, P.D.P., Kitagawa, A., Akita, J.: Finger robotic control use M5Stack board and MQTT protocol based. In: 2020 7th International Conference on Information Technology, Computer, and Electrical Engineering (ICITACEE), pp. 1–6. IEEE (2020). https://doi.org/10.1109/ICITACEE50144.2020.9239170

19. Adi, P.D.P., Kitagawa, A.: A Review of the blockly programming on M5Stack board and MQTT based for programming education. In: 2019 IEEE 11th International Conference on Engineering Education (ICEED), pp. 102–107. IEEE (2019). https://doi.org/10.1109/ICEED47294.2019.8994922

20. Nemlaha, E., Střelec, P., Horák, T., Kováč, S., Tanuška, P.: Suitability of MQTT and REST communication protocols for AIoT or IIoT devices based on ESP32 S3 presented at the (2023).https://doi.org/10.1007/978-3-031-21435-6_19

Unseen Obstacle Detection via Monocular Camera Against Speed Change and Background Noise

Kai Wang, Siming Lu, and Shenlu Jiang[✉]

School of Computer Science and Engineering, Macau University of Science and Technology, Macau, China
shenlujiang@must.edu.mo

Abstract. This paper proposes a novel obstacle detection system optimized for mobile platforms. The system uses a long-short step Recurrent Neural Network (RNN) for optical flow estimation in various speed scenarios, combined with a global direction filter that filters out background noise, resulting in more robust and accurate obstacle detection. The system is designed to maximize processing speed and resource efficiency on mobile platforms. Performance is demonstrated on own-collected YouTube videos, achieving a precision rate of 95.2%, recall rate of 94.3%, and a frame rate of 75 FPS, surpassing state-of-the-art optical flow techniques. The proposed method is also evaluated on a real robot platform, demonstrating robust performance in detecting and avoiding obstacles of varying sizes and speeds under different lighting and noise conditions. Overall, the proposed system offers a reliable and efficient solution for obstacle detection and avoidance on mobile platforms, with high confidence in obstacle detection and avoidance in various real-world scenarios.

Keywords: obstacle detection · robot application · optical flow

1 Introduction

Obstacle detection and avoidance are crucial elements in the development and deployment of autonomous systems, such as self-driving cars, mobile robots, and unmanned aerial vehicles (UAVs). These systems require the ability to perceive their surroundings accurately and efficiently, identify obstacles, and navigate through complex environments to ensure safe operation [1,2]. Over the years, researchers have proposed various approaches to address the challenges associated with obstacle detection, leading to significant advancements in the fields of robotics and computer vision [3,4].

Good idea to let folks know you are acknowledging them examples are a statistician who helped with analysis or a graphic artist who created images. [5–8]

The introductory paragraph, or introduction, should set the context for the rest of the paper. Tell your readers why you are writing and why your topic is important.

V. G. Duffy et al. (Eds.): HCII 2023, LNCS 14057, pp. 618–633, 2023.
https://doi.org/10.1007/978-3-031-48047-8_42

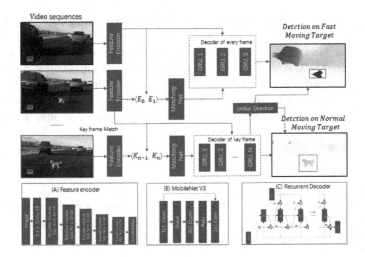

Fig. 1. The framework of proposed system. Red box is key frame, which is set by skipping a few of frames (Color figure online)

2 Related Work

Obstacle detection and avoidance have been extensively researched in recent years, with various approaches proposed in the literature. These methods can be broadly classified into four categories: (i) stereo vision-based methods, (ii) LIDAR-based methods, (iii) monocular camera-based methods, and (iv) motion camera-based methods. In this section, we review some of the key works in each category and discuss their limitations, which motivate the development of our proposed system.

Stereo vision-based techniques rely on the use of two or more cameras to estimate depth information by triangulating corresponding points in multiple views [9,10]. These methods have demonstrated success in a range of applications, such as autonomous vehicles [11,12] and mobile robotic systems [13,14]. However, stereo vision-based approaches often require complex hardware setups, suffer from high computational costs, and are susceptible to challenges related to camera calibration and synchronization. Moreover, these methods may be affected by varying lighting conditions, occlusions, and repetitive textures, which can lead to unreliable depth estimates [15].

LIDAR-based techniques employ laser range finders to obtain accurate depth measurements by calculating the time it takes for emitted light to travel to an object and back [16–18]. These methods have gained prominence in applications such as autonomous navigation [19,20] and 3D mapping [21,22]. Despite their accuracy in measuring depth, LIDAR-based approaches often come with high costs, bulky hardware, and high power consumption. Furthermore, LIDAR systems may struggle in adverse environmental conditions, such as fog, rain, or dust, which can attenuate the emitted laser signals.

Monocular camera-based approaches have gained traction as a lightweight and cost-effective alternative to stereo vision and LIDAR methods. These techniques typically involve estimating depth information from a single camera using cues such as motion parallax, perspective geometry, and shading [23]. In recent years, recent advances in deep learning have paved the way for improved monocular camera-based obstacle detection techniques, with a focus on optical flow estimation. Optical flow methods estimate the apparent motion of objects in consecutive image frames, enabling the tracking of obstacles in real-time [24,25]. However, monocular camera-based methods still face inherent challenges in accurately estimating depth and dealing with dynamic environments.

3   Method

In this section, we elaborate on the proposed architecture for the detection of unseen obstacles. The discussion is divided into three subsections: Long-short mobile RNN optical flow, global direction filter, and robot architecture description.

3.1   Long-Short Mobile RNN Optical Flow

We present a long-short step mobile recurrent neural network (RNN) optical flow algorithm designed to effectively detect targets with varying velocities. The proposed architecture, as depicted in Fig. 1, operates on image sequences with labels I_0 - I_n, and each image is decoded using a feature encoder based on the MobileNet V3 architecture with minor modifications (Fig. 1(B)). The architecture of the feature encoder is illustrated in Fig. 1(A).

Feature extraction is a crucial process for encoding information from image sequences. In many deep neural network (DNN) applications, pre-trained base networks such as ResNet or VGG, which are trained on large-scale datasets like ImageNet and COCO, are typically used as backbones for feature extraction. However, our objective is to deploy the DNN on mobile platforms, and using a pre-trained backbone network would increase processing time. Thus, we employ a self-encoding architecture to construct an end-to-end DNN. To achieve this, we utilize a cost-efficient encoder that balances efficiency and quality of feature encoding.

To begin, the input image (In) is filtered using a 1×1 convolutional layer to ensure a gradual transition from the RGB channel to the DNN. Next, 5×5 depth-wise separable convolutions are applied to further encode the features. To enhance feature extraction capabilities, we incorporate skip connections in the encoding model, taking advantage of the demonstrated efficiency of the residual architecture in MobileNet V3. Additionally, we employ two down-sampling scales to encode multi-scale features. In the original scale, a single encoding block with a D of 16 is used. In the second scale, two encoding blocks with a 5×5 convolutional layer and D = 32 are employed. The third scale utilizes three encoding blocks with D = 64. The encoded feature maps E_{n-1} and En are downsampled from $I^{H \times W \times 3}$ to $E^{H/4 \times W/4} \times D$ at a 1/4 resolution, and the final D is set to 64. This configuration allows the DNN to extract refined features while utilizing minimal computational resources, enabling an efficient feature encoding process.

3.2 Cosine Similarity Comparison

Once the encoded feature maps E_{n-1}, E_n (corresponding to keyframes k_{n-1} and k_n), a correlation volume is derived by integrating these two encoded maps. The volume enables a comprehensive comparison of the feature vectors originating from both maps. As illustrated in Fig. 4, the correlation volume C is computed via matrix multiplication, leveraging the pyramid architecture inherent to the feature maps.

$$C\left(E_0\left(I_0\right), E_1\left(I_1\right)\right) \in R^{H_1, W_1, H_2, W_2}$$

To address the multiscale detection of flow movement, the correlation volume encompasses a pyramid architecture. This structure consists of three distinct layers (C_0, C_1, C_2), pooled by utilizing kernels (1, 2, 4) concerning the last two dimensions. Through the execution of a similarity comparison across multiple scales, the architecture effectively discerns displacements of various magnitudes, while maintaining the integrity of the original flow pattern. The ensuing 4D correlation volume represents an initial flow map, which is subsequently passed on to the GRU for further decoding and analysis.

3.3 GRU Feature Decoding

The 4D correlation volume, derived from the multi scale cosine similarity comparison, serves as input for the recurrent flow decoding DNN. The GRU feature decoder, in conjunction with context information, systematically refines the pixel-wise displacement estimates in an iterative manner. As depicted in Fig. 4, the GRU feature decoder initializes the flow estimate f_0 to zero, and the current output g_0 is amalgamated with the correlation volume C and the previous output f_n to advance to the subsequent iteration, perpetuating this process n times. The correlation and context information are integrated and merged utilizing a 3×3 depth-wise convolutional layer, denoted as x_n. This x_n is subsequently fed into the GRU cell furnished with a forward gate g_n. The combined feature undergoes decoding via a duo of convolutional layers accompanied by a Sigmoid activation layer, while the tanh function operates as the activation function. Ultimately, the displacement prediction is procured through a softmax layer.

The output of the convolutional layer maintains a resolution of H and W, and a convex combination is employed to address minute displacements and background noise that may adversely impact obstacle tracking. In addition to the DNN, the camera's 120 FPS capture rate contributes to minor displacements (fewer than 5 pixels) between consecutive images, potentially culminating in the failure of detecting normal or slow-moving obstacles. Conversely, the standard refresh rate of optical cameras (30 FPS) may result in the inability to capture fast-moving obstacles. To effectively detect obstacles at disparate speeds, the RNN is optimally utilized, and two distinct paths are explored to cater to varying speed obstacle detection. The GRU upscaling is reused, involving a 3×3 grid of coarse-resolution neighbors, prediction masks, and an up-sampling procedure.

To address the aforementioned challenges in detecting obstacles in varying flow displacements, we have leveraged the power of recurrent neural networks (RNNs) and explored two distinct approaches to specifying different speed obstacle detection. Specifically, we have utilized the gated recurrent unit (GRU) component within the RNN and have incorporated key frames to overcome issues such as small displacements and background noise. Our methodology is illustrated in Fig. 1 and takes advantage of asynchronous system resources to ensure the robust operation of the architecture.

In detail, we have labeled key frames in red to serve for normal moving obstacles and have employed long iterations of GRU steps for their detection. Conversely, for fast-moving obstacles, we have used black-labeled key frames to alert the system, assuming that these obstacles move so quickly that they can be detected even at 120 FPS camera capture rates. In this case, we have utilized a small iteration of RCU. Moreover, we have incorporated a threshold to filter out background noise and ensure optimal performance.

Overall, our methodology has yielded a highly effective approach to detecting obstacles in varying flow displacements, enabling the use of RNNs and key frames to overcome the challenges posed by small displacements, background noise, and varying camera capture rates. The incorporation of global direction filtering and system resources management further enhances the performance and robustness of the architecture (Fig. 2).

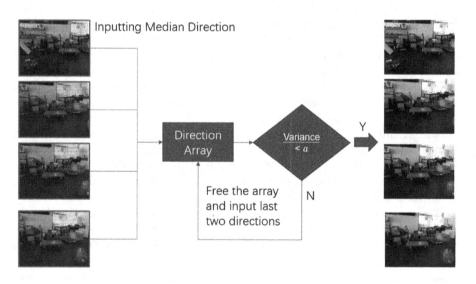

Fig. 2. The framework of using glboal direction filter on key frames.

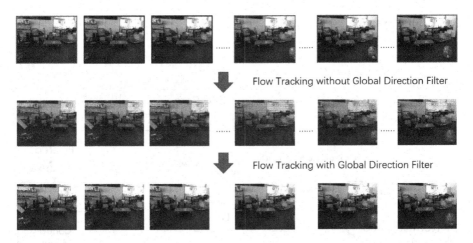

Flow Tracking without Global Direction Filter

Flow Tracking with Global Direction Filter

Fig. 3. Result on using the global direction filter. Arrows mean the displacement from last frame to current frame

3.4   Global Direction Filter

The detection of obstacles in dynamic scenes can be challenging due to the presence of background noise that can interfere with the tracking of objects, especially during rotations. To address this issue, we propose a global direction filter strategy that leverages the information from key frames to filter out background noise and focus on the detection of obstacles. For each key frame, we record and save the median direction in the x-y plane into the direction array. To detect changes in the rotation of the scene, we use the variance to calculate the array and identify significant increases or decreases. If the variance is smaller than a predetermined value, all encoded flow maps are increased by the vector of direction. Otherwise, we will free the array and input the last two directions into the direction array and generate a new direction filter to filter out background noise.

Our proposed global direction filter strategy is highly efficient, leveraging the use of discrete values and the median value to overcome global noise with very low computing resources. As seen in Fig. 3, our approach effectively filters out background noise during robot rotations and enables the detection of obstacles. The results of our methodology demonstrate its effectiveness in reducing the impact of background noise on obstacle detection, which is a significant issue in dynamic scenes. Our approach can be a useful tool in various applications, including robotics and autonomous driving, where the reliable detection of obstacles is critical for safe and effective navigation.

3.5   Robot System

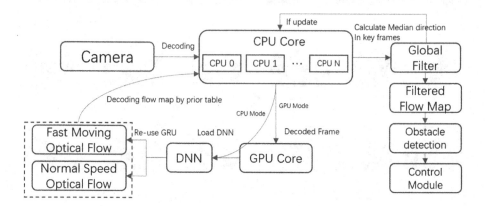

Fig. 4. The architecture of robot system

The robotic system architecture is illustrated in Fig. 4. The camera captures the image sequences and feeds them to the CPU core, which opens a thread to decode the images. The decoded frames are then inputted into a deep neural network (DNN), which is dependent on whether the frame is a key or a normal frame. The DNN utilizes the proposed long-short step GRU decoding to detect the fast-moving (short step) and normal speed (long step with key frames) optical flow. The optical flow is then sent back to the CPU core to calculate the global direction based on the key frames. Finally, the global direction filter is applied to denoise the background influence and output the obstacles' positions in the scene. The control module then operates to either brake or continue moving forward.

To ensure the system operates smoothly, multiple threads are utilized, and a priority list for each thread is set, as shown in Table 1. The priority levels are organized into real-time, very high, high, and normal levels, which are the same as those in a typical

Table 1. Priority list of threads' in OS

Thread Name	Thread Resource	Thread Priority
Ros System	CPU, 1 thread	Real time
Camera	CPU, 1 thread	Very high
Control module	CPU, 1 thread	Very high
Short step Optical flow	CPU, GPU, 1 thread	High
Global Direction Filter	CPU, 1 thread	High
Long step optical flow	CPU, GPU, 1 thread	Normal

operating system. The robot operating system acts as the backbone in real-time to guarantee that the other components can run without delay. The camera capture and control module are required to connect with hardware and are therefore set to a higher priority level than the other components. The short step optical flow and global direction filter are set to a third-level priority, while the long-step optical flow is set to a lower priority level, under consideration of asynchronous processing.

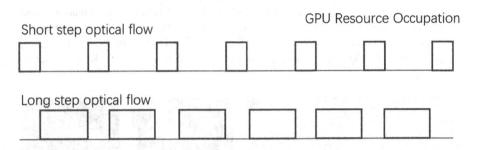

Fig. 5. Time-sharing operating on occupation of GPU resource

The resource timeline for GPU utilization is shown in Fig. 5. The timeline indicates that the short step optical flow occupies significantly less time than the long step optical flow due to the utilization of different step lengths of the GRU. However, the long-step optical flow does not require an immediate response, which is why the priority list ensures that both types of flow map generation are carried out asynchronously. When the thread of the short step optical flow is active, the long-step optical flow waits. After the long-step optical flow is operated, it sends its output to the final results and generates the global direction filter. This approach allows the system resources to be fully utilized.

4 Experiment

In this section, we describe the experiments conducted to evaluate the performance of the proposed method. We provide details on the implementation of the long-short step optical flow, the hardware used for the robot platform, and the evaluation of results on a YouTube video dataset. Additionally, we present the results of deploying the proposed system on a mobile robot in an indoor environment.

4.1 Implementation Details

To implement the proposed method, we first trained the long-short step optical flow as a supervised learning based DNN. We used a desktop with an AMD Ryzen 5900x CPU, 128 GB GPU DDR4 memory, and 1 Titan RTX to train the model. However, since optical flow datasets in the real world are limited, we utilized synthetic datasets including Sintel, Flying Things, and Flying Things 3D to train the model with an initial 100,000 steps. The model was then fine-tuned using the Kitti dataset with an additional 100,000 steps. We used the Adam optimizer with a loss function based on

$L = N \sum i = 1\gamma N - i||fgt - fi||1$, where the f_{gt} denotes the ground truth flow, and the difference between the prediction and ground truth was calculated. In particular, we set the value of the hyperparameter C to 0.8 for this experiment.

4.2 Animal Crashing Challenge

In order to demonstrate the effectiveness of the proposed method, we conducted experiments on three datasets and on a real robot platform. Firstly, the implementation details for training and testing the optical flow are provided. We trained the long-short step optical flow on synthetic datasets, namely Sintel, Flying Things and Flying Things 3D, for an initial 100,000 steps. Then, the model was fine-tuned on the Kitti dataset for

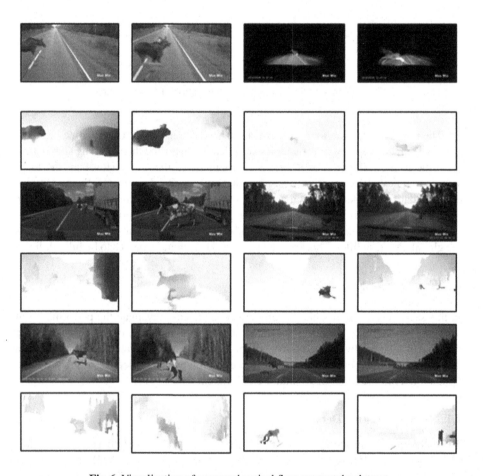

Fig. 6. Visualization of proposed optical flow on youtube dataset

another 100,000 steps. The optimization step was set using Adam and the loss function was based on the ground truth flow. The difference between the predicted flow and ground truth was calculated and C was set to 0.8 in this experiment (Fig. 6).

Table 2. Results of Unseen Obstacle Detection on Driver View

Method	Precision Rate	Recall Rate	Average FPS
LK Optical Flow [26]	62.5%	63.4%	12
FlowNet V2 [27]	89.4%	88.8%	32
RAFT-Net [28]	94.5%	94.3%	12
Long-short step Optical flow (O)	95.2%	94.3%	75
Long-short step Optical flow (H)	93.8%	94.1%	143
Long-short step Optical flow (I)	87.5%	88.2%	210

To evaluate the performance of the proposed method in detecting unseen obstacles, we collected a dataset of YouTube videos where animals were crushed on the road, which is a common occurrence on wilder western roads. The proposed system was employed to detect these incidents as obstacles. The results and ablation study are presented in Table 2.

Our proposed method was able to detect unseen obstacles in the road scene with very fast speed and with better flow tracking quality compared to state-of-the-art methods. Specifically, the LK optical flow achieved a precision rate of 62.5% and a recall rate of 63.4% with a frame rate of 14. This is mainly because traditional filters only utilize the CPU, leading to low FPS and human-crafted features that can be hard to apply to complicated targets. Meanwhile, FlowNet V2 and RAFT-Net achieved precision and recall rates of around 90%, but their frame rates were not very high (30 and 12, respectively). Moreover, they use dense feature extractors to extract features without any optimizations for various speed targets, leading to lower accuracy than the proposed method.

Our proposed method (O) achieved a frame rate of 75 FPS with 95.2% precision rate and 94.3% recall rate, which are higher than those of RAFT-Net, FlowNet V2 and LK optical flow in all aspects. Unexpectedly appearing animals were ideally detected as soon as they appeared on the road, and the system continuously tracked them as they moved. With half-processing enhancement and int 8 combining with speeding up based on TensorRTX, the method achieved a higher FPS (143) with just a 2% accuracy loss. With int-8, the accuracies decreased by 5%, but the FPS increased to 210.

The experimental results demonstrate that the long-short optical flow enables robust detection of obstacles at various speeds with limited background noise, and it maintains a high FPS during prediction. The visualization also shows the success of the proposed method. We can see that regardless of the scale of the obstacles, the proposed method successfully segmented the outline of the target and displayed them on the scene. Even when a deer appeared in very low illumination, the system was able to detect it as an obstacle on the scene. Overall, the proposed method has shown promising results in detecting unseen obstacles on the road and outperformed state-of-the-art methods in terms of accuracy and speed.

4.3   Evaluation on Real Robot Platform

Fig. 7. The first view of proposed method deployed on the mobile robot. Red boxes are with global direction filter, and others are without it. (Color figure online)

To evaluate the performance of the proposed system on a mobile robot platform, we conducted experiments using a stationary robot with obstacles of varying sizes and speeds placed randomly in a circular arena. The robot was equipped with the proposed system for obstacle detection and avoidance, and we evaluated its ability to detect and avoid obstacles under different lighting and noise conditions. We first evaluated the system's performance under normal lighting conditions for 2 h and 13 min. The experiment was set up with obstacles of different sizes and speeds, and the robot's performance was measured by the success rate of obstacle detection and avoidance. Table 3 shows the results of this experiment (Fig. 7).

Table 3 shows that the proposed system achieved a high success rate in detecting and avoiding obstacles of varying sizes and speeds under normal lighting conditions. The highest success rate of 100% was achieved for large obstacles at slow, medium, and fast speeds, indicating that the system can effectively detect and avoid large obstacles even at high speeds. The lowest success rate of 94% was observed for small obstacles at slow speeds, which is likely due to the small size of the obstacle making it easier to be recognized as background. However, the success rates for all obstacle sizes and speeds were consistently high, indicating the robustness and effectiveness of the proposed system under normal lighting conditions. The system's success in obstacle detection and avoidance demonstrates the effectiveness of the collaboration between short and long step optical flow techniques, as well as the overall performance of the system in detecting and avoiding obstacles.

Table 3. Performance under Normal Lighting Conditions

Obstacle Size	Obstacle Speed	Success Rate (%)
Small	Slow	94
Small	Medium	97
Small	Fast	98
Medium	Slow	99
Medium	Medium	99
Medium	Fast	98
Large	Slow	100
Large	Medium	100
Large	Fast	100

We then tested the system's performance under low-light conditions for 1 h and 12 min. For this test, we dimmed the lighting in the testing area to simulate nighttime operation. We then placed obstacles of varying sizes and speeds in the robot's path and tested its ability to detect and avoid them using the proposed system. Table 4 shows the results of this experiment.

Table 4. Performance under Low-light Conditions

Obstacle Size	Obstacle Speed	Success Rate (%)
Small	Slow	93
Small	Medium	96
Small	Fast	97
Medium	Slow	98
Medium	Medium	98
Medium	Fast	97
Large	Slow	100
Large	Medium	100
Large	Fast	98

Table 4 presents the results of the experiments conducted to evaluate the system's performance under low-light conditions. It can be observed that the success rates were slightly lower compared to normal lighting conditions for most obstacle sizes and speeds. The highest success rate of 100% was achieved for large obstacles at slow and medium speeds, and for all obstacle sizes at fast speeds. However, the lowest success rate of 93% was observed for small obstacles at slow speeds. This decrease in performance under low-light conditions can be attributed to the reduced visibility of the obstacles, which makes it more challenging for the system to detect and avoid them.

Despite the slight decrease in performance, the system was still able to detect and avoid obstacles with a reasonable success rate, with success rates ranging from 93% to 100%. This suggests that the system can effectively operate under low-light conditions, which is an important characteristic for a mobile robot system operating in real-world environments where lighting conditions can vary. Further analysis of the results indicates that the system's performance under low-light conditions was relatively consistent across obstacle sizes and speeds, indicating that the proposed system is robust and effective in detecting and avoiding obstacles under a wide range of conditions.

Next, we evaluated the system's performance with added noise reduction. For this experiment, we introduced background noise into the testing area to simulate a busy, real-world environment during rotation. We tested the robot's ability to detect and avoid obstacles under these conditions using the proposed system with the global direction filter and other noise reduction techniques. Table 3 shows the results of this experiment:

Table 5. Performance under Noise Reduction

Obstacle Size	Obstacle Speed	Success Rate (%)
Small	Slow	89
Small	Medium	95
Small	Fast	96
Medium	Slow	94
Medium	Medium	95
Medium	Fast	98
Large	Slow	100
Large	Medium	100
Large	Fast	100

However, it is worth noting that the success rates in Table 5 were slightly lower compared to the results obtained under normal lighting conditions in Table 1. This is because background noise can interfere with the accuracy of obstacle detection, making it more challenging for the system to distinguish between obstacles and noise. Nevertheless, the proposed system was still able to achieve high success rates even under noisy conditions, indicating its effectiveness in real-world environments where background noise is often present.

In addition to the success rates, the experiments in Table 5 also demonstrate the effectiveness of the proposed system's noise reduction techniques, including the global direction filter and other noise reduction techniques. These techniques enabled the system to maintain a high level of accuracy even in the presence of background noise, which further highlights the system's robustness in noisy environments.

Finally, we conducted experiments to compare the system's performance with and without optimizations. Specifically, we compared the system's performance with and without a priority list for computing resource allocation and with and without a time-sharing operating system. Table 4 shows the results of these experiments:

Table 6. Performance with Optimizations

Test Conditions	Success Rate(%)
Without Optimizations	67
With Priority List	91
With Time-sharing Operating System	96

Table 6 presents the results of experiments that compared the performance of the proposed system with and without optimizations in terms of obstacle avoidance success rate. The table shows that without optimizations, the system had a success rate of only 67%, indicating that the robot frequently failed to avoid obstacles. This highlights the crucial role of the optimization techniques in ensuring the smooth and reliable operation of the system.

The results also show that both the priority list for computing resource allocation and the time-sharing operating system contributed to improving the system's performance, with success rates of 91% and 96%, respectively. The time-sharing operating system demonstrated the highest success rate and therefore, the most effective optimization technique in ensuring obstacle avoidance. The experimental results demonstrate the effectiveness and importance of optimizing the system to achieve a high success rate in obstacle avoidance, which is crucial for the reliable operation of the robot in real-world environments.

The experimental results confirm that the proposed system can achieve high success rates in obstacle avoidance with the application of optimization techniques. The priority list for computing resource allocation and the time-sharing operating system have been shown to be effective in improving the system's performance, especially in terms of obstacle avoidance. These optimization techniques are crucial in ensuring the smooth and reliable operation of the robot in real-world environments, where the ability to avoid obstacles is essential.

Overall, the experimental results confirm the effectiveness and potential of the proposed system in obstacle detection and avoidance on a mobile robot platform. However, further studies are needed to investigate the system's performance in dynamic environments with moving robots and more complex obstacle configurations. Additionally, future research can explore the feasibility of implementing the system on different robot platforms, as well as integrating it with other autonomous systems to enable more advanced functionalities.

5   Conclusion

This paper presents a novel obstacle detection and avoidance system for mobile robots that utilizes a long-short step RNN for flow map estimation and a global direction filter for robust obstacle detection. The system's effectiveness and robustness were evaluated on a stationary robot with obstacles of varying sizes and speeds under different lighting and noise conditions. The proposed system achieved high success rates in obstacle detection and avoidance in both normal and low-light conditions and under noisy conditions. Optimizations, including a priority list for computing resource allocation and a time-sharing operating system, improved the system's performance significantly. The system outperformed state-of-the-art optical flow techniques, achieving a precision rate of 95.2% and a recall rate of 94.3% with 75 FPS on own-collected YouTube videos. The proposed system's visualization results indicate that it can successfully detect unseen obstacles in challenging environments. The experiments on a real robot platform demonstrate the system's high success rate in detecting and avoiding obstacles under various environmental conditions. The proposed system provides a lightweight, accurate, and efficient obstacle detection solution for mobile robots and contributes to the development of autonomous systems.

Acknowledgements. Thank for Mr. Haibo Ren and Mr. Xinpeng Du support the experiments in Beijing.

References

1. Jiang, S., Hong, Z.: Unexpected dynamic obstacle monocular detection in the driver view. IEEE Intell. Transp. Syst. Mag. **14**(1), 65–74 (2022)
2. Siegwart, R., Nourbakhsh, I.R., Scaramuzza, D.: Introduction to Autonomous Robots: Mechanisms and Sensors. MIT Press, Cambridge (2011)
3. Ren, S., He, K., Girshick, R., Sun, J.: Faster R-CNN: towards real-time object detection with region proposal networks. In: Advances in Neural Information Processing Systems, pp. 91–99 (2015)
4. Long, J., Shelhamer, E., Darrell, T.: Fully convolutional networks for semantic segmentation. In: Proceedings of the IEEE Conference on Computer Vision and Pattern Recognition, pp. 3431–3440 (2015)
5. Esfahlani, S.: Shabnam: the deep convolutional neural network role in the autonomous navigation of mobile robots (SROBO). Remote Sens. **14**, 3324–3324 (2022)
6. Li, Y., Liu, M., Tang, J.: Robust obstacle detection based on optical flow and SVM. J. Comput. Sci. Technol. **29**(1), 52–61 (2014)
7. Khan, A., Hamza, S., Li, X.: Luo: Obstacle avoidance and tracking control of redundant robotic manipulator: an RNN-based metaheuristic approach. IEEE Trans. Industr. Inf. **16**, 4670–4680 (2019)
8. Tian, L., Tu, Z., Zhang, D., Liu, J., Li, B., Yuan, J.: Unsupervised learning of optical flow with CNN-based non-local filtering. IEEE Trans. Image Process. **29**, 8429–8442 (2020)
9. Hirschmuller, H.: Stereo processing by semiglobal matching and mutual information. IEEE Trans. Pattern Anal. Mach. Intell. **30**(2), 328–341 (2008)
10. Scharstein, D., Szeliski, R.: A taxonomy and evaluation of dense two-frame stereo correspondence algorithms. Int. J. Comput. Vision **47**(1–3), 7–42 (2002)
11. Chuah, W., Tennakoon, R., Hoseinnezhad, R., Suter, D., Bab-Hadiashar, A.: Semantic guided long range stereo depth estimation for safer autonomous vehicle applications. IEEE Trans. Intell. Transp. Syst. **23**(10), 18916–18926 (2022)
12. Dodge, D., Yilmaz, M.: Convex vision-based negative obstacle detection framework for autonomous vehicles. IEEE Trans. Intell. Veh. **8**(1), 778–789 (2022)
13. Chen, G., Peng, P., Zhang, P., Dong, W.: Risk-aware trajectory sampling for quadrotor obstacle avoidance in dynamic environments. IEEE Trans. Ind. Electron. (2023)
14. Xu, Z., Zhou, X., Wu, H., Li, X., Li, S.: Motion planning of manipulators for simultaneous obstacle avoidance and target tracking: an RNN approach with guaranteed performance. IEEE Trans. Industr. Electron. **69**(4), 3887–3897 (2021)

15. Perumal, P.S., et al.: An insight into crash avoidance and overtaking advice systems for autonomous vehicles: a review, challenges and solutions. Eng. Appl. Artif. Intell. **104**, 104406 (2021)
16. Oroko, J.A., Nyakoe, G.N.: Obstacle avoidance and path planning schemes for autonomous navigation of a mobile robot: a review. In: Proceedings of the Sustainable Research and Innovation Conference (2022)
17. Hutabarat, D., Rivai, M., Purwanto, D., Hutomo, H.: Lidar-based obstacle avoidance for the autonomous mobile robot. In: 12th International Conference on Information & Communication Technology and System (ICTS), pp. 197–202 (2019)
18. Chen, K.: Mvlidarnet: real-time multi-class scene understanding for autonomous driving using multiple views. In: 2020 IEEE/RSJ International Conference on Intelligent Robots and Systems (IROS) (2020)
19. Wang, P., Gao, S., Li, L., Sun, B., Cheng, S.: Obstacle avoidance path planning design for autonomous driving vehicles based on an improved artificial potential field algorithm. Energies **12**(12), 2342–2342 (2019)
20. Pandey, A., Kashyap, A.K., Parhi, D.R., Patle, B.K.: Autonomous mobile robot navigation between static and dynamic obstacles using multiple ANFIS architecture. World J. Eng. **16**(2), 275–286 (2019)
21. Zhao, X., Sun, P., Xu, Z., Min, H., Yu, H.: Fusion of 3D LIDAR and camera data for object detection in autonomous vehicle applications. IEEE Sens. J. **20**(9), 4901–4913 (2020)
22. Hua, M., Nan, Y., Lian, S.: Small obstacle avoidance based on RGB-D semantic segmentation. In: Proceedings of the IEEE/CVF International Conference on Computer Vision Workshops (2019)
23. Zhao, C., Sun, Q., Zhang, C., Tang, Y., Qian, F.: Monocular depth estimation based on deep learning: an overview. SCIENCE CHINA Technol. Sci. **63**(9), 1612–1627 (2020)
24. Croon, D., Guido, C., De Wagter, C., Seidl, T.: Enhancing optical-flow-based control by learning visual appearance cues for flying robots. Nat. Mach. Intell. **3**(1), 33–41 (2021)
25. Fox, W., Burgard, S.: Thrun: the dynamic window approach to collision avoidance. IEEE Robot. Autom. Mag. **4**(1), 23–33 (1997)
26. Baker, S., Matthews, I.: Lucas-kanade 20 years on: a unifying framework. Int. J. Comput. Vision **56**, 221–255 (2004)
27. Ilg, E., Mayer, N., Saikia, T., Keuper, M., Dosovitskiy, A., Brox, T.: Flownet 2.0: evolution of optical flow estimation with deep networks. In: Proceedings of the IEEE Conference on Computer Vision and Pattern Recognition, pp. 2462–2470 (2017)
28. Teed, Z., Deng, J.: RAFT: recurrent all-pairs field transforms for optical flow. In: Vedaldi, A., Bischof, H., Brox, T., Frahm, J.-M. (eds.) ECCV 2020. LNCS, vol. 12347, pp. 402–419. Springer, Cham (2020). https://doi.org/10.1007/978-3-030-58536-5_24

Design of Equipment for Road Traffic Closure in Flooded Underpass

Cui Zhuang[1] and Jaime Alvarez[2(✉)]

[1] Graduate School of Engineering, Takushoku University, Tokyo, Japan
[2] Department of Design, Faculty of Engineering, Takushoku University, 193-0985 Tatemachi 815-1, Hachioji-shi, Tokyo, Japan
`a-jaime@id.takushoku-u.ac.jp`

Abstract. In order to deal with increasingly frequent accidents caused during underpass flooding, it is required to develop traffic control equipment that can stop vehicle traffic in a quick and effective way. In this research, design requirements for underpass traffic control equipment were clarified through literature review, analysis of existing equipment, and user research focused on road management authorities in Japan and China. Preliminary results of this work led to widening the scope of required functionality beyond stopping traffic, in order to include assistive functions such as traffic redirecting and warning. Based on this finding, the design proposal is composed by two main elements: a fixed barricade and a set of mobile assistive devices. At the present state of design development, a qualitative validation was carried out by applying questionnaires and conducting interviews with road managers. From an overall perspective, the proposal was positively evaluated. Specifically, characteristics such as efficiency, usage space, cost and aesthetic appealing were highlighted, while theft, safety enhancing and visibility were identified as points for future improvement.

Keywords: Flood · Underpass · Traffic control equipment

1 Introduction

Climate change is fueling conditions that rise water precipitation and intensity of hurricanes, leading to increasing occurrence of extreme rains that are causing flash floods in countries all around the globe [1]. These heavy rains are very difficult to forecast because they take place on a small spatial scale (less than 100 km) and over a short timespan (less than 12 h) [2] (see Fig. 1).

In recent times, the devastating power of torrential rains and typhoons has reached unprecedented levels, resulting in numerous fatalities, injuries and material loses, as well as paralyzation of important urban functions. Recent research using satellite imaging technology in flooded areas has revealed that the global population exposed to flood in the last decade is 10 times higher than previous estimates [4]. Furthermore, risk of floods is expected to rise, since several future scenarios that consider the planet climate and demographic change estimate that extreme rainfall will increase [5].

V. G. Duffy et al. (Eds.): HCII 2023, LNCS 14057, pp. 634–645, 2023.
https://doi.org/10.1007/978-3-031-48047-8_43

Fig. 1. Torrential rain in Tokyo [3].

Underpasses are among the most affected urban structure during floods due to their location below ground level. Even if drainage facilities and pumps are installed, underpass flooding will occur if there is an inflow that exceeds the drainage or pumping capacity, a scenario that can occur during extreme torrential rains.

Japan is prone to build urban underpass infrastructure, due to a geography characterized by rugged and mountainous terrain, as well as a highly developed road and rail systems. There are about 3,500 underpasses across the country cities [6]. Although road authorities have operation protocols for closing flooded underpasses, closure procedures take time and drivers attempt to make their way through a flooded underpass that has not being closed; resulting in fatal accidents [7–9]. Additionally, in recent years torrential rains have caused frequent cases of floods that are sudden and severe, known as "flash floods", that dramatically increases underpass hazard (Fig. 2).

Fig. 2. Accident in flooded underpass resulting in truck driver fatality [9].

Another issue that affects flooded underpass safety is driver's behavior. In underpasses that have not being closed yet, some drivers ignore warning systems in operation, and attempt to drive through; while in closed underpasses some motorists attempt to drive around barricades [10] (Fig. 3).

Fig. 3. Driver going through underpass by driving around barricades [11]

Based on the changing conditions of torrential rains and increasing number of accidents in flooded underpasses, it may be concluded that there is a necessity of improving traffic control solutions for better responsiveness, in order to close underpasses in a shorter time after a flash flood.

2 Research Objective and Methodology

The purpose of this study is to clarify design requirements, develop and validate a design proposal for underpass equipment that can quickly and effectively perform traffic control, in order to prevent accidents when the underpass is flooded. This objective will be achieved by the following research methodology.

- Analysis of existing equipment: Comparative analysis for clarifying present situation of traffic control devices.
- User research: Questionnaires and interviews for clarifying user requirements.
- Concept development: Brainstorming, sketching, and building physical and CAD models to support ideation, as well for evaluation of the design concept.
- Design validation: Questionnaires and interviews for validating design proposal.

Although this paper documents the overall design process of the proposed traffic control equipment, it pays special attention to a research-based design approach, showing how the findings of the user research stage were fundamental for clarifying the research challenge and setting a new design direction.

3 Analysis of Existing Equipment

Through literature review of traffic closure devices available in the market, this research identified and classified equipment in two categories: mobile equipment and fixed equipment. Mobile equipment -such as barricades- has to be carried to the site after flooding, while fixed equipment is already installed on the site. Table 1 shows mobile devices that are typically used for underpass closure.

Table 1. Mobile equipment for traffic control in flooded underpasses.

Product	Barricade	Traffic Cone	Cone bar
Image	(Source : Amazon)	(Source: Amazon)	(Source: Amazon)
Dimensions mm	W1200xH800	W380xH705	L200
Main function	Restrain entry Warn drivers	Warn drivers Assist redirecting traffic	Restrain entry (installed in traffic cones)

Since fixed equipment is installed at the expected flooding location, its operation may be manual or automatic. Table 2 summarizes manual and automatic devices for stopping traffic. Manual devices have no concern regarding power loss or electric system failure and do not require regular maintenance, but since an operator has to be dispatched to the

Table 2. Fixed equipment for traffic control in flooded underpasses.

Number	1	2	3	4
Type	Horizontal barrier (road transverse direction)	Horizontal barrier (road longitudinal direction)	Rope (chain) barrier	Balloon barrier
Image (source)	(Sanyo Road Industry Co., Ltd.)	(Sanyo Road Industry Co., Ltd.)	(M. of Internal Affairs and Communications)	(Advic Co., Ltd.)
Operation	Manual/Automatic	Manual/Automatic	Manual	Automatic
Blocking length (m)	≦6	≦7	N/A	3.0~3.5
Setting time (s)	18	40	N/A	20
Wind resist. (m/s)	40	40	N/A	10
Material	Column: Galvanized steel Barrier bar: aluminum	Column: Galvanized steel Barrier bar: aluminum	N/A	Polyester fabric Galvanized steel Super water repellent finish

site to perform manual closure, it takes time to complete the operation. Automatic type barriers can be operated remotely but their cost is higher and have a shorter service life that requires regular maintenance.

4   User Research

In order to clarify design requirements for the traffic control equipment, questionnaires (sent in advance) and interviews (based on questionnaire responses) were applied to officials of two road management departments, one in Japan (interview conducted online) and one in China (interview conducted face-to-face). Additionally, detailed information regarding their procedures for underpass closure was provided to authors. Both departments requested not to disclose their identity (Fig. 4).

Fig. 4. Interviews of road management officials in Japan (left) and China (right).

Table 3 summarizes the design requirements that were extracted from questionnaires and interviews, as well as a representative comment from the Voice of User (VOU) regarding each requirement. The most important design requirements were responsiveness (in terms of time to complete closure) and effectiveness (capability of prevent vehicle circulation).

A very important finding of user research was that even if fixed equipment is available on the site, underpass closure procedures also require using mobile equipment for assistive purposes, such as reinforcing closure, traffic deviation and warning. Furthermore, the presence of road workers is also necessary for performing these operations and monitoring flood and traffic status. Therefore, the scope of designing fixed equipment was widened to the design of a traffic control solution that is composed of a fixed traffic device and mobile assistive devices, in order to being able to perform traffic closure procedure (see Fig. 5).

Table 3. Summary of design requirements extracted from questionnaires and interviews.

V.O.U. (Voice of User)	Requirement
"Due to torrential rain and typhoons underpasses may be flooded in a short time, so we would like to complete traffic regulation soon as the water level reaches dangerous levels."	Responsive-ness
"After we implemented traffic blocking procedure, we want to make sure that cars are prevented from entering in underpass."	Effectiveness
"During rainfall and at night, the driver's visibility is poor, so traffic control equipment must be easy to see under these conditions in order to prevent collisions."	Safety
"Easy to operate the equipment, both when implementing and removing traffic restrictions."	Operability
"I want traffic control equipment that can handle bad climates such as heavy rain and strong winds."	Weather resistance

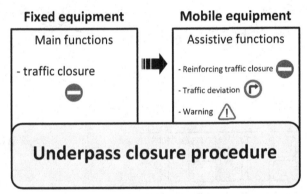

Fig. 5. Widening functional scope towards a concept that embraces both fixed and mobile equipment.

5   Concept Development

Based on the widened design scope, through brainstorming sessions several ideas for the initial concept design direction were produced, including different ideas for the location of such devices. Ideas were evaluated based on the clarified user requirements, and one idea was selected for further refinement. This idea consists on a traffic control device that can be installed in the road median strip and in the sidewalk buffer zone, as the guards shown in Fig. 6. Following this design concept, several sketches and rough models were produced for concept development of both fixed and mobile devices (see Fig. 7).

Fig. 6. Example of location of traffic control equipment (photograph by authors).

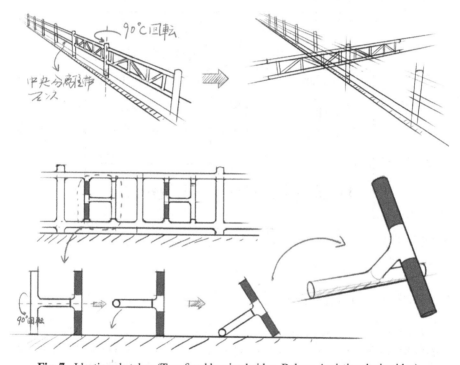

Fig. 7. Ideation sketches (Top: fixed barricade idea, Below: Assistive device idea).

After embodiment design, design CAD models of three proposals were built: A fixed traffic barricade that is part of the central road guard. Two design ideas were developed for this proposal, one "analog" barricade that functions as a traffic barricade (see Fig. 8), and a "digital" version that incorporates an electronic display that alerts underpass closure (see Fig. 9). In both solutions, the length of the barricades can be extended for the case of wider roads. These design proposals may be operated manually by staff or automatically by remote operation.

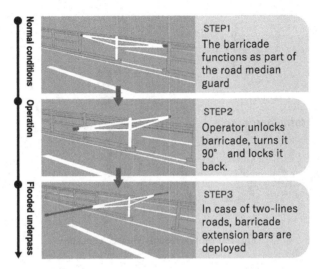

Fig. 8. Fixed barricade concept (operation of manual version).

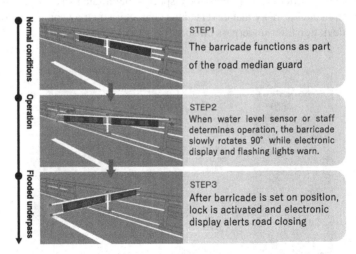

Fig. 9. Fixed barricade concept (operation of automatic version)

A third design proposal is a mobile assistive device that can be used reinforcing traffic closure or traffic deviation, in the same ways as road cones. These devices also may be part of the sidewalk road guard (see Fig. 10). A central characteristic of these proposals is that they can be integrated into the guards of the road median strip and sidewalk buffer zone. Hence, they don't require additional space for storage, neither use space for pedestrians.

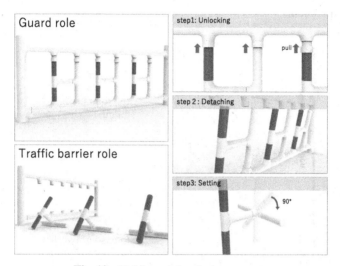

Fig. 10. Mobile assistive device concept.

Another advantage of this design proposal is that, by locating the traffic barrier in the central road guard, after closing operation a space is habilitated so cars can do a U-turn without complicated or risky maneuvers. This characteristic may contribute to ensure a safe traffic deviation after underpass closure (Fig. 11).

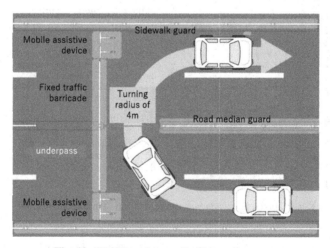

Fig. 11. Habilitated space for U-turn maneuver

6 Design Validation

Based on the proposed design, evaluation questionnaire targeting Japanese road managers was prepared. The questionnaire respondents were four road management departments (which requested not to disclose their identity), including participation of the road department from Japan that collaborated with this research during the user research stage previously described in Sect. 4 of this paper. After receiving overall evaluation of the design proposals, two of these departments agreed to conduct online interviews in order to collect detailed opinions (see Fig. 12).

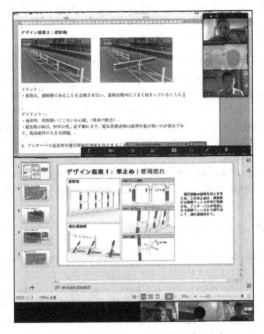

Fig. 12. Screen captures of online interviews

Through the design validation stage, the following aspects of the design proposals were summarized.

- There is no need to bring in the traffic control equipment, so efficiency can be improved.
- The proposal makes creative use of road guards, so there is no need for storage space.
- It fits well in the road space without making road users aware that it is a traffic control facility.
- Since the design proposal having a digital display doubles as a traffic barricade and a warning sign, the cost may be reduced as a whole.

As directions for improvement, the following issues were stated:

- It is necessary to consider measures to prevent mischief and theft.

- Automatic/remote-controlled traffic barriers need to consider collision prevention measures to avoid hitting cars of people.
- It is necessary to confirm the visibility of the mobile assistive device from the driver's point of view. In addition, it is necessary to reduce its weight to make it easier to carry, although not being light may be an advantage regarding wind resistance. It may be difficult to meet both requirements at the same time.

In addition, from the point of view of commercialization, the following issues were expressed.

- Since the automatic/remote control type road barrier has an electric display, it is necessary to consider the power supply and maintenance method.
- It is necessary to ensure that the function of the road guard is satisfactory fulfilled, from the point of view of structural strength.

From an overall point of view, the results of performed qualitative evaluation can be assumed as favorable, since positive opinions of the design proposals praised their responsiveness and effectiveness, which were central design requirements identified in earlier stage of the design process. Furthermore, the overall efficiency of underpass closure procedure can be enhanced since the need of bringing assistive traffic equipment can be eliminated. Although issues regarding safety, prevention of theft and visibility were negatively evaluated, these issues, as well as the ones regarding structural strength and maintenance, are not a central part of the proposed design concept and can be solved during further development stages, without compromising the novelty of the concept.

7 Conclusions

In this study, we first conducted a research using comparative analysis to understand the current status of fixed and mobile traffic control equipment. Then, by conducting questionnaires and online interviews the needs for traffic control equipment from the user's perspective were clarified. Responsiveness was identified as the most important design requirement. Furthermore, it was also clarified that adequate responsiveness of an underpass traffic barricade also encompasses assistive functions, such as reinforcing traffic closure, redirection of traffic and warning incoming traffic. Based on these findings, a design concept that is composed of a fixed barrier and assistive mobile equipment were developed. Both types of traffic control equipment can be integrated into the guards of the road median strip and the sidewalk duffer zone. Finally, by applying questionnaires and conducting interviews to road managers, favorable qualitative evaluation was earned, and issues that must be solved in further design stages were clarified.

8 Research Limitations and Future Studies

Secrecy concerns of road authorities' officials inhibited possibilities of having a greater number of questionnaires and interview respondents in order to perform qualitative validation using statistics tools. Additionally, further development requires building and testing full scale models and prototypes, and setting a location for installation and tests requires obtaining permissions from road authorities, police and others stakeholders.

References

1. Seneviratne, S. et al.: Changes in climate extremes and their impacts on the natural physical environment. In: Managing the Risks of Extreme Events and Disasters to Advance Climate Change Adaptation. Cambridge University Press (2012)
2. Torrential Rain. https://skydayproject.com/torrential-rain. Accessed 22 Mar 2022
3. Guerrilla Rainstorm' Caught on Camera from Tokyo Skytree. https://japantoday.com/cat egory/national/guerrilla-rainstorm-caught-on-camera-from-tokyo-skytree. Accessed 01 May 2022
4. Tellman, B., et al.: Satellite imaging reveals increased proportion of population exposed to floods. Nature **596**(7870), 80–86 (2021). https://doi.org/10.1038/s41586-021-03695-w
5. Hirabayashi, Y., et al.: Global exposure to flooding from the new CMIP6 climate model projections. Sci. Rep. **11**(1), 3740 (2021). https://doi.org/10.1038/s41598-021-83279-w
6. Roads in Japan 2021. https://www.mlit.go.jp/road/road_e/pdf/ROAD2021web.pdf. Accessed 30 May 2022
7. Woman Drowns After Entering Without Noticing Flooding (in Japanese). https://response. jp/article/2008/08/19/112728.html. Accessed 03 May 2022
8. Microbus Stuck in a Flooded Underpass due to Heavy Rain (in Japanese). https://response. jp/article/2008/09/26/114137.html. Accessed 06 May 2022
9. Call for Help to Work Place... Truck Submerged in Underpass (in Japanese), https://news. line.me/detail/oa-tokaitv-news/b9a8d3971cc0. Accessed 12 June 2022
10. EU Urban Transport Research Project: Safety and Accident Reduction. https://www.eltis.org/ sites/default/files/kt3_wm_en_pdf_ext_5.pdf. Accessed 24 June 2022
11. Far North Queensland on Flood Watch as Parts of State Prepare for 300 mm Rain. https://the newdaily.com.au/news/2021/04/19/queensland-flood-watch/. Accessed 19 July 2022

Author Index

© The Editor(s) (if applicable) and The Author(s), under exclusive license
to Springer Nature Switzerland AG 2023
V. G. Duffy et al. (Eds.): HCII 2023, LNCS 14057, pp. 647–648, 2023.
https://doi.org/10.1007/978-3-031-48047-8

Printed in the United States
by Baker & Taylor Publisher Services